W9-CCS-498

PATHS OF

AMERICAN THOUGHT

CONTRIBUTORS

Daniel Bell
McGeorge Bundy
Richard Chase
I. Bernard Cohen
James B. Conant
Marcus Cunliffe
Dwight L. Dumond
Donald Fleming
Seymour E. Harris
Louis Hartz
Richard Hofstadter
Irving Howe
Alfred Kazin
Melvin J. Lasky
Max Lerner
Everett Mendelsohn
Donald Meyer
William Lee Miller
Edmund S. Morgan
Eugene V. Rostow
Paul A. Samuelson
Arthur M. Schlesinger, Jr.
Edward Shils
Shigeto Tsuru
Lucia White
Morton White

PATHS OF AMERICAN THOUGHT

Edited by

ARTHUR M. SCHLESINGER, JR.
and
MORTON WHITE

HOUGHTON MIFFLIN COMPANY · BOSTON
1963

"Ideas and Economic Development," by Arthur M. Schlesinger, Jr.; reprinted in part from *American Economic History,* ed. Seymour E. Harris; copyright © 1961 by the McGraw-Hill Book Company, Inc.

"Pragmatism and the Scope of Science," by Morton White; adapted in part from *American Perspectives,* ed. R. E. Spiller and Eric Larrabee; copyright © 1961 by the President and Fellows of Harvard College.

"The Realist Tradition in American Law," by Eugene V. Rostow; reprinted in part from the *Rocky Mountain Law Review;* copyright © 1962 by the *Rocky Mountain Law Review.*

"Economic Thought and the New Industrialism," by Paul A. Samuelson; adapted in part from *Postwar Economic Trends in the United States,* ed. Ralph E. Freeman; copyright © 1960 by Massachusetts Institute of Technology; reprinted by permission of Harper & Row, Publishers.

"The Intellectual versus the City," by Morton and Lucia White; copyright © 1961 by Morton and Lucia White.

"America and Europe: Transatlantic Images," by Melvin J. Lasky; © 1961/62 by Encounter Ltd.

"The One Against the Many," by Arthur M. Schlesinger, Jr.; copyright © 1962 by Saturday Review, Inc.

An excerpt from "American Moderns" by Irving Howe appeared under the title "In Search of a Moral Style," in *The New Republic,* September 25, 1961. Copyright © 1961, by Harrison-Blaine, Inc.

An expanded version of "Modernity and Mass Society: On the Varieties of Cultural Experience" by Daniel Bell appeared in *Studies in Public Communication,* No. 4, Autumn, 1962. Copyright © 1962 by The University of Chicago.

An abbreviated version of "European Images of America" by Marcus Cunliffe appeared in *Encounter,* December, 1961. © 1961 by Encounter Ltd.

LIBRARY OF CONGRESS CATALOG CARD NUMBER: 63-14184

PRINTED IN THE U.S.A.

Contents

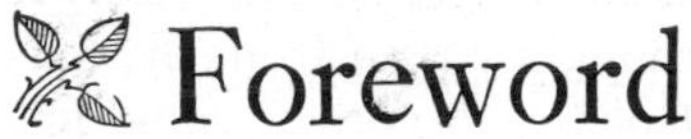

Foreword

American thought from colonial times to the present is so vast and ramified a subject that only the most intrepid explorer would venture to investigate it alone. Parrington sought to map its terrain and penetrate its recesses — with different degrees of success in different parts of the forest — and doubtless others in the future will try single-handedly to improve on Parrington's labors in a work of comparable scale. But we need not wait until these heroes appear before trying to order and absorb the great amount of research and writing on the history of American thought in the two generations since Parrington. Many hands have been at work in these years in the field of American intellectual history; and this has seemed to us an appropriate moment for a collective display of some of their achievements. We have accordingly invited a group of scholars and writers to deal with salient aspects of the evolution of the American mind. We have called on intellectual historians; and we have also in a number of cases called on men who are masters of particular fields and can give an insider's view of the historical development of their specialties.

We obviously have no pretensions to total coverage. This work is not only collective; it is selective. We decided to omit poetry, painting, and music — though we believe that strong arguments can be made for including all these in intellectual history — and we decided on grounds of space to omit essays on the details of scientific development. We have included contributions on technical subjects in philosophy or science only when the subject — like pragmatism or Keynesian economics — is of decisive cultural, political, or social significance and when its main elements may be easily communicated. In short, we have been primarily governed in our choice of topics by the desire to treat those chapters in the history of American thought that would be of interest to the historian of American social life as a whole. And to the rule that the ideas treated be in some sense American in origin, we have allowed two exceptions — namely the essays on European and Asian images of America. It seemed to us appropriate, as American thought passed from the federal to the national to the international phase, to convey some impression of the way America is perceived by people in other parts of the world.

We need hardly add that this volume represents a cooperative attempt by authors of independent minds and diverse views. Each contributor has expressed his own thoughts and is to be held accountable for these alone. The editors assume responsibility for the choice of topics and contributors. We are proud to include a posthumous essay by the distinguished critic and scholar, Richard Chase, whose brilliant writing did so much to illuminate the history of American literature. We would also like to take this occasion to express our appreciation to Perry Miller, whose counsel and companionship for many years has so effectively deepened our understanding of the problems of intellectual history. We wish to thank Lucia White for her incisive and discriminating editorial suggestions, and Stephen W. Grant of Houghton Mifflin for his patience and counsel.

ARTHUR M. SCHLESINGER, JR.
MORTON WHITE

PATHS OF

AMERICAN THOUGHT

Prologue: *Coherence and Correspondence in American Thought*

MORTON WHITE

At the very beginning of this volume it may be helpful to sketch a pattern that seems to emerge from the essays to follow. Parallel to the volume's division into sections on the colonial, federal, national, and international phases of American history, one may discern another division more directly connected with the ideas themselves. This intellectual pattern comes into view when we ask about the degree of internal coherence among leading ideas in each of the periods, and also about the extent to which these ideas correspond with the facts of social life. Just as a dream may be logically consistent and yet not be a record of reality or a guide to social action, so it is logically possible for a whole era of literature and philosophy to be internally integrated and yet out of touch with the major social problems of its age. And conversely, the thinkers and writers of an era may be engaged, as the existentialists say, but fail to produce a uniform climate of opinion.

If we approach the history of American thought with these possibilities in mind we can see an interesting evolution revealed in the essays to follow. In the colonial age the dominant ideas formed a unity and were in relatively close touch with the social and political life of the colonists. In the federal era that ideological unity declined, as did the ambition of intellectuals to be in touch with the major social and political issues of their day. In the national phase after the Civil War the American mind was once again dominated by a comparatively coherent set of ideas closely linked to the world and capable of guiding action. But in the present age that begins with the First World War we find something unique in our history: intellectuals close to a complex reality, yet unable to find intellectual coherence among themselves.

I

From today's perspective the thought of Revolutionary times seems eminently coherent and exceedingly realistic. While Americans fled from Europe, conquered a wilderness, and freed themselves from foreign domination, they forged a set of beliefs that helped them guide their revolutionary energies and form their new political structure. Colonial America was dedicated to a set of propositions, conceived in flight from political tyranny and religious persecution, and these propositions dominated and unified the age before Independence. There was not only a considerable degree of intellectual concord among thinking men, but what they thought was created and used in the crucible of action. Fear of nature and of threatening foreign powers brought the colonists together in spite of geographical and ethnic differences. They became a consciously united group whose internal disagreements, great as they were, seemed minor by comparison with their disagreements with the rest of the world. They had decided to live together under one government, and their collective decision was the result of long and serious reflection. They had fought hard for their precious liberties and were deeply suspicious of those — inside or outside of America — who might wish to take their liberties away.

Colonial consciousness of man's failings was a tough thread that bound together the sermons of Calvinist divines and the pamphlets of Revolutionary leaders. The divines had feared the depravity of individuals whereas their politically minded successors at the time of the Revolution were more exercised by the depravity of peoples and governments. And out of this second preoccupation there grew fundamental principles designed to guard against the effects of depravity in politics: that people of one region ought not to exercise dominion over those of another; that a people is distinct from its government and should protect itself from the dangers of tyranny inherent in all governments; and that even majorities could be tyrannical and hence should be checked.

II

Once independence had been achieved, the colonial intellectual unities began to dissolve. The dissolution of Calvinism and the controversy over slavery threatened the nation with serious division. The closest approximation to "the" Church in America was fragmented into churches, which were in turn separated from a State that promised to split up into states. Henceforth there was nothing like an Establishment in religion, and no agreement on slavery. The age of provincial community — or, as the German sociologists called it, *Gemeinschaft* — was over in America. If there was to be new spiritual unity, it would have to be on altogether different terms.

With the decline of religious agreement and with the growing conflict between Northern and Southern ways of life, the America of 1840 was understandably seen as Henry James saw it forty years later in his book on Hawthorne. Not only could New England writers find no sovereign, no court, no aristocracy, no church, no clergy, no army, no diplomatic service, no country gentlemen, no manors, and no ivied ruins, but as James also remarked, they found "no State, in the European sense of the word, and indeed barely a specific national name." And while the absence of all these things cannot explain the American writer's failure to produce an American *Madame Bovary*, it does help explain his failure to produce novels about those "items of high civilization" that James missed. American literature of the time was more interested in reflecting the emotions of a thwarted Calvinism and an ambiguous frontier. It expressed itself in the romance rather than the novel; it lacked a sense of history and culture, and was preoccupied with the Self. It found no high civilization to describe, and what it saw in the American city it feared or despised.

If one turns to the socio-political scene at the time — to that "simple, democratic, thinly-composed society" as James called it — one finds a poverty of abstract social thought. Understandably, Tocqueville said in 1835: "I think that in no country in the civilized world is less attention paid to philosophy than in the United States." The forces that united against Whiggery were not guided by any profoundly articulated political philosophy. Their movement was the result of a shrewdly managed, large combination of democrats operating without benefit of a unifying metaphysics or theology. The absent State, in that European sense of which Henry James spoke, could not have its theorists, just as the nonexistent Church and Society could not have their novelists. The life of the mind went its own transcendental way, more concerned with Nature and the Over-Soul than with the underbrush of Washington or the underworld of New York.

III

The Civil War officially ended a struggle between the Northern and Southern systems of value, but the old forces tending toward diversity continued to act and were augmented by others. The war that preserved the Union prepared the way for new forms of diversity and conflict in America by encouraging industrialization, urbanization, and immigration. After the Civil War, new social types entered American society and soon their ideals were described and espoused by intellectuals. A character of William Dean Howells succinctly portrayed the change in American society and values between Independence and the end of the nineteenth century. In reply to a Utopian traveler's question, "Who is your ideal great man?" Howells's character of 1894 said: "Before the [Civil] War, and during all the time from the revolution onward, it was undoubtedly the great politician, the publicist, the statesman. As we grew older and began to have an intellectual life of our own, I think the literary fellows had a pretty good share of the honors that were going. . . . When the war came, it brought the soldier to the front, and there was a period of ten or fifteen years when he dominated the national imagination. That period passed, and the great era of national prosperity set in. The big fortunes began to tower up, and heroes of another sort began to appeal to our imagination. I don't think there is any doubt but the millionaire is now the American ideal."*

* William Dean Howells, *A Traveler from Altruria* (New York, 1894), pp. 208–209.

The millionaire was not the only new social type on the American scene. He was accompanied by his opposite number, the industrial worker, and by the new European immigrant. Socially and economically the time seemed ripe for political and ideological conflict. Still, the seventy-five years following the Civil War witnessed an accommodation. Those seventy-five years were therefore very different from the seventy-five that had separated the Civil War from the Revolution. The national phase of America's history recorded dramatic progress toward a liberal, pluralistic society, and in this progress intellectuals played a prominent part. The period between Reconstruction and the First World War was, like the colonial era and unlike the federal era, doubly integrated from the point of view of the historian of ideas. Its liberal intellectuals formulated a coherent philosophy that was self-consciously and deliberately in correspondence with social reality and social action.

However, the emergence of that philosophy as the dominant philosophy of the age was not immediate. Although the millionaire — unlike the Revolutionary statesmen and the literary transcendentalist — was (except for Andrew Carnegie) too busy to give literary expression to his convictions and his aspirations, he did not lack for sociological and legal spokesmen. Social Darwinism (better called Social Spencerism) and the doctrine of laissez-faire provided the rationale and the apology for the accumulation of great fortunes, and for a period these two doctrines dominated the intellectual scene.

But soon the liberal and radical reply was presented, and the evils of unchecked capitalism were fully catalogued. The acrimonious contest between the Spencerians and those who rejected their social philosophy of fatalism was striking evidence of the intellectual's active interest in the world around him. Novelists might still contend with the traditional notion that literature required a moral purpose, and to some extent with the continuing paucity of Jamesian items of high civilization, but they found new excitement in the immense energy of the industrial society and their imaginations were set fire by it. Unlike the partisans of laissez-faire, the novelists did not defend the predatory aspect of the new society, but they were nonetheless fascinated by it. It stimulated them as it did the pragmatic philosophers, the institutional economists, the realistic lawyers, the new historians, and the sociologists and social workers who turned their sympathetic attention to the problems of a new urban world. It was the era of the revolt against formalism — of realism and naturalism in the novel, of pragmatism in philosophy, of practicality in science, of opposition to scholasticism in jurisprudence and the social sciences. The age's preoccupation with practical achievement afforded a climate more hospitable to the scientific technologist than to the scientific theorist; in philosophy it encouraged the pragmatists to reflect more seriously than Western philosophers ever had before on the relations between scientific theory and experimental practice. Universities and colleges were brought into closer contact with a society that was becoming more and more secularized. John Dewey urged that the education of the young be transformed as radically as social life itself had been transformed at the end of the nineteenth century. By the end of the First World War the liberal philosophy of society and social science had emerged as the typical expression of the American intellect at its best, unified within itself and in touch with reality.

IV

As we come to the present era, the lack of perspective makes it of course more difficult to fix the outlines. But having made this disclaimer we may say that whereas the American intellectual of the middle period of the twentieth century remains in touch with the realities of contemporary life, it is not easy to discover a unifying doctrinal theme in his response to it. A depression and two world wars diminished his confidence in the more optimistic messages of the earlier liberalism, and his brief encounter with Marxism left him hostile to totalitarian pretensions. The result may be a greater degree of toughness and heightened respect for technical expertise, but a failure to converge on a set of substantive principles comparable to those that guided the Founding Fathers, or to those that united Progressive politics and Progressive scholarship in the first half of the century.

Quite apart from whether one approves of it or not, one must acknowledge the presence of a principled aversion — outrunning even that of the philosophical pragmatists — to the formulation of general principles, an incapacity to put down in any simple formulae the aspirations and philosophy of the age, and a cautious skepticism that keeps today's intellectual from being lured into facile generalizations or towering systems built on quicksand. The three most admired literary figures between the two wars — Faulkner, Fitzgerald, and Hemingway — were, we are told, more in search of a moral style than of a moral system to replace what they saw pulled down in the First World War. From the thirties onward, the metaphysical urge was in great measure suppressed by philosophers as the methods of logical positivism and linguistic analysis superseded the more relaxed, more embracing reflections of the early pragmatists. In sociology, statisticians of market research and voting behavior gradually replaced the older, more philosophical sociologists. In foreign policy theory lagged cautiously behind the event.

Throughout American intellectual life today one detects not only a mystique of technique and toughness, but also a lack of any overarching world-view, moral philosophy, or political theory which may be said to embrace and articulate America's convictions on basic questions. Whether this is good or bad is a question that transcends history; it is a question on which serious and honest thinkers may differ. For some it is a sign of moral weakness, of a lack of intellectual originality, or of enervating agnosticism. For others the shunning of metaphysics and ideology represents the height of mature wisdom, a refusal to be trapped by a rigid system in an age that is more complicated, more dynamic, and more in need of intellectual resilience than any of its predecessors.

In any case, the adventure of American thought is still incomplete. In the three and a half centuries in which Western culture has existed in what is now the United States, the American mind has undergone a succession of moods and experiences. Along the way, if it has produced few major ideas, it has been shaped and stimulated by a number of vivid, arresting, and fertile thinkers; and it has accomplished with notable success — saving always the Civil War — the adjustment of the national society to changing economic and moral circumstances. As the world shrinks and the issues of life grow more complex, the demands on American thought become more urgent and intricate. Whatever the future, the past contains significant intellectual resources by which the nation has lived. We hope that the essays which follow will convey some impression of the abundance, diversity, and penetration of the life of the American mind.

PART ONE

Before Independence: The Colonial Phase

I

The American Revolution Considered as an Intellectual Movement

Edmund S. Morgan

In 1740 America's leading intellectuals were clergymen and thought about theology; in 1790 they were statesmen and thought about politics. A variety of forces, some of them reaching deep into the colonial past, helped to bring about the transformation, but it was so closely associated with the revolt from England that one may properly consider the American Revolution, as an intellectual movement, to mean the substitution of political for clerical leadership and of politics for religion as the most challenging area of human thought and endeavor.

The American colonies had been founded during the seventeenth century, when Englishmen were still animated by the great vision of John Calvin, the vision of human depravity and divine perfection. Every human being from Adam onward must be counted, Calvin insisted, in the ranks of "those whose feet are swift to shed blood, whose hands are polluted with rapine and murder, whose throats are like open sepulchres, whose tongues are deceitful, whose lips are envenomed, whose works are useless, iniquitous, corrupt, and deadly, whose souls are estranged from God, the inmost recesses of whose hearts are full of pravity, whose eyes are insidiously employed, whose minds are elated with insolence — in a word, all whose powers are prepared for the commission of atrocious and innumerable crimes." If a man did not actually commit such crimes, it was not for want of a desire to. God might furnish restraints of one sort or another to prevent "the perverseness of our nature from breaking out into external acts, but does not purify it within."[1]

The official church of England, born of a licentious monarch's divorce, had never fully shared in Calvin's vision. Though it absorbed much of his theology during the reign of Queen Elizabeth I, it retained a more flattering view than his of human capacities and priestly powers. The more thoroughgoing English Calvinists, the Puritans, were hopeful of effecting further reforms, but during the late 1620's and 1630's the Church and the king who headed it drew ever closer to old Roman Catholic doctrines. In the 1640's the Puritans resorted to arms, killed the king, purged the Church, and turned England into a republic. But in 1660 the monarchy was restored. Puritans, now called dissenters, were dismissed from office in both church and state; and the Church of England resumed its old ways, unimpeded by Calvinism.

It is no coincidence that England's American colonies were settled before 1640 or after 1660. Emigration offered a substitute for revolution to thousands of men and women who were discontented with the Church of England and with the government that fostered it. Puritans settled all the New England colonies, overran the Catholic refuge of the Calvert family in Maryland, and later furnished substantial numbers of settlers to New York, New Jersey, and the Carolinas. They came even to Virginia, where the majority of settlers, though remaining within the Church of England, did not share in its high-church movement. After the Restoration, the colonies attracted large numbers of English Quakers and Scotch-Irish Presbyterians, not to mention French Huguenots and German Protestants of various denominations. Anglicans came too, and the Anglican Church was supported by law in several colonies, but the flavor of American colonial life was overwhelmingly that of the Reformation.[2]

The intellectual center of the colonies was New England, and the intellectual leaders of New England were the clergy, who preached and wrote indefatigably of human depravity and divine perfection. These two axioms, for the Puritans as for Calvin himself, required the eternal damnation of most of mankind. And since God knew all and decreed all from eternity, it followed that He had determined in advance who should be damned and who should be saved. One of the principal tasks of the ministry was to explain to men how bad they were, so bad that they all deserved damnation. That God had chosen to save any was simply through mercy, another attribute of His perfection. No man deserved salvation, no one was less guilty than another, so that God's choice rested only in Himself.

To explain these doctrines was the easiest part of the preacher's task, for most of his audience were already persuaded of them. A more difficult assignment was to assist men in discerning where they stood in the divine scheme. No man could be certain whether he was saved until the day of judgment, but there were stages in the process of redemption that took place in this life; and ministers devoted much of their preaching and writing to descriptions of them. One of the first stages was conviction, a full recognition of man's helpless and hopeless condition. A man destined for damnation could reach this stage, but not the next one, conversion. Conversion was an act of God, infusing a man's soul with the Holy Spirit, "justifying" him through the attribution of Christ's merits. Conversion, for the Puritan, was so clear and precise an experience that a man who had undergone it could often specify the time and place. After conversion came sanctification, a gradual improvement in conduct, approximating, though only outwardly, the obedience which God had demanded of Adam. Sanctification could never be complete in this world, but it might be sufficiently marked to be discernible. Guided by the clergy, Puritans and other Calvinist Protestants became familiar with the morphology of redemption and expert in searching their own souls for signs of metamorphosis.

Just as the Puritans' theology revolved around human depravity and divine perfection, so did their political theory. And Puritan ministers instructed their congregations in politics as well as religion. They taught that society originates in a contract between God on the one hand and the people on the other, whereby if the people agreed to abide by His commands (though again, only outwardly, for true, inner obedience was beyond them) He would assure them outward prosperity. Having made such an agreement, the people, in another compact, voluntarily subjected themselves to a king or to other civil rulers. This was the origin of government; and the purpose of government was to restrain the sinfulness of man, to prevent and punish offenses against God. As long as a king enforced God's commands, embodying them in human laws, the people owed him obedience and assistance. If, however, moved by his own depravity, he violated God's commands or failed to enforce them, he broke the compact on which his political authority rested, and it was the people's duty to remove him lest God visit the whole community with death and destruction.[3]

These ideas had developed in England at a time when reigning monarchs exhibited (by Puritan standards) far too much depravity. Three generations of Puritans nervously scolded their kings and queens and momentarily expected God's wrath to descend on England. Finally, in 1649, they did away with both king and kingship. But even after monarchy ended, human depravity remained, and Englishmen faced the problem of controlling it in the new context of a republic. Ideas about the maintenance of purity, probity, and stability in a republic were offered by a number of men, the most influential of whom was James Harrington. In his *Oceana* (1656) Harrington associated republican government with widespread distribution — approaching equality — of property. He also advocated religious toleration, rotation in public office, and separation of governmental powers. With the restoration of the monarchy, Harrington's work continued for several generations to excite the admiration of a small group of British political thinkers, who probed the nature of government and speculated about methods of keeping it responsible to the people.[4] The best known of them, John Locke, reemphasized the idea of a compact between rulers and people in order to justify the exclusion of James II from the throne.[5]

The English republican writers were read in the colonies, and Locke's political doctrines were assimilated by American clergymen and dispensed in their sermons along with the older ideas. Every generation learned of its duty to pull down bad rulers and to uphold good ones. The colonists did not, however, develop a separate school of republican political theory. The clergy, who continued to be the principal exponents of political ideas and the most influential members of the community, devoted their creative intellectual efforts to theology, and their congregations continued to search souls. Every Sunday they attended at the meetinghouse morning and afternoon to hear the theological expositions that were always the principal ingredient in a Puritan church service. Then they went home to write in their diaries and measure their lives against what they had learned in the sermons. Daily they read their Bibles and prayed, in private and with their families. Theology was as much a part of their lives as meat and drink.

By the middle of the eighteenth century, however, a change had begun. A series of developments, culminating in the Revolution, combined to effect a weakening of popular interest in theology and a decline in clerical leadership.

The first development, and the most difficult to assess, was the growth in England and Europe, transmitted gradually to America, of a new confidence in human reason. The achievements of Sir Isaac Newton and of other seventeenth-century astronomers and mathematicians belied the low estimate hitherto entertained of man's capacity to understand, without the assistance of divine revelation, God's government of the universe. The Enlightenment, as the new attitude came to be called, promised to reveal the mysteries of creation simply through the application of human intelligence.

New England ministers at first perceived no threat to religion from the Enlightenment. Although they thought poorly of human reason, they were themselves assiduous in making the most of it. They had applied it primarily to the Bible, but they now welcomed every new piece of observational knowledge in the assurance that it would help to fill out the data derived from the Bible. With the success of Newton to spur them, they began to pay more attention to the physical world and made observations of plants and animals, of comets and stars; and they sent these observations to England to assist the progress of knowledge about God's wonderful universe.

It became apparent only gradually — first in England, then in America — that reason, instead of assisting revelation, might replace it. Though Newton himself retained a firm belief in the Scriptures and spent his later years unraveling Biblical prophecies, many of his admirers became deists, who believed that God reveals Himself only through the operation of His universe and not through prophets, priests, or holy scriptures. In America deism claimed few adherents before the last quarter of the eighteenth century; and it seems probable that the Enlightenment appreciably lowered the prestige of the clergy only after they had already lost much of their influence through the paradoxical operation of a religious revival.

The Great Awakening of the 1740's began when a young English minister, George Whitefield, showed American preachers how to convey the full meaning of human depravity. Traveling throughout the colonies, he preached wherever he could find an audience, whether inside a church or under a tree, and everywhere his message was the same: men deserve hell. Whitefield's talent lay in depicting the torments of hell dramatically and vividly. He could weep at will, over the fate of the men and women before him; he could impersonate God delivering the awful sentence against them. When he wept they did too, and when he pronounced the sentence against them, they fell to the ground in agony.[6]

Whitefield had already earned some notoriety by these methods before crossing the ocean. In the colonies his success was overwhelming. People flocked to him as to a new messiah. Though Anglicans remained largely unmoved, most Americans had been brought up on the doctrine of the depravity of man, and they could not find any expression of it too strong. Whitefield merely brought them a new and more emotional appreciation of truths they had known all along. Other preachers quickly imitated his methods and outdid him in the extravagance of their gestures. Gilbert Tennent of Pennsylvania made a specialty of roaring with holy laughter at sinners whom he had awakened to their helpless condition. James Davenport of Long Island liked to preach at night, when smoking candles and torches gave verisimilitude to his fiery denunciations.[7] These self-appointed apostles and dozens more like them imitated Whitefield not only in their manner of preaching but in wandering from place to place to deliver their fearful message.

Terror was the object; and terror was right. If a man faces eternal, unbearable pain, deserves it, and can do nothing to avoid it, he ought to be terrified. The preachers had another word for it, familiar to all Calvinists: they called it conviction, the awareness, denied to the complacent, of one's hopeless condition. The great thing about the new preaching was that it destroyed complacency and brought conviction to thousands. And the great thing about conviction was that conversion could be expected in many cases to follow it. Calvinist ministers for two centuries had described the divine process, and in the Great Awakening the course of conviction and conversion ran true to form. Not everyone who trembled in terror rose to the joy of conversion, but hundreds did.

As the churches filled with them, it seemed apparent that God approved the new method of preaching and the men who practiced it. Whether He also approved the older methods was questionable. Men and women who had worshiped for years without result under the guidance of an erudite but undramatic minister, found grace after a few hours at the feet of some wandering apostle. The itinerant was often a layman who had never been to college and knew no Greek, Latin, or Hebrew, but had a way with an audience. If God selected him to do so much without learning, was learning perhaps more a hindrance than a help to true religion? The thought occurred to many converts and was encouraged by the increasingly confident, not to say arrogant, posture of the itinerants. Whitefield had warned broadly against ministers who preached an unknown and unfelt Christ. His followers did not hesitate to name individual ministers as dead of heart, blind leaders of the blind.

After such a pronouncement, a congregation, or a substantial portion of it, might desert their old minister. If they were a majority, they could dismiss him; if a minority, they might secede to form a church of their own, with some newly discovered prophet to lead them. Congregations had left their ministers before, especially in New England, but never before had the desertions been so many or so bitter.

At first the deserted clergymen merely looked upon the Awakening with skepticism. But as its exponents (known to the time as New Lights) became more and more extravagant, skepticism spread and grew to hostility. Ministers who had spent their lives in the study of theology and who had perhaps been touched by the Enlightenment, were appalled at the ignorance of New Light preachers and dismissed their convictions and conversions as hysteria. Many of these opposers (Old Lights), though reluctant to recognize the fact, were already several steps down the road that led to Arminianism, Universalism, Unitarianism, and deism. The most outspoken of them, Charles Chauncy, eventually became a Universalist. But most of them pulled up short of these extremes, and those who went the whole way found few followers. The majority, clinging to the old doctrines of Calvinism, mitigated in some measure by the Enlightenment, were a humane and pious group, perhaps the most likeable of New England clergymen. Some of them retained or rewon the loyalty of large congregations. But they never regained the broad influence they had enjoyed over the colonial community before the Great Awakening.

The failure of the Old Light clergy to retain intellectual leadership was due partly to the fact that they failed to win the minds of the next generation of ministers. The New Lights, in spite of their ignorance, enjoyed the blessing of Jonathan Edwards, America's foremost intellectual. It was inevitable that bright young divinity students should follow his lead. Edwards, the most brilliant theologian the country ever produced, had already generated a minor awakening of his own at Northampton, Massachusetts, six years before the Great Awakening. By comparison with Whitefield his technique was muted: he talked almost in a monotone, and never resorted to dramatic gestures, but when he spoke of eternal torments in as matter-of-fact a manner as he spoke of the weather, the effect on a New England audience could be devastating. Observing the beneficial effects of terror, Edwards applauded when Whitefield and Tennent brought the fires of hell to New England.

In ensuing years Edwards wrote a series of treatises to demonstrate the importance of the emotions or "affections" in religion and to affirm, more rigorously than ever before in New England, the dogmas of divine perfection and human depravity. By the time he died in 1758, he had gathered a tight band of followers, who continued his doctrines and developed them into a theological system known as the New Divinity.[8] The high priest of the movement was Samuel Hopkins, who preached at Great Barrington, Massachusetts, and later at Newport, Rhode Island. Other leading figures were Edwards's son, Jonathan Jr., of New Haven, and Joseph Bellamy, who from the small village of Bethlehem, Connecticut, earned the title of pope of Litchfield County.

New Divinity men were often rough and domineering with their congregations, exploding in angry denunciations; and their doctrines matched their manners. It was wrong, they said, for the unregenerate to pray, since an unregenerate man, lacking real love for God, could not pray without hypocrisy and would anger God further by his futile efforts. The only way in which the unregenerate could contribute to the glory of God was to rejoice in their own damnation — an attitude which their very unregeneracy made improbable. The New Divinity also called for a restoration of the standards of church membership that had prevailed in New England before the Half-Way Covenant of 1662: a man could join the church only if he demonstrated to the satisfaction of the other members that God had predestined him to eternal salvation. Only such persons were entitled to take communion or to have their children baptized. The remainder of the community could only listen to the minister's preaching, in hopes that God would use this means to achieve a salvation already determined though as yet undisclosed.

The New Divinity had a consistency and rigor that young intellectuals found challenging. It was the fashionable, avant-garde movement of the seventeen-fifties, sixties, seventies, and to some extent the eighties. During these years many young men had already begun to find politics or the law more satisfying intellectually than religion, but insofar as religion continued to draw young minds, they gravitated to men like Bellamy and Hopkins for guidance. As a result, by 1792 the New Divinity claimed half the pulpits in Connecticut (and an increasing number in the rest of New England), together with virtually all the candidates for the ministry — this on the testimony of Ezra Stiles, president of Yale from 1778 to 1795, who despised the New Divinity and lamented its attraction for the young men he had educated.[9]

But the success of the New Divinity among the rising generation of clergy was not matched among the people at large. Its harsh doctrines could be sustained only by intellectual or religious fervor, and the religious fervor of Americans was already waning before the complexities of the system had been completely worked out. Even as Jonathan Edwards turned out his massive justifications of the Great Awakening, that movement subsided in the manner of later religious revivals. By the time Edwards had devised an intellectual foundation for emotionalism in religion, he had begun to lose his popular audience. When he announced that he would apply new standards of church membership, excluding all but the demonstrably regenerate from the sacraments, his church at Northampton dismissed him. America's greatest intellectual of his time spent most of his later years preaching, for want of a wider audience, to the Indians, who perhaps least of any group in America could understand him.

The careers of Edwards's disciples were somewhat more fortunate but not dissimilar. Samuel Hopkins, ministering to a large congregation at Great Barrington, saw it dwindle away until he was obliged to leave. At Newport, Rhode Island, he found another large congregation and again watched it decline. The history of New Haven's Second Church, formed during the Great Awakening by a seceding New Light minority from New Haven's First Church, reveals the same development. The new church prospered under the ministry of the Reverend Samuel Bird. But after Jonathan Edwards, Jr., took charge in 1769 and the relative simplicity of New Light gave way to the complexities of New Divinity, the congregation diminished until by 1795 there were not enough left or willing to support him.[10]

Hopkins and Jonathan Edwards, Jr., enjoyed the admiration of their ministerial colleagues, as did many other fearlessly consistent theologians of the New Divinity, but few of them could retain a popular following. Even while they justified emotionalism in religion, their sermons became complex, abstruse, metaphysical, devoted to details of theology that the layman found incomprehensible. During a revival of religion, their arid doctrines might still send shudders of horror through a receptive audience, but most of the time their congregations found them simply dull.

Their fault lay in addressing themselves more to each other than to their people. Engrossed in the details of their system, they delighted in exploring new elements of consistency in it and neglected the central problems of Christianity, until they scarcely knew how to deal with the elementary questions of salvation that their people put to them. Nowhere is the paradox of the New Divinity's intellectual success and popular failure more graphically demonstrated than in a letter from a young minister to his mentor. Medad Rogers, after graduating from Yale in 1777, had studied theology with Benjamin Trumbull, the New Divinity minister of North Haven. When Rogers began to preach, he discovered for the first time that he did not know the answers to the questions that Christians have always had to wrestle with.

"Sir," he wrote to Trumbull,

if you do not think I deserve more reproof than direction, some of your kind instructions, would be most timely to me — as also some directions how we should begin, spend, and end the day — What to say to those under concern for a future existence, when they enquire how they shall come to the foot of a sovereign God. They try to, but cannot. They would bow to Christ's sceptre but are not able. How are we to blame, say they? We would be saved but can't be saved. How are such to be dealt with? As also, if God hath decreed all things, why is he not the Author of sin? How can any man do otherwise than he does? If God hath elected a particular number, what is there for the others to do? Why had we not Just as good lie still and do nothing? Where is the criminality of their conduct in not embracing the Gospel offers, when they were not elected? What Justice, say they, in punishing those who miss of Salvation, for not accepting the offer, when they were not elected to it? Is not God partial? If we are to be saved we shall, if not we shall be cast away. Then, what good do our works do? Will persons who lived morally honest lives, have any respect shown them upon that account, in the day of Judgment, if they appear on the left hand of the Judge? Sir, if you could find yourself willing and at leasure Just to touch upon some, or all of these, you would do me a very great favour, and perhaps be a greater monument of glory to you, Kind sir, at last, than if you had written an hundred thousand volumes of Phylosophy, Rhetorick, Logick, and History.[11]

Trumbull's answer to Rogers is not preserved. But the very fact that a young minister should ask such questions speaks volumes about the state of religion in New England. The clergy for the first time in their history had lost contact with the people. In the seventeenth century when Roger Williams debated fine points of theology with John Cotton, or Increase Mather with Solomon Stoddard, people had not been bored. But the New Divinity ministers were unable to carry their congregations with them.

In earlier decades when a people became disgruntled with their minister, they had replaced him. But the American population had increased so rapidly that there were not enough ministers to go around; and since the New Divinity claimed such a large percentage of ministerial candidates, congregations were regularly faced with the necessity of taking a New Divinity man or leaving their pulpit vacant. The resultant discontent contributed in the last quarter of the eighteenth century to the rapid growth of

Anglicanism, Methodism, deism, and what people at the time called "nothingarianism," a total indifference to religion. The clergy, once the most respected members of the community, became the objects of ridicule and contempt, especially in Connecticut, the stronghold of the New Divinity. In 1788, when the ministers of the state published a rebuke to the people for their neglect of public worship, the newspapers carried some rude answers. "We have heard your animadversions," said one, "upon our absence from Sabbath meetings, and humbly conceive if you wish our attendance there, you would make it worth our while to give it. To miss a sermon of the present growth, what is it but to miss of an opiate? And can the loss of a nap expose our souls to eternal perdition?"[12]

Such indifference to religion, edged with hostility to the clergy, was the end product of the developments we have been tracing from the 1740's. But though the clergy could blame themselves for much of their loss of prestige and for much of the decline of popular interest in religion, it was Parliament's attempt to tax the colonists in the 1760's that caused Americans to transfer to politics the intellectual interest and energy that were once reserved for religion. This reorientation was directed partly by the clergy themselves. They had never stopped giving instruction in political thought; and (except for the Anglicans) throughout the 1760's and 1770's they publicly and passionately scored the actions of George III and his Parliament against the standards by which their English Puritan predecessors had judged and condemned Charles I.

Presbyterian and Congregational ministers also raised the alarm when a movement was set afoot for the establishment in the colonies of state-supported bishops. The American clergymen developed no new general ideas about government — there was no New Light in political thought, no New Politics to match the New Divinity — but the old ideas and those imported from English political theorists served well enough to impress upon their congregations the tyrannical nature of taxation without representation, and of bishops who might establish ecclesiastical courts with jurisdiction extending beyond their own denomination.

Although the clergy were a powerful influence in molding American political opinion during the Revolutionary period, they did not recover through politics the intellectual leadership they had already begun to lose. Their own principles barred them from an active role in politics. While they had always given political advice freely and exercised their influence in elections, most of them would have considered it wrong to sit in a representative assembly, on a governor's council, or on the bench. To them as to their Puritan ancestors the clerical exercise of temporal powers spelled Rome. A minister's business was, after all, the saving of souls. By the same token, however outraged he might be by the actions of the English government, however excited by the achievement of American independence, a minister could not devote his principal intellectual effort to the expounding of political ideas and political principles. As the quarrel with England developed and turned into a struggle for independence and nationhood, though the ministers continued to speak up on the American side, other voices commanding greater attention were raised by men who were free to make a career of politics and prepared to act as well as talk.

There had always, of course, been political leaders in the colonies, but hitherto politics had been a local affair, requiring at most the kind of talents needed for collecting votes or pulling wires. A colonial legislative assembly might occasionally engage in debates about paper money, defense, or modes of taxation; but the issues did not reach beyond the borders of the colony involved and were seldom of a kind to challenge a superior mind. No American debated imperial policy in the British Parliament, the Privy Council, or the Board of Trade. The highest political post to which a man could aspire in the colonies was that of governor, and everywhere except in Connecticut and Rhode Island, this was obtained not through political success but through having friends in England. Few native Americans ever achieved it or even tried to.

But the advent of Parliamentary taxation inaugurated a quarter-century of political discussion in America that has never since been matched in intensity. With the passage of the Stamp Act in 1765, every colonial legislature took up the task of defining the structure of the British empire; and as colonial definitions met with resistance from England, as the colonies banded together for defense and declared their independence, politics posed continental, even global, problems that called forth the best efforts of the best American minds. In no other period of our history would it be possible to find in politics five men of such intellectual stature as Benjamin Franklin, John Adams, Alexander Hamilton, James Madison, and

Thomas Jefferson; and there were others only slightly less distinguished.

Whether they hailed from Pennsylvania or Virginia, New England or New York, the men who steered Americans through the Revolution, the establishment of a new nation, and the framing of the Constitution did not for the most part repudiate the political ideas inherited from the period of clerical dominance. Like the clergy, they started from a conviction of human depravity; like the clergy, they saw government originating in compact, and measured governmental performance against an absolute standard ordained by God. Like the clergy too, they found inspiration in the example of seventeenth-century Englishmen. Sometimes they signed their own attacks on George III or his ministers with the names of John Hampden, William Pym, or other Parliamentary heroes in the struggle against Charles I. They read the works of Harrington and of Harrington's later admirers; and after the Declaration of Independence, when they found themselves in a position similar to that of England in the 1650's, they drew heavily on the arsenal of political ideas furnished by these latter-day republicans.

Indeed, most of the ideas about government which American intellectuals employed first in their resistance to Parliament, and then in constructing their own governments, had been articulated earlier in England and were still in limited circulation there. The social compact, fundamental law, the separation of powers, human equality, religious freedom, and the superiority of republican government were continuing ideals for a small but ardent group of Englishmen who, like the Americans, believed that the British constitution was basically republican and drew inspiration from it while attacking the ministers and monarch who seemed to be betraying it.[13] It is perhaps no accident that the work in which Americans first repudiated monarchy, *Common Sense*, was written by an Englishman, Thomas Paine, who had come to America only two years before.

But if Englishmen supplied the intellectual foundations both for the overthrow of English rule and for the construction of republican government, Americans put the ideas into practice and drew on American experience and tradition to devise refinements and applications of the greatest importance. That republican ideas, which existed in a state of obscurity in England, should be congenial in the colonies, was due in the first place to the strong continuing

Calvinist tradition which had been nourished over the years by the American clergy. But fully as important was the fact that during a hundred and fifty years of living in the freedom of a relatively isolated and empty continent, the colonists had developed a way of life in which republican ideas played a visible part. When Parliamentary taxation set Americans to analyzing their relationship to the mother country, they could not escape seeing that the social, economic, and political configuration of America had diverged from that of England in ways that made Americans better off than Englishmen. And the things that made them better off could be labeled republican.

England's practical experience with republicanism had lasted only eleven years. With the return of Charles II in 1660, Englishmen repudiated their republic and the Puritans who had sponsored it. Though a small minority continued to write and talk about republicanism and responsible government, they wielded no authority. The House of Commons grew more powerful but less common, and the main current of English national life flowed in the channels of monarchy, aristocracy, and special privilege. Americans, by contrast, though formally subjects of the king, had lived long under conditions that approximated the ideals of the English republican theorists. Harrington thought he had found in the England of his day the widespread ownership of property that seemed to him a necessary condition for republican government; but throughout the colonies ownership of property had always been more widespread than in England. Furthermore no member of the nobility had settled in America, so that people were accustomed to a greater degree of social as well as economic equality than existed anywhere in England.

During the 1640's and 1650's England had seen a rapid multiplication of religious sects, which produced a wide belief in religious freedom, but after the Anglican Church had reimposed its controls in the 1660's, the most that other denominations could hope for was toleration. In America, religious diversity had steadily increased, and with it came a religious freedom which, if still imperfect, surpassed anything England had ever known.

Though the English people had twice removed an unsatisfactory king, in 1649 and in 1688, the English government remained far less responsible and far less responsive to the people than any colonial government. While the members of Parliament disclaimed any obligation to their immediate constituents, the members of American representative assemblies knew that they were expected to look after the interests of the people who elected them. Nor were the voters in America only a small minority of the population as in England. In most colonies probably the great majority of adult males owned enough property to meet the qualification (which varied from colony to colony) for voting. In England, the government paid hundreds of office-holders whose offices, carrying no duties, existed solely for the enrichment of those who held them. In the colonies such sinecures were few. Americans thought that government existed to do a job, and they created no offices except for useful purposes.

Thus when the quarrel with Parliament began, the colonists already had what English reformers wanted. And the colonists were inclined to credit their good fortune not to the accident of geography but to their own superior virtue and political sophistication. The interpretation was not without foundation: since Calvinist traditions were still strong among them and since they had often learned of British republican ideas through the sermons of Calvinist clergymen, Americans retained what the Enlightenment had dimmed in England and Europe, a keen sense of human depravity and of the dangers it posed for government. Although their own governments had hitherto given little evidence of depravity, by comparison with those of Europe, they were expert at detecting it in any degree. They had always been horrified by the open corruption of British politics and feared it would lead to tyranny. When Parliament attempted to tax them and sent swarms of customs collectors, sailors, and soldiers to support the attempt, their fears were confirmed. In resisting the British and in forming their own governments, they saw the central problem as one of devising means to check the inevitable operation of depravity in men who wielded power. English statesmen had succumbed to it. How could Americans avoid their mistakes?

In the era of the American Revolution, from 1764 to 1789, this was the great intellectual challenge. Although human depravity continued to pose as difficult theological problems as ever, the best minds of the period addressed themselves to the rescue, not of souls, but of governments, from the perils of corruption. Of course the problem was not new, nor any more susceptible of final solution than it had been in an earlier time, but Americans in the Revolutionary period contributed three notable principles to men's efforts to deal with it.

The first principle, which evolved from the struggle with Parliament, was that the people of one region ought not to exercise dominion over those of another, even though the two may be joined together. It was an idea that overlapped and greatly facilitated the slower but parallel development of the more general belief in human equality. In objecting to British taxation in 1764 the colonists had begun by asserting their right to equal treatment with the king's subjects in Great Britain: Englishmen could not be taxed except by their representatives; neither therefore could Americans. Within a year or two the idea was extended to a denial that Parliament, representing the electors of Great Britain, could exercise any authority over the colonies. The empire, according to one American writer, was "a confederacy of states, independent of each other, yet united under one head," namely the king. "I cannot find," said another, "that the inhabitants of the colonies are dependent on the people of Britain, or the people of Britain on them, any more than Kent is on Sussex, or Sussex on Kent."[14]

It took varying lengths of time for other Americans to reach the position thus anonymously expressed in the press in 1765 and 1766. Franklin stated it later in 1766;[15] Jefferson, James Wilson, and John Adams had all expressed it by the beginning of 1775.[16] It was frequently buttressed by the citation of precedents from English constitutional history, but it rested on a principle capable of universal application, the principle stated in the preamble of the Declaration of Independence, that every people is entitled, by the laws of nature and of nature's God, to a separate and equal station.

Before Independence this principle offered a means of reorganizing the British empire so as to defeat the tyranny which Americans thought English statesmen were developing in the extension of taxation. If a British legislature, in which the colonists were not represented, could govern them, then neither British nor colonial freedom could be safe. Americans without a voice in the government could not defend their rights against corrupt rulers. Englishmen, relieved of expenses by American taxation, might rejoice for the moment, but their rulers, no longer dependent on them financially, would be able to govern as they pleased and would eventually escape popular control altogether. The only solution was to give each legislature power only over the people who chose it.

In the 1770's England was unwilling to listen to the colonial arguments, but ultimately adopted the American principle in forming the Commonwealth of Nations. The independent United States applied the principle not only in the confederation of states but in the annexation of other areas. When Virginia in 1781 offered the United States Congress her superior claim to the old Northwest, it was with the stipulation that the region be divided into separate republican states, each of which was to be admitted to the Union on equal terms with the old ones. The stipulation, though not accepted by Congress at the time, was carried out in Jefferson's land ordinance of 1784 and in the Northwest Ordinance of 1787 which superseded it. The United States never wavered from the principle until after the Spanish-American War, when it temporarily accepted government of areas which it had no intention of admitting to the union on equal terms.

The second contribution of the American Revolutionists was an application of the assumption, implicit in the whole idea of a compact between rulers and people, that a people can exist as a people before they have a government and that they can act as a people independently of government. The Puritans had distinguished between the compact of a group of individuals with God, by which they became a people, and the subsequent compact between this people and their rulers, by which government was created. John Locke had similarly distinguished between the dissolution of society and of government, and so, at least tacitly, had the Revolutionists. They would have been more daring, not to say foolhardy, if they had undertaken to destroy the bonds of society as well as of government. But in their haste to form new governments after the royal government in each colony dissolved, the Revolutionists followed a procedure that did not clearly distinguish the people from the government. Provincial congresses, exercising a *de facto* power, drafted and adopted permanent constitutions, which in most cases then went into effect without submission to a popular vote.

When the Massachusetts provincial congress proposed to follow this procedure in 1776, the citizens of the town of Concord pointed out the dangerous opening which it offered to human depravity. A *de facto* government that legitimized itself could also alter itself.

Whatever safeguards it adopted against corruption could easily be discarded by later legislators: "a Constitution alterable by the Supreme Legislative is no Security at all to the Subject against any Encroachment of the Governing part on any or on all of their Rights and priviliges." The town therefore suggested that a special popularly elected convention be called for the sole purpose of drafting a constitution, which should then be submitted to the people for approval.[17]

It is impossible to determine who was responsible for Concord's action, but the protest displays a refinement in the application of republican ideas that does not appear to have been expressed before. Concord's suggestion was eventually followed in the drafting and adoption of the Massachusetts constitution of 1780 and of every subsequent constitution established in the United States. By it the subservience of government to the people was secured through a constitution clearly superior to the government it created, a constitution against which the people could measure governmental performance and against which each branch of government could measure the actions of the other branches. The separation of governmental powers into a bicameral legislature, an executive, and a judiciary, which was an older and more familiar way of checking depravity, was rendered far more effective by the existence of a written constitution resting directly on popular approval. The written constitution also proved its effectiveness in later years by perpetuating in America the operation of judicial review, of executive veto, and of a powerful upper house of the legislature, all of which had been or would be lost in England, where the constitution was unwritten and consisted of customary procedures that could be altered at will by Parliament.

Thus by the time the Revolution ended, Americans had devised a way to establish the superiority of the people to their government and so to control man's tyranny over man. For the same purpose Americans had formulated the principle that no people should exercise dominion over another people. But the way in which they first employed the latter principle in running the new nation did not prove satisfactory. As thirteen separate colonies the people of America had joined to combat Parliamentary taxation, and the result had been thirteen independent republics. It had been an exhilarating experience, and it had led them almost from the beginning to think of themselves in some degree as one people. But the thought was not completed: they did not coalesce into one republic with one government. Instead, as thirteen separate and equal peoples, they set up a "perpetual union" in which they were joined only through a Congress in which each state had one vote. They gave the Congress responsibility for their common concerns. But they did not give it the ordinary powers of a government to tax or legislate.

Because of the straightforward equality of the member states and because the Congress did not possess the means by which governments generally ran to tyranny, the confederation seemed a safe shape in which to cast the new nation. Actually danger lurked in the fact that the Congress had insufficient power to carry out the responsibilities which the states assigned to it. After the British troops were defeated and the need for united action became less obvious, state support of the Congress steadily declined. Without coercive powers, the Congress could not act effectively either at home or abroad, and the nation was increasingly exposed to the danger of foreign depredations. At the same time, the state governments were proving vulnerable to manipulation by corrupt or ambitious politicians and were growing powerful at the expense not only of the Congress but of the people. Some undertook irresponsible inflationary measures that threatened property rights. Unless the state governments were brought under more effective control, local demagogues might destroy the union and replace the tyranny of Parliament with a new domestic brand.

Although a few men foresaw the drawbacks of a weak Congress from the beginning, most people needed time to show them. The Massachusetts legislature, perceiving that the experience of the state could be applied to the whole United States, in 1785 suggested a national constitutional convention to create a central authority capable of acting effectively in the interests of the whole American people. But in 1785, Americans were not yet convinced that what they had was inadequate. The Massachusetts delegates to the Congress replied to their state's suggestion with the same arguments that had in the first place prompted Americans to base their union on a weak coordinative Congress rather than a real national government: it would be impossible, they said, to prevent such a government from escaping popular control. With headquarters remote from most of its constituents, with only a select few from each state engaged in it, a national government would offer too many opportunities for corruption.[18] The fear was supported by the views of respected European political thinkers. Montesquieu, who had been widely read in America, maintained that republican government was suited only to small areas. A confederation of republics might extend far, but a single republican government of large extent would either fall a prey to the ambitions of a few corrupt individuals, or else it would break up into a number of smaller states.[19]

These sentiments were so widely held that they prevented any effort to establish a national government until 1787. And when a convention was finally called in that year it was charged, not to create a new government, but simply to revise the Articles of Confederation. The members of the convention, without authorization, assumed the larger task and turned themselves into a national Constitutional Convention. They did so because they became convinced that, contrary to popular belief, a large republic would not necessarily succumb to corruption. The man who persuaded the Convention, insofar as any one man did it, was James Madison, one of the delegates from Virginia.

In the month before the Convention assembled, Madison had drawn up some observations on the "Vices of the Political System of the United States." Following a hint thrown out by David Hume, he reached the conclusion that "the inconveniencies of popular States contrary to the prevailing Theory, are in proportion not to the extent, but to the narrowness of their limits." In the state governments that had operated since 1776, the great defect was a tendency of the majority to tyrannize over the minority. Madison took it as axiomatic that "in republican Government the majority however composed, ultimately give the law." Unless a way could be found to control them, the majority would inevitably oppress the minority, because the individuals who made up the majority were as susceptible as any king or lord to the operation of human depravity. The most effective curb, Madison suggested, was to make the territory of the republic so large that a majority would have difficulty forming. Men being hopelessly selfish would inevitably seek to capture the government for selfish purposes, and in a small republic they might easily form combinations to secure the necessary majority. But in a large republic, "the Society becomes broken into a greater variety of interests, of pursuits of passions, which check each other, whilst those who may feel a common sentiment have less opportunity of communication and concert."[20]

This insight, later given classic expression in the tenth *Federalist* paper, was the most fruitful intellectual achievement of the Revolutionary period, the third of the three principles mentioned earlier. It gave Madison and his colleagues at Philadelphia the courage to attempt a republican government for the whole nation. The constitution which they drew up would provide the American peoples with a government that would effectively make them one people. The government would incorporate all the protections to liberty that they still cherished from their British heritage; it would preserve both imported and home-grown republican traditions; and it would employ the political principles developed during the Revolution. It would be a government inferior to the people and one in which no people should have dominion over another, a government in which almost every detail was prompted by the framers' determination to control the operation of human depravity. Many Americans, doubting that the safeguards would work, opposed the adoption of the Constitution. But the character of American politics from 1789 to the present day has borne out Madison's observation: majorities in the United States have been composed of such a variety of interests that they have seldom proved oppressive, and the national government has been a stronger bulwark of freedom than the state governments.

The establishment of a national republic renewed the challenge which the contest with Great Britain had presented to the best minds of America. In the Constitutional Convention and in the conduct of the new national government, Americans found scope for talents that the Revolution had uncovered. Jefferson, Hamilton, Madison, and John Adams received from national politics the stimulus that made them great. The writings in which they embodied their best thoughts were state papers.

In the course of the nineteenth century the stimulus was somehow lost, in hard cider, log cabins, and civil war. Intellect moved away from politics; and intellectual leadership, having passed from clergy to statesmen, moved on to philosophers, scientists, and novelists. But during the brief period when America's intellectual leaders were her political leaders, they created for their country the most stable popular government ever invented and presented to the world three political principles which men have since used repeatedly and successfully to advance human freedom and responsible government.

PART TWO

From Independence to the Civil War: The Federal Phase

2

The Rise of the Democratic Idea

Louis Hartz

I

What accounts for the early triumph of democracy in America? In many ways this is the classic question of American history, the question which each of our major interpretations of the American past has sought most ardently to answer. And yet each of the answers has encountered difficulty because it has not been able to withstand the test of comparative analysis. The Germanic tradition stressed by Herbert Baxter Adams is of course to be found in Germany, hardly notorious for its democracy; the frontier cherished by Turner is to be found in many lands where democracy did not arise; the farmers and debtors discovered by Beard are a commonplace of Western politics in the early nineteenth century. Let us see if we can answer the question in another way: by a running analysis of America and Europe, of the part which came to the New World and the whole which it left behind.

In the Europe of the nineteenth century we see, first of all, an analogue of the early Whiggery of Hamilton and Fisher Ames, the chief obstacle in America to democratic success. It is a stern movement, marked on the one hand by a powerful capitalist ambition and on the other by an unchangeable fear of the people. We find it everywhere in the Western nations — in the English Whigs of the Reform Act era, in the French Liberals of the July Monarchy, in the conservative German liberals and Constitutionalists of 1848. But we must not assume that Whiggery in Europe serves merely the satisfaction of its own ambition, the ambition of the wealthier bourgeoisie. This drive, of course, comes out well enough when it assails the old European reactionary establishments, as in the liberal revolutions of the nineteenth century, ending up when victorious with severe limitations on the popular suffrage. But in the course of these upheavals, which utilize the people only to prevent them actually from coming to power, it performs an important educative function, serving to prepare the ground for later democracy. In a world of mass passivity and relative ignorance its exploitation of the people is the route by which they are in fact brought into the political arena. There is a striking contradiction between the splendid liberal slogans of the British bourgeoisie when it fights an unreformed Parliament and the almost hysterical fear of popular rule which immediately follows the issuing of these slogans. That is a contradiction which British democracy, as in the case of the Chartists, ultimately exposes. But the process of exposing it is one of the things which brings British democracy to consciousness.

In Europe, however, the opposition to Whiggery is not the simple, unified, and easily perceptible thing that it is in America. There, it is not a flat case of Jefferson versus Hamilton. And the reason is that the opposition to Whiggery is split up into various parts, some of them hating each other more bitterly than they hate Whiggery itself. There is first of all the peasant population which has strong affinities for the old feudal conservatism and which, if it is touched for a moment by the liberalism or the radicalism of the towns, can easily lapse back into reaction or into a Napoleonic authoritarianism, as in France. Next there is the lower middle class, which in Jacksonian America constitutes practically the whole of the democracy, but which is split off in Europe not only from the peasantry but from the workers as well. The painful relations between petit-bourgeoisie and labor are a part of the Marxian legend of the nineteenth century, documented in everything Marx and Engels wrote on the age. They may have drawn their categories sharply, and twisted them into a romantic proletarian pattern, but the facts they described were relevant.

Nevertheless, the American Whig and American democrat had analogues in the European setting from which they both ultimately derived. Why is it that the democrat wins out so easily here?

II

There are various ways of answering this question. One is to say what I have already implicitly said, that the democracy is vastly more unified in America and hence can rise up and with a single stroke bring Whiggery down. The notion that one of the central characteristics of American democracy is its unity of alignment is bound to come as a surprise to anyone studying the subject in the American context alone. For in that context what always seems impressive is the looseness of the popular combination. A political historian like Binkley will look at the elections of 1800 and 1828 and he will be struck with the hodgepodge of groups which brought the democracy to power: city wage-earners, small traders, landowners of a certain type.[1] From this angle, Jefferson and Jackson emerge as master politicians whose genius lay in their capacity to weld a unity out of a hopelessly disparate mass. But the truth of the matter is — and one does not need to deny the political genius of American democratic politicians to affirm this — that the unity was already there. The American farmer was hardly as alienated from the spirit of democracy as the German peasant of 1848, the American worker hardly in the same position as the British worker in 1832. Indeed the apparent looseness of the democratic combination is itself a clue to the point involved. For what the European scene presents us with is a series of sharp class breaks, involving deep mutual suspicions, and the bridging of these so effectively not even a master American politician could have accomplished. Could Jackson have done much better than Carl Schurz in the Germany of 1848?

But the unity of the American democratic alignment points to other things. Alone it is simply a matter of numbers, a wider combination of democrats overwhelming the Whig force, a matter of the Benthamite numerical majority. But this could not have come about if the mass of the American people were not capable of a very high degree of independent political activity. I have spoken of the function which Whiggery served in Europe of gradually leading the people into the political arena, educating them at the very moment it was making sure that they would not threaten its political or economic interest. Now we must not make the mistake of assuming that some such phenomenon did not take place in America too. The average American was not always the viable political unit that he appears to be at the hands of Jacksonian organizers. There is a background of political indifference, of submission to paternalism in the American people, which we are only now beginning to appreciate. The research of Robert E. Brown[2] and others has shown that electoral rights existed before they were fully used and that the rise of democracy in America is not simply a matter of obtaining the suffrage. It is a matter of political consciousness as well.

But this ought not to obscure the central fact that the shell of passivity and alienation cracked with comparative ease in the United States, bringing into existence the unified democratic alignment of American politics. There was from the outset no authentic feudal submissiveness; and if, during moments like 1776 and 1828, men of the type of Fisher Ames lamented that the average man no longer knew his place, those men did not have in mind the place of the European serf. In the agrarian sphere, for all of the delicate sense of status that may have prevailed in the South, the mood of the independent entrepreneur was a dominant one from the outset. Labor in the towns was never a mob in the European sense, despite the fears of Jefferson; and even before the arrival of the Loco-Foco movement in New York, the sense of political alienation and depression which characterized the urban proletariat almost anywhere in Europe was not to be found among the workers of that city. It is indeed a difficult matter to define the precise quality of American popular passivity prior to the outbreaks of democratic organization and passion in the nineteenth century. We are dealing with something midway between the European mood and the mood of a truly awakened democracy, something for which no precise category exists. But one thing is clear. Once the democratic organization began, a degree of mass political enlightenment was manifested which had no parallel in the world. Participation was continuous, and sentiment crystallized easily around the great democratic slogans of economic monopoly and the suffrage itself. Here again we find a place where our perspectives need to be altered when the European angle is considered. We do not ordinarily think of American democratic activity as continuous but are rather impressed with its cyclical character, rising and falling with the succession of democratic movements after the Revolution. But truly sporadic activity is what we find in the case of the French peasantry which leaps to a moment of glorious life in 1789 only to lapse back for a long period after that into shadows so deep that they can scarcely be dissipated by historical research. The American had a genius for political participation.

A wider and more unified majority, an enlightened electorate — these two factors were the woe of early American Whiggery. But they implied automatically a third which, in some measure, I have already touched upon: a simplification of political alignment. One cannot ever number with finality the forces in a political struggle, since any group can be broken down into other groups. But it is not wholly unfair to say that in the Europe of the early nineteenth century there were four major elements at work in the political arena: the feudal, aristocratic right, in various shades of strength and decline, ranging from a repatriated Bourbonism to the German princes; Whiggery, the analogue of the American right, fortified by industry in England, mainly by commerce and finance in France; the petit-bourgeoisie, sharply delineated on the Continent where big wealth is a class unto itself, much harder to find in England where the middle class has a more unified outlook; and finally labor, in different stages of political development and awakening. After one has taken all the shadings into account, these are the forces which stand out in the European world that the Americans left behind in the seventeenth century.

It is not hard to see what frustrates democracy in such a pattern. The fact that it is distributed in so many places, and lacks political confidence and awareness, means that it cannot assume command of the situation. It is an enemy of the right — but not quite, since on the land there is still a strong attachment to the aristocratic order. In the towns, where the press and industry are at work, democracy in its lower-middle-class and labor manifestations is clearly an enemy of the right. But even if it were powerful enough in these manifestations to lead the campaign against the right, it lacks the political education to do so, and in the end it follows Whiggery in that campaign. Limited reforms are made by Whiggery, and the natural instinct of democracy is to follow them up with wider demands for itself: a Jacksonian era in Europe. But this it cannot successfully do, first because Whiggery has turned around and joined the *ancien régime* against it, secondly because it thus loses its leadership, and thirdly because it begins to crack up itself as the leftward movement advances. On the Continent the lower middle class, not already incorporated into the Whig reform as in England in 1832, becomes terrified of labor as labor begins to increase its demands. Battles break out, and democracy is defeated. This is the old European story.

The situation is different in America. The very wideness of the democratic alliance is proof that the political situation has been simplified, and the very enlightenment of the American electorate is proof that in this simplified picture it cannot be defeated. The right is absent, never transported to America in the first place. Whiggery stands alone. But American democracy does not need it as an ally, or at least not for very long. Not only do the German princes not exist: even if they did, it is very likely that Jackson could take care of them without the help of Rufus Choate. But one thing is certain. It is not hard for Jackson to defeat Choate. The American farmer is Jackson's ally, not his sullen enemy; the small American trader is behind him; and the worker, however controversial his role may be in Jacksonian democracy, is not likely to strike out on terrifying revolutionary paths. The democracy has widened, and its capacity for political participation has insured the defeat of Whiggery. There are two contenders in America, as it were, not four, and one is vastly larger than the other, subsuming the two European contenders that are missing: an unenlightened peasantry and a threatening proletariat.

It is evident that the factors I have mentioned are analogues of each other. A wider and more cohesive democratic combination implies a larger degree of mass enlightenment, for it means that the predemocratic and antidemocratic dross in the European popular mind has been eliminated: the feudal spirit is gone from the land, the proletarian outlook from the towns. And this necessarily means a simpler political alignment, for the right is gone and the democracy has greatly grown. It was fortunate indeed for the democratic idea to find such a home, and Bancroft, for all of his nationalist piety, was right in terms of sheer political interactions when he said that a democratic Providence had fulfilled itself in the New World. But if one factor in the strategic rise of American democracy always turns out to be the analogue of another, there must surely be some deeper factor behind them all. What is it that works itself out through all the phases of the American political battle? What really is Bancroft's Providence?

III

The decisive moment in American history is the time of the great migration of the seventeenth century: this is our real "revolution," and what happened in 1776 is an aftermath, an experience determined by the earlier era. I do not mean this only in the sense that the American Revolution finally sundered the tie with England, completed, as it were, the original act of detachment. I mean it also in the sense that the domestic upheavals of the revolutionary age, which brought the democracy to power, prefiguring the victories of Jefferson and Jackson, were manifestations of the logic of the New World settlement. For it was precisely then that the complex world in which European Whigs and democrats moved was left behind, that the American political scene shrank at the moment that American democracy expanded. But more than complexity was left behind. There was the whole of the historic feudal culture, from which the liberal element, common to both antagonists in the American political struggle, was extricated. A liberal tradition arose in the New World, and this is the factor which, like some ultimate Hegelian force, keeps showing its face in the various aspects of American politics.

Now this was an idea, nothing more. In its Puritan form it was charged with immense passion; but on a more secular level, not unknown to the Puritans themselves, the level of land-hunger and economic ambition, it was still an idea. Elsewhere I have referred to Locke as a symbol of this idea,[3] but there is no need to overemphasize his significance, especially since in the actual historic sense there is much in his life and work which contradicts the

American scheme of thought. We must not forget that he was the author of the Fundamental Constitutions for the Carolinas, one of the historic ill-fated efforts to establish feudal relations in the New World. What is involved is a set of concepts concerning the social order which come out well, to be sure, in Locke's *Second Treatise* but which can be found in any of the classical liberal thinkers of the seventeenth and the eighteenth centuries. These concepts, transformed into operating modes of behavior, yielded the swift victories of American democracy.

They were responsible for the breadth of the democratic alignment. For what eliminated the barriers that divided European democracy into so many parts if not the sharing in America of liberal values? How did the English tenant or the German peasant become a vital part of the democratic force in the United States? How did the proletariat of Birmingham or Lyons become in the New World respectable members of the bourgeoisie? One can point to an abundance of land, which certainly aided the process, or to industrial conditions which were not so severe as those in Europe. But the explanatory power of these factors must be denied when one remembers that there was an abundance of land as well as comparable working conditions in other countries where the same results did not take place. Fundamentally we are dealing with a psychic matter, the transforming impact of an idea which, long before the American political manipulators got to work, brought both the farmer and the worker into the framework of democratic liberalism. Then a Jefferson could arise, and historians could marvel at his political genius. Then a Jackson could emerge, the wonder of students of political pressure groups. But from a European point of view there was an incongruity in this expansion of the experience of democratic liberalism. For in Europe that experience was the product essentially neither of farmers nor of workers; it was the experience of the small urban entrepreneur, the Jacobin. What happened by contrast in America was that this figure mushroomed to enormous proportions as the American political scene contracted.

The impact of the liberal idea is reflected also in the political activism of the American public. We must be careful not to be too idyllic here. It would certainly be false to portray the American democracy as a set of splendid citizens reading their Calvin or their Locke, and then rationally exercising individual responsibility. This was somewhat the image that Jefferson had of politics, and it did of course pursue American political thinking all the way into the Progressive era. The fact is that the slogans of democratic liberalism, whether they had to do with the natural rights of Samuel Adams or the popular will of William Leggett, were quite as irrational in their appeal as the deferential slogans of European feudalism or the proletarian outcries of the emergent working class of Europe. The issue is not one of rationalism, or at least of rationalism in the classical sense, but rather of the behavioral consequences of an allegiance to different types of symbols. The symbols of democratic liberalism produced a type of political participation which kept the people continuously in the political arena. Leadership was no less essential here than in Europe, ballyhoo, as it were, no less essential, but the public could be relied upon as a political force.

How the liberal idea simplified political alignments is obvious enough from what I have already said. When that idea is universal the politics of four dimensions becomes the politics of two dimensions, and the latter is contained within the bourgeois framework. We can lament, if we like, the missing components of the American experience, the European things that the seventeenth century in America left behind. We can long with the American Whigs of the eighteenth century for the aristocracy they could not lean on, or with the socialists of a later time for the proletarian outlook they could not find. America in the early nineteenth century might actually have been a more exciting place if Fisher Ames could have fulfilled his dream, or if Fanny Wright had had a better break. The simplification of American political alignments, which led to the burgeoning triumph of democracy, was a simplification also of cultural experience. It meant the elevation of the liberal idea to the rank of a national absolute. The virtue of this may be a debatable point. Some may prefer a quick democracy even if it means a contraction of perspective: others may not. Perhaps the question is whether one good experience is better than a multiplicity of experiences, some of them not so good. But there can be little doubt that the shrinking of the context of American politics, which yielded the giant figure of Jackson, was traceable to the dominion of the liberal spirit.

Wherever one looks, then, amid the excitement of early American political battles, one sees the power of the idea that was extracted from Europe and carried to the New World in the seventeenth century. The width of the democratic combination, the torchlight parades of the voters, the duality of the political struggle, all are traceable, in some final sense, to the *Mayflower*. Now one is tempted to be truly Hegelian, for the men in American politics do not really know this: they are victims of the universal mind. They call each other names — Tory, leveler[4] — which prove that they do not realize, or at least that they do not consciously care about, the process that is at work. But is not this the final proof of the process itself? When a unifying idea has sunk so far beneath the surface of a culture that it can support a raging hyperbole which contradicts it, then surely it has attained no mean victory.

IV

In such a world the search for "democratic theory," or even "political theory," is a beguiling quest. For it is the talent of such a world to take a single idea out of the conscious intellectual struggles of Europe and plunge it deep into unconscious behavior where it reigns, without philosophy, without criticism, as an operational absolute. This is the death of theory as theory is studied, the beginning of fetishism. A hundred books may be written on "American political thought," a score of "neglected American thinkers" may be discovered, but no amount of scholarly energy will ever, I think, alter this fact. Let us not then really search for "democratic theory" and confuse a social with a philosophic process. Let us try to find out rather how the thoughts of the Americans in the early nineteenth century disclose the actual process which brings democracy to power.

The amalgamation of the land and the workshop into the province of the small entrepreneur, which generated the greatness of the popular combination, and which was rooted in a universal liberal conception of life, is reflected in the multicolored character of the American democratic polemic. It has, to begin with, a strong agrarian strain, which in Europe is for the most part to be located in the theory of the reaction. Jefferson takes the rustic feudal philosophy of Bonald, with its picture of benign seigneurs and happy peasants, and dynamizes it with the image of countless independent bourgeois entrepreneurs. Of course the actual capitalist hunger among American landowners was far more intense than even Jefferson suggested, and we have to go into the story of land speculation to document it. But in contrast to Europe, Jefferson shows us enough, and so does John Taylor. There is a confusing issue here in the "anticapitalism" of democratic ruralism in America, the opposition to the Hamiltonian program which seems to link the American democrat with the hatred of commerce and industry that the European reactionary had. Indeed there is some connection, for the antagonism of city and farm cuts, in a sense, across all social alignments. But agrarian "anticapitalism" in America, for all of the grand historical concepts which Taylor mustered, and which give him a Marxian touch, is not really "anticapitalism." It is in fact a defense of the capitalist farmer against other capitalist interests.[5]

There is a comparable confusion which can hide the liberal nature of the American labor movement: the high-flown slogans of Stephen Simpson and Ely Moore about class struggle. During the thirties it used to be the fashion to find here a native American radicalism which had gone unnoticed before. Actually the thinking of the Jacksonian labor movement is shot through and through with individualistic aspirations. Its language is the language of natural right, and it is in the name of this concept that the whole range of labor demands, from lien legislation to shorter hours, is rationalized. The fate of true collectivists in the American labor movement was not a happy one, as the history of the movement in New York vividly shows. What touched labor, say, in the France of 1848 — Fourierism for example — was shoved out to the frontier in America, and the Lockean combination was not impaired.[6] Capitalist proletarianism united with capitalist agrarianism to make the Jacobin spirit, rather uninviting in its petty trader form, blossom into a many-splendored thing. The huge figure of Jackson moved amid the romance of log-cabin clearings and striking carpenters.

The issue of mass participation, however, as it comes out in American argument, has a comic rather than a romantic quality. For the Whigs conjure up a necessity for their existence which is false, while the democrats belabor the obvious to prove their right to power. There is John Adams with his mixed state in which the Senate was to represent wealth alone, in which an impartial executive was to mediate between rich and poor, all designed to keep the threatening mob under control. There is Thomas Jefferson ardently protesting that the people, at least the agrarian people, are fit for political participation. But in and through this argument, which does not really die until 1840, when the Whigs themselves have become log-cabin democrats, the Whigs are being defeated badly and the people are participating without catastrophic results. Whiggery dies a complete but easy death: it is laid to rest, not with an axe, but with a pat on the back. And this is of the very essence of the American story. For if the barricades had been thrown up in 1800 or 1828, the point of Whiggery about the people would have been proved, and the European pattern would instantaneously have appeared. Instead of democratizing itself, and generating the tradition of Lincoln and Grant, Whiggery would have made a triumphant return, displaying precisely that capacity for perpetual resurrection which the Whiggery of Europe manifested in the nineteenth century.

The spiritual transformation of American Whiggery in 1840 produces a duality of images which fulfills the democratic idea but confuses it forever in American thought. Who is the real democrat: the new Edward Everett or the old Van Buren; Harding or Wilson? It is rare in intellectual history that a nation has spent its time trying to disentangle two claims to the same principle, and surely there can be no better proof that this principle has succeeded. But for Whiggery, of course, this confusion is a much more fruitful matter than the false clarity of its earlier thinking. It is a method of seizing precisely those forces in the democratic combination which destroyed it, well worth the sacrifice of Fisher Ames to the egalitarian gods. Nor is everything given up. Big wealth is still there, and if the average man is linked to it by the magic of capitalist ambition, by the dream of Horatio Alger, that wealth has not been destroyed. There is only a psychological leveling, not an actual redistribution of goods. On the contrary — and this is one of the secrets of the Whig achievement — the elitism of the millionaire can be more openly flaunted now than in the age of Hamilton because he has become in origin and spirit an average man. Of course some gentility is lost, some Eastern hankering after an association of money and manners. But in America this is a luxury that Whiggery simply cannot afford, and Hamilton must be accounted lucky that there existed in American life that law of compensation which permitted him to live at least in the garb of Andrew Carnegie.

And this was indeed a law. For it was a matter of inevitable logic that the universality of the bourgeois spirit which isolated Hamilton should make the nation peculiarly susceptible to him when he preached the message of democratic capitalism. Actually throughout the entire earlier era the reality of Horatio Alger existed even if his novels had not yet been written in political thought. While Hamilton was sagely speaking in class economic terms, and embroidering the virtues of the employment of women and children in factories, American economic life was distinctly democratic in cast. While Jefferson was spinning out the virtues of the puritanical farmer, the speculative frame of mind, which reached vivid heights during the Jacksonian era, had already thrust itself forward. Alger was bursting beneath the surface of American life before he actually appeared. And if his appearance produced Whig victories, could the democratic politician complain? The Whig law of compensation works in reverse. What had given the democratic politician his success if not the unification of popular power that the individualist ethic had yielded? What had made him great if not the capitalist culture itself? Brownson might lament, but you cannot have the virtues of precapitalist and postcapitalist Europe and the virtues of capitalist America at the same time. If Jackson was to arise, he was bound in the end to be defeated too. But at least he was defeated by being enchanted with a millionaire's dream, not by being crushed beneath the complexities of the class politics of Europe. One may oppose that dream, and find it unsuitable as a way of life, but it was an inherent manifestation of the democratic idea in America.

Here then are the consequences of the liberal principle in American thought: the image of a many-faceted democrat proving his capacity to make and unmake politicians. But where in the American argument do we find the liberal principle itself? Where do we find a celebration of the historic act of the seventeenth century? Actually we do not find it. Folklore and ceremony will always of course remember the Pilgrims, but the significance of the middle-class extrication from Europe for the character of the American political struggle does not figure centrally in American thought. We are back again to the unconscious nature of the power of the liberal principle. One ought not to assume, of course, that overt political argument should always reflect actual political reality. Indeed this is almost never the case. English thought is Hobbesian but the English people are encrusted with a thick general will, French thought is Rousseauian but the French are individualists, German thought is nationalistic but Germany has had its problems with national unity. Political thought is as much the record of a yearning as it is the record of a reality. But the American case is not of this sort. American thought does not seek to reverse the liberal nature of American reality, although in a few cases of the Adams type this may be so. The hidden nature of the liberal premise is testimony, in fact, to its general acceptance, and what we are dealing with is not a misery the Americans seek to escape but a satisfaction so universal that they do not bother to mention it. The rise of American democracy, with its radical expansion of the small liberal, its popular activism, and its simplification of political culture, is traceable in the end to a bourgeois trip that was taken in the seventeenth century which everyone has forgotten.

V

This interpretation of American democratic success, based on the wider European context from which the American experience was extracted, is not wholly incompatible with other interpretations that have reigned in the past. The liberal idea could not have flourished so successfully unless there had been an open place to put it, and in this sense Turner was right. The American democratic combination did consist in large measure of farmers and workers, and in this sense Beard was right. But what this interpretation does is to place these factors in a perspective which comparative analysis cannot destroy. If there is a frontier in feudal French Canada, that need not now trouble us, for the liberal principle was not exported there. If there were farmers and workers in England, that is no problem, since they did not have the bourgeois mentality to unite them.

Indeed from the European angle, from the angle of the context and the part, the rise of American democracy is a fated thing, even though it is not duplicated there. For the analysis I have presented is based on the course of European history itself, and can be checked by it, so that if one were in a reckless mood, one might almost be tempted to say that if American history had not existed it could have been conjured up by an acute student of the European experience:

observe England, abstract the bourgeois element, put it on open ground, watch its democratic logic unfold. What is wrong with this view, however, is that abstraction is itself a process, yielding many of the crucial aspects of the American story, and it is not uniquely related to the liberal principle or for that matter to America itself. In any case the concept of a liberal tradition, if it modifies Turner and Beard, puts them on stronger ground. In American historical study, especially in connection with the rise of democracy, we have grown accustomed to a kind of cyclical excitement in which theories reign for a moment and then are dramatically "disproved." Actually all the major analyses of American democracy, from Bancroft's nationalism to Beard's proletarianism, seized on lasting insights. I believe that the idea of a liberal society puts these insights into a meaningful relationship to one another.

3

The Classic Literature: Art and Idea

Richard Chase

In assessing the relation of the classic American writers to the democracy they lived in and to its intellectual issues, one must first note that these writers — Cooper, Poe, Hawthorne, Melville, Emerson, Thoreau, Whitman — did not profess to be what we now call intellectuals. There are no Miltons or Shelleys among them, no writers, that is, whose poetry or fiction has a steady and direct relation to ideas and to the problems of the time. True, they were aware in varying degrees, some of them intensely, of the problems generated by the democratization of American life, by the first stirrings of a modern mass culture, and by slavery. They were aware of the changing religious tone of their time, brought about by the long decline of Calvinism and the rise of its poetic, secularized offspring, transcendentalism. And though they often spoke indirectly, in paradox, irony, or allegory, they made their positions clear enough so that we can say that, with the exception of the later Cooper, they were "liberal" in their views, favoring, though often with grave doubts, a popular and libertarian democracy, and that they were often religious in feeling and aspiration, but belonged to no church.

It is true that the American fiction and poetry of the first decades of the nineteenth century are relatively abstract when compared with the thriving concreteness and the sensuous richness of the European writing of the same period. It is true also that the American writers express the contradictions of their society and that this is, indeed, the key to understanding the special qualities of their prose and verse. But none of these facts means that their writings consistently respond, on the level of ideas, to the intellectual issues of the time; they do not. When they do respond on the level of ideas they do so, as a rule, in the broadest and most universal of abstractions. They ponder or more often allegorize and mythicize grand contradictions like the Self vs. Society or Good vs. Evil. They are "purer" artists than their European contemporaries, and they transmute the contradictions of their society into the aesthetic properties of their writing, rather than report social realities or make intellectual formulations. With the exception of Cooper (and lesser writers like Bryant and Whittier) they did not think of themselves as advocates in a public debate. If they did speak out, like Emerson, Thoreau, and Whitman, they spoke out as prophets, in the most inclusive language, delineating America and its democratic spirit, describing and exhorting the American and Man in general, speaking in the accents of homily and denunciation rather than of systematic argument. They were private empirics, and their task, like that assigned to the "literatus" in Whitman's *Democratic Vistas* (1871), was to create, not ideas, but archetypes of the American imagination and to find new languages in which to express these archetypes.

Thus there is a certain futility in the large and until recently dominant body of scholarship and criticism which has followed the "history-of-ideas" approach to American literature. Parrington's *Main Currents in American Thought* found no real place for the American imagination in its monumental account of religious, economic, and political ideas. And a work like Gay Wilson Allen's *Walt Whitman Handbook*, with its talk of immanence and emanation, acosmism and cosmotheism, pantheism and panpsychism, never gets around to a discussion of Whitman's real subject, which was the plight and destiny of the self. It is impossible to sympathize with Mr. Allen's statement that "an exhaustive comparative study needs to be made of the relations of Whitman's thought to the [Great] Chain of Being."[1] Poor old Walt, he had never heard of the Great Chain of Being. His leading conceptions are the self, equality, and contradiction — appropriate preoccupations for the poet of American democracy. What use had he, in a democratic culture, for the philosophic counterpart of European hierarchies?

The history-of-ideas approach works much better in studying European writers than it does in studying American writers. Melville, to be sure, had a strong and reflective mind; he was a thoughtful annotator of book margins. But compared with Dostoevski (let us say), who handles ideas with ease and skill, Melville seems to go at ideas with the desperation of the self-taught and isolated amateur. In later years, Emily Dickinson would not, like George Eliot, translate Feuerbach, and there is in fact no classic American novel with as much explicit intellectual content, or as much social observation, as *Middlemarch*. Hawthorne was incapable of abstract thought; his campaign biography of Franklin Pierce, for example, is, like its subject, remarkable for a nearly total absence of political ideas. Compared with the reflective Coleridge, Poe gives us the impression in a work like *Eureka* (1848), not of thought, but of a hallucinatory parody of thought. Emerson, great critic though he was, is intuitive, poetic, seer-like, not to say solipsistic, compared with the philosophical Goethe. Whitman, though inconceivable without the background of Jacksonian political thought, soon gave up an active interest in political practice and theory, and when he came to write *Democratic Vistas*, he wrote a work of prophecy and spiritual exhortation which takes much cognizance of the moral condition of Americans but little of the institutional realities of American society as these were evolving in history. And in general it may be said that the lack of a sense of history in the classic authors was in large part responsible for their lack of a direct connection with intellectual issues — though it is interesting that in his later years, in *Clarel* (1876) and *Billy Budd* written in his last years, Melville began to reflect on the meaning of history.

The classic writers lack not only a sense of history but, as I have said, a sense of society and culture. They are concerned primarily with the individual in his psychological and moral situation: Emerson and Whitman exult in the personal self with its vibrant creative power and its possible autonomy, whereas Poe, Hawthorne, and

Melville are concerned with the anguish and distortion of the isolated self. They all use the familiar contradictory terms: Solitude or Self vs. Society. Theoretically, they would all perhaps agree with Emerson's dialectical recommendation:

> Solitude is naught and society is naught. Alternate them and the good of each is seen. You can soon learn all that society can teach you. . . . After some interval when these delights have been sucked dry, accept again the opportunities of society. The same scenes revisited shall wear a new face, shall yield a higher culture. Undulation, alternation is the condition of progress, of life.[2]

But in classic American literature the self tends to outshine society. Society remains relatively undefined; it is either assumed to be a given quantity that exists outside of time and place or it is imagined as a random collection of persons who have come together more or less fortuitously in a town square, a forest bivouac, an old house, a whaling ship, or, as in Hawthorne's small allegory of society called "The Seven Vagabonds" (1837), in the covered wagon of a traveling puppeteer. One should add that the tenuousness of the social image in part accounts for the relative abstractness of the self, of the individual human being as we behold him in the fictions of Poe, Cooper, Hawthorne, and Melville, or in the poetry of Whitman.

To be sure, the works of these authors do contain from time to time significant social commentary. Cooper's political diatribes are often personally biased and have a hollow and sententious ring, but they do make a serious effort to confront the problems of a rising democracy. His championship of a landed aristocracy and the services it might render to democracy was by no means contemptible in its intellectual quality. Hawthorne, belying to some extent what I have said about the nonhistorical cast of mind, suggests in *The Scarlet Letter* (1850), with its account of the ordeal of Hester Prynne, the emotional and cultural values that are lost and gained in the liberalization and modernization of society, just as he suggests, though more vaguely, in the portrait of Holgrave in *The House of the Seven Gables* (1851) and of Dominicus Pike in "Mr. Higginbotham's Catastrophe" (1834), the passage from a precapitalist to a capitalist America.

In *Redburn* (1849) Melville etched in unrelenting detail the horrors of poverty and suffering as he had seen them in Liverpool in 1839, in a chapter which, as the politically pious were once wont reverently to remind us, was commended by Friedrich Engels. As in *Redburn,* so elsewhere Melville spoke out against injustice — for example, in *White Jacket* (1850), where he assails the inhumanity of martial law aboard an American navy vessel. Earlier, in *Mardi* (1849), he had broadly satirized in a farcical scene the American Congress. In "Benito Cereno" (1855), with its unforgettable account of the inability of either the effete European or the naïve Yankee ship captain to deal with the explosive situation brought about by an insurrection of Negro slaves, he was mirroring indirectly, though only indirectly, the apprehensions of many of his countrymen in the 1850's. And Emerson and Thoreau, of course, made their voices heard clearly on the slavery issue.

One ought to add that if the American writers had at best a vague conception of society, they were by no means incapable of realistic social observation or of realism in general. There has been a tendency to forget this among recent critics who have been interested in defining the characteristic American literary form as symbolistic or emblematic. And for the last three decades and more the standard anthologies and literary histories have given the impression that realism was something that "rose" (presumably from the ashes of romance) after the Civil War. (The conventional phrase, "the rise of realism," betrays a somewhat smug and superior attitude toward the classic American literature, suggesting, as it does, that that literature was backward and unenlightened—something we had to rise from. For myself, I find it difficult to believe that Sherwood Anderson, for example, is a marked improvement over Melville.)

Obviously, literary realism as a *program* did not appear until the age of Howells, but as a practice it was there from the beginning. Samuel Sewall saw Boston in his plain Puritan way, without translating everything he saw into a symbol. The Philadelphia scenes, especially those depicting the ravages of yellow fever, in Charles Brockden Brown's *Ormond* (1799) are strongly realistic, though Brown can also be the most fantastic of romancers. In "The Man of the Crowd" (1840) Poe created a haunting image of a mass society and suggested the problem of finding one's identity in it. In books like *Satanstoe* (1845) and *The Chainbearer* (1845) Cooper drew a rich portrait of aristocratic Westchester life. True, when

Hawthorne depicts Boston in "My Kinsman, Major Molineux" (1832) the city is nocturnal and unreal — a condition of the soul rather than a city (the same is true of Poe's "The City in the Sea" and even of Melville's picture of New York in *Pierre* — 1852), but Hawthorne can capture social reality in small units. For example, the socialist community in *The Blithedale Romance* (1852) is beheld momentarily with a realist's gaze, and everyone remembers effectively painted village and household scenes in Hawthorne's tales. Readers of Hawthorne who see only his allegories and symbols will do well to notice what a wealth of sensuously perceived detail, quite apart from *social* realism, there is in his writing. One might begin by reading the detailed description of a breakfast in Chapter 7 of *The House of the Seven Gables* (1851) and then reflect on the passage in Chapter 38 of *The Marble Faun* (1860) in which Hawthorne says that he prefers the Dutch painters, who "paint an over-ripe peach, with a fly upon it," to the more illustrious Italian masters, who, he thinks, catered to "a false intellectual taste" and too often took "dead mythology" for their subject.

But of course it was Whitman who brought into American literature for the first time the possibility, though by no means the fulfillment, of an uninhibited realism. Despite its spirited lyricism and transcendental flights, "Song of Myself" (1855) renders experience with a startling immediacy and concreteness:

> The blab of the pave, tires of carts, sluff of boot-soles, talk of
>   the promenaders,
> The heavy omnibus, the driver with his interrogating thumb, the
>   clank of the shod horses on the granite floor,
> The snow-sleighs, clinking, shouted jokes, pelts of snow-balls. . .[3]

Yet Whitman's larger social panoramas, in which he tries to encompass, in its vibrant and multifarious particularity, America itself, tend to become inchoate catalogues or else to be achieved by identifying the self with society in such a way that society becomes merely a rhetorical amplification of the self.

Reminding us that there was a pragmatic and realistic side to transcendentalism, as well as to Calvinism, Emerson in "The Poet" (1844) had called for realistic writing:

> I look in vain for the poet whom I describe. We do not with sufficient plainness or sufficient profoundness address ourselves to life,

> nor dare we chaunt our own times and social circumstance. . . . We have yet had no genius in America, with tyrannous eye, which knew the value of our incomparable materials, and saw, in the barbarism and materialism of the times, another carnival of the same gods whose picture he so much admires in Homer; then in the Middle Age; then in Calvinism. Banks and tariffs, the newspaper and caucus, Methodism and Unitarianism, are flat and dull to dull people, but rest on the same foundation of wonder as the town of Troy and the temple of Delphi, and are as swiftly passing away. Our log-rolling, our stumps and their politics, our fisheries, our Negroes and Indians, our boa[s]ts and our repudiations, the wrath of rogues and the pusillanimity of honest men, the northern trade, the southern planting, the western clearing, Oregon and Texas, are yet unsung.[4]

Whitman miraculously sprang up to answer Emerson's challenge and on occasion at least showed himself to have the "tyrannous eye" Emerson said the ideal poet would have to have (just as Henry James was to say many years later that to be great the American novelist who wrote about America would have to have a "grasping imagination"). In reading Emerson's exhortation, however, one may feel some doubt as to whether he was looking at banks, tariffs, and caucuses as realities or as symbols of hidden essences. One must note too that Whitman remained an incorrigible transcendentalist and that he specifically denigrates artistic realism in *Democratic Vistas.* The poet has pre-eminently "the image-making faculty," he says, and works with "analogies," "curious removes," and "indirection"; the poet does not make "the useless attempt to repeat the material creation."[5] But like his idea of the American "scholar," Emerson's idea of the poet, as Whitman embodied it, was a decisive step in making American writers receptive to the actualities of the national experience and in leading them to confront more directly, as many did after the Civil War, the intellectual issues of democracy.

Why do the older American authors write "romances," to use their own term, rather than "novels"? Why, indeed, did not Emerson and Thoreau, avid readers both, read novels, apparently having an incurable aversion to them? Thoreau prefers mythology, scripture, and fable, on the one hand, and, on the other, "true, sincere, human books . . . frank and honest biographies."[6] And he goes on to say (in *A Week on the Concord and Merrimack Rivers* — 1849), "I never read a novel, they have so little real life and thought in them." Later we find Henry James, in his essay on Emerson, shaking his head over the fact that Emerson, so much the man of letters, could see nothing in Cervantes, Jane Austen, or Dickens.[7] Why should it not have occurred to Emerson that perhaps the "poet" who beheld America with a "tyrannous eye" might turn out to be a novelist, the novel having long since established itself, in Europe, as the modern literary form best equipped to appropriate and express large areas of human experience? By contrast the romance, like Cooper's Leather-Stocking Tales and the fictions of Poe, Hawthorne, and Melville, takes its characteristic form by regarding actual experience at one or two removes and by assuming a freedom from psychological entanglements and social complexities which is at odds with our sense of the way human beings actually live.

The usual answer to the question why the novel properly so-called did not begin to flourish in this country until the time of Howells and James is "the poverty of materials." This is a phrase from Cooper's *Notions of the Americans* (1828), wherein he complains that the writer of fiction in America must face a social scene that is arid and featureless. "There is scarcely an ore," he says, "which contributes to the wealth of the author, that is found here in veins as rich as in Europe. There are no annals for the historian; no follies (beyond the most vulgar and commonplace) for the satirist; no manners for the dramatist."[8] He was echoing an earlier statement of Charles Brockden Brown and was echoed in turn in the prefaces to the romance-novels of Hawthorne, who explains that he is assuming the right to the fanciful practice of the "romancer." "When a writer calls his work a Romance," says Hawthorne in the preface to *The House of the Seven Gables,* "it need hardly be observed that he wishes to claim a certain latitude, both as to its fashion and material, which he would not have felt entitled to assume had he professed to be writing a Novel."[9] His implication seems to be either that the American scene does not furnish the requisite materials for a "novel" or that if it does he is not going to confront them directly. The poverty-of-materials argument is most eloquently expressed by Henry James in his biography of Hawthorne, where he laments in an oft-quoted passage the cultural thinness of his native land. "The negative side of the spectacle on which Hawthorne looked out, in his contemplative saunterings and reveries," James writes, "might, indeed, with a little ingenuity, be made almost ludicrous; one might enumerate the items of high civilization, as it exists in other countries, which are absent from the texture of American life." And then follows the inventory: "No sovereign, no court, no personal loyalty, no aristocracy, no church," and so on down to "no cathedrals, nor abbeys, nor little Norman churches; no great universities nor public schools — no Oxford, nor Eton, nor Harrow; no literature, no novels, no museums, no pictures, no political society. . . ."[10]

The poverty-of-materials argument has been invoked repeatedly by literary critics and historians in the last decade, so persistently indeed as to suggest a very parochial turn of mind. And it seems to me that Philip Rahv has done everyone a service by opposing this approach in an essay called "The Native Bias." In the first place there was a great deal of potential material for the novelist in the American scene; anyone to whom this is not obvious can confirm the fact by reading the historians who have written of the early republic. Pointing to the fact that there were doubtless a great many American Emma Bovarys, Mr. Rahv observes that, "after all, a pretty woman's boredom, adultery, and suicide are scarcely a monopoly of French life. Yet the sort of imaginative transaction represented by the story of Emma Bovary is unthinkable in mid-nineteenth-century America. It was not the absence of materials but the absence of writers prepared to cope with the materials actually at hand that decided the issue."[11] A civilization is not prepared at every point in its career to see itself with unvarnished truth through literature, and the classic American writers could not be expected to write like Flaubert or Balzac. They knew enough about the truths and dark realities, but they cloaked them in symbol, allegory, fable, and myth, submerging them deeply in the mind and allowing them to reappear only in transmuted form. Whitman (and in some ways Melville) presents American phenomena more directly than the others, exulting in their copious multiplicity, and his poems, surely, do not give us the sense of a poverty of materials.

Another objection to citing poverty of materials, in explanation of the characteristic form of the classic fiction, is that this explanation assumes that the authors were all born novelists of manners and morals, were frustrated because they could find so few manners and morals to write about, and therefore had to fall back on a second-best-form, which could be neither their nor any great writer's true vocation. This is the impression one gets, for example, from Marius Bewley's book *The Eccentric Design,* which attempts, unsuccessfully as it seems to me, to establish an American "tradition" of the novel consisting of Cooper, Hawthorne, Melville, Henry James, and F. Scott Fitzgerald. Mr. Bewley, a fine critic in many ways, is nevertheless an excellent example of the parochial conservatism that has overtaken literary criticism in the last ten or fifteen years. It was not so long ago — maybe twenty years — when hardly a critical voice was raised in behalf of the novel of manners, everyone agreeing that compared with the productions of the great romancers of the past and the radical realists of the present the kind of novel written by Edith Wharton, Ellen Glasgow, J. P. Marquand, and even Henry James was trivial and unrelated both to reality and to great acts of the imagination. All this has changed in recent years, and we have of course rediscovered genuine virtues in the works of Edith Wharton, James, and the others. But when we come to the point of assuming that all writers of fiction are born novelists of manners, something is wrong. Many influences might be cited as having brought about this state of mind. There is, for example, the criticism of F. R. Leavis, whose book called *The Great Tradition* (1948) finds pre-eminent places in the history of the English novel for Jane Austen, George Eliot, and James, but hardly any for Dickens and none for Emily Brontë. Lionel Trilling's criticism, with its insistence on the complexities of the cultural life, and its high estimate of the same authors Mr. Leavis exalts (though not of them alone), has had a wide influence. In general this is an age of sociology, in which Americans have been scrutinizing each other's manners and morals with a busy anxiety to find out what everybody's "status" is. David Riesman, for most thoughtful people outside the sociological profession, is *the* sociologist of the time, and he is read as a commentator on manners and morals. Veblen was that, but few readers are able to find in Riesman the delving into the human mind and the probing at the foundations of political and economic institutions that they once found in Veblen. In our age of sociology the literary slogans have changed. A few years ago the younger critics were dismissing America's greatest poet by saying, "Whitman? No sense of Evil." Now they seem to be well on their way to saying, "Whitman? No sense of Manners."

The "items of high civilization" enumerated by James were missing from the early republic. (Suppose they had been there, though — can one imagine Hawthorne or Melville writing witty social comedies about high-born people at a party in a country mansion or whatnot?) What was left? James himself, itemizing what he calls a "terrible denudation," says that "a good deal remains," but he specifies only "that 'American humor' of which of late years we have heard so much."[12] If we take the phrase "American humor" to mean what it means to Constance Rourke in her famous book of that title, we can see that James with his usual penetrating intuition has said something important. As every reader of Miss Rourke knows, she used the word "humor" to mean much more than jokes, quips, and tall tales. She used it to define the qualities not only of the American temperament, as that emerged after the Revolution, but of the characteristic preoccupations of the American mind whenever it expressed itself in art forms, either popular or sophisticated. For her, the emergence of the American imagination was not merely a negative event, the result of frustration because of the cultural thinness of American life; it was a positive and vigorous act of the mind, which in answer to a deep human need provided Americans with an imaginative counterpart to the growing political and economic life of the nation. As she herself realized, it is not always easy to state or understand just how this imagination is related to the institutional and intellectual growth of the republic. The relation is often one that seems well described by Melville when he writes in *The Confidence Man* (1857) that "it is with fiction as with religion: it should present another world, and yet one to which we feel the tie."[13]

Although we often have to "feel" rather than clearly perceive this tie in reading the older American authors, we can at least be specific about the native origins of what they wrote. One might ask, for example, a rather simplistic question: What did the American imagination need, after the arid eighteenth-century rationalism and cosmopolitanism of Benjamin Franklin? It needed depth, mystery, beauty, a sense of evil, images of innocence and escape, dramas of violence and anguish, an emotional enrichening of the self in its plight and destiny, a renewed sense of the manifold variety of the natural world. There were two major native sources of a richer imaginative experience: the American mind could recapture some of the imaginative qualities of Calvinism and it could respond to the beauty and violence of the frontier.[14] Neither of these sources of imagination would be likely to inspire a novelist of manners, but they could and did inspire writers who were by vocation and avocation romancers. These were writers who brought a new profundity, beauty, and significance to romance and created a characteristically American form. They were not, needless to say, practitioners of the insipid, escapist fiction we are likely to think of first when we hear the word "romance." *Moby-Dick* and *When Knighthood Was in Flower* (1899) may both be labeled "romances," but there the similarity ends.

Unlike his successors among the classic writers, Cooper may have been — in fact he *was*, from time to time — a would-be novelist of manners. But he was entirely right in thinking that posterity would prize him most highly for the Leather-Stocking Tales: *The Pioneers* (1823), *The Last of the Mohicans* (1826), *The Prairie* (1827), *The Pathfinder* (1840), *Deerslayer* (1841). Read in the order in which they were written, they provide a fascinating study in the gradual discovery of the full imaginative resources of the frontier experience. The most novelistic of these fictions is the first one, *The Pioneers*, and the purest romance is the last, *Deerslayer*. Through the five books, in an irregular chronological order, Cooper proceeds from the realistic picture of his hero, Natty Bumppo, as an old man who has lived beyond his time, tracing back the story of his earlier years as soldier, woodsman, guide, friend of matchless Indian braves, and scourge of Indian "varmints," to his highly idealized youth and initiation as depicted in *Deerslayer*. Cooper's work was an important act in the furnishing out of a somewhat void national imagination.

To ask another simplistic question: What did the American imagination need after Cooper? It needed psychological subtlety, for Cooper was a crude psychologist. It needed a more supple, sensuous language, for Cooper's "Federal" style was often sententious and stilted. It needed dark or colorful imagery, texture and detail, for Cooper painted pictures that were often stiff, formal, and lacking in atmosphere and reality. It needed a sense of the mysteriousness of human motives and of the dark, hidden forces of the world, for although Natty Bumppo has his mysteries, Cooper attributed to him nothing more soul-stirring than a sentimental deism. With his Calvinist background, his feeling for place, his sensuous imagination, his interest in the dark reaches of the human soul, Hawthorne, no pastoral poet any more than Cooper was a Calvinist, was eminently equipped to bring many of the needed qualities into American fiction. This he did in such original tales as "Young Goodman Brown" (1835) and "The Birthmark" (1843), his genius finding its most perfect expression in *The Scarlet Letter.* Although they have no ostensible relation to Calvinism, Charles Brockden Brown and Poe also brought into the literature of a vigorous, pragmatic, and optimistic culture their dark imaginings. In works like Brown's *Wieland* (1798) and Poe's "Narrative of A. Gordon Pym" (1838) and "The Fall of the House of Usher" (1839) the machinery of Gothic romance was used with a new skill and beauty.

Like Hawthorne (and later Emily Dickinson) Melville appeared at a time that was propitious for the adaptation of Calvinism to literature — when, that is, Calvinism was no longer alive as a doctrine to be believed but was intensely alive as a source of the literary imagination. And so we find Melville writing in a review of Hawthorne's *Mosses from an Old Manse*, in 1850 (while he was composing *Moby-Dick*), about the "great power of blackness" which emanates from "that Calvinistic sense of Innate Depravity and Original Sin, from whose visitations, in some shape or other, no deeply thinking mind is always and wholly free."[15] In works like *Moby-Dick* and "Benito Cereno," Melville gave powerful expression to the Calvinist, or more properly Manichean, drama of irreducible moral contradictions in a texture of the imagery of light and dark. In *Moby-Dick* Melville marshaled these moral, psychological, and spiritual contradictions into a grand if unstable synthesis with the more immediate contradiction of an equalitarian culture, that between the self and society — an aesthetic synthesis which is the culminating act of the American imagination before the Civil War. A part of Melville's great power is to be attributed to the fact that unlike the other classic writers he was able to draw on both the primary sources of American romance: Calvinism and the image of the frontier.

Reading *Moby-Dick* in 1851 it might have been easy to feel that what American literature needed was a bard who could dilate on some of Melville's own apostrophes to the grandeur of democratic man and the thriving vigor of the country he lived in. Whitman required for his purposes no Gothicism or Calvinism. In *Democratic Vistas* he was to write that one way to know a great poet is by the "absence in him of the idea of the covert, the lurid, the maleficent, the devil, the grim estimate inherited from the Puritans, hell, natural depravity, and the like."[16] And "Song of Myself" is full, on the one hand, of well-being and "loafing" and, on the other, of vaunting optimism and affirmation. Still, it would not be the great poem it is without the contradictions, paradoxes, and problems it expresses, nor without its awareness of death. If Melville is the culmination of the classic literature, Whitman is a transitional figure. He is a man of his time, but in his receptivity to experience, his literary experimentalism, his bohemianism, his utter rejection of puritanism and gentility is prefigured much of the modern literary movement. By the time of Whitman the classic American imagination had stated itself fully, and Americans, though few of them knew it, had a literature to match the material and intellectual development of their country.

I have noted above the obvious fact that this literature does not relate itself as directly to social actuality and to ideas as does the European literature of the time. One should add, however, that the remote or obscure qualities suggested by the word "symbolistic" are by no means always the qualities of this literature, although this seems to be a very common impression. For example, the *London Times Literary Supplement* devoted to "The American Imagination" (November 6, 1959) confidently declares that American literature, despite its considerable realism, is "symbolistic," and states that this insight is the fruit of modern literary criticism in America. This is wrong. True, there has been much talk of "symbols" among critics, from the middlebrow who automatically assails "symbol-hunting" whether or not there are any symbols to hunt, to an intensely erudite writer like Charles Feidelson, the author of *Symbolism and American Literature* (1953). Mr. Feidelson's influential book was perhaps inspired by earlier works like Edmund Wilson's *Axel's Castle* (1931) and F. O. Matthiessen's *American Renaissance* (1941), but on the whole it is a product of the "new criticism." Its contention that there is much in transcendentalist theory to support an aesthetic of symbolism is certainly correct, yet American literature does not seem to me on the whole to be symbolist.

Much of the literary to-do that has surrounded the word "symbol" could be avoided by an effort at definition. The word has come to mean two things, and unhappily they are confused in many people's minds. It has the ordinary meaning of a "sign," something whose function it is to stand for something else. But there is also what ought to be called for purposes of distinction the *poetic* symbol, which I take it is being referred to when people use the word "symbolistic." The poetic symbol stands for something else, but it also has a life, an autonomy, a mysterious integrity of its own which, we might say, it expresses. A further difference is that we know pretty well what the ordinary symbol stands for, but all we can say of the poetic symbol is that it expresses complexities and enigmas which we can never state accurately in any language but the symbol itself.

In Hawthorne's "The Birthmark" the stigma shaped like a small hand on the lady's face is an ordinary symbol. We would know what it means even if the helpful author had not told us, which he does; it stands for the moral taint of being human. Melville's white whale on the other hand is a poetic symbol — we can never quite paraphrase its meaning in our own words. Hawthorne is not a symbolistic writer, except in the sense that all writers in varying degrees use symbols; when he departs from realism he is an allegorist, and ordinarily there is nothing mysterious about what his allegorical signs stand for. Nor is Cooper a symbolist; when he departs from realism he does so via myth and legend. In the stories of Poe there are haunting and apparently complex symbols — the house, the ship, the tarn, the masquerades, the tombs, and the prisons. Yet so compulsive was Poe's neurosis and so limited is the experience his tales engross that he tends also to become an allegorist, as a judicious Freudian reading of him will show. The lilac in Whitman's "When Lilacs Last in the Dooryard Bloom'd" (1865) is doubtless a poetic symbol, but no more than Melville is Whitman to be unhesitatingly labeled a symbolist writer.

There is sufficient reason why the classic American literature is not primarily symbolistic: namely, that it is dialectical, like American civilization itself, and tends to rest among the unresolved contradictions it expresses. You cannot have a fully symbolistic (or for that matter tragic) work of art unless its tensions are resolved into the unity of its symbols. American literature is more nearly related to melodrama and farce — dialectical forms that do not come to an epistemological or aesthetic resolution — than it is to tragic and symbolist art, a fact which after all we do not have to engage in critical theorizing to perceive.

That the American writers both classic and modern embody, if often in ways not easy to see at first sight, the contradictions of their culture and that to understand this is the necessary first step in our understanding of their works — this may be taken as a fact established by contemporary criticism. Much of this criticism derives from Lionel Trilling's essay called "Reality in America." In this essay Mr. Trilling is opposing Parrington's ideas of realism, reality, and culture as these are expressed in *Main Currents in American Thought.* "Parrington's characteristic weakness as an historian is suggested by his title," writes Trilling,

> for the culture of a nation is not truly figured in the image of the current. A culture is not a flow, nor even a confluence; the form of its existence is struggle, or at least debate — it is nothing if not dialectic. And in any culture there are likely to be certain artists who contain a large part of the dialectic within themselves, their meaning and power lying in their contradictions; they contain within themselves, it may be said, the very essence of the culture, and the sign of this is that they do not submit to serve the ends of any one ideological group or tendency. It is a significant circumstance of American culture, and one that is susceptible of explanation, that an unusually large proportion of its notable writers of the nineteenth century were such repositories of the dialectic of their times — they contained both the yes and the no of their culture, and by that token they were prophetic of the future.[17]

Nearly all the best work of the last decade or so in American studies has been done by critics who elaborate in one way or another Mr. Trilling's formula. These dialectical critics have all but superseded the older realist criticism which was advanced in the 1920's or before by writers like Parrington, Edmund Wilson, and Van Wyck Brooks and which became the conventional academic view of our literary history and remained so for twenty-five years.

It is not quite true that Parrington and his fellow realists did not see culture as a "struggle" or "debate." Actually they did. They saw it as a struggle between the oligarch and the democrat, the conservative and the radical, the Puritan and the vitalist, the pessimist and the optimist, the religious man and the secularist, the romancer and the realist, the genteel writer and the plebeian writer, the highbrow and the lowbrow. With this the dialectical critic can agree. What he does not agree with is the assumption of the realist critics that the notable authors of the past and present must be in either one camp or the other, the assumption that they were repositories of either the first or the second terms of the above dualities, but not of both. The realists conceived of the struggle as being external, as a part of the evolving, progressive nature of democratic society, whose destiny it was to outgrow all that was conservative, Puritan, genteel, pessimistic, and religious and reach maturity ("come of age," the phrase was) in a culture of radical, secular, democratic realism. In some ways this view was naïve, being based on an unexamined faith in progress. And for any man of taste and judgment, it seemed to fly in the face of the facts, suggesting as it did that James T. Farrell and Dos Passos represent a higher stage of cultural development than Melville, Hawthorne, or Henry James.

The more recent critics have, so to speak, internalized the cultural struggle. They think of the most characteristically "American" writers as being, in Mr. Trilling's words, "repositories of the dialectic of their times." This view has led to a major reassessment of our "usable past" and of the continuity of the present with that past. But one must note, on the debit side, that this view is implicitly antihistorical. The trouble is not that the modern literary movement is now conceived of as "the fall of romance" rather than as "the rise of realism" (though some critics seem well on their way to that position). The real danger is the prevalent notion that if all our best writers have always embodied the contradictions of their culture, then there neither can be nor need be any real change of opinion, taste, style, or conviction. Instead of looking at our literature for evidences of progress, as did the old realists, the new dialecticians look for evidences of what is now called "the American imagination" or "the American tradition," as if these were not only clearly discernible from Jonathan Edwards to Jack Kerouac but as if they constituted a kind of monolithic and unchanging cultural phenomenon that was precipitated once and for all in its essential qualities at some early point in our history, if not in the Puritan period then in the days of the early republic. Nothing is more common in doctoral dissertations these days than uninhibited cross-references from Faulkner to Hawthorne or from Hemingway to Cooper as if all these writers existed contemporaneously, in some happy hunting-ground outside of history.

This attitude reflects the dull conservative temper of the time just as obviously as the older realist view reflected an unexamined and naïve progressivism. But for all its shortcomings, the realist criticism did propound a large and unavoidable truth: namely, that there began in the decades after the Civil War a modern movement in literature and that in certain basic ways modern American literature differs from classic American literature. If the criticism of the sixties is to advance it will have to be not only dialectical and adroit in describing the American-ness of our literature; it will also have to be a genuinely historical criticism.

Merely to reread the classic authors is to be struck by the fact that they were different from us. How should they not be? Hemingway could not possibly be a "symbolist" in the sense that Melville was. The pressures of convention, the unexpressed demands and needs of the culture, the attitude of the artist toward his art that made Melville a symbolist (in so far as he was one) had radically changed long before the time of Hemingway. The historical crisis can be seen most clearly in Stephen Crane. Crane is strikingly a modernist, a realist, and an ironist — not, as much criticism has tried to show, a symbolist in the older American manner. The source of symbolism, myth, and allegory in the classic writers was traced by D. H. Lawrence to what he called their "duplicity." Lawrence described this duplicity as arising from the fact that the older writers were outwardly conventional, even genteel, moralists but that inwardly they were impassioned destroyers of conventional morality. Their works, said Lawrence, show a "tight mental allegiance . . . to a morality which the passional self repudiates."[18] Given the temper of the times and the temperaments of the authors, this radical repudiation could be expressed only indirectly, in poetic modes of representation. But in the works of Crane this rich source of poetry has been largely lost. The morality that once inhibited the passional self has been openly rejected. The contrast between conventional morality and the dark actualities of the instinctual life is no longer a secret. It is an openly proclaimed fact; indeed, it becomes the main theme of Crane's writing and is the source of his ironic realism.

Of course there are other sources of poetry — of romance, allegory, and symbolism — than the one pointed out by Lawrence, and on these sources Crane and his successors have drawn. But this should not keep us from seeing that profound changes intervened between the classic and the modern literature. The classic authors had, at a given time, a historical destiny to fulfill. The great task they had to do, consciously or unconsciously, could not be repeated, nor would it need to be.

4

The Dissolution of Calvinism

Donald Meyer

I

At the end of his life, John Calvin in Geneva looked back — and ahead. "All was confusion," he said of the past. ". . . I have lived in marvelous combats. . . . Yes, I have been in combats, and you [who follow] will have more of them, not less but greater."[1] Calvin's descendants bred true — Knox, Cromwell, Winthrop. They intensified his combat against confusion; they insisted everywhere on the new structure of ordered clarity which he had imposed on traditional Christianity. But, if life was combat, what was to happen once Calvinism won its victories and no longer had confusion to assail?

In New England by 1730 the heirs of Calvin had expounded their theology freely and with authority for a century — an immense drama of sin and salvation centered on the unconditional omnipotence of God. Everyone accepted the triangle of orthodoxy, with its emphasis on the "inability" of men to repent their sins, on the "imputation" of Christ's merits to men, and on salvation through Christ's atonement "limited" to those elected by God. But triumph seemed to some Calvinists less a cause for satisfaction than for anxiety. Religion appeared to be growing routine, piety conventional. New England, indeed, was providing Calvinism its unique testing-ground; for in New England alone was Calvinism free to follow out its inner logic, distorted neither by a weight of inheritance from the past nor by strong external opposition.

And so in New England Calvinism confronted the dilemmas it had itself created. Now that the structure of intellectual order was established, how to prevent men from identifying that order with the omnipotence of God? How to remind men that, if God were in truth absolute sovereign, He could not be contained in any man-made system? For a time, the existence of a realm beyond order in daily life had made it easy to remember the uncontainable God; in the seventeenth century the Puritans had perilous seas, dark coasts, hard new land, wild Indians, wild animals, physical want, terrible sickness to remind them of God's unbounded will. But as civic order pushed back the natural wilderness, so intellectual order pushed back the metaphysical wilderness until Calvin's system began to seem not just an aspect of God but His total revelation.

Transformation in the sense of God flowed particularly from the doctrine of the covenant. Before ever coming to America, English Puritans had developed it. Since God the Absolute was blinding in His absoluteness, nothing but dazzle, how was He to be known? The answer was that God — of His own free choice, of course — had chosen to reveal Himself, above all in the Scriptures, and at the heart of this revelation were offers, agreements, bargains, contracts — covenants. If men, by the grace of God, would fulfill their side of the contracts, God would fulfill His. This was the "federal theology." Although it was never intended that God be conceived of only in terms of the covenants, it was natural that a main enterprise of Puritans should have been to fulfill them. Thus, when God showed the face of chaos, the Puritans began to interpret this as a sign, not of His illimitability, but of their own failure to live up to their obligations. Soon they took God's very freedom to confirm His self-limitation to the contracted goals. The doctrine of the covenant subtly and gradually petrified religious experience into religious legalism. As the sense of covenanted order expanded, it tended to reduce God to the magnitude of the orderliness — and, moreover, to suggest that it had always been His intention so to reduce Himself. If this were so, might not God have also intended that man have the powers of energy, diligence, reason, and morality necessary to fulfill his side of the contract? Might not man, without impiety, begin to speak of natural rights? And of earthly happiness?

Perry Miller has characterized New England in 1730 as a time-bomb with a burning fuse. The Puritan theocrats had begun to seek new motives for faith — to make religion vital through guilt or fright. But the theology of terror was provoking its own discontents. For one thing, people did not absolutely have to listen to the Old Calvinism any more. Royal governors had appeared in Massachusetts after 1692, tempering the authority of the theocracy. Baptists, Quakers, and other heretics could no longer be summarily purged or silenced. Even the Puritans themselves were beginning to rethink the basis of their faith. And so the fuse sputtered; and the contagion of revivals, the burst of religious renewal known as the Great Awakening, was the explosion. The Great Awakening cannot be traced solely to the internal build-up of frustrations and energies Puritan New England could no longer suppress; after all, the Awakening had its counterparts in England and on the Continent. But it struck in New England with exceptional force; and, by redefining the issues of Calvinism, it directed the flow of religious energy for the next century.

The impact of the Awakening was mixed and ambiguous. It tapped — and intensified — strong emotions, but these emotions were not part of the established style of religious sensibility. In the face of a threat to existing channels of order, a party of resistance crystallized, fearful that all the complicated and careful landmarks of sober Puritanism would be engulfed by undisciplined enthusiasm. And the threat of indiscriminate emotion precipitated out another party as well, the existence of which the Old Calvinists had already suspected and tried to keep in check: the Awakening liberated liberalism. The history of American Puritan Protestantism for the next hundred years was the history of the interplay between the Old Calvinism, the Calvinism of the Awakening, and the new liberalism.

II

The primary strength of the Old Calvinism had been its identification with social order. The Awakening came as a climax of a series of challenges to its social authority. With the explosion, Old Calvinism began to surrender its primacy, not just to Jonathan Edwards and his followers, or to the liberals, but to all the new energies of a secular, pluralistic, middle-class society. When Old Calvinism could no longer rely on the strength of social solidarity, then a chance lay in a revival of piety — but even this was stolen from it by the Awakening. All it could now do was hold on, marooned on islands of tradition buffeted by waves of reason, progress, and individualism.

Its death was long and lingering. The foundation of the Calvinist defense remained the federal theology. But the Edwardeans now qualified or rejected the old triangle of orthodoxy in all its aspects. If Edwards had not died before assuming his duties at Princeton in 1758, perhaps the story might have been different; his sheer personal and intellectual power might have brought together the two Calvinist tendencies which the Awakening had thrust asunder. But with the importation of John Witherspoon from Scotland ten years later, Princeton locked Presbyterian theology firmly into the Scottish common-sense philosophy. There it remained, safe from Edwardean idealism, safe from romanticism, safe from experience.

Politics helped stay its execution. The fact that orthodoxy was no less eager than liberalism to support the movement for national independence meant that New England congregations could hear about political freedom from the most respectable of pulpits. They did not have to turn to deism or go French to find sanction for revolution. But the day of reckoning was only delayed. By 1837 the Presbyterian community had split into the Old School and the New. Much of the Old School vote for expelling the heretics came from the South, where Calvinism still retained solidarity with society, firmly woven as it was into the maintenance of Southern institutions. Indeed, the Old Calvinism lived on longest where it found fewer logicians — and therefore fewer men to be seduced by polemics — to champion it. In the Presbyterian church, especially among the immigrant Scotch-Irish least associated with the old Puritan holy commonwealth of New England, Calvinism could feed on a folk passion — on the need of the Scotch-Irish to maintain identity in the loose circumstances of a new country and a baffling wilderness. But where frontier Presbyterianism insisted too strictly on the "Old School," it too suffered radical losses to popular evangelism — the Baptists, the Methodists, the Disciples of Christ, even the Church of the Latter Day Saints. Indeed, when in their General Assembly debates of 1889–91 some northern Presbyterians offered the last-ditch defense of the Calvinistic Westminster Confession of 1643, it was with undertones of protest against "individualism," of nostalgia for a stable God-supported solidarity of humanity and church. Following this line, one can find Old Calvinism that did not die at all in the nineteenth century, or since. Among the Dutch, especially the small Christian Reformed Church in southwestern Michigan, ethnic solidarity reinforced religious piety to keep alive an unflickering, forgotten flame.

III

The "New England theology" following Jonathan Edwards was really *the* American Calvinism. The early Puritans had not conceived of Calvinism as a creed requiring defense or reinterpretation. The impulse to rethink Calvinism came with the shift of focus in the Awakening — from contracts and social order to renewed piety and interior ecstasy. Edwards had experienced the shift in his own consciousness. In his precocious youth he had hated Calvinism. Then he came to love it. What had before seemed horrible — God's sovereign disposal of men as He chose — became holy, glorious, and above all endlessly sweet. How had this change taken place? Edwards did not know. It was not the result of speculative reason. It was not the result of searching Scripture. Then he concluded: this affection, this "relish," was the gift of God, a divine and supernatural light. What was important was not a mediatorial system of covenants, but the direct confrontation of man and God.

The New England theology was the rationalization of this emotion. Edwards did not see the divine light as a reward for good behavior. Love, he believed, was purest and most trustworthy when it depended on no merit whatever. No human being could ever believe that his strivings could be sufficient to deserve love; if one received love only as one had earned it, one would never have enough. The deeper one understood man's sin to be, the more ravishing one understood God's love to be. The more one understood that man had no claim on God, the more glorious His grace. In abandoning the federal system, Edwards revived and sharpened the pristine Calvinist and Augustinian doctrines of God's sovereignty.

The technical innovations of the New England theology followed from this freshened relish for the absolute God. Thus the Edwardeans saw every instance of salvation as a direct act of God. This required a reformulation of the older doctrines of atonement and imputation. Jonathan Edwards, Jr., carried on his father's work by reconstructing the atonement theory. Christ's atonement was necessary, yes, in order that God's justice be revealed. But Christ's atonement did not impute His merit to men; merit was not negotiable like a conveyance in law. Instead, Christ's atonement was not limited but was for all men (the senior Edwards himself had not understood this); Christ therefore made it possible, but not necessary, for God to save any man He chose. God's action was now direct; even more important, it flowed not from His justice but from His love.

This "governmental" theory of the atonement was one of the victories of the New England theology in the Congregational Church. And it also helped the disintegration of Calvinism into liberal Protestantism: the God who had divided mankind arbitrarily into the saved and the damned was now superseded by a God whose attribute was less power than love. The governmental theory of the atonement still supposed that the sacrifice of Jesus was required to satisfy God and win God to men. But it evolved painlessly in the early nineteenth century into the "moral influence" theory whereby the sacrifice of Jesus became the means, not of winning God to men, but of winning men to God; all who could learn to love through the example of Jesus were saved. The moral influence theory said little about God's sovereignty. The more it could talk about the Son, the less it needed to talk about the Father.

Jonathan Edwards used his most famous argument to deal with the third corner of the Old Calvinist triangle. Of course, he said, man had the ability to repent. Man had a will, and plainly he had the "power" to follow his will. Then Edwards asked the next question: did man have the power to "will" his will? If man repented, whence came the disposition, the inclination, the "heart" to do so? His answer was to recognize the will as involved in an infinite, unbroken series of causes, of determinations, in short, God. By a *tour de force* of logic, his demonstration of the sovereignty of God in salvation was inseparable from his demonstration that men were whole, unitary beings. This perception of the wholeness of man was the key to Edwards's reconstruction of Calvinism. From this standpoint one can say that the aim of the New England theology was to induce men to experience themselves in their wholeness of being — and to persuade them that this could not be done except as they experience the wholeness of being-in-general.

The task, one may say, was impossible. In a society in which change, commerce, rational techniques, rational philosophy, secular politics, and open land were cumulatively loosening bonds of unity and symbols of authority — and also, more tellingly, fragmenting men's lives into separate fields, separate interests, separate forms and levels of consciousness — such experience could barely describe itself to itself, let alone impress others. Edwards had cut his doctrine loose from the old theocracy; he had discarded the legalisms of the federal theology. He rested his new structure on the sweetness of the holy vision; but what had this to do with the confident energies of individual ambition and social progress which were remaking New England around him? When the Awakening subsided almost as quickly as it arose, it left the New England theology high and dry with no running stream of faith to tap.

IV

The fate of Edwards's successors was constantly to be expounding logic without full exposure of the heart. And so — a long thin line from Joseph Bellamy and Samuel Hopkins, whom Edwards trained in his home, through his son and Samuel West, Timothy Dwight, and Nathaniel W. Taylor, to Enoch Pond of Bangor and Edwards Amasa Park at Andover, late in the nineteenth century — they finally perished by logic.

Their faith in logic was strong and implacable. Thus Hopkins undertook to show that sin was actually an advantage to the universe, Bellamy to explain it as a display of the wisdom of God. For these Edwardeans, God revealed himself not simply in his justice but in his "vindictive" justice; man suffered not simply from sin but from an active "malice" toward God. In sharpening the ancient Augustinian dogmas, the New England theologians exhibited Puritanism's tough grandeur. But it was almost as if they were tricked into exaggerating their daring to the point where they became not logicians but acrobats. Certainly they reasoned themselves out of contact with most of the social realities of an expanding society.

Two modes of contact remained — terror and benevolence. The first was one to which Edwards himself, and Cotton Mather before him, had resorted with sporadic success. If men by themselves could not understand the necessity of whole and unconditional submission, then break down their pride and self-reliance through terror. The revivals became a means, transitory but vivid, of achieving wholeness, of groping for identity, among the endless dislocations and relocations of American mobility. The radical reduction of all the problems of the spirit into one of disloyal guilt opened the way to saving joy through reidentification with creeds, codes, and community — through conformity, in short. Sometimes the revivals were Calvinized, as among the Presbyterians and most Baptists, but with increasing frequency, as among the Methodists, they were founded simply on "the blood of Jesus," available to anyone for the desiring.

The notion of benevolence was developed by Hopkins with his argument that men could find their unity only in "disinterested benevolence" of which God himself was the culmination. Disinterested benevolence was a potent strain in the upsurge of reform in the generation before the Civil War. Hopkins himself was an early antislavery man. As usual, seduced by logic, Hopkins carried his reasoning to the limits of sanity and turned benevolence against itself. Not only should men be disinterestedly benevolent, but they should be "willing to be damned" for the greater glory of God. The two faces of this notion of benevolence suggest the ultimate tensions of Calvinism. Only men of a high degree of personal integration, deeply seasoned in a firm culture, could equably avow a willingness to be cast forever into the torment of hell. At the same time, if it took a strong sense of personal identity to be willing to be damned, it was this same strength which could so easily imagine itself self-sufficient. Thus New England produced both the extreme Calvinists and the extreme individualists, blood cousins if not brothers. And there was a third possibility: strength might submit to the divine sovereignty with no sense of sin but out of its ability to identify with the divine. This was to be Emerson.

A century's debate over infant damnation illustrated the growing unreality of sin in a century of benevolence. It was, in a sense, an improbable issue even for Edwards. His reconstruction of Calvinism plainly centered in consciousness, and therefore plainly concerned men the more centered in consciousness — the more mature — they were. But as early as 1757 Samuel Webster confronted the Edwardeans with the innocent, humane challenge that nothing, surely, in God's justice required that infants suffer damnation; and the issue would not down. The debate placed the Calvinist dilemma in compact form. If men said yes, they were hateful; and if they said no, then God's will was not quite so absolutely, arbitrarily, unconditionally sovereign as they had made it out to be. Well into the nineteenth century, Nathaniel Emmons, pastor of his flock at Franklin, Massachusetts, for over fifty years, could be found bravely arguing that infants could in truth be damned, since while sin was indeed a matter of conscious and "voluntary" acts, infants were guilty too. Other Calvinists, like Timothy Dwight, insisted that the spiritual nature of man was to be defined, not by his acts alone, but by the general disposition of his nature — a definition which qualified even babies for damnation. One would like to discover in these debates new frontiers in psychology, pushing into the territory of the pre- or sub- or un-conscious, where theological issues might have been refreshed by new concepts of psychological causation. But in all the arguments on infant damnation, no one looked at infants; the ultimate decision was left neither to logic nor to science but to the drift of social experience; and the nineteenth century pronounced clearly against infant damnation as absurd and horrible.

The final unraveling of logic could be seen in Nathaniel Taylor of Yale, the last inventor of a "system," the New Haven theology. Taylor solved the relationship of a Calvinist God to a humanitarian century by trying to affirm both. On the question of free will, he proposed shameless contradictions, no longer even paradoxes; he abandoned Edwards's commitment to the whole man by arguing that sin, while in some sense following the heart, counted only in acts (man sins by sinning); and he saved himself from the tough problems which obsessed Bellamy and Hopkins by contending that when man commits sin it may be that God cannot prevent it, thereby tacitly giving up the infinity of God. It would be nearly a century before Protestant theologians would debate plainly the question whether God was not perhaps finite, but the question waited silently in Taylor, as in William Ellery Channing — and as in every concept of a God whose benevolence is conceived purely in accord with the highest wishes of men.

At their National Council in Boston in 1865, the Congregationalists agreed not to include any reference to Calvinism in their declaration of faith. The Geneva combats had ended. The man whose ideas best revealed this new Protestantism was Horace Bushnell, one of Nathaniel Taylor's unpersuaded students. Like Edwards, Bushnell drew deeply on a personal religious illumination. His decisive point for Protestantism was that religion, as a special way of knowing, needed a language of its own. His primary debt here was to Coleridge, on whom the transcendentalists had already drawn. Coleridge had seen "reason" — or what today would be called intuition — as the special faculty for knowing religious reality. With this it was possible to dismiss legalistic intricacies about the Trinity, for example, justifying it now simply in the fact that men experience God in three ways. Religion was closer to poetry than to science; no more than poetry did religion prove itself through formal discursive reason.

Theology was becoming the psychology of religion; Bushnell's "instrumental" theories foretold the pragmatism of William James's *Varieties of Religious Experience*. Bushnell's approach also facilitated the incorporation of evolution into traditional Christianity. Harnessed into evolutionary images, Christianity was now justified as the highest stage of developing human experience; Darwinism, far from contradicting the power of God, was God's way of doing things.

Bushnell's theory of "Christian nurture" fitted in with his theory of religious knowledge and his view of nature, and it expressed the basic foundation of the liberal religious community. By nurture, Bushnell argued, men can become Christian without the necessity of conversion. Dismissing problems about sin, Bushnell postulated human beings as neither good nor bad to begin with, but rather sheer plasticity. Therefore the environment can help to damn or save; a good environment is itself the grace of God. The nurturing environment that concerned Bushnell was that of the family; but the liberal Protestantism of the last quarter of the nineteenth century, reaching its climax in the social gospel, could successively redefine the crucial environment as the community, the society, and finally the world.

V

In following this course, the Edwardean tradition, now transformed out of all recognition, finally began to follow once again toward the liberalism from which it had so sharply diverged after the Great Awakening.

The Awakening, we have noted, liberated liberalism. The story can be seen in the case of the Massachusetts minister, Charles Chauncy, moving from anonymous dissent to proud advocacy of the new spirit of reason, free will, and practical progress, able to come out in the open because the emotionalists provided him a foe feared equally by the orthodox theocrats. For the liberals, it was a prospect of divide and conquer — though in fact they had not done the dividing, nor were they truly to conquer. Pastors like Jonathan Mayhew and Ebenezer Gay joined Chauncy in urging ideas that had been filtering from liberalized English Presbyterian circles into the studies, if not yet the pulpits, of New England divines. These ideas, affirming the soundness of man's rational faculties, suggested that man might therefore be capable, in the light of that faculty, of advancing his own good. Was not this indeed the way God had arranged things, lawfully, so that man might take responsibility for himself? Was not law, the reasonable structure of existence, God's real contract with man? And, if this were so, was the federal theology, with the old covenants of redemption and grace, any longer necessary? Were those old schemes of mediation and atonement built around the Person of Christ essential after all?

The emergence of this spirit was slow. If the War for Independence helped stay the execution of the Old Calvinism, it also helped postpone the final showdown between it and liberalism. As the patriotic ardor of the orthodox saved the Revolution from identification with deism, so the patriotic ardor of the liberals saved the Revolution from identification with a folk orthodoxy to the right, as in the parochialized folk Calvinism of Scotland. The old Puritanism — twice in strange alliance with the liberalism it had spawned within itself, once against the Awakening and now against the British — really gathered itself in alarm only at the turn of the century. By then it was too late. The Unitarian schism was well under way. Beginning in Plymouth in 1799, Congregational church after church in Eastern Massachusetts ruptured, most of the time a majority of the parish renouncing Calvinism, rejecting total depravity, asserting the sufficiency of human reason and will, questioning the divinity of Jesus, and emerging as Unitarians. By 1826 the American Unitarian Association was formed.

The greatest of the Unitarians was not typical. William Ellery Channing objected to Calvinism because he believed that Calvinism degraded human nature. He condemned Calvin's insistence that salvation depended, not on man's works and character, but on the arbitrary and capricious predestination of God. Channing doubtless misunderstood Calvinism, but he understood all too well the Old Calvinists and their mechanical invocations of hell and Satan. Yet, in his reaction, he did not swing to an undue complacency about human nature. His faith centered rather in a perception of God, a love of God; it was in this love, Channing said, that the human spirit flourished. Channing's God was a perfect benevolence comprehensible to men and within their competence to emulate; nonetheless God, and not human free-will, defined man's orientation. It was as if Channing still retained the Edwardean sense that human coherence depended on more than the human personality. This sense led Channing into a social idealism which distinguished him from the Unitarian community.

The Unitarian community itself was Federalist, conventional, and aristocratic. The Unitarians shook off the past, not to exploit freedom, but to imitate a respectable, rational, classical eighteenth-century English culture — a culture which in England was already tired of itself and yielding to romantic impulses. Here was an American paradox: to ripen, to mature, was to end up more provincial and imitative than before, cut off by success from the perpetually verdant American mainstem. Almost from the start the typical heresy from Unitarianism was to be the conversion to Episcopalianism, usually high-church, if not to Rome. And when the Unitarians were later brought under fire by their transcendentalist rebels as too frigid, conventional, and orthodox, the Unitarian spokesmen back-pedaled rapidly into revelation, miracles, and the law, into a literal reading of Scriptures, into a security not Puritan but almost Fundamentalist.

Unitarianism thus failed quite to illustrate the secular potentialities of the liberal impulse. Those potentialities found their devastating expression in a worldly sagacity of which Benjamin Franklin was the archetype. Forsaking Puritan Boston for pluralistic Philadelphia — and Philadelphia for the great world beyond — Franklin, a man of genius, substituted for the old Calvinist predestination a plainer modern one. What has happened to me, he explained modestly in his *Autobiography*, happened because of what I made of myself. Training myself methodically in thirteen virtues, I equipped myself for every contingency. Anyone can do it; no one need feel overwhelmed by circumstance or defeated by mystery. The pervading implication was that God had arranged the world for men like Franklin. Thus Franklin represented the triumphant expansion of the federal theology of Puritanism to the point where the personal resources by which man fulfilled the covenant became the sum of self-consciousness. But though Franklin became a hero in American mythology, the mythical Franklin was not the real Franklin. The real Franklin remained a solitary genius; he created no tradition of the serenely self-sufficient ego. Men who saw themselves in his tradition expected help he never needed. Franklin earned his own money, but John D. Rockefeller was to explain that the Rockefeller fortune came from God.

VI

If the liberalism liberated by the Awakening reached its secular climax in Franklin, it reached its spiritual climax in Emerson, at once the leading son of Unitarianism and the leading rebel against it. Emerson returned to Edwards's perception of the oneness and beauty of being. Protesting against Unitarian anthropomorphism, he discerned the sovereign God once more, now as the creative energy of existence. But where Edwards saw the sweetness of sovereignty in a context of sin and salvation, Emerson saw it without a sense of crisis. (After all, who would feel guilty at deserting Unitarianism?) In Nature, both men saw the signature of the divine, but Emerson felt that signature already written in the heart as well. The individual fulfilled himself, not as he expressed his own vagaries, but as he expressed the absolute within him, as he surrendered himself to the Oversoul. Accordingly fulfillment exhibited a rigorous necessity; the artist does not "choose," is not "free," but "partakes of the precision of fate." "No room was there for choice; no play for fancy."[2] For his images of necessity Emerson drew on organic metaphors. This shift from the legal and mechanical metaphors of Calvinism saved him from those connotations of arbitrary tyranny which had doomed the Old School theologians.

Teaching communion without crisis, stressing the harmonies rather than the discontinuities between man and nature, soul and oversoul, Emerson's evangel suffered inevitable corruption in its transmission to liberal Protestant audiences. "Self-reliance" became the watchword of popular Emersonianism, only imperfectly protected by Emerson himself from serving as a sanction for any fool's complacency. In other cadences, Whitman's prodigious equations of himself-as-universal-poet with the "en-masse" risked the same invitation to everyone to accept himself complacently. The criticism of Emerson by Melville and Hawthorne derived its resonance from their sense that vital religion could not be so bland. Was man's integration, his wholeness of heart, to be won quite so cheaply as Chauncy, Bushnell, Emerson, and liberal religion generally seemed to imply? Was "malice" after all too strong a word to describe at least some human sentiments toward God, in view of a Chillingworth, in view of an Ahab? And was their malice so incomprehensible, in view of the way they had been treated by life? The emotions of Calvinism thus persisted in literature after the structure of theology had begun to fall to pieces. No one "theologized" *The Scarlet Letter* or *Moby-Dick* into "systems"; their power suggested what later theologians would begin to conclude, that religious "truth" was best expressed in terms of "myth," not of formal logic.

VII

The last version of Calvinism as social ideology may be said to be Social Darwinism. As in Calvinism, so in Social Darwinism man was to submit to the absolute. This call for submission could seem as harsh with one as with the other; the weak, even infants, were as liable to damnation; the absolutes of Darwinism seemed no less random, unfeeling, and categorical than the God that Channing criticized.

But the logic of salvation in Social Darwinism showed what was asserting itself. True obedience displayed itself in heightened individual purposefulness, in a willingness not to be damned but to forgo all other help for salvation except one's own energies. The greatest submission thus consisted of the greatest assertion, the purest dependence in the fullest self-dependence, the fullest independence. One best served God by being completely on one's own — and, at the same time, best served man, for by their submission to self-sufficiency men facilitated the selection — the "election" — of the fittest men. Men now elected themselves, taking over the role once assigned to God.

This paradoxical climax and degradation of Calvinist piety was appropriate in another respect as well. The vaunted "individualism" of Social Darwinism had nothing to do with individuals discovering themselves and their wholeness but rather with the necessity for the individual to respond on his own responsibility to the trials and pressures of a blind and materialistic nature. Here the Calvinist eagerness for order had turned itself inside out: men deliberately accepted a chaos of strife in order to fulfill a cosmic logic. In Franklin's case, drilling oneself for success had held the promise of an eventual freedom really to do what one's talents might suggest, whatever they were. In Social Darwinism no one was free to "be himself," only to be what survived.

5

The Controversy over Slavery

Dwight L. Dumond

I

Slavery in its individual relationship was the complete subjection of one person to the will of another by force, recognized and sustained by the statute law of certain American states. Slavery as a system was the complete and permanent subjection of Negroes, living and still unborn, to whites, justified by theories of biological inequality and racial inferiority. The basic features of slavery were inherent in these premises.

(1) The law denied to slaves all positive rights, both substantive and procedural. Slaves were personal property and real estate and were so taxed. They were confined to their master's domain by law. There were heavy penalties for teaching them to read or write. They could not assemble without supervision; nor legally marry; nor lift a hand in defense of themselves or their families. They were livestock; bred like cattle and hogs; sold with cattle and hogs. Work supervisors were drivers; mothers were breeders; children were surplus for the market.

(2) The law largely ignored individual relationships between master and slave. It placed no restrictions on slave ownership. Ability to pay the purchase price alone determined who might be a slaveholder. There were no standards of character, or responsibility. The master possessed absolute authority. He could hurt slaves cruelly and work them to the limits of human endurance. He could allow family relationships; or he could destroy them by sale and invasion. He could whip, brand, breed, castrate, otherwise mutilate or kill slaves almost wholly at his own pleasure. He could sell them in the marketplace by choice; and they could be sold by law in satisfaction of debts and settlement of estates. The master could delegate his authority. He could leave them in the care of overseers, hire them out as contract labor, send them to the public whipping posts, shoot them if they ran away. There was no machinery for supervising the master-slave relationship, no agency to which the slave could appeal for protection. The courts, established for protection of the most elementary rights, did not exist for the slave. Slaves could not testify against white men. The thinking of slaveholders, legislators, and judges was conditioned by the concept of slaves as less than human beings.

(3) The law itself victimized the entire race of slaves. They were expected to obey the law, but were denied the means of knowing the provisions of the law. Allegiance was exacted without reciprocal protection. The law allowed every white person to intercept slaves at large, to demand evidence of permission to be abroad, and to chastise delinquents. White men could rape female slaves, subject only to action for trespass by the master. The law punished by death exercise of the basic right of self-preservation. It restricted, then forbade manumission without removal from the state, and children begot by white men upon their female slaves were no exception. Thousands of men held their own children in slavery and sold them as late as 1860.

II

If these features were inherent in the system, it took time and circumstance to draw them to their full prominence and to clothe them with respectability. In the late eighteenth century, slavery was increasingly on the defensive in American society. It was condemned by leading statesmen and churchmen of Europe and America as the antithesis first of moral law, then of natural law, and finally of the fundamental law of the nation. It seemed equally incompatible with the social teachings of Jesus and the natural rights of man.

Quakers, as particular devotees of freedom of the human will and equality of all men in the sight of God, had seen no choice but to purge themselves of the evil. They did so, beginning in the mid-seventeenth century under the inspiring leadership of men like George Fox, later of John Woolman and Anthony Benezet. They freed their own slaves. They abandoned their homes in the slave areas and migrated to the non-slaveholding mountain areas of North Carolina and Tennessee or to the Old Northwest. They were the first to suffer from the arrogance of slaveholders, who sought to suppress freedom of inquiry and discussion, and to intimidate by charges of incendiarism and by invective all who opposed slavery, and all who sought to educate, Christianize, or otherwise meliorate the condition of the slaves.

The Quakers wrote an imposing chapter in man's long struggle to be free. They stated five theses and upheld them faithfully. (1) Slavery violated the principles of the Christian faith, and was an outrage against humanity and justice. (2) Slavery cultivated the false notion of racial superiority and the love of unrestrained power in the master race; and no person was mentally or morally competent to rule others independent of restraints. (3) There was no basis for the theory of mental and moral inferiority of Negroes, or for doubts about their ability to be useful and creative members of society. (4) All inconveniences, financial losses, and burdens connected with emancipation must be borne by those who had robbed the slaves of their birthright. (5) The slaves, when freed, were entitled to retributive justice. The Quakers founded schools in New York and Philadelphia. They gave guidance, protection, and economic aid to their former slaves. They aided fugitives and fought vigorously against kidnapping. The United Brethren, the Reformed Presbyterians, the Wesleyan Methodists, and the Free Will Baptists followed the example of the Quakers, renounced slavery and purged their churches. So, too, did a high percentage of the Congregationalists. All of this was well under way by 1776.

III

The American Revolution was a paradox in relation to slavery. Men gave to the world the incomparable statement of natural rights in the Declaration of Independence, the first sentence of which is the greatest condensation of antislavery philosophy ever written. They restated these principles in their state constitutions; and they sought to justify their stroke for political freedom by subsequent pronouncements to the world — all in such terms as to leave little seeming question that, if these principles were applied, American slavery would have to be abolished. Antislavery men insisted that the Constitution must be interpreted in the light of those principles, and that no branch of the government could ever do violence to them.

Despite this, neither Church nor State in the Revolutionary period completely divorced itself from slavery. Powerful men among the Founding Fathers opposed its continuance; but instead of forthright abolition, they applied the principle of gradualism. The Constitution does not contain the words "slave" or "slavery," but rather "person" or "person held to service or labor" — the delegates being ashamed to admit a property right in human flesh and unwilling to give slavery a national character. The Constitution gave to Congress the power to make all needful rules and regulations for the territories; and, in fact, the Congress of the Confederation forbade slavery in the Northwest Territory by legislation passed while the Convention was in session. Congress was also given control over interstate commerce and discretionary power to admit new states into the Union. It had power to prevent importation of slaves, and migration of slaves, but was restrained for twenty years in the use of that power contrary to the wishes of the then existing states. It was believed that slavery would be restricted and would quickly disappear. It was so stated freely in ratifying conventions.

Yet if the Founding Fathers looked forward to the ultimate abolition of slavery *by congressional restrictions*, they behaved in a most irrational manner. They added three-fifths of the slaves to the whole number of free persons in apportioning representation (Art. 1, Sec. 2); gave to slaveholders the right to recapture alleged fugitives in non-slaveholding states (Art. 4, Sec. 2); and allowed the several states to import slaves for twenty years if they cared to do so (Art. 1, Sec. 9). Slavery had always been a social and economic system. Colonial law, changing its basis from heathenism to race, had made it also a system of racial adjustment. The Constitution now made it the foundation of tremendous political power, 20,000 free whites with 50,000 slaves, for example, having as much power as 50,000 whites in a non-slaveholding state. This system gave the remaining slave states more than twenty extra votes in the House of Representatives and in the Electoral College at all times before 1860. Not a single victory for slavery, such as the admission of Missouri as a slave state, the Kansas-Nebraska Act, or the Fugitive Slave Act of 1850, could have passed without the extra votes based upon slaves. Such was the consequence of a philosophy which rewarded men with political power for enslaving their fellow men and in proportion as they did so. Little wonder that Wendell Phillips said of the Founders: "I love these men; I hate their work. I respect their memory; I reject their deeds. I trust their hearts; I distrust their heads."[1]

IV

There were 104,000 slaves in South Carolina at the close of the Revolution, only 16,000 in Georgia. There were approximately 350,000 in Virginia and Maryland. North Carolina, between the tobacco and rice growing areas, had 60,000. New York, New Jersey, and Pennsylvania had 36,000; the four states in New England had 16,000. In the years of the Revolution and after, the Northern states gradually got rid of slavery, by legislative action, court decision, or individual manumission.

Even Virginia, with its large slave population, contained many who looked forward to abolition. South Carolina and Georgia, however, placed economic interests in opposition to the broad humanitarian liberalism of the Revolution and matched the intellectual brilliance of the Masons and Wilsons with their own intransigence. Georgia did not prohibit importations until 1798. South Carolina prohibited the trade in 1787, but brought in 40,000 between 1803 and 1808. Then the cotton gin, invented in 1793, and the three-fifths rule of apportionment, provided a combination of economic and political power for slaveholders that seemed indestructible.

It was now possible to make enormous profits by growing cotton with slave labor in the vast interior region of the Southern states. Within a decade after the Constitution, the development of the Black Belt and Cotton Kingdom had begun. Profits from slave breeding ended the flutter of doubts in Virginia and Maryland. The plantation owners did not emancipate their slaves. Instead, their plantations took the place of Africa as the breeding ground for labor, and the interstate slave trade carried their produce to market as the African slave trade had done. All the original slave states of the South could not supply the swelling demand for slaves in the Black Belt. Slavery, in all parts of the South, was developing from a labor device into a system — an economic system, a social system, a system of racial adjustment, the basis of extraordinary political power, and the source of an increasingly comprehensive social philosophy. In this system, slaves (3,500,000 by 1860) were denied opportunity to cultivate intellectual and moral progress; denied incentive to develop creative talents; robbed of dignity and self-esteem. Society deprived the slave, so far as possible, of all human attributes, then argued a natural inferiority from the artificial inferiority it had created. Slaveholding thus confirmed the notion of Negro inferiority, as well as the practice of exploitation, and projected both into an interminable future. No admission of the evil was now made, no anticipation of its extinction was countenanced.

V

By 1840, the philosophy of slavery and the philosophy of human rights were fully committed to a contest for control of the nation — a contest which ended in the greatest civil war in all history. The first broad area of conflict was in religious and moral philosophy.

Quakers like Woolman; Congregationalists like Jonathan Edwards and Samuel Hopkins, who stand pre-eminent among the country's Calvinist theologians; John Wesley, founder of Methodism; William Agguter of Oxford, James Beattie of Aberdeen, and Charles Follen of Harvard; these and many other intellectual leaders, such as the famous physician Benjamin Rush, presented the moral case against slavery. All men, they said, were created equal in the sight of God, in His own image, and endowed with inalienable rights, rational minds, and immortal souls. Slavery destroyed the dignity of man, reduced his spirit to abject misery, denied him mental and moral improvement, and prevented the development of reason, judgment, conscience, and aspiration. In short, slavery sustained itself by compelling ignorance and destroying accountability. It became in consequence a violation of the Christian principle of human brotherhood. Jesus had commanded: "Thou shalt love the Lord thy God with all thy heart, with all thy mind, and with all thy strength, and thy neighbor as thyself"; and again, "All things whatsoever ye would that men should do to you, do ye even so to them." "Where the spirit of the Lord is, there is liberty." John Wesley said, "Liberty is the right of every human creature as soon as he breathes the vital air; and no human law can deprive him of that right which he derives from the law of nature."[2]

Slavery was the offspring of violence. The butcheries in Africa and the brutalities in America were inseparable in fact and in the sight of God. The peoples of Africa had offended no one. To make war upon and enslave unoffending people without cause was an outrage against humanity and justice. Slavery was at war with the Christian faith; and this lack of respect for the teachings of Jesus was leading to a breakdown of human relationships and corruption of the human spirit in the slave country.

VI

The defense of slavery in moral and religious terms was nearly as old as slavery itself. It was said that slavery was a Christian institution of divine origin, which stood uncondemned in the Bible and praiseworthy as a means of Christianizing the heathen; that the Negro was an inferior being, doomed to servitude by God's punishment of Cain, lacking in intellectual and moral attributes, and incapable of making advancement even if given an opportunity; and that slavery was essential to the cultural and economic development of southern regions, as it always had been to prosperous and cultivated peoples. These were familiar arguments by 1776. Later it was asserted that slavery was a positive good to both races because it had brought heathen Africans to America and given them the elements of Christian civilization, and had enabled the slaveholders to develop a superior culture.

Later still, slavery was said to be a political question. Having once taken that position, Southern churchmen shunned like the plague all discussion of the sin of slavery. The theory was that sins which pertained to society or to which the civil government gave sanction were not personal sins; individuals could not be held accountable for evils created by or allowed by the civil government.

Having surrendered their time-honored function of condemning both private and public immorality in this area, the Southern churches sprang to the defense of the system by denouncing antislavery activities and approving mob violence. They supported colonization. They did not discipline members for cruelties to slaves, nor bar slaveholders from Christian fellowship. Three-fourths of all Presbyterians, Methodists, Baptists, and Episcopalians in the South embraced slavery without reservation. Slaves in the South, and free Negroes in the North, were segregated in church services and in the burial grounds. The Baptist churches in their corporate capacities owned 125,000 slaves that were hired out to support their pastorates and foreign missionaries.

That the Christian churches could have held a race accursed because of the color of its skin, sanctified a system lacking in justice and equity, and then surrendered up the duty to direct moral reform by condemning sin in individual conduct and public affairs is worthy of note. Antislavery people had at first believed that moral condemnation of slavery, conviction of sin, and repentance by slaveholders would be enough to bring slavery to an end. Nothing, they thought, was to be gained for human rights by buying the freedom of the slaves, or by constitutional amendments, or by the use of force. The failure of the churches finally forced antislavery people to turn to political action, and secession forced them to coercion, but it was with reluctance because the hope was dashed of repentance, manumission, and retributive justice.

VII

The second broad area of conflict was in the area of natural rights and the relation of government to them. Antislavery men drew from the moral law and the natural law a conception of right relationships among persons and between persons and God. Freedom to perform all obligations arising out of the relationships constituted the natural rights of man. These rights derived from the creative act of God. Men were born with them. Governments did not create them, and could not destroy them. The Declaration of Independence stated them as the foundation of the government; the Constitution called them privileges and immunities of citizens.

Slavery was as antithetical to the natural rights of man as it was to Christianity. The slave power savagely suppressed all discussion of the evils of slavery in the slave states, then reached out to suppress it in the nation. The majority of antislavery writers and lecturers were reared in the midst of slavery, but no man or woman was ever permitted to speak against slavery and long remain in a community dominated by slaveholders. Men like John Woolman, Anthony Benezet, Benjamin Franklin, George Mason, Benjamin Rush, Samuel Hopkins, Noah Webster, Thomas Branagan, David Cooper, John Jay, Timothy Dwight, David Rice, and Alexander McCleod spoke against slavery only because the slave power in their communities was too weak to prevent it, or because, like Mason, they were too powerful to be touched. Wherever slaveholders were able to consolidate their power, they silenced dissent. John Rankin, David Nelson, Sarah Grimké, Angelina Grimké, George Bourne, James G. Birney, and a host of others were exiles by 1835. Most had to leave the slave states before 1820.

Having driven out of the slave states all who refused to be silenced on the slavery question, the slave power then imposed a reign of terror by mob violence and criminal law upon all who were suspected of introducing antislavery literature. A mob in Charleston invaded the post office, burned the mails in the public square, and thereafter censored all incoming mail, removing and destroying antislavery literature. State laws in some states compelled postmasters to do so. President Andrew Jackson suggested that postmasters publicize the names of all persons to whom such literature was addressed that they might be made the victims of public wrath. He requested legislation excluding antislavery literature from the mails. Congress, on the contrary, imposed penalties upon postal officials who failed to deliver the mail. The slave power, under the leadership of Calhoun, then secured from the Postmaster-General a complete subordination of federal power to state authority, and postmasters were instructed, despite federal law, to abide by all state regulations regarding the destruction of such mail. This situation continued to 1861, making every postmaster the guardian of the morals and minds of his community. The slave power then demanded, through the channels of grand juries and governors, the extradition to the slave states for trial, under the laws thereof, of the publishers in non-slaveholding states of antislavery literature sent into the slave states.

The slave power, and its strong right arm, the colonization societies, also sought to suppress antislavery activities in the North. Mobs were encouraged to sit in judgment upon and punish men who had violated no law. They disrupted peaceable assemblages; destroyed printing presses, homes, schools, churches, public buildings; and beat, stoned, hanged, and shot prominent men. It was lynch law, complete in all its refinements; and, as it turned out, a desecration of constitutional guarantees and a surrender to anarchy. Public officials, from the President down, complimented mobs for supplying by violence what they regarded as deficiencies of the law. Leaders of the mobs were frequently rewarded with United States judgeships. Law enforcement officials stood by and watched without interference the destruction of life and property on the theory that they had discretionary power to enforce the law or not in accordance with the best interests of society.

Finally the slaveholders demanded positive action by the federal and state governments. The legislatures of slave states requested those of non-slaveholding states to pass laws suppressing antislavery societies and publications. The House of Representatives enacted a gag resolution in 1836 which silenced discussion of slavery for eight years in that branch of the Congress, and which prevented the printing of any and all antislavery petitions presented to that body. The gag resolution was part of a report containing an elaborate eulogy of slavery, condemnation of antislavery activities, and endorsement of mob violence. The United States Attorney for the District of Columbia arrested and brought to trial for publishing and uttering a libel an unoffending Quaker who had in his possession some antislavery publications on which was written the words "read and distribute." Then as a capstone to this conspiracy of silence, Calhoun presented in the Senate his Resolutions of 1837 asserting that the federal government must use its full power to suppress antislavery activities, and that no person or group of persons dare speak against slavery. His argument was that the Union was formed to strengthen and preserve the domestic institutions of the several states; slavery was at that time, and remained, a most important domestic institution of the slave states; and continued agitation against it would destroy the bonds of Union.

VIII

The third broad area of conflict was in regard to the constitutional status of Negroes, and incidentally of all persons, involving citizenship, privileges and immunities, and due process. The debate was inseparable from that involving the nature of the national government. The slave power insisted that the Constitution was a compact among equally sovereign states which had never surrendered their sovereignty; that each state was the judge of the limits of its own powers; and that national citizenship was derivative from state citizenship. Its spokesmen argued that Negroes were not citizens of the United States; and that they were not party to the Constitution, which was framed by and for white men. This was fully argued by Andrew T. Judson in the Prudence Crandall Case (1835), was accepted as the basis of his decision by Judge David Daggett, and was reargued, and was accepted by Chief Justice Taney in the Dred Scott decision.

The defenders of the system insisted that color was a presumption of slavery; this was the prevailing philosophy in the slave states, and of the federal courts after 1831. They insisted, also, that slaves were property by law and might be recovered in the same manner as a horse which had strayed away, the only requirement being that the claimant maintain his right of ownership against any counter claim (not including that of the slave). Color as a presumption of servitude and the unobstructed right of recapture won in federal courts — in the Fugitive Slave Act of 1850 and the Dred Scott Decision of 1857. The slave power not only insisted upon the right of slaveholders to go into the free states and seize Negroes, but to invade homes without permission; and after 1842 they did so without legal process. The federal courts therefore, in substance, agreed that Negroes were not and could not be citizens, that slaves were property, not persons, that Negroes were presumed to be slaves and had no constitutional rights.

Antislavery men argued equality of all persons with regard to the nature of their faculties, their moral agency, and their legal rights. Negroes, they asserted, were citizens of the United States, and slaves, fugitive or otherwise, were persons and were so recognized in the Constitution. Legislatures and courts must recognize them as such and abide by the principle that every person was free until proved otherwise by positive evidence. As persons, they were entitled to all constitutional guarantees under federal law and were slaves only under state law. Negroes born free were citizens, and all slaves born here were citizens when they became free, if indeed they were not citizens while slaves. Citizenship was not dependent upon recognition of right but upon place of birth. Slavery had no national character, was not recognized by the Constitution, and was not entitled to protection by the government. It was an exercise of force, recognized and sustained by state law, and could have no existence outside of a slave state. The natural state of man being one of freedom, the instant the exercise of force over the individual slave was broken, by the flight of the slave beyond the limits of a slave state to a free state, to foreign soil, or to the high seas, or by the flight of the master, he was free and could not be re-enslaved by any process. In short, wherever physical force or social force or municipal law failed, status fell and the slave was free. Freedom should always take precedence over slavery in doubtful cases. This was not a matter of theory, but of practical necessity. States which had adopted gradual emancipation, or had freed all slaves, could not uphold and could not countenance the doctrine that color was presumptive of servitude.

IX

The public debate of these questions began in Congress in 1804 on the basic question of whether a state, in pursuing its own interest, might disregard the general interest of the nation. Antislavery spokesmen affirmed that a state could not operate against the general interest of the nation because the latter was paramount to the Constitution itself. This was later refined into the doctrine that the Constitution must be interpreted in the light of the principles stated in the Declaration of Independence. Calhoun then put into classic form the opposing doctrine of concurrent majority which would have given to any state the power to determine the limits of the powers of Congress.

The debate in Congress grew more intense in 1820 when Missouri sought admission as a state with a constitution excluding free Negroes from its sovereignty. Antislavery men insisted that the Constitution created a national government whose powers were derived from the people in their collective capacity as citizens of one great republic; that the states were limited sovereignties, incapable of interfering with the high prerogatives of the general government and restrained from any action for their own interest which injured the nation; and that new states grew out of the Constitution, were created by Act of Congress and derived their powers directly from the Constitution. They also maintained that all persons born or naturalized in the United States were citizens of the United States; that privileges and immunities as used in the Constitution meant the natural rights of man; and that citizenship constituted a compact in which allegiance on the one hand and protection on the other were necessary incidents. In arguing the proof of Negro citizenship, they stated its attributes as place of birth, contribution to society, rights and privileges, and protection. Negroes had been born in the United States, had fought in its armies, had contributed to its wealth, and had exercised the franchise, in some congressional districts with decisive power in elections. They owned property, pursued their own economic and religious interests, enjoyed the protection of the law, were enumerated in the Census, paid taxes, sued in the courts, conveyed property, enjoyed the rights of jury trial and *habeas corpus*, and might attain to the highest public offices so far as the law was concerned, all equally with whites; and no denial of equality on the basis of color or race could be found in any of the nation's foundation documents.

The final great debate in this area came on the amendment in 1850 of the Fugitive Slave Act of 1793. No law passed by the federal Congress probably was ever more drastic in its consequences than this new statute, and none was more widely and systematically disobeyed. The law authorized a slaveholder or his agent to go into a non-slaveholding state and seize an alleged fugitive, take him before any federal, state, or local justice, present testimony that the person owed him service or labor, and receive a certificate of return to his home state. There were no safeguards against disturbances of the peace. Due process — *habeas corpus,* legal counsel, trial by jury, witnesses — was ignored in the original law, specifically denied in the amendment.

The 1850 amendment placed the main burden of enforcement upon United States commissioners and marshals. No part of the law was ever declared unconstitutional by the federal courts, and every decision was based in part on the assertion that Negroes were not party to the Constitution, and that no restraints must be placed upon slaveholders in recovery of their property. Every man, woman, and child, of color, so far as the provisions of the law were concerned, was liable to be seized, dragged before a justice of the peace or commissioner, and carried into slavery — all on the testimony of a stranger. Justices might well be venal, ignorant, or prejudiced; commissioners were nonjudicial officials and were bribed by a multiple fee to surrender the alleged fugitive. The arrests were actually seizures without warrants. The trials were summary hearings by one person. The testimony was *ex parte.* There was no provision for consideration of extenuating circumstances. *Habeas corpus,* testimony of witnesses, and legal counsel were denied. Anyone who aided a fugitive was in violation of the law and subject to fine and imprisonment; and law enforcement officials could command the assistance of citizens in enforcement of the law.

The citizens of the free states insisted that this was not a question of recovering fugitives, but of protecting free persons against enslavement, and it could not be done without *habeas corpus.* They would not concede color as a presumption of slavery, or narrow application of the law of property in fugitive slave cases. All persons caught up in the peculiar operation of the law, they said, must stand before the bar of justice fully clothed with constitutional safeguards of individual freedom. In 1861 this question was still moot.

X

The fourth broad area of conflict embraced the power of the federal government to contain slavery and to abolish it. The slave power insisted that slaves were property; that the definition of what was property was an exercise of sovereign power pertaining only to a state constitutional convention; that the states had not surrendered their sovereignty, but had retained, each to itself, the power to determine the nature of its grievances and the mode and measure of redress even to the point of secession; that the territories were the common property of the sovereign states; and that any person might go to the territories with his slaves, and be protected in their enjoyment by the federal government until a constitution was framed for admission into the Union. Northern Democrats were willing to agree that Congress could not abolish slavery in the territories, and that the people going there must be allowed to determine the nature of their own institutional development, but insisted the decision could be made by a territorial legislature.

For their part, antislavery men agreed that Congress could abolish slavery in the District of Columbia and in the territories which belonged to the people of the nation, not to the slaveholders. The doctrine of congressional exclusion, they said, was the oldest and most venerable of antislavery principles. They held that Congress had broad powers to protect the general welfare in bestowing statehood upon the people of a territory; could demand emancipation as a condition of admission; and could prohibit migration of slaves, thus compelling such state to remain forever free. They stood solidly for restoration of the prestige of the federal government, maintenance of the Union, and denial of local autonomy to any section by any means whatsoever.

The conflicting theories were stated in classic form before the presidential campaign of 1848. The Congress of 1850 made its decision as to policy. It was a complete victory for the slave power, again by virtue of the votes based upon slave representation. There was no admission of the evils of slavery. Negroes, citizens or not, were now to be surrendered to slaveholders and kidnappers as a matter of national policy. The federal government would use all of its powers to quiet the slavery controversy and to condemn resistance to the return of fugitives as treasonable. The territories were open to slavery. Slavery might not expand but Congress was not going to prevent it. The Kansas-Nebraska Act, reversing the 1820 exclusion of slavery from the Louisiana Purchase north of 36°30′ except for Missouri, followed as night follows the day.

The hard core of the Republican party in 1860 consisted of the veterans of the thirty-year contest to wrest control from the slave power. They had been unable to penetrate the South with their campaign of education and moral suasion. They now had three possible courses of action. They could reorganize the Supreme Court, or change its philosophy by normal process of appointments, to find in the Constitution congressional power to contain slavery. They could abolish slavery by amendment to the Constitution. They could abolish it under the war powers. Soon the war brought a vindication of the antislavery claim that, when the exercise of force in the master-slave relationship was broken, slavery ceased. Hundreds of thousands of slaves were abandoned by their owners and invaded the army camps as the armies moved into the slave country.

XI

The final broad area of controversy was not entirely sectional, nor yet entirely racial. It was a question of human relationships and attitudes unrelated to government but inseparable from slavery. It pertained to the free Negro, and to labor.

A major item in the "positive-good" thesis of slavery was the assertion that slavery had permitted the white race to develop a superior culture. Spokesmen for the slave power defended slavery as the most stable foundation for free institutions, and the best organization of society. They invoked the example of ancient Athens to prove that the highest culture required a slave basis. They insisted that whites and Negroes could not live together except on the basis of slavery.

Finally some Southern spokesmen began to insist that slavery was best, not only for the South, but for the whole country. George Fitzhugh in his book of 1854, *Sociology for the South; or The Failure of Free Society*, defined slavery as "a form, and the very best form, of socialism." Socialism, he said, "proposes to do away with free competition; to afford protection and support at all times to the laboring class; to bring about, at least, a qualified community of property, and to associate labor. All these purposes slavery fully and perfectly attains. . . . A Southern farm is the beau ideal of Communism." Free society having succeeded in producing only social conflict, class oppression and mass unemployment and misery, the answer — for the North as well as for the South — was slavery.

The logic of slavery apologetics thus concluded in a total repudiation of the philosophy of free society.

Antislavery writers accepted the challenge, and condemned slavery as the deadly enemy of free labor. As Walt Whitman put it in 1856, "You young men! American mechanics, farmers, boatmen, manufacturers, and all work-people of the South, the same as North! you are either to abolish slavery, or it will abolish you." They admitted the injustices and inequalities of wealth, but emphasized the equality of rights, the enjoyment of legal protection, freedom of movement, of expression, and of education, and participation in public affairs. The debate was not too important from the standpoint of Northern labor because free-born, intelligent artisans and farm boys were not much impressed by the argument that slavery was a positive good, not alone for Negroes but for all laboring men. It did react violently upon the South because the appeal to non-slaveholding whites of the South to overthrow a system which gave complete control of public affairs to a small minority of aristocrats and kept the region one of ignorance, poverty, and unbalanced economy disturbed the slave power almost as badly as an appeal for slave insurrection.

XII

Finally, no aspect of the slavery controversy was more revelatory than that having to do with the free Negroes. Beginning about 1817, intense controversy arose over the subject of colonization. Support for the idea of removing free Negroes from the country came from those who believed in the doctrine of biological inequality. In slaveholding communities, free Negroes were thought to be a potential source of insurrection and an ever-present source of unrest and disquietude among the slaves. Worst of all, from the slaveholders' view, they were proof of the Negroes' ability to make progress — a denial of his animal status. In non-slaveholding communities, they were thought to constitute a permanently degraded and undesirable element in the population. The American Colonization Society was organized in 1817 to remove them to Africa. Non-slaveholding states passed legislative resolutions in the middle twenties favoring the use of the proceeds from public land sales to finance a vast program of compensated emancipation and colonization.

Negroes, who now had some able leaders in the Eastern cities, held mass meetings and quickly demonstrated that they had no intention of going anywhere of their own free will. Few ever did go except as an alternative to remaining in slavery. The furor created by the movement, however, bore heavily upon the free Negroes. Humanitarians, in the tradition of Franklin, Woolman, and Benezet, quickly realized that an invasion of man's natural rights was involved in tearing people away from their homeland, friends, and property, and transporting them to another continent. The colonization program was a monumental endorsement of the doctrine of the immutability of Negro inferiority.

The struggle for equality, justice, and economic opportunity for Negroes, however, was made manyfold more difficult by the thousands of assertions and reiterations by colonizationists of Negro depravity. They did nothing to secure repeal of repressive legislation, or to educate the Negroes, or to protect them against abuse, or to promote emancipation. Their philosophy was not one of assisting the Negro, but of putting him out of sight; not to improve society by aiding the downtrodden and underprivileged but by getting rid of them. Only a capable people could have fled, as thousands did, from the depths of degradation in slavery, adjusted to freedom, educated themselves, and become intelligent citizens. Many attained high rank in the professions and in scholarship here and abroad. Thousands went to Canada as temporary refugees, but retained their devotion to the United States, and returned to sustain the nation in its hours of trial.

It was a cold wind that came out of the slave country; one which chilled the lifeblood of democracy nigh unto death. Basically, it grew to be a totalitarian philosophy which would have held three and one-half million people in perpetual slavery; which used both law and mob violence to suppress free inquiry and discussion; sought to seal the South against contamination by antislavery arguments; struck down the right of petition; condemned universal manhood suffrage; advocated enslavement of all laboring men; glorified its fancied racial superiority; sought to drive into exile all free Negro citizens; made war on its neighbors to acquire more slave territory;

and proclaimed the superior virtue of a society founded on human bondage. In the light of eighteenth-century liberalism, it was a deep and powerful current of reaction, which flowed through the churches, the schools, the legislative halls, and the courtrooms, staining everything it touched. And the end is not yet.

6

Ideas and Economic Development

Arthur M. Schlesinger, Jr.

The economic experience of the United States provides a compact example of the growth of an underdeveloped country into a great and rich industrial state. When the thirteen colonies gained their independence toward the end of the eighteenth century, they joined together to form a weak and diffuse nation of some four million people, living in a confederation of states straggling along the Atlantic seaboard. Contemporary students of economic development would find the pattern of 1790 familiar enough: four-fifths of the American labor force were farmers; capital, technology, and finished goods came predominantly from overseas; and the prevailing vision of the nation's economic future was agricultural. Today, a century and three-quarters later, the United States is a vast continental nation, with a population of nearly 170 million living in an opulent industrial society, ceaselessly generating its own capital and its own technology, dedicated to the objective of an ever-expanding economy.

I

One must hastily add that this experience offers little comfort in the middle of the twentieth century to the new nations of Asia and Africa struggling to overcome the torpor of centuries and to achieve economic and social modernization in a single generation. While America in 1790 possessed certain features of what we call in the 1960's an underdeveloped country, it also enjoyed certain advantages denied to most underdeveloped countries today—advantages that enormously facilitated the processes of economic growth on the North American continent.

Some of these advantages derived from America's natural situation. The new nation had available for exploitation a fertile subcontinent well supplied with resources. A brisk and temperate climate preserved health and stimulated energy. A wide ocean provided relative freedom from foreign aggression; national defense did not have to become a consuming claim on resources. But what was perhaps the decisive advantage lay in the character of America's population and in the ideas and institutions that this population brought with them.

The first conspicuous fact about the American people was that there were not many of them. The young republic had no problem of overpopulation; it was free from the curse of Malthus. Hungry masses were not pressing on resources and preventing the accumulation of capital. Public health was a spur, not a threat, to economic growth. Indeed, the relative scarcity of labor hastened development by creating a need for technological advances designed to render labor unnecessary.

Not only was the population scant in relation to land and resources; it was also fairly advanced, culturally, politically, and morally. The legacy of Calvinism and the rising faith of democracy joined in producing respect for learning and reason. Most Americans could read and write. They understood about the rule of law and had had significant experience in self-government. They believed in education and were prepared to invest a tolerable share of resources in schools and libraries. Calvinism had instilled in them the determination to work and to save; democracy was developing in them the capacity to consume and to enjoy. The combination made economic progress almost irresistible.

American society, moreover, having skipped the feudal stage of development, escaped many of the social rigidities and economic inequalities that bottled up talent and energy in contemporary Europe. The decision of the ex-colonies to federate after independence meant the beginning of an internal market and thus a developing stimulus to economic growth. Here was a nation where opportunity prompted men to develop latent abilities, where social mobility became the vehicle of economic energy. The ever-beckoning, ever-receding western frontier confirmed the inherent social mobility, intensified the instinct for swift adaptation to novel problems and circumstances, and promised a continental fulfillment of the American destiny. Americans were thus endowed by birthright with a spontaneous and spacious belief in opportunity and equality as the ends of society and in social, political, and technological invention as the means.

Work, democracy, innovation, education — these were particular sources of the national talent for economic growth. The commitment to work beyond the need for subsistence (a rarer thing in history than one might imagine) made it possible for individuals to begin the long labor of capital accumulation. The commitment to democracy, with the "pursuit of happiness" formally avowed as the national goal, expressed and encouraged the national passion for individual economic betterment. The commitment to innovation, the never-ending fascination with new methods, new materials, and new machines, provided the methodology for national abundance. The commitment to education, enlarging both the common fund of knowledge and the individual's access to it, assured the efficient use and the steady improvement of human resources. The mobility of American life thus stimulated the productive ambitions of millions of individual Americans, and egalitarian democracy assured a wide diffusion of the resulting benefits. The consequence of this fortunate alliance of ideas and institutions was a release of social energy which remade a continent and which has not yet been exhausted.

II

The challenge of economic development for the new nation involved two essential problems: the expansion of agricultural production; and, concurrently, the increasing shift of capital from land to trading, commerce, and industry. The first objective was shared by all the Founding Fathers. The second, however, raised crucial questions about the shape of the American future.

Some leaders of the young republic wished to preserve the new nation as a primarily agricultural society. This was the view of Thomas Jefferson, at least in his more doctrinaire moods. "Those who labor in the earth," Jefferson wrote, "are the chosen people of God, if ever He had a chosen people." The integrity of the national future required that the husbandman, secure under his own vine and fig-tree, remain the center of the American economy. "While we have land to labor then, let us never wish to see our citizens occupied at a work-bench, or twirling a distaff." It was far better, Jefferson thought, for the United States to export raw materials to Europe for manufacture than to bring an industrial proletariat to these virgin shores "and with them their manners and principles." "The mobs of great cities," Jefferson concluded, "add just so much to the support of pure government, as sores do to the strength of the human body."

Though Jefferson remained, in a general way, the champion of the agricultural way of life against the impending financial and industrial revolution, he was too astute a statesman to remain a doctrinaire defender of the agrarian economy. That role fell rather to his Virginian friend John Taylor of Caroline, who condemned all paper money and tariffs as means by which the agricultural sector was drained of money for the benefit of financial and industrial capitalism. Jefferson himself, especially during his periods of administrative responsibility, was more equivocal on these issues. He welcomed commerce; in time he regarded manufacturing as inevitable. To the end, however, he remained deeply suspicious of banking and stockjobbing; and if the role of activist government was nothing more than to upset the natural order of things in which the producer (i.e., farmer) enjoyed the fruits of his own labor, then, Jefferson concluded, that government was best which governed least. His conception of laissez-faire, it is to be noted, was more closely allied to that of the physiocrats, who favored an agricultural economy, than to the followers of Adam Smith, who were thinking in terms of a commercial and industrial nation.

The Wealth of Nations and the Declaration of Independence were both phenomena of the year 1776 — a coincidence that has led some to suppose that the stars of laissez-faire and of the American republic rose in unison and shone forth jointly on the world. But it was not so simple as this. The characteristic economic philosophy of Western Europe in the late eighteenth century was mercantilism. Most Americans in the early republic who thought at all about economic matters were raised in the mercantilist tradition.

Mercantilism was essentially the means by which predominantly agricultural countries in the seventeenth and eighteenth centuries set to work to change themselves into modern industrial states. The great mercantilist statesman was Colbert, under whose direction France took European leadership in economic development; and mercantilist ideas and policies soon spread wide through the states of Western Europe and their colonies. In time, the new economic classes helped into prosperity by mercantilism began to find mercantilist constraints irksome and, in consequence, mercantilist economics fallacious. The rising protest against mercantilism was given its most comprehensive and trenchant statement by Adam Smith. Still, as Adam Smith wrote, many people, while impressed by the aspirations of the laissez-faire economy, were yet unwilling to surrender cherished mercantilist objectives, especially those concerned with the development of national power.

This was essentially the state of mind of Alexander Hamilton, who dominated economic policy in the United States in the first years of the republic. For Hamilton, Colbert remained the *beau ideal* of an economic statesman. Hamilton's own dream was to transform sleepy rural America into a great industrial nation, and he saw in the national government the instrument to attain this goal. Yet he recoiled from Colbertian notions of minute governmental supervision of the economy. He had deep faith in the dynamics of individual acquisition, if tempered by a measure of public control; his countrymen had, as he wrote, "a certain fermentation of mind, a certain activity of speculation and enterprise which, if properly directed, may be made subservient to useful purposes but which, if left entirely to itself, may be attended with pernicious effects." The essence of Hamilton's policy was to transfer capital to those most likely to make use of it to increase the national productive power; in a series of notable reports, he spelled out the tactics of this policy. His Report on Manufactures was the first grand expression of the industrial vision of America; and the Hamiltonian program — the United States Bank, the assumption of the state debts, the protective tariff — was precisely designed to give capital to those who could be relied on to put it to vigorous economic use. The task of government, as he saw it, was to guide economic activity while at the same time inciting individual energy.

Where the Jeffersonians thus detested banks, paper money, stocks, bonds, and the other contrivances of capitalist finance, the Hamiltonians saw them as indispensable to economic progress. Where the Jeffersonians rejected the notion of a national debt, Hamilton wrote that a "national debt, if it is not excessive, will be to us a national blessing." The Jeffersonians, in short, envisaged an essentially static economy with an essentially passive government. The Hamiltonians saw government as a benign and indispensable agency in the exciting adventure of acquisition and growth.

III

The necessities of development were on the side of Hamilton — and one must emphasize this in face of the conventional interpretation of American economic growth as the result of the motive power of the unfettered individual. While this interpretation is fundamentally sound, it has been exaggerated into a mystique of national economic development through the unassisted workings of rugged individualism and free competition. In this view, American economic growth owes nothing to public activity or to outside assistance; it has been entirely the result of the unaided genius of the American enterpriser.

No one can deny the enterpriser his brilliant and central role in American economic history. Yet to make his the exclusive role is to ignore fundamental points about the developmental process. The first stages of transition from an agricultural to an industrial economy require a vast expansion of what economists call "social overhead capital" — roads, canals, bridges, habors, railroads. The need for such expansion came in the United States at a time when there was no great surplus of private domestic capital for investment, and when such capital in any case tended to find its outlet in lucrative but nonproductive fields like trading and land speculation. Once the process of economic growth got under way, then sagacious enterprisers might themselves save and reinvest a sufficiently high ratio of the annual addition to national income to fuel the economic machine. But until the moment arrived when private decisions produced a sufficiently high ratio of savings to incremental income, it was necessary to uncover other sources of capital in order, so to speak, to prime the pump. Where was the capital for pump-priming and social overhead to come from? For the United States in its infancy, as for underdeveloped nations today, the answer was from abroad and from the state (and to some extent from the inflationary stimulus induced by public and private operations).

Thus early American development could not have come about nearly so rapidly without the aid of the London capital market. Consider, for example, the creation of the transportation net — an example of singular importance, since railroads not only constituted the largest capital-investment outlet during most of the nineteenth century but also played the central role in galvanizing the entire economy. Foreign investment was heavy from the start; between 1860 and 1880 — years of particularly dramatic railroad expansion — more than half the railroad capital probably came from overseas. In its overall accounts, the United States was a capital importer for nearly all the nineteenth century and, indeed, until the First World War. Nor does calculation in strictly monetary terms allow for the even greater debt American development owed to foreign nations: the debt in crafts, techniques, technologies, ideas, and, above all, in people — in workers, enterprisers, and inventors. In providing economic and technical assistance to underdeveloped nations today, the United States is, in a sense, repaying its own early debts to others; it is staking other new nations, as Europe staked it in its own first years.

Government on all levels — local, state, and national — also served as indispensable sources, direct and indirect, of capital. To take the example of railroads again, local and state governments, under the authorization of nearly 2,200 special laws, furnished a third of a billion dollars of assistance. Of the $245 million required to build the 9,000 miles of Southern railroads of 1860, public authorities furnished, according to the best estimates, 60 to 70 per cent of the capital. National aid included direct subsidies to the transcontinental railroads as well as lavish indirect assistance through grants of the public land. Far from being a vindication of unassisted private enterprise, the American transportation net was the result of an ingenious, if often discordant, collaboration among private, public, and foreign agencies.

Nor was government assistance confined to railroads, canals, turnpikes, and the like. State governments made loans to a wide variety of productive enterprises. In some states — notably Pennsylvania and Virginia — systems of mixed enterprise developed, in which the state government bought shares in private corporations and installed its own men on the boards of directors. A number of states undertook direct public projects, of which New York's Erie Canal was only the most celebrated. Bounties, franchises, tax exemptions, grants of monopoly privilege, support of education — in all these ways the state stimulated and subsidized economic growth.

In so doing, it necessarily served to a degree as the planner of economic development. The very idea of *commonwealth* implied that the state had distinctive interests that were more than simply the sum of the interests of its citizens. Indeed, the corporation itself, which became in later days the stronghold of business freedom from government interference, came into use in America primarily as an instrument of state activity — as a means by which the commonwealth could guide and promote economic growth. Early corporations were set up by specific legislative enactment and, in the main, to provide social overhead for quasi-public purposes; the stipulations in the charter assured detailed legislative approval of all aspects of the resulting enterprise. In every decade before the Civil War (except for the thirties), over 50 per cent of new incorporations fell into the classification of "public utilities." The state supplemented this control over the foundation of an enterprise by a variety of laws designed to regulate its subsequent performance — licensing systems, inspection systems, public-utility rate control, trackage specifications for railroads, specie-paper ratios for banks, rudimentary factory legislation, and so on.

In short, the necessities of development, as Hamilton well understood, required public authority to take the responsibility for the creation of social overhead capital and even to some degree for the provision of capital for banking and manufacturing and for the determination of social and economic priorities.

The project of national economic expansion, based on the United States Bank, the tariff, internal improvements, and the national debt, soon acquired a name — the American System. Henry Clay was its most thrilling spokesman and John Quincy Adams its most far-seeing and philosophical advocate. "The great object of the institution of civil government," said Adams in his first message to Congress,

> is the improvement of the condition of those who are parties to the social compact, and no government, in whatever form constituted, can accomplish the lawful end of its institution but in proportion as it improves the condition of those over whom it is established. . . . To the attainment of the end — the progressive improvement of the condition of the governed — the exercise of delegated powers is a duty as sacred and indispensable as the usurpation of powers not granted is criminal and odious.

So, at the start of the republic, because men like Hamilton regarded public initiative as necessary to induce capital formation and industrial development, the economic philosophy of the business community tended to be interventionist. On the other hand, because men like Jefferson could conceive of no government action other than that which transferred wealth from the actual producers, "the plundered ploughman and beggared yeomanry," to the businessmen, the economic philosophy of the opponents of business rule was that of the negative state. The history of economic policy in the next century was the history of the gradual exchange of these positions.

IV

The age of Jackson marked the first stage in this process of exchange. The United States was now entering the period of take-off. This meant that there was a measure of self-generating economic activity, and, in this situation, the relationship of the government and the private enterpriser began to undergo significant changes. Thus, as private capital formation began to supply a larger share of capital needs, government was no longer playing so indispensable a role as the supplier of capital. The expense and the administrative confusion and graft in state-supervised developmental programs further encouraged what Carter Goodrich has called "the revulsion against internal improvements."

The change in the corporation itself was symptomatic. As the number of corporations multiplied, the link between each specific corporation and the state became more tenuous. In consequence, as the Handlins have pointed out, a distinction began to arise between public and private corporation, in which the profit-making corporation began to lose its original character as a public instrumentality and became increasingly exempt from public regulation (an exemption rapidly transformed into immunity by judicial action). The agitation of the Jackson period for general laws of incorporation was a recognition of the extent to which the state had lost control over the corporative process.

Without at first being aware of it, the business community was growing away from the Hamiltonian conception of publicly guided private enterprise. Then the politics of the Jackson period shocked businessmen into a conscious change of their attitude toward the state. The business community of the 1830's was angered not only by Jackson's aggressive conception of the presidential power but even more by the use to which he put this conception in disciplining and ultimately dispossessing the great contemporary symbol of American capitalism, the Second United States Bank. In the states too, Jacksonians displayed an irritating penchant for economic regulation and administrative experiment. If Jackson's own economic ideas were naïve and obsolescent, the political philosophy behind them was not. He was contending in effect that in a free society the democratic state had to be more powerful than any private concentration of wealth within that society. Hamilton had perhaps implied the same point, but Hamilton always saw government as the ally of business, and so the business community never had to face the latent issue. Jackson now demonstrated that strong government could easily turn into the regulator, if not the foe, of business. The issue of the interventionist state could no longer be avoided.

The politics of the Jackson period was in consequence a traumatic experience for businessmen. The result was to make business reconsider the whole mercantilist assumption that positive government was a good thing. In the new economic context, businessmen no longer saw an economic need for governmental activism. Under the stern eye of Jackson, they began to discern a belated charm in the Jeffersonian proposition that that government was best which governed least. Their perception was still confused by the fact that they wanted government action in specified realms, especially in tariff protection, and the validation of bank paper money as legal tender; they were not quite ready for a full-blown anti-statist declaration. But mercantilism was beginning to be left behind.

By 1837 it was clear to John Quincy Adams that his nationalist vision was fading away. A decade before, "the principle of internal improvement was swelling the tide of public prosperity," but now it was vanishing before the mischievous new appeal to free trade and state rights. As a consequence, he predicted, the United States would be condemned "to live from hand to mouth, and to cast away instead of using for the improvement of its own condition, the bounties of Providence." "I fell," cried the despondent statesman, "and with me fell, I fear never to rise again in my day, the system of internal improvement by means of national energies."

Actually the responsibility for the decline of the Hamiltonian dream lay neither with Jackson nor with the businessmen now flirting with the idea of laissez-faire. That dream was more fundamentally a casualty of the development process. After take-off, the private sector of the economy began to assume an increasingly important role. It could now relieve the public sector of responsibilities often inadequately discharged. The essential need was no longer the provision of social overhead capital; it was rather the maximization of production and innovation; and here the private sector came into its own.

V

The implications of all this for economic thought were not at once clear. The American System had gone, but nothing was rising to take its place. As the business community was dimly retreating from mercantilism, so those who sought to limit business power were dimly retreating from laissez-faire; but neither side was prepared to redefine its principles and policies. This was particularly true for the Jacksonians, whose commitment to Jeffersonianism was more explicit and doctrinaire than that of the business community to Hamiltonianism. Most Jacksonians, for example, saw the activism of the Jackson administration not as a prelude to positive government but as a means of restoring government in its pristine simplicity. It was necessary for government to hew away the Hamiltonian excrescences in order to recover the old Jeffersonian purity; the state had to become strong in order to become weak. Few Jacksonians perceived the implications of the Jacksonian drift. Roger B. Taney might say in a judicial decision:

> The object and end of all government is to promote the happiness and prosperity of the community by which it is established; and it can never be assumed, that the government intended to diminish its power of accomplishing the end for which it was created.

But in the main the Jacksonians resisted any such codification of their practice and instead clung to the Jeffersonian maxims which so badly interpreted their own experience.

Economic thought was suspended in the confusion of transition. Laissez-faire manuals were now being imported from abroad and attracting followers. Thus Say's *Catechism of Political Economy* was published in the United States in 1817, and John McVickar's *Outlines of Political Economy*, the first significant American laissez-faire text, came out in 1825. On the other hand, Friedrich List powerfully defended the American System during his American interlude, while the Jacksonians, if laissez-faire in theory, were interventionist in fact. Nearly everyone professed an indiscriminate mixture of economic ideas, drawn from both mercantilist and laissez-faire sources. The economist who perhaps came nearest to giving these ideas some shape and order was Henry Charles Carey.

Carey's effort was to reconcile Hamilton and Adam Smith — to provide enough scope for government action to vindicate at least the protective tariff (and perhaps a measure of social legislation) but not enough to hamper capitalist accumulation. Like Hamilton, Carey admired Colbert. He constantly insisted on "the necessity for the exercise of the social body, of that same coordinating and regulating power, we see to be so constantly exercised in the physical man." He was savagely critical of contemporary British economists, especially Ricardo, and sought to relieve Adam Smith from responsibility for the wage-fund theory and other hard-hearted doctrines of the Manchester school.

> Adam Smith did *not* believe in the abdication, by the governments, of the power of so co-ordinating the movements of the individual members of a society, as to enable all to become more productive. His successors do — the result exhibiting itself in the fact, that "markets have become fields of battle," strewed with the corpses of slaves and paupers. . . . Each and every step must be in the direction of declining civilization and approaching anarchy — that being the point towards which tends the doctrine of laissez-faire, and at which all communities must inevitably arrive, that allow themselves to adopt it for their guide.

Against the economics of despair Carey asserted an optimistic economics, centered on man rather than production and dedicated to the thesis that social intelligence could outwit Manchester's iron laws.

> Look where we may, we shall find evidence, that the necessity for the application of intelligence to the co-ordination of the movements of the various members of the societary body, grows with the growth of wealth and numbers, and that the more wisely it is exercised, the greater is the growth of production — the more rapid is the progress of accumulation — the more equitable is the distribution — the longer is the duration of life — the more perfect is the development of the local centres of action — and the greater is the tendency towards the creation of a sound morality, and towards the development of the real MAN, master of nature and of himself.

It was doubtless this strain in Carey that led Marx to call him "the only American economist of importance." But in detail Carey was much closer to Manchester than he would have liked to concede. The point of national coordination, as he saw it, was to remove obstacles to "association and combination," in other words, to set free the corporation, which he saw as the providential agency of economic change. The corporation itself became the operative center of his economics: anything which strengthened the corporation, from the high tariff to limited liability, was good; anything which weakened it, from trade unions to factory legislation, was bad. The corporation was both the product and the proof of "the harmony of nature." Having thus expelled the international version of laissez-faire, which served the purposes of the British economy, Carey devised a national version which fitted what he conceived to be the needs of his own land. The old Hamiltonianism was reduced to a few phrases and a single issue — the high tariff. By thus identifying protection with free enterprise, Carey assisted the process which won the tariff immunity from the general laissez-faire upsurge after the Civil War. He himself was the key figure in the transformation of the economics of the business community from Hamilton to Herbert Spencer.

VI

The Civil War completed this transformation. It provided stimulus to American industrial development both through direct government demand and through the capital reserves created out of greenbacks and war profits. More than this, it eliminated the main political forces opposing business control of the economy: the slaveholding aristocracy of the South, the foundation of whose power was destroyed, and the Jackson–Van Buren "radical democracy" of the North, whose energies, diverted for a generation to the crusade against the slave power, could not now reorganize to cope with the new power of business. The result was to enable the business community, entering an epoch of tremendous economic growth, to command the most potent resources of politics and ideology in making sure that this growth took place on its own terms.

Those terms were "sound" money, the protective tariff, and, above all, a ban on all forms of unsolicited government intervention, from regulation to taxation. This meant a repudiation of Hamiltonian notions about the economic leadership of the state, even in the diluted form espoused by Henry Charles Carey. Instead, the corporation and the enterpriser came to the forefront as the sacrosanct agencies of economic activity; the ideological problem was now to move beyond Carey in making America intellectually safe for private economic enterprise. In this venture, American economists drew on elements in their own tradition; they drew even more particularly on the great European exponents of laissez-faire, especially on Herbert Spencer, and on the new evolutionary philosophy derived from Darwin. Both Ricardian economics and Darwinian biology seemed to conclude with the doctrine that the survival of the fittest through free competition was the necessary condition to the progress of the race. With this, American economic thought entered a new phase.

Through American history ideas have served as a means of releasing economic initiative and then as a means of chastening economic arrogance; as a means of stimulating private energy and then as a means of reasserting public responsibility. One set of ideas helped to launch American economic growth. Another assisted in the great phase of private accumulation. When the passion for private accumulation threatened the values of democracy, another set of ideas prepared for public supervision and regulation. When private enterprise proved inadequate to maintain national growth, further ideas accustomed the nation to a new national commitment for economic development. What has mattered has been the philosophical flexibility, the intellectual resilience, of the people — the capacity to face new problems relatively unencumbered by the cults and clichés of the past. One must say "relatively": America, in the face of every new crisis, has had to fight its way out of the "conventional wisdom" (in the valuable phrase of J. K. Galbraith) which would otherwise condemn it to repeating the same old mistakes. Yet in the end reality has generally triumphed over dogma. The ability to change one's mind turns out, on last analysis, to be the secret of American economic growth, without which resources, population, climate, and the other favoring factors would have been of no avail. If the American experience bequeaths anything to nations facing today even more formidable problems of economic self-development, it is that nothing counts more than a faith in thought combined with an instinct for empirical reality — and an understanding that reality is forever changing.

PART THREE

From Reconstruction to the First World War: The National Phase

7

Social Darwinism

Donald Fleming

In all but name "Social Darwinism" antedated Darwinism. Its prophet was the Englishman Herbert Spencer (1820–1903), a civil engineer turned cosmic philosopher. In his *Social Statics* of 1850, he already displayed the unfamiliar amalgam of familiar ideas which lay at the heart of Social Darwinism: the harnessing of Malthusianism to the doctrine of progress which Malthus had been trying to explode. The lopping off of excess population did not lead in Malthus's system to any permanent improvement in the human race. He did think that weak people living in bad conditions would be the first to go under, but in the pendulum-swing of history between bad times and less bad, the class of such people would be continually reconstituted and as continually pruned by adversity. He did not deny that there had been progress in the arts of civilization, but mankind did not become progressively better fitted by heredity to practice these arts. Spencer on the contrary argued that the weeding out of inferior specimens would produce a cumulatively better race of men.

The ideal mode of life toward which Spencer thought the cosmos was hastening was the exercise by each man of his natural right to fulfill himself in freedom without encroaching upon the right of others. In Spencer no fewer than four lines of early Methodists met to produce a fierce resentment of external restraints, matched only by the inner constraint of Nonconformity by which all solicitations to Byronic hedonism were put down. If Spencer cannot be imagined living a rich, vivid, or abandoned life, he, no less than Byron or Shelley, was a doctrinaire of freedom in the great English tradition, a fanatic for independence. He had much to say about ever-enlarging sympathy among men as both the means and end of social evolution. But sympathy must never tip over into willingness to do anybody else's work or save him from the necessity of keeping his head above water by his own exertions. Sympathy did not even mean that people could contribute to the enlargement of each other's personalities; for the only basis of sympathy was a conviction that other people must be exactly like yourself. Awareness of others could not give a man any new perspective upon himself from their vantage point. The self for Spencer was precisely a kind of freestanding essence susceptible of infinite expansion but only from within. By no accident, the only American writer known to have influenced Spencer in his formative days was Emerson of Self-Reliance.

Given this philosophy of life, Spencer could only look with distaste upon the growing power of the state over the individual. Accordingly he gave in *Social Statics* a famous enumeration of things that the state must not do. It must not regulate industry, impose tariffs, bestow subsidies, establish a church, print money or mint coins, regulate entry into the professions, carry the mails, establish colonies, build or operate lighthouses, or maintain schools. Above all, it must not succor the poor, it must not improve sanitation, and it must not minister to the public health except to prevent general contamination of the atmosphere. At this critical point, Spencer's vindication of individual rights passed over into anxiety for the community without in any way reinstating the prerogatives of government. Society advances, in Spencer's most reverberatory phrase, by survival of the fittest. "The poverty of the incapable, the distresses that come upon the imprudent, the starvation of the idle, and those shoulderings aside of the weak by the strong, which leave so many 'in shallows and in miseries,' are the decrees of a large, far-seeing benevolence" — the same kindly dispensation that "brings to early graves the children of diseased parents, and singles out the low-spirited, the intemperate, and the debilitated as the victims of an epidemic."[1] "Under the natural order of things society is constantly excreting its unhealthy, imbecile, slow, vacillating, faithless members" to leave more room for the deserving. The only thing that stands in the way of this beneficent purging of the social organism is the maudlin impulse of the fit to prolong the lives of the unfit. Here the cosmic plan is frustrated in three directions: the unfit are kept alive; the fit are diverted from their proper task of self-realization and propagation of their kind; and the ranks of the dependent are swollen by marginal people who might have been scared into redeeming themselves by a close swipe of the pruning hook. Spencer was probably the greatest skeptic of modern times about the value of formal education, but one teacher was sovereign or there was no instruction to be had: "a sharp experience" of "the really salutary sufferings that surround us." Nothing must come between a man and his sufferings — neither public assistance from the state nor private charity from individuals. Private benefactions, he said, are no better than poor relief when they enable the recipients to "elude the necessities of our social existence." Must there be no charity at all? Only the charity of "helping men to help themselves."

This was the social teaching of Herbert Spencer, set forth almost a decade before publication of the *Origin of Species* in 1859 and two decades before Darwin discussed *The Descent of Man* in 1871. But Spencer's social philosophy, however independent of Darwin in origin, would never by itself have taken on the compulsive plausibility, the ineluctable relevance to the real world, which Darwinism retrospectively lent to it. It has often been said that Darwin himself was too bland and kindly to be a Social Darwinian. In point of fact, he struck in *The Descent of Man* the central note of the whole doctrine, that many forms of mutual help and sympathy are dysgenic — do private good at the expense of cosmic harm by impeding the maximum efficiency of natural selection. He gives a list of dysgenic factors in civilized life by which those who would otherwise go under in the struggle for survival and procreation are kept afloat by the rest, often at the direct expense of the latter: exemption of the physically inferior from warfare, with conscription of the strongest young men to die in battle and leave few or no heirs; public assistance to the poor; organized solicitude for the "imbecile" and "maimed"; and universal extension of medical benefits, so that, to take only one example, thousands of people who would have died of smallpox owing to weak constitutions have been spared by vaccination to become fathers of the race. Except for the policy on conscription, which was partly pragmatic as well as compassionate, all these dysgenic factors arose out of tenderness for the weak. The implication was clear that in Darwin's view tenderness had become a clog upon evolution. The only difference between Spencer and Darwin on the social bearing of evolution was that they did not have the same stake in their common opinions. Darwin could dispose of the matter in a few brisk pages as peripheral to his main accomplishment. Spencer's whole reputation was involved.

He projected more and more cosmic syntheses of absolutely everything — a complete "Synthetic Philosophy" — but the turgid current of his prose was almost choked at the source for want of subscribers. His early American admirers, led by the popularizer of science E. L. Youmans (1821–87), came to the rescue, invested $7,000 in his name in public securities, and enabled him to complete his intended shelf of Synthetic Philosophy. Youmans also induced Spencer to write a volume outside of his basic scheme but destined to become his most popular work, *The Study of Sociology* of 1873; and got Spencer's American publisher, D. Appleton, to start the *Popular Science Monthly* in 1872, partly as a puffing organ for Spencer's "big" books. The other principal figure in stirring up American interest in Spencer was the thin-spread "philosopher" and historian John Fiske (1842–1901), author of the vast Spencerian *Outlines of Cosmic Philosophy* (1874). Fiske was not primarily a popularizer of the social implications of evolutionary thought but an advocate of its compatibility with religion. Though Spencer gradually became a great figure in England as well as the United States, he always remained culture-bound to the English-speaking world.

A man who commanded little serious attention on the Continent but seemed to many Americans to be the greatest philosopher since Aristotle could not fail to have diagnostic value for understanding American society. Spencer's variation upon the theme of inevitable progress fell in with the general optimism of American life, the sanguine views of a people who had won their independence and spread to the Pacific. When, at the close of the nineteenth century, the national aspirations were breaking upon foreign shores, John Fiske and others could invoke Spencerian formulas about the survival of the fittest to put the stamp of the cosmos upon the advance of the Anglo-Americans to world dominion over lesser breeds. Spencer not only proffered a hopeful philosophy to a hopeful people, he fixed his hopes upon the same object as theirs: to enlarge the area of freedom. He stood for a democratically oriented conception of social science by contrast with the only available alternative, the authoritarian sociology of Auguste Comte (1798–1857). It is inconceivable that social science could ever have taken root in America under Comte's auspices. One Anglo-American writer in the Comtian tradition, the chemist-historian John W. Draper (1811–82) of New York University, did acquire a considerable if spurious reputation as one of the prophets of Darwinism, but his conception of a severely planned society under a scientific elite made no impression. Draper was anti-Catholic and Comte a lapsed Catholic turned atheist, but the conception of social science for which they stood was profoundly Catholic — authoritarian, hierarchical, and requiring the imposition of external discipline upon the bulk of mankind. Herbert Spencer by contrast invoked the native self-discipline of Protestantism.

This was merely one aspect of the deep harmony between Social Darwinism and the cultural residues of Protestantism by which even the most liberated Americans were marked. The path of Darwinism was smoothed by the fact that, however much it imperiled theology, it reinforced the prevailing ethical climate of Protestant America. Where the Protestant ethic taught men to lay up riches to the greater glory of God, Social Darwinism taught them to fulfill themselves to the improvement of the species. Both turned self-concern into a social good. In the economic sphere, Spencer commended precisely the doctrinaire individualism which was being enfolded within the ark of the American covenant between Jackson and Cleveland. At a time when the states were abandoning many of their traditional controls over economic life and the federal government had not yet taken up the slack, nothing could have been more congenial to the American temper than Spencer's philosophy of liberation from the trammels of government.

If, in many respects, Spencerism appeared to be a cosmic ratification of actual American experience, neither it nor any other philosophy ever made its way by constituting a perfectly smooth fit to the existing body politic. A political philosophy to command disciples must serve to pare away excrescences, point to desirable new inclusions within the national ethos, or disclose a discrepancy between ideals and practice. This incentive to purification of the national life was the charm that Spencerism bore for William Graham Sumner (1840–1910), sometime Episcopal rector turned professor of political and social science and unrivaled prodder of the undergraduates at Yale. His father was an immigrant English workingman, largely self-educated, who inculcated the virtues of industry, thrift, self-denial, and self-reliance upon his children, and supplied them with an archetypically dour stepmother who economized upon expenditures and emotions alike. The family group was seclusive without being warm or united. The scholar who emerged from this background was a party of one, with a pungent style and a great contempt for popularity. When President Noah Porter objected to his assigning Spencer's *Study of Sociology* to undergraduates, Sumner without actually persisting in the use of the book seized the opportunity to endow his colleagues at Yale with a ringing charter of academic freedom.

The great evil of American life which Sumner hoped that Spencerism might cast out was egalitarianism, in the form of sour envy of abler men by less able and a desire to deprive the former of their substance to help the latter. Such "equality" so enforced made a mockery in Sumner's view of the only true and honorable equality. All self-supporting men (and no others) are entitled to participate equally in the political process and thereby contribute to the sole legitimate functions of government, to protect the property of men and the honor of women. The whole point, he says, in extending the suffrage to new groups is to contract the sphere of government to these dimensions. They are put upon an equal footing with everybody else, so far as this lies within human power — i.e., given equal access to the polling place and courts — precisely to ensure that the government shall have no further obligation to them. They are, in a word, set free. If, however, government is perverted to supply the ill-endowed with support at the expense of the well-endowed, both sides lose their freedom. The latter have the disposition of their means taken from them for the use of others — a modern tyranny of paupers to match the old tyranny of princes;

but the ill-endowed are also made radically unfree by yielding up their claim to fend for themselves. If it be said that to be free on the terms accessible to poor men is a harsh consolation, freedom *is* harsh. Sumner was prepared to grant that slavery conferred benefits upon the Negro and emancipation brought hardship with it. Hardship must be endured by the free Negro and the free white man alike; but that was not the worst evil, indeed the *possibility* of knowing hardship was the best good because the best touchstone of freedom. Men ought to rejoice in being Americans, the people of all peoples in history who have most thoroughly left a society of status behind and entered upon an age of contract. In a society governed by contract, unfavorable contracts will be made. This is the price that has to be paid for enabling the fittest men to contract their services to maximum advantage and the less fit to get as much, though poor, advantage as the cosmos will permit them. The reign of contract entails an end to all dependence of one class of people upon another or upon society as a whole. In Sumner's view, *What Social Classes Owe to Each Other* (the title of his little book of 1883) is nothing. If, however, the poor persist in looking for favors from government, they will keep alive the idea of the state as a favor-granting engine by which plutocrats and tariff-men will benefit more than anybody else. Sumner was a horrified spectator at the Great Barbecue and felt the need to cleanse and purify the national life. Spencerian individualism was his medicine against plutocracy. He thought it could be an instrument of national regeneration, recalling men from the sordid transactions of the Gilded Age to the old American ideal of equal standing under an incorruptible government of laws.

The injustice done by the favor-philosophy of government Sumner embodied in his famous conception of the "Forgotten Man." When *A* and *B* combine to make *C* give something unearned to *D*, *C* is the Forgotten Man, who by contriving to acquire enough substance to be levied upon is thereby rendered eligible to be victimized in behalf of the less deserving *D*. The figure of the Forgotten Man took on great pathos for Sumner as corresponding to his own father, valiantly struggling to keep afloat but too proud to look to anybody else for help. The community took the least thought for the welfare of its most deserving members and actually made them less capable of filling the role of Sumner's "hero of civilization," the savings-bank depositor, who by sacrifice of immediate satisfactions contributed to the accumulation of capital and the progress of mankind.

Sumner did not offer any general strictures on private charity, though why it should be any less injurious to society for the Forgotten Man to help the unfit out of his own pocket rather than by payment of taxes Sumner did not explain. The American who bearded private charity in its den and trimmed its claws was Josephine Shaw Lowell (1843–1905). A girl of eighteen in 1861, wishing to march off to war with the men but determined to pull her weight behind the lines, she became active in the New York branch of the United States Sanitary Commission, a private relief organization for soldiers and their families. Her sense of consecration, already strong, was deepened by the heroic death in battle of her brother and her husband. She had said before they died, and maybe she continued to believe, that there was something beautiful about men dying under discipline. This period of patriotic fervor, when spirited young women chafed at being mere women, left an enduring mark upon American institutions in the form of Clara Barton's American Red Cross and the founding of the first nursing schools in the United States. More generally, it raised up a group of wellborn women of means, best symbolized by Mrs. Lowell herself, who had found themselves in service to others and could never relapse into idle domesticity. This was a universal phenomenon of the Western world, reflected in the career of Florence Nightingale, but given a special American context by the crisis of civil war and the problem of living with the conscience of the rich in leveling America.

The whole situation, of rich, conceivably maudlin, and probably vague women casting about for some good to do to someone, was fraught with immense peril for the Spencerian philosophy. Mrs. Lowell had never been maudlin, even as a girl; she had been tempered to a steely hardness in wartime; and there was no vagueness in her. She proceeded to install Herbert Spencer as the presiding genius of American charities. She held that the day had passed when the rich could make their peace with the poor by indiscriminate alms to the most insistent beggars. In the matter of charity, society at large had its rights against rich and poor both — Spencerian rights of protection against the maintenance of a parasitical class of the unfit acting as a drag upon progress.

The institutional embodiment of this philosophical skepticism about charity was the Charity Organization Movement, begun in London in 1869 and first taking root in America at Buffalo in 1877. Mrs. Lowell herself founded the Charity Organization Society of New York city in 1882. Charity organization was an administrative device, based upon the keeping of common records by existing charitable bodies, to see that charity did not overlap from different sources and did not abound for anybody. Mrs. Lowell held that ideally all relief ought to be restricted to people "inside the doors of an institution" unattractive enough to make them want to get out. She acknowledged, however, that it was often necessary to relieve temporary distress in people's own homes. In that event, she said, never take a big basket of food, but just enough for one day — never money — so that they would be in genuine doubt about what they were going to eat the next day unless somebody promptly got a job. She was a strong opponent of soup kitchens and doles in time of depression. Useful work she would try to find for anybody who needed it, and even "made" work sooner than food or money. This philosophy had the triple merit in her eyes of getting all salvageable people back on their own feet, ridding society of an unnecessary drag upon evolution, and sparing the industrious classes the bitter reflection that nobody gave a thought to them but everybody loved to be at the beck and call of the shiftless. Mrs. Lowell spoke with deep feeling of the ordinary working people who "do not complain, or ask for sympathy," or get any; who struggle and work, live and die, "and very few people trouble themselves about them, little realizing that instead of helping them, they are often sadly hindering them, and even adding to their hardships by their vain efforts to help an entirely different set of people" — "the poor idlers, the failures, the broken-down men and women who could not stand the strain of the working life because of some special weakness either of body or mind or character."[2] The unregarded workingman who stumbled along under this burden of the unfit was Mrs. Lowell's version of the Forgotten Man and the true object of her sympathies in charitable work. She never did warm to the recipients of charity; but by taking them in hand she could get between the Forgotten Man and the unreflecting people of good will, shield him from the worst injuries they might otherwise inflict upon him by their susceptibility to beggars and weaklings. She gave unloving service to the charity cases in order to be of use to the Forgotten Man.

Though Mrs. Lowell lived on with unabated vitality into the twentieth century, she remained in essence a product of the Civil War period: the original motive-spring of her benevolence was patriotism. If the war could launch women like herself and Clara Barton on lifelong careers of service, it set the seal for American society at large upon the acquisitive instincts and every-man-for-himself philosophy which appeared to power the triumph of the industrial North over the agrarian South. It was precisely this self-regarding ethic which Spencer and Sumner were sanctifying in the name of the cosmos. For all her Spencerian leanings, Mrs. Lowell was proof against the virus of self-seeking. Many younger men and women, as they looked on in disgust at the behavior of the Robber Barons, also felt an urgent need for some kind of unselfish labor to perform. They did not have Mrs. Lowell's memories of wartime to validate the possibility of widespread devotion to the greater good; they did not want, even if they had the money, to be devoted amateurs of the unselfish life on her model, but learned professionals keeping in step with the advance of the experts to dominion; and oftentimes they did not have her secure foundation of religious faith to build upon. The characteristic professional outlet for unselfishness before Darwin had been the Christian ministry. But this was no answer for the growing number of women who were looking for careers. More profoundly, it was increasingly less eligible as a calling for intelligent men. That was the great change wrought by Darwin in the history of the professions. Yet the decline of orthodox religion among the intellectuals did not weaken their drive toward service, for they were eager to show that loss of faith need not be at the expense of decent human relations.

This was the psychological context for the founding of the first American graduate schools, as at Johns Hopkins in 1876, and the reform of medical instruction, begun at Harvard and Pennsylvania in the seventies and reaching a climax with the opening in 1889 of the Johns Hopkins Hospital (regarded from the outset as a teaching institution) and in 1893 of the Johns Hopkins Medical School. An exit from the acquisitive struggle had been found — for most American intellectuals a more acceptable exit than expatriatism, but partaking of the same revulsion from the main circumstances of contemporary American life. Attendance at the new graduate and medical schools was a form of internal expatriation from the Gilded Age.

Apart from the implied secession from the Spencerian ethic of individualism, scientific medicine as practiced in the university hospitals offered a grave challenge to other Spencerian values. Entry upon a career in medicine had always been a sign of concern for the weak, and correspondingly at odds with the main animus of Spencerism. The contradiction was sharpened by the introduction of anesthesia and modern narcotics. Medical science became the characteristic bearer of the nineteenth-century resolve to get rid of pain and suffering. Yet natural selection could achieve its maximum scope only by letting pain and misery take their toll of the unfit. John Fiske had said that the main theological bearing of Darwinism lay in inducing a reconciliation to pain as the means of evolutionary progress. Every new recruit to medical science automatically took up arms against this position. Medicine was the sworn enemy of pain and now at long last the about-to-be-triumphant enemy. New dimensions of tenderness among men were being opened up by the aid and example of scientific medicine. Even apart from the circumscription of pain, the state of medical knowledge had finally reached the point where doctors might hope to be of demonstrable use to an appreciable number of patients. Yet people who were mended and patched by the doctors would have in general less constitutional vigor than those who did not have to be. As the mending and patching became more ingenious, more people of inferior vitality would be returned to the breeding pool of the species and enabled to propagate their kind.

The hospitals of the new dispensation had been transformed not merely by an infusion of scientific medicine but also by a sweeping reformation of nursing. The hospitals of the mid-nineteenth century probably killed more patients by rampant cross-infection than they helped. To that extent, they contributed to Spencer's ideal of winnowing the race. Now, however, after the joint labors of Florence Nightingale, Lord Lister, and the founders of the Johns Hopkins Hospital, some hospitals were beginning to save lives. If this had been a matter of saving only those who could afford to pay for the care, that would have been doubtful enough by strict Spencerian principles. Any limitation to those who could pay was in fact precluded by the whole tradition of hospitals in the Christian world. Ample provision must always be made for charity patients. The new elements in the situation were the advance of medical knowledge and nursing skill, by which hospital care became more desirable, and the character of the best of the new hospitals as teaching institutions attached to university schools of medicine. Charity patients were an absolute necessity for medical students and interns to "practice" their art upon. A dearth of charity patients became a social evil in impeding the advance of medical science and instruction. The result was active competition for charity patients in cities with more than one teaching hospital and a warm welcome where there was only one. An institution historically committed to even-handed dispensing of charity was now bound more than ever to the charitable wheel. By so much, hospitals were actually performing what they had ineffectually aspired to perform in the past — the labor, dysgenic in Spencer's view, of enabling the dependent to stay alive and multiply side by side with the self-supporting.

The graduate school as the other principal institution by which young Americans were entering upon a secular form of the unselfish life was almost equally at odds with Spencerism. William Graham Sumner did participate in the transformation of Yale College into Yale University; and other men of his temper found a platform in the new or reformed universities from which to impress their views upon the next generation of scholars. On the whole, however, the situation in the graduate schools was inherently unfavorable to Spencerism. They were consciously striving for an orientation toward Germany and the Continent to complement the characteristic American absorption in England. For Ph.D.'s who piled study in Germany on top of their American training or at any rate studied in America under German-made professors, Herbert Spencer fell into perspective as a local writer of the English-speaking tribes and as no Aristotle. More specifically, young Americans who went to Germany, like the economist Simon N. Patten, or got a whiff of Germany from their professors, like Patten's student at the University of Pennsylvania, Edward T. Devine, were exposed to a conception of social science very different from Spencer's — above all, more receptive to statism and central planning.

The native American who crystallized the opposition to Spencer was Lester F. Ward (1841–1913). His father was a mechanic with an inventive turn of mind. The son went to work for the Treasury Department in Washington in 1865, acquired academic degrees on the side, and by ferocious self-application qualified for appointments as geologist and paleontologist to the United States Geological Survey. In the process he worked his way into the close-knit circle of career scholars in Washington, the intellectual aristocracy of government employees, who could never think of the state as a mere restraint upon the liberty of the individual. They had found fulfillment in its service and an opportunity to do constructive work. Ward thought that one of the best of all words was "official." It was a judgment that epitomized his *Dynamic Sociology* of 1883.

Dynamic Sociology by its very title is a rejoinder to Herbert Spencer, a social dynamics of the positive state to counter the *Social Statics*. Ward's thesis is that sociology must begin where a narrowly conceived Darwinism leaves off. Evolution through natural selection as expounded by Darwin is merely "genetic," an invidious term for Ward which he used to mean change without direction, aimless dynamism which does not point to any end of human choosing. Artificial selection, as of livestock but also susceptible in Ward's opinion of application to breeding a better species of men, is "teleological," marked by conscious advance toward chosen ends and correspondingly more desirable. The great accomplishment of natural selection was to bring men to the point where they had the brains to escape from its domination. Civilization is artificial and ought to be more so. That was the kind of purposive evolution that had a future.

In his contempt for mere passive submission to nature, Ward showed himself to be more a disciple of Francis Bacon, whom he often praised, than of Charles Darwin. Ward was proclaiming for the social sciences the doctrine that Bacon had pronounced for the physical and biological: that pure science is barren without practical applications. The use of discovering natural forces is to master them. As the physical sciences ought to result in new mechanical inventions, so the science of society ought to lead on to new social contrivances for the organization of greater happiness. Inventors were the cutting edge of the human race for Ward, whose own father had the right instincts even if his inventions did not amount to anything.

The unpardonable offense of Herbert Spencer, as Ward saw it, lay in trying to construct a science of society that was self-stultifying, with a built-in prohibition upon using it to improve the quality of life. By his espousal of the do-nothing philosophy, Spencer sought to turn the discovery of social forces into an argument against harnessing them. For Ward it was as if Newton had laid a ban upon applying the principle of gravity. It was both possible and wise to harness gravity and other physical forces and not let them run to waste. Equally the cosmos did not forbid men to apply any social forces they could discover to the manufacture of greater happiness.

In this sphere, the great invention for generating inventions would be scientific government — not, says Ward, "the present empirical, anti-progressive institution, miscalled the art of government," but an agency of "amelioration," such as the world has never seen, seeking to confer positive benefits upon the people rather than merely holding them in check.[3] The organs of ameliorative government would constitute "a central academy of social science, which shall stand in the same relation to the control of men in which a polytechnic institute stands to the control of nature." Government ought to be a feat of civil engineering, by which the native instincts of men would no longer be repressed or hindered, as by all present governments, but diverted into socially useful channels and made to do good work. Ward did not give any clear prescription as to how this project was to be carried out except by prodigious quantities of public education. Others would have to create the science of government by which the positive state would be guided. Ward was the prophet of its coming to pass.

Though slow to attract general attention, from the end of the eighties forward *Dynamic Sociology* was exerting a profound influence upon young academic sociologists like Albion W. Small of Chicago and the "Populist" Edward A. Ross of Stanford, Nebraska, and Wisconsin, who spoke of Ward as "master, pioneer, and pathfinder in sociology." Ward's doctrines when expounded by instructors to graduate students were bound to fire some of the latter to get out and actually perform constructive labors. In human terms, the matter went much deeper than that. Some men and women who had been drawn to graduate school as a refuge of unselfishness in a grasping society and secular age found that the life of mere scholarship was empty. They had recovered the minister's exemption from self-seeking but not his mission to be of direct help to people in trouble. At the point where scholarship did not seem to be enough, the still unfulfilled students joined the contemporary assault upon pain and suffering. This was not merely a matter of chloroform and morphine but of personal and social relations. The introduction of anesthesia and modern narcotics coincided with the birth of movements for kindness to animals and children and the abolition of serfdom and slavery. In the process men and women alike were humanized and made more sensitive to suffering. Yet it was inevitable that as women began to look for a career outside the home, they, even more than men, would try to become agents of the new tenderness, to show that they had not lost their essential womanhood. This had been no great problem for Mrs. Lowell, who always retained her posture of a public-spirited society woman, the least provocative category of feminine expression outside the home. For younger women who could not afford this posture or did not hold with it, and for some men besides, a new profession of social work was crying out to be born.

The general historical sequence of unselfish careers in America — from the Christian ministry for men only before the Civil War, through trained nursing for women as a legacy of the war, to scholarship, scientific medicine, and social work for both sexes as a form of revulsion from the Gilded Age — can actually be seen telescoped in the life-experience of certain individuals. The classic instance is Jane Addams, wrought upon by many of her teachers and college-classmates to become a missionary; beginning and breaking off the study of medicine; attending but not relishing lectures in the graduate school at Johns Hopkins; and only finding her true career in 1889 at Hull House in Chicago, as the leader of the settlement house movement in America. Nobody else tried on as many roles as Jane Addams, but the same general pattern is discernible in others. Lillian Wald went to nursing rather than medical school, on her way to founding the Henry Street settlement in New York and the tradition of visiting nurses in America; Edward T. Devine had been a graduate student of Simon Patten's in economics at the University of Pennsylvania before he found his appointed niche in Mrs. Lowell's Charity Organization Society of New York; Mary

Kingsbury Simkhovitch had been a graduate student in Berlin and at Harvard before founding West End House in New York; and Robert A. Woods had attended Andover Theological Seminary before setting up South End House in Boston.

Of these, the greatest, because most intelligent and least parochial, was Jane Addams (1860–1935) of Hull House. She became at once the philosopher of the settlement movement in America and eventually Mrs. Lowell's successor as chief interpreter of the charitable enterprise in general. In early days, she tried to go along with Mrs. Lowell's own ideas. In the desperate depression winter of 1893, an unemployed clerk whom she knew to be of good character came repeatedly to Hull House for relief. She finally told him that she did not think he ought to keep coming back when there were jobs to be had digging on the drainage canal. He protested that he was not up to manual labor out of doors in winter; but she could not take back her advice — that was what an up-to-date, scientific charity worker was supposed to say. He worked on the canal for two days and died of pneumonia within a week. Jane Addams always kept an eye out for his children. She said she had learned a bitter lesson at their expense. The charity movement had become pervaded by a "pseudo-scientific spirit" of which the whole wisdom was negative: "don't give," "don't break down self-respect," don't trust effective intelligence and constructive action, don't *act*.[4]

In time Jane Addams evolved an entire counter-philosophy, more hopeful of human nature and of active intervention in problematical situations, which is best understood as an inversion of Sumner's glorification of the Forgotten Man. She used to tell a story about a Forgotten Woman, a widow in the Hull House ward, with a neat little house and many stringent economies, who sent her daughters east to college and held herself severely aloof from the engulfing tide of Italian immigrants. The woman asked nothing of her neighbors and proffered nothing in return. In particular, she would have no part of the efforts to obtain a better code of tenement house sanitation. In 1902 typhoid broke out in the ward, did not understand that she was to be spared the experience of her neighbors, and killed one of her fine college-bred daughters. Jane Addams had no gentle verdict to pass upon the mother. She was an object-lesson in "the futility of the individual conscience which would isolate a family from the rest of the community and its interests."[5] So much for a woman who was a veritable type of the Spencerian ideal, self-contained, self-reliant, and tight-fisted of spirit.

What had come to seem intolerable in Spencer's and Sumner's philosophy was the narrow, almost secretive isolation which it commended — a hoarding up of the self and house-detention of all vivid emotions and outgoing sympathies. Sumner lauded the savings-bank depositor as a hero of civilization; but his philosophy did not allow for maximum investment of the self in human relations. Sumner's ideal man would live to himself in his own family, and the unextended Anglo-Saxon family at that. No style of life could have been less satisfying to Jane Addams. She, without being strident about it, was a great believer in the liberation of women and found the chief obstacle to this in the idea that a woman after having her sympathies enlarged by education ought to sink back into the family and contract her range of interests accordingly. A philosophy which appeared to sanctify the same attitude for men undercut the whole feminist strategy of demanding for women what men demanded for themselves. Jane Addams's distaste for confining the emotions within a small domestic circle fell in to perfection with her exposure to the extended family and village unit among her clients at Hull House, the "new" immigrants from southern and eastern Europe. She was fascinated by these gregarious people who appeared to have their whole being in the open and in throngs, where the most remote relationships were kept in repair, and all the immigrants from a village in Sicily would crowd into the same tenement and put the social organism back together as well as they could. Native Americans asked why these peasants did not fan out over the farm country. Jane Addams knew the answer: they could not imagine living as American but few other farmers did, each family to itself, in the middle of a big plot of land, and rattling about in an empty social space. They would let their immemorial calling go by the board before they gave up whetting their social instincts upon a large group of companions.

To Jane Addams this was not perverse but wise and sane: one of many admirable qualities which she discovered in her neighbors at Hull House. She and other people in settlement houses had the advantage of Mrs. Lowell in seeing the life of the poor in the round. Charity workers saw them in one context only, the economic, at the moment when the machinery of their ordinary lives had broken down. The charity agent found herself lecturing them upon the economic virtues as if these were the only good thing under the sun and none of their own. Jane Addams at Hull House did not always see the poor at low tide, gasping for breath and devoid of graces. One woman whom she did visit in extremities burned with embarrassment till the family got back on its feet and Jane Addams could be asked to supper to see that they were not always down and out. A neighbor who lived in a settlement house could trace the whole arc of a family's excursion from bad times to good. In this situation of seeing people close up from day to day over long periods of time, no imaginative person could judge the poor as mere deficient specimens of economic man. Jane Addams and other settlement house leaders took in the many-sidedness of the poor and perceived that there was no one fitness but a whole gamut of fitnesses spread out through all classes of men and ranks of society.

Her capacity for detecting the positive values of life among the poor was bound up for Jane Addams with an effort to see herself as they did. It seemed to her that while she was ticking them off for lack of economic foresight and general slackness of tone, they would be entitled to sour reflections upon her pampered state, cramped horizons, and lack of a husband. She thought all social workers ought to try this exercise of imagining the figure they cut in the eyes of their clientele; but for a dweller in a settlement house it was absolutely essential. The people around Hull House did not have to avail themselves of its facilities, they had to be coaxed into coming, and the staff members had to project an image that would not put them off. The best settlement worker was the one who could get out of himself and into the character of the poor as they gingerly approached these strange people who did not have to live in the slums but wanted to.

The role-taking was not all on one side. All the activities and forms of self-expression provided by the settlement houses — classes, debates, parties, theatricals, arts and crafts — were so many opportunities for the poor to step out of their ordinary selves and "try on" the style of life of the settlement workers. No activity was more popular than putting on plays, but the whole process of entering a settlement house, on whatever errand, constituted a dramatic performance from the moment of coming in off the street to going out again — the assumption of a new role with new modes and models of existence. Jane Addams did not think that this exchange of roles had to be a process of self-estrangement for either the social worker or the poor. A slum girl might have to stand back and look at her family through a settlement worker's eyes to perceive that her old peasant mother's skill in making lace was a thing to be admired; but henceforth the daughter would take more, not less, pride in her background. The social worker need not shrink into herself on perceiving what graces she lacked and the poor possessed: she could expand to fill the occasion of her contacts with them and become a more generous personality. The good that Jane Addams had in view was not the humiliation of either side but the enlargement of their perspectives.

She had been moving in her first twenty years at Hull House toward a new conception of the growth of personality, not by hugging one's identity tight and jealously fending off incursions but by incorporating other people's selves and perspectives into one's own nature. No challenge to the prevailing animus of Spencerism could have been more profound. By no accident, a consciously anti-Spencerian science of social psychology was being reared on the very same foundation by certain of her contemporaries, of whom the great pioneer in America was the sociologist Charles H. Cooley (1864–1929) of the University of Michigan. To show that this was no merely ideal relationship, Cooley cited Jane Addams more often than any other American in his book *Social Organization* (1909). Cooley, as befitted a more systematic thinker, addressed himself to the technical issue of the nature of the "self." William James in his great *Principles of Psychology* of 1890 had dwelt upon the capacity which men have of regarding their own "self" as an external object with the same general status as other objects and susceptible of a surprisingly cool contemplation by the possessor. Cooley came forward to argue that nobody is born with a self but only acquires one in a process of interaction with other people, above all in the form of pretending to *be* other people and in this character actually eliciting a definition of the self. Every child, said Cooley, goes through an extended period of make-believe in which he is never alone but always able to conjure up a whole group of imaginary companions, to him vivid, circumstantial, and undeniably "other," in fact, often grown up, who "talk" to him, give him orders, raise difficulties for him, and in general constitute so many self-incorporated points of resistance to the mere unconstrained flow of his elemental being. They are vehicles, in short, of the process by which he delimits a self. Cooley did not think that the self was ever completed or the necessity dispensed with as long as life endured to exchange selves with other people. His general position was elaborated upon by various Americans and often juxtaposed with the social teaching of John Dewey. In Europe Sigmund Freud was converging with a different terminology upon the same proposition, that other selves and a collective social self are taken up into the personality of the individual as an inclusion within his own ethical apparatus. The celebrated "ego" of Freud was a reasonable facsimile of Cooley's "self," charged with mediating between the primeval urges of the "id" and the constraints of the "superego" or body of social opinion.

If, as men were now coming to believe, the self was socially conditioned, indeed socially generated, it became something of a mystery why Spencerism had ever taken hold. One explanation that was widely canvassed at the opening of the twentieth century was that the Spencerian ideal did correspond more nearly to the reality of many people's lives at this point in history than the anti-Spencerians liked. Jane Addams and other students of society thought that the circumstances of urban existence were paradoxically consigning many people of the old American stock to a more secluded style of life than they or their forebears had ever known in the village or small town. Jane Addams even began to think more kindly — at a safe distance — of village meddling, as an acknowledgment of common humanity, the other side of the coin of mutual help, and more acceptable than chilly aloofness. Spencer's and Sumner's philosophy of isolation within the unextended family could never really be acted out on Main Street. In the sprawling anonymous city, there was ample opportunity to become the ideal Spencerian, forgetful of others and forgotten, till typhoid or some other natural force beat down the walls of seclusion.

Even where the will to socialize was strong, as among the new immigrants, many problems of urban life in the twentieth century — street cleaning and lighting, purification of the water supply, improvement of tenement housing, reduction of mortality from tuberculosis and other "crowd" diseases, provision of parks and playgrounds — resisted mere informal neighborliness. Jane Addams called for a higher level of social consciousness, a new magnitude of awareness that would take in the entire urban community and invoke its collective strength. If social concern could once break through to this new level, she thought that the promise of the city would begin to be fulfilled. By the same token, Spencerism would be dead; for the two chief things required were appropriation of tax money for ends anathema to Spencer and Sumner, and irreversible strengthening of the powers of government. Though Jane Addams did not shrink from these implications, the chief apostle of having continually more recourse to legislation to mitigate the evils of city life was Florence Kelley (1859–1932), who summed up her own career in the title of one of her books — *Some Ethical Gains through Legislation* (1905). After a period of graduate study in Europe, Florence Kelley lived for a time at Hull House, agitated with Jane Addams and Governor John Peter Altgeld for passage of the first Illinois law (1893) for inspection of factories and workshops, and served as first inspector till turned out by the next governor for political reasons. She attacked Spencerism upon its weakest side, its failure to recognize that women and children suffered from a form of biological inferiority which could not be regarded as unfitting them for survival. As Ward's disciple Edward A. Ross put it in 1901, even the "fittest" women are weaker than virtually any man; and "the fittest children are weaker than the unfittest adults."[6] To equate governmental protection of women and children with the coddling of adult males was mere unreflecting laissez-faire, with no biology to redeem it. Florence Kelley in her long campaign to stamp out child labor repeatedly came back to the point that by failing to protect the children one was eroding away any biological fitness they might have had before they could turn it to the advantage of the community by conceiving strong children of their own.

When the political wars turned against her in Illinois, Florence Kelley took her philosophy off to New York and affiliated with Lillian Wald's Henry Street settlement on the Lower East Side. In Lillian Wald (1867–1940), she found a powerful new ally, who from the vantage point of a graduate nurse and the pioneer in America of the idea of visiting nurses could link up the concern for children with the urge to put better nursing and medical care within reach of everybody. In this context Lillian Ward singlehandedly touched off a permanent expansion of the functions of government by supplying the city of New York gratis with a school nurse in 1902. Dr. Hermann Biggs, public health commissioner for the city, promptly built the idea into the structure of city government at public expense. Florence Kelley and Lillian Wald, working in tandem, went on to call forth a new fact-finding organ of the federal government, the United States Children's Bureau (1912) — a riposte conceived over the Henry Street breakfast table to a news item announcing that a large-scale campaign was being launched by the government against the ravages of the boll weevil, at a time when the crop of city children could be annually decimated without any notice being taken from Washington at all.

For Florence Kelley to join forces with Lillian Wald was natural. Less predictably, she also fell into step with the now legendary Mrs. Lowell, still dressed in black for her Civil War dead and still tramping tirelessly through the city in good causes, or taking a streetcar, but never keeping a carriage of her own — that would have been money ill-spent on herself. As the years wore on, Mrs. Lowell, without abandoning the Charity Organization Society, more and more shifted the weight of her endeavors elsewhere. The characteristic Spencerian disdain for paupers had grown upon her till she could no longer bear the sight of them. She was tired, she said, of fishing people out after they were half drowned, she would try to keep the good swimmers afloat. In this cause, she began to work for peaceful solution of labor disputes (though not opposing strikes as a last resort and sometimes going to the aid of strikers) and above all improvement in the working conditions of women. Her second great social foundation was the Consumers' League of New York city, begun in 1890, in which she enlisted well-to-do women to put pressure upon shopowners with whom they dealt, to improve the wages, hours, and rest-facilities of the clerks. Yet though private exertions remained the native medium of her social efficacy, Mrs. Lowell had never been a doctrinaire antilegislationist. She had approved of factory inspection and now she went along with the League's campaign for state inspection of retail stores as well. As if to symbolize the grave flaw in Mrs. Lowell's Spencerism, the National Consumers' League, an offshoot of the New York group, installed as its executive secretary the apostle of more government regulation, Florence Kelley.

The whole Spencerian matrix of Mrs. Lowell's lifework was

breaking up fast. She lived to observe with no recorded protest a profound reorientation of her own Charity Organization Society of New York, the most Spencerian of all social contrivances in its original conception but now increasingly devoted to anti-Spencerian ends. In 1896 she and other leaders of the Society recruited as general secretary the economist and disciple of Simon Patten, Edward T. Devine (1867–1948). In 1898 Devine took under the wing of the Society the whole burgeoning movement for regulation of tenement housing by the city and state. He followed this up in 1902 by building into the structure of the Society a campaign to bring tuberculosis under control, nominally a voluntary enterprise of private citizens but inevitably entailing demands for more government regulation and expenditures.

If anybody thought that these were mere pragmatic responses to particular problems, a close observer of Devine's private life would have known better. At least once every month Simon Patten (1852–1922) came over from Philadelphia to spend a day with his old student. Devine's work in the Charity Organization Society was the deliberate enactment in practice of a broad social philosophy conceived by Patten. Fittingly enough, Patten gave classic expression to this philosophy in a series of lectures Devine got him to deliver under the auspices of the Society in 1905 — published in 1907 as *The New Basis of Civilization.* Without even bothering to mention Herbert Spencer, Patten mounted the most devastating attack that could be made on the overt content and the underlying moral animus of Spencerism. Patten argued in the now-familiar vein that "the weight of the city" made it impossible for "a few poor folks to reinstate their smitten neighbor" in the rural and village tradition.[7] That was the old "service-altruism" of actually taking a broom, trowel, or pitchfork in hand, and a good thing in its time and place. Now, however, the only sufficient form of mutual aid was "income-altruism," including the payment of substantial taxes to supply social benefits like pure water and public health services to all. As an accompaniment to this, Patten advocated legislation for minimum wages and maximum hours. He wanted society to put a floor under existence for all its members.

To magnify the role of the state for impeding the operation of natural selection would have been bad enough from the point of view of Spencer or Sumner, but this was not the end of Patten's offenses.

He attacked the whole instinct for the hoarding of goods and of the self, the niggardliness of spirit, which lay at the heart of Spencerism. Once a floor had been put under men's conditions of life, he wanted people on all levels of society to adopt a more expansive and hopeful style of existence. They must rebel against slogging drearily along, learn to spend more freely, and make themselves a consumption economy directed toward a steadily higher standard of living. Patten did not exactly disparage Sumner's hero of civilization, the savings-bank depositor, but cut him down to size and defined alternatives to the saving-hoarding-sacrifice-and-worry ideal which social workers thrust upon the poor and yearned after in the Forgotten Man. Devine, to show that he had learned his lessons well, said that worry about the future was one of the chief causes of dependence rather than a preventive — the best advice that could be given to many poor people was to forget about tomorrow and live confidently today. As if to ratify the shift that such talk represented, Mrs. Lowell died in the same year that Patten delivered his lectures, and William Graham Sumner five years later in 1910. By one of the jokes of history, in less than a generation Franklin D. Roosevelt would campaign for the Presidency on the slogan of helping the Forgotten Man and then proceed to act upon the philosophy of Simon Patten.

8

The Triumph of Laissez-Faire

Max Lerner

I

THE NATURE OF THE TRIUMPH

One of the paradoxes of American social and intellectual history is that laissez-faire reached its height as a system of economic thought and judicial decision at the very time that its doom as a system of economic organization was already clear. Its triumph as an ideology came about in the period between Reconstruction and the turn of the nineteenth century, especially in the last two decades of that century. Yet as a matter of economic and legislative fact the system had its nearest approach to reality some forty years before — in the 1840's and 1850's, after the mercantilism of the early republic had faded away and before the rise of the "trusts" had constricted the workings of free competition and begun to centralize the economy. Paradox as it is, it is not unusual in history that an idea-system should reach its "triumph" exactly when its base of social reality is crumbling away.

The difficulty with writing of laissez-faire in any period of its history is that it is only a shorthand abbreviation for a whole complex of economic and social thought, economic organization, political policy, judicial theory and decision, and popular belief. To make the difficulty worse, the term itself has changed in meaning and is treacherously dependent upon the uses to which it is put. As formulated by the physiocrats and the early classical economists in Europe, it was a term used to fight a system of mercantilism and its restrictive controls in the interests of a rising class of free farmers and business enterprisers: one can still detect this spirit in the militant laissez-faire thinking of John Taylor of Caroline, who as a good Jeffersonian was also a good physiocrat. But the later champions of laissez-faire, after the Civil War, were fighting not mercantilism but welfarism. Where the thinkers of the first laissez-faire system stressed the virtues of competition and the economic harmonies which transmuted self-interest into the good of the whole community, the later defenders — who could not shut their eyes to the facts of the new economic combinations — stressed mainly the negative virtue of the absence of government intervention. Theirs was the philosophical anarchism of the rich and successful.

On the side of economic reality, the period of early American industrialism (as witness the three key state studies by Louis Hartz, the Handlins, and James N. Primm) saw state governments involved in licensing, inspection, incorporation, canal and railroad ventures, agricultural and manufacturing bounties, and even dabbling in banking. The America in which Henry Clay worked for the "American System" of governmental encouragement of the transportation revolution, and Henry Charles Carey saw salvation in protective tariffs, was not a laissez-faire America. Yet, as Sidney Fine notes, the governmental intervention was not based on any comprehensive theory of an affirmative state. Even the Jacksonian reformers were mainly concerned with the practical issues of educational extension and money and banking reforms, and built no welfare theory.

After the Civil War, with its victory for the Northern-Western alliance of the free farmer, the free businessman, and the free worker, laissez-faire came to be knit more tightly at once into an intellectual system of economic and constitutional theory and into a militant element in governmental policy — or rather, non-policy. But the economic historians also note that the sweep of economic reality moved faster and more insistently — and moved more sharply to undercut the validity of the laissez-faire theory. The march of invention became a massive fact of American life, and the new technological revolution accelerated a revolution in industrial organization. The concept and fact of the large corporation transformed the American economy. The spreading power of corporations produced a new corporate elite, with a talent for combining formerly independent operations and a knowledge of how to make the strategic advantage of the "trusts" pay off. By the time of the eighties and nineties the paradox I have mentioned reached its sharpest form: the invoking of an idea-system of an idyllic self-regulating society governed only by moral individualism, as a rationale for the power of a business collectivism.

It is not too hard to resolve the paradox. The development of enterprise had broken through to a new stage in the history of American capitalism. The swagger and militancy of this new capitalism may best be seen in the type-figures of the era. They were no longer the toolmakers, the inventors, the industrial pioneers — although one finds examples of each group who were glowingly successful. The new type-figures were (in John Moody's phrase) the "masters of capital." It was Thorstein Veblen who, in the 1890's, most clearly defined the difference when he drove his intellectual wedge between the "industrial" and the "pecuniary" occupations. Much of the glamour and clangor attaching to the names of the Masters of Capital was exactly due to the fact that their contemporaries did not distinguish between the two roles of industrial production and the profit-making which was due to corporate organization and reorganization.

Thus the victory of laissez-faire must be seen as the superbly effective effort of these men to dominate the imagination and action of their era, and to use the ideas of the past in protecting their present power and future growth. One phase of their effectiveness lay in the spirit of what Louis M. Hacker has called the "triumphant American capitalism" — the assertion of its power in both peace and war, of its boundless confidence in its own push and resourcefulness, in its irrepressible energy and its irreversible course. A second phase of the triumph lay in the knowledge of the members of the new elite that they must meet and even anticipate the inevitable resistance of the groups and classes whose power they were displacing or curtailing — the independent farmer, the small-scale businessman, the new labor organizations; and that this would mean hammering out an armor of economic and social theory and constitutional interpretation — the required orthodoxies to meet the felt needs. That they were able for a time to accomplish it — and this is the third phase of their triumph — was due not only to a complacent intellectual and legal elite which was swept up in the *élan* of their energy, but also to the firm hold they had on the legendry of the people, which gave them roots of strength in the popular myth.

II

THE ANATOMY OF LAISSEZ-FAIRE

What I have said is, in effect, that to achieve its "triumph" laissez-faire had to invoke the whole panoply of the American Establishment of the day, and the mystique of a popular religion as well. That it managed to do this at all is a remarkable fact; that it carried it off with so much success, for at least two generations, is a problem in American intellectual history worth some inquiry.

It is a study in "Dichtung and Wahrheit," in poetic abstractions on the one hand, and in rather tough realities on the other. The men of the academies saw and presented not the economic and social reality but the picture-in-the-books. The men involved in the legal and court processes — before the bar, on the bench, in the law classes and libraries — saw and presented not the economic and legal reality but the picture-in-the-law-reports. And both together, along with other shaping forces, helped to create a picture-in-the-mind which the ordinary American cherished, despite the fact that it jibed badly with the everyday realities of American life.

Clearly these three sets of abstractions from reality could not have triumphed except for the operation of impalpable and intangible but nonetheless powerful strains in the laissez-faire idea, or better, what I have called the laissez-faire complex. This essay is committed to tracing some of these strains. Let me start by mapping the major lines of direction in the anatomy of laissez-faire, and at the same time try to get at the sources of its effectiveness.

(1) I start with the *idea of Nature*, and of the immutable social laws and legal and moral ("higher") laws in it to match the immutable physical laws in its design. European economic theory had stressed the idea of the economic harmonies, and Adam Smith had assumed a hidden hand-of-God to make individual decisions congruous with the general good. But Americans brought a special passion to the doctrines of Adam Smith and Sir William Blackstone — an intensity about *natural law* which blended with the proud image of a vast continent on which it operated, and with a self-reliant individualism somehow linked with the order of Nature.

(2) The *Calvinist ethic*, with its emphasis on the economic virtues and on individual self-interest as a prime mover both in the life-history of the individual and in the community prosperity and welfare. The tradition of a *moral individualism*, which had come down from the Protestant thinkers, and from the moral philosophers of Adam Smith's day, had become established in the American schools and colleges, and was deeply part of the American consciousness.

(3) The *tradition of a weak state* as the most desirable one, and the fear of governmental tyranny which carried over from the standard accounts of the Tudor and Stuart monarchs and from European dynastic wars during the time when the migrations to America began.

(4) The *efficacy of competition*, as a carry-over of the Darwinian idea of *conflict and competition in Nature*, and as a carry-over also from the successful competitive nation to the successful competitive individual. In an intellectual climate which stressed natural selection and the survival of the fittest in the social as well as the natural order, the *élan* of capitalism seemed proof of its untrammeled competitive character—even at a time when competition was in fact being shrunk and trammeled. In such a climate also the economists who defended the competitive system became something more than economists. They became transcribers of the eternal verities, and portrait painters of the lineaments of a natural order.

Extracting the essence of these elements, one may speak of laissez-faire as the idea and belief that the state must keep its hands off the economic life of the community and that only through this autonomy, sanctioned by positive and moral law, can economic activity flourish, society be healthy, and the individual reach his best effectiveness. It should be clear that this was meant as a self-contained system, moved by its own prime mover, suspended in its own aether, functioning in an admirable equilibrium — if only it were not disturbed from without.

The materials for this laissez-faire complex came from the intellectual history of liberalism in England, France, and Germany and formed the philosophy of the rising class of entrepreneurs in the Europe of the eighteenth and nineteenth centuries. They crossed the ocean in the writings of John Locke, Sir William Blackstone, and Adam Smith, and gave a strong direction to American thought. But the chief architect of the house of laissez-faire, and the weightiest force in its acceptance in the United States, was the English sociologist Herbert Spencer. To Spencer laissez-faire was more than a doctrine: it was a religion. His *Social Statics* appeared in an American edition in 1865, and its influence was so great that forty years later Justice Holmes had to remind his colleagues (in the Lochner case) that "The Fourteenth Amendment does not enact Mr. Herbert Spencer's *Social Statics*." To industrialists and college professors, liberals and conservatives, Spencer was a name to conjure with. His visit to America in 1882 was a triumphal procession, and a public banquet in his honor was attended by an impressive array of the economic, political, and academic members of the American Establishment of his day.

Spencer had two main facets of his thought — his basic evolutionary approach to history and society, and his doctrine of laissez-faire. It was possible for someone like William James, who had little use for Spencer's broader philosophy, to identify for a time with his laissez-faire doctrine. Yet it is a mistake to believe there were two Spencers: they were one, and his doctrine of the negative state and his extremist individualism fitted exactly into his adaptation of Darwin's evolutionary doctrines to social theory. Because he believed that social legislation harmed individual development and did violence to the laws of nature and history, Spencer was alarmed at the increase of welfare legislation. "We are on the highway to Communism," he wrote in a pessimistic mood in 1882, "and I see no likelihood that the movement in that direction will be arrested."

III

THE ACADEMIC BATTLE-LINE

For a closer look at the elements of the laissez-faire complex we enter the groves of Academe, which had become most un-Arcadian, and were conscripted as the first battle-line of defense for the laissez-faire idea and ideal. The two established departments of the universities from which these defenders were drawn were "Political Economy" (the conjoined subjects had not yet been split away from each other) and "Moral Philosophy." While there were a few from the departments of "Public Law," who would today be called "political scientists," the "Sociology" departments were slow in emerging: when they did emerge, largely in the era of Progressivism and social protest, the new "sociologists" (William Graham Sumner was a notable exception) came largely as critics of the idea of a self-regulating economy, and flirted dangerously with notions of governmental and social activism. Men like Lester Ward and E. A. Ross thus marked the beginning of the end of the era.

In the interval, however, the academic and popular economists held sway in the republic of the mind. By 1870, says Joseph Dorfman, "the main theses of economic theory had been so long reiterated and accepted that they had the character of a tradition." The fact that new currents of thought were coming up in the eighties and nineties does not mean that the conventional wisdom of the academic Establishment could be dispensed with: it kept a considerable hold on the American mind. Yet under the stress of controversy on the grand economic "questions" of the day — the tariff, currency, the trusts, the railroads, the relation of capital and labor — there were shifting orthodoxies. The characteristic economist of the eighties and nineties was likely to be a man caught between the picture-in-the-books and the mounting evidence from the economy-in-action.

Amasa Walker was such a man: one is almost tempted to call him a dangling man of his era. He was a Yale professor who had formerly been Superintendent of the Census and something of a statistical expert, so that he had picked up enough of the inductive approach to economic reality to trouble his deductive serenity. His critical attacks on the laissez-faire system, including the wage-fund doctrine, came largely in the 1870's. The wage-fund doctrine — that there is a fixed amount of income available for wages, and that any effort to increase the fund is a violation of the iron law of economics — was constantly used to show the futility of trade unions and strikes. Walker insisted that the crucial factor was what happened to the value of the product, and that an increased value could be used as a basis for increased wages. He was thus, in the seventies, an opponent of anti-trade-union laws, in which he saw "a cruel advantage . . . by class legislation" given to "a domineering employing class." But in the eighties, as the fear of Socialism grew stronger, and as the Utopian vision of Edward Bellamy caught the imagination of many, Walker retreated from the logical consequences of his own position, and attacked the reformers as vigorously as he had earlier attacked laissez-faire. He continued, however, to draw a distinction between the "perfect competition" in the books and the "imperfect competition" of industrial reality.

He is best seen as a mirror of the conflicting currents of his time. His ambivalence of thought and emotion on the great question of the condition of the workers was an expression of the conflict between the American conscience and the strength of an ascending corporate elite which sought to use economic orthodoxy as a shield against opponents. It was not his conscience that won in the end. Even his argument for increased wages ran only in terms of the increased value of the product which the new technology made possible: he sternly rejected wage increases made "merely under the impulse of compassion, or philanthropy, or the enthusiasm of humanity."

This attests to the strength of Spencerism and Social Darwinism in the American climate. In England there was another and a greater dangling man, John Stuart Mill, caught between classical economics and the new tremors of socialist thought, who in his *Political Economy* had delimited the "province of the government" but had not refused to grant it a province, and had increasingly moved toward a social economics and a social politics. Mill and the radical English thinkers of the 1880's were able to take Darwinism in their stride. In fact, in the running debate on the nature of Nature, Mill's famous essay on that subject in his *Three Essays on Religion* described a Nature of savage cruelty from which he recoiled. But in America the empathy with the strong as against the weak was more powerful.

As a self-contained system, laissez-faire scorned the inductive and the historical, preferring the symmetries of deductive reasoning from first principles. Hence the new current which crossed the Atlantic from the German "Historical School" of Wilhelm Roscher was a disturbing one. It was not only Roscher's heterodox rejection of free trade that troubled the American economists, but his whole view that every historical era develops its own characteristic society and its corresponding economic system. This undercut the very foundations of universal economic law by bringing in a doctrine of historical relativism. Edwin L. Godkin, editor of the *Nation,* who was a free-trade anti-union Mugwump political liberal, orthodox in his economics, pointed out that the new German economists were young university teachers without experience, who came from a militarist-bureaucratic tradition and were at bottom Socialists. The pages of the *Nation* rang with the controversy.

The relativism of the historical approach was suspect from the start, and did not penetrate into the academic world until Thorstein Veblen, Simon N. Patten, and John R. Commons developed their "institutional" economics at the turn of the century. As one studies the economic controversies of the seventies, eighties, and nineties, it becomes clear that the defenders of laissez-faire were making their stand behind a disembodied doctrine which was forbidden contact with historical and social reality. This made economics vulnerable to what Morton White has called the "revolt against formalism." It also, however, made an appeal to the organic optimism of the American people. The appeal to the harmonies of a self-regulating economic system was strongly linked with the belief in national as well as individual progress. "I have hit the economic harmonies pretty hard," wrote Amasa Walker in a letter: it was the most dramatic sin he could recall in his career. Any departure from the harmonies was a surrender to pessimism, and a betrayal at once of progress and of the nation. Thus the corporate elite and their academic defenders had hold of a powerful mystique which the newer and more troubled economists could not muster. The best that writers like Bellamy and Henry George could do was to summon a counter-mystique of Utopian possibility, but this got little response from those who considered themselves hardheaded and practical.

The impact of laissez-faire thought cannot be understood without some discussion of three great American teachers and writers who were largely instrumental in formulating and spreading the doctrine.

From the angle of social theory the most active American figure was William Graham Sumner of Yale, a bristling hard-bitten mind, a salty writer, an eloquent and dramatic teacher who spread laissez-faire individualism like a gospel. Unsentimental and tough-minded, Sumner was merciless in flaying the humanitarian ideas that were challenging a market economy and a jungle society. "The fact that a man is here is no demand upon other people that they shall keep him alive and sustain him." Addressing himself to the argument "that we ought to see to it that everyone has an existence worthy of a human being," Sumner dismissed it: "this noble sentiment is simply a bathos."

But he did not delude himself into a belief that laissez-faire was built into the natural universe or even into the structure of the social universe. He saw that it "is a maxim of policy. It is not a rule of science." As a maxim of policy, he argued, it is supported by the history of civilization. Every high civilization has been built on the talent and energy of individuals, whose best efforts are evoked by the security of what they have made theirs — their property. Remove that spur and security and you remove the dynamic of advance. "The reason why I defend the millions of the millionaire is . . . that I know no way to get the defense of society for my hundreds, except to give my help . . . to protect his millions." He believed in the "natural monopolies" of men of talent, but not in the "artificial monopolies" which were the product of such abominations as the protective tariff and imperialist adventures. He fought every departure from laissez-faire as a betrayal of history, civilization, and the constructive skill of great individuals. While he made much of the "Forgotten Man" — the middle-class man who "prays and pays" and as a taxpayer always foots the bill — the society he thought best was run by an elite of talent.

From the angle of economics the crucial theorist of laissez-faire was a mild, scholarly Columbia professor, John Bates Clark. He too reflected the ambivalence of his era. Trained in Germany, under the Historical School, Clark returned to America as one of a little "new school" band of economic reformers. For a time, along with Richard T. Ely and Simon N. Patten, he tried to make these new winds of doctrine the prevailing ones. In *The Philosophy of Wealth* (1886) he developed a kind of Christian Capitalism, inspired by religious conceptions, attacking the extreme form of "economic man" which lay at the heart of laissez-faire economics, and arguing for a fusion of economics and ethics. "Nothing could be wilder or fiercer," he wrote, "than an unrestricted struggle of millions of men for gain, and nothing more irrational than to present such a struggle as a scientific ideal."

But by the turn of the century he had changed. In his major work, *The Distribution of Wealth* (1899), he insisted that impersonal forces were at work to fix the norms to which profits, wages, interest, and prices conform; and that in effect each agent of production gets as reward what it contributes to the productive process. Clark became the foremost American champion of the Austrian school of "marginal utility" economics, which in terms of technical theory was the extreme expression of man as a highly rational "lightning calculator of pleasures and pains," as Thorstein Veblen was to put it. In terms of economic policy he was only a qualified laissez-faire adherent, since he believed (unlike Sumner) that the state does have a function in the economic area — to remove the obstructions which keep competition from functioning perfectly. What he advocated, he said, was "a new and higher type of laissez-faire." But Clark's religious emphasis, while obscured by his later development, was still there. He deified "beneficent Nature," saw "the powers of evil" in man's presumptuous interfering hand when he tried to intervene. "Hinder not the grand dynamics of nature," he admonished his generation, "but lay hands on whatever perverse agent may now presume to offer hindrances." In his earnest way he too sought a universe governed by divine law, and he helped lend a mystique to the power and profits of men whose zeal for them was more often profane than sacred.*

As a prototype of the teachers of public law of the period, the

* For a further development of the theme of the mystique of laissez-faire, see section V below.

third great figure, John W. Burgess, stands out for his influence on thousands of his students. He served in the Civil War, went to Amherst, completed his academic studies in Germany, formed the Faculty of Political Science at Columbia, and published his great work, *Political Science and Comparative Constitutional Law*, in 1890. What was remarkable about his thought was his celebration of the state, in German fashion, as "the perfection of humanity . . . the perfect development of the human reason and its attainment over individualism," and at the same time his attack upon state intervention as "socialistic" meddling with "private rights." It was a tribute to the hold which laissez-faire theory had upon the time that it could capture the mind even of a German-oriented worshipper of the abstract state.

IV

THE LEGAL AND BUSINESS ELITES

One reason for the impression of a solid phalanx which one gets from the intellectual history of the laissez-faire period is that the academic elite and the legal and business elites maintained a united front until the academics began to break away in the 1890's. To be sure, the legislators were restive, but on the executive side Democrats like Samuel J. Tilden and Grover Cleveland did not noticeably differ from the Republicans in their view of the economic cosmos. The accepted wisdom was of government by the judiciary, in the interests of a corporate collectivism, within the frame of a self-regulating economy, with the theory of a higher law of Nature and of individual liberty as the rationale of the whole cosmos.

It was a revealing fact about Burgess that he looked upon the legal elite as the last line of defense for American civilization. "I do not hesitate," he wrote, "to pronounce the aristocracy of the robe the truest aristocracy for the purposes of governing that the world has yet produced." Tocqueville had of course noted a half-century earlier how important was the place of the lawyers in American political life. But the masters of capital preferred not to use Burgess's term "aristocracy" for their allies of bar and bench. John Taylor had once flung at Alexander Hamilton the epithet "aristocrat," and Hamilton had made the mistake of using the premises of the European aristocracy in his defense of conservatism. The new corporate elite knew better. They knew that they could best get the support of the middle class, the small farmer, even the worker, by talking not of aristocracy but of property, freedom, law. For this they needed the lawyers, judges, and legal commentators who formed an interlocked legal elite in America. The alliance was struck, and it proved far-reaching in its effects.

Two post-Civil War cases — the Slaughterhouse cases (1873) and *Munn v. Illinois* (the Grain-elevator case, 1876) — stand out in melancholy solitude as part of the "road not taken" when two paths diverged for the Supreme Court in the constitutional wood. In the first case, the problem was whether to apply to corporations the guarantees of the Fourteenth Amendment which had been intended for the protection of the ex-slaves. Justice Miller refused to make the shift. In the second case Chief Justice Waite accepted the doctrine that certain utilities were "affected with a public interest" and therefore subject to state regulation despite the constitutional limitations on state power. But while the laissez-faire opinions of Justices Field and Bradley were those of dissenters in the two cases, they became the doctrine of a Court minority triumphantly turned into a majority a decade later, and remained thus well through the dissenting opinions of Justices Holmes and Brandeis, and into the early years of the New Deal.

Justice Stephen J. Field, whose career of rugged conservative individualism on the California frontier stands as a one-man denial of Turner's thesis of the moving frontier as a source of democracy, deserves whatever credit is due him in making a fight for attaching substantive property values to the "due process" clause of the Fourteenth Amendment. Yet the constitutional history of the period shows that the trial lawyer, in his brief and argument, was as often the creative figure as was the judge who wrote the opinion. In the Slaughterhouse cases John A. Campbell, a former Supreme Court judge from the South who returned to legal practice after the Civil War, is the really dramatic figure. Campbell at first tried to use the "privileges and immunities" clause as a refuge for unregulated corporate powers; thwarted here, he shifted to the "due process" clause. His powerful, almost mystical, historical survey of the struggle to protect individual freedom by the rule of law made its way into Field's opinions and those of other judges in later cases. "Leave it to God and Mr. Campbell," was the slogan among lawyers and their clients in the South of that time. God clearly took a hand, but Mr. Campbell must be held to have done his share.

The Field dissent in the Slaughterhouse cases became constitutional doctrine in a case decided in New York — the Jacobs or Tenement House Cigar case, where the state's police power was effectively whittled down. A railroad lawyer called John W. Cary was influential in the Granger railroad case, while two lawyers called Goudy and Jewett gave Field the substance of his dissent in the Munn case. William Maxwell Evarts, the "Prince of the American Bar," was also a counsel in that case, and later in the Jacobs case. John E. Parsons was influential in the Sugar Trust case, and Joseph H. Choate in a succession of cases.

They used to the full the powerful specter of Socialism, and the parade of the imaginary horribles which would follow if the protection of individual (and corporate) property were relaxed in the slightest. Their recital of the constitutional and political past of America and Europe came to be known as "lawyer's history." Their florid style gave its tone to the period, and the hyperbole of their discourse grows tedious as it is reread today. One of the less highflown examples, taken from Justice Field, who reflected the thinking of the great lawyers, will serve for the rest. In a concurring opinion in the Pollock case (1895), holding the income tax unconstitutional, Field wrote: "The present assault upon capital is but the beginning. It will be but the stepping-stone to others, larger and more sweeping, till our political contests will become a war of the poor against the rich." They were able and forceful men, these lawyers and judges. John R. Tucker, a lawyer for the Baltimore and Ohio and later a professor at Washington and Lee, called them (in a speech in 1892) a "priestly tribe." It is true that they came to make their pronouncements in a hieratic manner, as though they had just had a communication from the oracle at Delphi.

Any good history of American constitutional law will list the Supreme Court decisions in which the power of the new corporate elite was given this sanction by the legal-judicial elite. After the Jacobs case (1885) came *Stone v. Farmers Loan and Trust* (1886), where Chief Justice Waite drew boundaries around his own Munn decision ("the power to regulate is not a power to destroy") by ruling against the "taking of private property without just compensation, or without due process of law." In 1890 *Chicago, Milwaukee and St. Paul v. Minnesota* declared a police power statute unconstitutional on substantive grounds. In 1895 the Pollock case invalidated the income tax, the E. C. Knight (Sugar Trust) case crippled the Sherman Antitrust Act, and *In re Debs* gave impetus to the court injunction against strikes. In 1897 the Allgeyer case first applied the substantive concept of due process to a case involving liberty of contract. In 1898 *Smythe v. Ames* laid down the "rule of reason" in revising or rejecting rates set in regulating public carriers. The cases cited are only the barest outline of what the courts were able to accomplish in the effective limitation of the legislative will. The fact that six new Justices took their place on the Supreme Court in the 1890's gave the new court an almost unchallenged scope for its chosen work.

But more meaningful than the individual Justices were the judicial doctrines they evoked and shaped. One was the doctrine of "implied limitations" on state power, for which Thomas M. Cooley, the most renowned constitutional commentator of his time, was largely responsible. Cooley, a self-made and self-educated man, one of a family of fifteen children on a farm in western New York State, believed in the Calvinist doctrine of hard work, and in the accompanying creed of individualism and success. He became in time dean of a law school, a member of the Michigan Supreme Court, and (in 1894) president of the American Bar Association. His great work rests on his treatise on *Constitutional Limitations*, which disowned a "higher law" than the Constitution, but premised certain pre-existing basic rights of the individual which are protected in the Constitution, not expressly, but by *implied* limitations on state power.

Other judicial doctrines must be placed alongside this one. I have mentioned the doctrine which sees in the "due process" concept a substantive as well as a procedural meaning. There was the doctrine of a "higher law" than the Constitution, whose source is natural law, and by which exercises of constitutional power must be tested. There was the doctrine that individual property rights have priority over the state's police power, and over a federal police power under the "general welfare" clause, and that the one must therefore be allowed to expand while the other must be made to shrink. There was the doctrine that a corporation is a "person" under the meaning of the Fourteenth Amendment, thereby giving a fateful twist to the Amendments which grew out of the Civil War. There was the doctrine of a limited federal commerce power. There was the doctrine of liberty of contract, as between an employer however powerful and an employee however powerless, which served as a roadblock against the further progress of trade-union organization and social legislation.

Just as important as the judicial doctrines themselves was the way they were used in the alliance of the legal and corporate elites in order to maintain the power of both. If it be asked why the interlocking legal elite (of bar, bench, and commentator) threw its skills toward the new corporate elite rather than toward the support of the legislative majorities, the answer must be that the greater money and prestige lay with the rulers and organizers of the economy; and that with them also the legal elite felt a greater affinity. But that merely postpones the basic question: why the affinity? I believe it goes beyond legal and judicial doctrine, to the freedom-property-higher law nexus which has served to hold together much of American thinking over the generations.

V

MYSTIQUE AND POPULAR RELIGION

At the point where we speak of the freedom-property-higher law concept we have moved beyond both economic and constitutional theory to a mystique. I have talked about the academic thinkers and the legal and corporate elites. But while they go far toward explaining the "triumph" of laissez-faire, they give the structure of ideas, power, and decision, but leave out the cement. It is the interrelated elements of the great mystique of the time which furnish the cement.

One way of putting this mystique is to speak of the Constitution itself as a symbol with a powerful mythical appeal, and of the doctrine of the Supreme Court as the guardian of the Constitution.

Partly because it seemed an element of permanence in a world of change, partly because it became linked with the success of the whole American experiment, the Constitution became the keystone of the popular iconography. Remember that the intensity of religious revivalism — the phases of Puritan belief, of the Great Awakening, of the frontier religion — was pretty much spent, and a vacuum was left. Now the overtones of deeply religious feeling attached themselves to a successful capitalist order, identified with an awesome order of Nature and of natural law, and linked with both Constitution and Court. Something like a popular religion or myth was born. Add the freedom-property-higher law complex I have talked about, and a sense of the sweep and vigor of American energies as they have poured into the continent, and you get the culminating mystique.

But the human mind, even on the level of a mystique, must operate with concrete symbols. One can mark best the lineaments of an era by the personality-structure and ethos of its type-men. In the laissez-faire era one can think of men like Andrew Carnegie, John D. Rockefeller, and J. P. Morgan, along with the lesser men like Frick, Phipps, Flagler, Rogers, Harriman, and Hill. Charles Beard called them the "barons of the bag" who were the successors to the "barons of the crag"; Matthew Josephson called them the "Robber Barons"; Brooks Adams, closer to the truth, saw them at once as the great Plunderers and the great Centralizers. Without their centralizing they would not have been able to plunder, nor would their plundering have been forgiven; without their plundering, however, they would not have taken the American imagination as they did. Perhaps the common element in their plundering and centralizing together was a single-purposed — and to some degree constructive — energy, and it was toward this energy that their contemporaries were drawn.

Morgan and Rockefeller represent the twin aspects of these Titans — the Magnifico and the Puritan; Carnegie tends more toward the Rockefeller pole than toward the Morgan. Morgan's gestures were more sweeping, his vision perhaps grander, his tastes those of a Renaissance prince, and his motto "Never sell America short." But it was John D. Rockefeller who — exactly because of his lack of the magnifico glamour — distilled the essential personality-structure of the emerging industrial Titan. He was only one of a number of oil refiners, but by 1868 he had the idea of bringing the whole oil business under a single control; in the 1870's he saw his first real chance and made his start; and at the end he had not only 90 per cent of all refining capacity but also a vertical combination of pipelines, railroads, and smelters. His was the first great American trust. After Standard Oil came steel, telephones, utilities, agricultural machinery, tobacco. Rockefeller's qualities of single-minded determination and ruthlessness are clear enough. But equally important were organization and his capacity to plot the whole drama of manipulative moves in his mind.

The question now is not whether he was a moral man: most of the Titans, for all their piety, were amoral in method. It is why these qualities of his polarized at once the hatred and the belief of most Americans. Even the hatred was a grudging form of belief. To understand this, one must understand the gospel not only of work and shrewdness and saving, but of survival and success — that "Bitch-Goddess Success" which William James spoke of when the Progressives recoiled from the exasperating façade of the laissez-faire system.

The strength of the "Bitch-Goddess" lay in the persisting American dream of the self-made man — what Irvin Wyllie has called "the myth of rags to riches." A whole school of popular writers came into being, mainly in the 1890's, to push the gospel of the paradise of success which awaited those who prepared themselves, who seized their chance, who used their qualities to the full, who persisted despite adversities. William Makepeace Thayer wrote "guides to success" in the form of popular biographies of successful men. Orison Swett Marden's *Pushing to the Front* (1894) went through 250 printings, and its message that what counted was the "will to succeed" sustained many a faltering spirit. The great figure in the cult of success, however, was not an essayist or economist but a writer of boys' fiction in the form of "dime novels" — Horatio Alger, Jr., whose succession of rags-to-riches stories formed a great American saga, embodying the Protestant ethic in its most consummate form since the "Poor Richard" of Benjamin Franklin.

America, seen in terms of its effective survival, was primarily an energy-system which brought people from every corner of the world, and gave them a chance to stretch themselves to the utmost of profit and glory. It was not just the academic economists and philosophers and the aristocracy of lawyers and judges who held together the laissez-faire mystique. It was also the immigrants who came pouring in during every decade, who were driven hard and often exploited as workers, but who fed on the dream of success and never lost their sense of possibility.

VI

DECLINE AND FALL

It was this sense of possibility which held the whole thing together. When the trusts could no longer masquerade as a force in a natural order, the plunderers and centralizers wrecked their own system. The sense of possibility gave way to the sense of loss of the original American promise. The Social Gospel appeared with a new message of compassion, a new set of economic thinkers came in with a new relativism in place of the economic verities, new social and psychological thinkers took a hard look at the idea-system camouflaged behind natural law and the economic harmonies and moral individualism. The whole structure took on an unreal quality, as of a dream. Like a dream, in time it dissolved.

For one thing, in the area of social reality, the actual legislative trend turned ever more strongly against laissez-faire. The changing forces in the American economy forced the federal and state governments to take on a variety of functions never dreamed of in the philosophy of a naturally functioning economic order. This was especially true of the state governments, which began to regulate railroads, banks, grain elevators, insurance companies, business and labor, public utilities, the exploitation of natural resources, working hours and conditions. The perceptive British observer of American governmental reality, James Bryce, noted in his *American Commonwealth* (1888) that while Americans had the fantasy of living under a system of laissez-faire they were actually living under one in which the government was extending its intervention "into ever-widening fields."

But this was taking place largely under the stimulus of social protest and new social thought. The questioning of competition reached from its effects on the economy to its effects on the individual personality and the whole society. One of the most thoughtful essays in this area, Charles Horton Cooley's *Personal Competition*, appeared in 1894. The 1890's saw also a sweeping political movement in Populism. But that movement in turn expressed a far-reaching inner revolt in the American consciousness. It took a number of forms: a revolt against absolutism in the "eternal verities" upon which several generations had been sustained; a revolt against a dry-as-dust formalism in academic categories; a revolt against the concept of "Nature" when used to restrain the affirmative actions of men to better their conditions; a revolt against a jungle Tory Darwinism (although some of the rebels, as Eric Goldman has suggested, substituted a "reform Darwinism" for it); a revolt against the alliance of elites which ran the whole American show in its own way; a revolt against the moral smugness which held that nothing could be done to improve things in the best of all autonomous natural systems.

What emerged from that revolt was the start of a new concept of a welfare economy, a welfare state, and a welfare society. This concept had to wait until the ground had been cleared for it further by the Muckrakers — a band of devoted and impassioned journalists, led by Ida Tarbell, Lincoln Steffens, Thomas W. Lawson, and David Graham Phillips, whose effectiveness came between the turn of the century and the election of Woodrow Wilson as President in 1912. But once the idea was set in motion that the economy, the state, and the welfare of the people were indissolubly interlinked, its march to triumphant affirmation (which came in Franklin Roosevelt's New Deal) became one of the grand themes of American history.

9

Science in America: The Nineteenth Century

I. Bernard Cohen

I

A historian of science contemplating the role of America in the advancement of the sciences during the nineteenth century cannot avoid a profound sense of disappointment. After a colonial period notable for a vigorous contribution to scientific theory and information, the century following Independence appears devoid of clear and incisive progress in science. This situation may most easily be seen in the domain of physics: between the time of Franklin in the eighteenth century and Gibbs in the later years of the nineteenth — two Americans who won the highest possible international distinction for their theoretical achievements — the record in physics shows no truly significant American contribution. Joseph Henry was, without question, the ablest physical scientist produced in America in the first half of the nineteenth century, and he had a real talent for electromagnetic science. But he was not in the same class with such men as Faraday, Kirchhoff, or Clerk Maxwell; he was not made a foreign fellow of the Royal Society of London or a foreign associate of the French Academy of Sciences. And therefore we must recognize that the major scientific ideas of the nineteenth century — associated with such men as Helmholtz, Liebig, Pasteur, Claude Bernard, Gauss, Darwin, Mendel, Weierstrass, Mendeleeff — did not originate in the New World. For this reason, the development of science in nineteenth-century America is of minor importance to the general history of scientific ideas. But this subject is fundamental for any student of the social history of science or the intellectual history of America. The social history of science as an aspect of the history of science is today only in an infantile state; presumably as it becomes a major part of sociology it will gladly consider the nineteenth-century American scene from such points of view as the diffusion of scientific knowledge, the kinds of environmental conditions that seem to inhibit scientific research, the relation of science to government, the role of scientific institutions in the advancement of science, and the connections between pure science and its applications. As to the cultural and social history of America, the history of science may here add a new dimension to studies in this area.[1] The very failure to produce men who by a single commanding idea dominate a whole segment of future scientific activity poses a profound question for anyone who would claim to understand fully the growth of the American nation.

Physics was not the only science in which, up to the end of the nineteenth century, progress in America was slow. If we look at mathematics, we find one significant American innovation, the "linear associative algebra" of Benjamin Peirce. Yet it is clear that the only genius in pure mathematics in America in the nineteenth century was J. J. Sylvester, an Englishman who twice came to America to teach. In astronomy things appear a little better. At the close of the century America had some of the world's major observatories, as well as able astronomers like Newcomb and Pickering. America was the site of early photographic astronomical experiments — the daguerreotype being used in conjunction with a telescope — and of the work on spectral classification of stars by Draper. But this was paltry in comparison with the great work done in Europe. In chemistry there were two American contributions recorded in European annals: Hare's blowtorch and plunge battery, and at the century's end the work of Josiah Parsons Cooke toward the periodic classification of the chemical elements.

In geology, American contributions were greater; at least, descriptions of American geological formations made by native scientists were praised by Europeans. And the same is true of the biological sciences to an extent which may inflate the reputation of such botanists as John Torrey and Asa Gray out of due proportion. In one science a first-class contribution may have come from America — I refer to the work of Matthew Fontaine Maury, a founder of the science of oceanography — but that field is not central to our understanding of matter or life. One can have only the highest admiration for the brave pioneering work of William Beaumont, who made so much of an extraordinary opportunity to study the physiology of digestion. But the pitiful state of American science in his day can be seen in the enormous difficulties Beaumont encountered in attempting to do research and the lack of appreciation of his magnificent achievements, which fortunately were esteemed in Europe.[2] When all is said and done, so far as the great new scientific ideas are concerned, or even major ideas of the next lower rank, the contributions of nineteenth-century America were few at best and tend to enter the world's literature largely by courtesy.

A very different picture emerges from a consideration of colonial America. It was in America in late colonial times that the first experiments on controlled plant hybridization were performed and the phenomena of dominance, xenia, and metaxenia recorded; soon afterwards the methods of detasseling corn used today for breeding and genetic experiments were set forth clearly.[3] In colonial America the first controlled test of the new method of inoculation for smallpox was tried out. Newton reported in his *Principia* that two Americans had produced splendid and reliable cometary observations. On our shores it was discovered that northeast storms come from the southwest. And it was in colonial America that the modern theory of electricity was formulated and the law of conservation of charge applied to such phenomena as the condenser or capacitor.[4]

In colonial colleges science formed an important part of the curriculum. The bills for purchase of scientific equipment in the late eighteenth century appear often to have been greater than in the early part of the nineteenth. When in the 1760's a great fire at Harvard destroyed the library and the "Philosophical Apparatus," the first steps taken were to replace the instruments of science.

When the onset of the Revolution made it impossible for the senior class to do their experiments and observations, with the removal of the college from Cambridge, Commencement was delayed so that no man would graduate who had not had opportunity to use the scientific instruments.[5] I have looked carefully through the records of science in our colonial colleges for any evidence of an organized antiscientific spirit and have found none. Natural philosophy was generally held to be the friend and not the enemy of revealed truth; from the sermons of the colonial divines one can easily make a compendium of the science of the times; and in every recommendation for a program of preparation for the ministry there is a recommendation for the study of science.

Further evidence of the scientific interest of colonial America may be found in the fact that the second endowed professorship established in the New World was the Hollis Professorship of Mathematics and Natural Philosophy (1723), and that as early as the seventeenth century the first scientific society in the New World was founded. In the eighteenth century were established two major scientific societies or academies that still flourish: the American Philosophical Society and the American Academy of Arts and Sciences. More Americans were elected Fellows of the Royal Society of London in the eighteenth century than in the nineteenth.[6] Finally, as evidence of the importance of pure science, recall that for two days the Revolutionary War was suspended so that an expedition could be sent from the American side into British territory to observe a total eclipse of the sun. Even the debates on the Constitution of the United States were held up by questions of the meaning and possible applications of Newtonian physical principles. Could not one have therefore expected that the tradition so established would continue and that in the nineteenth century there would be an even greater scientific movement?

II

It is often held that the failure of the young republic to establish a continuing scientific tradition arose from the tendency of Americans toward applied rather than creative science. Thus Tocqueville wrote in *De la démocratie en Amérique*, "It must be confessed that among the civilized people of our age, there are few in which the sciences have made so little progress as in the United States." Had America been alone in the world, he held, then she would have had to learn that to apply science one must first have science to apply. As things were, America was merely drawing on the accumulated scientific resources of Europe without adding anything of her own save the uses to which existing knowledge could be put. Tocqueville concluded by asking whether "the passion for profound knowledge, so rare and so fruitful," which had produced the theoretical European science, could "be born and developed so readily in democratic societies as in aristocracies." While only the future could answer the question, he concluded, "As for me I can hardly believe it."[7]

The next half-century in the United States seems to have proved the correctness of Tocqueville's prediction with regard to pure science, though the record shows a generous overestimate on his part of the role in America of applied science, at least at the time of his visit in the 1830's. The forties and fifties were the decades of new mechanical inventions like the reaper, the sewing machine, and the six-shooting pistol or revolver — inventions based on superior mechanical ingenuity rather than on knowledge of recent scientific advances. The telegraph was devised as a practical embodiment of the newly discovered laws of electromagnetism, but among the chief inventions of the antebellum period it was atypical if not unique. Indeed, in the first fifty years of the republic, there was about as great a want of applied science as of pure science. Thus any failure of America to have produced a great scientific tradition by mid-century can hardly be ascribed to a concentration on application rather than on theory. In the second half of the nineteenth century — and even in the twentieth century when the pure sciences had begun to prosper in America — our men of science complained that America so overvalued the applications of science that the advancement of knowledge for its own sake aroused little financial support and intellectual enthusiasm. But plainly we must exercise caution lest we read back such statements into the conditions of early-nineteenth-century American science.

It is true, nevertheless, that during the first half of the nineteenth century the religious impetus to the study of science faded away and was eventually replaced by an emphasis on science as the servant of technology and the agent of human welfare. In practice this shift meant a declining fascination with the dynamics of celestial systems, the wonders of microscope and telescope, and even the beauties of nature. The nineteenth century saw the rise of interest in chemistry as the science of matter, in scientific biology (physiology) rather than natural history, in medicine and the arts allied with health, and in practical physics and engineering. Typical of this change in orientation is the introduction of such college courses as nineteenth-century Harvard's required lectures on the applications of science to the useful arts. Students were informed that if anyone were to try to draw a dividing line between science, "so-called," and the practical arts, the result would be a set of "distinctions which are comparative rather than absolute." In many branches of knowledge the pure and applied branches were said to be "so blended together, that it is impossible to make their separation complete." At Yale, at about the same time, the students were told by Benjamin Silliman that ". . . art furnishes hands and science eyes; science without art is inefficient, art without science is blind. The philosophical chemist must understand the *principles* of the chemical arts, and the more of the *practice* the better."[8]

By the mid-1840's the stress on practicality produced schools of science at both Harvard and Yale in which a dominant theme was the *utility* of the sciences. Harvard's Lawrence Scientific School was founded in 1847 specifically for those men who intended

> . . . to enter upon an active life as engineers or chemists, or, in general, as men of science, applying their attainments to practical purposes, where they may learn what has been done at other times and in other countries. . . .
>
> Inventive men laboriously reinvent what has been produced before. Ignorant men fight against the laws of nature with a vain energy, and purchase their experience at great cost. Why should not all these start where their predecessors ended, and not where they began? Education can enable them to do so. The application of science to the useful arts has changed, in the last century, the conditions and relations of the world. It seems to me that we have been somewhat neglectful in the cultivation and encouragement of the scientific portion of our national economy.[9]

This statement by Abbott Lawrence about his proposed school is extraordinarily interesting to the historian, because its propagandistic tone makes clear that in the late 1840's Americans had not yet come to a full appreciation of the importance of the practical applications of science. Furthermore, Lawrence evidently conceived the major problem to be that of finding new applications rather than new principles that might some day be applied. The problem was only to "educate our engineers, our miners, machinists, and mechanics." Special schools already existed where one could study law, medicine, and surgery, but where, Lawrence asked, "can we send those who intend to devote themselves to the practical applications of science?"

In New Haven, the Sheffield Scientific School began also in the 1840's, the initial steps being the appointment of John Pitkin Norton as Professor of Agricultural Chemistry and Animal and Vegetable Physiology, and of Benjamin Silliman, Jr., as Professor of Practical Chemistry. It was Silliman's specific obligation to give instruction "in respect to the application of chemistry and the kindred sciences to the manufacturing arts, to the exploration of the resources of the country and to other practical uses." The new department at Yale called itself the School of Applied Chemistry; it combined with the School of Engineering in 1854 to become the Yale Scientific School, later renamed the Sheffield Scientific School in 1861 in honor of a benefactor.[10]

Prior to the 1840's, when Harvard and Yale established "scientific schools," there was not in our country even a strong tradition of engineering. The surveys of the West, the planning of the railroads, and kindred jobs were assigned to military men, because the United States Military Academy at West Point was the only higher institution of learning in the country which even had an engineering department. On a somewhat lower level Rensselaer Academy, now the Rensselaer Polytechnic Institute, made brave beginnings in this direction. So great was the need of engineers in the 1840's that Harvard's modest scientific school could not at first fill the post of Professor of Engineering, the president observing year after year that the engineers were too busily employed "in superintending the railroads and other public works in progress throughout the United States" to give up their important work for teaching.

III

While there was a decline in emphasis on Newtonian natural philosophy during the first half of the nineteenth century, the subject of natural history did flourish — which is not so surprising when one thinks of the terrain, not fully explored, stretching out between the oceans. During the first half of the nineteenth century, America was most productive of naturalists, geologists, oceanographers, and explorers, and least productive of physical scientists of equal rank. Indeed, the major native American scientist prior to the Civil War was a naturalist, Asa Gray, professor at Harvard, to whom Charles Darwin communicated his early ideas about the theory of evolution. And it is certainly significant that the chief organization of scientists in the United States, known since 1848 as the American Association for the Advancement of Science, began in 1840 as an organization of geologists, which soon after added "naturalists" to its membership. The first American scientific society devoted to a single branch of science was an American Geological Society, founded at Yale in 1819, and having a national membership.

The major scientific emphasis in the first half of the nineteenth century in America was on a kind of natural history, and this emphasis also came to an end in the fifth and sixth decades of the century; by the time of the Civil War the great age of the naturalists was past. Typical in this regard is the career of Asa Gray. Gray's achievement had been, as befitted the major disciple of John Torrey, to compile a *Flora of North America*. But by the end of his academic life in the early 1870's, Gray himself had organized a botanical laboratory and could see that "a magnificent new era in world botany — the transitional era — was dawning." The shift has been described by Andrew Denny Rodgers as one from an "observational" botanical natural history based on morphology to a "physiological" botany based on experimentation. Gray's last lectures in 1872 show the trend away from the old natural history in such topics as "reproduction among algae," "the sun and vegetation," "general principles of classification," "reproduction among fungi," "reproduction among mosses," and "characteristics of selected families of flowering plants." The new age of experimental biology was well along into the twentieth century before Americans began to make their mark by significant contributions to either botany or zoology on the highest level of scientific generalization.[11]

IV

American science in the first half of the century displays its quality in the list of men chosen to be *associés étrangers* of the French Académie des Sciences. Benjamin Franklin had been given this honor at a time when there were only eight such foreign associates, in 1773, an honor not given again to an American for another century — until Louis Agassiz was so designated in 1872, though on the basis of research done in Europe before he had come to America in the mid-forties. Up to the twentieth century only one other American, the astronomer Simon Newcomb (elected in 1895), achieved this honor, but eight Americans did become *membres correspondants:* Alexander Dallas Bache (1861), James Dwight Dana (1873), Asa Gray (1878), Lawrence Smith (1879), Newcomb (1874), Alexander Agassiz (1887),[12] Henry A. Rowland (1893), and Josiah Willard Gibbs (1900).[13]

From the founding of the republic until the end of the nineteenth century only a dozen Americans entered the foreign list of the Royal Society of London; eight of them achieved this distinction after 1873, a good group which includes Asa Gray (1873), Simon Newcomb (1877), James Dwight Dana (1884), Benjamin Apthorp Gould (1891), Alexander Agassiz (1891), Hubert Anson Newton (1892), Samuel Pierpont Langley (1895), and Josiah Willard Gibbs (1897). For the period from the Civil War to the century's end this is a rather generous selection of America's creative scientific talent, and although the group is small, each member of it made somewhat notable contributions to science. But compared with Germany or France, the outstanding aspect of the group is that it is so small. Furthermore, of these eight men only one (Gibbs) was a scientist of the highest genius, and only two others (Gray and Langley) are still remembered in the annals of science for significant contributions to scientific knowledge. James Bowdoin, whose election to the Royal Society in 1788 constituted a formal recognition of the new American nationality, made no true contribution to scientific knowledge and was probably chosen merely to honor the new

American Academy of Arts and Sciences of which he was the inaugural president. Nathaniel Bowditch achieved fame for his *Practical Navigator* and his translation of Laplace's *Mécanique céleste*, and was elected in 1818. The first American on the foreign list of the Royal Society, therefore, to win this honor for true scientific distinction may have been Benjamin Peirce, a Harvard mathematician of some quality. Yet one suspects that Peirce was chosen because of his editorship of the *American Nautical Almanac*, which he directed from Cambridge, and that his election was thus similar to that of Bowditch, and perhaps also to that of Alexander Dallas Bache (elected in 1860), who won a kind of small renown for his geomagnetic observatory and his directorship of the Coast Survey.[14]

The impotence of American science in the decades prior to the Civil War can be seen dramatically in the successive failures either to interest the federal government in supporting a program of scientific research or to obtain federal sanction for a truly national academy of sciences. Both failures were in some measure related to the great debate concerning states' rights and the limitations of federal power, and to a fear, dating from Jefferson's time, of establishing aristocratic or monarchical institutions. As a result, the first national scientific establishment within the government was the Smithsonian Institution, which was supported by private funds willed to the United States by an Englishman, and no National Academy of Sciences was founded in our country until Civil War days.[15] Organized when the national pattern of life was already well established, the Academy has never played the major role in either national affairs or organized science that its European counterparts did. Although formed in time of war, in part to serve as official adviser to the government, the Academy — from the end of the Civil War almost to the close of the century — was rarely called upon for such service. As late as 1902 the Academy's want of even a permanent headquarters with a library and rooms for meetings or conferences was cited among "conditions which discourage scientific work in America," for one "hardly knows where to look for a spectacle less befitting our civilization than that of such a body of men searching through Washington to find a suitable place for their meeting . . . grateful to one of their officers when he has a spare corner in which to keep their records; wondering what shall be done with an invitation from a foreign organization."[16]

In 1913, when the National Academy of Sciences celebrated its semicentennial anniversary, President Ira Remsen spoke of the "most eminent or most conspicuous" of the founders: "those whose names are most familiar to the present generation." The group he cited consisted of Louis Agassiz, James D. Dana, Wolcott Gibbs, B. A. Gould, Asa Gray, A. Guyot, Joseph Henry, J. Leidy, J. P. Lesley, Benjamin Peirce, R. E. Rogers, W. B. Rogers, L. M. Rutherford, Benjamin Silliman, Jeffries Wyman, and J. D. Whitney. To the historian in the mid-twentieth century this list is extremely valuable as an index to the place of science in American culture and the status of our American science a hundred years ago. For the fact of the matter is that probably not a single American historian knows why every one of these men was "eminent" or "conspicuous"; nor could any general historian of science identify each member of the group and state his contribution to the advancement of scientific knowledge.

V

In the decades following the Civil War, several new features are discernible in the American scientific scene. One of these is the rise of agricultural research. Henry L. Ellsworth, first U. S. Commissioner of Patents (appointed after Congress created a Patent Office as a branch of the State Department in 1836), was interested in agricultural problems and had published a newspaper column called "The Farmer's Repository." As Commissioner he sought to collect new seeds and plants from all possible sources, enlisting the aid of naval officers, consular officials, and travelers. By 1839, he had obtained funds for agricultural statistics and was pleading for studies of the applications of chemistry to agriculture. In 1848, Congress appropriated $1,000 for "chemical analysis of vegetable substances produced and used for the food of man and animals in the United States." The study was made by Lewis C. Beck of Rutgers, and dealt with such matters as the effect of soil and climate on grains, and the problems of sea voyages and "other storages" on flour and meal. By 1862, a full-scale department was established, organized by Isaac Newton, who succeeded in gaining the appointment as department chemist of Charles Mayer Wetherill, a graduate of the University of Pennsylvania who had done graduate work in France and Germany and had obtained his Ph.D. under Liebig at Giessen. But it was not until a decade later that the scientific work of the Department of Agriculture became established, and grew and expanded, accompanied by the rise of state agricultural experiment stations which had been aided by the Morrill Act and even more substantially and directly by the Hatch Act of 1886.[17]

By the 1860's, scientific work was being conducted not only in the Department of Agriculture, but also in the Coast Survey, which had had an abortive start in the days of Jefferson and a new career under the guiding hands of Alexander Dallas Bache.[18] The federal government formally recognized geology in 1834, when G. W. Featherstonhaugh, under direction of the War Department, was authorized to make a geological and mineralogical survey of the Ozark Mountain region. In 1830, the first state geological survey was undertaken by Massachusetts, and within ten years there were sixteen others.[19] A national observatory had been established — although without direct sanction — in 1842 when provisions were made for a permanent depot of charts and instruments for the Navy. Astronomical observations were begun in 1845, and within three years the depot was designated the "Naval Observatory," which name it still bears.

At the end of the Civil War, science was conducted within the federal government in the Smithsonian Institution, the Coast Survey, the Naval Observatory, and the Department of Agriculture. The way was open for that expansion of scientific bureaus which became characteristic of late-nineteenth-century America. With the improvement of scientific training, and with a general rise in the standards of American scientific work, it was inevitable that the level of activity within these bureaus should also rise. By 1884, science within the government had assumed proportions of such magnitude and complexity that a Joint Commission of the Congress (known generally as the Allison Commission, after its chairman, Senator W. B. Allison) was appointed to study the actual organization of a number of federal agencies concerned with science in an attempt "to secure greater efficiency and economy of administration in the public service." In the end no action was taken on the Commission's proposals for reorganization, stemming from a report prepared by the National Academy of Sciences. The reasons for the refusal to act are complex and relate more to the nature of the political scene than the state of science. Yet the refusal to accept even the recommendation that a Department of Science be established in the executive branch of the federal government demonstrated an obvious failure to appreciate the economic importance of such applications of science as photography, telegraphy, the electric light, and the electric railway. Neither congressmen nor senators were much moved by the Academy's conclusion that "none who have ever lived with open eyes during the development of these results of purely scientific investigations doubt that the cultivation of science 'promotes the general welfare.' "[20]

If a first feature of the post-Civil War era is the rise of science in government bureaus, a second is the growth of applied science and the beginnings of industrial scientific research. A concomitant of the phenomenon was the founding of scientific schools and the development of polytechnic institutes on the European model, including special institutions for roads and bridges, mines, forestry, and so on. Mention has already been made of Rensselaer, West Point, and the Sheffield and Lawrence scientific schools. The Massachusetts Institute of Technology — proposed by William Barton Rogers, Professor of Natural Philosophy in the University of Virginia, in a letter to his brother Henry in 1846 — was established in 1861; by 1899 there were two thousand graduates. In 1864 Columbia had a school of mines that was endowed with $3,000 and had a faculty of three nonsalaried professors who lived on students' fees. Eventually the school embraced chemistry, civil engineering, sanitary engineering, and architecture. In 1868 the Worcester Polytechnic Institute was founded on a model of similar schools in Moscow and St. Petersburg. Other engineering schools founded before 1900 include Lehigh, Stevens Institute of Technology (Hoboken), Case School of Applied Science (Cleveland), Rose Polytechnic Institute (Terre Haute), Throop Polytechnic Institute (now California Institute of Technology, at Pasadena), and Armour Institute of Technology (Chicago). At the same time major scientific schools grew up at Princeton, Pennsylvania, Dartmouth, and Rutgers, while the scientific departments became more and more important in other colleges and universities.

Probably the first industrial laboratory in the United States was established by Samuel Luther Dana, a Harvard graduate of 1813 and an M.D. who found practical chemistry more to his taste than the practice of medicine. His own laboratory, which he built to manufacture sulfuric acid and bleaching salts, eventually merged with the Newton Chemical Company, of which he was the manager until 1833, when he went abroad for further study. On his return he became research chemist to the Merrimac Manufacturing Company, where he worked on methods of calico printing, improving on Mercerization until his own methods became standard. Dana's research was a major contributing factor to the rise of the New England textile industry. Another pioneer industrial scientist was Charles B. Dudley, who taught science at the Riverside Military Academy at Poughkeepsie, New York, until 1875, when he quit to go to work for the Pennsylvania Railroad. Although practical men at first regarded his scientific approach with skepticism, he eventually made his point by working out methods of increasing the life of valves used on steam locomotives and by demonstrating the importance of careful rendering of tallow and the use of fresh tallow to reduce corrosion. He gained fame from a work entitled *Chemical Composition and Physical Properties of Steel Rails*, in which he tried to set up standards for the steel rails being introduced as a substitute for iron.[21]

VI

It is difficult to conceive of the small number of American scientists a century ago. In 1860 the American Association for the Advancement of Science could boast only 644 members, a figure which dropped during the Civil War and rose again to only 536 by 1870. Although the membership of the Association included many doctors, clergymen, teachers, and laymen interested in science who were not scientists at all, the rolls did not pass even the two-thousand mark by 1900. One can easily imagine, therefore, the great concern of American men of science to improve both the quantity and the quality of the scientific movement in the United States. In 1872, twenty-five frustrated American men of science began a movement to improve the state of American science by inviting to our shores one of England's most renowned lecturers on science, John Tyndall, on the specific ground that "a course of experimental lectures would materially promote scientific education" in the United States. Tyndall's success netted him so great a profit that he decided to place the "surplus over expenses" in trust for the advancement of science in America. Specifically, Tyndall directed that the income from the fund he was establishing be used "in aid of students who devote themselves to original researches."

At a farewell banquet given in his honor, at Delmonico's Restaurant in New York in 1873, Tyndall analyzed the American scientific scene. Like Newcomb, he was disturbed by the emphasis on applications of science rather than on the cultivation of science "for its own sake, for the pure love of truth, rather than for the applause or profit it brings." He recommended that America honor the man whose research created new ideas as well as the man who devised new things or new ways of making or doing things. He urged the founding of chairs "which shall have original research for their main object and ambition." Above all, he warned against the evils of the scientist seeking public acclaim, of the "investigator who is fond of wandering from his true vocation to appear on public platforms."[22]

VII

From the time of the Civil War to the end of the century, the applications of science to industry, agriculture, medicine, and communication were definitely a part of the national scene. The emphasis on practice, even in the old established colleges, may be seen most clearly in the early career of J. Willard Gibbs, whose eventual contribution to pure science was of so abstract a nature that few of his countrymen could understand his publications, much less see their profound significance and long-range effects on both theory and practice. Gibbs won his Ph.D. at Yale in 1863, the third year in which that degree was offered. Having demonstrated an unusual talent in mathematics, he was led — naturally enough in those days

— to a career in engineering. The subject of his thesis was the design of gears, and he invented a "center vent" hydraulic turbine and a railroad brake (patented in 1868); he was also the author of a study of governors for steam engines. After a few years as tutor at Yale, Gibbs went abroad and studied mathematics and physics in Paris and Berlin. Stimulated by the European scientific environment, his focus of interest shifted from brakes, gears, and governors to higher mathematics and pure physics, and his career was thenceforth marked by his contributions to abstract science rather than technology as such. Given the post of Professor of Mathematical Physics at Yale in 1871, he was not paid any salary, and his reputation grew in Europe but not in America, although he was approached by Johns Hopkins in 1879 and had also been offered a salaried post by Bowdoin — both of which he refused.[23]

Reviewing the state of science in America in 1883, the physicist Henry A. Rowland particularly deplored a distinction that he found between scientists or mathematicians and sculptors, painters, novelists, poets, or musicians. The latter group, he found, "have wealth before them as the end of a successful career. But the scientist and the mathematician have no such incentive to work: they must earn their living by other pursuits, usually teaching, and only devote their surplus time to the true pursuit of their science. And frequently, by the small salary which they receive, by the lack of instrumental and literary facilities, by the mental atmosphere in which they exist, and, most of all, by their low ideals of life, they are led to devote their surplus time to applied science or to other means of increasing their fortune."[24] Many careers could be cited to exemplify these remarks. Perhaps the most striking is that of Eben Norton Horsford, a native of upstate New York who studied under Amos Eaton at Rensselaer and then went to Giessen to become a pupil of Liebig's. There he not only learned the principles of the new organic chemistry and the methods of research, but also was introduced to the revolutionary method of science instruction by student laboratory work. To this day there is no better account of mid-century scientific-academic Germany than the letters written by Horsford for publication in *The American Cultivator*. On his return to America, Horsford became in 1846 the Rumford Professor at Harvard and soon was one of the major figures in the new Lawrence Scientific School, where he introduced student laboratories in chemistry on the German model. Horsford's reputation, however, was made not as teacher or as researcher, but as applied chemist. Only older readers may remember "Horsford's acid phosphate" (a good "tonic" in the spring); but who does not know of the "baking powder" he invented, a product which is still being manufactured by the company he founded and named after the Rumford professorship he was forced to resign.

VIII

Although the close of the nineteenth century was characterized by the expansion of colleges and universities, the inauguration of graduate schools on Continental models, and the founding of engineering and technical institutes, these centers of higher education did not become firmly established as the homes of disinterested scientific research. There are at least two apparent causes for this situation. One is the relatively low estate in which college and university teachers found themselves; far from being a title of honor, as in Europe, "professor" in America was apt to indicate the master of a flea circus or even a weight-lifter in a side show. Another is the tradition of young men choosing a college without reference to the particular distinction of those individuals comprising the faculty. These aspects of American science were stressed in a pair of articles which Simon Newcomb, the astronomer, one of the distinguished scientists in America in the nineteenth century, wrote for the *North American Review.*[25] In the first of these, published in 1874, called "Exact Science in America," Newcomb expressed his deep concern that Americans, despite their faith in the "future greatness of their country," had an opinion of its "intellectual development [which] is modest in the extreme." All that Americans had learned, according to Newcomb, led them to believe that first-rate men of science were necessarily of transatlantic origin. Not only did Newcomb find this belief widespread, but he found also that the American citizen had "a theory which explains the deficiency to his entire satisfaction, and, indeed, reconciles him to it, namely, that the activities and energies of this country are all directed toward material development, and that the atmosphere produced by this development is unfavorable to the production of the highest intellectual qualities. He therefore waits for the intellectual development of his country with the same philosophic patience with which he looks forward to the day when our infant manufactures will no longer need protection against European labor and capital." Newcomb, an astronomer, confined himself to the exact or physical sciences, as contrasted to the biological sciences, and to the pure rather than the applied aspects of science. He was quite aware that he thus brought to light the greatest weaknesses of America, knowing full well that if the survey were extended "into other fields, we could find things more pleasing to our national pride than those we expect to find in the field we have chosen." Yet even in the sciences of nature, he held, apart from collecting and systematizing, "Were we to look at the philosophic side of natural history, as exemplified by the works of such men as Darwin and Huxley, we might find here nearly as great a dearth of activity as in the exact sciences." How different the result were we to examine "the application of even the exact sciences to the arts of life," for in applications we "should find our country in the front ranks of progress." The most notable change that had occurred in the American scientific scene by the 1870's was evidently the emergence of America as one of the primary nations engaged in the applications of science, on a scale and of a variety not encountered in other countries. The success of those who had campaigned in the 1840's for the needs of applied science had been great indeed.

Searching for possible causes of America's low scientific state, Newcomb called particular attention to "the relative inducements to scientific research here and in Europe." He found that in Germany scientific activity was located in the universities while in France and England the learned societies were the fostering institutions of pure scientific research. He also contrasted the universities of Germany and America to the detriment of the latter. Newcomb observed that students did not go to Berlin because the university was old, celebrated, and good, but rather because in Berlin they could attend lectures by such men as Helmholtz and Virchow. In America, people asked of a professor, "What does he know?" But in Europe, people asked, "What has he discovered that is new?" A European professor who was an original investigator would thereby increase his income, because he would then attract large numbers of students, and his salary was based on the fees paid by the students.

The American professor did not have to show a genius for research to become eminent among either his colleagues or the public at large. This American professor was described by Newcomb as follows:

> Among the large number of our so-called universities, in fact at all outside of the Eastern States, nothing more is expected of a professor than acquaintance with a certain defined curriculum, and ability to carry the student through it. He has nothing to do but to satisfy the appointing power that he understands what is found in a certain text-book, and that he can teach what he knows to others. Even at our highest institutions of learning, Harvard and Yale for instance, we find nothing like the German standard. However great the knowledge of the subject which may be expected in a professor, he is not for a moment expected to be an original investigator, and the labor of becoming such, so far as his professional position is concerned, is entirely gratuitous. He may thereby add to his reputation in the world, but will scarcely gain a dollar or a hearer at the university.

In short,

> The various deficiencies in the incentives to scientific research which we have described may be summed up in the single proposition, that the American public has no adequate appreciation of the superiority of original research to simple knowledge. It is too prone to look upon great intellectual efforts as mere *tours de force*, worthy of more admiration than the feats of the gymnast, but not half so amusing, and no more in need of public support.

Thus Newcomb deplored the fact that many Americans made a scientific reputation not so much for having done significant original research as for having had success at popularization. He was not opposed to popularization as such, holding it a necessity to have an enlightened citizenry for the adequate support of scientific research. But he did insist that "popular lecturing is something entirely different from scientific research" — and the very fact that it was necessary to discuss this distinction proves how unappreciative of the true nature of science he found the American public to be.

Two years later, in a centennial review on "Abstract Science in America, 1776–1876," Newcomb especially emphasized the great gulf which separates "the so-called 'practical men' of our country" and "the investigator in any field which deserves the name of science or philosophy." As to the latter, the true genius, who knows under what conditions he may be produced? Thus Newcomb did not find it too surprising that America had not during her early history produced a Lavoisier, a Cuvier, or a Jussieu, "but why should we not have had plenty [of men of talent] to adopt, to criticize, or to develop their ideas? . . . The fact is that our science was little more than a timid commentary on European science, in which certain models, supposed to be standards, were followed in the same way that the schoolmen of the Middle Ages followed the philosophy of Aristotle." American science had improved considerably but was still impotent. Lacking financial support from the government, American scientific societies were too small to support themselves adequately. The journal founded by the elder Silliman was still the only journal in America devoted to pure science. "When we inquire into the wealth and power of our scientific organizations, and the extent of their publications, — when, in fact, we consider merely the gross quantity of original published research, —" Newcomb exclaimed, "we see our science in the aspect best fitted to make us contemplate the past with humility and the future with despair." The chief deficiencies of the national scientific enterprise were seen to be interrelated, each "both a cause and an effect of the others." Chiefly he found us "deficient in the number of men actively devoted to scientific research of the higher types, in public recognition of the labors of those who are so engaged, in the machinery for making the public acquainted with their labors and their wants, and in the pecuniary means for publishing their researches."

These comments were written by a thoughtful man who was both a keen observer of the scientific scene around him and a distinguished man of science working at the Naval Observatory. For more than a quarter of a century he pondered the failures of American science and their causes, and to this day his analyses have not been surpassed in either acuteness or awareness of the whole situation. Lest his pronouncements seem too pessimistic, they may be buttressed by somewhat similar sentiments of other American men of science. In 1883, for instance, Henry A. Rowland entitled his address as vice-president of the American Association for the Advancement of Science "A Plea for Pure Science." Rowland, professor at Johns Hopkins and at that time America's only experimental physicist of established first rank, told his audience quite frankly that "American science is a thing of the future, and not of the present or past." Chief among the causes of this condition he placed the confusion between pure science and its applications. Another reason he found was the lack of concentration of scientific resources. As an example he cited the growing number of well-equipped observatories, each lacking sufficient endowment or other financial support to maintain adequate research staffs. Spreading the scientific resources of the nation thinly could result only in "mediocrity," he believed, a mediocrity which he found the "curse" of America.

Rowland also held that scientists in universities often were overburdened with excessive teaching loads, lacked the needed corps of laboratory assistants and mechanics, and were not esteemed for whatever contributions to knowledge they might make. A decade and a half later, in 1899, Rowland returned to these subjects in his presidential address, "The Highest Aim of the Physicist," delivered at the New York meeting of the newly founded American Physical Society. Alas, he said, he must decry the fact that the condition of American science was in many ways as bad as he had found it "fifteen years ago, . . . much of the intellect of the country is still wasted in the pursuit of the so-called practical science which ministers to our physical needs and but little thought and money is given to the grander portion of the subject which appeals to our intellect alone."

But there were signs that the situation was improving. Rowland in 1899 referred to the "experiment of Michelson to detect the etherial wind" which failed to "find any relative motion of the matter and the ether";[26] little could he know that this experiment — performed in concert with Morley — was to become one of the most famous experiments of all time and thus bring true renown to American exact science. In 1875 the Johns Hopkins University had been founded, an event of enormous consequence to science and to all American higher learning, because this university — established firmly on Continental models — was dedicated to advanced training and research and set a standard to be followed by other institutions. Gifts of private capital had begun to endow great instruments of research, notably in astronomy (e.g., the Lick and Yerkes observatories), and it was becoming clear that finances would be available to support research. Within two years after Rowland's address to the physicists, a native American professor, the chemist Theodore W. Richards of Harvard, achieved the unheard-of distinction of being offered a regular professorship in a German university, Göttingen, which he declined. He set the seal on the growing scientific eminence of America by winning the Nobel Prize in chemistry: the second such American award, the first having been gained by A. A. Michelson in physics.

IX

By the time of the First World War, American science had certainly achieved a respectable position in the world scene, but had not yet reached a level of greatness commensurate with America's size and strength. The day was still far off when an American scientist could consider himself well prepared for research without a period of training in Europe, and a still longer time would have to pass before it would become generally customary for Europeans to require similar training in America as the necessary condition for becoming successful investigators. Undoubtedly, the failure of the scientist to achieve the same place in nineteenth-century American cultural life as his European counterpart is related to the more general situation of intellectuals and particularly of college professors. But the history of the sciences in nineteenth-century America also demonstrates one of the special aspects of science as an enterprise. The establishment of a scientific tradition, it would appear, requires more than the production of able individual scientists. There is needed a group of men working in either loose or close association, attracting still others who are fired by the pride of continuing, extending, revising, and perhaps in the end finding substitutes for the original concepts, experiments, or procedures. Such a level of activity, given financial support and intellectual respectability, perpetuates itself and may even incite similar activity in other fields. In this sense the failure of American science in the nineteenth century was not so much the lack of individual men of high order as the failure to produce the conditions under which a true scientific tradition could become established at all. And it is precisely the nature of such questions, lying in the *terra incognita* of the social history of science, that causes the subject of the development of the sciences in nineteenth-century America to be of greater interest and concern than would be warranted by the sum of the contributions to the advancement of science made by Americans during that century.

10

Pragmatism and the Scope of Science

Morton White

The problem of defining the scope of science has been more fundamental and more persistent than almost any other problem of philosophy. Is the method of checking statements by observation and experiment the only method of achieving knowledge of the truth, or are there others? Are there disciplines which validly arrive at truth by means fundamentally different from those used in empirical science? Is there such a thing as knowledge of the truth which may be reached without recourse to experience? Like their European predecessors and contemporaries, American philosophers have struggled with these questions, and like European philosophers they have offered no one answer to them. Neither American philosophy as a whole, nor pragmatism, the most distinctive American philosophical movement, has described the scope of science in a uniform manner. America has been the home of Emerson and Thoreau as well as of Franklin and Jefferson; and from the eighteenth century onward, American philosophy has oscillated between deflationary and inflationary conceptions of the scope of science.

The path from the Enlightenment to transcendentalism, and from transcendentalism to evolutionism in the nineteenth century, may be represented by a cyclical curve depicting the fortunes of science in American thought. And even more striking evidence of the lack of any monolithic attitude toward science is the fact that pragmatism — supposedly *the* scientific American philosophy — has been torn on the issue. Not all pragmatists have been, as it were, scientific imperialists; not all of them have maintained that all knowledge is scientific in the sense in which physics, chemistry, and biology are commonly said to be scientific.

Of course, pragmatism, as much as any philosophy in modern times, has proclaimed its respect for empirical science and its sympathy with the spirit of scientific method. The founder of pragmatism, Charles S. Peirce, was a logician who sometimes spoke of his doctrine as if it were nothing more than a theory of the meaning of scientific words; the great popularizer of pragmatism, William James, occasionally spoke of his theory of mind as a corollary of Darwinian biology; and John Dewey, the youngest member of the pragmatic trinity, devoted most of his long life to extolling the virtues of scientific intelligence and to urging its application to political, social, and moral problems. Nineteenth-century America, so unsuccessful in producing scientific thinkers of the first rank, did give to the world three of science's loudest cheerleaders. In fact, so loudly did they cheer that they did much to encourage the erroneous view that all pragmatists worship at the altar of something called "scientism" and believe that one scientific method rules as a god over all branches of human thought.

And yet, if one conceives of pragmatism as the doctrine originated by Peirce, popularized by James, applied by Dewey, and more recently refined by C. I. Lewis and W. V. Quine, one may safely say that whereas some pragmatists may believe that one and the same scientific method is applicable in all spheres of intellectual activity, other self-styled pragmatists do not. Some pragmatists may be called methodological monists; some are pluralists; and some think they are methodological monists when they really are not. Therefore, the historian of pragmatism cannot present a pragmatic catechism which will formulate a unified creed concerning the scope and limits of scientific method. This may best be seen by reflecting on the pragmatists' ambiguities and disagreements about the nature of metaphysics, theology, ethics, and mathematics. When one does reflect, one sees that pragmatism, more than any historical movement in philosophy, has had internal disagreements on one of the fundamental problems of the theory of knowledge. Let us turn first to the ambiguous status of metaphysics in the writings of Charles S. Peirce, the original pragmatist.

I

SCIENCE AND METAPHYSICS

The pragmatism of Peirce was basically a theory about the meaning of scientific beliefs. Confronted with assertions containing laboratory words like "hard," "heavy," and "lithium," to mention Peirce's own examples, a pragmatic logician must translate them into statements of practice. Peirce recognized, of course, that a scientific statement about the hardness or weight of an object is logically equivalent to what he described as a myriad of other statements, but he held that one type of equivalent is of special significance to the scientist, that which specifies certain experiences that an experimenter would have if he were to perform certain operations on the experimental object. Peirce held that if a statement could not be translated into such an equivalent, it lacked scientific or pragmatic meaning; and that two statements, no matter how different they might appear, meant the same thing if their pragmatic translations were identical or equivalent. One purpose of establishing such a test of translatability was to eliminate what he jeeringly referred to in some of his writings as "ontological metaphysics," but ironically enough his own pragmatic maxim led him to conclusions which were themselves metaphysical. For if every laboratory statement about a particular object is equivalent to a statement which asserts what would happen if one were to perform certain operations on it, then, Peirce held, every such statement covertly attributes a *disposition* to the experimental object. To say that Shylock would bleed if he were pricked is to attribute a disposition to Shylock; hence, Peirce said, to imply the existence of an entity which is a *universal*, a metaphysical entity. It was precisely this metaphysical implication of his version of pragmatism that led him to claim that medieval realism was the consequence of pragmatism, that pragmatism implied the existence of universals.

In saying this, however, Peirce created a puzzle, for how could a maxim dedicated to the elimination of "ontological metaphysics," lead to such a conclusion without violating itself?[1] On the one hand, Peirce urges us to present the pragmatic meaning of a laboratory statement in order to distinguish laboratory statements from pragmatically meaningless metaphysical statements; on the other hand, our very pragmatic translation supposedly implies the metaphysical conclusion that universals exist. But can we translate the statement that universals exist into pragmatic terms? If not, should we not conclude that this statement is scientifically or pragmatically meaningless? And if it has another kind of meaning, are we not led to think that two standards of meaningfulness and hence two criteria of truth are employed in Peirce's philosophy? Apparently Peirce is forced into the acceptance of two such criteria of truth, but he leaves the criterion of metaphysical truth very obscure indeed. Peirce's predicament, therefore, is not very different from one in which William James found himself when he came to discuss the method of theology.

II

SCIENCE AND THEOLOGY

James's sense of style led him to avoid the jargon of the schools, his racing intelligence made him impatient of logical minutiae, and his feelings inevitably brought him to religion. But James, like so many of his generation, was caught in the cross fire of science and theology, his sense of conflict exacerbated by his devotion to Darwin's biology. His *Principles of Psychology*, in applying scientific Darwinism to the mind, was of enormous strategic importance to those who sought to shore up something immaterial against the flood that followed Darwin's bombardment of conventional theology. On the other hand, although he shared their Darwinism in biological science, James could not line up with the agnostic W. K.

Clifford and T. H. Huxley on theological matters. James was too religious in temperament, too much the son of his Swedenborgian father, too quick to resent a short way with dissenters from agnosticism. In 1877 Clifford had said sternly: "It is wrong in all cases to believe on insufficient evidence; and where it is presumption to doubt and to investigate, there it is worse than presumption to believe";[2] and in the very same year Peirce had spoken scornfully of the man who might say, "Oh, I could not believe so-and-so, because I should be wretched if I did."[3] Yet James, the Darwinist, spoke up against Clifford in defense of what James called "the religious hypothesis." His first famous attempt in its behalf was his essay "The Will to Believe," which appeared in 1896; the second was his *Pragmatism* of 1907.

"The Will to Believe," as James pointed out, was essentially an answer to Clifford's agnosticism, an argument in justification of religious faith as a policy. According to James, we do have a right to believe a religious statement even though "our merely logical intellect may not have been coerced,"[4] even though neither the statement nor its contradictory has been scientifically verified. But, when one examines James's treatment of religious statements, one is struck by the fact that he does not bother to see whether they can be translated in accordance with Peirce's pragmatic maxim. The statement that God exists, is not — or at any rate James does not bother to persuade us that it is — a statement that is easily translated into one of Peirce's pragmatic "if-then" statements. It does not predict certain experiences after the performance of certain operations on an experimental object. For this reason, an application of Peirce's severe pragmatic test of meaningfulness might well yield the conclusion that such a statement was meaning*less.* And this is why James's predicament is similar to that in which Peirce found himself when he defended medieval realism. Just as Peirce consciously or unconsciously exempted the statement that universals exist from the need to satisfy the pragmatic criterion of meaning, so James seemed to exempt the statement that God exists. Once again a double standard of meaning and truth seems to emerge — one for science and another for theology.

Although the effect of James's "Will to Believe" was to encourage a dualistic view of the grounds of belief, in his *Pragmatism* James seemed to adopt a more unified approach to the problem. There he tried to present a theory of truth which would cover both scientific and religious beliefs; he tried to avoid concluding that the logic of theology and the logic of science are fundamentally different. Nevertheless, a careful examination of his *Pragmatism* shows that James continued to hold — by implication — that scientific statements and theological statements are justified in fundamentally different ways.

One plausible interpretation of James's theory of truth in *Pragmatism* is that it represents an effort to do for the word "true" what Peirce tried to do for laboratory words like "hard" and "heavy." For Peirce, to say that an object is heavy is to say that if one were to let it go, one would have certain sensory experiences; for James, to say that a statement is true is to say that if one were to believe it, one would have certain satisfactory experiences. Both translations are statements of the "if-then" form; both prescribe certain operations — in one case letting things go and in the other believing; both predict certain experiences upon the performance of these operations. However, before the Peirceian scientist may say that a statement is true, the statement must be meaningful. But in order for it to be meaningful, it must be translatable into something analogous to the statement, "If I let this body go, I shall see it fall." If a statement cannot be so translated, then there is, in Peirce's view, no scientific point in saying that the statement is true. One may pronounce with satisfying results the *words*, "I believe that God exists," or the *words*, "It is true that God exists," but if the statement that God exists is itself not capable of Peirceian translation, then according to a Peirceian one is not really believing anything when one utters the words "God exists"; one is not seriously attributing truth even though one thinks or says one is. And yet James in his *Pragmatism* did not insist that religious statements pass muster before Peirce's pragmatic theory of meaning. In effect, James by-passed the crucial rule of Peirce's pragmatism by not requiring that the statements of theology be pragmatically translatable in the manner of Peirce's laboratory statements. James went on, as it were, to the election of statements as true, without bothering to nominate them as pragmatically meaningful.

The conclusion that must be drawn is that neither Peirce nor James was fully consistent or thoroughgoing in his application of Peirce's pragmatic maxim. Peirce failed to apply it to his own realistic metaphysics, and James failed to follow its full implications in his discussion of theological belief. The result is the confusion in which they left the subjects of metaphysical and theological method. One clung to universals, and the other to God; but neither of them provided a rationale for their ontological or theological beliefs which is clearly consistent with the pragmatic theory of meaning set forth in Peirce's famous essay, "How to Make Our Ideas Clear."[5] Both Peirce and James, by implication at least, failed to adopt the view that all knowledge is scientific and empirical.

III

SCIENCE AND ETHICS

Whereas the use of a double standard of truth is implicit in Peirce's treatment of metaphysical assertions as well as in James's treatment of theological statements, the ambivalence of the pragmatic movement is much more explicit in the field of ethics. John Dewey was an ethical naturalist, who believed that all ethical statements are translatable into empirical statements; but C. I. Lewis, the most distinguished pragmatist of the generation after Dewey (Dewey was born in 1859, Lewis in 1883), emphatically disagrees. In the ethical writings of Lewis one finds an explicit defense of the view that not all ethical knowledge is based on empirical investigation. In particular, Lewis argues, knowledge of what is right and just can never be determined by empirical facts alone. Lewis therefore explicitly rejected the epistemology of "scientism," whereas Dewey insisted that the method of ethics was thoroughly scientific.

Dewey and Lewis were united in regarding statements of *value* as empirical, but they divided on the subject of obligation, of what ought to be done. On the subject of value, Dewey's view was close to that of Lewis, who says: "As a first approximation, we might say that attributing value to an existent, *O*, means that under circumstances *C*, *O* will or would lead to satisfaction in the experience of somebody, *S;* or it intends the joint assertion of many such affirmations."[6] Here both Dewey and Lewis follow Peirce's pragmatic maxim, applying its central idea to statements of value; indeed, Lewis points out explicitly that value is a disposition, and that therefore attributing value to a diamond is like attributing a specific gravity to it. In both cases, we imply that certain experiences would occur under certain circumstances, and in both cases we express scientific knowledge.

However, Lewis's distinction between value and obligation upsets any picture of pragmatic uniformity on the fundamentals of ethics. In his own words, "Valuation is always a matter of empirical knowledge. But what is right and just, can never be determined by empirical facts alone."[7] By contrast, Dewey was not prepared to grant that there is a class of moral statements or beliefs which are established by means that are fundamentally different from those used in science. For this reason, the historian of twentieth-century pragmatism must record its divided view in ethics. It is true that Lewis acknowledges a double standard, whereas Peirce and James seem to slip unconsciously into holding that metaphysics and theology have methods of their own which are distinct from that of empirical science. But, like Peirce and James in their respective treatments of metaphysics and theology, Lewis — in my opinion — fails to make clear just how we do justify judgments of right and wrong. His difficulty is related to his position on the nature of *a priori* knowledge, which is itself a subject on which pragmatists are in considerable disagreement.

Perhaps one of the most distinctive features of Lewis's work in epistemology is his theory of *a priori* knowledge, knowledge that we allegedly justify without reference to experience. The most distinctive characteristic of such knowledge is its necessity: statements expressing such knowledge must be true. By contrast, *a posteriori* knowledge is said to be contingent: statements expressing it may be false. If *a posteriori* statements are true, that is not because they *must* be true but because the world happens to be as they say it is. The classic examples of *a priori* statements have usually come from pure mathematics; whereas the most highly developed variety of *a posteriori* knowledge is to be found in the empirical sciences.

The problem of *a priori* knowledge has often been conceived as the problem of saying how there could be such a thing, and a number of answers have been offered in the history of philosophy. The answer given by Lewis is one of the most widely accepted in the twentieth century and is in broad outline similar to that given by logical positivists. He holds that all and only *a priori* statements are analytic; that is, they may be seen to be true merely by inspecting the meanings of their component terms. Therefore he rejects Kant's doctrine of the synthetic *a priori*. In Lewis's view, the truth of the statement that every horse is an animal is a consequence of the fact that the meaning of the word "horse" contains the meaning of the word "animal," and this is why we can discover its truth without engaging in experiment on or observation of horses. Therefore, analytic statements are sharply distinguished by Lewis from synthetic statements, whose truth we cannot determine merely by studying meanings. Moreover, according to Lewis and the positivists in Hume's tradition, all logical and mathematical truths are fundamentally like the statement that every horse is an animal in being analytic. The upshot of Lewis's theory is an exhaustive and exclusive division of knowledge into two kinds: logico-mathematical knowledge which requires no observation of the world for its justification, and empirical knowledge which does.

One can therefore understand why Lewis is involved in a serious problem over the status of statements about what is right and just. He contrasts them with value statements because he claims that value statements are empirical. Yet I do not think that he can successfully hold that *all* statements about the rightness or wrongness of actions are analytic, seen to be true merely by an inspection of the meanings of their component terms. Moreover, he seems to reject the view that ethical statements express no knowledge at all. Therefore, he has entered a quandary from which he has not yet successfully emerged. In one respect, therefore, statements about the rightness of action are to Lewis what ontological statements are to Peirce and theological statements to James. On Lewis's view their method of justification is not empirically scientific, but the positive nature of their method of justification is not made sufficiently clear.

IV

SCIENCE AND MATHEMATICO-LOGICAL TRUTH

This brief discussion of *a priori* knowledge leads naturally to the question of pragmatism's position on the nature of mathematical and logical truth; and once again, there is no uniformly held position. One of the most discerning expositors of Peirce's philosophy writes:

> Peirce's Pragmatism is, primarily, the logic of hypothesis; its aim is to prescribe and articulate the one essential condition to which every genuine hypothesis must conform; and broadly this condition is that a hypothesis must be verifiable experimentally. This being the case, it would be natural to assume that Pragmatism has a bearing solely on questions of matters of fact, questions about the world which is disclosed to us, ultimately through our sensations. It should therefore have no bearing whatsoever on our purely formal *a priori* knowledge, that is, our knowledge of logical truths and of pure mathematics. But, although Peirce's writings on this issue are distressingly scrappy, there can be no doubt that he did *not* wish the scope of his Pragmatism to be restricted to thoughts, statements, or hypotheses concerning questions of empirical fact. Pragmatism, he maintains, has an important relevance to those parts of our knowledge which are commonly described as purely formal, or apodeictic.[8]

But while Peirce's writing on this subject may be "scrappy" and even "confused," as Gallie says, the fact that Peirce did try to extend his pragmatism to the statements of logic and mathematics itself prefigures later pragmatic efforts to erase the sharp line between the analytic and the synthetic. Moreover, there is evidence that James too had serious doubts about the distinction between analytic and synthetic, especially in the last chapter of his *Psychology*. It is entitled "Necessary Truths and the Effects of Experience," and in one of its notes James says: "Some readers may expect me to plunge into the old debate as to whether the *a priori* truths are 'analytic' or 'synthetic.' It seems to me that the distinction is one of Kant's most unhappy legacies, for the reason that it is impossible to make it sharp."[9]

Contemporary reflection on the sharpness of the distinction between analytic and synthetic statements has led to a serious difference between pragmatists on the subject of logico-mathematical truth. Lewis espouses just such a sharp distinction as James disowns. On the other hand, W. V. Quine argues that his own refusal to make a sharp distinction between analytic and synthetic statements is more thoroughly pragmatic in spirit than the dualism of

Lewis.[10] Quine's attack on the distinction between analytic and synthetic is prompted by a number of considerations. It is mainly inspired by the negative conviction that the "meanings" appealed to by Lewis in his account of analytic statements are shadowy, obscure entities, and furthermore that the word "synonymous" as applied to linguistic expressions lacks the clarity to be expected of philosophical terms. Other considerations lead Quine to the conclusion that we must surrender the notion that for each kind of statement there is a separate and distinct method of validation. He advances this view in opposition not only to a sharp methodological distinction between logico-mathematical truth and truth in the natural sciences, but also to the contrast between ontology and natural science which seems implicit in Peirce's acceptance of scholastic realism. Quine contends that there is a basic similarity in the methods of justifying statements of mathematics, statements of physics, and statements which assert the existence of universals. In short, they are all justified pragmatically. Quine may therefore be called a methodological monist, at least so far as mathematics, the empirical sciences, and ontology are concerned. As he has not written on theology or ethics, one cannot say how far his monism would extend. But it is certainly safe to say that such a methodological monism has not been typical in the history of American pragmatism. Either half-consciously, as in the case of Peirce and James, or explicitly, as in the case of Lewis, pragmatists have tended to shy away from the view that Peirce's theory of meaning — or something like it — applies to *all* statements which express knowledge.

In fact even Dewey, who seems by intent to be the most thoroughgoing of all pragmatists in his methodological monism, has wavered in his treatment of questions surrounding the distinction between *a priori* and *a posteriori* knowledge. More than any thinker in modern times, Dewey viewed the history of Western philosophy as a fruitless quest for certainty, a misguided effort to discover a class of truths that would be stable, certain, and self-evident. And for this reason the notion of *a priori* knowledge was always suspect in Dewey's philosophy. For more than a half-century he campaigned against the view that there are two sorts of knowledge, one rational, necessary, and unchanging, and the other empirical, contingent, and merely probable. In his *Reconstruction in Philosophy* Dewey wrote: "Mathematics is often cited as an example of purely normative thinking dependent on *a priori* canons and supra-empirical material. But it is hard to see how the student who approaches the matter historically can avoid the conclusion that the status of mathematics is as empirical as that of metallurgy."[11] And a little further on in the same book Dewey says: "Logic is a matter of profound human importance precisely because it is empirically founded and experimentally applied."[12]

In such passages Dewey appears to be a methodological monist who puts logic in the same category as one of the most practical of empirical sciences; he adopts a position that is not unlike the extreme empiricism of John Stuart Mill in its methodological monism. And when we read the earlier pages of Dewey's *Logic*, we continue to think of him as a methodological monist, who does not make a sharp distinction between the methods of logico-mathematical science and natural science. But the *Logic* is a very long book, and by the end of it Dewey's monism seems to flag, and he seems to revert to a view which is strongly dualistic in its implications. Dewey makes a distinction between what he calls "existential" and "ideational" propositions, which is a version of the positivistic distinction between synthetic and analytic propositions. "Propositions," he says, "are . . . of two main categories: (1) Existential, referring directly to actual conditions as determined by experimental observation, and (2) ideational or conceptual, consisting of interrelated meanings, which are non-existential in content in *direct* reference but which are applicable to existence through the operations they represent as possibilities."[13] And this distinction, it would appear, serves to reinstate the sharp distinction between *a posteriori* and *a priori* knowledge that was apparently repudiated in *Reconstruction in Philosophy* and in the earlier pages of his *Logic*. In any case it is a far cry from the doctrine that mathematics is as empirical in its status as metallurgy, for it does suggest that whereas the "existential" truths of metallurgy are established experimentally, the "ideational" truths of mathematics are established by an examination of the interrelationships between "meanings." And it is hard to see how Dewey can view propositions about the interrelationships between meanings as experimentally verifiable. Once again we find a pragmatist speaking by implication of a kind of knowledge which is not experimental, and this time it is one of the most antidualistic of all pragmatic theorists of knowledge.

V

SCIENCE AND PRAGMATISM

One may sum up the situation as follows. Peirce seemed to exempt the statements of ontology from the need to follow the pragmatic maxim. James seemed to exempt the statements of theology. Lewis unquestionably exempted those ethical statements in which we assert that actions are right or wrong. And while Dewey professed to apply the canons of experimental science to all claims to knowledge, he seems at places to have fallen unwittingly into a variety of dualism. Quine is monistic in his approach to mathematics, logic, physics, and ontology, but through lack of interest fails to commit himself on ethics and theology. In short, no one of these five distinguished American pragmatists has seriously subscribed to the view that all statements by means of which men take themselves to express knowledge may be justified by the techniques commonly associated with experimental science. Because individual pragmatists have not all been consistent about the scope of science and because the movement as a whole has been divided on this question, pragmatism has never been able to present a single face to the world on one of the most central problems of modern philosophy. Whether this has been philosophically or socially fortunate is a matter beyond the concern of this essay. But it is a fact that must be acknowledged by any serious historian of ideas in America.

II

The Realist Tradition in American Law

Eugene V. Rostow

I

In 1883, Oliver Wendell Holmes, Jr., had just started a new career, that of Professor at the Harvard Law School. He had delivered *The Common Law* as Lowell Lectures in the winter of 1880 and had seen it through the press in 1881 — the year he reached forty. *The Common Law* was recognized from the beginning as a work of consequence, at least in England, although even there no one anticipated its future as one of the most influential books ever published in the United States.

Its author had been a studious young lawyer in Boston since his return from the Civil War and his graduation from the Harvard Law School in 1866. An incurably ardent intellectual, he had worked late nights to write articles and edit a legal journal, while actively engaged in the practitioner's life. But his interest in ideas, strong as it was, was weaker than his commitment to honor in the realm of affairs. In his own mind, at least, he was and remained more the brevet-colonel than the professor. As Mark Howe has shown, his self-doubts led him to an endless testing of his powers.[1] His experience in war confirmed his belief that the aim of life was life itself, and that its climax occurred in the arena, not the study. "Life is action and passion," he said in a famous speech. "I think it is required of a man that he should share the action and passion of his time at peril of being judged not to have lived."[2] He recurred often to the theme. He wrote elsewhere:

> I doubt if there is any more exalted form of life than that of a great abstract thinker, wrapt in the successful study of problems to which he devotes himself, for an end which is neither unselfish nor selfish in the common sense of those words, but is simply to feed the deepest hunger and to use the greatest gifts of his soul.
>
> But after all the place for a man who is complete in all his powers is in the fight. The professor, the man of letters, gives up one-half of life that his protected talent may grow and flower in peace. But to make up your mind at your peril upon a living question, for purposes of action, calls upon your whole nature.[3]

And on another occasion, he said,

> I know of no true measure of men except the total of human energy which they embody. . . . The final test of this energy is battle in some form — actual war — the crush of Arctic ice — the fight for mastery in the market or the court. Many of those who are remembered have spared themselves this supreme trial, and have fostered a faculty at the expense of their total life. It is one thing to utter a happy phrase from a protected cloister; another to think under fire — to think for action upon which great interests depend.[4]

This view of life led him to value the courtroom more than the classroom. When his former law partner, George D. Shattuck, came to him with the governor's offer of a place on the Supreme Judicial Court of Massachusetts, Professor Holmes did not pause. Indeed, he had anticipated the possibility of becoming a judge even when he accepted his chair at Harvard.[5]

In restrospect, it is fair to wonder whether Holmes's influence would have been greater if he had remained a professor. His achievements as a writer and as an intellectual critic of the law have survived better than his work as a judge. As a judge, by and large, he failed to carry out the precepts he taught as a writer of essays about law. In one branch of law after another, his judicial opinions have lost their power to lead. In the world of the law reports, Holmes no longer commands the field, as Brandeis does. It is rare to find in one of his opinions the germinal idea or the creative suggestion which starts a line of decisions and guides later judges in their quest. But his legal papers retain their relevance and vitality.

Be that as it may, Holmes did what he couldn't help doing. If as a professor he did not fully develop the view of law for which he remains famous, his glory and his legend as a judge helped to open many minds to the ideas he preached with such power.

For Holmes's book, and his professorial papers, and their echoes in his opinions, have decisively colored the intellectual universe in which the modern American lawyer is formed. They constitute the natural starting place for an attempt to review the turbulent streams of thought generally known as American Legal Realism.

II

It has always been curiously difficult to define law. The Romans regarded all such definitions as "periculosa," most dangerous. A recent book on legal philosophy concludes that a workable definition is impossible, and abandons the effort,[6] as Max Radin did many years ago.[7] Still, the word "law" carries reasonably familiar freight to most minds.[8] It conjures up a series of institutions — policemen, lawyers, judges, libraries of statutes and judicial opinions, witnesses and juries — and a series of ideas, procedures, and methods for reaching decisions. Some writers have stressed the importance of authority in law, and particularly the authority of the sovereign who can punish disobedience. They distinguish legal "laws" from those of games, or science, or art, by reason of the coercive sanction — the policeman's stick — associated with their enforcement. In law, Hobbes remarked, clubs are trumps. Others, recalling King Canute, observe the sovereign's inability to defy custom, and find the sources of law in the mores of each particular people, at each successive stage of its development.

We can think of law in terms of many competing and complementary formulae: as a code of rules laid down by a sovereign, as a process of social decision, a prediction of when the public force will be invoked, a pattern of approved social behavior, more or less effectively acknowledged by courts and legislatures — the number of such phrases is almost infinite. But whether we view law through the eyes of Hobbes or Hegel, of Montesquieu or Roscoe Pound, at least one intractable feature of the landscape will be almost universally acknowledged. We cannot ignore the fact that the law involves rules, articulated and rearticulated in more or less abstract form, and that these rules play a part in the outcome of legal controversies. The art of generalization has an indispensable role in the legal process, and is an indispensable feature of law as an institution both of order and of justice. The rationalizing and generalizing aspect of law derives from the basic moral principle, acknowledged by every legal system we know anything about, that similar cases should be decided alike. This principle of equality before the law is easy to recite, and infinitely difficult to apply. It lies behind the weight given to precedent in legal systems, and gives force to the yearning for certainty and predictability in law which each generation has expressed, in vain, since the beginnings of recorded time.

In the generation of lawyers and judges who prevailed in England and America about a hundred years ago, the rationalizing, system-building component of law became oppressive. Deference to precedent became not one wise principle among many in the growth of law, but a rigid and restrictive absolute, which is still considered to be at least the nominal rule of decision in England.[9] The men of that day, intoxicated by the notion of law as a science freed at last of its religious past, began to think of it as a self-contained body of rational precepts. Greatly influenced by the force and cogency of Blackstone's masterpiece, his *Commentaries on the Laws of England*, they treated the rules of law not as tentative hypotheses, advanced to explain shifting bodies of social behavior, but as fixed propositions, laws of nature and of "reason" in some magical sense, sustained by autonomous authority, and capable of surviving unchanged for indefinite periods of time. The so-called rules of law, which subsumed and organized groups and sequences of decisions, were invoked without reference to the purposes they had been called into being to serve, and without considering whether those ends were still appropriate. Orations at bar association meetings, and at the funerals of departed legal worthies, invoked the grandeur of "eternal principles" of law. The legal texts of the time, and the teaching in law schools, followed the same pattern. Whole areas of the law were reduced to the symmetry and consistency of logical order, with all their features clear and clearly derived from two or three general propositions deemed self-evident. Thus the dream was revived of law as a code of rules, and no more, so that with a little effort we could achieve its restatement in books that would not fill a single shelf. Then judgment could be found, not made, and society could at long last enjoy a stable, certain, and perfectly predictable legal order.[10]

I sometimes wonder whether the lawyers of the day really believed in the "mechanical jurisprudence" they professed, and against which Roscoe Pound's early articles inveighed with such vehemence. After all, we live by a philosophy of law even when we have no legal philosophers to tell us what it is, or when they describe it inaccurately. The centuries-old habits of the common law readily survived the strait-jacket of what Karl N. Llewellyn called the Formal Style of thought about law, which we still have too much with us. Professor Llewellyn described it in these terms:

> The Formal Style is of peculiar interest to us because it set the picture against which all modern thinking has played — call it, as of the last eighty or ninety years, "the orthodox ideology." That picture is clean and clear: the rules of law are to decide the cases; policy is for the legislature, not for the courts, and so is change even in pure common law. Opinions run in deductive form with an air or expression of single-line inevitability. "Principle" is a generalization producing order which can and should be used to prune away those "anomalous" cases or rules which do not fit, such cases or rules having no function except, in places where the supposed "principle" does not work well, to accomplish sense — but sense is no official concern of a formal-style court.[11]

But no doubt the Formal Style of the age and, perhaps more important still, the mediocrity and intense conservatism of many of the judges had their consequences in the realm of affairs. Many cases were decided mechanically. The common law process of creative change, through which the law meets and molds the flow of social experience, was slowed up. The law became too static, too resistant to pressure from without, cut off from the source of its vitality in the stuff of life.

The reaction of opinion was sharp and explosive, and it has continued in various forms to our own time. The need for the struggle remains, for the old orthodox idea of law as a fixed body of received rules, divorced from policy, has a tenacious hold on the minds of men. The battle cry of the counterattack was the opening page of *The Common Law,* still the rallying point and the point of beginning for most phases of the struggle to recover and reestablish effective methods for pursuing the reform of law and social reform through law.

> The object of this book is to present a general view of the Common Law. To accomplish the task, other tools are needed besides logic. It is something to show that the consistency of a system requires a particular result, but it is not all. The life of the law has not been logic: it has been experience. The felt necessities of the time, the prevalent moral and political theories, intuitions of public policy, avowed or unconscious, even the prejudices which judges share with their fellow-men, have had a good deal more to do than the syllogism in determining the rules by which men should be governed. The law embodies the story of a nation's development through many centuries, and it cannot be dealt with as if it contained only the axioms and corollaries of a book of mathematics. In order to know what it is, we must know what it has been, and what it tends to become. We must alternately consult history and existing theories of legislation. But the most difficult labor will be to understand the combination of the two into new products at every stage. The substance of the law at any given time pretty nearly corresponds, so far as it goes, with what is then understood to be convenient; but its form and machinery, and the degree to which it is able to work out desired results, depend very much upon its past.
>
> In Massachusetts to-day, while, on the one hand, there are a great many rules which are quite sufficiently accounted for by their manifest good sense, on the other, there are some which can only be understood by reference to the infancy of procedure among the German tribes, or to the social condition of Rome under the Decemvirs.[12]

These views and their reception measured deep movements in American and European thought. Great man though Holmes was, he did not strike off these passages, and others of like tenor, wholly through private revelation. The view he took emerged in large part from a collision between the static notions of law which prevailed among lawyers at the time, and the revolutionary new developments in historical studies. By 1880, the German, French, and English writers about history, sociology, and philosophy, after more than a century of effort, were beginning to transform our consciousness of the past, and of the nature of social development. Holmes's thought owed much as well to philosophy and the impact on philosophy of science. William James and Charles Peirce, both important philosophers of science and its methods, were his friends. These pillars of American pragmatism shared with Holmes and other young Bostonians the delights of the Metaphysical Club, a philosophical society founded in 1870, or thereabouts, to discuss "none but the tallest and broadest questions."[13] The development of science, and the ideas of Darwin and Huxley, were in the forefront of their thought. And, above all, by natural descent in the literature of law, Holmes and his fellow lawyers in the group were under the spell of the Utilitarians, and especially of Jeremy Bentham, that extraordinary figure, far in advance of his time, whose writings have not yet begun to exhaust their capacity to stir men into fresh thought.

For sixty years or so, following the publication of Holmes's book and his early articles, American law has been enlivened and illuminated by a Homeric series of debates addressed to the themes he had sounded.

The protagonists were a singularly colorful and often eccentric group of highly individual individualists. And their debate was lively, vigorous, and usually very combative indeed. As Felix Cohen wrote, "In the lists of jurisprudence, the champion of a new theory is generally expected to prove the virtue of the lady for whom he fights by splitting the skulls of those who champion other ladies."[14] If you run over their articles and book reviews, in the bound volumes of the old law journals, you can still catch an authentic whiff of cordite. They were, and some of them still are, a formidable lot. I hope the next generation can produce their equals. The lists included W. N. Hohfeld and Walter Wheeler Cook, A. F. Bentley, Roscoe Pound, Jerome Frank, Underhill Moore, Thurman Arnold, Morris and Felix Cohen, Albert Kocourek, Herman Oliphant, John Dickinson, H. E. Yntema, Max Radin, Arthur Corbin,

M. S. McDougal and H. D. Lasswell, L. L. Fuller, A. L. Goodhart, J. C. Hutcheson, Jr., and Hermann Kantorowicz. Many words have been used to describe the attitudes toward law which were expressed and applied in the course of this debate: pragmatism and positivism; functionalism and institutionalism; realism and idealism; jurisprudence sociological, operational, gastronomic, non-Euclidean, transcendental; the jurisprudence of values, of skepticism, and of cynicism. On the whole, none of the labels is of much use in describing either the terms of the debate or the prevailing state of thought which is its outcome.

III

I started by stressing a difference of view as to the place of legal rules in the legal process as the beginning of the modern American battle over the function and nature of law. The significance and propriety of these rules has remained a central issue in almost all phases of the discussion. The debate was part of a more generalized reconsideration of the respective roles of "reason" and "nature" in the process of learning, and in the creation of organized bodies of knowledge. In the legal literature, as in the literature about the philosophy of science, the words "rule" and "reason," "fact" and "principle," were used in a bewildering variety of denotations, which added to the excitement if not to the coherence of the argument. And in law, as elsewhere, there were tides in the conflict — first the stress on "facts" and "experiments," during the period of clearing away the tenacious authority of outmoded rules; then, after their discovery of Peirce, and of *Principia Mathematica* by Whitehead and Russell, some legal thinkers realized that propositions and propositional sets were indispensable to thought, although they were now viewed as hypotheses, not revelations. Every shade and nuance of the wider philosophical colloquy was reflected in the writing about law, from the discreteness or coherence of "facts" to the nature of logic and its uses in thought.

In the earlier years of the controversy over American legal realism, the reformers approached the citadel of the rules of law in an atmosphere of skepticism, often of mistrust. Almost all the realists agreed, by and large, on two propositions: first, that under legal customs all would accept, many and perhaps most of the cases which reached appellate courts could only be decided one way; and second, that in many instances the judge had a significant range of choice in deciding the case: choice in finding the facts, which Judge Frank stressed, or choice among the rules which might be chosen as major premise for the case, and in their interpretation. As Cardozo put it in his classical Storrs Lectures at Yale:

> My analysis of the judicial process comes then to this, and little more: logic, and history, and custom, and utility, and the accepted standards of right conduct, are the forces which singly or in combination shape the progress of the law. Which of these forces shall dominate in any case, must depend largely upon the comparative importance or value of the social interests that will be thereby promoted or impaired. One of the most fundamental social interests is that law shall be uniform and impartial. There must be nothing in its action that savors of prejudice or favor or even arbitrary whim or fitfulness. Therefore in the main there shall be adherence to precedent. There shall be symmetrical development, consistently with history or custom when history or custom has been the motive force, or the chief one, in giving shape to existing rules, and with logic or philosophy when the motive power has been theirs. But symmetrical development may be bought at too high a price. Uniformity ceases to be a good when it becomes uniformity of oppression. The social interest served by symmetry or certainty must then be balanced against the social interest served by equity and fairness or other elements of social welfare. These may enjoin upon the judge the duty of drawing the line at another angle, of staking the path along new courses, of marking a new point of departure from which others who come after him will set out upon their journey.
>
> If you ask how he is to know when one interest outweighs another, I can only answer that he must get his knowledge just as the legislator gets it, from experience and study and reflection; in brief, from life itself. Here, indeed, is the point of contact between the legislator's work and his. The choice of methods, the appraisement of values, must in the end be guided by like considerations for the one as for the other. Each indeed is legislating within the limits of his competence. No doubt the limits for the judge are narrower. He legislates only between gaps. He fills the open spaces in the law. How far he may go without traveling beyond the walls of the interstices cannot be staked out for him upon a chart.[15]

In short, the judge was inevitably concerned with policy, since law was "a means to social ends, and not an end in itself."[16] He makes law, and does not merely find it.

A considerable number of the writers who participated in the discussions concentrated on the artificial and unreal character of many legal rules. They were preoccupied with demonstrating that existing rules were meaningless, or circular, or self-contradictory, like the concept of "implied malice" which drew Holmes's scorn.[17] Some then went on, seeking to formulate new rules which would more accurately describe the law in action. Law, Sabine said, is "what it does,"[18] not what the judges say they are doing, or why. Others sought to investigate the effects of the existing law, as in court administration, bankruptcy, or divorce, or the relation between doctrines of law and patterns of custom or usage.

Many of the realists were heatedly accused of nihilism or worse, and charged with denying the presence of a generalizing element in law altogether. They were alleged to believe that decisions were based on unstated interests or value preferences, and that the reasons given for decisions were in fact afterthoughts, cynical rationalizations, representing the judge not as a conscientious lawyer, working within the permissible limits of his discretion, but as a wilful autocrat. By and large (although with several exceptional and occasional aberrations), the charge was not justified: the realist literature agreed with Pekelis's striking remark, amending one of Holmes's most famous quips, that "concrete cases cannot be decided by general propositions — nor without them."[19] The realists — or most of them, at any rate — were not trying to deny the inevitability of rules in a system of law that sought at any given time to decide like cases alike. Nor were they among those who used the battle flag of pragmatism to conceal the confusion, or sometimes even the absence of their systematic thought. The realists were trying to achieve an awareness of the relationship between rules and policy, viewing law as an instrument for social action in a society constantly in flux, "and in flux typically faster than the law, so that the probability is always given that any position of the law needs re-examination to determine how far it fits the society it purports to serve."[20]

During recent years, a significant reaction has occurred against this feature of the realist tradition: — that is, against the concept of judicial discretion it achieved, its stress on the inevitability of policy choices, and the limited and subordinate function it assigned to logical deduction from legal rules in its analysis of the judicial process.

Several factors have contributed to the counterattack.

In part, it derives strength from the natural democratic fear of entrusting political authority to judges, professionally remote from the people even when they are elected by them. The power of the judges did not seem so threatening when people believed that law was a technical matter, distinct from policy and politics, and that judges did not make law in any event, but merely applied the law they found in the books. The realists, however, changed all that. They stripped fig leaves away with gusto, and insisted on calling every possible spade a shovel.

Concern about the propriety of judicial lawmaking in a democracy has been enhanced by another aspect of recent experience: the prolonged battle over the powers of the Supreme Court, which has featured our political life in aggravated form almost without interruption since the early 1930's. The characteristic power of judges to interpret and develop the law is visible to a large public in the work of the Supreme Court, and it concerns issues about which intense feelings cluster. Many leaders of modern legal thought, anxious lest political reprisal altogether destroy the integrity of the courts, have counseled caution and abstinence in judicial lawmaking, and have advanced doubts about the existence or scope of many of the most controversial powers of the Supreme Court, particularly those derived from the Bill of Rights.[21] Others have reached comparable views about judicial lawmaking generally under modern circumstances, when legislatures function far more effectively than was the case in earlier periods of the law.[22]

A third element reinforcing the modern withdrawal from the view of law attained by the realists is the influence of analytical philosophy, and notably that of modern positivism, with its stress on precision and form and its preference for problems which can be studied in a quasi-mathematical way.[23] And, for the first time in more than a generation, legal thinkers who are not analytic or positivistic in orientation have made ambitious attempts to impose formal rules purporting to be those of logic on the judicial process.[24] Writers of this persuasion attempt to minimize the role of policy choice in the judge's task — that is, to minimize precisely the factor which Holmes and Cardozo were at pains to stress as primary. Seeking to guide the judicial process through neutral and a-political principles of general application, they propose rules of judicial action which would drastically confine the zone of judicial freedom so characteristic of the legal history we have thus far experienced and observed. They would make deduction from rules taken to be nearly fixed — both rules of judicial procedure and substantive rules of law — the central feature of judicial decision-making. In this regard, they reject the principal insight attained by the realists, that the judge's policy choice among alternative available premises is far more important to the judicial process than the logical application of the chosen premise to the particular case, necessary as that step is.

IV

When all the rules of law were re-examined and reformulated in the light of the tests and tenets of realism, when everyone understood and accepted the tentative nature of the rules, and their relation to the customs and morals and strong policy preferences of society, what then? Should modern lawyers, worthy to be welcomed as brothers into the fellowship of "realism," "liberalism," and "enlightenment," devote their attention to the law as it is, or to the law as it ought to be? In the early stages of the campaign, the rebels were anxious to concentrate — temporarily, in Llewellyn's phrase — on the law that is, and to set aside for the future the problem of the law that ought to be.[25] It was difficult enough, they thought, to show that the law recited in appellate decisions had lost contact with the mores of the community and with the law in action. The first job was to clear away the circular syllogisms and the meaningless concepts; to dispose of rules which had no other reason to support them than that so it was in the time of an ancient Henry; and to test, reformulate, and review all legal rules in the light of their factual background and their social effect.[26]

But was this the whole task of law and of legal scholarship? Was there no more to the job of lawyer and judge than to see to it that the law corresponds to the felt needs of the community, and maintains adequate means for knowing such needs, through its use of analytic procedures, and of methods and data drawn from economics, political theory, psychology, and sociology? Is the only end to be served that the law discover itself accurately, realistically, to make it the mirror of custom, rather than an instrument of higher values?

One of the most significant criticisms of the realist movement, that advanced at one time by Professor Lon L. Fuller of Harvard, stressed this thought — that the realists denied the problem of judging the goodness or badness of law, beyond the single issue of the correspondence between the law in the books and the law in action, that is, between positive law and custom.[27] Hadn't Holmes, following Bentham, laughed at the very idea of natural law, and favored the "separation" of law and morals?[28] Had he not said that justice was not his business as a judge, but only playing the game according to its rules?[29] And did he not remark that "the prophecies of what the courts will do in fact, and nothing more pretentious, are what I mean by the law."[30]

There is a paradox in this charge against the modern movement in American thought about law, for the legal realists were among our most devoted and effective reformers, both of law and of society. Professor McDougal commented on the charge in these terms:

> The American legal realism which Professor Fuller attacks is . . . a bogus American legal realism. John Austin, Kelsen, and others, from abroad and at home, may have done their bit to "separate the inseparable," but most of the men whose names appear upon Professor Llewellyn's famous list of American legal realists are innocent men. So also are most of their followers. They do not deny that the law-in-fact (rules and behavior) embodies somebody's ethical notions (how absurd it would be to deny it!); on the contrary, they are the people who have been most insistent that it has too often embodied an ossified ethics, inherited from previous centuries and opposed to the basic human needs of our time. More clearly than any of their critics, the realists have appreciated that legal rules are but the normative declarations of particular individuals, conditioned by their own peculiar cultural milieu, and not truths revealed from on high. Most of their writing has, in fact, been for the avowed purpose of freeing people from the emotional compulsion of antiquated legal doctrine and so enabling them better to pursue their hearts' desires. Not bothering to explain how judges can legislate, it is they who have insisted that judges do and must legislate, that is, make a policy

decision, in every case. The major tenet of the "functional approach," which they have so vigorously espoused, is that law is instrumental only, a means to an end, and is to be appraised only in the light of the ends it achieves. Any divorce they may at times have urged between is and ought has been underscored always as temporary, solely for the purpose of preventing their preferences from obscuring a clear understanding of the ways and means for securing such preferences. Directly contrary to Professor Fuller's charges, they have sought to distinguish between the is and the ought, not for the purpose of ignoring or dismissing the ought, but for the purpose of making a future is into an ought for its time.[31]

On the whole, Professor McDougal is right in his judgment, although there is a great deal on both sides of the debate about "the law that is" and "the law that ought to be" which is purely formal, inconclusive, and irrelevant.[32] There is more to modern American jurisprudence than the cheerful clatter of breaking idols, as we can see in the debate that is raging about the work of the Supreme Court. Holmes had put his definition of law into the future tense. It was never enough, he said, to discover what the law really was at a given moment. What would it become tomorrow? What forces would influence the law to change, and what fruit would come of the process of change? To answer that question, Holmes urged with equal zeal, the lawyer had to understand and consider the ideas playing on the formation of law — the pressures for social change in many areas, from banking and bankruptcy to labor law and the law of torts. He had to master all the sciences of society, from anthropology to statistics. And he had to know the judges, their prejudices and predilections, their zeal to participate in the growth of the law, or to resist it. After all, Holmes spoke of law not only as a prediction of what the judges would in fact decide, but also as the "witness and external deposit of our moral life," and of its history as "the history of the moral development of the race."[33]

During the last twenty years or so, the stress in the American literature about law has been on this part of the equation — the quest for standards and values in the process of guiding the evolution of "the law that is" into the law we think it ought to become. The formulation and acceptance of ends, these writers know, helps to fix the line of growth of the law. They have regained a general, if not universal acceptance for the thesis that the study of law properly includes the study of criteria for determining the goodness or badness of a given body of positive law at a given time and place. Of those who have contributed this feature to the body of our thought about law, I should mention particularly Felix Cohen, F. S. C. Northrop, Messrs. Lasswell and McDougal, Friedrich Kessler, Henry Hart, Jerome Hall, Lon L. Fuller, and Edmond Cahn. Their work has helped to correct and offset the relative neglect of the problem of values which characterized the early and more positivistic outlook of the legal realists.[34]

The emerging awareness of these three themes in their relations to each other constitutes a new synthesis of ideas about law, which tends to dominate the universe of American law today. (1) That synthesis accepts, and nowadays accepts without protest, the use of generalization, as a limited but essential part of the process of making legal decisions. (2) It stresses the links between the actual law and what Ehrlich and Northrop, following Montesquieu, call the living law of society, the mass of its customs and usages, animated by the existing Spirit of its Laws, the norm for law toward which it seeks to move in its day-to-day processes of lawmaking. This phase of the problem requires the lawyer and judge to go far beyond the traditional data of the law books, and to investigate the functioning of society, and the minds of men. And (3) it recognizes the need to acknowledge and to define the existence of standards of aspiration which govern the development both of the particular society and of its Spirit of Law. Some identify this third element in the legal process, a culture's ideal for the future of its law, as "natural law," a phrase of many ambiguities, and seek to study it objectively, with all the apparatus of modern scholarship.

V

The role of law is central to the life of all societies. In the United States, law has special significance because the American constitutional system requires judges to decide many questions which other democratic constitutions leave to legislators. This fact has suffused the literature and institutions of American law with a sense of drama and of acknowledged importance. And it has tended to sustain the vigor, independence, and capacity for initiative of the American judges, as compared with those in most other countries, not only on constitutional questions, but in all the areas of their work. American thought about law naturally reflects the distinctive quality and atmosphere of the American legal system. Its orientation has put more stress on judicial discretion and the inevitability of judicial policy choices than appears in most other national literatures of legal philosophy, and correspondingly less emphasis on precedent and precision. While the literature about law is an integral part of a widely shared intellectual and general history, its content in any given country is bound to be in part a function of that country's particular experience and outlook. Thus modern American thought about law includes a series of peculiarly vivid and peculiarly American variations on ancient and universal themes.

12

Economic Thought and the New Industrialism

Paul A. Samuelson

That the history of ideas can be written without paying *serious* attention to changing theories about economics is itself a preposterous idea. Yet, like Samuel Johnson's kicking of the table to disprove skeptics of reality, any doubter can convince himself of this remarkable truth by training his magnifying glass on a random page of a random book from the library shelf labeled "intellectual history."[1] It is not really that historians think economics is unintellectual, but rather that it strikes them as being too intellectual—that the esoteric ideas with which it abounds are too much for the ordinary man.

Evidently there are two fallacies here. First, as will not be evident to those who hold it, there is the mistaken belief that economics is really all that hard. When Carlyle called economics the Dismal Science, he was of course not referring to the mathematical complexity of modern economics or even to the Ricardian syllogisms and supply-demand diagrams of the nineteenth century; but for many learned men he might just as well have been. Here of course we have merely another problem of the two (or *n*) cultures: the real difference is not between science and the humanities, for both Saint Peter in heaven and Maxwell's Demon recognize that the savant who toils over vocabulary shifts in Tibetan is blood brother to the tireless collector of atomic spectra, while the big-picture man who can trace the rise and fall of civilizations is as incapable of mastering a nice point in literary philosophy as he is in quantum mechanics or growth economics.

The second fallacy renders the first gratuitous. For suppose it really did take a superman to understand basic economic principles. It would not then follow that the bulk of men carry around in their heads no economic ideas at all. Nature does abhor vacuums — a law of Sir T. Gresham, not Sir I. Newton. And simple economic notions, like weeds, homestead wherever they are not forced out by the cultivated flowers of the intellect. Moreover, many a flower is but a weed grown tame: unprune it and you discover its original sins. Just as every chairman of the board is a walking encyclopedia of economic theories, every barefoot econometrician has hidden inside him the full-blown prejudices of his high school civics teacher mingled among the Keynesian theories of deflation and the Paretian theorems on optimal competitive pricing.

All this can be illustrated by the present essay. I am concerned with the development of economists' thought in America, particularly in the period from the Civil to the First World War. While this is of interest for its own sake, I must confess that I began with the following vague hypothesis:

> Businessmen today — and for that matter congressmen, editors, and the American middle classes generally — have economic beliefs which keep the country from doing things that would improve profits, real wages, job opportunities, and living standards generally. The source of these archaic notions is perhaps to be found in the "conventional wisdom" laid down by academic economists in the half-century after the Civil War.

But the more deeply I study the evolution of thought, the less confidence I have in the attractive theory that today's popular beliefs are primarily vestiges of yesterday's science. For one thing, the best economic scholars of the past, even though deprived of access to a good M.I.T. training in economics and ignorant of the experiences of nations in the twentieth century, turn out upon examination to have had a much better understanding of economic principles *for our times* than does a present-day man of affairs. If the rock-and-roll music of popular fashion is not the same as Schoenberg, that does not mean it has to be the Bach or even the Chopin of some past epoch.

Too much, however, should not be read into my assertion that popular notions about economics are somewhat different from those of past and present economists. It does not follow that the history of popular economic notions has to be much like the histories of water closets or of sexual superstitions, which are perhaps best recorded by busy anthropologists working across time and space. Were that so, I suppose we would push the subject out of the category of intellectual history and into the category of "social" or some other kind of history. But to do this would, I think, be a mistake.

How a man feels about a balanced budget turns out to be closely linked with how he feels about the gold standard or minimum-wage legislation. This is merely to say that his various ideas in economics have *analytical and intellectual connections*, even if they do not form an integrated self-consistent system. "I rationalize; therefore I am" might well be the credo of everyman as economist. To be articulate it is well to have something articulated to talk about—which is more than a play on words. All this applies to the radical as well as to the conservative: it is not enough to express hate for a system and implore others to do likewise; one inevitably tries to explain why the hateful is hateful.

At this point of generalization an element of science does enter in at least crudely. If I manufacture dolls, and Japanese imports threaten my income, I do not have to convince my wife that free trade is a bad thing. But in asking Congress and the voters to do something about it, I require arguments that go beyond my own need or greed: so I find myself shopping among economic theories for new points of persuasion, thereby implicitly entering the realm of primitive economic science. Nor should rationalization be thought of as simple reflections of views already arrived at without the need for reasoning: rationalizations do take on a life of their own and do in some degree affect subsequent opinions and actions. Thus, if my wish to be left alone to run my own business convinces me of the virtues of laissez-faire and limited government, I may end up voting against governmental tariff protection for some other industry even though I do not overdo consistency by refraining from asking government to protect my own. One does after all owe something to one's wife!

In summary, while reviewing the developing economic thought among economists is not quite the same as giving a definitive history of American economic opinions, I believe such a review provides an indispensable aspect of the problem. Besides, as any survey of the history of ideas must show, there is more interest for its own sake in the story of connected thought than in a chronological listing of an inventory of notions. The portrait of a baby or a lobster is more memorable than the photocopy of a yeast colony in a washtub.

EARLY AMERICAN ECONOMICS IN BROAD VIEW *

Every textbook on the history of economic doctrines includes a separate section on American thought. Invariably the same names appear: Benjamin Franklin, Alexander Hamilton, Henry C. Carey, Henry George, Francis Walker, and John Bates Clark. Certain clichés and stereotypes about the character of American economics are repeated in every discussion. What are some of these?

American economics is first and foremost supposed to be "optimistic." Men living on a bounteous and yet unsettled continent during a time of rapid progress in population and real national product per capita could hardly be expected to take much stock in a gloomy Malthusian vision of diminishing returns and subsistence wages. And they did not. Henry C. Carey, writing just before the middle of the nineteenth century, rebelled against the dismal aspects of classical economics. His logic was often bad and his prolix style atrocious. But his fundamental empirical inferences seem correct for his time and place.

By virtue of technological developments in transportation the ef-

* The next three sections are adapted from my essay "American Economics," Chapter 2, pages 33–44 in *Postwar Economic Trends in the United States*, edited by Ralph E. Freeman; copyright © 1960 by Massachusetts Institute of Technology; reprinted by permission of Harper & Row, Publishers.

fective supply of land and natural resources, far from declining relative to labor and capital, was actually increasing.[2] Most important, real wages were rising as a result of technological change and capital formation, and in addition could confidently be expected to continue to rise. No wonder Henry C. Carey saw social harmony everywhere — and before Bastiat, as he himself bitterly pointed out. It is instructive that the economic theories which Carey used to deduce those glowing trends were not unlike the labor-theory-of-value models. Yet they were used to deduce predictions about real wages quite opposite from those of Karl Marx — predictions which we now know are more nearly in accordance with the historical record than Marx's expectation of an absolute or relative impoverishment of labor.

A second characteristic of nineteenth-century economics is its "theological" character. The typical textbook writer seems to have been an ordained clergyman teaching as an amateur economist in a college. As Cliffe Leslie pointed out in his essay, *Political Economy in the United States* (1881), anyone looking over the leaves of American treatises would be tempted to classify them as "Sunday" rather than "weekday" books: they take for granted that God designed the competitive economic system in a harmonious way, regarding this as an axiom rather than as a theorem proved by Adam Smith.[3]

A third characteristic commented on by most writers is the "protectionist" leanings of American economists. Since this seems hardly consistent with a belief in the harmonious nature of free private enterprise, most chroniclers have tried to explain protectionism in terms of aberrations of logic.

A better explanation of protectionist leanings will be found, I suspect, in a fourth characteristic of American economics, its "nationalistic" nature. Thus to the array of important American economists I would add the name of Friedrich List. Of course List would usually be considered the arch exponent of German nationalism; but Joseph Dorfman, in his monumental study, *The Economic Mind in American Civilization*, has convincingly argued that List's theories had already jelled prior to his returning to Germany from the United States, and that it was in the nature of an accident that he wrote his *National System of Political Economy* in German.[4] Native writers, such as Harvard's Francis Bowen, produced textbooks with such titles as *American Political Economy;* and as late as the First World War, Thomas Nixon Carver was writing elementary textbooks of an unashamedly nationalistic character.

As an ethical end, Carey and his followers wanted a diversified America. I suspect they were willing to pay an economic price for this,[5] but they were poor enough reasoners to be able to convince themselves that no price would be exacted. Instead of presenting their many specious arguments in favor of a tariff, they would have done better to concentrate on the "infant industry" argument. In retrospect, knowing as we do that America has developed a comparative advantage in many lines of manufacture, it seems to me a legitimate hypothesis that tariffs which speeded up their introduction and *initiated early experimentation* may have had some helpful role in accelerating the pace of American development.

Undoubtedly, however, the most powerful forces pushing economists toward arguments for protection were not the interests of industries yet unborn but the established coal and iron interests. Little wonder that Pennsylvania was a hotbed of protectionism and that no free trader could teach at the University of Pennsylvania.[6]

This brings me to a fifth characteristic of nineteenth-century American economics — its "pro-business, conservative" character. The harmonies of the economic system were the harmonies of ruthless competition. Whereas at the beginning of the century many writers thought that the result would be an equalitarian society, by the end of the century economists observed that the outcome did involve great disparities of wealth. Many followed Herbert Spencer in embracing a crude form of "Social Darwinism," in which the poor were blamed for their misfortune and the rich praised for their success. One such "forgotten man," who enthralled several generations of Yale men with this stern philosophy, was William Graham Sumner.

The final characteristic of earlier American economics that most writers have agreed on is its "untheoretical," even "antitheoretical," nature. This is summed up in the much-quoted view of Harvard's C. F. Dunbar, who said in his essay "Economic Science in America, 1776–1876": ". . . The United States has done nothing towards developing the theory of political economy. . . ." There is much to this, but two reservations must be made.

First, there is the fact that Dunbar was pretty much satisfied with theoretical economics as laid down by the classical economists. (He was the person Eliot picked to teach sound free-trade economics in place of Bowen.) So he could hardly be regarded as an unbiased judge of the newer doctrines of Carey and other Americans.

Second, there is the neglected American theorist John Rae. Rae developed a sophisticated theory of capital and interest and put forth many interesting notions concerning invention and progress. Not only was Rae a theorist of international caliber, but in addition it can be argued that most of what is valid in Carey he might have found in his reading of Rae.

But, all in all, we must accept the charge that early American economics was on the primitive side where economic theory was concerned. Perhaps nothing more could have been expected of amateurs writing in a provincial backwater. The tendency of American thought to be derivative and doctrinaire — as seen by the popularity and repeated imitation of the textbooks of Jean Baptiste Say and John Ramsay McCulloch — fits in with such a pattern too. There may be something also in the notion that Americans are peculiarly pragmatic, content to stay close to the facts and untempted toward long chains of deductive reasoning.

A more flattering interpretation of this untheoretical trait may be found in the nature of the subjects in which American economics excelled. Around the turn of the century Americans did a great deal of work on business cycles, which culminated in Wesley C. Mitchell's magnificent book published in 1913. The fact that American fluctuations were always so much bigger than those abroad led naturally to an interest in this subject. Even those of us who are fondest of economic theory will not argue that cultivating the economic theories of the classical and neoclassical writers would have been an optimal way of then advancing knowledge of business fluctuations.

The second subject that American economists can be said to have been studying with special vigor comprises what would today be called "growth and development economics." Thus the early writers were interested in promoting thrift and capital formation, were stressing progress and technological change, and were emphasizing the economies of large-scale production. It is true that they did not succeed in formulating a simple and comprehensive theory to cover growth and development. But modern economists of the 1960's are least likely to blame them — since in our own day the philosopher's stone that would unify and illuminate this area has long been sought, but the search has as yet produced only a catalogue of important but not unobvious tendencies and countertendencies.

THE TRANSITION TO MODERN ECONOMICS

Does this survey of American economics throw much light on the present position of the subject? I am not sure.

From it one would hardly be prepared for the fact that abstract mathematical economics and statistics are being avidly studied today here in the United States. (That economists should be busily engaged in operations research and programing for large corporations and the armed services fits in a little better with the earlier pattern.)

Nor would reading a survey of the nature of early American economics lead one to guess that today large parts of the business community look on economists with suspicion — as impractical "eggheads" bent on criticizing private enterprise and putting it in fetters. The intervening years of trust formation at the turn of the century and of mass depression in the 1930's substantially changed characteristic patterns of the earlier economics.

The evolution of American economic thought would, however, have prepared one for the emergence in the first part of this century of the *institutionalist* school of economics. This was associated with the names of Thorstein Veblen, John R. Commons, and Wesley C. Mitchell. For the most part this school has not succeeded in reproducing itself and today it seems to be almost extinct. But at the University of Wisconsin and the New School for Social Research in New York in the years after the First World War, this school, with its rejection of abstract "equilibrium" economics in favor of a concentration on economic institutions, did appear to be the wave of the future.

It is hard today to see what such diverse men really had in common, that is, aside from their all being critical of the deductive economics promulgated by complacent classical and neoclassical theorists. Veblen — the American Karl Marx — was primarily an iconoclast and social critic, debunking in murky but brilliant prose the cherished beliefs and institutions of his time. The lasting achievements of Commons and Mitchell would not seem to reside in anything that they had particularly in common with Veblen or with each other but rather with the important work in applied economics that each was motivated to do — Commons in the field of labor economics and Mitchell in the field of business cycles.

Prior to the institutionalists, America was not without its critics of the existing order. About Henry George and his single-tax movement I shall say little, since so forceful a speaker and stylist was able to command for himself an amount of attention disproportionate to his intrinsic importance. The imputation of land income is unlikely to be considered by the economic historian of the future as a problem of the first magnitude, and the expectation by George's followers that the single tax would cure most of the ills of society seems merely crankish.[7]

One would have expected the deflationary decades at the end of the nineteenth century to have created a group of radical economists. In the political field itself we had the era of Populist agitation, and this did have its counterpart in the realm of thought. The young John Bates Clark was a kind of Christian socialist; and Francis Walker at the threshold of his career as an economist felt himself to be a militant critic of the harmonies of laissez-faire. The American Economic Association was founded in the 1880's by the younger economists — many of whom had studied in Germany under so-called "socialists of the chair" and exponents of the historical method — as a protest movement against the older conservative economists. It may not seem remarkable today but it was then a use of strong language for them to propose in their platform the assertion: "We regard the State as an educational and ethical agency whose positive aid is an indispensable condition of human progress." How different this was from the Jeffersonian notion that the best government was that which governed least!

In time the American Economic Association lost its radical tinge and embraced almost all the leading American economists. And it is interesting to observe how many of the men associated with its founding became less radical with advancing age and prestige. In the nineties Richard T. Ely, one of the leading spirits in the founding of the Association, was formally accused at the University of Wisconsin of being a socialist. Not only did he clear himself of this charge, but, what is more remarkable, he agreed that if the charge had been true, it would have been good grounds for disqualifying him from teaching. And Clark ended by formulating in his classic *Distribution of Wealth* the doctrine that the imputation of functional wages and interests by the specific productivity laws that prevail under free competition is *ethically* optimal.

Perhaps the pressures of what was on the whole an intolerant society can explain the increasing conservatism of the transitional generation of economists. Certainly some explanation for the relative unimportance of socialism in modern American thought is called for. As far as the changing ideas of economists themselves are concerned, I have this hypothesis to put forward. By the turn of the century economists were ceasing to be amateurs and were making their livelihoods as college professors. This professionalization of economics may have had as one of its by-products a toning down of radical feelings, for the university environment and the full-time study of economics may make for a reduction of Utopian ardor. (It is interesting to note that Alfred Marshall in England and Léon Walras in France and Switzerland went through similar developments, each starting and ending with warm social sympathies but in the course of time becoming more and more skeptical about proposals for the radical remaking of society.)

The professionalization of American economics greatly improved its analytical quality. Now articles and books were being written by men who had been taught by other economists, not by themselves. What was lost in originality was more than made up for in cogency. The two great figures from the standpoint of analytic contribution undoubtedly were John Bates Clark and Irving Fisher.[8] After the First World War this transitional period culminated in such world-famous economists as Frank H. Knight, John Maurice Clark, and Jacob Viner. These men, the sons of our grandfathers, belonged to the first generation of topnotch economists to have been completely reared by American graduate schools. They provide a fitting bridge to the modern generation of American economists.

THE MODERN SCENE

In giving a survey of American economics and American economists, I must not make the mistake of the patriotic Greek who insisted that the moon of Athens was different from the moon of Sparta. American economics is plainly in the tradition of Western economics generally. Indeed, to a Russian it would be indistinguishable from French or German economics. To a Latin American it would not seem different from English economics. (And even we American economists have our private little joke concerning our great advantage over the English. They read only their own writings, whereas we can get the benefit from reading their papers and our own too!)

Furthermore, by American economics one cannot mean economics as taught and discussed by persons *born* in this country. Scarcely one French professor in twenty was born outside of France. But of twenty outstanding American economists at the time of the Second World War, perhaps two came here from England and six to eight from Europe. (I do not even distinguish Canadian from American economists. Another of our jokes is that we are all Canadians!) An American university that tried to recruit its economics department from *Mayflower* descendants would, I fear, have a tough time of it.

These and other characteristics of the American economic profession would also be quite typical of other disciplines: mathematics, physics, chemistry, classics, sociology, medicine — and in some degree law and history. Many of my remarks then, though couched in terms of the concrete detail of economics, will be applicable to American academic life generally; and this essay can be considered a contribution to the general subject of *comparative academics*.

For about a quarter of a century now, American economics has been first-rate. What does this mean? It means what any competent observer means when he says that a particular university or person is in the forefront in creative research in the field of mathematics, physics, or medicine. Naturally there is an inevitable subjective element in any such appraisal. And there is an inevitable bias that predisposes any observer to magnify the accomplishments of his own town, province, and country. When I state that the *quantity* of economic thought in Cambridge, Massachusetts, is second to none anywhere in the world, I might be able to back this up by a count of the pages of articles published in learned journals, by measurement of the total inches of our theoretical and statistical curves, by the decibel count of the seminars at Harvard and further down the river. But when I go on to state that the *quality* of this thought is second to none, you must make allowance for the fact that Cambridge is where I sip my morning coffee.

In saying that American economics has been first-rate for a quarter of a century, I seem to be implying that prior to that time it was not. One can never be sure about such judgments, but I am inclined to risk the hypothesis that the scholarly research done by Americans in economics prior to, say, 1932 was generally not quite of the first rank. And I suspect this is a judgment that could be risked about mathematics, physics, and chemistry, too.

Let me illustrate by the case of mathematics and physics. Toward the end of the Second World War, when President Roosevelt set up the Bush Committee to survey science, I recall hearing I. I. Rabi, himself an American Nobel prize winner in physics, point out that in our history we had produced only one truly outstanding theoretical physicist (presumably Willard Gibbs). And the story is told that when the young G. D. Birkhoff proved in 1910 a famous conjecture of the dying J. H. Poincaré, the French mathematician C. E. Picard refused to believe that an American could have done it.[9]

It was not purely for reasons of fashion that at the turn of the century Americans went to Germany to do their graduate work. In the natural sciences the best work was being done there, and many Americans who studied abroad were frank to report that they found themselves less well prepared and creative than many of the fellow students they met in Europe.

Returning to economics, can we explain the earlier trek to Germany purely in terms of the world superiority of German *economic* scholarship? I think not. If American economics was years ago clearly inferior to some other economics, one would have to point to English economics as the clearly front-rank effort. So, I suppose, we must invoke the institutional factor that German universities were set up to give graduate instruction whereas Cambridge (and Oxford) were not. If an economist like J. B. Clark could have gained anything from his teachers — and there is little evidence that so self-oriented and original a man could — one would have thought that a W. S. Jevons might have given him more than could a Karl Knies or any other less theoretically oriented German scholar. But Jevons taught undergraduates in a university that was not yet even red brick. And even after the nineties, when Alfred Marshall was widely regarded as the world-leading economist, there was really no way for anyone to do graduate study in his Cambridge classroom — much less at his knee.[10] Had a young American been venturesome enough to break away from the German pattern, how could he get into an English college? And outside the college common room, whom would he have found to talk to? Worst of all, to cap his folly he would have had to return to our shores unanointed by the all-important Ph.D. degree, which was the necessary passport for a successful teaching career.

Demand creates its supply. We have seen that American universities increasingly began to process their own graduate students and to award domestic Ph.D. degrees. And yet, as we have seen, it was perhaps still not true that American economics was first-rate. This led many observers by the familiar *post-hoc-ergo-propter-hoc* reasoning to the inference that our second-rateness must be due to our horrible propensity to insist on doctor's degrees. Even today this view will take one a long way in many a common room of the British Isles, and there are *Gelehrten* here at home who think that the mere *absence* of a degree will convert a mediocre son of the Middle Border into a sparkling and omniscient don.

I must confess my own original predilections were against our Ph.D. until, under the impact of direct empirical observation, I was forced to the view that the absence of a comprehensive Ph.D. program may be the curse of economics abroad. This is not at all because our average doctoral dissertation is a substantial contribution to scholarship, a work of art, or even a literate document. To look at the thesis is to miss the point; it is only the exposed peak of a submerged iceberg. If the Ph.D. program had never existed, we should now have to invent it — for the simple reason that *it gives us the excuse to carry on advanced instruction in economics.*

For, make no mistake about it, modern economics has become a complicated subject — one which takes a long time to learn. Gone are the days when one could give a bright undergraduate a copy of Alfred Marshall's *Principles* to take along with him on his vacation trip to the mountains and expect him to end his undergraduate days as an accomplished economist. True, such a system may generate clever essays about Marshall's use of the representative firm or his concept of quasi rent. But that is not the sort of thing that economists today regard as important work — nor would similar clever essays by Marshall on Mill's use of "derived demand" have earned him *his* world reputation.

AMATEURS AND PROFESSIONALS

My survey has given primary emphasis to the economic ideas of economists rather than of noneconomists. Increasingly as the years went by, being an economist meant being a professor. But the two terms are by no means identical: neither David Ricardo nor John Stuart Mill was an academic teacher or even a college undergraduate; in America people like Rae and Carey were more important *as economists* than academic figures like Bowen and Dunbar, and for this reason I have paid more attention to them. On the other hand, someone like Edward Bellamy, through his novel *Looking Backward* (1888), had a far greater political impact on socialist sentiments in America than did Karl Marx or even Thorstein Veblen. Yet though Bellamy deserves a full treatment in the history of Utopias, I do not think he rates a major place in the history of economic ideas as developed by economists.

Elsewhere I have written at some length on the different rating we in the economics profession give to economic ideas of the past as compared to the rating used by professional historians of ideas and cultivated men of affairs generally.[11] The present essay further illustrates this divergence. Consider Henry Ford. The man in the street attached some importance to the ideas of Henry Ford, and perhaps the eclectic historian of social thought will give him a few paragraphs. Yet in the catalogue of economic ideas and principles, professional economists will spare him scarcely a footnote. His ideas about mass purchasing power are not new or particularly well phrased: his pronouncements about production and about tapping a mass market through price reduction seem not of the importance of an Eli Whitney or even a Frederick Taylor. While Shaw may be right in saying that "Those who can, do; those who can't, teach," it is the latter who survive in books of intellectual history. For history is written, after all, by writers.

The point about Ford is a trite one. More subtle are the examples provided by Henry George and William Graham Sumner. Henry George was long a force to reckon with in the political world and in the marketplace for general ideas. Yet, as I have indicated, he really was not much of an economics scholar. The example I use to illustrate this is a conversation at the Harvard Society of Fellows that I once had before the war with Frank W. Taussig, then the dean of venerable American economists. He told me that a recent remark by John Dewey praising George as the greatest economist America had ever produced simply filled him with despair: in terms of economic analysis — and I am not here referring to any conservative doubts Taussig might have had about the land-tax movement — George appeared to Taussig to be like a confused child. This same Taussig has somewhere written that William Graham Sumner, however important his polemical eloquence might have been, added nothing essential to economic knowledge, not even to the principles a conservative might want to appeal to. Lest I give the impression that Taussig was by temperament a stuffed-shirt and an overcritical judge, let me add that as editor of the austere *Quarterly Journal of Economics* Taussig had encouraged publication of papers by Thorstein Veblen, whom he regarded as a genius, albeit not necessarily a faultless economic reasoner.

One is not surprised that an unoriginal vulgarizer should carry more political weight than a subtle creator of important economic ideas. Part of the hard-sell involves repetition and oversimplification. To be persuasive one should often ignore objections to a thesis: and one way to ignore an objection is to be unaware of it. Yet it can be argued that the advocate of a special view is best armed with the most complete knowledge about the strengths and weaknesses of his own arguments. If this be the case, I think it definitely true that by shopping around among contemporary and past economic scholars, a Machiavellian advocate can construct his most powerful brief. Economic scholars come in all opinions; and since, by definition, they are the ones who have devoted the most time to the pursuit, they are the ones in the best position to enunciate the intrinsic merits (and demerits) of a particular view. As an illustration of all this, consider the dictum of my old teacher and friend, Professor Jacob Viner of Chicago and Princeton. Like most economists, he would regard himself as pretty much of a free trader; and yet he would claim, "The best arguments for tariff protection have been thought up and described by free traders."

Yet, I must confess to lingering doubts. Viner would no doubt have in mind arguments like J. S. Mill's that a temporary protective tariff may enable an "infant industry" to get started and develop into a competitively viable national asset. That is one of the best arguments for a tariff. But in what sense "best"? Best in the sense that free traders, or rather economists generally, will be most likely to deem it best. Evidently there is a danger here of circularity: economic scholars provide the best analysis of important matters, if you use their criteria as the test. Now, the best arguments in this sense are not necessarily the most persuasive ones politically. Thus, the argument for a so-called "scientific tariff" — one that *merely* serves to equalize costs of production at home and abroad! — perhaps had as much political sex-appeal a third of a century ago as any argument. Yet it is widely regarded by economists as a tissue of nonsense, which if taken seriously would wipe out *all* trade and all the benefits of trade. Was it developed by a free trader, or for that matter by a professional economist? I do not know, but if it was, it was probably developed in a fit of absentmindedness. Unless a political protagonist is very Machiavellian indeed, is he not better off *not* realizing how illogical is his use of the scientific tariff argument? I realize it may be argued that in the long run logic will win out over illogic and correct description of reality will win out over incorrect. But as we survey the history of popular ideas, just how confident are we of that?

CONCLUDING REMARKS

Does the history of economic ideas in America fit into any simple patterns? To a first approximation, it seems to me the data can be usefully described in terms of the familiar interpretations.

American economics has, on the whole, been on the conservative and laissez-faire side prior to 1933. The fact that America has always enjoyed about the highest standard of living in the world, and has tended to enjoy a rising standard, does seem important in explaining this. The fact that America started with a clean slate and abundant natural resources does make it seem likely that ours would be a relatively classless society, and hence not too favorably disposed toward interventionist or socialistic ideologies.

This is, of course, a banality. But better a correct banality than an ingenious sophistry. As soon as one proceeds to a closer examination of the record, the shortcomings of a first-approximation description become evident, along with doubts about further theories purporting to "explain" America's thought. Here are a few doubts.

First, why this American prosperity? Climate and abundant resources? No doubt a part of the explanation. Good racial stock? Mm. The perfection of our Constitution and mores? Luck? What kind of an explanation is that? Yankee ingenuity? An answer that raises a new question, albeit possibly a fact as solid as a table and not to be ignored merely on the ground that it is simply a description.

Second, why should Australia and New Zealand, also sparsely settled regions of considerable prosperity, have developed a kind of Fabian socialism that America shunned? At this point one may argue, as Paul Sweezy and others have argued, that radicals were rooted out of American colleges and converted by pressure to conformity. The troubles of Scott Nearing, Thorstein Veblen, Richard T. Ely, and more recent scholars are indeed facts that cannot be ignored. But to the degree that we accept this thesis, we undercut another: thus, the clear-slate freedom from feudalism is widely used to explain our lack of class consciousness; yet it is that same absence of feudal traditions which left American universities at the mercy of their businessman trustees — all this showing the subtlety needed in appraising simple interpretations.

Third, how good is the Max Weber view that the Protestant Ethic and Capitalist Spirit are significantly related? Certainly many religious sermons have a Chamber of Commerce ring about them. But, as Kurt Samuelsson has been the most recent to point out, capitalism has flourished with and without Protestantism and vice versa — so that the historian must turn quantitative in a way he has been reluctant to do. If Weber can use Benjamin Franklin as a prototype of a religious man, then his thesis has been widened into emptiness. (If Adam Smith and David Hume are Protestants, then I am the Pope.) And how does the American observer treat the radicalism inherent in the "social gospel" movement that grew up in the pre-1914 Protestant ministry? Is Herbert Spencer to be given honorary baptism, and W. G. Sumner to be equated with John Wesley? Thus, there is truth and untruth in the Weber thesis; and if a Talcott Parsons should charge that it is a vulgarization of the subtle Weber position which is being attacked, one must reply that the vulgarization of an idea sometimes contains its cash-value in the Bridgman-Carnap sense of operational meaningfulness, while its subtle qualifications may be the antidote that emasculates its empirical dote.

While Charles Darwin lent false respectability to Herbert Spencer, the causal direction between the notions of evolution and economic progress are far from simple. Progress in the sense of size and real-income growth was a solid fact to every Wisconsin schoolboy, and it may be as correct to say that belief in progress led to belief in evolution as vice versa. Certainly it is ironical that both Darwin and Wallace were led by Malthus to natural selection, and yet the America that was so hospitable to Social Darwinism was the same America that thought Malthus just plain wrong. It is partly because Social Darwinism is such a jolly good story, aside from its merits, that it has had its vogue with historians. Sumner spoke to his age, not for it. To ignore what he felt a need to rebut is like reporting one side of a telephone conversation. Also we must not forget that economists as diverse as Mill and Schumpeter and Milton Friedman do attach the greatest importance to "competition" — not the rivalry of Dan'l Drew and Cornelius Vanderbilt so much as the erosion of profits for those who put their noses to the wrong grindstone. The man who builds a better mousetrap makes grass grow in his neighbor's road.

Hardly more satisfying are the attempts to link up American philosophies with economics. The transcendentalists founded collective colonies of good chaps, it is true. But is there not also much of the Horatio Alger, Jr., and Dale Carnegie kind of individualism in Ralph Waldo Emerson? And was not America a natural place for experimental colonies for the same prosaic reason that one does not plant a nudist colony in the high-rent district? To link Veblen with pragmatism because he overlapped with John Dewey at the University of Chicago is as superficial as identifying the know-nothing attitudes of practical businessmen with the ideas of William James and Charles S. Peirce. The facile explanation of Dewey's radicalism in terms of his father's being a rural Vermont merchant of limited means must seem a fine joke to those who knew Davis R. Dewey, the conservative economist who was John's brother: perhaps Freudian historians can explain this by Davis's sibling envy!

I desist from continuing this list of points and counterpoints. If history is not to be an impressionistic arrangement of descriptions that happen to please the historian and his friends, I think one has to be critical of a book like J. F. Normano, *The Spirit of American Economics* (1943), which, along with a review of the troops, includes the usual interpretations of American economic thought together with a few new ones. My point is not that I happen to like a different emphasis, since why cater to my tastes rather than Normano's? My point is that such a book, written within the last twenty years, would lead its readers to expect in the postwar era an entirely different kind of American economics from the mathematical and New Dealish economics that Professor Harris correctly describes elsewhere in this volume. But the latter came as no surprise to competent observers of the 1930's. Good history does not pretend to create accurate predictions, but it should not serve to make its readers' batting average worse than that of a pair of dice.

13

The Realistic Novel

Alfred Kazin

Ralph Waldo Emerson did not care for fiction; he felt "a little uneasiness about these novels."

> Why should these sorceries have a monopoly of our delicious emotions? — The novel still weakly uses the cheap resource of property married away instead of earned, and that is the chief conjuring stick it has; for the instincts of man always attach to property, as he knows what accumulations of spiritual force go to the creation of that, and sobs and heartbeats and sudden sacrifice very easily result from the dealing with it. But the novel will find the way to our interiors one day, and will not always be novel of costume merely. These stories are to stories of real life what the figures which represent the fashions of the month on the front page of the magazine are to portraits and inspired pictures.
>
> Are you fond of drama? say the Gods. Said you so my fine fellow? Verily? Speak the truth a little, and truth on truth, and to every man and woman; try that a few hours, and you shall have dramatic situations, assaults and batteries, and heroic alternatives to your heart's content.[1]

The condescension of this language even more than the thought behind it marks off two literary generations. Emerson could not read novels; Henry James was not much interested in anything else. To James, William Dean Howells, Mark Twain, all born between 1835 and 1843, young enough to fight in the Civil War or to remember ever after that they had not fought, literature *was* the novel (and what came with an interest in the novel, the theater and "theatricals"). Theirs was the first literary generation generally to take to the novel as a form, to see it as the indispensable modern form. For them the novel was as a matter of course "the book of life," as D. H. Lawrence was to call it. And the novels or near-novels or writings on the novel by James and Howells and Mark Twain were to establish that emphasis on the social novel which in the twentieth century, with Theodore Dreiser, Sinclair Lewis, and Willa Cather, Ernest Hemingway, Scott Fitzgerald, and William Faulkner, was to make realistic fiction the most popular and influential side of American literature.

Yet when Emerson complained that the novels he looked into were romantic trash, closer to fashion pictures than "to stories of real life," he was saying no more than what Howells and James would say to each other about the unreality of American fiction when, in the late 1860's, they discovered their common ambition to be modern *novelists*, portraitists and critics of their time, rather than the oracles and poet-priests that Emerson and Thoreau had tried to be. Howells and James were to the end of their lives to dislike the usual run of American fiction, and each in his way came to think that he had paid a penalty for his devotion to realism and psychological truth.

The fact is that, as a form, the social novel has never had an established place in America, for such a novel is always identified with a society deeply settled, a society that knows itself thoroughly, that takes itself for granted and has a definite image of itself. In all the great European novels society itself — class restrictions, social usages and forms, intense social ambition — is the great daily stuff of reality in which people live and to which they look for their satisfactions. In the America described by Emerson and Thoreau, Poe and Melville and Hawthorne, society does not intervene between man and nature, between man and his cosmic loneliness; the world is relatively unpeopled, unhumanized, ridden with harsh abstractions. The tendency of the American storyteller was to take abstract human nature for his subject. He was not a novelist but a "romancer," in the different styles of Poe, Melville, Hawthorne; such writers preferred the "tale" (essentially moral variations on an anecdote) or the "epic" (the poetic inflation of ordinary experience) to the social novel, which takes its prosaic dimensions from the world around it. Even the "realistic" novelists who came up after the Civil War, and who may be said to have inaugurated the novel as a usable American form, were always impatient with it. Mark Twain's books were always breaking down into chatty oral performances; the novels of Henry James's last period — *The Wings of the Dove* (1902), *The Ambassadors* (1903), *The Golden Bowl* (1904) — though still, in James's nineteenth-century style, theatrical in their calculated effects, were suspended on a style fundamentally so uneasy and strained that the passionate personal urgency behind it would have bewildered those social novelists, like George Eliot and Ivan Turgenev, whom James most admired.

Even the sudden fascination of American writers at the end of the century with "naturalism," the literary conception of society as necessarily harsh and impersonal, betrays the fundamental lack of attachment in this country to the social novel. For "naturalism" replaces a living society with the iron law of society; instead of human association, we get human frustration and despair. The English, the particular masters of the social novel, have always distrusted naturalism as theoretical. American writers have tended to be stronger on theories of society than on the actualities of society. Wherever, as in the novels of Theodore Dreiser and Frank Norris and Stephen Crane, society is portrayed as implacably the enemy of men's hopes instead of being the reasonably hopeful ground of their association, an essential part of the realistic novel, the good-humored depiction of manners, is lost to us.

The generation that turned to the novel — and this includes Henry Adams, who not only published two novels but wrote history, biography, and autobiography with the sure instinct of a literary artist — were, then, working in a form that was essentially new to American literature and self-conscious; and they found themselves up against the usual unbelief that a novel could be significant literature. The American tended, as perhaps he does still, to expect of literature a tangible moral purpose — otherwise it was a slightly covert entertainment. When a man bought a book, he demanded value for his money. Novels were "sorcery," "frippery." European visitors often commented on the sober and even solemn attitude that Americans brought to books. Yet at the same time "romantic" fiction, especially in magazines, provided one outlet for normal human impulses in a highly moralistic culture. The enormous popularity of Sir Walter Scott's romances, especially in the South (where they helped to fill out the Southern gentleman's picture of himself as a chivalric knight) gave no encouragement to the would-be realist, like Howells or James; the suspicion of European "immoralism" in the novels of Balzac was to drive Henry James to say bitterly that "It is not open to us, as yet, to discuss whether a novel had better be an excision from life, or a structure built up of picture cards, for we have not made up our mind as to whether life in general may be described."[2]

But the greatest difficulty for the realists to overcome was the prejudice that America was not "interesting" — that it was too new, too raw, too prosy, too uniform. Emerson's condescension to novelists in general, as vulgar contraptionists always working up effects, was a shrewd criticism of the often desperate straits to which the American "romancer" was forced — he was a melodramatist in his means even when, like Herman Melville, his vision of life was above melodrama. The admiration of a Balzac for a James Fenimore Cooper was based on the latter's access to the wilderness: America was still a myth to European writers. American *society* as a subject, however, still seemed vaguely unworthy to Henry James, who knew Europe so well, and to Howells, who had spent the Civil War as American consul in Venice and had come home with a scholarly knowledge of Italian literature. It was only when such writers seized upon the witty and even comic possibilities of contrasting American plainness with European complexity, when, like Mark Twain in his first book, *The Innocents Abroad* (1869), they were able to capitalize on those native folkways and prejudices that had been highlighted by their travels, that the social novel in America, the novel of contrasting manners, could get off the ground. All these novelists, even Mark Twain who struck the pose of the country rube, were likely to feel the superiority of the European and finely wrought old British literary tradition to the glaringly empty sunlight, the bareness, the boring provincial complacency of American life — that life which drove Henry James to his much quoted lament in his book on Hawthorne:

> No sovereign, no court, no personal loyalty, no aristocracy, no church, no clergy, no army, no diplomatic service, no country gentlemen, no palaces, no castles, nor manors, nor old country houses, nor parsonages, nor thatched cottages, nor ivied ruins; no cathedrals, nor abbeys, nor little Norman churches; no great universities nor public schools — no Oxford, nor Eton, nor Harrow; no literature, no novels. . . ![3]

James wrote that the America called up by reading Hawthorne's *American Notebooks* "is characterized by an extraordinary blankness — a curious paleness of color and paucity of detail. . . . We are struck with the large number of elements that were absent . . . , and the coldness, the thinness, the blankness, . . . present themselves so vividly that our foremost feeling is that of compassion for a romancer looking for subjects in such a field."[4] James constantly associated emptiness with New England; *bare* and *bareness* are always among the first words that spring to his mind. In *The Bostonians* (1886), where he satirized the busybody reformers and virginal idealists like Elizabeth Peabody (Hawthorne's sister-in-law) left over from transcendentalist days, James wrote that "the bareness of her long, loose, empty parlour told that she had never had any needs but moral needs, and that all her history had been that of her sympathies. The place was lighted by a small hot glare of gas, which made it look white and featureless."[5] And earlier, in *The Europeans* (1878), James's prevailing sense of bareness and featurelessness is immediately expressed in the Baroness Munster's impressions of her Boston hotel room. "She glanced about her — the room had a certain vulgar nudity; the bed and the window were curtainless." James, who of course had seen more of Europe in his youth than most American writers, felt that "the primitive New England character" of Emerson's time had lived in a society so empty that there had been a "queer search for something to expend itself upon."

By contrast, James could not keep up with his many literary projects, and Howells, with his keen editor's sense of what was going on and his strong attachment to his own kind, people from small Western towns firmly making their way up in the East, was to find stories on every hand. Henry Adams was to complain that "Howells cannot deal with gentlemen or ladies; he always slips up."[6] In the mid-eighties it was common among the literary Brahmins and their descendants to say that "Mr. Howells . . . has never known anybody who has a soul among buttons."[7] The association of realism with the socially "common" certainly troubled Henry James, who in his letters from Europe calculated the risk of taking middle-class America as his subject. But the decline of New England as *the* American center, the transfer of vital influence to the Middle West, is cruelly revealed in the literary custodians and museum-keepers of New England's literary tradition who to the rising realistic novel opposed abstract considerations of "Beauty." To the literary imagination of Howells and James and Mark Twain, reality itself — the actual life of society — was now the great romance. What made possible the very career of a writer like Howells, by no means a literary genius, was the fact that he found the social aspirations of the period so exciting. All the great nineteenth-century novelists were to catch fire from the immense energy of industrial society, from the new scope that it gave human ambition. At the center of the new fiction, as Howells said, was "the man who has risen." "Westerners" like Howells discovered the imaginative possibilities in "ordinary" life because this life now had promise for them.

This confident attachment to reality is always the mark of a class in the ascendency. Howells of Ohio, who as an editor and business man of letters was linked to many influential circles in America, represented an exemplary middle-class morality, a proper fear of the flesh. He spoke out of a particular pride of place, of class, for what he called "the region-effect." That remarkable line of realistic novelists and poets who were to come out of the Midwest in the next forty years — Sinclair Lewis and Scott Fitzgerald from Minnesota, Willa Cather from Nebraska, Sherwood Anderson from Ohio, Edgar Lee Masters and Vachel Lindsay from Illinois, Ernest Hemingway from Michigan — identified itself with the West as the upsurging, as yet unspoiled part of American life. So Henry James of New York tended to portray Americans from the eastern seaboard as more "beautifully innocent" than Europeans, and it was this sense of Americans as being more virtuous because they were less experienced that was perhaps the "secret," as James put it in his book on Hawthorne, that made up for the American writer's lack of tradition and society. A new and ambitious class naturally portrays itself as young and innocent. As late as 1925, F. Scott Fitzgerald was to claim in *The Great Gatsby* that "this has been a story of the West, after all — Tom and Gatsby, Daisy and Jordan and I, were all Westerners, and perhaps we possessed some deficiency in common which made us subtly unadaptable to Eastern life."[8]

In respect to the East, the older America, the Westerner always thought of himself as more "natural," closer to the essence of things. As late as 1901, reviewing Mark Twain's fabulous career, Howells explained it in terms of the "region-effect"; he thought that the Westerner as a type had been far more dramatically "the creature of circumstances, of conditions . . . than any other prior man":

> He found himself placed in them and under them, so near to a world in which the natural and primitive were obsolete, that while he could not escape them, neither could he help challenging them. The inventions, the appliances, the improvements of the modern world invaded the hoary eld of his rivers and forests and prairies, and while he was still a pioneer, a hunter, a trapper, he found himself confronted with the financier, the scholar, the gentleman. They seemed to him, with the world they represented, at first droll, and he laughed. Then they set him to thinking, and, as he never was afraid of anything, he thought over the whole field and demanded explanations of all his prepossessions — of equality, of humanity, of representative government, and revealed religion. When they had not their answers ready, without accepting the conventions of the modern world as solutions or in any manner final, he laughed again, not mockingly, but patiently, compassionately. Such, or somewhat like this, was the genesis and evolution of Mark Twain.[9]

This statement is remarkable as an affirmation of the Western writer's favorite myth — he was entirely the "natural" man who, "as he never was afraid of anything, thought over the whole field and demanded explanations of all his prepossessions" when he saw his primitive Eden overrun. Actually, of course, Mark Twain was at times hysterically enthusiastic about material progress and inventions, and was intimately associated with more than one financier and gentleman. But like so many other Americans who became quickly and to themselves uncomfortably successful in the Gilded

Age, Mark Twain could not really assimilate success into his established idea of himself. The mobility of American life had made no provision for a philosophy suitable to the times. The American thought of himself as a frontiersman even when he lived like a millionaire. As Henry James was to say in a later preface to *The American* (1877), the theme of the innocent American was the enduring "romantic" element in realism. And certainly the career of Mark Twain, who uncovered his best literary material in a world that ended with the Civil War, whose deepest literary motivations were in what he called "Old Times on the Mississippi," was shaped by the dilemma success presented to a man who always equated goodness with the raw world of his youth. The tradition of Western humor that Mark Twain took over had been based on the device of jeeringly contrasting homegrown prejudices with "culture." The contrast between the natural man and civilization was to remain Mark Twain's literary philosophy; it became the secret of his enduring success as a public entertainer — in and out of his books. For the legend that Mark Twain brought with him, the expectant delight that fell on an audience as soon as he appeared before it in the character of the benign but sly American funnyman, was based on his suggestion that the old, rustic, jeeringly lower-class America represented an unchanged and unchangeable value. There was an ancient simplicity about Americans which he could always invoke for them, and its symbol was his old home town, Hannibal on the Mississippi. What a time that had been, what a time! When Mark Twain spoke, that time seemed never to have passed, and its values were as good as ever. No wonder that to Mark Twain being a humorist was often a strained business, that he thought of it as being the "mask" he had to wear, the public posture and imposture. He felt himself held to a role, a pseudo-oracular way of looking and pronouncing on things always in jest. The duplicity which Mark Twain increasingly felt about American political ideals in the age of economic oligarchy he increasingly felt about himself.

The creative genius of this writer, who leaned so much on autobiography and anecdote, can be heard in the use he made of his single voice. In Mark Twain ended the solipsistic tradition of American style, so much the work of writers who lacked familiar communication with their public and who wrote as if they despaired of being heard. It was not the "Western humorist" in him that gave Mark Twain his ease and cleverness; the language of Western humor, on the whole, was deliberately crude, not natural. But in playing the breezy anecdotalist, the after-dinner speaker, Mark Twain discovered his genius for the spoken rhythm. This was *his* realism. No other American writer has brought home to us so vivid a taste of man in the open air, man at home again with earth, water, and sky:

> . . . The first thing to see, looking away over the water, was a kind of dull line — that was the woods on t'other side — you couldn't make nothing else out; then a pale place in the sky; then more paleness, spreading around; then the river softened up, away off, and warn't black any more, but gray; you could see little dark spots drifting along, ever so far away — trading scows, and such things; and long black streaks — rafts; sometimes you could hear a sweep screaking; or jumbled up voices, it was so still, and sounds come so far; and by-and-by you could see a streak on the water which you know by the look of the streak that there's a snag there in a swift current which breaks on it and makes that streak look that way; and you see the mist curl up off of the water, and the east reddens up, and the river, and you make out a log cabin in the edge of the woods. . . .[10]

This is from *Huckleberry Finn* (1885) — the book, said Ernest Hemingway, with which modern writing in America begins. No one else since Mark Twain has had a gift of style secure enough to attempt a sentence so easy yet tricky in its rhythms (". . . which you know by the look of the streak that there's a snag there in a swift current which breaks on it . . ."). *Huckleberry Finn* is the book which more than any other in America justifies the legend that the American was once at home with nature. It is of all American novels the closest to the actual sensuous life of humanity — to the whole range of man's senses. And above all is it close to man's stubborn sense of freedom. As a boy wants to be free, simply free, free for himself, not responsible to older people's conventions, so Huckleberry Finn seeks, to the end, freedom from all those who would plan his life for him. At key moments in the book this purposive flight from society is fused with a boy's first speculative questions about the nature of things. In our industrialized and militarized society, it is impossible to read certain pages of *Huckleberry Finn* without a shiver of longing and despair. Everything which once made man feel at home with the earth is still present to our imagination because of this book. At the heart of it lies not Huck's passage to "maturity," as we say so admiringly these days in stressing Huck's care for a runaway slave, but the web of earth and water and sky, the contrast between the natural world and its human corruption.

This contrast is always behind the American realist's concern with society. Holding to the style of natural speech, writing with the ease that belongs to an age of comedy, Mark Twain created a lasting idyll of the world that was past yet pointed to the social world that Huck must flee again when, near the end of the book, Tom Sawyer turns up again and puts Jim through the tortures of an unnecessary captivity so that he can be rescued according to the storybooks. Tom Sawyer is a conventional boy who only plays at freedom. Huck's flight ends in another flight; for Jim the slave has his legal freedom at last, but Huck needs more than ever to escape civilization. "But I reckon I got to light out for the Territory ahead of the rest, because Aunt Sally she's going to adopt me and sivilize me and I can't stand it. I been there before." This is the great last line of *Huckleberry Finn*, and expresses suspicion not of a particular society but of *all* society. And it is characteristic of American realism that the best material about society in it should be at the expense of Victorian gentility, for when Huck is taken in by the Grangerfords, his pathetic admiration establishes the meretriciousness of their taste.

In Mark Twain the loner, the natural man, incarnated in a boy, is always right, while society is usually false. This stark opposition of self and society would have astonished the European realists, for society supplied such values as man could find for his life. Even in Henry James the solitary and untouched individual is the source of moral plenitude, and the power of society, though very great, is morally in contrast with him. A novelist like Howells, who taught himself to be a novelist of manners, kept to a carefully limited scale of observation, and had no such commanding sense of the necessary division between the individual and society, inevitably has not much significance for another generation.

Still, Henry James's peculiar sensitiveness to the individual is now so cherished that it is proper to remember how very much of a "realist" of the European type he tried to be. James's great admirations — Balzac, George Eliot, Turgenev — help us to understand why his actual disciples have always been writers like Joseph Conrad and Graham Greene. James's whole aim as a novelist was to dramatize, to represent, to make us see. James's extraordinary sense of scenic values makes his powerfully vibrating literary imagination the greatest thing of its kind in American literature. In our day, when the often insignificantly complex language of James's last works has been seized on to score a point against realism itself, one has forgotten what a beautifully old-fashioned artist of "verisimilitude" James was. All his first novels, the shadowy but intensely felt *Roderick Hudson* (1876), the exquisite and richly symbolic *The American* (1877), *Daisy Miller* (1879), *Washington Square* (1881), reveal his gift for re-creating the solid surfaces of society in the long Victorian afternoon. James's ability in his early travel essays to summon up a place, a moment, had astonished Emerson. Now that James was concentrating on the novel with the same sense of "fact," of the "moment" cherished, he made these first novels fresh and precocious classics of the realist's art. James was the first of the American realists to identify representation with painting, and his sense of color explains why Lewis Mumford was led to describe this period as "The Brown Decades." The contemporary student, who has been taught to regard Henry James as a subtle "mathematician" of art, as the companion-in-arms of symbolist poets and critics, has a deep satisfaction in store for him when he turns to such witty and solid performances as *The American*, *The Bostonians*, and to James's masterpiece of this period, *The Portrait of a Lady* (1881), which renders great English country houses and Tuscan villas with a loving exactness, a particular feeling for the rich human tone of European society. James's work is always delightful and stimulating in its passion for the weight and color and "feel" of things.

One reason why James's novels are so rich in detail, so avid to catch every surface of the visible, hard, external world, is that such descriptions put "fine consciences" into relief. The vulnerable goodness of his heroines makes a very American contrast with their dazzling surroundings. Our present esteem for James as an artist has blinded us to the extraordinary innocence of his own mind. Henry Adams once complained that "James knows almost nothing of women but the mere outside; he never had a wife."[11] James indeed knew very little of the human heart, for he identified it with emotion, not action; but because he knew so little, he could speculate endlessly. The great subject of his novels, first to last, is the ordeal of goodness in a world of greater complexity than it has any reason to expect. His favorite protagonists were adorable young American women, as intellectually "sophisticated" as they were emotionally inexperienced. It can be said of him that he identified America itself with these lofty but all too bruisable souls. It was always because Henry James, as his brother William said, was "under all his rich sea weeds" so "powerless-feeling,"[12] so enamored of the upper-class English surface of things, that his novels are so charming but involve one so little. As a moral critic of society, he is rather helpless. Like all true realists, he was in love with his material, and it is this that gives the lasting polish to James's descriptions. As he once confessed, looking around a rich man's waiting room, "I can stand a great deal of gold." If John Singer Sargent was in one respect court painter to the *haute bourgeoisie*, Henry James was its novelist. He was so bewitched with the ostentation and pride of English society that he thought it more lasting than did any other writer of his stature in England. When war broke out in 1914, James cried out to a friend "that to have to take it all now for what the treacherous years were all the while really making for and *meaning* is too tragic for any words."[13] Only in his extreme sensitiveness to personal tragedy did James have, as he said he did, "the imagination of disaster — and see life indeed as ferocious and sinister."[14] He saw experience riding down innocence, but he saw it as if he were at a play, from a distance, bemused by the color and pageantry of the great world. James had every quality that goes to make a great writer except that quality of commitment which comes to a writer from having been violated, as it were, by life itself.

James was perfectly right to consider the American novelist, as a type, genteel; and he was more than right when, as a beginning novelist, he prophesied that America as a "literary field" would "yield its secrets only to a really *grasping* imagination. This I think Howells lacks."[15] Howells lacked this "grasping imagination" because he was altogether too much of the prudent middle-class world; he did not have the sense of American society as a power, whether for good or evil, that Mark Twain and Henry James did. He tended to think of "realism" as a doctrine rather like "free enterprise" — a distinctly American point of view proper to the decent middle class of the most successful country in the world. The papers in defense of realism on which Howells's fame as a critic rests defend not "truth to life" in the universal sense, but the experience of a particular class:

> Our novelists . . . concern themselves with the more smiling aspects of life, which are the more American, and seek the universal in the individual rather than the social interests. It is worth while, even at the risk of being called commonplace, to be true to our well-to-do actualities; the very passions themselves seem to be softened and modified by conditions which formerly at least could not be said to wrong any one, to cramp endeavor, or to cross lawful desire. Sin and suffering and shame there must always be in the world, I suppose, but I believe that in this new world of ours it is still mainly from one to another one, and oftener still from one to one's self.[16]

What is still so peculiarly chilling about this famous declaration of literary principle is the petty range of experience it talks from. To write "lawful desire" as if the courts or churches or newspapers had established for all time the bounds of human passion does not argue a high degree of curiosity or literary imagination. And when Howells speaks of the need "to be true to our well-to-do actualities" he misrepresents the artistic intent behind realism by making the novelist simply a copyist of external life. The realism that Howells practiced in his better novels, such as *A Modern Instance* (1882) and *The Landlord at Lion's Head* (1897), represents invention and choice, as does every artistic method. No literary work can ever be simply a copy of actuality, for the writer is dominated by an idea of what reality is before he even chooses his examples of it, and a book represents an effort at organization that life, as life, never possesses.

Howells, in speaking for "actuality" and "lawful desire," was speaking for certain social controls, for the quiet elegance of style that is synonymous in his novels with elusiveness of mind and restraint of the flesh. These class values of morality and style fell to pieces at the hands of a Theodore Dreiser, who, brought up as a Catholic, in an immigrant and proletarianized family, wrote as if he simply was not aware of the scruples that had provided the drama and the moral frame of Howells and James and Mark Twain. Dreiser was perhaps the first substantial American writer who was not of Anglo-Saxon descent and who was brought up outside the Protestant middle class. In his personal ambition for success and in his lifelong hope to find salvation in a literary philosophy, he was very much part of his agnostic generation in the Middle West. But there was always about Dreiser a quality of unassimilated personal bitterness, a lack of ease and even of correctness in his style, that would have perplexed not only so wholly literary a mind as Henry James but so urbane a literary celebrity as Mark Twain. Many American writers have been labeled "barbaric" in the light of European tradition. But in Dreiser we feel the literal meaning of the term — the outsider, the stranger to our ways, the man from a different world. This unassimilated and perhaps unassimilable quality comes home to us when we compare Dreiser with two other famous "naturalists," Stephen Crane and Frank Norris, who were almost exactly his age. Crane in particular was inexpressibly more gifted as a literary artist than Dreiser, but in his original and perverse poems, in his famous novel *The Red Badge of Courage* (1895), and in his greatest story, "The Open Boat" (1897), the theme is always on the surface. There is nothing left over in any work of Stephen Crane's that can affect our minds as belonging to life itself. The moral of every story becomes one with the story. There is no providence; if anything, there is an anti-providence that mocks human hopes. Even in Crane's most powerful single prose work, "The Open Boat," the terror of the men trying to reach land is never allowed to be a fact in itself, but is constantly being interpreted to us in ironic prose as a fresh symbol of the universe's indifference to human needs.

In Dreiser, however, certain experiences, many dumb and dim apprehensions of things, reach the reader from those stupefied and inarticulate people who live on the periphery of our society. One becomes aware of a class which our culture, our schools, our religion, does not touch. Dreiser is himself one of these people for whom society does not avail, who try to find their strength in the life-force itself. As there is no providence, so there is no anti-providence; life simply *is*, and man is strong only as he gets access to its sacred fire.

It was exactly Dreiser's "barbaric" appreciation of sex as a force beyond the moral calculus of middle-class Protestant morality that so shocked Dreiser's first publisher, Frank Doubleday, who was outraged by the fact that in *Sister Carrie* (1900) there is no system of rewards and punishments that corresponds with the sexual behavior of the characters. Up to Dreiser, American realism had not been much concerned with sexual passion. The power of sex is felt in James's novels always as guilty and esoteric. That the most famous disclosure in James's novels should be the moment in *The Ambassadors* where a character modeled in part on William Dean Howells realizes that a man and woman who have constantly been in each other's company are lovers, is itself a commentary on the timidity of American realistic fiction about so fundamental a human interest. In Stephen Crane's *Maggie: A Girl of the Streets* (1893), the story of a girl forced into prostitution is suggestive of real life only because of the irony with which Crane handles so trite and sentimental a plot. In *McTeague* (1899), the one novel by Frank Norris which still has purely artistic interest, one sees the influence of Victorianism in the "brutish" quality of McTeague's passion for a girl whom he slavers over when she is under gas in his dentist chair.

In Dreiser's *Sister Carrie* (1900), *Jennie Gerhardt* (1911), *The Financier* (1912), *The Titan* (1914), and above all in *An American Tragedy* (1925), sex is matter-of-factly represented as a power which can rip people's lives out of their usual secure patterns. Dreiser showed that young women like Carrie Meeber and Jennie Gerhardt, innocent, unsophisticated, and kindly women, possesed this power as a wholly unconscious attribute, and that although it changed men's lives, they wore this power half-dimly as one of those accidents which determined individual lives. In *The Financier* and *The Titan*, both dealing with the barely disguised life of a famous capitalist, and in *The 'Genius,'* his most explicitly autobiographical novel, Dreiser insisted on the connection between passionate sexual desire in certain men and their longing for power in society. In this Dreiser gave a peculiar distinctness to the vitalism current in his generation. It was not so much the pseudo-scientific attempt to show determinism in fiction as it was the old romantic idea of "nature" as the ultimate ground, the term identical with God, that gave the naturalists their peculiar confidence and aggressiveness. The closer they got to the "primitive," to what Frank Norris liked to call "the beast," the more they felt they were reaching that core of truth, beyond human concept, beyond the illusory human will, which was the raw fact of experience that middle-class society never got to. It was out of this essentially romantic concern with the "brute facts," with nature-in-the-raw, that Frank Norris, who wrote about these things as young men today write about space ships, blusteringly cried out: "The enormous, the formidable, the terrible, is what counts; no teacup tragedies here."

Naturalism could not last; it was too literary and romantic. It played at the primitive. Inevitably, in the next generation, naturalism dissolved into the normal realism of middle-class writers being ironic about their own class. In the twenties, this realism became the popular literary medium of a people who had grown rich so fast that they felt they had left conscience behind. The conscience was picked up by the writers, and in the next generation — Sinclair Lewis, Sherwood Anderson, Willa Cather, Scott Fitzgerald, Ernest Hemingway — realism was so much in the air that it was no longer "Realism." It had been absorbed into the very texture of American literature.

14

The Intellectual versus the City

Morton and Lucia White

Although the city has become one of the most absorbing and most intensively studied social problems in America today, and although it is now fashionable for intellectuals to express an almost tender concern for its future, to hope that its decay can be arrested, and to offer plans for its revitalization, this has not always been the attitude of our greatest American thinkers. For a variety of reasons they have expressed different degrees of hostility toward urban life in America, hostility which may be partly responsible for a feeling on the part of today's city planner and urban reformer that he has no mythology or mystique on which he can rest or depend. We have no tradition of romantic attachment to the city in our highbrow literature, nothing that remotely resembles the Greek philosopher's attachment to the *polis* or the French writer's affection for Paris. And this fits very well with the frequently defended thesis that the American writer has been more than usually alienated from the society in which he lives, that he is typically in revolt against it. Throughout the nineteenth century our society was becoming more and more urbanized, but the literary tendency to denigrate the American city hardly declined in proportion. If anything, it increased in intensity.

Faced with this fact about the history of American thought, the contemporary student of the city can take one of two opposing attitudes. He, at his peril, can turn his back on the tradition of Jefferson, Emerson, Thoreau, Hawthorne, Melville, Poe, Henry Adams, Henry James, Louis Sullivan, Frank Lloyd Wright, and John Dewey. In this case he will treat some of the American city's profoundest critics as irresponsible literary men or as idle metaphysicians who fled the city rather than face its problems. Or he can regard this critical tradition as a repository of deep, though troubling, wisdom, one which raises basic questions for any urban reformer, and some of whose premonitions and fears have been more than justified by the passage of time. There is no doubt that the second is the wiser course. He who would improve the American city can only profit by an awareness of what some of our greatest minds have said, felt, and thought about one of the most conspicuous and most troubling features of our national life.

One cannot deny, of course, that there were pro-urban literary voices like Whitman's, or that there were urban sociologists like Robert Park who tried to speak up for the city. But they are voices in "the city wilderness," never comparing in volume with the anti-urban roar in the national literary pantheon. The urbanist must face the fact that the anti-urbanist does not live only in the Kentucky hills, in the Rockies, in the Ozarks, in the Cracker country, or the bayous. He lives in the mind and heart of America as conceived by the intellectual historian. The intellectual, whose home is the city, according to some sociologists, has been the American city's sharpest critic. Everyone knows that Jefferson once hoped to discourage the development of the city in America, but he was only the first of a long and varied list of critics of the city.

Jefferson despised the manners and principles of the urban "mob" as he knew it in Europe and he hoped to keep it from crossing the Atlantic intact. He certainly did not think of the city as "The Hope of Democracy," as some Progressive theorists did at the turn of the twentieth century. He adopted a conciliatory tone about the city in his old age when he said in 1816 that we could not possibly depend on England for manufactures, as he had originally thought, and therefore we *needed* cities. But this does not show any *love* for the city. The country and its yeomen Jefferson loved all his life; in his old age he grudgingly accepted the manufacturing city as a necessity.

The same War of 1812 which led Jefferson to reassess his views was followed by a great expansion of the American city. It inaugurated a major phase of urban civilization between the Revolution and the Civil War. By 1860 the urban population was eleven times what it had been in 1820. The early decades of the nineteenth century saw the decline of Jefferson's empiricism among American intellectuals, and the emergence of philosophical transcendentalism, but a distaste for the city persisted among American writers.

The growth of the city in the North produced an even sharper reaction in Ralph Waldo Emerson than the European city had produced in Jefferson. Emerson's first philosophical work, *Nature*, appeared in 1836, in the middle of that interval which witnessed an eleven-fold increase in our urban population. Its very title was a protest against what he thought was happening. Partly under the influence of English romanticism, Emerson and some of his friends took to deprecating manufacture, art, and civilization, and so it was not long before they took to criticizing the city, the greatest of artifacts. The distaste for the city as an artificial creation was associated in Emerson's mind, as it was in the case of many romantic thinkers, with doubts about the value of science as an avenue to truth. And yet Emerson agreed with the scientifically minded Jefferson about the nasty manners and principles of the city. Whereas Jefferson was given to arguing the defects of the city in common-sense political terms, Emerson sought to buttress his feelings by a metaphysical theory. Hence we may label his period as the metaphysical period of anti-urbanism. To be is to be natural for Emerson. In the wilderness he said he found "something more dear and connate than in streets or villages." The life of the city was "artificial and curtailed"; it destroyed solitude, poetry, and philosophy.

One will find passages in which Emerson extolled the application of science and the virtues of civilization, the need for sociability to educate a man's sympathies, and the advantages of specialization that allow each man to develop his own talents. This suggests a more friendly view of the industrial urban society which was emerging in his own lifetime. But he always harped on the human failings of State Street and commercialism. At times Emerson could celebrate the artifice of pure technology, but he persistently attacked the debasement of moral standards by those who pursued nothing but wealth in the cities as he knew them. One is reminded of Thorstein Veblen's praise of urban industry even as he attacked its financial captains, for it was Veblen who saw the modern industrial city as the *locus classicus* of conspicuous waste.

Thoreau went even further than Emerson in his distaste for civilization and the city, for Thoreau also attacked the village and the farm. *Walden* is a bible of anti-urbanism, in which Thoreau celebrates the life of the isolated individual, living in Nature and free of *all* social attachments. No wonder that Thoreau refused to visit the Saturday Club, which provided one of the few values of Boston in Emerson's eyes: intellectual conversation. And when Thoreau refused, Perry Miller reminds us, he put his refusal in no uncertain terms: "The only room in Boston which I visit with alacrity is the Gentlemen's Room at the Fitchburg Depot, where I wait for cars, sometimes for two hours, in order to get out of town."[1] No wonder Henry James said that Thoreau "was essentially a sylvan personage."[2]

If Jefferson attacked the city on political grounds, and if Emerson and Thoreau may be represented as criticizing it from the point of view of transcendental metaphysics, what shall we say of Poe, Hawthorne, and Melville, all of whom may be added to our list of pre-Civil War critics of the city? They were far from political theorists or metaphysicians but all of them saw the city as the scene of sin and crime. Speaking of them, Harry Levin says: "For our dreamers, America was a garden, an agrarian Eden, which was losing its innocence by becoming citified. Melville had located his City of Woe in London or Liverpool; Poe had tracked down imaginary crimes in the streets of an imagined Paris; and Hawthorne had exposed sins most luridly among the ruins of Rome."[3] As in Jefferson's case, the urban models of extreme crime and sinfulness were not located in the United States by most of our pre-Civil War anti-urbanists, but they saw dark omens in the streets of American cities which made them fear that they might become like Paris, London, Liverpool, or Rome.

The observant Tocqueville expressed his worry about the American city in 1835, one year before Emerson's essay *Nature* appeared. He said that the fact that America as yet had no dominating metropolis was one of those circumstances which tended to maintain a democratic republic in the United States and to counteract that great danger to which all democracies are subject — the tyranny of the majority. But Tocqueville thought that the "lower ranks" which inhabited Philadelphia (pop. 161,000) and New York (pop. 202,000) in the 1830's "constitute a rabble even more formidable than the populace of European towns. They consist of freed blacks . . . who are condemned by the laws and by public opinion to a hereditary state of misery and degradation. They also contain a multitude of Europeans who have been driven to the shore of the New World by their misfortunes or their misconduct; and they bring to the United States all our greatest vices, without any of those interests which counteract their baneful influence. As inhabitants of a country where they have no civil rights, they are ready to turn all the passions which agitate the community to their own advantage; thus, within the last few months, serious riots have broken out in Philadelphia and New York."[4] So seriously did Tocqueville treat this matter that he said: "I look upon the size of certain American cities, and especially on the nature of their population, as a real danger which threatens the future security of the democratic republics of the New World; and I venture to predict that they will perish from this circumstance, unless the government succeeds in creating an armed force which, while it remains under the control of the majority of the nation, will be independent of the town population and able to repress its excesses."[5]

If this could be the conclusion of the most astute foreign observer ever to visit our shores, it is not surprising that some of our great literary figures might have developed less than an admiring view of our urban culture between the Revolution and the Civil War. Optimistic empiricists like Jefferson, optimistic transcendentalists like Emerson, pessimistic believers in original sin like Hawthorne and Melville, all forgot their philosophical differences when they looked upon the American city, even before it developed into the industrial jungle it was to become between the Civil War and the end of the nineteenth century.

Between 1860 and 1900 the urban population quadrupled while the rural population only doubled; and, what is more staggering and significant, between 1790 and 1890, while the total population of the country increased sixteen times, the urban population increased 139 times.[6] The great exodus from the countryside was in full force, and New England became the scene of deserted hill and village farms, while the city's problems became the great social problems of the nation. The city became the home of the elevated railroad, the trolley car, the cable car, the subway, the apartment house, the telephone, and the skyscraper, while it continued to encourage what one physician called "American nervousness."

Among the most influential and most fastidious observers of this development were Henry Adams and the younger Henry James. Both were men of literary genius, both were members of cultivated families with wealth in their backgrounds, and for both of them the American city provided a profound spiritual problem. Because Henry Adams and Henry James lived in the age of the city's supremacy, they did not speak of it, as Jefferson had, as a remote future phenomenon or as something existing in Europe alone. And, unlike Thoreau, they did not feel as though they had only the American city and the American wilderness to choose between. Adams and James were both refined, civilized, indeed urban men whose animadversions on the American city are made more significant precisely because they were not opposed to cities in principle. They demonstrate what a hard time the American city had at the hands of nineteenth-century intellectuals. For here at last were two *city* types who also found the American city sadly wanting. Their reaction to the American city is more esthetic, more literary, more psychological than that of their predecessors Jefferson and Emerson.

The two most important documents for an understanding of the views of Adams and James are the former's *Education* and the latter's *The American Scene*. It is significant that the great problem of *The Education of Henry Adams* was to steer a course between the poles of town and country, between the Boston and Quincy of his childhood. "Town," Adams tells us, "was restraint, law, unity. Country, only seven miles away, was liberty, diversity, outlawry, the endless delight of mere sense impressions given by nature for nothing, and breathed by boys without knowing it."[7] Adams also tells us that he spent his life trying to choose between the ways of life they represented without ever making up his mind. And yet, in a sense, he did make up his mind, or the social forces of America made it up for him. He could not go back to the Quincy house of his grandfather Adams. And, being no Thoreau, he had to live in the American city if he was to live anywhere in America. But what was *the* American city in his mature years? Surely not Boston, but New York. And when Henry Adams looked at the New York of 1868, he tells us in a book which he wrote in 1905 that he felt swept aside by the forces pushing the country in a new direction. "His world," he lamented, "was dead. Not a Polish Jew fresh from Warsaw or Cracow — not a furtive Yacoob or Ysaac still reeking of the Ghetto, snarling a weird Yiddish to the officers of the customs — but had a keener instinct, an intenser energy, and a freer hand than he — American of Americans, with Heaven knew how many Puritans and Patriots behind him, and an education that had cost a civil war."[8] Adams felt like the dispossessed Indian and the buffalo in America after 1865, for it was a banker's, and neither a buffalo's nor a Bostonian's world. To Henry Adams, New York symbolized the spiritual confusion of America at the end of the nineteenth century.

Henry James, as one might expect, also complained about his birthplace, New York, after a period of flirtation with it. James attacked it most explicitly in *The American Scene*, published in 1907 as the report of an expatriate revisiting the country of his birth. He, too, spoke of the city's chaos, and even the New York skyline insulted his very expressively complex sensibilities. He complained of the lack of history and of the lack of time for history in a way that reminds one of his early critical work on Nathaniel Hawthorne. The buildings, he said, "never speak to you, in the manner of the builded majesties of the world . . . towers, or temples, or fortresses or palaces with the authority of things of permanence or even of things of long duration."[9] History had given way to commerce: "The great city is projected into its future as practically, a huge continuous fifty-floored conspiracy against the very idea of the ancient graces."[10] The city lacked order, structure, dignity, history. James speaks of it as a "heaped industrial battlefield" and as a scene of "the universal will to move — to move, move, move, as an end in itself, an appetite at any price."[11] He missed what he called "organic social relations,"[12] and he felt some pleasurable relief when he visited Philadelphia, because it didn't "bristle," and because "it went back."[13] In this spirit he warned: "Let not the unwary . . . visit Ellis Island,"[14] as Henry Adams might have warned in *his* snobbish way. James was upset by what he called "that loud primary stage of alienism which

New York most offers to sight."[15] And he dreamed "of the luxury of some such close and sweet and *whole* national consciousness as that of the Switzer and the Scot."[16] His final head-shaking conclusion was "that there was no escape from the ubiquitous alien into the future or even into the present; there was no escape but into the past."[17]

Of course, one must not forget that Henry James was a cosmopolite, a lifelong inhabitant of cities, a man who is reputed to have dined out more than any resident of London in his day. One must be mindful of the fact that his novel *The Princess Casamassima* represents an effort to penetrate the depths of London, as does his famous admiring essay on that city. But James viewed the American city in an entirely different way. After his harsh handling of the Boston reformers in *The Bostonians,* the American city did not provide him with any serious material for a full-length novel because he found neither the uptown nor the downtown of the American city sufficiently interesting, as F. O. Matthiessen has pointed out.[18] And even *The Princess Casamassima* shows a greater interest in the bizarre doings of weirdly inspired misfits and aristocrats, whose philanthropic concern with the slums James satirizes, than a sustained interest in the typical life of London. With characteristic delicacy and insight he saw the crushing, oppressive defects of the British metropolis of his day, but he could never bring himself to the same sympathetic concern for the American metropolis.

Although we are primarily concerned with recording the theme of *anti*-urbanism in American writing and thinking, it would be absurd to argue that *every* great writer or thinker in the American pantheon was hostile to urban life. The fact is that at the end of the nineteenth century there emerged a tendency to view the American city in a more friendly manner. By contrast to his brother Henry, William James had very little desire to escape from the American city into the past. His philosophy was one of hope, of optimism, of possibility — indeed, a little bit too much so — and this allowed him to view the urbanization of America in a way that might encourage Americans to do something about urban problems. Unlike Henry, he did not adore the great cities of Western Europe. For ten days after his arrival in Florence in 1875 he "was so disgusted with the swarming and reeking blackness of the streets and the age of everything, that enjoyment took place under protest."[19] As for London, during his visit of 1889 he wrote his sister that he was "thoroughly sated" with it, and "never cared to see its yellow-brownness and stale spaciousness again."[20]

William James loved the country, but his love of nature was tempered by a fondness for general sociability; he was unable to subscribe either to Thoreau's primitivism or to the ultracivilized sentiments of his brother. With Emerson he looked to the future, but unlike Emerson he did not think that the future excluded the possibility of a decent life in the cities of America. Many of William James's reactions to the buzzing confusion of New York of 1880 and 1900 had been unfavorable because of "the clangor, disorder and permanent earthquake conditions" which he experienced on his customary daylong visits. But in 1907 he spent a longer time there and, as he says, "caught the pulse of the machine, took up the rhythm, and vibrated *mit*, and found it simply magnificent."[21] He spoke of it as an "*entirely* new New York, in soul as well as in body, from the old one, which looks like a village in retrospect. The courage, the heaven-scaling audacity of it all, and the *lightness* withal, as if there were nothing that was not easy, and the great pulses and bounds of progress, so many in directions all simultaneous that the coordination is indefinitely future, give a drumming background of life that I have never felt before. I'm sure that once *in* that movement, and at home, all other places would seem insipid."[22] This was written to his brother, of all people, after the appearance of the latter's *The American Scene*, but William had evidently read parts of it, since he says: "I observe that your book — 'The American Scene,' — dear H., is just out. I must get it and devour again the chapters relative to New York." William would not have liked them upon rereading them, and one can imagine how Henry must have winced when William exclaimed, "I'm surprised at you, Henry, not having been more enthusiastic, but perhaps the superbly powerful subway was not opened when you were there!"[23]

William James, like Walt Whitman, saw virtue and promise in the American city. Both William James and Whitman not only accept the city as an inescapable part of America, but they *enjoy* it, as Jefferson most certainly did not. The year of William James's discovery of what he called "the new New York" was 1907, when he delivered his most famous set of lectures, entitled *Pragmatism*, at Columbia. James thought his philosophy would mediate between the views of those whom he called "tenderfoot Bostonians" and those he labeled "Rocky Mountain toughs" in philosophy. It is not too fanciful to suppose that James identified the great future city, along with his pragmatic philosophy, as a blend of, a compromise between, the insipidity of Boston and the craggy brutality of the Rockies. A livable city on earth, one is tempted to say, is the social counterpart of James's pragmatism, and therefore he is one of the first great American writers to associate himself with the effort to accept what is good and to root out what is bad in the American city. He does not escape to the country with Emerson and Thoreau, or to the past with his brother and Henry Adams. He revives the wisdom of the older Jefferson after a century of transcendentalism, Brook-farming, and expatriation, and adds to it a love of the city. In doing so he becomes the herald of a pragmatic phase in urban thinking.

But this pragmatic phase, in which the city was joyfully described by Frederic C. Howe in 1905 as "The Hope of Democracy," did not last very long. Indeed, Howe's book contained within itself the classical argument for the central city's impending destruction. "The open fields about the city are inviting occupancy," Howe said, "and there the homes of the future will surely be. The city proper will not remain the permanent home of the people. Population must be dispersed. The great cities of Australia are spread out into the suburbs in a splendid way. For miles about are broad roads, with small houses, gardens, and an opportunity for touch with the freer, sweeter life which the country offers."[24] Howe calls the city the hope of democracy, but he is, it would appear, a suburban booster rather than a city-lover. He shares the basic inability of much greater American intellectuals to go all out in their admiration for the modern American city.

A more striking illustration of the same thing may be found in the writings of William James's disciple, John Dewey, who sympathized with so much of James's interest in the American city. In his earlier writing Dewey expressed a typically progressive interest in the city. This was part of the political liberalism of the period, with its interest in urban planning, social work, socialism, the single tax, and muckraking. The city was not regarded as a perfect form of life, but it was seen as having promise. And, to the extent to which it showed promise, it became the concern of all sorts of people who could criticize it in a constructive spirit quite different from that which dominated the work of militant anti-urbanists from Jefferson to Henry James. For a variety of reasons Chicago became the most conspicuous locale of this new way of looking at the city. It was the home of a great university, which had opened its doors in the nineties and which became a center of urban sociology and, it might be said, of urban philosophy. One can understand, therefore, why William James looked to Dewey and other Chicago intellectuals as his friends, and why they regarded him as their spiritual leader. For Chicago at the turn of the century was the home of James's pupil, Robert Park, his worshipper, Jane Addams, and his disciple, John Dewey.

As early as 1899 Dewey was urging that the congregation of men into cities was one of the most conspicuous features of the modern world and that no theory of education could possibly disregard the fact of urbanization. Indeed, *the* problem of education, as Dewey saw it in his *School and Society,* was how to adjust the child to life in the city. The earlier kind of rural environment, in which he had been raised as a boy in Vermont, had its virtues, he admitted. It encouraged habits of personal orderliness, industry, and responsibility; it led to a firsthand acquaintance with nature. But, Dewey said in 1899, "it was useless to bemoan the departure of the good old days . . . if we expect merely by bemoaning and by exhortation to bring them back."[25] The problem, as Dewey saw it, was that of retaining some advantages of the older mode of life while training the child to cope with the new urban world. The school, therefore, was to be a miniature urban community, a microcosmic duplication of macrocosmic Chicago, much as Hull House was in Jane Addams's eyes. The essence of society, said Dewey — and in this he was joined by Robert Park and other sociologists — was communication — and therefore the school was to encourage and develop this peculiarly social phenomenon, this salient feature of the urban age. Dewey's progressivism in educational theory was defined by his broad conception of communication, his idea that it takes place while children are building blocks, dancing, and cooking, as well as on the more formal level of asserting propositions.

Soon, however, a new and more critical attitude toward the city began to enter Dewey's writing. In *The Public and Its Problems* (1927) he concluded that steam and electricity, the very forces that had created modern society, that had provided it with the means of transportation and communication that made urban concentration possible, were creating a situation in which communication at its most human level was being destroyed. The very forces which brought Bangkok and Chicago closer to each other and which brought people from isolated farms to urban centers had diminished the possibility of "face-to-face" relationships. The primary group, in the phrase of the sociologist Charles Horton Cooley, was disappearing rapidly. And while Dewey did not use our current jargon, he said, in effect, that modern society was becoming a lonely crowd of organization men.

Dewey warned: "Unless local communal life can be restored, the public cannot adequately resolve its most urgent problem: to find and identify itself."[26] But the local communal unit of which Dewey spoke now was not the enormous city as it was coming to be known in the twentieth century. It was more like the University Elementary School at the University of Chicago, or Hull House. "Democracy must begin at home," Dewey said, "and its home is the neighborly community."[27] As a result, a curious reversal takes place in Dewey's thinking. Instead of taking the city as the model *for* the progressive school, he almost speaks as though the urban community should be modeled *on* the progressive school. Jefferson wrote at the end of his life: "As Cato concluded every speech with the words, 'Carthago delenda est,' so do I every opinion with the injunction, 'Divide the counties into wards.' " At the end of his life Dewey seemed to conclude every speech with the words, "Divide the cities into settlement houses."

It is ironic to find the most influential philosopher of the urban age in America reverting to the localism of Jefferson, but no more ironic than the anti-urbanism of Louis Sullivan and Frank Lloyd Wright, our most distinctive architects. For functionalism, like pragmatism, is one of a complex of American ideas that could not exist in a nonurban society, and yet its greatest spokesmen seem to hate the American city. Sullivan's *Autobiography* records his distaste for Boston in his childhood, and in his *Kindergarten Chats* he fulminates against New York and Chicago. "Lieber Meister," as Wright called Sullivan, bequeathed this hostility to his disciple, and the disciple, as everyone knows, added his own powerful spice to the brew of anti-urbanism. John Dewey may have reverted to Jefferson's localism, but Wright was a little more partial to Emerson.

Not only are there copious references to Emerson in Wright's books, but he adds as a red-printed appendix to *The Living City* a long excerpt from Emerson's essay, "Farming," which concludes with a typically transcendental warning: "Cities force growth and make men talkative and entertaining, but they make them artificial." And so the great American architect of the twentieth century went back spiritually to Concord, while the great American philosopher retreated to Monticello.

One moral of this tale is that city-loving urban reformers will not find much boosting or sentimental admiration of city life in the writings of those who have been canonized in our national literature and philosophy. A brief flurry of pro-urban sentiment in the late nineteenth and early twentieth century under the encouraging eye of Walt Whitman and William James was swiftly buried by the exploding megalopolis, but after it our most sensitive and gifted intellectuals went on criticizing the American city. Readers who may feel that this story is based on an excessively narrow selection of writers and thinkers should remember that other readers will find in these pages the names of our greatest political thinker, our greatest essayist, our greatest philosopher, our greatest theorist of education, our greatest novelist, our greatest autobiographer, and our greatest architect, all of them throwing up their hands about the most distinctive and most pressing features of our national life. If *their* views should not be typical of the nation's view on this topic, that in itself would be a fact that is worth recording and pondering. Moreover, it is impossible to produce a list of *pro*-urban American thinkers who remotely approach this collection in distinction and intellectual influence.

In spite of the anti-urbanism of our literary and philosophical tradition, the city planner would make a grave mistake if he were to dismiss that tradition, if he were to treat it as a point of view from which nothing could be learned, if he were to forget it and disregard it. Those who must live in today's American city or who like to live in it can profit by taking seriously the urban criticism of our great writers, for it was deep and many-sided. It was not only esthetic but also moral in character. Henry James spoke most persuasively for those who saw the city as a scene of chaos as it presented itself to "the painter's eye." It lacked order, structure, history, and dignity in 1907, and God knows that these virtues have not been miraculously supplied in the age of urban sprawl and suburban slums. But the city, as Robert Park said, is a state of mind as well as an esthetic object, and the profoundest critics of the American city have found other faults with it.

When Jefferson warned of the dangers of what he called the city mob, when Emerson complained of the city's artificiality and conventionalism, when John Dewey lamented the decline of neighborliness, all of them thought of the city as a place in which certain basic human values were being subverted, values which are cherishable today as they were in the eighteenth century of Jefferson, the nineteenth century of Emerson, and the twentieth century of Dewey. And what are these values? Jefferson's worry about the mobs of the city arose from doubt about the American city's capacity to educate its inhabitants in a way that would preserve and extend the democratic process. And when Emerson worried about the growth of artificiality and conventionalism in the city, he was thinking, as were his contemporaries, Kierkegaard and John Stuart Mill, about the increase in conformity, about the decline of individuality which was proportional to the increase of urbanization in America. Dewey's main concern was with the improvement of human communication within the city; and by communication he did not mean the exchange of information alone. He valued the capacity to share feelings and experiences, the capacity to discuss with, to learn from and intelligently persuade others, and to *live* with them in the profoundest sense.

Who can deny, then, that today the great problem of the American city is to demonstrate at least three things: first, that it can solve the problem of education for the millions of people who are entering its gates, that it can absorb the Puerto Rican and the Negro, as it has other groups, into the democratic process; second, that it can foster individuality, the capacity and the right of the human being to develop into a rounded personality who is concerned with more than merely commercial values; and third, that it can be more than a vast prison of unconnected cells in which people of different occupations, color, class, or creed fail to understand one another on the basic human issues of social life, let alone agree with one another.

The moral message of the intellectual critic of the city today is not fundamentally different from what it was in the age of Jefferson, Emerson, and Dewey. For today's serious thinker must also build upon a respect for the fundamental values of education, individuality, and easy communication among men. But, unlike his predecessors, he cannot deceive himself about the *place* in which those values must be realized today. The wilderness, the isolated farm, the plantation, the self-contained New England town, the detached neighborhood are things of the American past. All the world's a city now and there is no escaping urbanization, not even in outer space.

15

The Revolution in Higher Education

Richard Hofstadter

I

In discussing the revolution that took place in American higher education between 1870 and 1910, it is impossible to meet the expectations created by the currently fashionable set of mind, which demands that the cultural situation be portrayed as constantly in a state of decline. One is obliged to report that this era was one of impressive achievement. We take for granted, as elements in our cultural inheritance, the existence of universities and an academic profession. But before the Civil War the United States had neither, in any respectable degree. They were created within one generation, in a country that previously had not much more than a scattered brood of small colleges in various stages of inanition.

To assess this academic revolution, it is necessary first to look at the old college without sentimentality or illusion. Troubled as we are by our present sense of educational failure, we may be too ready to imagine the old college to have been far better than it was. We think of the impersonality of so much contemporary college instruction, and long for that log with Mark Hopkins at one end and a student at the other; we think of the disorders of the modern curriculum, and long for the old classical course; we contemplate the half-literate products of many modern colleges, and long for graduates reared on Horace, Demosthenes, Cicero, and Tacitus. We tend to forget that the college that offered its undergraduates President Hopkins (himself on some counts intellectually retrograde)[1] offered them otherwise all too little; that the great writers of antiquity were commonly taught as exercises in grammar; and that students were frequently bored into disorderly reaction against the picayune discipline and unimaginative pedagogy of the old regime.

If the graduate of the old-time college sometimes turned out to be a well-educated man it was only in small part because of the contents of the college curriculum itself. Obsolescent mathematics, a smattering of science, and poorly taught classics no doubt had their disciplinary values; but whatever the typical old-time college student may have learned of modern literatures, including English, of modern languages (except in some colleges a little French), or of history or political economy came to him either through informal and extracurricular sources or by virtue of some rare local accident. The status of history may serve to illustrate this curricular poverty. As late as 1884, even after leaders of the university movement had begun to overhaul the undergraduate colleges, Charles William Eliot pointed out that "the great majority of American colleges . . . make no requirements in history for admission, and have no teacher of history whatever."[2] Nor can it be imagined that this was the case only with the inferior colleges; Eliot remarked that Dartmouth had no teacher of history — not so much as a temporary instructor — and that Princeton had only one professor of history (who doubled in political science), as compared with three professors of Greek.

On occasion the old-time colleges were sentimentalized by their alumni; but rarely by their teachers or their presidents. Most of the serious literature of college reminiscence is a literature of complaint: the mordant criticisms of Harvard College in the 1850's that have been etched on the memories of countless readers by Henry Adams's *Education* were exaggerated and unfair; but they were no more than hyperbolic statements of what dozens of other graduates and many educators had to say of their schools. As to the educators themselves, one must of course remember that a large portion of the writing in their field has always been an expression of discontent; but when this allowance has been duly made, one is still impressed by the volume and the cogency of their criticisms. Outstanding pre-Civil War teachers and presidents — men like George Ticknor, Francis Wayland, Philip Lindsley, Henry P. Tappan, F. A. P. Barnard, and others — echo in their educational writings the reminiscent complaints of graduates and anticipate the tart critiques of later university-builders like Charles William Eliot, Andrew D. White, and Daniel Coit Gilman.

With the exception of a few so-called universities, feebly maintained by the states, the colleges of the old regime were creations of various religious denominations. Sectarian competition, compounded by local competition, had prevented the educational energies of the country from being concentrated in a limited number of institutions of adequate size and adequate sustenance. Instead, the country was dotted with tiny colleges, weakly founded; only one out of five created before the Civil War survived — it is an incredible rate of failure. Those that did survive were frequently too small to be educationally effective; they lacked complexity; they lacked variety. We are too much tempted to think of the old college as being represented by the larger, better, and more famous institutions like Harvard, Yale, and Dartmouth, that had, by the 1850's, faculties ranging from fifteen to twenty-five officers and student bodies of from three to four hundred. But much smaller and more obscure and inefficient schools with faculties of six or eight and student bodies of 50 to 100 are far more typical of the 200-odd colleges of 1860, many of them inferior in quality to the best academies. Sectarian competition kept such institutions small and inadequate; the indifference of parents to good instruction, so long as their sons could emerge with degrees, made it unnecessary for these schools to do better than totter along from year to year. "What has heretofore been the idea of an University with us?" asked Longfellow. "The answer is a simple one: — Two or three large brick buildings, — with a chapel, and a President to pray in it!"[3] This was in 1829; a generation later the situation was but slightly changed, except in a few fortunate institutions.

Diversity of performance in the old-time college makes it difficult to make a universally fair appraisal of its work. Of course there were, as there always are, exceptional teachers with a gift for arousing the minds of the young. The classical curriculum, competently taught, could develop the capacity for work, instill a feeling for rhetoric, and inspire passion for learning. A not inconsiderable number of learned men came out of the old colleges, among them the leaders and scholars of the postwar university movement itself. The undergraduate literary and debating societies, whose libraries were often better and always more accessible than the college libraries, made it possible for the self-education and the mutual education of the undergraduates, always one of the most fruitful aspects of college life, to be carried on to good effect. Sometimes the capstone course in moral philosophy, given to seniors by the college president, was a source of genuine intellectual illumination.

But in good part, the old-college classroom was a dreary place. The students were subjected to a curriculum which rarely gave them any choice of courses, hardly ever a choice of teachers. They were submitted to a teaching routine consisting almost entirely of tedious daily recitations, and governed in detail by disciplinary rules that were excessively demanding. Since their instructors were set over them as policemen,[4] outbursts of mutual hostility were a perennial motif. Term time was frequently punctuated by student riots, and putting the cow in the chapel was a standard college prank. In the atmosphere of tension and irritation created by rigid discipline and nagging boredom, the instructor who achieved an affectionate or inspiring relationship with his charges represented a triumph of personal kindliness and ingenuity over poor institutional arrangements.

It was neither gratifying nor particularly useful to go to college. Earlier, in the latter half of the eighteenth century, the American colleges, still few in number, had done a bit to modernize their curricula, to put education into step with science and the thought of the Enlightenment, and to surmount the limitations of sectarian control. Their achievements in educating the revolutionary generation had been considerable. But in the early decades of the nineteenth century, the excessive diffusion of the nation's educational resources and the tightening grip of the sects crippled the colleges' capacity for further advances. They became less and less related to the intellectual life of the country; or, after the rise of industrialism, to its vocational and practical life. To be sure, for those interested in the ministry a college degree was always of vocational value; and the accoutrements of a college education, not least the formality of the degree itself, continued to give cachet to anyone in the professions and to confer social prestige. But a college degree was not necessary for law or medicine, and most of the engineers in the country were trained at West Point. Some parents, resigned to the modest accomplishments of the colleges, took them cynically as inexpensive custodial institutions — for it must be conceded to the colleges that they charged even less for their services than they were worth. Francis Wayland, the president of Brown, remarked in 1842: "Parents have assured me that they were obliged to send their sons to college because they could not afford to bring them up in a good counting house."

Cheap though they were, the colleges had ceased by the time of the Civil War to attract students in proportion to the growth of the population. In 1826 one in 1,513 young men of college age went to college. By 1855 it was down to one in 1,689; by 1869 to one in 1,927. The colleges were falling behind the birth rate, and at an accelerating pace. "The sad fact stares us in the face," said Charles Kendall Adams, "that the training which has long been considered essential to finished scholarship has been losing ground from year to year in the favor of the people."[5] But even as he spoke, the university revolution was under way, and the educational scene was undergoing drastic transformation.

II

After years of what seemed to be fruitless agitation, the university era began abruptly. It is true that some preparation had been made in the 1850's, a decade notable for lively educational criticism and new plans; and that a few leading institutions, notably Yale and Harvard, had made prewar gains that brought them to a stage of development something like that of the smaller German universities. But nothing could have prepared observers of the educational scene for the sudden explosive change of the post-Civil War years. The years 1868 and 1869 stand out — the first for the opening of Cornell under Andrew D. White, the second for the election of Charles

William Eliot to the presidency of Harvard. Seven years after Eliot's inauguration, instruction began at Johns Hopkins under the presidency of his friend Daniel Coit Gilman. These men led the university revolution, created its models, and set its tone; and while they were rapidly building modern universities and fostering advanced studies in the East, James Burrill Angell was working, though with less success, to carry the impetus of the university idea into the largest of the state universities at Michigan.

The first surge of reform, represented by these four men and institutions, was followed by others. Minnesota and Wisconsin made marked progress in the 1880's. Between 1889 and 1891, G. Stanley Hall, William Rainey Harper, and David Starr Jordan launched Clark, Chicago, and Stanford. Around the turn of the century Arthur Twining Hadley, Woodrow Wilson, and Nicholas Murray Butler, taking over Yale, Princeton, and Columbia, helped to bring these older institutions more fully into the swing of the university revolution.

Harvard, though not quite so innovative as Cornell or Johns Hopkins, was the leading institution of the university movement, partly because it brought the prestige that no newly founded school could bring. The achievements of Eliot were a measure of what a great administrator could do with adequate support. When Eliot became president, Harvard, consisting of the College, the Divinity, Law, Medical, Dental, and Scientific schools, had about a thousand students and sixty teachers. At the close of his reign in 1909 it had added the graduate schools of Arts and Sciences, Applied Science, and Business Administration, had some 4,000 students and about 600 teachers, and had increased its endowment from $2,500,000 to more than $20,000,000. Size is no measure of quality; but Harvard had also developed advanced study and had transformed and immensely improved undergraduate and professional studies — had grown, in short, from a small fledgling university to a great one. Other institutions, less daring, began to imitate her.[6]

No doubt the Civil War, by giving an impetus to science and technology, had something to do with quickening the university movement. In 1861 the legislature of Massachusetts chartered M.I.T., and the following year the Morrill Act made millions of acres available as a subsidy to state universities and agricultural and mechanical colleges. But it was mainly private funds, supplied on an unprecedented scale, that touched off the movement, and private institutions that showed the way. The work of sponsoring universities in which the states had failed and the sects had been no better than a hindrance, was at last taken over successfully by the postwar millionaires.

The contrast between the massive postwar donations and the poverty of the old college can hardly be overstated. When Princeton, for instance, had been revivified by her alumni in the middle 1830's, the largest single gift was $5,000, and the overall goal of this unprecedented drive was only $100,000. Williams was founded on $14,000, Amherst on $50,000. The largest single cash bequest received by Columbia before the Civil War was $20,000. With these figures one must compare Ezra Cornell's $500,000 for his new university at Ithaca, which was augmented to $2,500,000 in twenty years by the sale of land scrip allotted to New York under the Morrill Act; Johns Hopkins's $3,500,000; Vanderbilt's $1,000,000; Rockefeller's $30,000,000 for Chicago; Stanford's $20,000,000; or the endowment of over $20,000,000 that Harvard had built up at the close of Eliot's regime. In the twenty years after 1878, private donors gave at least $140,000,000 to all branches of higher education.

When the rich began to give their money, the people began to send their children, and the relative numerical decline of students before the year 1869 was at last reversed. Between 1870 and 1910, while the nation's population doubled, the number of students enrolled in higher education nearly quintupled. American parents were taking greater interest in sending their sons to college, and were beginning to send their daughters.[7] Graduate education, as well as coeducation, was entirely the creation of this forty-year period: the first Ph.D. was granted by Yale in 1861; total graduate enrollment rose from 198 students in 1871 to 2,382 in 1890 and 9,370 in 1910. The sources of undergraduate recruitment also grew, as the number of public high schools rose from about 1,000 in 1870 to 6,000 in 1900. In 1898 there were five times as many pupils enrolled in secondary schools as there had been twenty years earlier.

The great universities were launched with generous minds as well as generous purses. For decades farsighted educators had pleaded with very little success to get the yoke of sectarianism lifted from American higher education. Suddenly, within the span of a few years, it was lifted; almost, it seemed, without effort. In the main, the new donors, though far from impious men, were content to let the work of inquiry go on untrammeled by sectarian restraints. They were prepared to give away immense sums without interfering unduly with the manner in which their money was spent. Abruptly, the paternalism of the small college was abandoned, along with its sectarian atmosphere.

The same generosity of mind was brought to bear upon the debate over the curriculum and the competing claims of the disciplines. One thinks of Ezra Cornell's famous statement, "I would found an institution in which any person can find instruction in any study"; or of the opening of Eliot's inaugural address:

> The endless controversies whether language, philosophy, mathematics, or science supplies the best mental training, whether general education should be chiefly scientific, have no practical lesson for us to-day. This University recognizes no real antagonism between literature and science, consents to no such narrow alternatives as mathematics or classics, science or metaphysics. We would have them all, and at their best. . . .
>
> It were a bitter mockery to suggest that any subject whatever should be taught less than it now is in American colleges. The only conceivable aim of a college government in our day is to broaden, deepen, and invigorate American teaching in all branches of learning. It will be generations before the best of American institutions of education will get growth enough to bear pruning.[8]

III

The university revolution broke the institutional grip of sectarianism on American education; at the same time the Darwinian revolution broke its intellectual grip. While the needs of postwar industry gave science practical prestige, Darwinism gave it a preeminent prestige in the realm of thought. The response of American scientists to Darwinism was prompt and hearty. By 1873, when Louis Agassiz, the last major scientist who opposed evolution, went to his grave, Darwinism had swept the scientific profession. Darwin himself was accorded the honor of election to the American Philosophical Society as early as 1869; it was ten years from that date before his own university, Cambridge, gave him an honorary degree.

The flexibility of the more enlightened clergy before the Darwinian challenge was impressive. However, insofar as clerics active in academic life resisted Darwinism, their resistance only discredited their old dominion over education, and underlined the truth of Eliot's observation, "A university cannot be founded upon a sect." That scientists found occasion to attack the conservative ministers was not so fatal as the fact that they began to laugh at them.

Scientists and ministers alike had moved into an altogether different intellectual milieu. In the old-time sectarian college, orthodoxy had been a major test of the eligibility of an academic to his job. A professor had to be, in many places, a Christian of the right denomination or theological persuasion. For instance, in 1854 Oliver Wolcott Gibbs, a distinguished chemist, had been denied appointment at Columbia because the Episcopalian trustees, including several ministers, could not stomach his Unitarianism. This incident, one of many such throughout the country, caused the few enlightened trustees to despair of making Columbia into a genuine university. But all of this was quick to change. In the postwar decades, evolutionary science and the dominant scientific ideal enlarged and aggrandized the claims of *competence* as a criterion for faculty appointments. As competence displaced orthodoxy, the new university promoters began quietly to ignore sectarian criteria in choosing professors, and they found themselves upheld by their boards of trustees. Enlightened men knew that there was only one way to realize the dream of creating great universities equal to those of Europe — above all, those of Germany — and that was to recruit men on the basis of distinguished learning, without regard to other considerations.

The strategy of such promoters of the secular university as Gilman, White, and Eliot was not one of militancy but of quiet persistence and partial accommodation. These men were not interested in making the tension between science and religion the source of unnecessary antagonism and struggle. Being administrators and promoters rather than agitators, they went on their way firmly and steadily, avoiding polemics, quietly ignoring religious interests or thrusting them into the background, counting upon the passage of time and the undeniable usefulness of their enterprises to carry them through. They preferred by-passing the major religious strongholds rather than carrying them by assault — and not surprisingly, for they were themselves by no means devoid of religious feeling. It is true, of course, that Andrew D. White wrote a two-volume *History of the Warfare of Science with Theology*, but to him the last word of this title was essential: it was not, as he saw it, true religion but dogmatic theology that had stood in the way of science. In any case, the book was not published until 1896, when White's university-building work had been done and he had been eleven years retired from Cornell's presidency. In practice, White had not been excessively bold. For instance, he had brought Felix Adler (later the founder of the Society for Ethical Culture) to lecture on Hebrew and Oriental literature; but when Adler's latitudinarian ideas aroused widespread criticism in the local religious press, the university refused to renew an expired three-year appointment. White seems to have interposed no objection when Vice-President William C. Russel cashiered Adler.

The secularization of the new and more dynamic institutions proceeded from the top down, beginning with the donors. It is significant that of the three vanguard institutions in the university revolution, two were endowed by millionaires with Quaker backgrounds, who well understood the evils of sectarian oppression, while the third was Harvard with its relaxed Unitarian tradition. Moreover, donors of large fortunes preferred to have their gifts and bequests managed by businessmen and men of affairs rather than by clergymen. As the universities came to be less concerned with matters on which the clergy were deemed authoritative, the ministers seemed less competent to run them. The development of institutions large enough to be considered great enterprises suggested the need for business and promotional skills. Quietly, with the passage of time, clergymen began to disappear from governing boards. At Harvard the combined boards, Overseers and Corporation, had seven clergymen out of thirty-six members in 1874; by 1894 there was only one. Earl McGrath's study of the boards of fifteen private institutions shows that while in 1860 39 per cent of the trustees were clergymen, the figure had dropped to 23 per cent by 1900 and to 7 per cent by 1930.

Boards increasingly dominated by men with an eye to the needs of business and the development of research began to think naturally of laymen for college presidencies. By solemn tradition, the presidential office had gone to clergymen, and it was secularized at the same time as the trusteeships themselves. Columbia, choosing the chemist and naturalist F. A. P. Barnard in 1864, was one of the pioneers; and took as his successor in 1889 Seth Low, a businessman and politician. Harvard, which had already had two nineteenth-century lay presidents — Josiah Quincy in 1829 and Cornelius C. Felton in 1860 — turned from a minister, Thomas Hill, to a scientist, Eliot, in 1869. Cornell and Johns Hopkins began their existence with laymen as their presidents, as did Clark with G. Stanley Hall, a psychologist, and Stanford with David Starr Jordan, a biologist. Yale's first lay president was Arthur Twining Hadley, an economist, in 1899; Princeton's was Woodrow Wilson, a political scientist, in 1902.

A final phase in the induced secularization of the colleges came only after the turn of the century. The Carnegie Foundation for the Advancement of Teaching, established in 1906 to provide retirement allowances for professors in private, *nonsectarian* colleges, excluded from its bounty all colleges having intimate relations to religious denominations or requiring that trustees be members of a stated church. Many good colleges suffering from sectarian affiliations were happy to use their need for the foundation's bounty as an excuse to throw off church control. A number renounced their sectarian connections and revised their charters or by-laws to qualify for aid. At first only fifty-one institutions satisfied the foundation that they were nondenominational; but within four years twenty more managed to qualify, and others did so soon afterwards. Several hundred colleges still held the sectarian line, to be sure, but by and large these were the weakest colleges at the bottom of the educational ladder. Sectarianism was left mainly with the rearguard of American education.

IV

If we look for the educational convictions underlying the university revolution, we find ideas that may now seem so obvious as to have little compelling interest — ideas, moreover, so clearly anticipated by men like Jefferson, Ticknor, Wayland, Tappan, and others that they could hardly have been considered new in the years after 1869. The novelty lay in the means and the determination to implement them. Still, the convictions had to be reasserted in the university era and to be established against a tenaciously held counter-philosophy. During his first twenty years of service as Harvard's president, Eliot once said, he was "generally conscious of speaking to men who, to say the least, did not agree with me." President Hyde of Bowdoin remembered him as having been "misunderstood, misrepresented, maligned, hated," for his first twenty-five years.[9]

As education had been understood in the Anglo-American college tradition, the formation of character was held to be more important than the development of intellect, the transmission of inherited knowledge more important than the search for new knowledge, and discipline more important than stimulation. Of course these are not necessary antinomies. Few spokesmen either of the old or the new regimes would have been prepared to say that there is some inevitable antagonism between character and intellect, or between conserving past knowledge and acquiring new knowledge. But there was an undeniable difference in emphasis, a difference that, carried far enough, aroused real antagonism. For this reason men like Eliot, Gilman, and White could not simply assert their ideas, but had to campaign for them. If cultivating intellect was to become their central business, colleges devoted to character and discipline must undergo important changes. Again, to foster research was not to challenge the importance of conserving the past; but it did lead to an upheaval in a curriculum and in teaching methods that had been based almost entirely upon the ideal of conserving knowledge. To exalt the ideal of secular knowledge in the age of Darwinian science constituted, whether one was looking for controversy or not, a subversive movement against institutions reared upon sects.

The new generation had a strikingly untraditional sense of what higher education should be, derived in the main from their experience with the German universities.[10] Since the early nineteenth century, American students returning from Germany had brought with them a conception of university work altogether at odds with their American college experience. In the German university two things were central: scholarship and freedom. Scholarship was specialized and advanced, so that it was possible for students and faculties to go beyond the elementary stages and reach depth of understanding in special subjects. Freedom for the students meant not only the chance for a choice in one's studies, but also the opportunity to form one's habits and goals of conduct independently. The German idealization of scholarship gave to the professor a position of social importance unheard of in America. The German ideal of educational freedom (not to be confused with the modern conception of political-academic freedom) stressed the free pursuit by the professor of his scholarly interests without regard to curricular limitations. Where the American college had fitted its faculty to a curriculum, the German university tended to fit the curriculum to its faculty. The established German professor taught what he wished. The student too was free to choose among professors and even among universities in the pursuit of a self-determined and specialized scholarly goal. The German emphasis on *Lehrfreiheit* and *Lernfreiheit* was translatable (though in the process of translation it was substantially altered) in the Anglo-American conceptions of democracy, competition, and laissez-faire.[11] As the new open curriculum crept into the American college, all academic subjects were thought to have been created equal, and all teachers and pupils entitled to the pursuit of intellectual happiness by exercising their free choice among subjects. Professors and curricular offerings were to engage in a measure of open competition, thus realizing more closely the model of economic behavior portrayed in classical economics. It would be exaggerating to suggest that this is what was done, but this was the ideal toward which changes were directed.

The canons of university education were, then, in some sense new. They embraced the following propositions. First, education must be freed from sectarian and political domination. Moreover, it must be freed from paternalistic domination: trustees must leave educational, curricular, and disciplinary matters almost entirely to the faculties. Trustees should consider themselves business managers and general overseers; but must largely forgo control of the educational process itself.[12]

Secondly, the faculties were now recognized, not in law but surely in fact, to constitute the universities. Not grand buildings, not imposing presidents, not respectable church sponsorship, not large and well-behaved student bodies — none of these was any longer assumed to be the important thing. A university was an aggregate of intellectual talents. Illustrious teachers — recruited from at home or abroad without serious concern for anything but their scholarly or scientific achievements — were understood to be the heart and soul of the university. To attract them an institution must be prepared to pay well, and the whole community must be willing to make the academic profession roughly commensurate with other professions in salaries, in dignity, and in freedom.

Thirdly, a university must make advanced study its main concern. The graduate school was not an afterthought or an adornment, but a necessity and a model. Not only must advanced scholars be recruited to teach in graduate schools, but good students must, in effect, be hired to attend them — i.e., fellowships must be provided. It was assumed that *all* instruction, including professional and undergraduate instruction, would be improved in the atmosphere created by advanced research and experimentation. When opponents of a graduate school at Harvard suggested that it was useless to compete in this respect with Johns Hopkins, and that a graduate school would weaken the College, Eliot replied: "It will strengthen the College. As long as our teachers regard their work as simply giving so many courses for undergraduates, we shall never have first-class teaching here. If they have to teach graduate students as well as undergraduates, they will regard their subjects as infinite, and keep up that constant investigation which is necessary for first-class teaching."[13]

Fourthly, the resistance of the old college to the scientific and vocational demands of the community gave way. Scientific and technical education were no longer frowned at, or isolated in separate "scientific" schools, but were made an integral part of the educational process.

Finally, undergraduate teaching and the undergraduate curriculum were overhauled. Science was given an increasingly important part in the course of studies. But even more drastic was the enlarged place of the social sciences and modern languages and literature, hitherto but slightly represented. Under the elective system the undergraduate was given a high degree of freedom to choose his course of studies. Now the disciplines had to compete with each other for enrollment — which could put a premium upon fresh and interesting teaching (as it could also, unfortunately, upon the easy course). The tedious recitation session lost favor, and ultimately disappeared, in favor of more imaginative methods of instruction: the lecture, the small discussion group (borrowed from the graduate seminar), and, in science, demonstrations and laboratory work. The elective system, while making more specialized courses available to undergraduates, made it possible for teachers to teach subjects of vital interest to themselves. The consequent improvement in the morale of instructors contributed substantially to the liveliness of teaching.

The greatest single weakness of the old colleges had been neither their curriculum, however archaic, nor their faculties, however limited, but their hopelessly dull recitation method of teaching, which could deaden the most interesting subjects and convert faculty men of genuine intellectual and scholarly distinction into drillmasters.[14] James Freeman Clarke's ironic remark at the Harvard commencement dinner of 1886 may be taken with entire seriousness: "Formerly, the only business of a teacher was to hear recitations, and make marks for merit. Now, he has the opportunity of teaching. This is one of the greatest educational discoveries of modern times, — that the business of a teacher is to teach."[15]

V

Before the university era, men had spent their lives teaching in colleges, but there was nothing that could be called an academic profession. There were no well-recognized and generally maintained standards of competence in scholarly subjects; professional and intellectual specialization was not generally recognized as a prerogative of the college teacher; there was no lively academic marketplace in which competing institutions could or would regularly bid for the skills of eminent men; there were few opportunities or facilities for specialized research or experimentation; there were few scholarly organizations or publications. With these elementary prerequisites of professional life so conspicuously lacking, there could be no such spirit of professional solidarity as began to manifest itself in informal ways after 1870 and finally found formal expression in 1915 in the organization of the American Association of University Professors.

The lack of specialization was only slowly overcome in the

university era, except in the vanguard institutions. We need not, perhaps, concern ourselves overmuch with such institutions of the educational underworld as Florida State College of Agriculture, with its professorship in agriculture, horticulture, and Greek. But distinguished men were often reduced to drillmasters and petty disciplinarians, tormented by the tedium of underspecialization. James Burrill Angell, president of the University of Vermont in the 1860's, finding that the institution lacked the funds to round out its faculty, taught all the missing subjects himself — including rhetoric, German, history, and international law. David Starr Jordan, as late as the 1870's when he taught at Lombard University in Illinois, had classes in natural science, political economy, evidences of Christianity, German, Spanish, and literature, and pitched for the baseball team. Eliot well knew the costs of this system — or lack of system — for he had suffered from it as a young assistant professor at Harvard in the 1850's. To Charles Eliot Norton he wrote in 1860:

> I generally experience a slight disgust at recitations at the beginning of a term, particularly at Mathematical recitations. I wish I could teach the science in which I am most interested, and in which I work during leisure hours, but at present I have four recitations in Mathematics for one in Chemistry, and I see no reasonable hope of any change. . . . And yet the College demands so much of my time that I can do original scientific work only by working up to the very limit of physical endurance and sometimes going a little beyond it.[16]

The feebleness of the libraries was almost as great an obstacle to professional work in the old colleges. A privileged scholar like George Ticknor might build a private library, mainly in his own specialty, of 13,000 volumes; but it was upon such efforts, or upon inconvenient resort to general libraries not maintained by their own schools, that American academics did what important scholarly work was done. Ticknor had pointed out when he joined Harvard that its library, then 20,000 volumes, was only one-tenth the size of Göttingen's. By 1839, when Harvard's library had grown to 50,000, Yale's was the only other college library with more than half as many; and in the country at large there were only sixteen colleges that could claim more than 10,000 books. As late as 1873 the library of the University of Pennsylvania, with 20,000 volumes, was dwarfed by the Philadelphia Mercantile Library with 125,000. This poverty persisted into the post-Civil War period. In 1869 Gilman, who had only recently ceased being Yale's librarian, pointed out that "Yale College has not a dollar on hand to buy books for the next two years, its scanty library income having been expended two years in advance."[17] To scholars familiar with these conditions of the pre-university era, the growth of libraries was immensely heartening. By 1900 Harvard's, the leading library, had 560,000 volumes and 350,000 pamphlets. Such lesser libraries as that of Pennsylvania had grown to respectable size with about a third as many.

The situation of laboratory science in the old colleges had been still worse. American colleges provided no laboratories for teaching, or even, normally, for the experiments of faculty members. At Yale, pre-eminent in science, Benjamin Silliman, Sr., could do no more for his students in this respect than perform some experiments for them in the lecture room. He disliked having students in his private laboratory for fear they would "hinder me and my trained assistants, [or] derange or break the apparatus."[18] The younger Silliman, as his father's assistant, was able to get a room at Yale in 1842, in which he could give practical laboratory instruction to a few students, but this was an unofficial arrangement having no functional connection with college instruction. The foundation in 1847 of Sheffield Scientific School at Yale and Lawrence at Harvard represented a step toward academic laboratories, but adequate support for scientific teaching and research had to await the more substantial endowments of the period after 1870.

Professionalism moved from the institutions to the disciplines. There had been professional organizations before the Civil War, but usually they had been either local organizations, like the Massachusetts Historical Society, the American Academy of Arts and Sciences, and the American Antiquarian Society, or comprehensive and unspecialized, like the American Association for the Advancement of Science. Now the various disciplines, many of them being taught for the first time in the universities, began under the stimulus of Gilman and Johns Hopkins to form their own specialized societies. Learned societies began to proliferate with rapidity in the 1870's and 1880's; by 1908 there were 120 national societies and countless local ones besides. Again spurred by Johns Hopkins, professional journals began to develop, led by the mathematicians, chemists, and philologists. Chicago followed the example of Johns

Hopkins in becoming a major center for the publication of professional journals.

The development of graduate studies and professional standards spread from academic studies to the professional schools. Legal and medical education, as they had been carried on in the United States during the nineteenth century, were hardly professional. Law schools had little to offer that was better than the informal apprentice training available in the office of a good lawyer. Eliot found the law school at Harvard in disgraceful condition, unchanged for the past twenty years, staffed by three lawyers busy with their own private practices, and attended by students less than half of whom were college graduates, and none of whom had to pass examinations in order to get the LL.B. degree. The new president forced Christopher C. Langdell into the deanship in 1870, and thus instituted a series of changes that in good time set the pace for legal education throughout the country. A capable faculty was recruited, law study was extended from eighteen months to three years, written examinations were required, and the case method of study replaced the old textbook method. These reforms, much resisted at first, paid off within a little more than a dozen years. By then the student body had doubled, and the *Harvard Law Review* had been founded. After 1893 none but college graduates were admitted. Harvard set a pattern that was widely imitated.

Where legal education had been lax, medical education had been lethal. The old proprietary medical schools were essentially profit-making institutions, devoid of laboratories and hospital connections, in which teaching was done by lecture and a rare dissection. The course of study was normally one academic year; the tuition income was divided among the local medical practitioners who did the teaching. "Chairs" in medicine were sold to their occupants. Examinations were brief and oral. Even at Harvard the candidate who could pass with five out of nine examiners was qualified for medicine. There were no state boards to impose standards. Eliot considered that "the ignorance and general incompetency of the average graduate of American Medical Schools, at the time when he receives the degree which turns him loose on the community, is something horrible to contemplate." [19]

Harvard Medical School began its reforms under Eliot simultaneously with the reforms in the law school. A three-year course of study was set up, and written examinations established, with the requirement that all fields be passed by those who were to receive their M.D.'s. Johns Hopkins opened its great medical school in 1893 requiring a bachelor's degree for admission. When Abraham Flexner made the famous investigation in 1910 that launched a general reform in medical education, he took Johns Hopkins as the model of what an American medical school should be, and graded other institutions by measuring their distance from the Johns Hopkins standard. Twenty years earlier there had been no school in America good enough to serve as a standard.

But quite as important as the effects of the university revolution on the other professions was its effect on the academic profession itself. Now, for the first time, the profession developed the capacity both for large-scale innovative work in scholarship and for social criticism and practical contribution to the political dialogue of American society. If one considers only philosophy and the social sciences, the roster of men reared in the university movement is impressive enough: Oliver Wendell Holmes (one of Langdell's first recruits) and Roscoe Pound in law; Thorstein Veblen and John R. Commons in economics; John Dewey and William James in philosophy; Charles A. Beard, Carl Becker, James Harvey Robinson, Frederick Jackson Turner in history. The important and original movements in thought and scholarship — pragmatism, legal realism, institutional economics, the "new history," which are all products of this era, stand in refreshing contrast to the earlier borrowings from Scottish realism and classical economic doctrine.

Pragmatism itself, the most significant product of American academic work, was in part the result of applying to philosophical problems certain insights derived from Darwinian evolution and from Anglo-American case law. It became, in a sense, almost the official philosophy of American liberalism. It was ideally adapted to a time when the academic man was beginning to overcome his traditional civic passivity and take an active part in the shaping of political events. A long-standing estrangement between the life of the mind and the life of politics was overcome at the turn of the century, and in the new synthesis of academic life and politics, scholars like John Dewey, J. Allen Smith, and Charles A. Beard were to play a signal part. Among the consequences of the empirical specialized skills that had been fostered by the university movement, academic men had not only prestige but some real marketable advice to bring to public life. It was not surprising that they played an important part in the Progressive era, both on the national level and in the states. In Wisconsin, under La Follette, the idea of the university in the service of the reformist state received a remarkable consummation. In the nation at large, the participation of professors in government had become a thing familiar enough not to cause exceptional notice. In 1918, when Woodrow Wilson, himself a product of the university movement, took to Paris a team of about 150 scholars to give technical advice on the making of the peace, the employment of experts seems to have been sufficiently taken for granted to elicit only faint hostile comment.

VI

Every revolution has its excesses, its disappointments, its Thermidor; the university revolution was no exception. Its leaders, who were familiar only with the underspecialization and impracticality they had to surmount, could not very well anticipate or prevent the new evils of overspecialization and excessive vocationalism. The modern university brought with it the defects of its merits. If the old college had preserved too much of what was dead in the past, the new university became in time all too responsive to trivial innovations of the present. Limited though it had been in the quality and range of its achievement, the old college had had a clear form and mold and a firm sense of purpose. The university often lost its center and became a diffuse federal union whose parts seemed to work at cross purposes. It replaced underspecialization with overspecialization, overdiscipline of the young with excessive indulgence, archaism with a restless and sometimes indiscriminate passion for novelty, impracticality with a crass surrender to vocationalism, neglect of science with obtrusive scientism and crude positivism, stubborn resistance to change with complaisant response to the demands of an anti-intellectualist society.

The history of the elective system is a perfect case of the difficulties of change. By 1910 it was recognizable that those institutions which had made the elective experiment too fast and carried it too far had invited curricular chaos. Students, freed from set courses of study, sometimes chose courses largely because they were easy or entertaining; some were capable of devising for themselves strange collections of courses aggregating enough credits to earn the B.A. but hardly constituting a liberal education. Much of the curricular planning of the twentieth-century college has been an attempt to surmount this tendency toward formlessness, to devise meaningful core curricula, and to conform once again to the old-college ideal of giving the student a minimum base in general education preliminary to specialization.

Although the old college subordinated intellect to character and discipline, it never doubted that education was basically concerned with the mind. The modern university, with its multiple concerns and its effort to meet a variety of needs, has at times degenerated into a kind of cultural filling-station. This tendency has reached its peak among the state universities, one of whose presidents once declared: "The state universities hold that there is no intellectual service too undignified for them to perform."[20] By 1930, when Abraham Flexner published his famous survey, *Universities: American, English, German*, his account of the trivialities to which the universities at their worst had descended — the correspondence courses, the offerings in advertising, judo, food etiquette, and home laundering, the graduate theses on ways of washing dishes, on the bacterial content of cotton undershirts, or on "the origin and nature of common annoyances" — matched in scorn his earlier account of the inadequacies of the medical schools.

These things must be said as a caution against claiming too much for the university revolution. But no one who looks carefully into the old college and the work of the university reformers would propose that we simply set the clock back. We go on, trying to strike a balance between the vocational and the intellectual, between the general and the specialized, between the "two cultures" of science and humanities with an uneasy awareness that the problem is not susceptible to perfect solution. No doubt there is something missing and something wrong in every educational dispensation. Education is a field in which everyone is, in his own mind, an expert;

a field in which everyone cherishes a Utopia which he imagines to be realizable. We think of men or women whom we consider well educated, and we demand that somehow institutions be created that will turn out such products wholesale; but a good education depends upon an uncommon, happy conjunction between institutional excellence and personal capacity and desire.

PART FOUR

From the First World War to the Present: The International Phase

16

Foreign Policy: From Innocence to Engagement

McGeorge Bundy

Foreign affairs are the last and greatest task of modern American thought — the last, in that the others have had a deeper and more natural connection with our own history in the latter part of the nineteenth century, and the greatest, in that it is now reasonably plain that we shall not survive in our "new world" if we do not survive in the world as a whole.

Thought about world affairs, in the last sixty years, has been dominated by events, and not the other way around. It was not American thought which produced the two world wars and the cold war with Russia; even the little war with Spain was more a cause than a result of American thinking about foreign affairs. This relative balance of forces is not in principle a happy basis for an essay in intellectual history. It is more comforting, somehow, to say that this or that event grew out of these and those habits of mind. Such tracings can be valid and important, and certainly international history is not a wholly unmoved mover, in its relation to American thought. But the prevailing fact of our international life since 1900 is that it has been one long series of great surprises (more often than not unpleasant), in which it has regularly been demonstrated that the theories dominant among us — whether descriptive or purposive in cast — have been quite inadequate to deal with the world's realities.

At the same time that they have regularly destroyed our expectations, these enormous events have been the quarry from which thought has come. We have not had a theory of imperialism, but a set of arguments responding to particular opportunities in the Philippines, or Puerto Rico, or the Panama Canal. In the First World War we did not work out a clear theory of neutrality; instead we slowly developed a series of propositions aimed at stating and maintaining a certain diplomatic stance. A theorist's image of the new international society did not lead to the debate on the League of Nations — rather the arguments for forming the League were hammered out in the political process of the season after victory. It is a familiar point that the isolationism of the 1930's was a delayed reaction to the terrible costs and unrewarded hopes of the first war, and the idea of a great common interest with Western Europe owes more to the impact of the fall of France in 1940 than to any theorist of the Atlantic Community writing before that date. We have had global war, cold war, and limited war, in practice, before we have had influential theories about any one of them.

Thus in this field we ride close to the ground. No decade of this century, except perhaps the first, has been without its cataclysmic shift in the scene. Sometimes these shifts have been predicted in a general way (mainly by those who have profited from the fact, which Walter Lippmann has noted, that prophets of doom are usually right). But even those who have warned of war or of depression have never penetrated the veil of the future to foretell how drastically all our expectations would be upset by such convulsions. The pictures in men's minds, for the most part, have been produced by the impact of immediate and enormous events on their traditional attitudes.

The dominance of the event has as one notable consequence the importance, for thought as well as action, of political leaders. Students of American thought about the world must concern themselves closely with the words of such Presidents as the two Roosevelts and Woodrow Wilson, of such Secretaries of State as Root,

Stimson, Acheson, and Dulles, and of such special advisers as House and Hopkins. The rush of events has repeatedly forced upon our statesmen a requirement of exposition that has automatically made them the framers, not merely of policy, but of the terms of discussion and even reflection. This fact in itself has once again enmeshed the analysis in the event.

Nor does the scholar, in this subject, have the usual countervailing advantage of the detached observer in other fields of inquiry. The economist has tools the businessman lacks; the art historian does things the artist does not; the critic has a function apart from that of the poet. But when international relations are conceived as a whole, the subject is quite literally too big for theory, except in the form of propositions whose generality equals their lack of immediate relevance, while at the working level of applicable propositions the event, as already suggested, has tended to outrun the theorist.

Yet at the same time that events have shaped thought, the American response to events has of course been strongly affected at each stage by existing attitudes and sentiments. Thus at the beginning of the century the dominant force is *not*, as we often think, the process of response to the great new challenges of American power and possession, dramatized in the Spanish-American War. The dominant force is rather a persisting and essentially unbroken conviction that the central destinies of Americans are within the great continental country itself. Archibald C. Coolidge, a pioneer in the study of modern American foreign policy, wrote of his countrymen before 1898 that "The American people as a whole were wrapped up in their home affairs,"[1] and that their attitude toward the rest of the world was one of proud and secure independence. The most important rule of foreign policy was George Washington's warning against foreign alliances, strengthened by a century of practice even beyond its original purport. And what is remarkable is that the same basic attitudes persisted even after the Spanish-American War. Certainly that curious contest, with its consequences in the Caribbean and in the Philippines, led to new responsibilities and new speculations. But it did not change the main structure of national attitudes.

We can test this conclusion by considering the meaning of the debate which was precipitated by the war of 1898 and settled, in a measure, by McKinley's second election — the debate between "expansionists" and anti-imperialists. Just because theory and action, events and attitudes, are so little separated, the history of our thinking about foreign affairs is sketched with startling clarity in what we have done and thought at moments of political decision.

In form and in immediate result, the debate of 1900 turned on the wisdom or unwisdom of holding the Philippines and adopting a certain posture of concern for and participation in other activities beyond our shores. But in relation to the deeper national interest and purpose, this was no great debate at all. To neither side was it really very important what happened to the Philippines. To both the issue was there because accident had put it there (if accident had been given a push by Theodore Roosevelt's orders to Dewey, still one cannot find here a vast cosmic force, and still less a coherent theory of policy). To both sides, moreover, the problem seemed capable of a fairly easy solution — each was urging a way of ending the problem, not a way of adjusting to its long-term meaning.

Finally, by a charming irony, the main reason for the acceptance of McKinley's view instead of Bryan's was the country's contentment with its domestic situation. In the sense that matters, the sense that reflects what citizens really thought important and what they themselves were touched by, the election of 1900 was a victory for isolationism. Isolationism dominated the decade and a half that followed, and there was no need for a definition of American policy more complex than John Hay's in 1901: "The Monroe Doctrine and the Golden Rule."[2]

Theodore Roosevelt believed in foreign affairs, and still more important, he enjoyed them. He was ceaselessly active, and in three ways his activities affected real issues: he changed the posture of the United States in Latin America; he ably continued the work begun in the new possessions; and his personal diplomacy was occasionally a useful element in negotiations primarily affecting other powers. But he did not commit his country to international politics as the European powers were committed; he did not himself put international affairs at the head of the agenda. Though he was President, soldier, and spokesman for realism, he did not and could not see America as engaged in the way that history would inevitably engage her a generation later. He was no isolationist, but his country was. Walter Millis is right to remind us that one of Roosevelt's most famous gestures, his dispatch of the Great White Fleet around the world, was possible only because it had no real meaning.[3]

The debate over neutrality in 1914–17 is remarkable largely for having generated large amounts of feeling among men who did not deeply disagree. It seems doubtful whether American entry into the war would have been significantly different in shape if Hughes, or Taft, or even Theodore Roosevelt had been President in these years. But when the divergence was real, as between Wilson and Bryan, one feels that the latter was somehow trying to escape history; the issue has more intellectual clarity than political life. For Bryan's willingness to avoid war by a gradual abandonment of traditional rights was not at all acceptable to the people; in this sense the America of 1812 had survived all the years of isolation. Bryan's hope was as irrelevant as the opposite view — so little expressed before 1917 and so often afterward — that the United States should intervene in Europe because of her vital national interest in the European balance of power.[4] The United States got into the first war because Germany pushed her in; that this point was always clear to the Germans has lately been shown again, in high style, by Ernest May.[5]

The next great moment of political decision came, of course, in the contest over the League of Nations. Here the difference of policy became so entangled with personal and partisan feeling that the immediate result tells very little about what the country really wanted. Students of the League controversy usually find their final problem in the purpose and character of Woodrow Wilson: his certainty of righteousness and his identification of his own pride with the general will probably are at the center of the failure here. It is quite wrong to suppose that the American people rejected the League of Nations and still worse to draw large conclusions from this supposition. Wilson rejected a compromise that he should have accepted, and then, certainly, in the election of 1920, the people voted for peace and quiet under Harding.

Yet Wilson's purpose and character are not limited to a tragic flaw. His strengths and weaknesses were representative of those which great numbers of Americans of his generation brought to the new challenges of world affairs. Professor Langer summarizes his failings thus: "exaggerated idealism, superiority complex, ignorance of world affairs resulting from isolation, failure to recognize the true national interest and to assume the obligations demanded by it." And against this list he sets out these strengths: "his adherence to principle, his conception of morality, his faith in his country's mission to advance freedom and justice, his advocacy of a conciliatory peace, and his devotion to the idea of a new world order to provide security and exorcise war."[6] Certainly in the depth of his perception that isolation was impossible Wilson was ahead of his people as a whole, just as he never showed much of the simple nationalistic pride that was symbolized in Theodore Roosevelt. But on balance he remains an American of his time — displaying in heightened form the tension between moral aims and practical problems which was the necessary accompaniment of the end of isolation.

What we can say of the debate of 1919 we can say also about discussion of America's role in the world during most of the two decades that followed: that the framework of such discussion had moved from the innocence of 1900 to a new level, which combined an awareness of the general problem with a startling optimism about its size and shape. After the First World War it was hard to think that international affairs were self-regulating or unimportant (though many Americans managed it); what was easy, however, was to suppose that a sound general solution was available in this new situation. In this, the isolationists and the partisans of collective security remained more alike than different between the two world wars. Each side developed great skill in satirizing the false hopes of the other — but neither transcended the framework of unspoken belief that there *must* be a policy that would solve the general problem.

Thus the League of Nations, to its ardent believers, was less an instrument of than a substitute for policy, and its opponents urged not a coherent theory of behavior but a solution by rejection. Later, in the 1930's, a small but articulate minority began to urge a policy of collective security, and while the form was one of responsible participation, the underlying expectation was that virtuous commitment to peace would be a self-executing solution. Of course many men knew better, but the capacity for self-deception on all sides was very great in these decades — most notably in the real hopes which men had for paper instruments of moral protestation like the

Kellogg-Briand Pact. Statesmen could and did explain later that such weak reeds were all they had, but until the test came the weakness was not much discussed by these same men. We are driven to the conclusion that in the two decades between the wars Americans gravely misconstrued the power and hazard of the forces they aimed to control, or avoid. It is hard to know whether this error of estimation is the more remarkable among those who relied on the moral force of world opinion to deter aggression or among those who supposed that legislated neutrality could insulate the United States from a wicked world.

The Second World War brings the second Roosevelt — the most important as he is the most complex of all actors and spokesmen for America on world affairs. Both the importance and the complexity derive from Franklin D. Roosevelt's crucial role as a transitional figure. On the one hand he maintained — and reinforced — the simple expectation that eight points or four freedoms were somehow to be made real by the mere negative act of removing international villains like Hitler. He dramatized and defended a policy of alliance in which the American purpose was — or seemed to be — to paper over the differences of style and commitment that separated the United States from such powers as Stalin's Russia or Chiang's China. Roosevelt's United Nations was Wilson's League with the tactical errors avoided; both its theorists and its early support from public opinion betray a wondrous revival of faith in the instrument of policy as a policy in itself.

But Franklin D. Roosevelt was also the first twentieth-century President to use real power, in peacetime, as an instrument of policy beyond the Western Hemisphere. He plainly understood, as he eloquently explained, the depth and strength of the American interest in Western Europe, and he never himself believed that organization was a substitute for policy. Swept up by forces larger than himself, confidently ignorant of much that lesser men understood, reflecting to the end something of that belief in easy answers which was never possible after his death, he yet remains great, in our affairs as in our thinking about them, for having led his country strongly out of one age and into another. More than any other one man he symbolized and made permanent the entry of the United States upon world power as an operational responsibility, and he did it while holding clearly before the world a high and credible image of the American purpose.

It is the fate of transitional figures to be obscured for a while by time, and the world of the last fifteen years has distressingly little connection with the hopes and thoughts of Franklin Roosevelt. Its great debates have turned on new questions, harder and more searching than any of his time. Most of these new issues have posed again the old issue of isolation as against involvement — but on the whole this is no longer the central question. Broadly speaking there is now agreement on two simple propositions: that we cannot isolate ourselves, and that participation is not in itself a sufficient policy. Echoes of older debates and outdated hopes still color what is said and written, and the subcontinent is still populated by a people to whom private life is the most immediately interesting sphere of existence. But what our wits did not do for us, events have done: we know that world affairs matter.

Before we turn to these more recent and more relevant theories, we can sharpen our general survey of twentieth-century attitudes by a close look at the special problems of economic and military thought. Both display the same basic progression from innocence to engagement, and then, after the Second World War, from black-and-white to gray in the assessment of the problem.

Economic foreign policy, before the First World War, was nearly nonexistent. Economic forces there were of course, and their influence was great. But it is remarkable that those forces were not usually assessed within a framework of national policy. The foreign activity of the American businessman was seen as an independent enterprise; there was argument on the degree to which the government owed him diplomatic support and encouragement, but it was rare indeed that his activity as such was considered against the test of national interest. The governmental policy most relevant to international affairs, the tariff, was not seen as an issue of "foreign" policy at all. Economic policy as an instrument of foreign policy did not exist.

The First World War, with its vast loans and its drastic rearrangement of the financial balance of power, changed all that, and Americans were forced to have an opinion on economic forces in foreign affairs. As in political affairs, two main lines of thought developed. One was that all this could and should be managed to produce sound and enduring results, and the other was that it was a vicious business, essentially beyond the control of the United States Government, something in which the main object of policy must be to avoid new costs and cut losses.

The problem-solvers have come in many shapes. There were the financial rearrangers of the twenties, carefully adjusting small pieces of a machine they understood in detail but never in its whole; to them the balance-of-payments problem, in its narrow and almost literal sense, was the center of concern. The age of Cordell Hull produced a thin but fierce commitment to peace by tariff-reduction. And the planning for peace that was done in the Second World War showed again, in somewhat more sophisticated form, an expectation that with new institutions and a modest amount of pump-priming the world's economic well-being could become virtually self-regulating.

In opposition were those who felt that international economic forces were no proper concern of the United States — that bankers were bad, or that lower tariffs were a sign of softness, that international economic instruments were, at the very best, useless entanglements, and that pump-priming abroad was even worse than the same activity at home. Obviously interest as well as opinion was at work in many of these positions, but we must not discount the force of the basic attitude of rejection. Here was an unpleasant problem, to be dealt with by denying its importance.

Rarely and exceptionally an opponent of economic involvement and responsibility would add to his rejection a coherent alternative policy. The most notable such effort was made in the mid-thirties by Charles A. Beard, who sketched, in *The Open Door at Home*, a plan for controlled and limited trade, organized in subordination to a national policy of insulation, the whole directed less *against* foreign involvement than *for* the cultivation of our own garden. It was a remarkable speculative flight, and in its combination of good temper and affirmative purpose it is still rare among isolationist writings. But it had no discernible influence, and it remained exceptional even in Beard's own work, the dominant tone of which, on international affairs, is better portrayed by a better-known title, *Giddy Minds and Foreign Quarrels*.

It is only in 1947 that new economic issues, larger and more demanding than ever before, begin to tilt the balance away from black-

and-white responses toward more complex and accurate analysis. The first great act is the Marshall Plan, and ever since, with an ebb and flow of energy, there has been an increasing understanding that economic questions are lasting and endlessly varied forces in the world's affairs and also in American policy. Crudeness of theory still exists; the Marshall Plan itself was too much conceived and presented as a lasting solution, and in the field of aid to underdeveloped countries simple views do not easily give way to the beginnings of more subtle and accurate analysis. Even the tariff, though now widely understood to be relevant to world affairs, is not always handled on this basis, and the level of American thought on the political meaning of business activity abroad remains remarkably primitive. Yet we have at least reached a point where economics is recognized as a permanent and major force in affairs and in policy.

In turning to military policy we shall do well to recollect that national defense is never an easy topic for a democracy, and that in the twentieth century it has been an easy topic for no one. With rare and always partial exceptions no state has had adequate theories of the role of force, and hardly any has successfully anticipated the decisive elements of a major conflict. The difficulties in American thinking about these matters do not have to be contrasted with any great triumphs of others.

Yet there are remarkable special features in the American situation. The first and most notable is the military element of the basic expectation that the rest of the world would not bother us. Whether we consider the amateur warriors of Theodore Roosevelt's time and spirit, or the eager pacifists who opposed them, we can see that in the end and in essence no one believed the problem of national defense was urgent or real. It is this unreality that makes for the extraordinarily narrow and artificial patterns of military and naval thought as such. The Army found it particularly difficult to make a good theory of its role — for in the basic strategic situation of the United States, as the country understood it in 1900, there was quite literally no room for a major army. Thus the best that we can find are new theories of military organization, borrowed largely from Germany, and persuasive mainly by contrast with the bureaucratic somnolence of the nineteenth-century War Department.

But what is surprising is that naval theory is not much better. A

Navy did at least exist — but what it should be and do was far from clear. Mahan was the great figure in the field. From the maritime history of modern Europe he distilled a powerful theory of sea power, in which aggressive tactics aimed at the enemy's fleet were combined with bases, commerce, and colonies to make a self-sustaining general policy of power: the bases and the merchant marine make possible the Navy, which in turn protects them both, and works with them to enlarge the colonies. This was a most ingenious interpretation of the British past (and Mahan achieved an extraordinary success in Great Britain), but it really did not describe the American present or future. Certainly Mahan was right in asserting the importance of sea power, but neither colonies nor foreign commerce were central in American affairs, and the real needs of the later Navy were never foreseen by Mahan or his followers. Thus in essence a misleading general theory gave prestige and surface plausibility to a navalism which was never closely articulated to the realities of national position and purpose.

Whatever else it was, the First World War was real, and so was the American role in it. As Walter Millis has perceptively noted, the efforts at "preparedness" which went before it were only dimly related to what actually happened, so that the war actually led to an abandonment of the naval program of 1916.[7] But the war was real, and its consequences for military thought were powerful.

For here we have the first modern war in which victory was allowed to become an end in itself. This happened to the European belligerents too (and the Russians under Lenin were not really exceptional, save in that their own unlimited war had an internal target), but it happened with especial clarity and completeness to the United States. Military men were cut loose, as Lincoln's generals never had been, to think in terms of military problems and purposes alone. The soldiers, and warfare itself, were isolated more than ever from politics; the war was an event with political causes, political consequences, and political purposes, but it was never understood this way by military men.

They were not alone. Those who hated war were equally unable to see it in the context of policy. "War is an abomination," cried Oswald G. Villard's *Nation* after the First World War — and no one could disagree — but it was another matter to think one's way to a course of action that would render the abomination less probable, and at least in retrospect it appears that American pacifists and antimilitarists were quite unable in this period to mesh their powerful argument against war with any connected view of the political purposes and proper international policy of the United States. Pacifists and military men alike were proceeding in a vacuum, from the standpoint of the political analyst.

In this, again, they reflected the nation. For war was indeed detached from political purpose in the national attitudes of the 1920's. Military debates were sharp — but they were about the future of specific weapons and branches of the service, not about force and policy, and in any case the debates took place in a budgetary desert. The host of 1918 evaporated; the weapons aged; the promotions stopped, or even reversed; and warfare, discontinuous from policy while it was going on, became an unconsidered off-stage actor once the fighting had stopped. There was thus bred into the professional soldiers of one more generation that deep-seated sense of material undernourishment and personal deprivation which has helped to make many of our military men gluttons for material, and self-indulgent in personal privilege, in times when the desert has bloomed.

The beginning of maturity in our modern thought about military matters dates, again, from 1940. Until then no one, not even the second Roosevelt, the Navy's friend, had closely connected the military position of the United States to real issues of international policy. Since then the process of examination and re-examination has been almost continuous, as events have gradually demonstrated beyond the power of doubt or dissent that military policy and policy as a whole are not only fully intertwined, but also decisive of the nation's future. Circumstance no longer makes the United States safe, and victory is no longer its own justification.

It is true that a part of the demonstration of these propositions has come from great events in which they were ignored. It is now hard to doubt that the Second World War was fought by the United States too much for victory as such, and too little for the fruits of victory. That in partial consequence of wartime attitudes the country disarmed with foolish haste after 1945 seems equally plain. That it is hard to limit war by policy was demonstrated in Korea, and that we really know how to think continuously and pertinently about the relation of force and policy is still far from clear. But the discourse is real now, as it very seldom was in earlier years.

In the last decade, for the first time in our modern history, thinking about foreign affairs has begun to keep pace with events — not in the sense that everything has been predicted or even understood, but in the sense that the gap between what is happening and what is thought about it has been significantly narrowed. As political, economic, and military analysis have forsworn easy answers, and as the overwhelming and enduring importance of foreign affairs has become self-evident, it has been possible for both statesmen and theorists to think and write about these matters with a new clarity and depth.

If a single prophet must be chosen, among statesmen, to exhibit this development, I believe it should be Dean Acheson. In 1946 he put it this way:

> Our name for problems is significant. We call them headaches. You take a powder and they are gone. These pains [of foreign relations] are not like that. They are like the pain of earning a living. They will stay with us until death. We have got to understand that all our lives the danger, the uncertainty, the need for alertness, for effort, for discipline will be upon us.[8]

Construed in these terms, policy becomes a continuous task, and thought about it can escape static generalities.

It is true that notable recent writers on American foreign policy have too often tried to set their observations in a framework of general and universal applicability; by a curious paradox this sort of excessively stern categorizing has frequently occurred among men whose first purpose was to root out the simple-minded follies of earlier periods. Thus George Kennan has correctly criticized the legalistic-moralistic tone and temper of such statesmen as Taft, Wilson, Kellogg, Stimson, and Hull. Treaties of arbitration, treaties renouncing war, reliance upon forms and not on real forces, have drawn his searching fire. Yet he has sometimes seemed to write history as a morality play of his own, in which only blindness and folly prevented sound tactical solutions of interesting political problems like the role of Germany after the First World War. And Hans Morgenthau, ably restoring the problem of power to the center of textbook concern with international relations, and replacing a generation of writers who overemphasized problems of law, organization, and peaceful collaboration, has sometimes sounded as if there were no problem of purpose behind the slogan of "the national interest." Reinhold Niebuhr, probably the most influential single mind in the development of American attitudes which combine moral purpose with a sense of political reality, has sometimes seemed so impatient with visionaries as to be in effect an opponent of all idealism; his analysis of "The Illusion of World Government," for example, undid the intellectual pretensions of a group of fervent zealots active in the years immediately following the Second World War, but it also seemed — a little — to downgrade the importance of searching continuously for some line of action that might lead out of the anarchy of the international world.[9]

Yet on balance the "new realists" have contributed greatly to understanding, and it is notable that their keenest critics are men who do not reject the problem of power or the need for realism, but who insist only that the problems are even harder than the "realistic" analysis suggests.[10] And such men as Kennan, Morgenthau, and Niebuhr have themselves shown repeatedly on all sorts of immediate practical issues that their realism does not exclude a deep concern for the quality and direction of political purpose.

Certainly we have had debates on "realism" and "idealism" in which overstatement has provoked misunderstanding. But these debates have been a surface ripple, compared with the underlying main current of increased understanding, and in the end the common premises of the debaters are, as usual, more illuminating than their differences.

Economic and military thought too have begun to come of age — especially in the sense that increasingly analysis of both sorts of problems occurs within a concern for policy as a whole. Foreign economic policy is no longer seen merely as an instrument of commerce, and economists concerned with foreign affairs are increasingly — necessarily — political economists. It is no longer seen as merely a temporary or accidental matter that the United States should have an active political concern with the impact of its economic decisions abroad, and economic development as much as economic exchange is now well within the purview of thought about our foreign affairs.

Military thought has taken similar strides forward. While clear statement from men still on active service is rare — so much is it cast in terms of the justification of this arm or that — a high level of analysis has been attained by such critics as Bernard Brodie, Klaus Knorr, and (more boldly, if somewhat less convincingly) Henry Kissinger. A similar sophistication begins to appear in the thinking about control and limitation of weapons, mainly in occasional pieces from men who have been close to the problems involved. Military analysis continues to have its extreme positions. Not all soldiers have connected their new and fearful weapons to a rational policy for their management, and the pressures of terror have revived a new neo-pacifism in which unilateral disarmament is urged as the lesser evil. But the main line of thought is between these dangerous and politically unsupported wings.

As other improvements in our work are noted, it is proper to cast a respectful eye backward at the studies which went forward in earlier decades. Circumstances may have limited the impact of the sober and intelligent work which went forward on all these topics, and great events may have shattered particular frames of reference, but it would be quite wrong to suggest that there were no good students of these matters before 1950. All that is argued here is that the students of the last decade have the great advantage of facing a world situation from which the false hopes and shallow assumptions of an earlier age have been largely removed. Moreover, it is likely that our own efforts at understanding also rest on assumptions not all of which will prove durable, and the areas of ignorance and inescapable uncertainty remain very great.[11] Surprises still occur, and most of them, still, are unpleasant. The future comes at us more rapidly than ever, and each year precipitates into the cauldron of world politics new states, new weapons, new pressures of population, and new notions about all of them.

There remains a deeper difficulty in our national situation. Let us suppose it to be true that we have outgrown the simple errors of our fathers, and that we know the world is real and our role in it big and hard. Suppose that in a measure at least we accept the inevitable trials of power, and the responsibilities of economic cooperation and military defense in a world which has made both kinds of effort complex beyond the imagination of earlier centuries. But do we, as a people, combine them in an image of the national purpose which we can understand and by which we can act? The answer must be negative, and the reasons for it are of two kinds.

The first is a general one, and all of us can work at it: It is simply that these matters are very difficult indeed — complex, varied, constantly changing. Weapons alone have undergone a number of revolutions since the Second World War, and even the most backward general no longer expects to replay the Normandy landings. But it is hard for even the most forward-looking to be right about the ways in which force and purpose will connect ten years from now. And in political and social affairs whole continents — like Africa — can appear onstage overnight, to play a role which none dares to predict and few claim to understand. The age of the general "expert" in foreign affairs has only begun, and it is over. We must learn to learn in little bits and to put them together modestly. Yet we must also learn fast.

Large as these tasks are, there is a larger one. Concrete and timely assessments of specific complex questions will not of themselves combine to form "an image of the national purpose." That can only be done by a man, and only one man can do it. Elements of a general policy can come from hundreds of sources, both theoretical and empirical. Preachers and philosophers have as much to suggest as diplomats, economists, and strategists. But the national purpose in the world can be crystallized and communicated, at any given time, only by the President of the United States. Three men in the twentieth century have had this power in greater than ordinary measure: Wilson and the two Roosevelts. Mr. Truman had the gift of practical decision, but his sense of the meaning of what he did was limited. General Eisenhower had good will and basic soundness of instinct, cabined by fiscal timidity and muffled by cloudy perception and statement. Secretaries of State have been variously handicapped — Marshall by soldierly restraint, Acheson by unpopularity partly of his own making, Dulles by self-righteousness and obsession with one enemy. But in any case the task is one for the President — and it is now as urgent as it is large.[12]

17

American Moderns

Irving Howe

I

"I went to the woods," wrote Henry David Thoreau, "because I wished to live deliberately, to front only the essential facts of life, and see if I could not learn what it had to teach and not, when I came to die, discover that I had not lived." It is no mere fancy to suggest that in this one sentence Thoreau released the dominant concern of nineteenth-century American writing, especially that segment of it composed in New England under the influence of the transcendental philosophers. Not many American writers have cared, literally, to go to the woods: Hawthorne would have preferred a warm study. But in the mid-nineteenth century most of them believed that, by discovering a new freedom in the openness of the natural world, man could reach out toward both God and his inmost self — the two were not always kept distinct in Emerson's New England — without having first to be greatly concerned about the intervening barriers of society. The first major outburst of American writing, as it comes to us in the work of Emerson, Hawthorne, Melville, and Whitman, is at once intimate, dealing with problems of personal being, and metaphysical, seeking to establish a fresh sense of man's relation to the universe. But of social forms, conventions, institutions, ambitions, and burdens there is very little.

Only during the last decades of the nineteenth century does the idea of society as an overwhelming and inescapable force appear in American literature. The important writers of this period differ radically in their responses to society: Mark Twain looks upon it as insidiously enclosing and asphyxiating, Henry James regards it as both the solvent of innocence and the necessary theater for high drama, William Dean Howells treats it simply as the neutral and sometimes benign medium of daily existence, and for Frank Norris it becomes a mysterious agency dispensing pleasure and destruction with promiscuous brutishness. But all of these writers, both those who announce their contempt and those who relax in acceptance, confront society with a vigilance that is new to American literature.

In two later novelists, Theodore Dreiser and Edith Wharton, the idea of society becomes a central preoccupation. Though utterly different in literary method and social opinion, Dreiser in *Sister Carrie* and Mrs. Wharton in *The House of Mirth* rely on the same assumption: that values, whether traditional or modernist, desirable or false, can be tested in a novel by dramatizing the relationships between fixed social groups and mobile characters. Neither writer would so much as think to question the presence or impact of these social groups as they form part of the examined structure of class society. In both novels "the heart of fools is in the house of mirth," the heartbreak house of the modern city; and as Carrie Meeber and Lily Bart make their way up and down the social hierarchy, their stories take on enormous weights of implication because we are ready to assume some relationship between the observed scale of social place and the evolving measure of moral value. It is this assumption that has been a major resource of most modern novelists: for without some such assumption there could hardly occur that symbolic compression of incident, the readiness to suppose that event *X* stands for meaning *Y*, which is a prerequisite for the very existence of the novel.

In their desire to amass social detail and their commitment to the view that the power of circumstance is a power over the human soul, Dreiser and Mrs. Wharton are closer to the central tradition of the nineteenth-century European novel than to the American writers who preceded or followed them. Unlike the Melville of *Moby-Dick* or the Hemingway of *The Sun Also Rises*, they believe that the web of society is the true locale of man's destiny and that his salvation can be found, if found at all, within society. But Dreiser and Mrs. Wharton are not mere passive recorders, mere photographers of the world as it is. Like every other sensitive writer of the past hundred years, they also need to question — even if, in some of Mrs. Wharton's novels, strongly to reaffirm — traditional views governing our moral existence. They too are involved in that peculiarly anxious and persistent search for values which forms so prominent an aspect of the moral history of our time — the search for secure assumptions, unbroken justifications, which can give direction and coherence to human conduct.

II

That search is by now not only a familiar but an expected component of the serious novel; a tradition has been established in which it figures conspicuously and often omnivorously, so that readers have come, with a certain loss of historical perspective, to regard it as a necessary part of literary experience.

For the generation of American writers, however, that began publishing shortly after the First World War, the crisis of traditional values was no longer a problem in quite the way it had been for writers in the late nineteenth century. By now the crisis of values was an accepted fact, and therefore not so much a painful conclusion toward which their novels and poems might reach as a necessary assumption from which their novels and poems had to begin.

This attitude found an important anticipation in the stories of Sherwood Anderson, a writer who began to publish only a few years before Hemingway and Fitzgerald but who was clearly a man of an older generation, his mind and temper having been formed in the rural Midwest. The younger writers would soon be brushing Anderson aside as a sentimentalist, which in part he was; but at his best, in the haunting tales and sketches he wrote about American loneliness, he helped prepare the way for the modernist writing of the twenties.

Anderson did this through the example of his life, particularly that moment of climax, soon to become a legend in our culture, when at the age of thirty-six he abandoned his paint factory, wife, and children to strike out for the bohemia of Chicago, devote himself to the cult of art, and thereby, as he might have said, "front only the essential facts of life." His work, too, set a significant example. *Winesburg, Ohio* is a classic American portrait of human bewilderment, a parable about the loss of love conveying a vision of the native landscape cluttered with dead stumps, twisted oddities, grotesque and pitiful remnants of human creatures. Confronted with this world of back-street grotesques, for whom nothing can happen because everything is too late, one hardly feels it enough to speak of a crisis of values. Things have gone beyond that, and what *Winesburg* reveals is the debris of crisis, the cost of collapse. As it abandons the naturalist impulse of a Dreiser to represent society in overwhelming detail and moves toward an expressionist tableau of human deformity, *Winesburg* helps to confirm the younger writers in their sense of American life and their desire to find, through their fiction, a way of imaginatively transcending it.

Perhaps the most vivid account of this new generation of writers, a generation that begins to publish after the First World War and reaches its finest achievement during the mid-twenties, has come from the poet and critic John Peale Bishop. In his essay "The Missing All" — the title is taken from an Emily Dickinson poem that begins "The missing All prevented me/ From missing minor things" — Bishop described how the young literary men returning from the war felt they had been cheated not merely of health and time but, more important, of truth and honor. They formed "really the first literary generation in America. There had been groups before, but they were not united by a communion of youth, a sense of experience shared and enemies encountered. . . ." They felt themselves to be cut off from the world of all who had come immediately before them, all who held power and spoke with authority. They were not in rebellion against the political order of Western capitalism, but in revulsion from its moral disorder. As Bishop wrote:

> The most tragic thing about the war was not that it made so many dead men, but that it destroyed the tragedy of death. Not only did the young suffer in the war, but every abstraction that would have sustained and given dignity to their suffering. The war made the traditional morality inacceptable; it did not annihilate it; it revealed

> its immediate inadequacy. So that at its end the survivors were left to face, as they could, a world without values.[1]

This sense of having been betrayed and left adrift was powerful among young people in all the Western countries, where it formed the psychic foundation for that "communion of youth" Bishop so keenly observed. It is one of the strongest feelings behind the writing of the twenties, and nowhere has it been expressed so poignantly as in the suppressed introduction T. E. Lawrence would write for *The Seven Pillars of Wisdom:*

> We were wrought up with ideas inexpressible and vaporous, but to be fought for. We lived many lives in those whirling campaigns, never sparing ourselves any good or evil: yet when we achieved and the new world dawned, the old men came out again and took from us our victory and remade it in the likeness of the former world they knew. Youth could win, but had not learned to keep, and was pitiably weak against age. We stammered that we had worked for a new heaven and a new earth, and they thanked us kindly and made their peace.

When Emily Dickinson spoke of "the missing All," she meant the God of her fathers, the God of Christianity; when Bishop borrowed her phrase, he had in mind not merely the image of God but a whole way of life that had been the heritage of classical Christianity, even if hardened and distorted in America by Puritanism, and that was now clearly in the process of crumbling. This perception — it is more a perception than a belief or idea — is seldom the dominant subject in the work of Hemingway and his contemporaries, but it is the dominant fact that needs to be known about their work. It is the premise from which they start, a premise that strikes them as so entirely obvious they feel no need to demonstrate or dramatize it. They do not even discuss it — only their critics do. The hopelessness of the familiar social world, the pointlessness of trying to change it, and the necessity for some credo of private disaffiliation (Hemingway's "separate peace") are assumptions in their work quite as the need to grapple with inherited but fading Christian pieties forms an assumption in the work of Hawthorne and Melville.

For writers like Hemingway, Fitzgerald, Cummings, and the early Dos Passos there could no longer be any question of clinging to traditional values. But more important, there could not even be a question of trying to find a new set of values: they were beyond such ambitions or delusions, they knew it was their lot to spend their lives in uncertainty, and the problem that troubled them most was how to do this without violating their feelings about courage and dignity. To be sure, the very desire to find an honorable style of survival in a time of moral confusion indicates a certain strength of moral intent, and the hope of preserving courage and dignity while experiencing a crack-up of values implies the continued hold of certain values. Even these, however, become extremely problematic when they are raised to the level of a troubled self-consciousness.

The writers we are here discussing went through just this kind of crisis. Almost by instinct they backed away from large-scale beliefs or ideals: they had had enough of rhetoric, enough of "idealism," and lived in a magnified fear of platitudes. They had given up, if they had ever had it, the hope of achieving a coherent and ordered moral perspective; they were concerned with something more desperate, more fragmentary, more immediate. They were struggling to survive, as men of sensibility who had lost their way and knew it. They saw their task as a defensive one: the preservation of residual decencies even when they could not quite provide sufficient reasons for wishing to preserve them. And if that seemed too ambitious, they were ready to settle for a severe insistence upon keeping honest among, and with, themselves. Though often bohemian and sometimes dissolute, these writers nourished a sense of their calling as austere and finally as monastic as Flaubert's. It was as if they had taken upon themselves the obligation to keep alive an undefiled word, not because they grasped its full meaning but because they felt that to keep it alive would allow others, later on, to grasp it.

The best of these writers were in search of what I propose to call a *moral style*. I mean by this improvised phrase: a series of tentative embodiments in conduct of a moral outlook they could not bring to full statement; or a series of gestures and rituals that would be made to serve as a substitute for a moral outlook that could no longer be summoned; or a fragmentary code of behavior by which to survive decently, as if there were — the drama consisting in the fact that there is not — a secure morality behind it. The search for a moral style, which I take to be fundamental to the best American writing between the First World War and the depression years, is a search undertaken by men who have learned that a life constricted to the standard of *faute de mieux* can still be a rigorous, even an exalting obligation. Or to put it in more homely terms, the idea of moral style is a twentieth-century equivalent — only far more urgent and desperate — of the New England notion of "making do." How one "makes do," whether with grace or falsity, courage or evasion, is the great problem.

III

The great problem, above all, in the work of the most influential American novelist of our time, Ernest Hemingway. Of all the writers who began to appear in print after the First World War, Hemingway seems best to have captured the tone of human malaise in an era of war and revolution; yet it is noteworthy that, while doing so, he rarely attempted a frontal or sustained representation of life in the United States, for he seems always to have understood that common experience was not within his reach. By evoking the "essence" of the modern experience through fables of violence that had their settings in Africa and Europe, Hemingway touched the imagination of American readers whose lives, for all their apparent ordinariness, were also marked by that desperation which would become his literary signature and which is, indeed, central to all "modernist" writing. These readers, in turn, often tried to endow their lives with meaning and value by copying the gestures of defiance, the devotion to clenched styles of survival, which they found in Hemingway's work. Because he had penetrated so deeply to the true dilemmas of the age, Hemingway soon began to influence its experience — not for the first time, life came to imitate art.

Who, by now, is not familiar with the shape and colors of Hemingway's world? His recurrent figures are literary expatriates in the wastes of *nada*, bullfighters who have lost their nerve and skill, rich young men without purpose, wounded soldiers who would sign "a separate peace" in order to withdraw from the world's battles, distraught young women grasping at physical sensations as if they were a mode of salvation, tired gangsters, homeless café-sitters, stricken Spaniards: men and women always on the margin, barely able to get by from day to day. There emerges from this gallery of figures the characteristic hero of the Hemingway world: the hero who is wounded but bears his wound in silence, who is sensitive but scorns to devalue his feelings into words, who is defeated but finds a remnant of dignity in an honest confrontation of defeat. In almost all of Hemingway's books there is a tacit assumption that the deracination of our life is so extreme, everyone must find a psychic shelter of his own, a place in which to make a last stand.

But note: to make a last stand — for if defeat is accepted in Hemingway's world, humiliation and rout are not. His fictions present moments of violence, crisis, and death, yet these become occasions for a stubborn, quixotic resistance through which the human capacity for satisfying its self-defined obligations is both asserted and tested. "Grace under pressure": this becomes the ideal stance, the hoped-for moral style, of Hemingway's characters. Or as he puts it in describing Romero's bullfighting style in *The Sun Also Rises:* "the holding of his purity of line through the maximum of exposure." All of Hemingway's novels and stories can be read as variants upon this theme, efforts to find improvised gestures and surrogate codes for the good, the true, even the heroic.

The Hemingway hero is a man who has surrendered the world in order to remake a tiny part of it, the part in which he can share honor and manner with a few chosen comrades. Jake Barnes, Frederick Henry, most of Hemingway's heroes, are men who have seen too much, who want no more of this world and now seek to act out the choreography of heroism as a kind of private charade. The bullring becomes, for some of them, a substitute for the social world; the combat with the bull, a version of the manly testing which this world does not allow; the circle of *aficionados*, a monastic order of crippled heroes.

It may be true, as Edmund Wilson claims, that Hemingway shows a taste for scenes of killing, but at his best he wishes to squeeze from them some precarious assertion — or perhaps more accurately, some credible facsimile — of value. The Hemingway hero turns to his code, a mixture of stylized repression and inarticulate decencies, so that manners become the outer sign of an inexpressible heroism and gestures the substance of a surviving impulse to moral good. And what is this code? The determination to be faithful to one's own experience, not to fake emotions or pretend to sentiments that are not there; the belief that loyalty to one's few friends matters more than the claims and dogmas of the world; the insistence upon avoiding self-pity and public displays; the assumption that the most precious feelings cannot be articulated and that if the attempt is made they turn "rotten"; the desire to salvage from the collapse of social life a version of stoicism that can make suffering bearable; the hope that in direct physical sensation, the cold water of the creek in which one fishes or the purity of the wine made by Spanish peasants, there will be found an experience that can resist corruption (which is one reason Hemingway approaches these sensations with a kind of propitiatory awe, seldom venturing epithets more precise than "fine" and "nice," as if he feared to risk a death through naming). Life now consists in keeping an equilibrium with one's nerves, and that requires a tight control over one's desires, so that finally one learns what one cannot have and then even not to want it, and above all, not to make a fuss while learning. As Jake Barnes says in *The Sun Also Rises:* "I did not care what it was all about. All I wanted was how to live in it."

A code pressing so painfully on the nervous system and so constricted to symbolic gratifications is almost certain to break down — indeed, in his best work Hemingway often shows that it does. After a time, however, his devotion to this code yields him fewer and fewer psychic returns, since it is in the nature of the quest for a moral style that the very act of approaching or even finding it sets off a series of discoveries as to its radical limitations. As a result the later Hemingway, in his apparent satisfaction with the moral style he has improvised, begins to imitate and caricature himself: the manner becomes that of the tight-lipped tough guy, and the once taut and frugal prose turns corpulent.

At first glance F. Scott Fitzgerald's novels seem closer to the social portraiture of Edith Wharton than to the moral fables of Hemingway. Few American writers have commanded so fine a sense of social gradations, not merely in terms of class relationships but even more in the subtle nuances of status which in our country often replace or disguise class relationships. Fitzgerald is a writer very much of the historical moment, the laureate of the twenties, the *wunderkind* of the jazz age, and his talent, profligacy, and tragic personal fate seem symbolic tokens of that historical moment. But in addition to the Fitzgerald who made of his "extreme environmental sense" a foundation of his gift for rendering social manners, there was the Fitzgerald who had been seized and driven by a vision of earthly beatitude which allowed him, all through his life, neither rest nor fulfillment.

Fitzgerald was an eternal adolescent infatuated with the surfaces of material existence. He worshiped money, he worshiped glamour, he worshiped youth, but above all, he worshiped the three together in a totality of false values. Like Keats before the candy shop, he stared with a deep yearning at the blessings of the rich, the ease and security with which they moved through the years, apparently free from the tyranny of work and the burden of circumstance, and thereby enabled to cultivate their own sense of what life might be. He thought that in the American dream of money there lay imbedded a possibility of human realization, because money means power and when you have power you can do anything — you can even, as Jay Gatsby supposes, obliterate the past. He felt that youth was the greatest of human possessions, indeed a kind of *accomplishment* for which the young should be praised. His work was a glittering celebration of immaturity, the American fear of aloneness and limitation.

The preceding paragraph condenses the kind of critical attacks to which Fitzgerald was subject during his career: it is true, all of it true, but not the whole truth about his writing.

For the man who composed *The Great Gatsby* and *The Last Tycoon* was a writer who had gone to war against the unexamined convictions of his youth, and at a terrible price in suffering and blood, had triumphed. This writer noted that "all the stories that came into my head had a touch of disaster in them — the lovely young creatures in my novels went to ruin, the diamond mountains of my short stories blew up, my millionaires were as beautiful and damned as Thomas Hardy's peasants." Fitzgerald knew — it was to anchor this knowledge that he put Nick Carraway into *The Great Gatsby* as narrator — that the vitality and ambition of Jay Gatsby were lavished on "a vast, vulgar and meretricious beauty." He knew — it was to release this knowledge that he created the looming figure of Monroe Stahr in *The Last Tycoon* — that "life is essentially a cheat and its conditions are those of defeat, and that the redeeming things are not 'happiness and pleasure' but the deeper satisfactions that come out of struggle." As one of Fitzgerald's critics, Andrews Wanning, has remarked: "his style keeps reminding you

. . . of his sense of the enormous beauty of which life, suitably ornamented, is capable; and at the same time of his judgment as to the worthlessness of the ornament and the corruptibility of the beauty."

The preceding paragraph condenses the kind of critical praise with which Fitzgerald was honored in the years after his death: it is true, all of it true, but only if one also remembers how accurate were the attacks against him.

Yet there is more to Fitzgerald than this counterposition of early illusion and later self-discovery. In his best writing — which consists not merely of one or two novels and several stories but also of a succession of extraordinary passages appearing almost anywhere in his books, like sudden flares of beauty and wisdom — Fitzgerald confronted both early illusion and later self-discovery from a certain ironic distance. ("The test of a first-rate intelligence," he once wrote, "is the ability to hold two opposed ideas in his mind at the same time, and still retain the ability to function.") Supremely American that he was, Fitzgerald tried to preserve something of the sense of human potentiality which had first led him to be enticed by the vulgarity of money and the shallowness of youth. He knew how impotent, and finally irrelevant, was that depreciation of material values in the name of some moralistic ideal which had become a set attitude in American thought and writing; he sensed that, endlessly rehearsed, this depreciation had actually come to reinforce the power of material values, partly because it could not come to grips with the society that drove men to concern themselves with money and partly because any claim of indifference to such a concern was in America likely to be a mere Sunday pose. As Fitzgerald had worshiped wealth, youth, and glamour, they were surely false; as he later turned upon them, his turning was true; but even in his turning he kept some essential part of his earlier worship, and — one is inclined to say — he was right to do so.

Where Hemingway had tried to salvage a code for men at the margin of society, Fitzgerald tried to construct a vision of human possibility at its center. He enjoyed neither doctrinal support in religion nor a buoying social goal nor even a firm awareness of traditional culture that might have helped him sustain and enlarge this vision. Necessarily, it was sporadic, marred and precarious, more a series of flickering intuitions than assured values. Fitzgerald was struggling to achieve something of vast importance for our society, even though he could hardly have named it and we, in turn, can seldom enlarge upon it. He tried to create a moral style out of the sheer urgencies of desire and talent, and finally it came to a search, at the very least, for a mode of gracefulness in outer life and, at the very best, for some token of grace in a world where grace could no longer be provided by anyone but man himself.

William Faulkner, last of the three major American novelists to begin writing in the decade after the First World War, enjoyed a more secure sense of social place and moral tradition than either Hemingway or Fitzgerald. The impact of the fundamentalist Protestantism of the South was still fresh to his imagination, even if more as a discipline than a dogma; the power of a commanding historical myth, the myth of heroic Southern resistance and defeat in the Civil War, was everywhere to be felt in the world of his youth; and the idea of kinship, a deep tacit awareness of the bonds of family and clan, was still a reality in his early experience, as it would later be in the series of novels set in his imaginary Yoknapatawpha County.

In one major respect, however, Faulkner began as a thoroughly "modern" writer, caught up with the same emotions of uprootedness and uncertainties of value which afflicted Hemingway: his early novels *Soldier's Pay* and *Sartoris* reflect, though not nearly so well as those of Hemingway, the belief of a generation that it is adrift, "lost" in the aftermath of a terrible war. Provincial though the early Faulkner was, he had nevertheless been bruised by the troubles of the outer world, and for all his attachment to the Southern homeland he always retained a lively conviction about the pervasiveness of malaise in modern life. But as a man and writer he had available resources which both Hemingway and Fitzgerald lacked. Where Hemingway turned in his novels and stories to a marginal world he had partly observed and partly imagined, and Fitzgerald tried to impose his vision of human possibility upon such recalcitrant material as the lives of the very rich and very young, Faulkner could still turn back to a living segment of American society — back to the familiar places of the South, the homeland he knew with an intimacy beyond love or hate. Until shortly before he began to write, the South had possessed a compact and homogeneous culture, and the exploration of the virtues and guilts of this culture, as well as the testing of its myth, became for him a lifelong preoccupation.

Each of Faulkner's novels written during his great creative outburst — from *The Sound and the Fury* in 1929 to *Go Down, Moses* in 1942 — represents an increasingly severe and fundamental criticism of the homeland. Not merely of the South alone, to be sure; for when Faulkner composed his despairing estimate of social loss in *The Sound and the Fury* he was also portraying some of the central disabilities of modern civilization. But the foreground subject in the Yoknapatawpha novels is the immediate present and recent past of the South: the way in which its claims to grandeur prove to be aspects of delusion, its pretensions to gentility elements of corruption, and its compulsive racialism a poison coursing through its whole moral life. In the novels written during this period Faulkner ranged through almost every area of Southern life, beginning with a wish for nostalgia and ending with the bleakness of accepted truth.

At every point in these novels Faulkner had available — or wrote as if there were still available — persons, places, and principles to which he could look for moral support and standards. He *turned back*, as neither Hemingway nor Fitzgerald could, to the hillsmen, the poor farmers, the Negroes, and the children, all of whom seemed to him apart and pure, surviving in the interstices of a decadent society, unable significantly to change its course, yet vital enough to serve him as figures of moral and dramatic contrast. The MacCallums, Dilsey, Cash Bundren, Lena Grove, Ike McCaslin, Lucas Beauchamp, Miss Habersham, Ratliff — these are some of the characters in Faulkner's world who embody in their conduct some portion of goodness and charity. Defeated as they may often be, they are nevertheless *there*, and because they are there Faulkner did not yet need to invent a moral style in the sense that Hemingway and Fitzgerald did.

Now, in what is obviously a simplification, one can regard the whole development of Faulkner's Yoknapatawpha saga as a gradual discovery that these figures, whatever their attractions and virtues, prove less and less competent as moral guides for the contemporary world. That Faulkner clearly sees as much is suggested by the history of Ratliff, the choric figure in the Snopes trilogy who is so marvelously self-assured in *The Hamlet* but so fumbling in *The*

Mansion when he must approach the modern South. Slowly, Faulkner has been exhausting the psychic and moral resources he had supposed to be present for him in the world of Yoknapatawpha; slowly, he has been emerging to the same needs and bewilderments that other writers now feel. The idea of a return to primitive simplicity retains its strength in Faulkner's books insofar as it is kept by him at a certain distance from the present, or can be recognized as metaphor rather than prescription. In his later books Faulkner still turns for moral contrast and support to the kinds of characters he had admired in the earlier ones — the back-country saints, the earthy madonnas, the Negroes, the children, the good simple men. But now it is with very little of the old conviction: you need only contrast his use of Nancy in *Requiem for a Nun* with Dilsey in *The Sound and the Fury*. He turns to such figures because he has nowhere else to go, but he turns to them, I would suggest, not with any firm conviction as to their moral power but simply in the hope of imposing on and through them his hopes and standards. With the figures who had once been for him the bulwarks of life he must now try to "make do," late in his career, and not very skillfully, learn to improvise a moral style.

IV

The concern with moral style is also notable in modern American poetry. But there is an important difference: a theme which in a work of fiction must be represented through an action, can be the very substance of the poem itself. One is always aware that a work of fiction is "about" something, for there is always a distance between the representation and that which is being represented; while in a poem this distance is frequently less visible and sometimes not at all. A poem is more likely to approach self-sufficiency; it incorporates its subject through style, meter, rhythm, and image, and is thereby less available to paraphrase than a work of fiction.

In a poem the search for moral style, if it occurs at all, is likely to be evident not so much in the subject as in the writing from line to line. In Hart Crane's poetry there is neither explicit statement nor representation of the theme I have been discussing here, yet a number of poems in *White Buildings* and parts of "The Bridge" would seem inordinately opaque unless one read them with the assumption that Crane is searching for some supportive mode of valuation, some tentative myth for deracinated men. T. S. Eliot's poetry contains brilliant vignettes of moral failure and inadequacy, but the idea of moral style is present neither as subject nor solution, for in Eliot, particularly in his earlier work, the poem itself becomes an act equivalent to moral style. And in Allen Tate's poetry much of the violence of language is due to a recognition that moral style, which cannot be had, would be inadequate even if it could be: so that his work strains, as it were, toward an anticipation of disappointment.

But it is in the poetry of Wallace Stevens that the idea of moral style, though not of course the term itself, seems to be employed with some deliberateness. At the base of Stevens's work, as a force barely acknowledged yet always felt, lies a pressing awareness of human disorder in our time — but an awareness radically different from that of most writers. Rarely does it emerge in his poems as a dramatized instance or fiction; Stevens seldom tries and almost never manages to evoke the modern disorder through representations of moral conduct or social conflict. Lacking that "novelistic" gift for portraiture-in-depth which is so valuable to a good many twentieth-century poets, Stevens does not examine society closely or even notice it directly for any length of time; he simply absorbs the "idea" of it. A trained connoisseur in chaos, he sees no need to linger before the evidence: other writers have long accumulated it, sorted it and passed their judgment. And that is why it seems neither a paradox nor a conceit to say that in Stevens's poetry the social world may be dimly apprehended, yet a perspective upon history is brilliantly maintained: history as it filters through his consciousness of living and writing at a given time. The disorder that occupies the foreground of so much modern literature is calmly accepted by Stevens, appearing in his work not as a dominant subject but a pressure upon all subjects.

Stevens is sharply responsive to the crisis of belief which has troubled so many sensitive persons in the twentieth century, but he is not himself directly involved in it. He knows and feels it, but he has begun to move beyond it. When he writes that

The death of Satan was a tragedy
For the imagination. A capital
Negation destroyed him in his tenement
And, with him, many blue phenomena . . .[2]

the force of these lines is clearly secular, releasing an attitude of humane comedy that lies beyond any deep or continuous involvement in the crisis of belief. The lines are a little blasphemous, since it is hard to imagine a religious writer making quite this complaint about the consequences of the death of Satan. Here, as elsewhere in Stevens, a secular imagination measures with notable composure the losses it has suffered from the exhaustion of religious myths and symbols, and then hopes that emotional equivalents can be found in

One's self and the mountains of one's land

— which is very much what Hemingway and, less directly, Fitzgerald were hoping for.

Accepting the uncertainties and confusions which in other writers cause so much anxiety, Stevens poses as his ultimate question not, what shall we do about the crisis of belief, but rather, how shall we live with and perhaps beyond it? To answer — perhaps to ambush — this question, he keeps returning to the theme of the relation between reality and imagination. Not because he is interested in epistemological forays as such — though he is; nor because he is fascinated with the creative process — though that too; but because his main concern is with discovering and, through his poetry, *enacting* the possibilities for human self-renewal in an impersonal and recalcitrant age.

How recalcitrant that age can be Stevens knew very well. The fragmenting of personality, the loss of the self in its social roles, the problem of discovering one's identity amid a din of public claims — all this, so obsessively rehearsed in modern literature, is the premise from which Stevens moves to poetry. The elaborate conceptual maneuvers of his longer poems have as their objective not any conclusions in the realm of thought but revelations in the realm of experience. They are written to rediscover the human gift for self-creation; they try to enlarge our margin of autonomy; they are incitements to sharpening our sense of what remains possible to us even today. For Stevens the writing of poems becomes a means of wresting convictions of selfhood; and when he writes about the writing of poetry, he needs to be read as if the idea of poetry were a force able to liberate us from the tyranny of mechanical life and slow dying — as if the act of poetry were itself the sought-for moral style. Stevens is a revolutionist of the imagination, demonstrating through poetry the possibilities of a renewed consciousness, the way the mind can reach out toward fresh modes of awareness and thereby "make" its own life from moment to moment.

The search for moral style is recurrent in modern writing. It places a tremendous burden upon literature, almost the burden of demanding that literature provide us with norms of value we find impossible to locate in experience. It tends to demand from literature a kind of prophetic gratification which would have seemed decidedly strange to earlier generations of readers. Yet precisely this aspect of the work of such modern figures as Hemingway, Fitzgerald, Faulkner, and Stevens makes them seem so close to us, so very much the spokesmen for our needs and our desires.

18

The Rise of Neo-Orthodoxy

William Lee Miller

Religion in America in the 1920's appears, from the standpoint of the theology of the 1960's, to be a strange and uncongenial phenomenon. That was another world. There is a greater change, from then until now, than can be explained just by the passage of time. A contemporary religious person may feel a greater affinity with more remote periods: with the Puritans (now restudied and rehabilitated); with Jonathan Edwards (no longer the dark anachronism of Parrington's chapter); with the earlier and more serious proponents of the Social Gospel. The vast gulf between the twenties and the sixties is not made by time alone, but by a deep opposition in the currents of thought. The twenties symbolize what much of contemporary religious thought sets itself firmly against: a religion comfortably and uncritically accommodated to the thought and life of the bourgeois society around it.

If we ask what historical fact most explains this change, this gulf between then and now, the primary answer lies in the realm of ideas.

It is the profound reconstruction of Protestant theology that, for want of a better term, goes by the name of "neo-orthodoxy."

In this essay we examine this "neo-orthodoxy" (or "post-liberalism") in its American setting. First, we indicate the historical shape of religion in America — perhaps seen especially clearly in the twenties — into which this new theological current came; second, we indicate some characteristics of this movement and look at its most American and interesting representative, Reinhold Niebuhr; third, we examine the contemporary shape of religion in America, of which this theological movement is the most important part. Finally, we comment critically on the whole development, especially in its relation to American society.

I

Characterizations of decades, of course, are always a little suspect; they are "impressionistic," and plenty of evidence to contradict the generalization can usually be found. No doubt religion in America in the 1920's exhibited somewhere most of the characteristics of religion in other times; no doubt many devoted people found something real and deep in the religion of the American twenties; no doubt the negative picture one now gets is influenced by the present angle of vision. But, still, that picture is clear. One historian of the twenties writes: "With the possible exception of the great religious depression of the Revolutionary epoch (1770–1800), there was probably never a time in American history when less heed was paid to the message of the churches." He adds: "At no time did it so deserve to be ignored."[1]

To interpret what happened in this period, and before and after, one might look at the best book on religion in this country, H. Richard Niebuhr's *The Kingdom of God in America.* Niebuhr, writing from within the Christian community, and interpreting its inner history in its own terms, sees the history of Christianity here as a *movement* (not an organization or idea) described by the phrase that is the title of his book and appearing only partially — inadequately — in the institutions and ideas "in which men seek to fix it." In the pattern of this movement in American Christianity (and throughout Christian history, in fact) periods of institutionalization, crystallization, even petrification, follow upon the prophetic, dynamic new departures that recurrently appear. These phenomena of institutionalization are seen to have an ambiguous character: "On the one hand they are genuine efforts to conserve for postrevolutionary generations the gains made by a revolutionary movement. . . . Yet institutions can never conserve without betraying the movements from which they proceed."[2] These alternations cannot be exactly identified, of course, or neatly set off from each other, or given precise dates; they overlap and mix with each other. But perhaps we can use this framework of Dr. Niebuhr's to understand, in a very general way, what happened in the twenties. The prevailing movement, liberal Protestantism, had by then become institutionalized and conventionalized; the revolutionary movement of a previous generation, it had become static. The gains it had made in a break from the literalism and narrowness of a conventional orthodoxy were consolidated and made secure, but the liberalism that made those gains had lost its punch.

This liberal Protestantism had by then a considerable history. In a drastic oversimplification, one may see the mainstream of American Protestantism as a Puritanism turning first into an evangelical free-church Protestantism and then into this liberal Protestantism. This last turn came, here in the United States, at some time in the second half of the nineteenth century, later than liberal Protestantism came to the fore in Europe. One indication of the date of the change here is this observation by an older historian of the "New England Theology" (i.e., the Calvinism, modified by revivalism, following in the line of Jonathan Edwards): "In 1880 the chairs of theology at all the Congregational and some of the Presbyterian seminaries were occupied by adherents of the New England school, and fifteen years later every one had been filled by some one of an entirely different temper."[3] The new temper was liberal. Throughout the later nineteenth century this new liberal or "modern" perspective was growing; by the turn of the century it had become centrally important; in the first two decades of the twentieth century it was in its heyday.

The picture one now gets of "liberal Protestantism" within many Protestant theological circles is overwhelmingly negative; "liberalism," in reference to theology, is almost an epithet. Liberalism sometimes appears as the first, and only, break in a straight, doctrinal line from the Reformation, or maybe from Biblical times; it appears as a great falling off, the single detour in the straight road of orthodox Protestant Christian history. The reasons for this attitude are these: that liberalism is the immediately previous position against which minds are now in reaction; that the liberalism against which the reaction comes is that of a late, static, complacent phase; and that American liberal Protestantism was peculiarly prone to appear to be, and perhaps to become, the "culture religion" against which contemporary neo-orthodoxy most vigorously contends.

But perhaps it is better to see this movement not as the one falling off, but, as Richard Niebuhr does, as another in a series of positive new developments in Protestant history. Originally this liberal Protestantism must have been dynamic, powerful, needed — in the words of the movement itself, "prophetic." As over against a mechanical revivalism that was running downhill toward Billy Sunday, it must have come as a great new insight to think instead of the Christian nurture that carefully trains for the person's whole life. As over against an obscurantist Biblicism, it must have been a great liberation to accept the "higher criticism" — that is, the application of critical intelligence and scientific method to the Bible itself. As over against wooden dogmatisms it must have been a great discovery to see Christianity not in terms of abstract creeds but of ethics, of life, of the real world. The new liberal awareness of the "ethical teachings" and the humanity of Jesus, must have been a revelation to those who had heard only of the supernatural Christ of the creeds; the idea of a Kingdom of God *on earth* must have been a powerful vision to those who had heard only of an otherworldly, individualistic religion.

As these characteristic themes of liberal Protestantism (the immanence of God, the humanity of Jesus, the compatibility of Christianity with science and the modern world, the priority of ethics over doctrine) became conventional, however, they came to have quite another significance. Richard Niebuhr wrote: "In the course of succeeding generations the heritage of faith with which liberalism had started was used up. The liberal children of liberal fathers needed to operate with ever diminishing capital."[4] Liberalism, in protest, built on pre-liberal substance; liberalism triumphant, institutionalized, became empty, and defensive. The period of the twenties may be a sample of the latter.

An indication — and perhaps also a cause — of the lack of vitality and creativity in the Protestantism of the period was the preoccupation with the Fundamentalist-Modernist controversy. Fundamentalism is the movement that is explicitly and centrally built on a total rejection of liberalism. It is the reactionary movement that responded negatively to modern thought, especially to scientific thought and to the critical examination of the Bible. It held on to revivalism and to a moralistic, legalistic, individualistic ethic, and to a rigid doctrinal core (the fundamentals) in a wooden, mechanical way; the movement, separated off, by definition, from all liberal and modernizing tendencies, became the twentieth-century precipitate of all that was backward-looking and anti-intellectual in the evangelical Protestantism of the nineteenth century. Ironically, this "old-time religion" is really very modern: it requires the modern liberal, scientific opponent to come into being. It has come to be, through an affinity of mind and through monied sources of support, reactionary in social and political as well as in religious matters. The Scopes trial in 1925 symbolizes the rather irrelevant battles that had to be fought with Fundamentalism in the period. Liberal Protestantism, facing that opponent, was much less meaningful than the liberalism that fought its way against a more vital earlier evangelical faith. In many areas then — and now — a rather rigid Fundamentalism and rather empty Liberalism feed on each other.

Another indication of the state of Protestantism in America prior to the rise of neo-orthodoxy is the Prohibition experiment. Temperance and antisaloon crusades have a long American history, of course, but in the fight to maintain Prohibition once it was enacted, something new appeared: Prohibition as "a surrogate for the social gospel."[5] As historian Paul Carter shows, Prohibition did grow — in part — out of the latter days of that most dynamic, reformist part of liberalism, the Social Gospel movement. The connection is hard for many contemporary minds to make, but in the twenties Prohibition was a cause in which social gospel liberals could join conservatives and fundamentalists in a kind of united free-church Protestant front. The liberals could see the defense of Prohibition as a humanitarian effort, opposing another "interest" (the liquor interest) and another "social" evil. In a prosperous, conservative period of "normalcy" this issue could drain off much of the reforming zeal that had once asked fundamental questions about the whole structure of the society.

Thus liberal Protestantism followed the course of most historical movements, once new and radical, becoming tame and well domesticated in later years. The domestication of this particular movement, however, proceeded much further than in the ordinary case, since it found itself in such an extraordinarily congenial environment. The characteristic themes and attitudes of liberal Protestantism coincided almost perfectly with characteristic themes and attitudes of American secular culture. Liberal Protestantism is "tolerant" and inclined to deprecate creedal-doctrinal distinctions; it is "democratic" and humanistic in ethics and strongly inclined to reduce religion to ethics; it is optimistic and progressive, taking a sanguine view of man and society: in all this it fits very well into American ideas. Liberal Protestantism, which explicitly intended to be hospitable to secular culture, was also implicitly quite in tune with this particular secular culture; therefore its rapprochement with the American ethos proceeded very far. From the point of view of those who want Christianity to show forth a dimension beyond and critical of the society, there came to be a need for a new movement to challenge liberalism.

II

Beginning in the thirties, and increasingly ever since, there has come a fundamentally different atmosphere, if not in all of religion, at least in theology. The usual name for this new theological atmosphere is "neo-orthodoxy."

The word is inadequate and may mislead; it is usually rejected by those to whom it is applied. There is no unified "school" of thought that it fits; the thinkers to whom it is applied — most of the outstanding theologians of the recent period — differ widely among themselves, and to them and their followers the very large differences (between Paul Tillich and Karl Barth, say, or between Reinhold Niebuhr and Barth) are much more important than any general characteristics taken over from the whole climate of opinion that they may share. Moreover, even if one term is to be applied to the phenomenon, some doubt that anything involving "orthodoxy" really fits a group and period and impulse with many heretical and radical tendencies within it; conservative and fundamentalist Christians often challenge the connection of the group with "orthodoxy" as they understand it. The term "post-liberal" has sometimes been used to describe this group, or fact, and that term is all right as far as it goes: there has come a climate of thought that is very much "after" (and to a considerable extent opposed to) liberal Protestantism. But it is not only "after" liberalism; it has specific, positive characteristics of its own. If there is not a single, relatively unified "school," there is something much more important: a large and fundamental change, in a specific direction, of the whole climate of theological opinion within which various, divergent "schools" and thinkers operate. For shorthand, with some reservations, "neo-orthodoxy" will do as a name for it.

What is the new climate? To describe it one must refer to developments abroad. American Protestant thought, of course, has never been separately or purely American; liberalism and all that went before liberalism had connections with European Christianity. But the neo-orthodox reconstruction depends more especially upon European developments. Indeed, its struggle with liberalism has often been seen — especially in the American middle and far West — as a struggle of "Continental" theology with characteristic "American" ways of thinking.

In Europe immediately after the First World War there began to appear a "dialectical" theology, a theology of "crisis," whose outstanding spokesman was Karl Barth. There were other representatives (Emil Brunner); the line reached back to minority, protest figures in the nineteenth century (Kierkegaard) and out to other movements opposed to "bourgeois complacency" (existentialism). It was aided and accompanied by new, more theologically-oriented research into Reformation thought, especially into Luther's; and most important of all, by a whole new orientation — theological and "confessional" rather than liberal and "objective" — in Biblical scholarship.

The core of the movement was a radical reorientation of the Christian's starting point, directly challenging liberalism: one started not with the subjective religious experience, but with the presented Word of God; not with a long path from man and society somehow up to God, but with God's self-disclosure to man; not with what is best in "Christian" civilization, but with the "strange new world inside the Bible"; not with man, his needs, his reasoning, his society, his morality, his religion — but with God; not with the inspiring ethical teachings of Jesus, the man, but with the "saving act of God in Christ." Thus to some extent this neo-orthodoxy was a recovery of the classical way the Christian has looked at the world. But that is only part of the story. The movement of thought in the history of Christianity, as elsewhere, does not follow simple pendulum swings from a right to a left, from conservatism to liberalism, but rather moves in complex, unbalanced spirals. This new orthodoxy is far from the old; it is "post-liberal," and absorbs much of liberalism at the same time that it sets itself against liberalism as its chief opponent. Its doctrinal emphases (the transcendent "otherness" of God; the freedom of God over the world and over all categories of thought; the doctrine of man as sinner, for example) stand in direct contrast to characteristic themes of liberal Protestantism. At the same time, however, there is much in the current temper that is continuous with the liberalism it denounces: an acceptance of Biblical criticism; a rejection of Biblical literalism; a toleration of varieties of faith; a critical, intellectual spirit rather than a pious celebrational one.

In the late twenties and early thirties there began to be translations and presentations of Barth and Kierkegaard for American readers, but the moment "neo-orthodoxy" made a real impact on American thought came in 1933 with the publication of a book called *Moral Man and Immoral Society*. The writer of this book, Reinhold Niebuhr, had been for a dozen years a pastor of a church in Detroit and had recently come to teach at Union Seminary in New York. He was to be both the most effective American mediator and the most important critic of European neo-orthodoxy.

We will set aside for the moment the way in which Reinhold Niebuhr differed from, and was a critic of, neo-orthodoxy. That difference was not as apparent, or as important, at first as it has come to be later. In the environment of American liberal Protestantism his work appeared to be continuous with the new European theological mood, a part of one single big new — and antagonistic — movement.

Although *Moral Man and Immoral Society* was almost entirely a political-ethical treatise, it nevertheless had an important theological significance because liberal Protestantism had almost reduced Christian theology to the kind of simple unpolitical social idealism the book refuted. Niebuhr followed that book with others, like his

Rauschenbusch lectures called *An Interpretation of Christian Ethics,* in which a more explicit theology appeared. Meanwhile, other Protestant thinkers — mostly from a liberal background — were changing their thought and elaborating also a more "realistic" and "orthodox" theology.

Although we have emphasized the influence of intellectual developments abroad, as a key to the American development, it would not do of course to ignore the major effect that historical events had upon religious thinking in both Europe and America. The older liberal outlook was challenged not only by the trenchant criticism of Reinhold Niebuhr, but also by the events of history that made that criticism compelling: the Great Depression and the rise of demonic totalitarian political movements, later the Second World War and the development of nuclear weapons.

At the center of the new theological point of view, especially in the early period, especially in America, and especially in the broader public understanding of it, was the doctrine of man as sinner. This was the doctrine with which Dr. Niebuhr was most widely associated and which he elaborated in his major theological work *The Nature and Destiny of Man.* This was the doctrine to which the liberals most often and most vigorously objected. This was the doctrine which most often led men over from the older, liberal perspective to the neo-orthodox perspective.

Liberalism had been "optimistic" about history and about man. Usually explicitly and always implicitly, it had emphasized what man can do in the world: make a progressive development toward a better society. Man was seen to be at least potentially reasonable and disinterested, susceptible to the appeals to goodwill in which liberal Protestantism abounded. As we have said, the contemporary polemical picture of that liberalism may be too negative, and the presentation of the doctrines of man appearing in it may be a caricature. But the tendency of those doctrines is clear: man can respond to the ethical ideals of Jesus and thereby make a better world.

Neo-orthodoxy sharply contradicted the liberal picture of man. To some extent it was recovering the older, classically Christian position against what, in different forms, had been called Pelagianism and Arminianism in ancient doctrinal controversies: that is, the positions that in various ways had held out for man's freedom and ability in respect to his own "salvation." But in challenging the liberal view of man the neo-orthodox movement embraced more than the old orthodox Christian understanding. Partly interpreting orthodoxy in modern terms and partly qualifying it, neo-orthodoxy absorbed much of modern thought: an awareness of the psychological fact of rationalization, of the sociological fact of ideology, and of the cultural-historical fact of relativity. Then too, much of the existential awareness of the unique problems of the self was assimilated in the neo-orthodox view of man. The new view held, against the liberals, that man's reason and conscience were heavily corrupted by his self-preference; the mind and true will were — if not absolute tools — at least continual servants of the passion and interest of the self. Out of this new (or recovered) view, reinforced by events, came a new "realistic" theology.

III

Much more has happened, of course, to religion in America than the intellectual change we have so far discussed. Among other developments are a new religious pluralism and a new religious revival. These two, which came to be central after the Second World War, have helped to set the frame within which the newer theology has spread and changed in the United States.

As to the new religious pluralism, we mean that Americans have recently come to think of their country not as fundamentally Protestant but as Protestant-Catholic-Jew.[6] Roman Catholics, after the Second World War came fully into the national consciousness as a major influence in the central institutions of the nation. Before that time, although of course there was a long American Catholic history, Catholicism could be thought of as being somewhere on the periphery of the national life. But there are now nearly forty million Roman Catholics, increasing in income, status, and power. They are no longer recent arrivals, and the whole movement is more self-confident. The Jewish community, too, though much smaller in numbers, is unmistakably a part of the central stream of American life in a way that may not have been true in days nearer to the waves of immigration. The American today is conscious of three major religions, all of them "American."

Where thirty years ago observers, whether Protestant or Catholic, or nonreligious, would describe the American nation as "fundamentally Protestant," now Americans and others, of whatever point of view, see in the nation a three-faith, "pluralistic" society.

This change has meant a considerable psychological readjustment on all sides. The Protestant no longer can think, as he once tended to do, of an America in which he is the one who fundamentally is at home. Now he must, so to speak, move over, and give place to Catholic and Jewish Americans as fully "American" as he. The American Catholic, sometimes inclined to be aggressive in a minority's self-defense and in an overly nationalistic "Americanism," may now lose this minority psychology and enter into the "dialogue" about the religious and ethical foundations of American life in a new way.

This new consciousness of religious pluralism has its connection with the second major development, the religious revival. As Martin Marty has pointed out, this "revival" of the late forties and the fifties is the first in American history that has not been a revival of evangelical Protestantism, but rather of "religion-in-general."[7] America's religious pluralism operates, along with other forces, to create a kind of neutral inclusive religiosity that eliminates the distinctive claims of particular groups but is "religious" in general, amalgamating with that religion a kind of national patriotic piety.

Religious pluralism is connected with the "revival," too, in being one of its sociological sources. If one were to try to explain the renewed interest in religion historically and sociologically, one would probably refer to the following: to the disillusionment with political movements and ideologies and to the raising of profound life problems as a result of the historical events of the twentieth century (totalitarianism, war, nuclear weapons); to the pressures in modern organized life that make for adjustment to group norms which tend to include religious allegiance as one aspect of the adjustment; to the impersonality of life in modern technical society that increases the yearning for a community of personal warmth; to the kind of amalgam of patriotism and religion that appears in popular culture, in response to the Communist threat to the nation; and also to the dynamics of religious pluralism. The increased awareness of the presence of other religious groups has tended to create in reaction an increased affiliation with one's own religious community. None of these social influences, of course, wholly "explains" the mysteries of this kind of phenomenon, but they are important.

This religious revival, or revived interest in religion, can be analyzed into three rather distinct parts: (1) an increased place for religion as a part of popular culture; (2) an increased membership and participation in the churches; and (3) an increased intellectual (theological) interest within the religious communities and an increased place of theology in general American intellectual life. Thus there is a popular revival; a churchly revival; and a theological revival.

The statistics on the second of these, the revival of church membership and participation, are impressive. Americans of the 1920's would be startled to know that by 1956 there would be a hundred million members of churches and synagogues; that six out of ten Americans would have a religious affiliation; that church membership would be increasing twice as fast as the population; that there would be a tremendous increase in church building and giving to churches, and even that more regular church attendance would be reported in some polls and analyses.

They would be startled, also, by the other two phenomena — the theological and the popular revival — that help to feed the churchly revival.

Perhaps the popular religiosity — the aspect of the whole complex most commented on in the fifties — would really be the least surprising to the American of the twenties. A popular utilitarian religion has been a part of the American scene for a long time; it did not start with the chief representative of the mid-century era, Norman Vincent Peale. Dr. Peale's most successful book, *The Power of Positive Thinking*, the national best seller in 1953, '54, and '55, is not fundamentally different from Bruce Barton's *The Man Nobody Knows*, the best seller in 1925 and '26. His books are not really different from those of one Orison Swett Marden ("How to Get What You Want"), who worked the same vein in the first decades of the century. William James's *Varieties of Religious Experience* refers to a "mind-cure" movement at the turn of the century that sounds very much like "positive thinking." No doubt one could find evidences of the same thing clear back to the popular preachers of the post-Civil War period, and Tocqueville reports as early as the 1830's a strong utilitarian element in religion in American democracy. Thus this tendency of popular religion in a democracy to justify itself, in very sentimental and obvious terms, as *useful* for nonreligious ends of living — for peace of mind, for national strength, above all for personal success — is no new thing.

The "cult of reassurance" in the 1950's simply put forward with a new prominence and in a new context (basically more secular and also much less self-confident) some old themes. At the height of the development, in the early and middle fifties, this kind of religiosity was an important aspect of American popular culture, appearing in extraordinary measure in Biblical movies, on news stands, on television, on the best-seller lists, in the speeches of public men, even on the juke box. But perhaps the independent significance of this phenomenon has been exaggerated; too often, in fact, this aspect of the revived interest in religion has been taken to represent the whole. Actually, this is simply the mass-culture wing of the larger development, with the oversimplicity, sentimentality, vulgarity, and commercial manipulation that characterize mass culture generally.

The churchly revival, as well as this mass-culture revival, is to be distinguished from the theological revival. One notable aspect of the whole development since the Second World War, distinguishing it from times past, may be just the sharpness of the separation among these parts of the religious scene. In other times a Jonathan Edwards could be simultaneously a churchman, a preacher of the popular awakening, and a great theologian. Today the theologians mostly speak to other intellectuals, in and sometimes out of the church, and the popular religiosity hears quite different voices. The separation of the intellectual, the institutional, and the popular worlds that marks the modern advanced technical society generally affects also the religious sphere.

It is in this setting that the new theological interest has grown and developed. The relation of that interest to the other aspects of religious revival is complex. Partly it shares with them the characteristics of one large religious development, but partly it stands over against them in reaction and criticism. Where the popular revival is religiously utilitarian, making religion an instrument for the uncriticized goals of the self and the society, the new theology inclines to be sharply anti-utilitarian, insisting emphatically and centrally upon the transcendence of God and the independence and priority of His claims, apart from any alleged contributions "religion" may make to cultural or personal life.

Both the religious pluralism and the post-Christian secularism of the society have further encouraged the tendency already present in neo-orthodoxy to insist sharply upon the *distinctive* claims of faith, apart from and even over against any generally and rationally discoverable truths and any shared cultural values and objectives.

It is true that the two best-known figures in the American part of neo-orthodoxy, Paul Tillich and Reinhold Niebuhr, had each had a fundamental interest in the connection between religious faith and contemporary life — Niebuhr more to politics and Tillich more to culture and personal psychology. But this interest has not been developed very far by their theological students and followers. In fact, gradually in the fifties the influence of Tillich and Niebuhr came to be greater outside the seminaries and theological circles than within. The neo-orthodox movement came to have a single-mindedly scriptural and doctrinal and even anticultural atmosphere quite different from the one in which, in the thirties, Niebuhr and Tillich first spoke effectively to the American religious community. By the 1960's something new had come, about which the older generation — again — would have real doubts.

IV

The neo-orthodox reconstruction in theology has been extraordinarily relevant and necessary, but it also may have dangers in it for American society. It has been, of course, a world-wide movement, touching at least Protestant Christianity throughout the world; but its meaning differs with each of the different cultures environing the Christian communities it has touched.

The key to the particular relation of this intellectual development to American society may be found in this: here it stood in its most thoroughgoing opposition to the ethos of the nation. To put this point oversimply, we may say that neo-orthodoxy and "Americanism" were almost polar opposites.

The relevance of this movement (or atmosphere) to American

society springs from this opposition. One might say America stood most in need of this reinterpretation of Christianity.

We are all quite familiar with the characterization of the American as too much the optimist, the activist, the very practical and this-worldly believer in the goodness of man, in the unrestrained freedom of the individual, in the great goal of success, and in an automatic progress in history. The American society has been dominated by these themes without much challenge or restraint. What was in Europe but one movement (liberal-democratic) became here the whole spirit and basis of the society. To classical political-economic liberalism, with its emphasis on freedom as the central value and the individual as the social unit, we Americans added our additional elements of practicality and vitality, and an increase in the optimism about man and history. In addition, we are, and have increasingly become, not only a liberal-individualist society but also a popular-democratic society, and one that has carried modern technology to its highest peak of development. These last two elements — the populist and technical — have heightened some characteristics already present in America's liberal culture and added others. As a result of the whole combination, we may be a rather shallow culture, lacking in explicit attention to the qualities and profundities of life. We may be a complacent, optimistic, bourgeois society that believes too much in the self-made man (so the story goes, and it is partly right). We may concentrate on the obvious, tangible, quantitative, material, and external — so it is said — and miss the depths and refinements. American life may be dominated by a thoroughgoing pragmatism that does not know enough about the ends of life. Sometimes it may incline toward anti-intellectualism. It may be filled with a kind of popular democratic relativism or skepticism that challenges all truths and values in the name of numbers or of sheer individual opinion.

To such a society the neo-orthodox movement has been particularly relevant. The older evangelical and free-church Christianity and the later liberal Protestantism, in America, were deeply involved in the faults as well as the merits of this American ethos. The neo-orthodox movement can be seen as having in it a corrective to American inclinations first of all within the churches and then also in the society in general. To this pre-eminently liberal society, this "post-liberal" movement has spoken a needed word.

When we specify the points of correction and contribution that neo-orthodoxy makes in this society we would begin with the contrast, already mentioned, between the extraordinary American optimism about human nature and the neo-orthodox recovery of a Christian or Reformation Protestant pessimism about human nature. Where American society, particularly recently, has had in it a large trust in the goodness of man, in his reason and conscience, and has tended to believe that democracy requires such a view, the theological revival has recovered a needed awareness of man's wilfulness, pride, and self-interest. This familiar point is important, but it is not the whole story.

In addition, the theological reconstruction has stood in fundamental opposition to the "moralism" and "legalism" of American society. These characteristics, often connected with Puritanism, probably derive at least as much from the sectarian strand in America's religious history; in any case, they are familiar to every reader of books about American character and American values. We Americans are inclined, to an extraordinary degree, to think in terms of sharp, clear, simple lines of right and wrong, of "moral law," and of relatively easily realized moral ideals. Neo-orthodoxy has just now brought to the United States a generation of young ministers, if not of lay Christians, who are opposed to this "moralism," including that of their predecessors. The theological revival has affirmed again the Biblical and Reformation teaching about salvation by God's grace alone, and in so doing has recaptured the opposition to legalism and "works-righteousness": to the assumption that man can "save" himself by fulfilling laws or doing moral acts. This has resulted in a considerable change in the atmosphere in the Protestant churches, with much less of the simple moralism (Purity against Evil, as in the Prohibition movement) than was once prevalent. There may also have been some effect upon the society generally on this point.

To a lesser extent, the theological revival has stood in opposition to the pragmatic and relativistic currents of American society and of modern mass society. We say "to a lesser extent," because Protestant neo-orthodoxy has not stood exactly with Catholicism or idealistic philosophy, affirming some "absolutes" against the modern sea of relativity; on the contrary, many representatives of newer Protestant theology (both of the Niebuhrs, for example) have a deep awareness of relativity in their own position. But, if the neo-orthodox attack upon the modern world in which "whirl is king" has been oblique, it has nevertheless been an attack. Though much neo-orthodoxy joins modern man in his criticism of "Objective Values" or "Absolutes" or Natural Law, it does not stop with that criticism. It does not leave man in a relativistic morass. Neo-orthodoxy gets out of the morass and provides (or receives) a starting point for thought and ethics and life, not by affirming absolute truths accepted by the mind, but by a "leap of faith" made by the self. At its best it may provide a way to avoid the ills of skepticism and relativism without falling into those on the other side associated with the quest for certainty.

But then we said there are also dangers in this movement. The dangers appear most clearly — as with liberal Protestantism — when the movement reaches its later, conventionalized phase. There are signs already of what neo-orthodoxy is like in that phase. In reaction, or overreaction, against the antidoctrinaire and anti-intellectual characteristics of liberalism and of a pragmatic American culture, it may become too intellectualistic, insisting on Right Doctrine as the key to life's problems. In reaction against the moralism of liberalism and of American society, it may become too antimoralistic, swallowing up ethics in theology (it will indeed be a curious thing when America's Protestant preachers are heavily antimoralistic, but the day may come).

We may refer here once more to Reinhold Niebuhr, because he represents neo-orthodoxy at its best but not at its worst. He has disagreed continually with Karl Barth and with main tendencies in the developing neo-orthodox theology, and his disagreement has given him a different relation to liberalism and to American society. The differences are these: Niebuhr's Christian thought is fundamentally ethical, political, practical; the new theology generally has come to be quite otherwise. Niebuhr has had a real sense of the limits of thought and language in dealing with the ultimate mysteries; neo-orthodoxy, as it has developed, has not.

Niebuhr's *Moral Man and Immoral Society* may be seen as a critique of the liberal social gospel from one who carries on its interests while rejecting its analysis. The new theology generally has not carried on those interests.

Niebuhr's books all have a strong ethical, political, even topical aspect; they are about democracy (*The Children of Light and the Children of Darkness*), international affairs (*The Structure of Nations and Empires*), America's ethic and ideology (*The Irony of American History*). The doctrines he has dealt with at length are those about man (*The Nature and Destiny of Man*) and history (*Faith and History*) that have the most immediate ethical-political significance. Niebuhr is the most powerful and effective critic of all that was sentimental and superficial in the American liberal Protestantism of the twenties and earlier, but at the same time he is the most important representative of the continuity of its social-ethical interests.

Neo-orthodoxy in general does not necessarily continue those interests, and therein lies an important point. For Niebuhr, Christian theology illuminated politics; for many of the neo-orthodox, Christian theology supplanted politics. They spoke of a Word of God over against the "world," and became much more detached from the merely "ethical" than Niebuhr ever was. Moreover, the reconstruction of theology became much more technically doctrinal, much more speculative, much surer that it spoke of events, not myths, than Niebuhr was.

One might say that Niebuhr had in him a much more "American" mind and much more of liberalism than his early critics, attacking him for his "Continental pessimism" and his orthodoxy, ever discerned. Niebuhr, like most Americans (religious and secular), has been mostly concerned with practical, historical effects, not with logical analysis, systematic intellectual construction, abstract speculation, or "religious" questions in a separate, narrow sense. But neo-orthodoxy has come to differ from that. Maybe it has also become conventionalized in its opposition to liberal and "American" ideas.

The conventionalized neo-orthodoxy may score easy theological points against this American society without recognizing (as liberalism, especially in its social gospel phase, did) the merits built into the actual social-political life of that society.

Despite its insistence upon a transcendent, "wholly other" God, Lord of the world and Judge of all cultures, this neo-orthodoxy may in the end have its own subtle kind of capitulation to the prevailing currents of the society. It may so much insist on a strictly and abstractly doctrinal answer to all of life's problems as to leave their concrete detail in fact untouched, especially when the problems are those we easily overlook, the social ones. Men who insist as the answer to all questions that "Christ is Lord," without making any connection between that claim and concrete social-political life, may be iterating an empty formula, leaving their ideologies unexamined. If neo-orthodoxy should reach that point, it would be time for yet another movement of protest.

19

The New Economics

Seymour E. Harris

I concentrate here primarily on Keynesian economics, and secondly on the advance of mathematical economics; these seem to be the most important developments in economics in the United States since the First World War. Keynesian economics has made not only substantial theoretical advances, but also has had almost revolutionary effects on public policy. Mathematics, aside from its contribution to advances in statistics and econometrics, has so far primarily advanced basic economics, not its engineering aspects.

THE KEYNESIAN SYSTEM

Why, some may ask, so much space to John Maynard Keynes and Keynesian economics when Keynes was an Englishman? The answer is that Keynesian economics has dominated American economics in the last generation, and has influenced especially those economists born after 1900. Moreover, not only have American economists contributed much to Keynesian economics, but American policy-makers have also applied Keynesian economics. In his macro-economic approach, to be explained below, Keynes built on the national income work of Kuznets and others; and in the clarification and supplementation of Keynes's *General Theory*, American economists and econometricians played an important role: Kuznets, M. Gilbert, R. Nathan, Jaszi, and others in the development of national income statistics; Hansen, Lerner, Samuelson, L. Klein, Bryce, and many others in improving and clarifying Keynes's ideas; Samuelson, Galbraith, Harris, and many others in disseminating Keynesian economics. Samuelson's famous textbook on economics is now approaching the millionth copy; this means that about one in every four students studying elementary economics uses this book, and the ratio is much higher for students in the better colleges and universities.

I disagree with my former colleague and friend, the late Joseph Schumpeter, one of the most brilliant social scientists of the twentieth century, when he writes that "practical Keynesianism is a seedling which cannot be transplanted into foreign soil: it dies there and becomes poisonous before it dies . . . all of this applies to every bit of advice that Keynes ever offered. . . ."[1] The fact is that Keynesian economics and the policies which follow from it have received at least as large acceptance in the United States, Scandinavian countries, and many other countries, as in the United Kingdom.

I remind the reader that this essay is not a history of economic thought in the United States. In two weighty survey volumes sponsored by the American Economic Association one may find authoritative summaries of recent contributions in economics, including advances both in this country and elsewhere. The major space is given to economists in this country and in Great Britain, but others have also contributed much — Scandinavian, Dutch, and Italian economists especially. In these two volumes, experts in their fields cover 23 categories of economics. Among the areas where important progress has been made are theories of value and distribution, monopoly, price and production policies, theory of international trade, dynamic process analysis, econometrics, socialist economics, welfare economics, theory of the firm, national economic planning. That I fail to mention my colleague, Edward Chamberlin, and his important work on monopolistic competition, does not in any sense mean, for example, an unawareness of his very important contribution to economics. But I assess other advances as more important.

All of this contrasts sharply with the economics of seventy-five years ago. In a world where Adam Smith's "invisible hand" guided the activities of those seeking their own ends in a manner to further those of society, economists had very little to do with the formation of policy. Until the late nineteenth century, economics remained a branch of moral philosophy and economists were few indeed. But by 1960, economics had become a career for about 20,000 men and women in the United States, while those who should be called economists probably numbered from 10,000 to 15,000. Today economists are as numerous as airplane pilots and navigators, authors, chiropractors, mining engineers, and veterinarians. Whereas in most countries economists still seem to be a luxury, the United States, with roughly half the world's telephones, automobiles, and television sets, seems to have about one-half the world's supply of economists. I would not argue from this that this country provides one-half of the contributions to the economics of the world, though it undoubtedly writes more than one-half of the number of words. Yet few would deny that the contribution of American economists has greatly increased, both absolutely and relatively, since the First World War.

It is a fair question to ask how this country has come to have so many economists. Undoubtedly the increasing complexity of our economic life called forth increased efforts at understanding and explanation; and the ten-fold rise of our college population from 1910 to 1960, with the accompanying demand for teaching students about the material aspects of our life, also played a role in the expansion of economics. But before this increase in the number of economists could come about, the teaching of economics had to overcome many obstacles, not the least of which was the suspicion of college trustees who considered economics impractical or potentially critical and reformist in temper. Moreover, "classicists, philologists and philosophers frequently regarded economists as vulgar fellows — much as they are apt today, sometimes in alliance with the now-entrenched economists, to regard sociologists."[2] On the other hand, and much more important, was the growing realization that the Adam Smith–Spencer approach was no longer acceptable. Socialists in the nineteenth century had already raised many perplexing questions concerning the validity of the classical premises, and even Alfred Marshall, the great British economist of the era preceding the First World War, paid respectful attention to the outcry of the Socialists. But the Socialists "seemed to him to underrate the difficulty of their problems, and to be too quick to assume that the abolition of private property would purge away the faults and deficiencies of human nature. . . ."[3]

It was left to John Maynard Keynes to revolutionize economics and to give the economist an increasingly important role in modern life. Keynes assumed that the classical economists had solved the major problems involved in the allocation of resources, but argued that they had erred in their assumption of full employment, in their neglect of demand, and in their acceptance of the view that employment responds to wage cuts. As late as 1933, Marshall's successor, Professor Pigou, in a book on unemployment, proved to his own satisfaction that a reduction of wages of *X* per cent would bring such a rise in the number of people employed as to increase the wage bill by 3*X*. However, he had left out of account the fact that against the favorable effect of a decline of wages on the employer-incentives is to be put the unfavorable effect of a decline in the employee's demand for goods because of the reduction in wage rates.

Above all, Keynes destroyed the myth of Say's Law, which dominated nineteenth-century economics: namely, that supply creates its own demand. This is equivalent to saying that what is produced will be sold, and at satisfactory prices, and what is saved will be invested. Flexible interest rates will assure this in the classical system; and with flexible wages and prices, except temporarily, the sellers will find adequate markets.

Keynes attacked laissez-faire and appealed for a modified capitalist system. He gave the economist a vital task: to study the functioning of the economy, to estimate the probable gaps (or excesses) of private spending; to suggest the extent, the manner, and the timing of governmental intervention. This was not to be intervention for intervention's sake. In fact, Keynes's point was essentially not to interfere in the millions of markets or billions of transactions, but rather to treat the system in a broad general attack which interferes as little as possible with incentives.

He had little faith in specific planning such as that supported by the Socialists. Those who identify Keynes with Communism either do not understand the ABC of Keynesian economics or are just malicious. It is true that he shared with Marxists the view that in the absence of some intervention, markets may well become saturated. But the objective of the Marxist was to destroy capitalism; that of Keynes, to save it. The approach of the Marxist was purposeful meddling with every aspect of the economy; that of Keynes was an overall monetary and fiscal therapy, leaving complete freedom to the businessman, worker, consumer, and farmer in their daily transactions. He wanted to know "how a doctrine [Marxist] so illogical and so dull can have exercised so powerful and enduring an influence over the minds of men, and, through them, the events of history." "How can I adopt a creed which, preferring the mud to the fish, exalts the boorish proletariat above the bourgeois and the intelligentsia . . . ?"[4]

What were the crucial advances for which Keynes was responsible? Perhaps most important was the shift of emphasis from micro- to macro-economics. As I have written in a study of Keynes's work: ". . . The [present] concern of theoretical economics and the economic engineer with high or full employment is largely Keynes's doing. This shift of emphasis from studies of cost, demand, value, and prices of the individual enterprise or industry, of the degree of monopoly, of productivity, of the optimum size of the business unit, . . . the shift from almost exclusive consideration of these problems to that of employment, and wastages associated with less than full employment, is the contribution, directly, and, indirectly, through those he inspired, of J. M. Keynes."[5]

This shift of emphasis greatly facilitated the use of statistics to suggest the theoretical framework and also to test the validity of the assumptions. Keynes's formula, Y (income) $= C$ (consumption) $+$ I (investment), became the foundation of the New Economics. Kuznets's work on national income helped Keynes formulate his theoretical underpinnings, and in turn Keynes's system inspired tremendous advances in the area of national income statistics. A striking example of Keynes's impact appears in the economics of consumption. Keynes assumed that the consumption function (the relation of consumption to income) was relatively stable. It followed that, if income rose, there would be the problem of finding an outlet for the part of the additional income that would not be spent on consumption goods. Concern lest the additional income not be invested, but rather be hoarded and thus contribute to inadequate spending (e.g., goods without a buyer) and rising unemployment, led Keynes to make a frontal attack on thrift. Perhaps nothing in the writings of Keynes shocked the defenders of the capitalist system so much as the statement that there could be too much thrift or savings. Even as early as 1923 he wondered whether saving is always desirable, and in his *Treatise on Money* (1930) he said that it "should be obvious that mere abstinence is not enough by itself to build cities or drain fens. . . . Thus, Thrift may be the handmaid and nurse of Enterprise. But equally she may not. And, perhaps, even usually she is not." In 1931, he urged the people to spend more money, and thus put people to work and hence bring "a chance and a hope to Lancashire, Yorkshire and Belfast."[6]

All of this does not mean that Keynes would limit savings and thrift at all times. But he would generally associate prosperity with periods when thriftiness was not excessive, even to the point of arguing that an excess of investment over savings was a condition for the great cultural advances. "We were just in a financial position to afford Shakespeare at the moment when he presented himself."[7] I shall not enter here into the rather sterile debate on whether investments can exceed savings. Though Keynes defined investments as savings in his *General Theory*, for our purposes he still was aware that there were lags in adjustment of savings and investments. In periods of excess spending, for example during both world wars, Keynes was eloquent on the need of additional savings. It was Keynes, not the defenders of thrift, who fought so strenuously for compulsory savings to help finance the Second World War, and who created a new measure, the inflationary gap, an understanding and treatment of which would exclude inflation. The gap is measured by the excess of spending over the flow of goods and services at a fixed price, the excess then pushing prices up.

To get some idea of the impact of Keynes's macro-economics, one has only to examine superficially the economic policies of the Western economies. They all now present a national budget, the ingredients of which are expected investment, consumption, export balance, government purchases of goods and services. Thus for 1960, for this country, the forecast was as follows:

	$ Billion
Gross National Product	504.4
1. Personal Consumption Expenditures	328.9
2. Gross Private Domestic Investment	72.4
3. Net Exports of Goods and Services	3.0
4. Government Purchase of Goods and Services	100.1
a. Federal	52.9
b. State and Local	47.2

Almost every Western nation, in addition to its usual budgetary presentation, will offer a national income projection. On the basis of past experience and estimated values for, say, 1964, the government will draw up the national accounts for 1964. Indeed, the revenue for 1964 will be related to the estimates of gross national product, national income, etc.

Following Keynes, the econometricians will be interested especially in the projected investment, for this is the most volatile item. Indeed in the United States, investment runs from 20 to 25 per cent of gross national product; but its fluctuations are relatively much larger than those of consumption. Where the economy declines, it is investment which especially reflects the adverse trends. Thus, in the eleven years 1949 to 1960, consumption expenditures increased every year, despite three recessions, and the average gain was $14 billion, or 5½ per cent. But investment is only ¼–⅕ of consumption; in six years of gains the rise of investment averaged $9 billion (21 per cent) and in five years of decline (inclusive of one year of no change) the reduction averaged $4 billion (6 per cent).

Using as a basis the estimates of consumption, investment, export balance, and government purchases, the authorities can then project gross national product, and they can then also estimate unemployment. For example, with expected productivity rising 2 to 3 per cent per year, and with an annual rise of numbers on the labor market of 1 to 1.5 million, the government estimates the needed rise in gross national product which would preclude any rise of unemployment or which would bring unemployment down to, say, a minimum of 3 to 4 per cent.

The way to bring about the needed rise in gross national product is the Keynesian one: either to raise investment or to increase the contribution of government through increased spending or reduced taxes. In the early years of the formulation of his position, Keynes was very hopeful that strong measures to stimulate investment might help greatly. He was particularly impressed by the possibilities of bringing the rate of interest down, with the result that investment would respond to a reduction of the rate of interest vis-à-vis expected earnings on capital. But with time, he became more pessimistic even as he sensed a growing pessimism of investors and great uncertainty about future earnings, which could not easily be treated through the creation of money. In the gloomy atmosphere of the 1930's, the additional money manufactured, instead of being used to put men to work, satisfied the rising desire for liquidity. Oddly enough, in recent years economists have tended once more to stress the importance of inducing investment through a reduction in the rate of interest. Perhaps the explanation is a change of psychology accompanying almost a generation of reasonably prosperous conditions.

In a world where an adequate response of investment to declining rates of interest is not to be had, the way out is likely to be governmental intervention. For Keynes, this meant public investment. He could not agree that government was more inefficient than the private economy or than his frequent target, the Bank of England, which spent 2 shillings for each transfer of cash on its books (one-half hour contemplating each transfer). In 1931, he asked: "Why not pull down the whole of South London from Westchester to Greenwich, thus providing housing near where the people work, more comfortable buildings, areas of parks, and public spaces. Something magnificent to the eye, yet useful and convenient to human life as a monument of our age."[8] The unemployed "are not storing up reserves of energy and enthusiasm which will enable them to work triple when finance permits."[9]

No one can reasonably argue with Keynes's arithmetic. When the spending of the private economy is deficient, the contribution of government should increase. This is the germ of modern fiscal theory which stresses not the financial aspects of government activity, but the economic repercussions. Keynes was puzzled that wholly wasteful forms of expenditures were preferred to productive ones. Why should mining gold, which in its major uses adds nothing to the real wealth, be acceptable? "If the Treasury were to fill old bottles with bank-notes, bury them at suitable depths in disused coal-mines which are then filled up to the surface with town rubbish, and leave it to private enterprise on well-tried principles of laissez-faire to dig the notes up again . . . there need be no more unemployment. . . ."[10]

Many have criticized Keynes for his underestimation of the practical difficulties involved in public spending. Would not a rise of public spending impair confidence and reduce private spending? Would the public spending come when needed, or when the depression was over? Was the counter-cyclical or counter-stagnation expenditure reversible or would it continue through periods of prosperity as well as depression? Keynes was more aware of these problems than many assume. "With the confused psychology which often prevails, the Government programme may, through its effect on 'confidence,' increase liquidity-preference or diminish the marginal efficiency of capital, which, again, may retard other investment unless measures are taken to offset it."[11]

What Keynes knew, but did neglect, was the possibility that the most effective approach might well be tax cuts rather than increased government expenditures. In fact the former approach has gained ascendency — in part because of its greater popularity, in part because it is easier to introduce, and in part because of the difficulty of fitting public investment to fluctuations in private spending. Largely on noneconomic grounds, the trend has been toward tax cuts. Yet on purely economic grounds, a stronger case can be made for public investment. For a given cost to the Treasury, public investment yields larger income gains than a tax cut, as Kaldor, in Beveridge's *Full Employment in a Free Society* (1944), has proved.[12]

The appeal of public investment derived in part from a new tool, the Multiplier, forged by one of Keynes's students, Professor Richard Kahn. But Keynes gave it a new role "by transforming it from an instrument for the analysis of road building into one for the analysis of income building."[13] A rise of investment yields an increase of income that is a multiple of the original increase of investment. Let us see why. If we increase our investment, say in a certain factory, the income of the workers and owners of that factory will increase. But an increase of income will have a different effect on the spending habits of different people, and to express this fact the economist speaks of their different marginal propensities to consume. When some of them receive a dollar of extra income they spend more of it on consumption goods than others do, and hence are said to have a higher marginal propensity to consume. Suppose we invest $10,000 in a factory and all the money goes to people who have a marginal propensity to consume of ½, which means that they spend half of their new income on new consumption goods. They will spend $5,000 on such goods. Suppose now that the people to whom *this* money comes as extra income also have a marginal propensity to consume of ½; they will spend $2,500 on consumption goods. And now suppose that this chain of expenditure continues through a group with the same marginal propensity to consume. The original increase in income of $10,000 (which we may represent as "1" for the sake of simplicity in the formula that follows) will swell to $(1 + \frac{1}{2} + \frac{1}{4} + \frac{1}{8}\ldots) = 2$. If the marginal propensity to consume had been $\frac{9}{10}$, the increase of the income would have been given by the formula $(1 + \frac{9}{10} + 9^2/10^2 + 9^3/10^3\ldots) = 10$. In the first case the multiplier is 2; in the second, 10.

Now the multiplier is seen to be greater when the marginal propensity to consume is higher, and the marginal propensity to consume is generally higher when people are poorer. Poor people spend a greater part of their new income on consumption goods than rich people, and hence put a smaller part of that income into savings. Therefore the more unemployment, the higher the multiplier is likely to be; the more of the additional income that is saved or spent on foreign goods, the less the multiplier. (Keynes's estimate for Great Britain was a multiplier between 2 and 3.) Moreover, it is clear why the gains we have described above are in general possible only when we drop the assumption of full employment. We now see that conventional economics is soaked with presuppositions "which are only applicable to a society which is in equilibrium with all its productive resources already employed."[14]

With the development of Keynesian economics came a rash of econometric models, many of them used not only for the analysis of the economy, but also for forecasting. The econometric model "is the statistical embodiment of theoretical relationships that are every economist's stock in trade."[15]

The econometrician observes and measures the relationship of numerous variables: prices, costs, incomes, savings, etc. These relationships derive from transactions of tens of millions of consumers, millions of firms, and thousands of governmental units. Their complete presentation would require billions of equations. D. B. Suits condenses his model to 23 equations which are fitted to data drawn from the period 1929–59 (1941–47 omitted). The 23 equations contain variables representing consumption of automobiles and parts, demand for other durables, demand for nondurable goods, demand for services (these four constitute the demand sector); plant and equipment expenditure, housing starts, housing expenditures, inventory investments, foreign balance, private gross national product, wage and salary workers, unemployment, private wage bill, property income, corporate profits, dividends, personal income, disposable income, personal taxes and social insurance contributions, corporate benefits tax, individual business taxes, and depreciation and transfer payments. These 23 items include consumer demand, investment demand, income and taxes.

> The econometric model approximates the economy by a system of equations in which the unknowns are those variables — income, automobile demand, unemployment, etc. — whose behavior is to be analyzed. The knowns are variables such as government orders, labor force, lagged nondurable expenditures, etc. When projected values for the "knowns" are inserted in the equations, the system can be solved to forecast the values of the unknowns.[16]

Let us consider briefly two of these equations. Consumer expenditures for new and used automobiles and parts depends on disposable income, stocks of cars already on the road and the average number of months' duration of automobile credit contracts. Of course this is a highly simplified presentation. Actual results may vary from those given by this equation if, for example, new models have an unusual appeal.

The equation for housing starts relates the number of nonresidential housing starts (ΔT) to (Δi), "defined as the gap between the average of the FHA and VA ceiling interest rates on the one hand, and the Aaa bond yield on the other. . . . This interest rate differential reflects the substantial influence of credit availability on the volume of FHA and VA financed residential construction. . . ."[17] But the use of this equation may not yield accurate forecasts because some of the important factors are omitted — for example, modifications of down payments required and mortgage duration may greatly influence the number of new starts, because they may greatly reduce the monthly payments and may even contribute more to a rise of starts than to a substantial cut in the rate of interest.

Estimating the results of forecasts for the next year made each year since 1953, the author concludes "that the direction of movement was correctly forecast each year, and the levels were generally well predicted."[18] Actual gross national product was less than one per cent at variance with the forecast gross national product in 1953, 1954, 1956, 1957, and 1958. In 1955 the underestimate was 7 per cent; in 1959, 4 per cent; and in 1960, 2 per cent. For 1961, a forecast of $515 billion in 1960 was only $4 billion off, and the variance explained by the Berlin crisis, a factor not easily allowed for in a forecast.[19]

Having presented an econometric model which springs from the Keynesian approach, I return to Keynes's system. And here I present the main facets of the system and its relevance for economic policy.

An emphasis on general demand is one of the crucial aspects of Keynesian economics. It is not enough to produce; it is necessary to assure adequate markets. Keynes would not accept Mill's statement that "could we suddenly double the productive powers of the country, we should double the supply of commodities in every market; but we should by the same stroke double the purchasing power."[20] Keynes was much more sympathetic with Malthus, who argued that excessive accumulation would reduce unproductive consumption and "by greatly impairing the usual motives to production must prematurely check progress of wealth."[21] No wonder Keynes wrote that "the obliteration of Malthus's line of approach and the complete dominance of Ricardo's for a period of a hundred years has been a disaster to the progress of economics."[22] I should add that Keynes greatly underestimated Ricardo. Even Marshall, the great figure of Anglo-Saxon economics in the half century preceding the First World War, had failed to deal with the issue of demand. Indeed Marshall had advanced economics through his contribution to the marginal* and substitution† principles, both of

* "We must go to the margin to study the action of the forces which govern the value of the whole."

† "In every phase of any branch of production there is some distribution of resources between various expenditures which yields a better result than any other."

which are essential in an understanding of how to achieve the most effective use of the factors of production. But, like most of Keynes's predecessors, Marshall had assumed employment and income as given — and hence had failed to deal with demand and unemployment. Keynes, on the other hand, as we shall see, was too ready to assume that the problems of the most effective use of the factors of production had been solved.

Keynes's dissatisfaction with an analysis that neglected demand in turn led him to a steady attack on laissez-faire. As late as 1939, he had said that "the intensification of the trade cycle, and the increasingly chronic character of unemployment, have shown that private capitalism was already in its decline as a means of solving the economic problem." Only if spending could be kept on a high plane could capitalism survive.[23] Yet to suggest "social action for the public good to the City of London is like discussing the *Origin of Species* with a Bishop sixty years ago."[24] Keynes reminded us that, under laissez-faire, giraffes with the longest necks would indeed get the most leaves; but, he asked, what of those with short necks, and what of the waste as the sweet leaves are trampled on the ground in the hot pursuit?

In reassessing his views in 1937, Keynes summarized his position as follows:

> The theory can be summed up by saying that, given the psychology of the public, the level of output and employment as a whole depends on the amount of investment. I put it in this way, not because this is the only factor on which aggregate output depends, but because it is usual in a complex system to regard as the *causa causans* that factor which is most prone to sudden and wide fluctuation. More comprehensively, aggregate output depends on the propensity to hoard, on the policy of the monetary authority as it affects the quantity of money, on the state of confidence concerning the prospective yield of capital-assets, on the propensity to spend, and on the social factors which influence the level of the money-wage. But of these several factors it is those which determine the rate of investment which are most unreliable, since it is they which are influenced by our views of the future about which we know so little.
>
> This that I offer is, therefore, a theory of why output and employment are so liable to fluctuation. It does not offer a ready-made remedy as to how to avoid these fluctuations and to maintain output at a steady optimum level. But it is, properly speaking, a theory of

employment because it explains *why*, in any given circumstances, employment is what it is. Naturally I am interested not only in the diagnosis, but also in the cure; and many pages of my book are devoted to the latter.[25]

In evaluating Keynes's contribution, the great econometrician Jan Tinbergen stressed his singling out of the important problems of shrinking output and employment for which mankind needed a solution and for which traditional theory had offered none that was adequate. That is also why the econometricians came to apply macro-economic concepts. "Our limited mental power — and perhaps even more the limited mental power of the 'public' — make it a necessity to use macro-economic concepts."[26]

Keynes, more than anyone else, emphasized the need of monetary expansion as a means of reducing the interest rates. The struggle continues between those who would allow the free market to determine rates (e.g., the predominant view of the Federal Reserve in the 1950's) and those who would manipulate the market. Yet Keynes was also aware of the difficulties of getting the rate down, and particularly of the obstacle of rising preferences for liquidity when economic prospects are not good. He knew that during an economic decline more money encourages more hoarding. Once adequately low rates of interest were achieved, he would deal with inflation through rising taxes, increased imports, and control of investment.

But even when there were low interest rates, Keynes was not overly optimistic that the employment problem would be solved. The marginal efficiency of capital (crudely, the anticipated return on capital) may be low and uncertain, and hence make for an inadequate response of investment to reduced rates of interest. Moreover, as we all know so much better since Keynes, rising employment may be blocked by wage and price inflation.

In his discussion of the relation of money and prices, Keynes went far beyond the simple quantity theory of money. "So long as there is unemployment, *employment* will change in the same proportion as the quantity of money; and when there is full employment, *prices* will change in the same proportion as the quantity of money."[27] But this was an oversimplification. Keynes was aware of the possibilities of wage inflation and the emergence of bottlenecks long before full employment was reached.

In his system the inflexibility of wages was crucial. In the depression, prices tended to fall and real wages to rise, a development that was the opposite of what was required. When reduced real wages were needed and when the large amount of unemployment was evidence that many more would like to work at current or lower wages, the system functioned in such a manner as to raise real wages.

I have tried to outline the Keynesian system and to suggest the major contributions. The emphasis put on macro-economics, on employment and unemployment, on national income and its determinants, on effective demand, on the use of fiscal and monetary policies to achieve higher employment, on the determination to escape the tyranny of gold (the supporters of gold envelop it "in a garment of respectability as densely respectable as was ever met with, even in the realms of sex or religion . . . and [consider it] the sole prophylactic against the plague of fiat moneys"),[28] on the emphasis of international trade in its relation to output and employment, on the concern with international liquidity as a means of giving economies more freedom to maneuver — these are among the great achievements of Lord Keynes. They are contributions to economics not matched in the twentieth century, and perhaps not since the days of Ricardo. Keynes well wrote in 1935 that "we are . . . at one of those uncommon junctions of human affairs where we can be saved by the solution of an intellectual problem and in no other way."[29] But his recommendation was that government take action at the general level and not interfere with individual decisions. If Keynes would not condone do-nothingism, he also refused to accept catastrophism and revolution as the way out.

The Keynesian system has had its critics as well as its disciples. For example, Keynes was held to underestimate the significance of technological change (Hansen); to exclude the impact of variations in the production function, that is, new combinations of factors of production (Schumpeter); to overdo the elasticity of the liquidity function, that is, the tendency to absorb additional supplies of money to satisfy a rising liquidity preference (an increasing preference for cash or close substitutes for cash as against other assets), and hence to overdo the obstacles to reductions in the rate of interest (Haberler); to underestimate the responsiveness of investment to a reduction in the rate of interest (Terborgh); and to be wrong in his assertion that real wages rise in depressions (Dunlop and Tarshis). These are all debatable points; and insofar as they are valid, the Keynesian assumption of a faulty functioning of the free enterprise system and the need of government intervention is weakened.

More recently, in his brilliant and influential book *The Affluent Society*, J. K. Galbraith has also urged a rising contribution by the public sector, but his main argument was unlike Keynes's. Though Galbraith had absorbed and advanced Keynesian economics in the forties and fifties, in his *Affluent Society* he stressed especially the practical difficulties of fiscal policy. For Galbraith, what was important for the advanced countries was the restraint of private consumption and the increase of public consumption, not to stimulate the economy primarily, but rather to induce an improved use of the large and growing annual output.

Galbraith expressed his concern over current allocation of resources as follows:

> . . . The family which takes its mauve and cerise, air-conditioned, power-steered, and power-braked automobile out for a tour passes through cities that are badly paved, made hideous by litter, blighted buildings, billboards, and posts for wires that should long since have been underground. They pass into a countryside that has been rendered largely invisible by commercial art. (The goods which the latter advertise have an absolute priority in our value system. Such aesthetic considerations as a view of the countryside accordingly come second.) . . . They picnic on exquisitely packaged food from a portable icebox by a polluted stream and go on to spend the night at a park which is a menace to public health and morals. . . .[30]

In less colorful language, from 1952 to 1960, while the gross national product rose by $156 billion, the federal government's take of goods and services was unchanged, and vis-à-vis gross national product dropped from 20 to 15 per cent.

Perhaps the most important criticism that may be made against Keynesian economics is of the failure of Keynesians to bridge the gap between ideas and action. Although Keynes and his disciples have greatly changed policies in the Western world, and to some extent in underdeveloped areas in the West and elsewhere, there is still stout resistance to Keynesian ideas among those responsible for legislation. This is partly the result of the failure of economists to devote their energies adequately to persuasion and dissemination. No economist (I would class Marx as a sociologist) has ever been more persuasive than Keynes. But too many Keynesians are satisfied with model building, often of the sterile type, and too few are prepared to devote their energies to persuasion and dissemination.

If economists were all that Keynes had demanded of them, this problem would have been solved.

> The study of economics does not seem to require any specialised gifts of an unusually high order. Is it not, intellectually regarded, a very easy subject compared with the higher branches of philosophy and pure science? Yet good, or even competent, economists are the rarest of birds. An easy subject, at which very few excel! The paradox finds its explanation, perhaps, in that the master-economist must possess a rare *combination* of gifts. He must reach a high standard in several different directions and must combine talents not often found together. He must be mathematician, historian, statesman, philosopher — in some degree. He must understand symbols and speak in words. He must contemplate the particular in terms of the general, and touch abstract and concrete in the same flight of thought. He must study the present in the light of the past for the purposes of the future. No part of man's nature or his institutions must lie entirely outside his regard. He must be purposeful and disinterested in a simultaneous mood; as aloof and incorruptible as an artist, yet sometimes as near the earth as a politician. Much, but not all, of this ideal many-sidedness Marshall possessed. But chiefly his mixed training and divided nature furnished him with the most essential and fundamental of the economist's necessary gifts. . .[31]

But the absence of total acceptance stems not only from an unsatisfactory distribution between thinkers and activists, but also from administrative and political difficulties, and disagreements on creed. Those who are suspicious of, and antagonistic to, government are not likely to be persuaded by the logic of the Keynesian system.

The economist must seek knowledge with no ulterior motive. Much economics is of that kind; indeed, in my view we tend to invest excessively in basic economics. The economist must also seek ways of achieving rising output, full employment, stability of prices, etc. Undoubtedly the 10,000–15,000 economists in this country earn their bread merely because the Hoover policy of more taxes and less public spending to treat a depression is not likely to be invoked again — even by a Republican administration. The acceptance of the Keynesian principle of more spending and less taxes in depression means gains of billions of dollars annually — many, many times the hundred million or so the economists of this nation cost the country. For all of this our greatest debt is to Lord Keynes, with an assist from many British and American economists.

Keynes's impact is evident in the large controversies of the day. His important writings of the period between 1925 and 1936 first announced the issues over which the economists were to battle in the generation after that. They are probably the issues which economists will debate so long as a modified free-enterprise system endures. Full employment and full utilization of resources were the targets of the Keynesian system. They still are today, and the Employment Act of 1946 in the United States is a monument to Keynes. Keynes concentrated on employment. He left out of account a number of variables that are now receiving increasing attention. The first is the size of the labor market. The second is the problem of productivity. Recent discussion of growth stems from Keynesian economics, both because of the relevance of unemployment and because of the impetus Keynes gave to macroeconomics and econometrics. But the level of output and its rise depend not only on the amount of unemployment, but also on the numbers on the labor market (in turn related to the amount of unemployment), and also on productivity, e.g., man-hour output of given factors of production. The importance of the omissions from the Keynesian system of these two variables is suggested by the following comparison of two peak years for the United States, 1948 and 1959 (in the British economy, where growth of number is much less, the omissions in the Keynesian system related to rising numbers are less):

	$ Billion
1. The rise of gross national output in stable dollars	= 169
2. Losses due to rise of unemployment	= 11
3. Gains due to increase of employment (related largely to increase of numbers on labor market)	= 50*
4. Remainder — rising productivity	= 108

* We should allow here also for any rise in the amount of capital.
SOURCE: Calculated from *Economic Report of the President*, January, 1961.

MATHEMATICAL ECONOMICS[32]

I come now to the second of my main concerns in this essay. In the last generation, one of the most striking developments in economics has been the increasing recourse to mathematics. When Paul Samuelson, aged 19, came to Harvard as a graduate student in 1934, he was assigned to the writer for advice on his program, in the thought that we shared a common interest in mathematical economics. My qualifications apparently were that I had just struggled through the algebra in Pigou's *Theory of Unemployment.* (A few years later, at age 40, I took a course in calculus.) The small part played by mathematics in American economics is suggested by the fact that, in seventy years, only two presidents of the American Economic Association were competent mathematicians — Irving Fisher and, in 1960, Paul Samuelson. But my guess is that in the next generation the exceptional president will be one incapable of understanding and using mathematics in his economics. Yet even in 1952, teachers of graduate students revealed that only 2 per cent of the Ph.D. candidates were good in the use of mathematics for economic analysis, and 41 per cent fair; and only 9 per cent of the teachers of graduate students in economics held that mathematical economics or econometrics was being underemphasized.

But much has changed even in the last ten years. The generation of economists now in the age group of the 20's and 30's has a command of mathematics and a capacity to use mathematics far beyond that of my generation. The economists of my generation tend to be critical of the use of mathematics in economics.

They are disenchanted for various reasons. Many believe that the mathematical economists claim more for their results than is justified. But this is generally due to misunderstanding by the nonmathematical economist. The good mathematical economist knows that he does not prove anything; but rather that the mathematics helps provide a criterion for the provisional acceptance of the theories, and of course he knows that the propositions are valid in the framework of the premises. Moreover, he also knows that a particular theory may be replaced by another which more nearly accords with the facts, or has an increased predictive power, or logical implications covering a wider range of phenomena. As

Samuelson has said (quoting Ernest Mach), ". . . every general principle brings . . . disillusionment as well as elucidation."[33] That is to say, the critics of mathematical economics are wrong to assume that the mathematical economist claims proofs for his propositions. Indeed, errors are made, as Cournot, the first great mathematical economist, revealed long ago in his study of foreign trade. But we can leave it to the mathematicians to discover one another's errors. The case for mathematics is that it is a powerful and efficient tool for discovering the logical link between basic premises and observable phenomena and other relevant implications. For many problems, literary economics will not be adequate. As Professor Schumpeter once said, "It is of course possible to argue that any particular result or even the general vision of a system of interdependent economic quantities could also have been attained by methods not mathematically articulate, just as it is possible to argue that a railroad cannot take us to any place which we could not also reach by walking. . . ."[34]

I would not go so far as to say that mathematical economics does not raise problems. For the older generation, often the victim of "technological" change, feels a resentment as great as the railroad worker who is being displaced by the airplane pilot and hostess, and by the automobile mechanic. Again, the nonmathematical economist senses that there are some genuine costs involved: a tendency to concentrate on problems that lend themselves to symbolic manipulation, irrespective of their importance; a tendency to divert too much of the energies of the bright young men from the large issues of public policy to what is often sterile model building; an excessive concentration on model building as against seeking out the facts to test assumptions and conclusions; a tendency to use assumptions which reduce empirical content to a minimum; and a reluctance of the mathematical economists to state their premises and the main elements of their argument in language that the nonmathematician can understand. I am convinced, however, that full translations are not to be expected, both because of the energies required and the impossibility as a rule of translating the mathematics into literary language.

Years ago Keynes, an able mathematician who turned to economics when he became convinced that he could not excel in the higher reaches of mathematics, wrote as follows:

Mathematical economics often exercise an excessive fascination and influence over students who approach the subject without much previous training in technical mathematics. They are so easy as to be within the grasp of almost anyone, yet do introduce the student, on a small scale, to the delights of perceiving constructions of pure form, and place toy bricks in his hands that he can manipulate for himself, which gives a new thrill to those who have had no glimpse of the sky-scraping architecture and minutely embellished monuments of modern mathematics.

Professor Planck, of Berlin, the famous originator of the Quantum Theory, once remarked to me that in early life he had thought of studying economics, but had found it too difficult! Professor Planck could easily master the whole corpus of mathematical economics in a few days. He did not mean that! But the amalgam of logic and intuition and the wide knowledge of facts, most of which are not precise, which is required for economic interpretation in its highest form is, quite truly, overwhelmingly difficult for those whose gift mainly consists in the power to imagine and pursue to their furthest points the implications and prior conditions of comparatively simple facts which are known with a high degree of precision.

. . . Too large a proportion of recent "mathematical" economics are mere concoctions, as imprecise as the initial assumptions they rest on, which allow the author to lose sight of the complexities and interdependencies of the real world in a maze of pretentious and unhelpful symbols.[35]

Marshall, a first-class mathematician, also had warned against the undue use of mathematics. In fact, he would use mathematics only for help in putting down thoughts "quickly, shortly and exactly" for his own use. As late as 1906, Marshall wrote "that a good mathematical theorem dealing with economic hypothesis was very unlikely to be good economics."[36] He was doubtful that anyone could make good use of lengthy translations of economics into mathematics.

Marshall's criticism derived in part from the scraps of elementary algebra, geometry, and differential calculus which then made up mathematical economics. The great advances of mathematical economics in recent years spring in no small part from the use of more advanced mathematics. With the mathematics used by economists until recent years, it was impossible, for example, to solve the diet problem — "to determine the cheapest diet by which a minimum intake of given nutrients can be achieved . . . [and] the transportation problem — to determine the cheapest pattern by which given demands of *m* markets can be supplied by *n* sources with given unit costs of transport from any source to any market. . . ."[37] As Koopmans observes, mathematical economics has recently exploited "matrix algebra, set theory, difference equations, stochastic processes, statistical inference, and the axiomatic method. . . ."[38]

Dorfman tells us that "no one has succeeded in exploring the existence theorems and welfare implications of general equilibrium without a liberal application of fancy mathematics . . . ,"[39] and that "only recently the non-contradictory character of the premises of the theory of competitive economic equilibrium was fully established, and . . . this was done through . . . using the tool of topology which had hitherto not been used in economics."[40] In activity analysis, linear programming, input-output, the interaction of the multiplier and accelerator, the inventory cycle, the fundamental equation of value theory (Slutsky equation), analysis of Keynes's *General Theory*, analysis of the business cycle (Frisch on *Propagation Problems and Impulse Problems in Dynamic Economics*) — these are all important advances made possible by the use of mathematics. I do not pretend to understand all these contributions. I have even published some in a journal without being able to follow the arguments fully. This is my misfortune. But I take heed from a remark by Pigou, namely, that he who does not read Chinese should not criticize Chinese literature. I am also impressed by the fact that Samuelson, Frisch, Arrow, Dorfman, Leontief, Koopmans, Tinbergen, Solow, and other contributors to mathematical economics are the top-flight economists of their generation. It is not necessary to understand the most advanced mathematical economics to realize this fact. Even without mathematics, these economists are among the foremost anywhere. We may be sure that with mathematics they are even better.

What does mathematics bring to economics? It is, of course, a language, and one can say some things more effectively in one language than in another. Mathematics offers an opportunity to express in an elegant and concise manner what is often not available in literary language. As Dorfman has said, ". . . mathematics is the technique of expressing relationships, usually symbolically, in such a way as to bring out their formal structure and then of taking advantage of accumulated knowledge about the properties of such formal structures to reveal further relationships which are not immediately evident."[41] It is, in short, a branch of logic. Even the effective use of econometrics, with its limited factual base, to test hypotheses and generalizations, depends upon the proper use of mathematics.

Some economists have compared the present impasse in economics with the situation of the physicists before the Second World War. The increased use of matrix algebra and group theory by the creators of quantum mechanics stimulated dissent by experimental and even some theoretical physicists. But now quantum theory is accepted by all.

The use of mathematics in economics is especially troublesome to both the literary and mathematical economists when the assumptions chosen and the variables introduced result in the treatment of a problem and its solution that does not seem to check with the real world — for example, Professor Pigou's variables in relating employment to wage rates are an example of the dangers. Should the mathematical economist, in an attempt to be realistic, introduce more and more variables, he would complicate the problem beyond the comprehension of most. The large contributions will come from the model with a few assumptions and variables and yet suggesting a picture of the real world. Unfortunately, often the assumptions convenient for the model are not appropriate for the real world, and the result is a shadow of reality. In the choice of assumptions and variables, a high level of intuition is required.

Tinbergen has well presented the requirements for the treatment of an economic problem:

1. A listing of the phenomena in order to define the realm of the analyses.
2. The attachment of symbols to achieve clarity and brevity. This is especially important because of the many variables involved and the limited capacity of the mind to memorize.
3. Hypotheses that suggest the causal and other relationships of the phenomena.
4. Putting the hypotheses in the form of equations of a general form, "using function symbols yet unspecified to indicate relations which theory is not able to specify *a priori*. . . ."[42]

5. It is then necessary to give specifications through numerical determination of certain functions.
6. Then combine the specified partial theories in order to solve the problem.[43]

Linear Programming, Input-Output, etc.

Until recently, under what Professor John Hicks calls the Walras-Cassel prototype of general equilibrium, economics was solely concerned with the allocation of given factor supplies in the production of numerous products, each requiring factor supplies in proportions technically given. The great mathematician, John von Neuman, in his model of general equilibrium contributed greatly toward moving beyond the solution of this type of problem. It was now possible to introduce variable proportions of factors, joint supply, and intermediate products. In order to move to Linear Programming, which has been one of the great advances in economics in recent years, it was necessary first to realize that there are problems "other than the straightforward 'economic' maximization of the value of output from given resources, which are formally equivalent to economic optimization."[44] Second, it was necessary to find solutions of these problems. Here the Simplex method discovered by Dantzig in 1947 was especially important. This advance helps us recognize an optimum when we reach it. Under Linear Programming the objective is to cast the problem in appropriate form for solution. Most problems of the public sector are of the minima cost type. It is also possible to apply Linear Programming to the private sector — e.g., determination of maximum profit combinations of inputs and outputs. When the market mechanism is not available — for example, in some public sector problems for noneconomic reasons — Linear Programming offers an alternative manner of treatment. We do not have to depend on fixed technical coefficients, and this type of analysis informs us of products that will not be produced and of factors that will not be used. But, like the earlier analysis, it is not very helpful when we abandon the assumption of perfect competition or convexity, constant costs, and have to deal with increasing returns.

In this general area, Professor Leontief's creation, the Input-Output economics, is one of the most fruitful. "Essentially it is a method of analysis that takes advantage of the relatively stable pattern of the flow of goods and services among the elements of our economy to bring a much more detailed statistical picture of the system into the range of manipulation by economic theory."[45] In 1951 Professor Leontief analyzed 42 major branches of production, distribution, transportation, and consumption, arranged in a matrix of horizontal rows and vertical colums. Thus sector 14, for primary metals, shows in the vertical column the inputs of each of the various goods and services needed for the production of primary metals (in dollars) and hence the economy's outlay for these metals. The horizontal column (14) reveals the distribution of the output of this sector. More recently the analysis has been extended to 500 branches of the U.S. economy.

This is essentially a static formulation. Leontief and his disciples have, however, gone much further and have introduced dynamic elements into the matrix. Leontief has compared the ouput in three different years, 1919, 1929, and 1939, thus showing how the combination of factors of production has changed: ". . . a reduction in any one or more coefficients, with the rest of the structural matrix remaining the same, will always result in a more efficient utilization of resources."[46] The Input-Output technique has been widely used the world over. In the summer of 1961, 218 experts attended a five-day conference in Europe on Input-Output. A British study "presents an analysis of the purchases of each of the 46 industry groups in terms of 44 groups of commodities . . . and the sources of supply of each of the 44 commodity groups."[47] Many other countries, including the U.S.S.R., have produced Input-Output studies.

Leontief's approach lends itself to many interesting uses. According to the *London Economist*, the Input-Output table "should be able to tell industry a lot of new facts about its customers . . . [it] reveals intermediate as well as final demands in detail . . . one has a reliable map of the interconnections of the whole economy . . . but [national income analysis] does not trace how these changes may cumulatively affect the country's industries, services and agriculture . . . [as Input-Output does]."[48]

An example of the application of the Input-Output technique is given by a study by Leontief and Hoffenberg on the economic effects of disarmament. What is required is to find out what industries provide the input for the military outlays. Hence, should these be greatly reduced or eliminated, we would know what substitute outlays would be required if we are to avoid serious economic disturbances. It is obviously unlikely that the purchases for Cape Canaveral will soon be reflected in the shopping list of the average housewife. It is not merely a matter of total demand. A $10 billion cut in military outlays will mean reductions in demand for some products and workers, and a $10 billion rise of civilian expenditures would not necessarily result in the desired employment of those excluded by the drop of military outlays. For example, as the authors point out, a large road program may result in inflationary prices of cement and similar products. In studying this problem the authors estimate how an $8 billion cut in military outlays would affect employment accordingly as the $8 billion are spent on various categories of outlays — e.g. government, exports. The results vary greatly. The study ". . . shows the effects upon employment in the 58 industries that follow from a more reasonable assumption: the projected $8 billion cut in the military budget is here transferred pro rata to the various categories of civilian demand. . . . As can be seen, a total of 253,815 jobs would be eliminated in 19 industries and a total of 591,855 new jobs would be created in the other 38 industries — a gain of 288,040 jobs. . . ."[49]

The emphasis in this paper has been on Keynesian economics first and on mathematical economics second. I have not tried to cover all developments in American economic thought since the First World War; Keynesian economics has been selected for special consideration because it has introduced a brand of economics which allows treatment of the overall economy, and corrects the overemphasis on micro-economics, and especially the stress on the economics of the firm. Keynes built to some extent on income analysis developed in this country, and American economists in turn have applied and implemented Keynesian economics. The attention that is paid to national income, gross national product, consumption, investment, the public sector — these are all products of Keynesian economics. Application of Keynesian economics is an acknowledgment that the government has special responsibilities through tax, spending, and debt policies to offset deficiency of demand and output as well as to correct excess demand, with its inflationary threat.

The 1964 federal budget, with its stress on tax cuts to stimulate the economy suffering from sluggishness, is a tribute to Keynes's theories, his persuasiveness, and the large contributions of American economists to advancing and applying this theory. Keynes failed to reach the White House in the nineteen-thirties despite several talks with President Roosevelt; but in 1963 the spirit of Keynes has greatly influenced the government.

As much cannot be said of mathematical economics as a tool of policy. In fact the excessive diversion of minds fascinated by the manipulation of mathematical symbols reduces the net contribution of economists to the solution of the great public issues of the day. The techniques are novel, and the potential contribution to the solution of some problems is great; but there is danger that excessive resources will be spent on problems that lend themselves to this treatment, irrespective of the substantive content of the problem.

20

Sources of the New Deal

Arthur M. Schlesinger, Jr.

In the background of any historical episode lies all previous history. The strands which a historian may select as vital to an understanding of the particular event will vary widely according to his interest, his temperament, his faith, and his time. Each man must unravel the seamless web in his own way. This essay does not propose any definitive assessment of the sources of the New Deal. No such final assessment is possible. It seeks rather to describe certain social and intellectual tendencies which helped give the New Deal its identity.

I

It is first important to investigate the origins of the New Deal in the psychology of American society. What were the preoccupations which urged the nation into a cascade of reform in the years between 1933 and 1938? One obvious answer to this, of course, is the collapse of the American economic system in 1929. Yet one must wonder whether that shock, devastating as it was, was the whole story of the psychological sources of the New Deal. To sharpen the issue, consider the question: would there have been a New Deal if there had been no depression? Without a depression, would we have had nothing but a placid continuation, so long as prosperity itself continued, of the New Era of the twenties?

One must answer that there would very likely have been some sort of New Deal in the thirties even without the depression. Contemporary thinking has come too unreflectively to assume depression as the necessary prelude to reform. Students of American history know better. The fight against depression was, to be sure, the heart of the New Deal, but it has not been the central issue of traditional American reform: it was not the heart of Jeffersonian democracy nor of Jacksonian democracy nor of the antislavery movement nor of the Progressive movement.

What preceded these other epochs of reform was an accumulation of disquietudes and discontents in American society, often noneconomic in character, and producing a general susceptibility to appeals for change — this and the existence within society of able men or groups who felt themselves cramped by the status quo and who were capable of using the spreading dissatisfaction to advance policies and purposes of their own. This combination of outsiders striving for status and power and a people wearying of the existing leadership and the existing ideals has been the characteristic model of American reform.

The official order in the twenties presented perhaps the nearest we ever came in our history to the identification of the national interest with the interest, values, and goals of a specific class — in this case, of course, the American business community. During the generation before Harding, the political leaders who had commanded the loyalties and the energies of the American people — Theodore Roosevelt and Woodrow Wilson — expressed strains in American life distinct from and often opposed to the values of business. They represented a fusion of patrician and intellectual attitudes which saw in public policy an outlet for creative energy — in Walter Lippmann's phrase, they stood for mastery as against drift. In the service of this conception, they led the people into great national efforts of various sorts, culminating in the convulsive and terrible experience of war. Two decades of this — two decades under the glittering eyes of such leaders as Roosevelt and Wilson, Bryan and La Follette — left the nation in a state of exhaustion.

By 1920 the nation was tired of public crisis. It was tired of discipline and sacrifice. It was tired of abstract and intangible objectives. It could gird itself no longer for heroic moral or intellectual effort. Its instinct for idealism was spent. "It is only once in a generation," Wilson himself had said, "that a people can be lifted above material things. That is why conservative government is in the saddle two-thirds of the time." And the junior official to whom he made this remark, the young Assistant Secretary of the Navy, noted after his unsuccessful try for the Vice-Presidency in 1920, "Every war brings after it a period of materialism and conservatism; people tire quickly of ideals and we are now repeating history." John W. Davis, the Democratic candidate in 1924, said a few years later, "The people usually know what they want at a particular time. . . . In 1924 when I was a candidate what they wanted was repose."

A nation fatigued with ideals and longing for repose was ready for "normalcy." As popular attention receded from public policy, as values and aspirations became private again, people stopped caring about politics, which meant that political power inevitably gravitated to society's powerful economic interests — the government of the exhausted nation quite naturally fell to the businessmen. And for nearly a decade the business government reigned over a prosperous and expanding country.

Yet, for all the material contentment of the twenties, the decade was also marked by mounting spiritual and psychological discontent. One could detect abundant and multiplying symptoms of what Josiah Royce, after Hegel, used to call a self-estranged social order. The official creed began to encounter growing skepticism, and even opposition and ridicule, in the community at large. Able and ambitious groups, denied what they considered fitting recognition or opportunity, began to turn against the Establishment.

If the economic crash of 1929 astonished the experts, a spiritual crash was diagnosed well in advance. "By 1927," reported Scott Fitzgerald, "a widespread neurosis began to be evident, faintly signalled, like a nervous beating of the feet, by the popularity of crossword puzzles." In the same year Walter Lippmann pointed more soberly to the growing discrepancy between the nominal political issues of the day and the actual emotions of the people. If politics took up these real issues, Lippmann said, it would revolutionize the existing party system. "It is not surprising, then, that our political leaders are greatly occupied in dampening down interest, in obscuring issues, and in attempting to distract attention from the realities of American life."

What was wrong with the New Era was not (as yet) evidence of incompetence or stupidity in public policy. Rather, there was a profound discontent with the monopoly of power and prestige by a single class and the resulting indifference of the national government to deeper tensions. Those excluded from the magic circle suffered boredom, resentment, irritation, and eventually indignation over what seemed the intolerable pretensions and irrelevances of their masters. It is an error to underrate the power of boredom as a factor in social change. Our political scientists have pointed out convincingly how the human tendency toward inertia is the enemy of liberalism; they might spend equal time showing how the human dislike of boredom is the enemy of conservatism. The dominant society of the twenties was exceedingly boring, neither bright nor witty nor picturesque nor even handsome, and this prodded the human impulse to redress the balance by throwing rocks at stuffed shirts and top hats.

All this encouraged the defection of specific groups from an official order which ignored their needs and snubbed their ambitions. Within the business community itself there were dissident individuals, especially in the underdeveloped areas of the country, who considered that opportunities for local growth were unduly restrained by Wall Street's control of the money market. The farmers felt themselves shut out from the prevailing prosperity. Elements in the labor movement resented their evident second-class citizenship. Members of foreign nationality groups, especially the newer immigration and its children, chafed under the prevalent assumption that the real America was Anglo-Saxon, Protestant, middle-class, and white. In time some of the younger people of the nation began to grow restless before the ideals held out to them; while others, in accepting these ideals, acquired a smug mediocrity which even depressed some of their elders.

Gravest among the symptoms was the defection of the intellectuals: writers, educators, newspapermen, editors — those who manned the machinery of opinion and who dominated the transmission of ideas. Their estrangement guaranteed the articulation, and thus, to a degree, the coordination of the larger unrest. The intellectuals put the ruling class in its place by substituting for its own admiring picture of itself a set of disrespectful images which an increasing number of people found delightful and persuasive; the insiders, who had before been seen in the reverent terms of Bruce Barton and the *American Magazine*, were now to be seen less reverently through the eyes of H. L. Mencken and Sinclair Lewis. Satire liberated people from the illusion of business infallibility and opened their minds to other visions of American possibility.

The next function of the intellectuals was precisely to explore and substantiate those other visions. They did so with ingenuity and ardor; and the result was that, beneath the official crust, the twenties billowed with agitation, criticism, and hope. Dewey affirmed man's capability for social invention and management; Beard argued that intelligent national planning was the irresistible next phase in history; Parrington insisted that Jeffersonian idealism had a sound basis in the American past, and indeed expressed a truer Americanism than did materialism. Together the satirists and the prophets drew a new portrait of America — both of the American present and of the American promise — and the increasingly visible discrepancy between what was and what might be in America armed the spreading discontent.

The well of idealism was rising again; energies were being replenished, batteries recharged. Outsiders were preparing to hammer on the gates of the citadel. The 1928 election, in which an Irish Catholic challenged Yankee Protestant supremacy, illustrated the gathering revolt against the Establishment. And though Hoover won the election, Samuel Lubell has pointed out that "Smith split not only the Solid South but the Republican North as well." Smith carried counties which had long been traditionally Republican; he smashed the Republican hold on the cities; he mobilized the new immigrants. In losing, he polled nearly as many votes as Calvin Coolidge had polled in winning four years before. He stood for the vital new tendencies of politics; it is likely that the prolongation of these tendencies would have assured a national Democratic victory, without a depression, in 1932 or certainly by 1936. And such a Democratic victory would surely have meant the discharge into public life of able and ambitious people denied preference under a business administration — much the same sort of people, indeed, who eventually came to power with the New Deal. It would have meant new opportunities for the outsiders, for the groups that had seen the door slammed in their faces in the twenties — labor, the farmers, the ethnic minorities, the intellectuals.

The suspicion that a political overturn was due even without a depression is fortified, I think, by the calculations of Arthur M. Schlesinger in his essay of some years back "The Tides of National Politics." In this essay he proposed that liberal and conservative periods in our national life succeed themselves at intervals of about fifteen or sixteen years; this alternation takes place, he wrote, without any apparent correlation with economic circumstances or, indeed, with anything else, except the ebb and flow of national political psychology. By this argument, a liberal epoch was due in America around 1934 or 1935, depression or no.

In short, the New Deal was, among other things, an expression of what would seem — to use a currently unfashionable concept — an inherent cyclical rhythm in American politics. The depression did not cause the cycle: what the depression did was to increase its intensity and deepen its impact by superimposing on the normal cycle the peculiar and unprecedented urgencies arising from economic despair. One might even argue that the depression coming at another stage in the cycle would not necessarily have produced a New Deal. It is certainly true that depressions did not induce epochs of reform in 1873 or in 1893. I think myself, however, that the magnitude of the shock made a political recoil almost certain after 1929. Still, the fact that this recoil took a liberal rather than a reactionary turn may well be due to the accident that the economic shock coincided with a liberal turn in the cycle.

II

The defection of the intellectuals not only gave disquietude a voice: it gave it a philosophy. The more sustained and conscientious thinkers among the rebels were not satisfied with throwing custard pies, in the manner of Mencken, or with drawing cartoons, in the manner of Lewis. Rejecting what James Truslow Adams called the "business civilization," they diligently applied themselves to the analysis of alternatives. John Dewey, Herbert Croly, Thorstein Veblen, and Charles A. Beard dominated the search for a better society. Dewey's instrumentalism supplied the liberal synthesis with its philosophy; Croly's progressivism with its politics; Veblen's institutionalism with its economics; and Beard's nationalism with its history. Together the four men, operating as the intellectual *maquis* of the twenties, prepared themselves to offer the thirties an ideology of social regeneration.

Dewey was perhaps most comprehensive in his impact. Of all the figures in what Morton White has called "the revolt against formalism," he was the most committed both to laying down general principles and to pursuing their implications for a variety of specific fields. His instrumentalism was an organized and public formulation of the pragmatism of which William James's radical empiricism was the brilliant, searching, and private statement. Armed with instrumentalist presuppositions and methods, Dewey ventured forth with serene confidence to redefine aesthetics and logic, educational theory and political theory and social philosophy. His wide sweep, combined with his manifest sensitivity to the issues of disquietude and his intensely earnest, if often groping, style, made him the pervasive influence among the social ideologists of the twenties.

Dewey gave James's pragmatism an activist and collective bent. If, as James said, theories became instruments, then, in Dewey's view, they were instruments to be used. The logic of pragmatism was action; and the logic of action, Dewey believed, was experiment and education in a social context. His hope was that a philosophy of experience, absorbing the findings of science and technology, adjusted to the harsh requirements of industrial society, could issue in an organized social intelligence, capable of superseding a nation of Babbitts by a new Utopia.

Dewey moved steadily forward in his approach to social problems through the twenties. In *Human Nature and Conduct* in 1922, he emphasized the plasticity of human nature. In *The Public and Its Problems* in 1927, he waved away the abstract questions which preoccupied the older political theory and contended that the application of the scientific method to society could produce a community capable of making rational plans for the future. In *Individualism Old and New* in 1929, he said that the old American ideal of individualism had been corrupted by capitalism, that America had already entered "the collective age," and that the choice lay between the anarchic collectivism of profit and the benign collectivism of planning. Only a democratic collectivism, he concluded, could create the conditions for a new and authentic American individualism.

The pressure of depression drove Dewey to push this philosophy to its conclusion. His book of 1935, *Liberalism and Social Action,* was suffused with contempt for social effort which fell short of comprehensive ideology. "Experimental method," he wrote, "is not just messing around nor doing a little of this and a little of that in the hope that things will improve. Just as in the physical sciences, it implies a coherent body of ideas, a theory, that gives direction to effort." The exponent of pragmatism in philosophy had become the stern foe of pragmatism in politics. " 'Reforms' that deal now with this abuse and now with that without having a social goal based upon an inclusive plan, differ entirely from effort at re-forming, in its literal sense, the institutional scheme of things." The piecemeal approach was hopeless; central social planning, Dewey said, was "the sole method of social action by which liberalism can realize its professed aims." The old liberalism was obsolete; its ends, he said, could be achieved "only by reversal of the means to which early liberalism was committed."

The key was the "inclusive plan" — and Croly, Veblen, and Beard, from different starting points, reached the same conclusion. Croly, indeed, had long anticipated Dewey in enthusiasm for a supreme national authority. In 1909 his *Promise of American Life* had given the case for national planning powerful support in historical and economic analysis. In the twenties Croly's influence came more from his writings of the past than from his reflections of the present. Successive disenchantments had destroyed his interest in politics, and he was resting hope increasingly on education, psychology, and finally perhaps religion.

Veblen, on the other hand, was more "practical" than ever before. The translation from a harried existence on university campuses to life as editor in Greenwich Village gave his writing new clarity and his recommendations new concreteness. The basic frame of his thought had long since been established. He had exposed the presuppositions of laissez-faire economics a quarter of a century before; and this had led him to a general rejection of equilibrium economics — of classical model-building — as a means of delusion if not of deliberate deception. The business of economists, he believed, was to describe and explain economic institutions as the actualities of economic society.

His own analysis of the institutions of the American economy centered on two contrasting concepts — "industry," the maximization of production, and "business," the maximization of profits. The drama of American capitalism, as Veblen saw it, was the struggle on the part of industry to fulfill itself by producing more and more as against the determination of business to subordinate the making of goods to the making of money. The price system was the means by which capitalism sabotaged technology and business thwarted the potentialities of industry. "In any community that is organized on the price system," Veblen wrote, ". . . habitual unemployment of the available industrial plant and workmen, in whole or in part, appears to be the indispensable condition."

There was much more to Veblen than that. He was a thoughtful economic historian, an astute spinner of economic and sociological theory, and a biting satirist. But, so far as social reorganization was concerned, his determination was to liberate industry from its bondage to business. This meant essentially the replacement of the price system by a system of centralized physical planning. In *The Engineers and the Price System* in 1921, Veblen tried to show how the economy could be organized "as a systematic whole." His basic proposal was the supersession of the market by a "soviet" of technicians with authority to make direct allocation of resources through the economy.

So Veblen, the economist, ended too with a demand for the "inclusive plan." Beard, the historian, soon joined him. Like Croly, Beard had been under the spell of the New Nationalism a quarter of a century earlier. His great work of 1927, *The Rise of American Civilization*, surveyed the transformation of America from an agricultural to an industrial state in accents both romantic and ironic. The work culminated with the onset of what Beard called the Machine Age; society was now poised, he thought, between integration and catastrophe. The future, he believed, lay in following out the logic of the machine. Beard busied himself in trying to see how modern technology could "extend its area and intensify its characteristics" until its concepts of order and control determined public policy. In 1928 and 1930 he edited two symposia — *Whither*

Mankind and *Toward Civilization*—which hailed "the imperative necessity of planning" and saw science "controlling unlimited power, mastering the nature of materials, adapting them to mankind and mankind to them, conscious rationality triumphant."

The ideology of social regeneration was, in short, the ideology of national economic planning. This was an entirely indigenous faith. It had no relationship with the experiments in totalitarian planning currently in operation in Italy and Soviet Russia and soon to come to Germany. It was, if anything, a reversion to the Utopianism of Edward Bellamy and *Looking Backward.* "Bellamy's epic dream," wrote Beard, "served as a torch from which were lighted the aspirations of multitudes in the United States." And Dewey found it "encouraging" in 1934 that "Bellamy Societies are starting almost spontaneously, but with the aid of a central organization, all over the country." This native progressivism opposed fascism and communism as brutal and false; it opposed traditional conservatism as a façade for business tyranny; it opposed piecemeal liberalism as inadequate and fraudulent. The existing system was rotten; it had to go; and it must be replaced by a system of intelligent central control, a planned society, a democratic collectivism, a new social order, "conscious rationality triumphant."

III

If the New Deal was the expression of an activist phase in a recurrent rhythm in American politics, it was also a concrete response to the breakdown of the traditional economic order in the United States. Whether or not a progressive period would have come about anyway without a depression, this particular progressive period took its specific character from efforts to deal with mass unemployment and economic privation.

It approached these problems in the spirit of Theodore Roosevelt and Woodrow Wilson—the two men whose progressive ideals had inspired many of the leaders of the New Deal, including especially Franklin Roosevelt himself. T. R. and Wilson had accepted the capitalist system, had rejected Utopian change as well as standpat conservatism, and had believed that the answer to revolution was reform. Though moralists in their rhetoric, they were pragmatists in their performance. Their faith was in limited and piecemeal change.

But they left behind a political mood and style rather than an economic policy. The New Nationalism and the New Freedom had assumed the inevitability of economic growth; its disciples were therefore unprepared for economic collapse. And in confronting this unprecedented challenge, the New Deal was confronting a good deal more than merely an American problem. The depression was world-wide. Economic collapse threatened the roots of free institutions everywhere. "This problem of unemployment," as Winston Churchill said in England in 1930, "is the most torturing that can be presented to civilized society." The urgent issue was whether representative democracy could ever deal effectively with it.

Churchill, in the same Romanes lecture at Oxford in 1930, questioned whether it could: democratic governments, he said, drifted along the lines of least resistance, took short views, smoothed their path with platitudes, and paid their way with sops and doles; parliaments could deal with political problems, but not with economic. "One may even be pardoned," Churchill said, "for doubting whether institutions based on adult suffrage could possibly arrive at the right decisions upon the intricate propositions of modern business and finance." These problems required specialist treatment. "You cannot cure cancer by a majority. What is wanted is a remedy."

The movement of discussion in the United States as well as in Britain in the early depression underlined Churchill's doubt whether parliamentary capitalism could meet the economic challenge. Communists and socialists, of course, rejoiced in the depression as the fulfillment of the Marxist prophecy; fascists saw it as the consequence of capitalist degeneration; and even the non-Marxist, democratic planners of the twenties, apparently vindicated by the breakdown of the system, called for the total replacement of capitalism. As for the capitalists themselves, baffled, impotent, and scared, they were capable only of mumbling ancient clichés and incantations. In the years after 1929, a sense spread through the intellectual community that the democratic impulse was drained of vitality and that liberalism was spent as a means of organizing human action. Consider a selection of statements from American writers at the time, and their mortuary resonance:

> The rejection of democracy is nowadays regarded as evidence of superior wisdom. (Ralph Barton Perry)
>
> The moral and intellectual bankruptcy of liberalism in our time needs no demonstration. It is as obvious as rain and as taken for granted. (Nathaniel Peffer)
>
> To attempt a defense of democracy these days is a little like defending paganism in 313 or the divine right of kings in 1793. It is taken for granted that democracy is bad and that it is dying. (George Boas)
>
> "Liberalism is dead." So many people who seem to agree upon nothing else have agreed to accept these three sweeping words. (Joseph Wood Krutch)
>
> Modern Western civilization is a failure. That theory is now generally accepted. (Louise Maunsell Fields)
>
> Why is it that democracy has fallen so rapidly from the high prestige which it had at the Armistice? . . . Why is it that in America itself — in the very temple and citadel of democracy — self-government has been held up to every ridicule, and many observers count it already dead? (Will Durant)

It is hard now to reconstruct the creeping fear that the free system itself had run out of energy, that America had reached, in a phrase Reinhold Niebuhr used as a part of the title of a book in 1934, the "end of an era." What this pessimism implied for the realm of public policy was that democracy had exhausted its intellectual and moral resources, its bag of tricks was played out, and salvation now lay in moving over to a system of total control.

Nor was this in the realm of theory alone; the fate of a moderate socialist government in Great Britain seemed to furnish practical proof that democratic evolution was inadequate. It would have been hard to select a better place than Britain to test the possibilities of a tranquil advance from laissez-faire capitalism to a managed society. Here was a Labour government, sustained by a faith in the "inevitability of gradualness," ruling a nation committed by tradition and instinct to the acceptance of empirical change. How did the British Labour government exploit its opportunity?

The central figures were Ramsay MacDonald, now Prime Minister for the second time, and Philip Snowden, his Chancellor of the Exchequer. Both were classical Socialists who saw in the nationalization of basic industry the answer to all economic riddles. Yet in the existing situation, with a slim Labour majority, nationalization was out of the question. With socialism excluded, MacDonald and Snowden — indeed, nearly all the Labour party leaders — could find no alternative to all-out socialism but nearly all-out laissez-faire. A capitalist order had to be operated on capitalist principles. The economic policy of the Labour government was thus consecrated as faithfully as that of Herbert Hoover's Republican administration in the United States to the balanced budget and the gold standard — and, far more faithfully than American Republicanism, to free trade.

Socialism across the Channel was hardly more resourceful. As the German Social Democrat Fritz Naphtali put it in 1930, "I don't believe that we can do very much, nor anything very decisive, from the point of view of economic policy, to overcome the crisis until it has run its course." In this spirit of impotence, the democratic Socialists of Europe (until Leon Blum came to power some years later) denied the possibility of a middle way and concluded that, short of full socialization, they had no alternative but to accept the logic of laissez-faire.

The assumption that there were two absolutely distinct economic orders, socialism and capitalism, expressed, of course, an unconscious Platonism — a conviction that the true reality lay in the theoretical essences of which any working economy, with its compromises and confusions, could only be an imperfect copy. If in the realm of essences socialism and capitalism were separate phenomena based on separate principles, then they must be kept rigorously apart on earth. Nor was this addiction to Platonism — the belief that the abstraction was somehow more real than the reality, which Whitehead so well called the "fallacy of misplaced concreteness" — confined to doctrinaire capitalists and doctrinaire socialists. The eminent Liberal economist Sir William Beveridge, director of the London School of Economics, braintruster for the Lloyd George welfare reforms before the First World War, spoke for enlightened economic opinion when he identified the "inescapable fatal danger" confronting public policy in the depression as "the danger of mixing freedom and control. We have to decide either to let production be guided by the free play of prices or to plan it socialistically from beginning to end. . . . Control and freedom do not mix." Beveridge, encountering Donald Richberg in Washington in the glowing days of 1933, asked a bit patronizingly whether Richberg really believed that there was "a halfway between Wall Street and Moscow." As for Britain, "there is not much that anyone can do now to help us," Beveridge said. "We must plan to avoid another crisis later. We shall not by conscious effort escape this one."

So dogma denied the possibility of a managed capitalism. Some Englishmen, it is true, dissented from the either/or philosophy. In the general election of 1929, John Maynard Keynes provided the Liberal party with the rudiments of an expansionist policy, based on national spending and public works. As unemployment increased in 1930, so too did the pressure for government action. But Keynesian proposals made no impression on the capitalist orthodoxy of the Socialist leaders. When a minister suggested leaving the gold standard, Snowden covered him with scorn. To the party conference of 1930, MacDonald said, "I appeal to you to go back to your Socialist faith. Do not mix that up with pettifogging patching, either of a Poor Law kind or Relief Work kind." In other words, socialism meant all or — in this case — nothing.

To Snowden and the Labour government little seemed more essential than staying on the gold standard. To keep Britain on gold required American loans; American loans would not be forthcoming unless satisfactory evidence existed of a determination to balance the budget; and the evidence most likely to satisfy the American bankers was a cut in unemployment benefits. In August 1931, MacDonald and Snowden confronted the cabinet with this dismal logic. Arthur Henderson made it clear that the whole cabinet absolutely accepted Snowden's economic theory: "We ought to do everything in our power to balance the Budget." But the proposal to do so through a cut in the dole was unacceptable; the Labour government fell. MacDonald soon returned to office as head of a coalition government. The new government, slightly more adventurous than its predecessors, took Britain off gold in a few weeks. Sidney Webb, Labour's senior intellectual, provided the Labour experiment with its obituary: "No one ever told *us* we could do that!"

The Labour government having immobilized itself by its intellectual conviction that there was no room for maneuver, no middle way, now seemed through its collapse to document its major premise. Thus the experience of 1931 appeared to display the Left as too impotent to achieve reform short of revolution and the Right as too hardboiled to acquiesce in even the most gradual change. "The attempt to give a social bias to capitalism, while leaving it master of the house," wrote R. H. Tawney, "appears to have failed."

If piecemeal reform was beyond the power of the Labour government, as it was beyond the desire of a Tory government, then the only way socialism could be achieved seemed to be through ruthlessness on the Left as great as that on the Right. Such reasoning produced the lust for catastrophism that suffused the British Left and infected a part of the American Left in the early thirties. No one drew more facile conclusions than Harold Laski. The fate of the MacDonald government, Laski wrote, was "tantamount to an insistence that if socialists wish to secure a state built upon the principles of their faith, they can only do so by revolutionary means."

From this perspective Laski and those like him quite naturally looked with contempt on the advocates of the middle way. In December 1934, for the perhaps puzzled readers of *Redbook* magazine, Laski debated with Maynard Keynes whether America could spend its way to recovery. Public spending, Laski said with horror, would lead to inflation or heavy taxation or waste; it would mean, he solemnly wrote, "an unbalanced budget with the disturbance of confidence (an essential condition of recovery) which this implies"; it would bequeath a "bill of staggering dimensions" to future generations. "Government spending as anything more than a temporary and limited expedient," he concluded, "will necessarily do harm in a capitalist society." This was, of course, not only the argument of Ramsay MacDonald but of Herbert Hoover; Laski's novelty was to use it to defend, not a balanced budget and the gold standard, but — socialist revolution.

One way or another, the British Left, persuaded of the impossibility of reform under capitalism, began to vote against liberal democracy. All peaceful roads to progress seemed blocked. Sidney and Beatrice Webb abandoned Fabianism for the mirage of a new civilization in the Soviet Union. After a visit with Roosevelt in Washington, Sir Stafford Cripps wrote, "My whole impression is of an honest anxious man faced by an impossible task — humanizing capitalism and making it work." "The one thing that is not inevitable now," said Cripps, "is gradualness."

IV

Thus, by 1932, both the ideological Left and the ideological Right stood with fierce intransigence on the comforting solidity of dogma. The appearance of the New Deal in 1933 — an enterprise based on a belief in pragmatic experiment and reform — could only excite derision in both camps. Proponents of individualism and proponents of collectivism rejected with equal certitude the doctrine that anything was possible between total free enterprise and total planning.

Herbert Hoover's last Secretary of the Treasury, Ogden Mills, spoke for American conservatives: "We can have a free country or a socialistic one. We cannot have both. Our economic system cannot be half free and half socialistic. . . . There is no middle ground between governing and being governed, between absolute sovereignty and liberty, between tyranny and freedom." Hoover himself was equally vehement: "Even partial regimentation cannot be made to work and still maintain live democratic institutions." In such sentiments, Mills and Hoover would command the enthusiastic assent of Stalin and Mussolini. If the critical question was whether a middle way was possible — a mixed system which might give the state more power than conservatives would like, enough power, indeed, to assure economic and social security, but still not so much as to create dictatorship — then to this question the Hoovers, no less than the Stalins and Mussolinis, had long since returned categorical answers. They all agreed on this, if on nothing else: No.

As for the non-Marxist, indigenous Left in the United States, which had developed an ideology of democratic planning in the twenties, their reaction was equally categorical. John Dewey, conceding that Roosevelt showed a commendable desire for a "controlled and humanized capitalism," pronounced "the necessary conclusion . . . that no such compromise with a decaying system is possible." Where the conservatives said that any attempt to modify the capitalist system must mean socialism, so the radicals said that any attempt to maintain the capitalist system must mean fascism. Laski had made clear in *Democracy in Crisis* that the American ruling class would be as tough and hopeless as any other:

> What evidence is there, among the class which controls the destiny of America, of a will to make the necessary concessions? Is not the execution of Sacco and Vanzetti, the long indefensible imprisonment of Mooney, the grim history of American strikes, the root of the answer to that question?

"Roosevelt's policies can be welded into a consistent whole," concluded I. F. Stone, "only on the basis of one hypothesis . . . that Mr. Roosevelt intends to move toward fascism." "The essential logic of the New Deal," wrote Max Lerner, "is increasingly the naked fist of the capitalist state." In 1934 Sidney Hook, James Burnham, Louis Budenz, V. F. Calverton, James Rorty, and others addressed "An Open Letter to American Intellectuals." "We cannot by some clever Rooseveltian trick," the letter warned,

> evade the unfolding of basic economic and political developments under capitalism. . . . Let us not deceive ourselves that we shall not have to face here also the choice between reaction, on the one hand, and a truly scientific economy under a genuine workers' democracy on the other.

When Professor Rexford G. Tugwell of the Columbia University economics department, on leave in Washington, revisited his campus in 1933, he rashly bragged of the New Deal's freedom from "blind doctrine." The *Columbia Spectator*, then edited by a brilliant young undergraduate named James Wechsler, seized on this boast as the fatal weakness of Tugwell's argument and of the whole New Deal. "This is the crux of the problem," the *Spectator* said; "the blind stumbling in the most chaotic fashion — experimenting from day to day — without any anchor except a few idealistic phrases — is worthless. It is merely political pragmatism." *Merely political pragmatism* — to ideologists, whether of Right or of Left, this seemed conclusive evidence of intellectual bankruptcy. In 1935 *The New Republic* stated with magistral simplicity the argument of the radicals against the New Dealers, of New York against Washington, of the central planners against the pragmatists.

> Either the nation must put up with the confusions and miseries of an essentially unregulated capitalism, or it must prepare to supersede capitalism with socialism. *There is no longer a feasible middle course.*

Both radicalism and conservatism thus ended in the domain of either/or. The contradictions of actuality, which so stimulated the pragmatists of Washington, only violated the proprieties and offended the illusions of the ideologists. While the ideologists, Right or Left, saw themselves as tough-minded realists, in fact they were tender-minded Platonists, preferring essence to existence and considering abstractions the only reality.

The great central source of the New Deal lay precisely in the instinctive response of practical, energetic, and compassionate people to dogmatic absolutes. The compulsion to sacrifice reality to doctrine presented a profound challenge to the pragmatic nerve. Many Americans, refusing to be intimidated by abstractions or to be overawed by ideology, responded by doing things. The whole point of the New Deal lay in its belief in activism, its faith in gradualness, its rejection of catastrophism, its indifference to ideology, its conviction that a managed and modified capitalist order achieved by piecemeal experiment could combine personal freedom and economic growth. "In a world in which revolutions just now are coming easily," said Adolf Berle, "the New Deal chose the more difficult course of moderation and rebuilding." "The course that the new Administration did take," said Harold Ickes, "was the hardest course. It conformed to no theory, but it did fit into the American system — a system of taking action step by step, a system of regulation only to meet concrete needs, a system of courageous recognition of change." Tugwell, rejecting laissez-faire and communism, spoke of the "third course."

Roosevelt himself, of course, was the liberal pragmatist *par excellence*. His aim was to steer between the extremes of chaos and tyranny by moving always, in his phrase, "slightly to the left of center." "Unrestrained individualism," he wrote, had proved a failure; yet "any paternalistic system which tries to provide for security for everyone from above only calls for an impossible task and a regimentation utterly uncongenial to the spirit of our people." He constantly repeated Macaulay's injunction to reform if you wished to preserve.

Roosevelt had no illusions about revolution. Mussolini and Stalin seemed to him, in his phrase, "not mere distant relatives" but "blood brothers." When Emil Ludwig asked him his "political motive," he replied, "My desire is to obviate revolution. . . . I work in a contrary sense to Rome and Moscow." He said during the 1932 campaign:

> Say that civilization is a tree which, as it grows, continually produces rot and dead wood. The radical says: "Cut it down." The conservative says: "Don't touch it." The liberal compromises: "Let's prune, so that we lose neither the old trunk nor the new branches." This campaign is waged to teach the country to march upon its appointed course, the way of change, in an orderly march, avoiding alike the revolution of radicalism and the revolution of conservatism.

It would be a mistake to underestimate the extent to which this pragmatic attitude was itself a major source of New Deal vitality. The exaltation of the middle way seems banal to a later generation. Yet the tyranny of dogma was such in the early years of the Great Depression that infatuation with ideology blocked and smothered the instinctive efforts of free men to work their own salvation. In a world intoxicated with abstractions, the New Deal stood almost alone among governments in a stubborn faith in rational experiment, in trial and error. No one understood this more keenly than the great English critic of absolutes; Keynes, in an open letter to Roosevelt at the end of 1933, defined the hopes generated by the New Deal. "You have made yourself," Keynes told Roosevelt,

> the trustee for those in every country who seek to mend the evils of our condition by reasoned experiment within the framework of the existing social system. If you fail, rational choice will be gravely prejudiced throughout the world, leaving orthodoxy and revolution to fight it out. But, if you succeed, new and bolder methods will be tried everywhere, and we may date the first chapter of a new economic era from your accession to office.

V

The question remains: why did the New Deal have the pragmatic commitment? Why, under the impact of depression, was it not overborne by dogma as were most other governments in the world? The answer to this lies, I suspect, in the point proposed earlier — in the suggestion that the New Deal represented, not just a response to depression, but also a response to pent-up frustrations and needs in American society—frustrations and needs which would have produced an activist, practical mood had there been no depression at all. The periodic demand for affirmative government in American politics, the periodic breakthrough of new leadership—these were already in the works before the depression. Depression, therefore, instead of catching a nation wholly unprepared, merely accelerated tendencies toward change already visible in the national community. The response to depression, in short, was controlled by the values of experimentalism, rather than by those of ideology. The New Deal, rejecting formalism and dogma, was thus able to conduct a fight against economic collapse without destroying the continuities which held American life together.

21

The Contemplation of Society in America

Edward Shils

I

ASPIRATIONS TO ESTABLISHMENT

Our ancestral social scientists of forty years ago were worthy men who believed in the dignity of their calling as university professors. Some of the elders were men of great erudition on the old German and French model, who had read all the literature in their own fields and much else as well. They were scholarly men; they regarded written and printed paper with the critical reverence characteristic of the German and French erudition of the preceding century. They inclined toward the descriptive and statistical concreteness of historical scholarship, toward the *Staatswissenschaften*, the social survey and the ethnographic monograph. They came from a tradition of Darwinism and the German historical and philological disciplines. Almost to a man, they wished their subjects to become more scientific because it was right to be scientific, and because they wished to partake of the respect which the natural sciences received from their university colleagues. They also wished that social science would possess the precision, the reliability, and the power of prediction attributed to the natural sciences. The newer generation, which they formed, did not share their erudition, but it was one with them in the ambition to be scientific.

Their desire has not been fulfilled. The social sciences have not yet become sciences according to the simplified model which they held. But even if their goal — toward which some of the best minds in social science still aspire — has not been realized, the work of the four decades separating us from them has disciplined our understanding, enriched our conception of the social world, and become a vital sector of contemporary culture.

An inspection of the best and the average literature of the early 1920's shows how much more sophisticated and subtle the understanding of individual action and social structure has since become; how much more intimate, observation; how much deeper and more systematic, analysis. Sociology and its companions, anthropology, political science, and psychology, have become more concerned, in a disciplined way, with the great problems of the age and its epochal trends. The treatment of almost any subject forty years ago seems very callow by contrast with the treatment it now receives. The older treatment was obviously much cruder in its techniques of observation and analysis, more simplistic in its theory, more slipshod and unsystematic. Its theory was mainly a prolegomenon to theory rather than theory about the working of particular classes of social things; declaratory aspirations, definitions, and classifications were its stock in trade. *Aperçus* and discursive reflections were most of its best substance. Its practitioners' writings reveal only a distant relationship to vital realities.

Most of the sociology of the older generation of the 1920's has disappeared from the memory of sociologists, and rightly so. Some of it still lives on and is still relevant to present-day interests and the present-day idiom. Much of what has happened since, however different it is, would be inconceivable without the laborious efforts of that serious generation. The fundamental outlook of Robert Park, W. I. Thomas, Charles Cooley, John Dewey, and George Herbert Mead has been assimilated into the intellectual line of the succeeding decades. The conception of man as a restless, outgoing, instrumentally rational, end-seeking, value-internalizing organism, developed by Dewey from a Darwinian inspiration, has continued at the center of American social science. Every new influence has had to adapt itself to this initial point of departure, which despite limitations has been rich in its capacity for extension. At the other side, the conception of a consensual moral order, an order of shared values, from an ultimately Hegelian inspiration, has provided a framework which — however complicated, differentiated, and even transformed by subsequent criticism, research, and theory — has endured into the present. The conception of an individual capable of conformity, withdrawal, rebellion, intelligence, and creativity within a moral order — loose and multifarious, but an order nonetheless — was a great achievement, which has been steadily developed. Even more important, the conception of contemporary society as a state of nature — which the sociologists of forty years ago used as a guide line for their understanding — has survived in a more fashionable translation.

There were few sociologists forty years ago; they were isolated bands of newcomers in the American university. This made them solicitous about the legitimacy of their subject; and it caused them to engage in activities which no longer retain any interest for us. But not all their efforts were spent in self-justification. They attended, as men with a sense of civic responsibility and some concern about the well-being of their society, to a variety of public problems. Immigrants, from abroad and from the American countryside, were much on their minds; like other conservative and liberal intellectuals, they wished to see the newcomers well and happily assimilated, in an orderly and seemly American society, egalitarian, democratic, hard-working, and law-abiding. The Negro, too, became an early object of their interest. Juvenile delinquency and broken families attracted a curiosity which was impelled by compassion and abhorrence. These came together in urban sociological studies at the University of Chicago. In the state universities of the Middle West, the society of the agricultural population was inventoried: church attendance, family budgets, educational composition, club memberships, in studies rather more quantitative and less empathic than the urban studies. Despite their moral earnestness, drawn from an austere

American Victorianism, the sociologists were all in favor of expelling moral judgments from their view of the working of society. They were against Aristotle and Plato; they wanted to understand society as it actually was, not as it should be.

Eager to delimit an autonomous territory of their own, they deliberately eschewed the political. There was another reason for the avoidance: sociologists did not really believe in the efficacy of politics. They regarded society as a part of the process of the natural order of things, controlled by forces deeper than the human will. Power and authority, as part of this natural process, did not impress them much. The sociological social science of the early 1920's was a part of the general revolt — humanitarian, anti-authoritarian, and even realistic — against the ascendancy of kings and rulers. The "New History" had pulled down the monarchs and the conquerors as the determinants of life and had installed the workaday activities of mankind as ethically and empirically more worthy of the scholar's attention. Social scientists were too close to an older and fruitless contest between the "individual" and "society," or, as it was termed then, "social forces," and they were, in the main, on the side of "social forces."

Universities were small by present standards. Postgraduate students were relatively few. Teachers, in so far as they did research, did so with scarcely any assistance other than that of students working on their dissertations. For these reasons and because of the sparseness of financial provision for research, there was a low density of work on any particular subject. The social map was only faintly explored, and the exploration deliberately eschewed the aid of the humanistic and literary contemplation of society. Forty years later it was possible to see that Dos Passos's *Manhattan Transfer*, Scott Fitzgerald's *The Great Gatsby*, Dreiser's *An American Tragedy*, and Eliot's *The Waste Land* were part of a common culture in which sociology grew. Social scientists were attempting then to free themselves from the inhibiting burden of the puritanism and idealism of the Victorian age, to which they were so deeply attached. But before the First World War they made their attempt shyly, awkwardly, and provincially.

II

EXPANSION AND SOPHISTICATION

America's participation in the First World War started the chain of events which ultimately transformed the style of the sociological sciences. The employment of psychologists in the Adjutant General's Office of the U.S. Army during the war was a great turning point. Psychology had become established as a science with pertinent things to relate about human beings; and mental testing went forward at a great rate in the following decade. Psychologists began to regard the industrial working force as a fit object of their ministrations; and the popularity of Taylorism made the psychologists feel that they had discovered their calling.

Another extra-academic influence — ultimately of intellectual importance — was long-standing concern with the welfare of the rural population. Rural sociology, in the second decade, had made unspectacular progress. One part of its concern was carried on by the Institute of Social and Economic Research — the concern for the health of the church in the countryside and in small towns. In the early 1920's, the Institute decided to extend its interests to a somewhat larger community and engaged a young divine-turned-sociologist for the job.

The result was the Lynds' *Middletown*, the first sociological inquiry to attract wide and enduring public attention. It was factual, comprehensive, courageous, and pedestrian. It vaguely conceived of itself as an anthropological monograph, on the Boasian model. It ignored, for all practical purposes, the ideas and the procedures of the urban sociology instituted at the University of Chicago by Professors Park and Burgess, and used by them in studies of Chicago social life. *Middletown*, as an "anthropological" inquiry, studied for the first time the full round of life of all sectors of the population of an entire urban community with the techniques which had been in the process of formation from the time of Eden's *Condition of the Poor*, Le Play's *Les Ouvriers européens*, Engels's studies of family budgets, the *Reports of H. M. Poor Law Commissioners*, and Charles Booth's *Survey of London Life and Labour*. *Middletown*'s comparison between a town as it was at the time of the study and the same town a half-century earlier helped to give clear definition to the growing historical consciousness of the transformation of American society. It fixed the image of an urban society — later to be called, with horrendous implications, a "mass society" — in which hedonism and *anomie* were common. Like much of the sociology of the next decades, it postulated an idyllic epoch of American society which it contrasted with the harsh, conflict-laden, man-destroying, urban society of the present. *Middletown* was in another respect, too, a prefiguration of the future. It espoused and adhered to the claim that prosaic, patient quantitative analysis was the road to progress.

This feature of *Middletown* was further developed by a very different and somewhat later work, which also owed much to extra-academic initiative and patronage: the *Report of the President's Committee on Recent Social Trends.* Its genius was Mr. Herbert Hoover, the factually minded engineer. As Secretary of Commerce, he had already sponsored the earlier survey of *Recent Economic Changes.* As President, he invited a committee, with W. F. Ogburn as its research director, to inquire into the major changes which had occurred in all spheres of American life since the latter part of the nineteenth century. It was an ideal theater for Ogburn's talents — no theoretical adventures, a minimum of generalization, and an ideal of rigorous documentation and quantitative demonstration. No comparably large or thorough investigation — past or present — of "political arithmetic" has ever been undertaken and successfully carried out. Like *Middletown*, but for different reasons, *Recent Social Trends* was the culmination of a great line of inquiry. But the intellectual climate changed, and aspirations went in other directions. *Recent Social Trends* had no successors; it was the last and the greatest instance of its species. Nonetheless, it had a pervasive influence; it contributed mightily to making sociological research more solid and sober. Like *Middletown*, it too purported to describe the new American society, the society in which the family had lost most of its functions, in which religious belief was evaporating, in which power was being concentrated. It too worked within the shadow of the fundamental romantic distinction between the small solidary society with a soul, *Gemeinschaft*, and the large, impersonal, dehumanized, market-centered society which the Germans called *Gesellschaft.*

III

EUROPEAN INFLUENCES

When American sociology entered the second third of the century, its first European contact was behind it. It still retained the European sociological distinction between *Gemeinschaft* and *Gesellschaft;* but in its open, pragmatic, active curiosity about the immediate environment, American sociology had gone far beyond its European forebears. In the course of the twenties and the first years of the Great Depression, the lines between American and European sociology had become attenuated. The older generation had known the writings of their German teachers and colleagues, but to their pupils these learned men were little more than names, having little connection with what the new stage of the subject demanded. The concerns of their elders were too archaic, too remote from the work which American sociologists wanted to do in this period. The older generation had been preoccupied with the establishment of sociology as a separate, self-sufficient discipline; and they selected from Europe what they thought would accredit this claim. What they selected was mainly "methodology," i.e., the location of sociology in the classification of the sciences, and the definitional propensities of German sociology. Therefore, although most of the older generation for a time continued to be viewed with a distant respect, they left no impact on the subsequent growth of sociology.

In their failure to concern themselves seriously with the substance of European sociology, the older American sociologists were not alone, for that substance had scarcely been taken up in Europe. Few Germans had read much of Max Weber beyond the first chapter of *Wirtschaft und Gesellschaft,* the first essay in "Die Protestantische Ethik und der Geist des Kapitalismus" in the first volume of *Aufsätze zur Religionssoziologie,* and a few of the essays from *Wissenschaftslehre.* Americans did no more. Theodore Abel, Louis Wirth, Howard Becker, and, above all, Pitirim Sorokin were well-acquainted with a wide range of European sociological literature. Yet in one way or another, the fruitful but insufficient distinction between *Gemeinschaft* and *Gesellschaft* dominated their outlook and determined what they saw in contemporary society. Thus in the 1920's practically nothing was known by sociologists of the "daring" ideas in which Robert Michels challenged the feasibility of democracy in large societies, of Carl Schmitt's conception of politics as an engagement of irreconcilable enemies, of Marx, Weber, Pareto, Sombart, Mannheim. Practically nothing was known of those who deal with class structure and conflict, with revolution and violence, with oppression and hierarchy, with intellectuals and ideologies, and who, whether they were right or wrong, at least looked over the whole terrain of society and out over a broad horizon. The substantive writings of these European sociologists did begin to become known in the thirties, but they did not penetrate widely into sociological research or theory. Only Professors Lasswell and Parsons, in different ways, took up the lead of European social science and went beyond the distinction between the solidary folk society and the urban *Gesellschaft*.

Among American-born social scientists who became productive in the 1930's, Harold Lasswell was practically alone in absorbing European ideas and seeking to apply them to substantive problems. His interests lay in the great macro-sociological questions of political and social order, and their connection with the interior life of the individual. From psychoanalysis he elaborated a conception of political attachments and antagonisms as extensions of the child's original dispositions toward his parents and siblings. From Marx and Pareto he developed a conception of political life as a struggle over the distribution of wealth, power, income, and deference. With Pareto and Sorel, he envisaged the political process on a world-wide scale as the generation, spread, and retraction of the great political myths. He brought a deliberately tough-minded approach to subjects which American social scientists had not studied previously. He was one of the most influential teachers of the decade, who encouraged his students and others to go beyond legalism and administrative charts in their analysis of national and international politics.

Talcott Parsons was the other American sociologist who drew into a single channel the various streams of thought from which the ideas of the Europeans flowed. He worked at a deeper level and with greater generality. In the thirties he had still to interest himself in concrete, substantive problems. No American or European had mastered so thoroughly and so fundamentally the main lines of European sociological and proto-sociological thought; and no one had or has approached the depth, coherence, and elaboration of his synthesis. Eventually he transformed the traditions which he inherited; and in so doing, he took sociology beyond the reiteration of the *Gemeinschaft-Gesellschaft* scheme and the tension between idealism and utilitarianism which that scheme had left unresolved. Parsons's interest in motives and in personality was balanced by a deeper appreciation of the cultural order. His transforming influence on American sociological thought became more effective, however, only with the beginning of the second half of the century.

IV

EMPIRICISM AND RADICALISM

The Great Depression and Hitler were the most important events in American social science of the 1930's. They changed the field of attention of the student generation both by the force of their disclosures and by their impact on the more open-minded of the generation born around the turn of the century. The depression renewed the faded radicalism of the social sciences. By the middle of the 1930's a new spirit was abroad, and Robert Lynd became one of its leaders. *Middletown in Transition* was a new beginning. Conceived as a documentation of further changes, it turned from a study of society adapting to technological change by jettisoning its traditions, to an analysis of class structure and dynastic power — features of the life of the community which had been accorded no prominence in the earlier study, although they must have been as important then as later. Marx and Veblen were joining Tönnies in the canon of American sociology.

The radicalism of American social scientists had gone into hibernation during the twenties, together with muckraking, municipal reform, and Wilsonian liberalism. Social scientists had not become mere yea-sayers to their society. They continued to be aware of its shortcomings; but the growing scientific aspiration of sociology and the evaporation of radical sentiment and action throughout the country had diminished preoccupation with the righting of social wrongs. Unemployment and poverty in America and the growth of National Socialism in Germany awakened the sleeping tradition. With this awakening came greater sensitivity to inequalities in income, status, and power. The more than academic interest in Marxism, particularly among the youngest generation of social scientists, was a response to the depression, and to the crisis in Europe. The vicissitudes of this contact with Marxism are among the most important factors in the development of sociological studies in the ensuing decades.

Hitler was important to American sociology because National Socialism gave to sociologists a model of total society different from any conceived of previously — namely, the "mass society." He was important also because he presented America with the intellectual refugees, who brought to America a touch of the excitement of Central Europe. They brought awareness of the possibilities of decay of a whole social order. They also brought with them the great names of Marx, Weber, and Freud.

Even if these external agencies had not intervened, American social science of the 1930's would probably not have continued to be what it had been. The subject was making progress. Its acceptance as a respectable academic discipline had diminished the need for self-justification by methodological arguments. The decline in European immigration resulting from the First World War and the xenophobic legislation following it had pushed to one side the theme of assimilation of newcomers into a dominant society and its culture. The subject was ready to move into a more generalized analysis of the cultural consensus and its vicissitudes. The growing sophistication and specialization of intellectual life in the country at large would, in any case, have made academic social scientists less ready to see their subject as one with the concerns of social workers, probation officers, and municipal reformers. The depression and the European intellectual immigration only sharpened this disinclination. They made social scientists more pessimistic and gave them a more inclusive perspective.

In the years between the publication of *Recent Social Trends* and the American entry into the Second World War, interest in the working of the democratic process as expressed through the public opinion poll and the study of voting, and concern with inequality and class conflict as expressed in the study of social stratification, political behavior, and industrial relations, gave a new appearance to American sociology.

The public opinion survey, the creation of a psychologist who had entered market research, was the prototype of a new development. Sociologists proper played a negligible role in its development, but few techniques have had a more profound impact on sociology. It has caused sociologists to think of whole national populations as their subjects, rather than of those accidentally at hand, and it greatly enhanced the statistical sensitivity of sociologists. It set a relatively high standard of precision in the description of the present, so that the disregard for history, so common among sociologists in America, was reinforced. As the scientifically most advanced part of the subject, public opinion (and electoral) studies also defined the image of sociology within and outside the academic world.

The techniques of interviewing began to receive much more attention than in the previous decade. The larger number of interviewers who had to be trained, their lack of previous sociological experience, and the need to treat the records of their interviews statistically rather than impressionistically, accentuated the pressure to standardize interviewing procedures. Participant observation and the study of life history documents, which had been among the finest contributions of the generation which ruled the twenties, declined in favor of the more superficial and more simplifying, but more rigorous methods of the survey.

Much of the responsibility for this turning, within the academic community, rests with Professor Paul Lazarsfeld. His interests, as a psychologist who was one of the earliest market research workers in Europe, his pleasure in technical virtuosity, and his collaboration with Robert Merton — the heir of all that academic sociology had hitherto presented — transformed the social and intellectual structure of American sociology, and with it the other social sciences which were capable of becoming sociological.

When Lazarsfeld settled in the United States in the first half of the thirties, market research was just beginning to soar with radio broadcasting and advertising. New York City was the center for these activities because it was the major commercial and communications center of the country. It was inevitable that one of the universities there should, in so far as sociologists could respond to the new possibilities of research into the outlook and responses of listeners and buyers, become the locus of the new type of research. New York City, Columbia University, and Lazarsfeld were the optimal combination of place, institution, and man.

Within a relatively short time, the most prominent part of sociological research changed, from a subject individually cultivated by university teachers as one part of their general academic responsibility and by postgraduate students doing research, into a more highly organized activity with an elaborate division of labor carried out by a large staff under central direction. There had been collaborative research before — the collaboration of equals, or of teachers and their advanced students, or of a handful of research assistants, usually students submitting some part of the research in the form of a dissertation. There had been team research ever since the first great urban surveys. But this type of team research had not assumed a stable institutional form, with continuous administration and staff employed on a long-term basis without regard to particular research schemes. And although most sociologists still work in the traditional mode, with the cooperation of a few students or student assistants, large-scale institutionally planned and executed research, and the sample survey in particular, have become increasingly important.

In a sense, therefore, the vague and misformulated aspiration of forty years ago, the desire to become a science, has finally begun to be realized — but the realization is rather different from the aspiration. The intellectual skills which sociologists have thought worthy of cultivation, the ideal ends, have changed. Sociology has become a discipline demanding more exact procedures, more self-consciously and more reliably applied than in the past. Techniques of sampling, interviewing, and analyzing have therefore become much more rigorous. Training and experience have become more specialized, and with specialization has come a considerable increase in the number of technically proficient sociologists with a sense of professional dignity. The general standard of technical competence has risen, accompanied by a sense of self-sufficiency and even complacency. In certain centers, this institutionalization and specialization have been accompanied by an indifference to "deeper" variables and to the formulation of more general, more theoretical themes.

Yet the most notable empirical research, despite its descriptive and analytical crudity, has always remained close to the interests of a theory of society. Public opinion polling and market research have always hovered around the problems of the formation of a consensual order. The interest in class structure showed similar traits. It was Professor Lloyd Warner who brought the study of social status and class stratification into American sociology in an idiom appropriate to the empirical and radical temper of the times. Professor Warner came to the subject of social stratification not by the usual, more or less Marxist course, not through any contact with the German sociology, which had sought to cope more adequately with the Marxian problems than had its American counterpart. His inquiry into Yankee City was vast, heterogeneous, and graceless. It too, despite its new accent, bore strong traces of *Gemeinschaft*-sentimentality. The new accent on inequality of status, though not very rich, was forcefully emphatic, and as a result, American sociology acquired a new sensitivity to inequality.

Professor Warner opened the way to a treatment which touched more deeply on the pains of indignity and the gains of ascendancy. John Dollard's *Caste and Class in a Southern Town* followed Warner's path, with the complication of a more or less psychoanalytic interpretation which, though simplified, was a more serious approach to the misery of inferiority and subordination than the hitherto prevailing psychological schemes. Dollard's was the first of a series of studies of the situation of the American Negro; its psychological sensitivity had never been equaled in the study of the stratification of American white society.

The series of inquiries into the conditions affecting industrial output at the Hawthorne plant of the Western Electric Company were conceived in the mode of industrial psychology as an instrument for the management of men. The inquiries themselves were cumbersomely performed — they were begun before the creation of the more rigorous techniques arising from market research and the more penetrating techniques of psychoanalysis, and they were also isolated from the rather amorphous but fertile field-work techniques of the Chicago school. The first schemes of interpretation were likewise very primitive; but as the research progressed, Elton Mayo began to produce a coherent version of the nature of industrial society and the sources of conflict within it. The upshot was a picture of society which, drawing more on Durkheim than on fact, corresponded very closely with what German romanticism and Marxism had envisaged as the essential features of modern society — a society in which there was no moral unity, in which personal ties had broken down, and in which conflict between classes, restless individual ambition, and apathy were all that could be expected.

This Hobbesian conception of modern, and particularly contemporary American, society received considerable reinforcement from the second entry of psychoanalysis into the social sciences in the last part of the thirties and in the beginning of the forties. At the end of the thirties, Erich Fromm, who had already essayed an amalgamation of Marxism and psychoanalysis, came upon the scene with an interpretation of the deeper sources of National Socialism. Fromm's *Escape from Freedom* presented an appealing explanation of a cataclysmic event of modern history, and his explanation was in harmony with the enhanced and widened political sensitivity of the new generation of sociologists. It too was a critique of the social order of capitalism, and it seemed applicable to the United States as well as to Germany.

By the end of the inter-war period, the sociological sciences had established themselves as academic disciplines. They had found an adequate subject matter. They had developed techniques of observation, and they had found an appreciative if narrow public outside the academic world. They had no demonstrated propositions to offer; but in a society which valued information about itself, social research seemed to offer a more reliable sort of information than casual experience and random and occasional reflection. For those who thought that they must manipulate their fellow-men and who believed in science as the instrument of manipulation, social research appeared to be an appropriate handmaiden. Furthermore, the results of social research, uncertain as they were, began to exercise and to gratify that fascination which psychoanalysis had generated earlier in the century. Sociology had actually come to talk about ourselves and our fellow-men, in an age curious about and sensitive to the nuances of motive and conduct. The Second World War drew all these impulses together and quickened them.

Edward Shils

V

THE POLITICS OF SOCIOLOGY

The muses may be silent in wartime — but not the muse of the social sciences. The First World War helped to create the confidence of psychologists; the Second World War enhanced the confidence of the sociologists and those who shared the culture of sociology. Sociologists and their like were nearly everywhere active in the national exertion. Moreover, the end of the war did not slow down their extraordinary range and diversity of activities. The deeper causes of the vitality of the social sciences after the Second World War are manifold. Increased openness about our own experiences and an enhanced empathy with the experience of others have greatly benefited sociology. Still, the subject would have remained meager and amateurish if it had not been for the great productivity of the American economy, the tradition of educational philanthropy, and the great expansion of the foundations.

Self-confident readiness for large undertakings, ample resources, and a more potent technical preparation have all contributed to bring to fruition what was scarcely more than prefigured before the war. The establishment of sample survey institutions — affiliated to universities and supported by income from market research, government contracts, and contracts with private and civic bodies — has also helped to change further the face of sociological research. The conception of the right procedure of research has narrowed, as has probably the imagination of many of its younger practitioners. The level of technical proficiency of the average young sociologist has been raised, and a standard of proficient workmanship has been created where one scarcely existed.

The substance of our thought about society has been enriched by these more precise techniques. The results of their use are not unambiguous. Sociology, however, now talks more frequently of interesting things, and it talks of them in intellectual terms, which, despite jargon and the deformations of technical necessity, touch more and more on what is important in life. Authority, bureaucracy, ambition, tradition, civility, love, fanaticism, and much else on which previously only philosophers, historians, and novelists spoke, are now the common coin of sociology.

Much of the best of the new sociology derives from Max Weber, with a small contribution from Mannheim, a little of Simmel, Michels, and Marx. It is a sociology concerned with the problems of a large-scale democratic society, with civic responsibility, and with "bureaucratization"; it is concerned with power and authority, with man in the modern social machine. Like Max Weber's own work, it is a reformulation of what is living in Marxism and an alternative to what is dead in it. The fundamental lines of this reformulation are largely the achievement of Talcott Parsons, whose book *The Structure of Social Action* was published in 1937. Its influence began to be felt as a guide to European sociological thought only when, after the Second World War, American sociology became interested in problems which transcended the interests of the generation dominant between the wars. When race relations, urban sociology, human ecology, and social disorganization, which had been the inherited idiom and subject matter of American sociology, were replaced by political action, mass communication, fundamental attitudes toward authority, military organization, private and public bureaucracy, and social stratification, then a hitherto hidden European sociology was discovered. Sociology became more political.

The events of the great world played their part in this extension of the horizon. The political emergence of Asia and Africa — previously the concern only of students of mandates and trusteeships, of colonial administration, and of anthropologists seeking real existence in a tiny village — has led to a dramatic turning point in this development. The problems of formation of a society from separate tribes and kinship groups have made social scientists reflect more than hitherto on the nature of a whole society and not just on the conduct of its parts.

This broadening of horizon and the deepening of penetration have not been confined to present-day American society, nor to the new states of Asia and Africa. The contemplation of whole societies and of the fundamental elements of social life has gone backward in history and has ascended in abstraction. In the former movement, comparative analysis has reappeared without the encumbrance of evolutionist prejudice. American social scientists who were for so long history-less and, outside contemporary

America, familiar only with the recent history of Western Europe and a few primitive societies, have, in a few outstanding instances, greatly extended their reach into the depth of human experience. George Homans was the first sociologist of the new breed who interested himself in the domains outside the Western present and the then ostensibly timeless primitive; and he was the first to do original research up to the level of proficiency of the technically trained historian. Many have followed him on the former trail and a few on the latter.

VI

SOCIOLOGY AND OPINION

In a society which does not believe in the efficacy of prayer and divination, and yet retains the needs which both these practices once expressed, sociological research can aspire to be a prelude to action, a means of strengthening the resolution of those who have to make decisions. The manipulation of other human beings on the basis of a knowledge of sociologically formulated "laws" or on the basis of particular empirical observations remains slight, not only because manipulation itself is both difficult and inhibited, and human beings recalcitrant, but because the laws and the observations are nonexistent in the former case and equivocal in the latter. Between its functions of ritual reassurance and its technological function lies the vast body of sociological research. Much of it conducts its small life entirely within academic and professional confines. If it has any impact at all — much of it is still-born — it is on the opinion and the subsequent teaching and research of other sociologists. These now form, within the United States and increasingly on an international scale, a numerous body, and they are enough to satisfy the need for an environment which consumes attention and loyalty. This moral self-sufficiency of the sociological profession runs hand in hand with the isolation, partly necessary and partly self-indulgent, imposed by specialization of techniques and terminology.

This is, however, no unilinear march. Especially at its upper reaches, sociology extends beyond its boundaries into intimate contact and even fusion with other academic subjects and further beyond the academic boundaries into the deeper opinion of contemporary public life. Sociology has been accepted as an organ of the illumination of opinion, as qualified as journalism or literature to illuminate and criticize the condition of man and the state of contemporary society. It was the aspiration of the first generation that sociology should play a part in the enlightenment of opinion and therewith in the improvement of social arrangements. The early social surveys were viewed as society's taking inventory of itself, and field research was intended to contribute both to the remote ideal of a scientific sociology and to the sympathetic awareness in educated circles of the conditions and problems of other sections of society less likely to be perceived through direct experience. It was fitting that this current of hope should have found its fullest realization in Myrdal's *The American Dilemma.* This was the culmination and fulfillment of the classical period, in which the study of ethnic groups and their relationships to the dominant white, English-speaking America was the major theme. Myrdal's work was built upon the sociology which had been cultivated at Chicago, and his collaborators to a large degree either were Chicago sociologists or had been trained under their influence. Its effectiveness lay in the enlightenment of opinion, in making the citizenry more aware of the condition of the Negro in America and of the discrepancies between that condition and the standards of American life. It heightened sensitivity, clarified minds, and reinforced the courage of critics of the inherited situation of the Negro.

The more sophisticated sociology which has since developed in America has no comparable achievement. But whatever the intellectual value of the propositions of *The Lonely Crowd*, *The Power Elite*, *The Authoritarian Personality*, and *Yankee City*, they have made the opinion of educated Americans more subtle and more responsive to the social structure of America than was the opinion of their predecessors of about half a century ago. The complications of authority and inequality are now more finely and sympathetically understood than they were at the beginning of our period; the complexities of personality and the varieties of response in family, school class, play group, workshop, and office are now seen in a more just complexity than they were forty years ago. The more compassionate attitude, now so much taken for granted, the more appreciative perception of the worlds in which our contemporaries live, are at bottom a result of a transformation of consciousness and of the sense of affinity which human beings feel toward each other. The sociological outlook has grown up in this gradually emergent shift in our most fundamental orientations, in an epoch of a more widespread social sensibility. But as it has grown up, it has acquired an independent force of its own, moving in the same direction. This remains its chief significance so far, and such it promises to be in what remains of the present century.

22

Modernity and Mass Society: On the Varieties of Cultural Experience

Daniel Bell

I

THE GREAT SOCIETY

Who Knows Whom

In 1789, when George Washington was inaugurated as the first President of the United States, there were less than four million persons in all thirteen states of the Union, of whom 750,000 were Negro. It was a young population — the median age was sixteen, and there were only 816,000 males older than that. Few persons lived in cities. New York, then the capital of the country, had a population of 33,000. In all, 200,000 individuals lived in what were defined as "urban areas" — meaning, at that time, places with more than 2,500 inhabitants. Because it was a small country, members of the American political elite knew each other well, as did the thin stratum of leading families. But most people lived in small communities or in sparsely inhabited areas, rarely traveled great distances, and considered a visitor from afar a rarity. News meant local gossip, and the few news sheets concentrated on parochial events. The ordinary citizen's image of the world and its politics was exceedingly circumscribed.

Today the United States numbers over 180,000,000 persons. The median age is over thirty, and 130,000,000 persons are over fourteen years of age. About forty million people live in rural areas, but only half of these live on farms. More than a hundred million Americans live in metropolitan areas (i.e., within a county that contains at least one city with 50,000 residents). If one thinks today of the number of persons each of us *knows*, and, even more striking, of the number of persons one *knows of*, the change in dimensions becomes extraordinary.[1] With multiplication of contacts, increased geographical and social mobility, and disintegration of folk and regional patterns, America in recent years has become, perhaps for the first time, truly a national society.[2]

But only in a most tenuous way have there been truly *national institutions*, other than the specifically political ones. A hundred years after Henry James complained of the thinness of American culture, institutional ties are still vague and fitful. There is no established church, no legal or military caste, no Society.[3] There is a national party system, but few commanding national figures. There is a burgeoning intellectual class, tied together by the major large universities; a managerial elite, yet one that recognizes itself more through formal ideology than personal ties or acquaintance; and national groups of scientists, military figures, and journalists. Yet these do not provide American society with a clearly identifiable Establishment.

Rather the emergent national society has been pulled together primarily by popular culture. With the rise of movies, radio, and television, and with the simultaneous printing in different cities of the weekly magazines, to provide uniform national distribution on the same day, for the first time in American history there exists a common set of images, ideas, and entertainments, presented simultaneously to a national audience. American society is woven together precisely through the mass media.

The Mass as Equal

This distinctive character of the times is best conveyed by the phrase *mass society*. Although the term has been used variously and has become entangled with an assortment of judgments and feelings about modern society,[4] it does help one communicate the fact that modern society differs from all previous societies — call them folk, traditional, aristocratic, hierarchical, or organic. And just as the word *culture* has been redefined in our time, so that what once signified refinement of a moral and intellectual nature and the cultivation of the arts, has been expanded to include the total codes of conduct of a group or a people, so, too, the idea of *society*, which once meant a group of genteel people of refined manner, has been broadened to include all the individuals who form a particular social unit. The theme of equality — the fight for political, economic, and social rights, symbolized most strongly in the nineteenth century by the demand for political suffrage and equality of opportunity — the fact that the masses will no longer permit their "exclusion" from society, becomes one of the distinguishing characteristics of the mass society. The style of life, the rights, the norms and values, the desires, the access to privilege, the culture that was once the exclusive property of an elite, are now extended to everyone. In a *democratic* mass society, to belong *in* society means other things as well — not only to share the fruits of society but to have the right — and the chance — to choose: to choose lawmakers, to choose an occupation or profession, to choose where one lives, to choose one's friends, to choose what to buy; in short, to have the right to make and pass judgments in all areas of life, from politics to the arts.

All of this has been made possible by the rise of mass production and mass consumption, and the consequent leveling of distinctive class styles of life. Since 1920, the distinctions between rich and poor have been either modified or glossed over. The great estates have shrunk, and society has been replaced by celebrity. Distinctive modes of dress and travel have been in large part erased. Differences remain, but they are more a matter of degree than of kind, of multitude rather than quality.

Many of the changes that lie behind the rise of a national society and the creation of a mass culture have been due in great measure to the structural transformation of the country's labor force: the change-over from an agrarian to an industrialized urban population, and the end, with the spread of cheap auto transport and radio, of rural isolation; the transformation of the industrial working class from a predominantly immigrant group, speaking languages and leading lives unrelated to American culture, to one largely native-born, speaking English and possessing at least a grade-school education; the entry of women into the labor force, creating vastly different kinds of markets; and, finally, the growing *embourgeoisement* of the work force, with the spread of white-collar jobs. Hand in hand with all this has gone both a reduction of hours worked and a rise in the number of years spent in school by the population as a whole.

With this rapid process of "upgrading," there arises the problem of who becomes the arbiter of taste, the guide to "culture." A society undergoing rapid change inevitably spawns confusion about appropriate modes of behavior, taste, and dress. Victorian and post-Victorian society assumed the task of initiating a rising commercial class into "good manners," through its books on etiquette. Today, this function is performed by the mass media — the guides to behavior are the movies, television, and advertising. In this respect, the mass media do not, like advertising, merely stimulate wants; they play a more subtle role in the changing of habits. The mass media "upgrade" taste, and then a whole series of specialized agencies begins to take over for the new culture-hungry public. The new "tastemakers" — the women's magazines, house-and-home journals, sophisticated periodicals like *The New Yorker* or *Esquire*, prestige institutions like the Museum of Modern Art — teach people style in clothes, home furnishings, standards of design, taste in art, the right wines to stock, the cheeses to buy; in short, the style of life appropriate to the new-found status.

Though these changes initially influence the surface of life — manners, dress, tastes, food habits, and standards of entertainment — sooner or later the metamorphosis affects more basic patterns as well: the structure of authority in the family, and the values of the society as a whole. Where culture was once the "superstructure" of society, shaped by patterns of work and family and religious life, the greed for culture now becomes the foundation; its drives and modes shape the other patterns of life. All of this should add up to a glowingly positive achievement. And yet this new culture has more detractors than defenders. In the very years of this new culture's boom its critics have become increasingly vocal. What is the nature of their indictment?

II

THE IMPEACHMENT OF THE MASS

From Politics to Culture

The preoccupation with the effects of mass culture was one of the distinctive features of the cultural scene in the 1950's. There were many reasons for this. One was the extraordinarily rapid spread of television — the true *mass* medium and the most potent agency available for reaching the largest number of persons simultaneously. And the fact that so much television time was consumed by witless comedy and stereotyped stories of violence, either cowboy-western or big-city gangster, led to concern that the national taste was being debauched.

A second reason for anxiety about mass culture, more diffuse in its effects but sociologically more potent, was America's altered relationship with the rest of the world, particularly Europe, following the Second World War. For the first time, America was claiming, albeit awkwardly and self-consciously, the moral leadership of the world. This evoked an increasing fear, particularly among the European intelligentsia, of an "Americanization of Europe" and a breakdown of cultural standards and of cultural homogeneity. Americans' self-consciousness about their own past and present, and European intellectuals' scrutiny of the key features in contemporary American life, focused most intensely on the nature of mass culture.

Extraordinary social changes became manifest after the war — the cultural absorption into American life of the children of the immigrant generation; the *embourgeoisement* of the working class; the spread of suburbia; the increase of income — involving, in turn, a growing desire on the part of the lower middle class to live conspicuously well; the new affluence, symbolized by the acquisition of television sets, dishwashers, automobiles, even by a taste for "gourmet" foods; the rising curve of higher education, which was given a strong push by the G. I. Bill of Rights for veterans of the Second World War. Yet the self-consciousness generated by these changes, the uncertainties about taste and behavior, created an anxiety about "self" and a concern about "identity" unique in socio-cultural history. The very titles of such best sellers as *The Lonely Crowd*, *The Organization Man*, *The Status Seekers* — each of which sold over 200,000 copies in paperback editions — underline the pre-occupation with popular sociology. And these self-examinations about the validity of American life focused upon mass culture as the inescapable product and symbol of the new age.

Finally, in seeking to account for the nervous preoccupation with mass culture in this decade, one must also take into account the changes in the character of political liberalism, and particularly of political radicalism. The number of political radicals in the United States has never been very large, but radical critics have always had an influence far beyond their numbers. For one thing, the charges they made — about poverty, unequal opportunity, injustice, corruption — found their mark; and these charges were, to a considerable extent, accepted by the society. For another, American intellectual culture, particularly in the last thirty years, has been predominantly liberal, and radical critics have formed a large proportion of the intellectual community as a whole — the large universities, the publishing houses, the "small" magazines. In the 1930's, the major radical criticism of American life centered on economic and social injustice. But in the succeeding decades, which saw the rise of the welfare state and the disenchantment with Communism, radical criticism lost much of its impulse and impact. By the 1950's, political criticism had turned to cultural criticism. In part this was a carry-over of the critical stance in general. Having defined a role for himself as critic, the radical intellectual, once the most extreme economic ills had been meliorated, turned his attention to the quality of American life.[5]

At the same time, the mass media themselves were reaching out for the avant-garde intellectual. In 1959, the *Saturday Evening Post*, for example, began running a feature series entitled "Adventures of the Mind," composed of articles by, among others, the poet Randall Jarrell, the art critic Clement Greenberg, and the novelist C. P. Snow. A magazine like *The New Yorker*, which in the forties was attacked by *Partisan Review* as being too slick, now regularly printed *Partisan Review* writers such as Edmund Wilson, Dwight Macdonald, and Mary McCarthy. The terms "highbrow" and "lowbrow"—which had been coined in 1915 by Van Wyck Brooks, in his famous essay *America's Coming of Age*, to distinguish between the intellectual ("who . . . in his isolation was out of the stream") and the philistine businessman ("who knew nothing but acquisition")—were now resurrected, and in between the high and the low brow was added the new category "middlebrow." Cultural criticism had become a game, and the game caught on.

But even though cultural criticism became a game, it was also a serious problem for the intellectual, who now found himself invited to play some role, albeit an ambiguous one, in a culture he had always spurned. Many of the radical critics felt that the purpose of their being invited into the mass media was to provide "window-dressing," or a spurious prestige, for the mass magazines and television, or because the ideas and themes of serious writing would now be exploited for their "shock value." An even more sinister motive was suspected—the blunting of radical criticism altogether. The relationship of the serious critic and intellectual to the burgeoning mass culture of the fifties became an anxiety in itself, and the source of many a solemn essay and symposium.

High-Low-Middle

The multifarious critique of American mass culture may be divided into four kinds of charges. The first is that genuinely creative work is insufficiently encouraged. Various reasons are cited: that there does not exist an audience to support new and experimental work; that since popular art pays better than serious art, the creative artist is diverted from his true task of producing high culture; and that since the market is the arbiter of taste, large-scale production—whether in the theater, television, movies, or the world of music—has to be diluted to please the lowest common denominator, which means that serious work cannot find a producer or sponsor on its own terms.

The second charge is that serious work, particularly of the past (the so-called high culture), has been debased by being made glibly popular and too readily accessible—as when *Life* or *Look*, for example, prints a reproduction of a serious painting alongside a flashy photograph of a Hollywood starlet. Thus T. W. Adorno has argued that, although radio and hi-fi have permitted people to listen to more records of Beethoven than ever before, they listen to them in order to hum or whistle a melody, and not to appreciate the complex structure of the symphony itself. The mass audience, by accepting slick oversimplifications as serious art, has cheapened our most precious cultural legacy.

The third argument, reversing the second, is that mediocre and middlebrow works become acclaimed as serious art because in purpose, theme, or even in style they seem difficult — though in fact they are not. Dwight Macdonald, for example, singles out Hemingway's *The Old Man and the Sea*, Thornton Wilder's *Our Town*, and Archibald MacLeish's *J.B.* as such speciously serious writing. "Technically, they are advanced enough to impress the middlebrows without worrying them. In content, they are 'central' and 'universal,' in that line of hollowly portentous art which the French call *pompier*, after the glittering golden beplumed helmets of their firemen."[6] The "real" enemy is therefore not the vast sea of self-evident trash but meretricious middlebrow culture — or, as Macdonald labels it, "midcult."[7] In "Masscult," Macdonald writes, "the trick is plain — to please the crowd by any means. But Midcult has it both ways: it pretends to respect the standards of High Culture while in fact it waters them down and vulgarizes them." To critics like Mr. Macdonald, the special danger of "midcult" is that in the upgrading of American taste and standards, the lines between high culture and midcult have been blurred, and midcult standards, precisely because they seem to advance culture, now predominate.

And, finally, there is the argument that most of the run-of-the-mill material that fills up the main bulk of television and the mass magazines is cheap, vulgar, titillating, inciting to violence, prurient and debasing. The material aimed at the mass audience directly, with no pretensions to seriousness, is thus corrupting in itself.

The Root Criticisms of Mass Culture

If these complaints reached the heart of the matter, one might deal with the problem by taking several remedial steps: by greater encouragement of serious work by foundations, such as the Ford

Foundation's program to provide support for novelists, dramatists, painters, and other artists who have already demonstrated their talent; by strengthening the Federal Communications Commission rules toward giving more network time to public-service programs; and by more intensive scrutiny of critical standards and of cultural products by detached agencies such as universities.

But beyond criticism such as Mr. Macdonald's lies an analysis that challenges the possibility of any improvement at all, and denies the possibility of serious culture in a mass society. Such a viewpoint is the basic source of much of the attack on mass culture.

Perhaps the most sweeping indictment of mass culture comes from Ortega y Gasset's *The Revolt of the Masses*, a book written by a Spaniard in 1930, at once humane and aristocratic, culminating a century of Continental thought, fearful since the French Revolution of the impact of the masses on traditional society. For Ortega, mass society meant that the qualified members of society lost authority. Ortega equated culture with classical studies; in his view only the humanist was cultivated. Specialization became the main "enemy" and science was believed to have undermined the authority of the humanities. This defense of classicism as the heart of the traditionalist position, is also to be found in the work of the Catholic theologian Josef Pieper and the Anglican T. S. Eliot. In the United States it has been most strongly echoed in the quondam school of Southern Agrarians, especially in the work of its historical spokesman, Donald Davidson, and sporadically of its literary spokesmen, such as John Crowe Ransom and Allen Tate.

Hannah Arendt, a thoughtful and disquieting social critic, takes this argument one step further and blends it with a historical-Marxist analysis. She argues that "society"—that relatively homogeneous unity of educated and cultivated persons—had always treated culture as a commodity, and had gained snob value from its production and dissemination. But, she continues, there are two crucial differences between the past and the present. First of all, in the past individualism was made possible through an escape *from* society into rebel or bohemian worlds. But in mass society these avenues of escape are closed because such a society incorporates all the strata of the population. Secondly, although society in the past coveted culture largely for its snob appeal, it did not corrupt culture, even if it abused or devaluated it. But mass society does not want culture, it wants entertainment, hence the wares offered by the entertainment industry are consumed by society just as are any other consumer goods.[8]

This charge that mass culture is a form of distraction, and therefore a surrender of standards, is as old as Juvenal's despairing cry that the once proud Roman race now "limits its anxious longings to two things only — bread and the games of the circus." The argument that the mass media simply reformulate the reactionary strategy of social restraint was given its most elegant modern statement by Thorstein Veblen. *Panem et circenses* — "the formula for the politicians of Imperial Rome on which they relied to keep the underlying population from imagining vain remedies for their own hard case" — Veblen rendered as "The Breadline and the Movies."[9] But Veblen pointed out sardonically that modern industry as a form of commercial exploitation is superior to the old Roman imperium. Whereas "the Roman *circenses* appear to have cut somewhat wastefully into the ordinary 'earnings' of those vested interests for whose benefit the Roman imperium was administered . . . the movies of the twentieth century are a business proposition in their own right." And if the manufacture of "pomp and circumstance" and the "rant and swagger" is expensive, since the function of such display is to relieve the common man "of afterthought," it is "only reasonable that the common man should pay the cost."

But contemporary mass culture, the French sociologist Edgar Morin has argued, goes beyond the age-old purpose of social control. Its essential function is "mythic" — to provide, since religion no longer can do so, a giant stage on which the new heroes and gods can be deployed. The authentic mythological hero, M. Morin claims, is the movie actor James Dean. In his brief explosive life, Dean fulfilled the classic requirements. He was an orphan, he ran away, he sought many different experiences ("labors"), and he became, at last, "what in the modern world incarnates the myth of a total life, a film star." Seeking the "absolute," unable to realize this in a woman's love, he found it instead in the ersatz absolute of "speed," and finally, meeting death in an auto crash, he gained immortality. On the first anniversary of his death, three thousand people visited his grave, and for almost a year after his death, two thousand letters a week were written to him in the belief, apparently, that secretly he was still alive, or that somewhere his spirit was accessible.

The distinctive feature of modern society, Morin argues, is that it has invented a new age of man — adolescence.[10] In archaic societies, a boy was often violently initiated into manhood. In modern societies, youth refuses to be absorbed, and seeks, either through nihilism, delinquency, or beatnikism, to drop out of society. Rimbaud pointed the way, with his nostalgia for childhood, his refusal to be "corrupted" by the adult world, by his desire "to live." In contemporary society, adolescents form their own world and elect their own heroes. With its "insatiable demand for personalities," mass culture today feeds upon this youth culture, Morin argues, and in doing so it has made heroes out of adolescent stars. "Anti-culture," he writes, "is not the 'massification' of culture, nor even its vulgarization — on the contrary, anti-culture is the metaphysic of success. . . . Of course, mass culture welcomes the damned, such as Rimbaud and Lawrence, but only to confer posthumous success upon them."

III

MODERNITY AND HIGH CULTURE

The Varieties of Cultural Experience

The difficulty in dealing with such "root" criticism of mass culture is that its spokesmen formulate the problems in all-or-nothing terms. They seek to penetrate to the Platonic essence of modern society, to discover some transcendent principle — the "judgment of the unqualified" or "culture is being destroyed to yield entertainment" — which singularly defines and annihilates the character of mass society. While some specific observations, notably Miss Arendt's and M. Morin's, are dazzlingly brilliant, the question nevertheless arises whether mass society can be defined by any single formula. For the most striking aspect of mass society is that, while it incorporates the broad mass into society, it creates diversity and variety and sharpens hunger for experience, as more and more aspects of the world — geographical, political, and cultural — come within the purview of ordinary men.

At the heart of the problem is the meaning of culture. When one speaks of a "classical culture" or a "Catholic culture" one thinks of a long-linked set of beliefs, traditions, rituals, and injunctions, which in the course of its history has achieved something of a homogeneous style. But modernity is, distinctively, a break with the past *as* past, catapulting it into the present. Mass society contains "the tradition of the new," in Harold Rosenberg's phrase. Under such conditions, not even an avant-garde is possible, for it is by its very nature a rejection of a specific tradition. The characteristic avant-garde tactic is scandal. In modern culture, scandal is eagerly pursued only as still another sensation. Modernity castrates an avant-garde by quickly accepting it, just as it accepts, with equal flexibility, elements from the Western past, the Byzantine past, the Oriental past (and present) in its omnium-gatherum of cultures. The old concept of culture is based on continuity, the modern on variety; the old valued tradition, the contemporary ideal is syncretism.

Little more than a hundred years ago, the Anglo-American world of cultivated discourse was bounded by the classical writers, Latin poets, Greek and Renaissance art, the French *philosophes,* and some German literature introduced mostly through the translations of Carlyle. Today the boundaries of the world, geographically speaking, have been broken, and the range of the arts, both within the traditional frames of literature, painting, sculpture, and music, and outside those frames, is almost limitless. It is not only that the art market has become international, so that Polish painters show in Paris and American painting is bought in England, or that the theater now ignores national frontiers, so that Chekhov, Strindberg, Brecht, O'Neill, Tennessee Williams, Miller, Giradoux, Anouilh, Ionesco, Genet, Beckett, and Osborne are performed simultaneously in Paris, London, New York, Berlin, Frankfurt, Stockholm, Warsaw, and a hundred other cities on several continents. Even more, the range of culture is so diffuse, the "topics" of interest so proliferated, that it is almost impossible to find a center of gravity that can truly define the contemporary "cultivated" man.

The Lack of a Center

It is not only the bewildering variety of cultural demesnes and the vast multiplication of practitioners — serious, semiskilled, or amateur — that create a sense of diffuseness. There is also, in America, the lack of a *center*, spiritual or geographical, which can provide both authority and a place where the leading painters, musicians, and novelists might meet and get to know one another. In the past almost all societies with a "high culture" had some center — the agora, piazza, marketplace, or club located in a national capital — where, in the concentration, exchange, competition, and jousting, each stimulated the other, creating and deriving a sense of vitality from the interchange. Paris, in the early decades of the twentieth century ("the banquet years," as Roger Shattuck has called them) and later, in the 1920's, was such a center. A ballet by Fokine might have decor by Chagall or Picasso and music by Stravinsky or Satie. Through its public schools and the tight triangle of Oxford, Cambridge, and London, England has had an elite whose members could count on direct literary and social acquaintance with each other.

The United States has lacked such a center. In the second quarter of the nineteenth century, Boston provided a unifying ground and, through the mingling of church, wealth, and culture, created a style of sorts. But its very unity was self-defeating in that it was a New England style, and could never dominate the country as a whole. Toward the end of the century, New York became a center for aspiring and parvenu Society, and to some extent a cultural center as well, but it could never quite encompass the different American regional cultures — the Midwest, the Border States, the South, and the Southwest — that had begun to manifest themselves distinctly. Even with the burgeoning of Greenwich Village as topography and symbol, in the years shortly before the First World War and after, New York caught but one element of American culture, the avant-garde, and that only for a while, since it turned out to serve mostly as a way station on the road to Paris.

Given the sheer size of the country, the heterogeneity of ethnic and religious groups, American intellectuals, as Irving Kristol has put it, "meet one another in the dark, so to speak."[11] The United States is probably the only major country in the world (with the exception of Germany) that lacks a national center where the various elites can mingle. The men who edit the large magazines usually lack the opportunity to meet anyone of distinction in politics, drama, or music. The political people are in Washington, the publishing and theater people in New York, the movie people in Los Angeles, and the professoriat is scattered across the country in the large universities. The universities have become the dominant force in the American cultural world today: many novelists, composers, painters, and critics find their haven in the far-flung universities, and many of the major literary and cultural quarterlies are edited there.[12]

Even when, as in New York, there does exist an acknowledged, large center for publishing, theater, music, and painting, the enormous numbers who congregate there, plus the great stress on professionalism, make for a compartmentalization that isolates serious artists from one another. Few painters know theater people or musicians or writers. Composers talk to composers, painters to painters, writers to writers. And where the audience resists compartmentalization, it does so at the expense of the distinctive qualities of the separate arts. A voracious audience of sophisticates quickly snaps up and adopts any avant-garde before it even has a chance to proclaim its rebellion, and the increasingly technical nature of experimentation in the arts, whether it be serial composition in music or *Tachisme* in painting, seems to deny the possibility of a common aesthetic.

The Visual Culture

But the most important way in which modernity confronts high culture is in its denial of the unity of culture. Traditional culture made the distinction between the creative and utilitarian arts. Literature and music, as the contemplative arts, stood at the highest rungs of culture. The status of painting, or sculpture or architecture, because they involved artisan skills, was more ambiguous. Modernity refuses to create any hierarchies. If anything, the "dominant outlook" is visual. It is "sight and sound," and particularly sight, which organize the aesthetic and command the audience. It almost could not be otherwise in a mass society. Mass entertainments (circuses, spectacles, theaters) have always been visual, but today two distinct facts about contemporary life necessarily place the visual element in the forefront: first, that the modern world is an urban world, providing a preponderance of occasions for people to *see* and *want to see* (rather than read and hear) things; the other, that the modern temper, with its hunger for action (as against contemplation), its search for novelty, and its lust for sensation, invites the visual element in the arts as the means of appeasing these compulsions.

The cityscape, man-made, is etched in its architecture and its bridges. The key materials of an industrial civilization, steel and concrete, find their distinctive use in these structures. The use of steel, replacing masonry, allowed architects to erect a simple frame on which to "drape" a building, and to push that frame high into the sky. The use of reinforced concrete allowed the architect to create "sculptured" shapes that have a free-flowing life of their own. In these new forms, one finds a powerful new comprehension and organization of space.

There is an inherent "eclipse of distance" in modern life. Not only is physical distance compressed by modern modes of transportation, but the very techniques of the new arts, principally cinema and modern painting, eclipse the psychic and aesthetic distance between the viewer and the visual experience. The emphasis in cubism on "simultaneity" and in abstract expressionism on "impact" are efforts to intensify the immediacy of the emotion, to pull the spectator into the action, rather than allow him to contemplate the experience. Such is the underlying principle, as well, of the cinema, which, in its use of montage, goes the farthest of any of the contemporary arts in this direction of the "regulation" of emotion: to select the images, the angles of vision, the length of time in viewing a single scene, and the "synapse" of composition. This central aspect of modernity — the organization of social and aesthetic responses in terms of novelty, sensation, simultaneity, and impact — finds its major expression in the visual arts.[13]

IV

THE MARKET AND MASS CULTURE

Audiences: The One and the Many

Today, the "mass" is part of society, and constitutes the largest audience for culture known in history. But reaching such an audience — or audiences — is a costly affair, and in a society that expects culture to pay its own way, rather than be subsidized, the problem of marketing becomes crucial.

A mass society, however, implies not only the great audience — the largest in human history — but equally, the growth of many, differentiated audiences, of varying tastes and interests; and the problem of how to reach such audiences is also one of marketing. In a crucial sense, television has pre-empted the mass market, and in so doing has changed the pattern of magazine audiences and of movie-making in America. As a result of television, the large "general circulation" magazines in the country are losing out. Advertisers are not interested in the sheer size of the magazine audience, since on this count, television can always do better. Despite its four million circulation, *Collier's* folded because it could not attract sufficient advertising, and *Coronet*, despite a record circulation of more than three million, suspended publication because it could not keep up with rising production costs.

But the magazines based on specialized markets do very well indeed. *The New Yorker* has become the national arbiter of sophisticated reading taste. *Esquire,* with Dwight Macdonald as its film critic, and novelists like Norman Mailer and Saul Bellow as contributors, has established itself as the highbrow magazine of the new junior-executive sophisticates. Magazines such as *Harper's* and *Atlantic,* which seek to discuss socio-political issues, have been growing. And, with less fanfare, the range and varieties of new cultural experience are strongly reflected in smaller, specialized magazines that catch the enthusiasms of their special audiences — in painting, in music, the dance, jazz, photography, cinema, and criticism — and in little magazines as well.

As in the theater, the problems of costs are particularly crucial for the large commercial endeavors that, as on Broadway, depend on large audiences. For Broadway, the high rentals in the midtown areas, the high salaries of the stars, and the make-work practices of the unions all combine to kite the costs of production. But the influx of a new, younger generation of theater entrepreneurs, along with the emergence of an audience for experimental plays, has spurred the extraordinary phenomenon of the off-Broadway theater — usually small out-of-the-way lofts or converted neighborhood movie houses — where Beckett, Genet, Ionesco, Brecht, as well as Tennessee Williams, Edward Albee, and younger playwrights are produced. It takes between $50,000 and $125,000 to mount a Broadway play (triple that cost for a musical), while the average off-Broadway show costs, on the average, $5,000 to $12,000.

In the cinema, which, before television, had been the prime mass medium, the competition of home-viewing has produced a similar transmutation. On the one hand, Hollywood has sought to produce huge "spectaculars" (*Spartacus, Exodus, Ben-Hur*), exhibited on a road-show basis of two-a-day screenings at high prices; on the other hand, the breakup of the old studios has released a host of independent movie-makers who produce films aimed at particular audiences. The growth of "art houses" (the movie trade's name for small cinemas that show only "serious" or "foreign" films) from twelve to over six hundred since the end of the Second World War, according to *Variety*, has encouraged the production of semidocumentary and experimental films, such as Morris Engel's *The Little Fugitive*, John Cassavetes' *Shadows*, Sidney Meyer's *The Savage Eye*, and Jack Kerouac's beatnik joke, *Pull My Daisy*. Just as off-Broadway has become a permanent fact of the New York theater, so, too, off-Hollywood cinema promises to become a new dimension of cinema life.

Nowhere has the conquest of new audiences been as dramatic as in publishing. The so-called paperback revolution has been primarily a revolution in marketing. Until fairly recently publishing in the United States followed the nineteenth-century practice of selling books through bookstores. In a country as "small" as England, bookstores have concentrated markets. But in the United States, except for a few major cities and university towns, bookstores have been an inadequate means of reaching mass audiences. The marketing revolution consisted mainly in finding thousands of additional outlets — in bus and air terminals, cigar and candy stores, supermarkets, and the like — for the sale of paperbacks. As against the few thousand bookstores that sold books, there are today over thirty thousand outlets for paperbacks. Sales of paperbacks have risen from about six million copies in 1940 to an estimated five hundred million in 1960. Not only have sales of individual volumes been astounding but the variety of books brought back into print now makes it possible for nearly everyone to build a serious library.

Not only has the range of the arts and culture been widely extended, but in the last forty years there has been an extraordinary multiplication in the number of persons trying to make a living as painters, writers, actors, or holding jobs (e.g., in colleges) that allow them to produce novels, poetry, critical essays and books, or paint, sculpt, compose music, or put on experimental drama. In New York, for example, the Telephone Directory now lists about 400 art galleries, and the critics regularly cover about 250 of these. If one assumes that each gallery has between fifteen and twenty shows a season, and that a good many of these are group shows, then it is reasonable to assume that the work of about three thousand painters is displayed each year in New York. It is extraordinarily difficult to pin down, statistically, any comparative figures, but the very increase in population, the rise of an urban audience, the change-over in the labor force, and, most particularly, the spread of education would allow one to say that more persons are now engaged in producing and consuming cultural works than at any other time in world history.

Standards and Subsidies

The problem of numbers — either of producers of culture, or of audience — brings one back to the debate about standards: the argument that mass culture is necessarily a debauched one; that, as Nietzsche once put it, popular art "counterfeits" the serious arts and lowers standards of excellence.

The arguments drawn from history are inconclusive; we know little about the way the masses spent their time a hundred years ago.[14] From novels and from travelers' accounts, we know, for example, that the popular entertainments in England, as late as the early nineteenth century, consisted of cock-fighting, bear-baiting, and attending the public hangings of criminals.[15] How does one compare the effects of the direct viewing of violence and blood-letting with the vicarious viewing of such events today? "The major error of the analysts of popular culture," writes Edward Shils, "is their belief that it has succeeded to something which was intrinsically worthy, that man has sunk into a hitherto unknown mire because of it, and that it is a necessary prelude to the further degradation and perhaps ultimate extinction of high culture. . . . It would be far more correct to assume that mass culture is now less damaging to the lower classes than the dismal and harsh existence of earlier centuries had ever been. The reading of good books, the enjoyment of superior music and painting, although perhaps meager, is certainly more widespread than in previous centuries, and there is no reason to believe that it is less profound and less genuine."[16]

In the curious dialectic of the debate, popular sociology — the analysis of mass culture — has tried to replace literary criticism as the arbiter of taste. Popular sociology establishes categories like highbrow, middlebrow, and lowbrow, or masscult and midcult — based either on audience reaction or the presumed intention of the cultural work — and then judges by these categories, rather than by explicit literary or aesthetic standards. But this usurpation of function can help neither sociology nor literary criticism. In critical terms, a work is either good or bad, whatever audience it is aimed at. Many highbrow works are pretentious and empty, and many items of mass appeal, particularly in the movies, are skilled works of art. The judgment belongs to the critic and the creators, and their peers.

It is curious, too, that in a whole decade of writing about the vacuities of mass culture and the problem of maintaining standards of serious culture, almost no attention has been paid to concrete matters of public policy: to what can be done to eliminate some of the overwhelming vulgarity, particularly on television, what can be done to raise public taste and, through public subsidy, support composers, painters, writers, the opera, or serious dramatic productions. As Arthur Schlesinger, Jr., has pointed out,[17] the machinery for regulating television does exist. A television channel is a quasi-public utility; the number of wave lengths is limited, and a television license is a lucrative thing. The Federal Communications Commission does have the power, which until recently it has rarely exercised, to encourage better programs, to limit advertising, to increase the time for public-service presentations and the like. Whether the specific proposals Schlesinger makes are valid or not is less relevant than the fact that the problem remains singularly unexplored. One clear reason for this, as has been pointed out earlier, is that critics of mass culture, as part of their general political stance, prefer to be critics rather than doers.

If, however, one wishes to do something, one must distinguish the modest problem of improving the mass media from the more difficult and complex problem of how an age comes to create great art at all. The solution of the first depends in great measure on the willingness of the institutions of the community — universities, foundations, community groups, and government — to produce a competent audience and to channel moneys into the support of the arts. But the second is of a different magnitude and is not — and here is where I feel the critics of mass culture have gone awry — dependent on audience at all. The great art of any time is an act of decisive and solitary affirmation. It arises when, in the uneven development of styles, specific arts break the bounds of convention and develop new modes of expression, and this is as much an *immanent* problem in the nature of an art form as it is a response to social environment. The great art of the twentieth century — the modern movement — arose out of the hatred of bourgeois conventions (and, in part, was also a masked pastoral protest against the requirements of an industrial society). That art did not depend on a large audience, or even on a cultivated one, as much as it did on a community of its own, and on an attendant circle of sympathetic critics. As in many instances of the past, that defiant model — the artist as rebel, as alienated figure, as avant-garde — became the image that a later society has accepted almost as valid.[18]

Modernity, however, has in this respect run its course. The old rebellious styles have become the new academicism, and the artists have been absorbed and defeated by the audience.

As to the future of "mass culture" in America? The greatness of America has been its openness. Few Americans have "inherited" a culture or a style of life through the thread of tradition or family. In culture, as in politics, they have had to "make" their own way. Neither the immigrant boy from the New York slum nor the farm boy from the midwest prairie who sought art as an experience or as life, has been barred because of caste or class, though other difficulties — notably the scorn for the aesthetic or the emphasis on the practical — have stood in his way. Today, the paths are wider than ever before. The varieties of cultural experience are being matched by the diversities of audience. The philistinism of the past has been replaced by a hunger for culture; every critic can find his forum, and the American is anxious to say his *mea culpa*. The period of modernity, from 1910 on, has already provided an enormous capital for the future — in painting, architecture, and literature. Whether it is squandered or not depends upon the imagination and will of those who make public policy and on the audiences' concern, as shaped by the colleges and universities of the land.

23

Science in America: The Twentieth Century

Everett Mendelsohn

The pace of American science at the turn of the century was leisurely at best; some felt it cripplingly slow. In 1902 Carl Snyder, an economist, observed in the *North American Review* that, "despite much notable achievement, America's position in the world of science is inferior."[1] The world's scientific literature, Snyder said, could be searched in vain for reference to major American achievement.

The fault was not due in Snyder's view to the lack of educational opportunity. America outnumbered England and France, he wrote, in colleges and universities of the first rank; only Germany had as many or as well-supported institutions for higher education. The cause of the continued failure of America to develop basic science lay rather, Snyder and others thought, in the American cultural tradition. The situation had changed little from the day when Joseph Henry complained: "in this country, though many excel in the application of science to the practical arts of life, few devote themselves to the continued labor and patient thought necessary to the discovery and development of new truths."[2] In his Presidential Address before the American Physical Society in 1899, the physicist Henry A. Rowland declared: "Much of the intellect of the country is still wasted in the pursuit of so-called practical science which ministers to our physical needs and but little thought and money is given to the grander portion of the subject which appeals to our intellect alone."[3] Americans, Rowland felt, were still confusing invention with science. But he added that the growth of professional scientific groups indicated that a true scientific spirit must sometime emerge. And already Americans were beginning to carry out important work in certain scientific fields.

I

One field in which the United States evidenced leadership early in the century was the study of heredity, or genetics. The rediscovery of the Mendelian theories in 1900 provoked a new interest in experimental studies of heredity in laboratories throughout Europe. Why this area of biology became the first scientific field in which Americans were able to make a sequence of important contributions is hard to tell. The pattern of work may, however, hold the key. By 1909 Thomas Hunt Morgan, already a prominent American experimental zoologist, started investigations in genetics. The field was new and lively and no rigid tradition sent students to any single center for advanced study. Genetics must also have attracted those interested in transforming biology into a precise and analytical science. Certainly Morgan brought reputation and vitality to his new studies. The consequence was the gathering in the Morgan laboratories at Columbia (and at Woods Hole in the summer) of an active group of students and young associates engaged in collective stimulation and inquiry.

The chromosome theory of inheritance was only the first of the "classical" theories of genetics to come from the Morgan group. The names of the early associates, Herman J. Muller, Alfred H. Sturtevant, Calvin Bridges, are a roster of major innovators in genetics. During the years 1910–27 foreign geneticists went to the genetics center at Columbia University in the same way that American physicists and chemists flocked to European laboratories. Sex-linked heredity, the mapping of gene locations on the chromosome, genetic effects of imperfect cell division, all emerged from the Columbia investigation.

Other Americans, perhaps challenged by discoveries being made so close to home, extended the area of genetic research. George Beadle learned about the genetics of fruit flies from A. H. Sturtevant while on a postdoctoral fellowship at the California Institute of Technology. Working in later years with the chemist Edward L. Tatum, Beadle and Sturtevant confirmed an hypothesis of Sewall Wright, another early geneticist, that genes directly affect the metabolic activities of the cell. With this background, it is not surprising that major advances in genetics since 1945 continue to come from American laboratories.

II

The outbreak of war in 1914 helped to catalyze the efforts of those attempting to reform American science. Even before America's entry into the war, a committee under the chairmanship of George Ellery Hale persuaded President Wilson to form the National Research Council, a body "whose purpose shall be to bring into cooperation existing governmental, educational, industrial, and other research organizations" in order to strengthen the national defense.[4] Hale, who made his reputation as an astronomer and Director of the Mount Wilson Observatory, was at his best "as an initiator and promoter of scientific enterprises."[5] He helped re-establish the National Academy of Science and it was at his urging that the Academy in 1916 offered its resources to the President of the United States. Hale was among those who recognized that science could play a role in breaking the stalemate of trench warfare through the development of new and unconventional weapons. He felt that the gap between pure and applied research had to be closed. From the outset the National Research Council included engineers from the prominent industrial research establishments. "Experience has shown," Hale claimed, "that the investigator can adapt himself to the solution of the problems which the exigencies of the moment may have thrust upon him."[6]

As American relations with Germany grew worse in the winter

and spring of 1917 Hale was joined in Washington by the Chicago physicist R. A. Millikan, who shortly became the key administrative officer of the National Research Council. The major problem in the early years of the Council was financial. The Council was an arm of the National Academy of Science; and the government was accordingly prohibited from subsidizing its activities. The Carnegie Corporation and the Rockefeller Foundation made the initial grants. Although government funds later became available, private funds provided a large share of the total support given the N.R.C. during the war.

One of the most important acts of the N.R.C. was the establishment of the Research Information Service. Set up in early 1918 with funds made available by President Wilson, the Research Information Service placed two leading scientists in London and Paris as scientific attachés at the embassies. It was clear to the American directors of the Service, as it had been to prominent American scientists earlier in the century, that American science was dependent in large measure on European science and technology.

The research effort of the First World War has received mixed evaluation. Basic science was subordinated to the need for immediate results. But to some "the wonderful achievements of science under the pressure of necessity have demonstrated the economic possibilities of scientific investigation."[7] Even if this had been accomplished at the expense of training new men and continuing basic research, as some claimed, it opened up a new horizon for industrial exploitation of science.

III

With the liquidation of the wartime N.R.C. after the Armistice, the new peacetime N.R.C. emerged as a subdivision of the National Academy of Science with membership derived from the seventy-nine scientific societies which had participated in naming the governing boards. Although operating from Washington and enjoying semiofficial status, the N.R.C. was completely financed by private funds coming in large measure from the great foundations. But the N.R.C. was not a powerful central organization, and it could not effectively coordinate national scientific activity.

There were several appeals for the establishment of a research policy. Vernon Kellogg, the director of the N.R.C., urged the planning of concerted efforts for the resolution of certain scientific problems. Karl Compton called for the establishment of some means for effectively directing scientific research.

But such appeals fell on deaf ears. Government activity in the sciences during the decade of the twenties remained rather limited, and the traditional federal agencies within which research had been carried out showed little vitality. At no time during the postwar period did governmental expenditures for research and development exceed two per cent of the total. Herbert Hoover realized the importance of science but was more interested in channeling private than public funds into basic research. The case for research, he believed, rested on the self-interest of the business community. He made the point bluntly before one group of businessmen: "Our whole banking community does not do the public service in a year that Faraday's discoveries do us daily."[8] In absolute amount, the federal government was still spending less than $50 million per year on science by 1930.

The Great Depression, with the Hoover policy of government retrenchment, brought a further decline in government expenditures for science. Nonetheless Hoover retained his hope that scientific research, privately financed, might ultimately reverse the trend and provide productivity and prosperity.

The New Deal at first did not know what attitude to take toward scientific research. In the long run such research would obviously be beneficial; but with the economy in crisis the improvement of productivity promised only to shrink further the supply of jobs. It was the new Secretary of Agriculture, Henry A. Wallace, who furnished the New Deal with a policy. "Science," he pointed out, "has turned scarcity into plenty. Merely because it has served us well is no reason why we should charge science with the responsibility of our failure to apportion production to need and to distribute the fruits of plenty equitably."[9] The science Wallace talked of was social as well as physical. Its fields included human application as well as basic discovery. The laissez-faire approach to scientific discovery would not do, Wallace claimed; scientists and engineers must take the social implications of their work into account. American scientists were challenged to play a role in the social experiments of the New Deal.

The major instrument in the revival of organized scientific activity was the newly created Science Advisory Board whose first chairman was Karl Compton. Through a series of subcommittees the Board undertook a study of the governmental research establishment. The Board ultimately drew up a "Recovery Program of Science Progress" which laid stress on the social objectives of science and aimed to provide the scientific establishment a share in the New Deal. Although it succeeded in rationalizing the federal scientific bureaus, the Board's proposals for enlisting scientific talent in combatting the depression and providing employment for unemployed scientists and engineers were never carried out. By 1935, after two years of intense activity, the Science Advisory Board dissolved, never having been successful in convincing the government to invest in rebuilding the scientific establishment.[10]

It was during the later part of the New Deal, under new auspices, that many of the proposed aids for science were finally acted upon. Under the direction of the National Resources Committee a study was prepared, *Research — A National Resource*, which carefully examined all aspects of government research, placing it against a background of the scientific activities of industry and the universities.[11] With the outbreak of war in Europe, science, with its relationships to government and society more clearly understood, was called to wrestle with new problems.

IV

One factor, often overlooked by students of American scientific development, had its roots outside of the United States. This was the treatment of science in Nazi Germany. The great German universities, which had been world centers of scientific learning and to which several generations of Americans had gone for their advanced training in science, came under political control. Censorship was imposed; "non-Aryan" professors were dismissed, among them many of the great names in German science. Between 1933 and 1938, approximately 1,880 scientists of distinction left the universities of Austria and Germany. Fully one-fourth of the German Nobel prize winners were among those exiled. The number of science students in the German universities dropped by two-thirds between 1932 and 1937.[12] Many of the scientific exiles migrated to the United States, thus greatly strengthening the nation's scientific resources for research and training. Among them were Leo Szilard, Eugene Wigner, Edward Teller, Enrico Fermi, James Franck, and Emilio Segre, to mention but a few.

The European influence was particularly strong in the field of physics. The work of the physicist I. I. Rabi in developing the molecular beam techniques in 1929 led to the establishment at Columbia University of a group which explored the many ramifications of this discovery. Rabi himself had been trained at the Hamburg laboratory of the German physicist Otto Stern; but his insight and leadership brought talented American physicists into the fruitful field of molecular beam studies.[13]

Nonetheless, major innovations in modern physics came from the European laboratories. Copenhagen, Cambridge (England), and Göttingen were the centers of vibrant activity in the first three decades of this century. Americans went abroad to study with Bohr, Rutherford, Heisenberg, Born, and the other new interpreters of matter. Contributions from American physicists began to become more substantial in the thirties, and some new facilities, such as E. O. Lawrence's cyclotron at the Radiation Laboratory in California, began attracting attention. The onset of the Second World War administered a special stimulus to American physics.

V

Perhaps the most marked change brought about in science by America's involvement in the Second World War was the rise of the organization scientist. Teams of basic scientists were assembled for operations research — meeting complex military problems with collective scientific analysis. Other teams of scientists were brought together for the production of major new weapons.

A new series of agencies sprang into existence to coordinate the enormously accelerated scientific contribution to military research and development. The Office of Scientific Research and Development (OSRD) headed by Dr. Vannevar Bush had two major constituents, the National Defense Research Committee (NDRC) and the Committee on Medical Research. These agencies often subcontracted critical problems to groups of outside scientists, many within the universities. Among the better-known successes was the development of radar.[14]

The activity which ultimately provided the greatest public drama was the one least known during the course of the war itself. The Manhattan Engineering District of the Army Corps of Engineers organized the large-scale scientific and industrial undertaking which produced the nuclear bombs exploded over Hiroshima and Nagasaki. The idea for a uranium bomb was initiated by physicists and only reluctantly accepted by a government wary of spending large amounts of money on a project filled with uncertainties. But the scientists, with many refugees from Nazism among them, impressed others with their fears that Germany might already be at work on nuclear bomb development.

July 1941 marked the turning point in the invention of the atomic bomb. New developments reported from several laboratories made a bomb seem scientifically feasible. Furthermore, a report indicated that the British, who had treated the bomb project more seriously all along, had theoretically calculated that a bomb small enough to be carried in existing aircraft could be produced within two years. Laboratories at Columbia, Chicago, and Berkeley worked on the varied aspects of isotope separation, atomic-pile construction, bomb design, and so forth. Whole new scientific-technological cities were created. Oak Ridge, Tennessee, and Hanford, Washington, forest and mountain prior to 1942, became major centers of scientific activity. On a hill at Los Alamos, New Mexico, J. Robert Oppenheimer assembled as talented a group of physicists as existed any place in the world. Their success opened a new chapter in the history of science as well as a new epoch in international affairs.

VI

The mushroom cloud symbolized more than man's entry into the nuclear age. It did more than bring a heightened sense of social responsibility to the scientific community. It signaled the entrance of science into government affairs on a scale hardly even dreamed of in the tracts of earlier writers. An estimated two billion dollars was spent upon the development of the first nuclear bombs, representing a larger investment than the total of all previous federal expenditures for research and development. The most significant fact about these extraordinary funds was that the American scientific establishment had the capacity to absorb them. The United States could now claim a highly competent group of physicists, many of whom had received graduate training abroad but who were now teaching and researching in university laboratories in the United States: Arthur H. and Karl T. Compton, I. I. Rabi, J. Robert Oppenheimer, Vannevar Bush, James B. Conant, Ernest O. Lawrence, Glenn T. Seaborg, and others. The United States had entered the twentieth century without a large-scale scientific establishment. The Second World War left America with a scientific community large enough, varied enough, and talented enough to work miracles in scientific research and development.

VII

As late as 1945, Vannevar Bush's report to the President warned the nation:

> Our national pre-eminence in the fields of applied research and technology should not blind us to the truth that with respect to pure research — the discovery of fundamental new knowledge and basic scientific principles — America has occupied a second place.[15]

America's dependence on Europe for basic science and for the training of advanced scientists had existed since the first days of colonization. But after the Second World War the situation was beginning to change. I. I. Rabi's comment dramatizes the shift that has occurred in the last generation: "When I first went to Europe a quarter of a century ago I was provincial. When I went to Europe after the war, it was Europe that had become provincial."[16] Between 1901 and 1939 some 128 Nobel Prizes were awarded in the fields of physics, chemistry, medicine, and physiology. Americans won only fifteen. Of the 101 Nobel Prizes awarded from 1943 through 1961, Americans have received 48.

The characteristic feature of American science in the twentieth century has been growth — in size, in vitality, in excellence, and in a new concentration on basic research. The change in the quantity and quality of American science is made manifest in several ways. The number of men involved in scientific research and development has grown at the rate of 6 per cent per year and is expected to total about 2.5 million by 1970. The growth rate for the labor force at large has been only 1.4 per cent per year. Of the professionals in science and engineering the number holding doctoral degrees has risen from just under 4,000 in 1900 to approximately 87,000 in 1960 and is expected to reach approximately 168,000 by 1970, indicating a growth rate of 7 per cent per year.[17] Lest these figures be taken to mean that science has grown at the expense of other areas of scholarship, it should be noted that in 1914 some 48 per cent of those receiving Ph.D. degrees were in the sciences; while in 1959, although an increase is noticeable, the Ph.D. degrees granted in science represented only 57 per cent of the total. These data suggest that, along with science, the whole of learning has enjoyed a marked growth in the first half of the twentieth century.[18]

The increase in the total number of scientists has been matched by a steady increase in the membership of scientific societies and in the number of specialized scientific groups. The American Association for the Advancement of Science has sought to associate the many specialized science societies with itself. In the brief span of years from 1948 to 1955, the number of such associated organizations rose from 208 to 265; and in the latter year the aggregate memberships rose above 2,000,000, making the A.A.A.S. the largest scientific organization in the world.

The membership of the A.A.A.S. itself can serve as a barometer of the growth of science as a profession. At the time of its founding in 1848 the A.A.A.S. had 461 members. At its fiftieth anniversary the Association numbered under 2,000. Only twenty years later, at the time of America's entry into the First World War, the number had increased to about 9,000. By the time of its centenary in 1948, the A.A.A.S. had 42,000 members, exclusive of the associated groups.[19] By 1962 the membership had increased to 71,000.

A recent study of sixty of the leading engineering and scientific societies in the United States indicates that there has been, during the past twenty years, an average growth of 8 per cent per year in membership. Physics and electronics showed the most rapid acceleration, undergoing a six-fold increase. The other scientific groups had a 3.5-fold increase, or a growth of only 5 per cent per year in the past twenty years.[20]

The meaning of this rapid growth is not told in the numbers alone. For example, prior to the Second World War most physicists were involved in teaching and academic research; only a small portion of their work carried immediate practical implications. During the 1930's less than one-third of those who held Ph.D. degrees in physics went into government or industrial laboratories, the other two-thirds remaining in colleges and universities. By 1957 there had been a five-fold increase in the number of physicists while the total number whose primary occupation was teaching showed no significant increase. Thus a high proportion of the physicists now receiving their degrees are involved in full-time research under government or industrial sponsorship. Although the proportions are not the same for all fields of science, it is clear that a shift has occurred from the period during which the majority of scientists lived their lives within the university, to the present time, which finds a majority of professional scientists working outside of the university framework.

VIII

Perhaps the most startling phenomenon connected with the growth of science has been the rapid rise in the amount of money spent on research and development. In the past decade there has been a steady 15 per cent per year increase in funds expended for research and development as compared to an increase of only 3.5 per cent per year of the gross national product.[21] Expenditures in this area have been shared by several sectors of the economy, government, industry, and the universities. The most spectacular growth in spending occurred in the period after the Second World War. In 1938, for example, a total of $264 million was spent (government $48 million, 18 per cent; industry $177 million, 67 per cent; universities $28 million, 11 per cent; all other sources $11 million, 4 per cent). Since that date the total spending on scientific research and development has multiplied by more than forty-fold, with government funds accounting for well over half the total. In 1961 the federal government provided an estimated $9,000 million of the total $14,000 million spent on scientific research and development.

The amount of money allocated to basic research is approximately 8 per cent of the total expenditure for research and development, and again government funds predominate, although the major portion of basic research is still conducted in the universities.[22] The periods of rapid expansion in funds for research and development have coincided with military demand. Thus allocations rose from $74 million to $1.6 billion between 1940 and 1945, the billion mark being passed in 1943. The major portion of the increase — about one-half of the total research and development costs during the latter years of the war — can be attributed to the Manhattan Project.[23]

The outbreak of the Korean War produced another expansion in budgets for research and development. Military research and development expenditures increased by more than forty-fold in the years between the beginning of the Second World War and the end of the Korean War, while this same period witnessed only a four-fold rise in nonmilitary research.[24] Still another jump in funds for scientific work followed the launching of the Soviet earth satellite, Sputnik, in 1958. Although military demands continue to account for the bulk of expenditures in research and development, this expenditure goes for pure as well as for applied research.

Nor has weapons development been alone in receiving substantially increased budgets. Both the National Institutes of Health and the National Science Foundation have benefited from the enlarged public interest and have been able to develop major programs in basic and general science. The National Institutes of Health have enjoyed a nine-fold budget increase since being founded in the years just after the Second World War. In fact, medical research has proved so popular with the Congress that the Institutes have been given each year more money than the President has recommended in his budget message.

All indications are that the relative importance of the government in supporting research will continue to increase. The last twenty years have witnessed a fundamental shift so that in principle and by appropriation of funds the federal government has demonstrated that the conduct of scientific research and the training of new scientists have an important place in national policy.

IX

Even as American science has grown in stature and research facilities in the United States have increased in importance, science has become more rather than less international. Karl Compton's plea for the rehabilitation of those institutions of science and implements of learning destroyed during the war has in large measure been realized.[25] Scientific conferences have become increasingly international in nature. The new social problems of science are shared by all nations.

One such problem — dramatized by the novelist-physicist Sir Charles Snow in his influential essay *The Two Cultures* — is the proper relationship between the traditional culture of the humanists and the technical culture of the scientists.[26] Snow warned against the widening gap between the two and added that the humanist's ignorance of the laws of thermodynamics was no less a betrayal of a common cultural responsibility than the scientist's ignorance of Picasso or Proust. This scientific resentment of the monopolization of "culture" by the humanities is one aspect of the problem; the other is the humanist's fear that the heavy social investment in science is likely to downgrade and devitalize the humane studies. The increased allocation of funds, public and private, to scientific and technical training fills traditionalists with alarm at a time when Latin and Greek are vanishing from educational curricula. Even the lucrative fellowships available in scientific and technical areas are considered magnets to draw bright students away from the humanities and social sciences.

There can be no question that a tension exists between the "two cultures" — that, for example, laymen in even the most advanced technological societies are often abysmally ignorant of the most elementary scientific propositions and practices. Nonetheless, the influence of magazines like *The Scientific American* reveals a public interest in science not matched since the days of Huxley and Fiske. At the same time, scientists themselves increasingly recognize the indispensability of the humane studies not only to the health of a civilization but to their own fulfillment as individuals. While the gap between the "two cultures" remains, one notes a disposition on both sides to throw a bridge across the chasm.

This disposition is reinforced by the most pressing of all the social problems created by contemporary science — that is, the control of the destructive power unleashed in the modern laboratory. Modern science and technology have conferred on mankind the ultimate power — the power to blow up the world. A sense of responsibility and of guilt in bringing this situation about has taken scientists into the arena of public policy as never before; and at the same time the existence of this terrifying threat to human survival has compelled nonscientists to give unprecedented attention to scientific issues. The somber threat of annihilation commits the future of civilization to the future of science in terms not envisaged by the benign prophets of nineteenth-century scientism. The final irony would be if the gap between the two cultures were to be healed by the urgent necessity to insure the survival of both.

24

Contemporary Issues in Education

James B. Conant

Education is and always will be a controversial subject in a free society. The discussion of American public education which has taken place since the Second World War provides no exception to this statement. Quite the contrary. At least half a dozen books highly critical of our public schools have been published in the last decade and a half. One organization has been formed with the avowed purpose of re-establishing what the organizers declare are the principles of basic education. The voice of the critics grew louder after the Russian success with rockets in the fall of 1957, and articles about the alleged shortcomings of our public high schools were front-page news. The immediate demand was for the training of more and better scientists, but many proposals for radical changes in the pattern of public education were aimed at much larger objectives. The claim was made that our secondary schools were too soft, our able youth insufficiently challenged both before and after entering college.

The vigorous attack on those who were responsible for the

direction of the tax-supported schools was promptly answered. Both sides in the acrimonious debate which took place in the winter of 1957–58 quoted national statistics to support their claims. For example, the small percentages of high school pupils studying physics and trigonometry and a foreign language were cited to prove the inadequacy of our schools; comparisons with similar figures fifty years ago certainly showed a vast alteration in the pattern of studies of the teenagers attending school. The defenders of the public schools were quick to point out that fifty years ago the high schools were attended by only a small fraction of those of high school age; those who did attend had demonstrated interest in and ability to handle mathematics and foreign languages. The revolutionary transformation of the composition of the student body of our secondary schools which had occurred between 1900 and 1930 certainly invalidated the comparisons put forward by the critics. On the other hand, no state or national figures were available to show what fraction of the boys and girls who had the capacity to benefit from studying a full program of academic subjects were taking advantage of the courses offered.

The dubious value of arguments about American education (either pro or con) based on national statistics is obvious when one considers the number and diversity of our high schools and remembers the implications of local control. There were some 21,000 high schools in the 48 states of the Union in 1958; of those some 17,000 were small schools graduating each year less than one hundred boys and girls; many schools graduated as few as ten or twenty. Most of these small schools could not afford to offer courses in twelfth-grade mathematics, or physics, or a modern foreign language. To average together numbers from these small schools with the figures pertaining to the 4,000 or so high schools which graduate more than one hundred a year is to obtain a set of meaningless statistics. Furthermore, the differences in the nature of the communities being served have a large effect on the attitudes of the pupils and the pedagogic problems of the teachers. As the furor of the debate subsided in late 1958, it began to be admitted by both sides that there was no such thing as a typical American high school, and the less said in support or defense of such a mythical institution the better, if one wished to improve public education. And all hands admitted the need for improving at least some and probably most of our tax-supported secondary schools. Many likewise agreed that the number-one problem in many states was district reorganization and school consolidation, with the elimination as far as possible of the small high school.

When looking overseas, one saw that bitter controversies about education were not confined to the United States. Great Britain at the close of the Second World War introduced considerable changes in the educational system, and the period of adjustment and discussion is far from over. In France proposals for quite radical reforms have been discussed for a decade. When De Gaulle became President, some of these reforms were put into operation; the school-leaving age was raised by two years effective for the class entering in 1959. More than one European educator has said to me, "It seems as if we in Europe are talking about introducing a dose of American education in Europe just when you are talking about Europeanizing your schools." To this I have always replied, "The problems on both sides of the Atlantic are similar. They arise when a free democratic nation tries to adjust its educational pattern to a heavily industrialized society."

The slogan "equality of educational opportunity" is now widely proclaimed throughout the free world. The problems arise when one tries to translate this general phrase into concrete terms, and there are few specific measures applicable to all countries. The vast differences in history, tradition, and governmental structure of different nations make the importation or exportation of educational schemes usually impossible and almost certainly unwise. To try and decide whether education in one country is better than in another is like asking a comparative anatomist whether an elephant is a better mammal than a whale.

One European problem in education which has caused sharp differences of opinion among politicians as well as among educators is the adjustment of the relation of the state to the schools and to the church. Because of the American doctrine of the separation of church and state and the development during the last one hundred years of a pattern of locally controlled nondenominational public schools, the European church-state-school problem finds no parallel in the United States. Nevertheless, there is an issue as to the relation of organized religious bodies to American education, and, therefore, this is the first of the issues I shall treat in this brief survey of the current scene.

I

THE RELIGIOUS ISSUE

Nearly forty years ago the Supreme Court ruled that the Fourteenth Amendment guaranteed to every parent the right to send children to a private school; any laws of a state to the contrary were invalid. The right of an individual state to set standards for private schools, as far as I am aware, has never been questioned, but in practice the degree of supervision of private schools in most states is small. As a consequence, I may note in passing that there is very little information available as to the curricula and standards of private schools. About 15 per cent of the young people attending elementary and secondary schools are enrolled in private schools. The vast majority of these schools are church-connected, and Catholic, Lutheran, and Episcopalian parochial schools are to be found throughout the United States. In some cities as many as half the children are attending Catholic parochial schools.

The religious issue is primarily, then, an issue facing the parent. If a person believes that formal schooling cannot and should not be divorced from religious beliefs, then he sends his children to a church school. That many parents have such a conviction is demonstrated by the large attendance in parochial schools. At the college level the situation seems to be markedly different, and many graduates of parochial schools enter nondenominational institutions of higher education. Since the public high school serves effectively in many communities as a center for developing respect and understanding between different groups of children, I cannot refrain from expressing my regret at the spread of parochial high schools. I wish that those parents who insist that the education of their children be in a school of their own faith might be satisfied with sending their children to a church school for the first six or eight years and then be ready to enter them into a public high school. As a matter of fact, at present in a number of cities and towns a tax-supported high school is the only high school available, and many boys and girls enter after completing their education in parochial elementary schools.

Ten years and more ago a few churchmen in a number of different denominations repeatedly attacked the public schools because they were secular and, emphasizing their belief in a religious education, suggested that tax money should go to the support of church-connected schools. One hears few arguments along these lines today; rather the proponents of federal aid to parochial schools base their case on what they regard as the unfairness of the proposals to limit aid to public schools. The discussion seems to turn on whether the First and Fourteenth Amendments of the Constitution prohibit the use of either federal or state funds to pay for instruction in schools directed by a religious organization. On this subject, until a case is decided by the Supreme Court, people are entitled to diverse views, but to my mind those who oppose the granting of state or federal money to private schools have the better of the argument. It is perhaps significant that some denominations in certain localities provide daily religious instruction in buildings provided by the denomination. Such a combination of public education and denominational instruction appears to satisfy the considerable number of families which are involved.

II

CONTROL OF PUBLIC EDUCATION

The powers of the local school board are so great that the character of the members of the board may be the determining factor in regard to whether the local schools are good or bad. Where public apathy prevails for one reason or another, the school board may become purely political; those who seek election or are appointed by the mayor (a practice in large cities) may be aspiring politicians who regard schools only as an area for political patronage. Under such conditions teachers may be hired and promoted because of their friends and relatives, not because of their ability; school supplies and buildings may become sources of political power for a few members of the board.

A good school board will leave all personnel problems to the superintendent and the school principals. The details of the curriculum and the choice of textbooks will likewise be left to the administrative officers and the teachers. The board will confine itself to problems of general policy and the choosing of the superintendent. This last is a matter of supreme importance.

The shortcomings of more than one local school board have led frustrated citizens interested in public education to question the basic idea of local control. For some critics of the present situation, the continuation of local control is a real and vital issue. To my mind, the question is not whether local control is fundamentally a good scheme but what today are the alternatives. One possibility is for the state itself to exercise complete control as is the case in Hawaii and to a large extent in Alaska. The teachers could be employed by the state authorities and assigned to the local schools; salaries could be determined at the state capital and curricula and all other matters centrally controlled. If a first-rate state board of education were chosen and the board in turn appointed an excellent state superintendent, a state system might well be an improvement over the present situation in most states. But these are two very large "ifs" in the proposition. The remedy might very well prove to be worse than the disease.

I regard any debate over the merits of a state system versus local control as highly theoretical, for I cannot imagine the legislature in any large important state abolishing the local boards and centralizing authority for education in the capital of the state. Moreover, nothing short of an amendment to the Constitution would provide the basis for a positive federal policy on education. A national advisory body appointed by the President might conceivably recommend standards and a secondary school curriculum. But one's judgment of the wisdom of such recommendations would depend largely on the appraisal of the committee membership.

Real issues about the control of public education do exist, however, in every state. They turn on the extent to which the state authorities should limit the powers of the local boards. There is room for great differences of opinion as to what powers should be delegated by the state to the local boards and what powers retained by a state school board and its agents. New York is a state in which the state educational authority is exercised to about as great an extent as possible without setting up a system of state schools. In other states, the issue might be to what degree they should imitate New York.

III

FINANCE

The issues clustering about the problem of financing public education are not new. Traditionally for many years local real estate taxes provided the money to support the local public schools. Increasingly state aid has been used in many states to supplement the local resources, because in many communities the real estate base for taxation has been found to be totally inadequate. For at least a generation there has been a strong movement, supported by the professional educators, to persuade the Federal Congress to make large grants to the states to supplement those state funds which go to the local communities to support the local schools. The issue is generally called the issue of "federal aid to education," though more accurately it might be called "massive federal aid to the states in support of the local public schools." It has been pointed out often that Congress each year does appropriate considerable sums of money in support of education. The so-called land-grant colleges have received federal funds ever since the passage of the Morrill Act during the Civil War. The states receive federal funds in support of vocational education under the Smith-Hughes Act passed by Congress more than forty years ago. In response to the public pressures created by the excitement over the launching of sputniks, Congress passed the National Defense Education Act in 1958.

It has been estimated that in the country over something like six to eight billion dollars a year should be spent on increasing the current annual expenses of the local public schools. In addition, in some states the construction of school buildings has failed to keep pace with the rapid increase in the size of the school-age population. If one takes into account this deficit in school construction, the total educational deficit is still larger. Where is the money to come from?

The proponents of massive federal aid to the states for school construction and the payment of teachers' salaries point out that (*a*) Congress has over the years appropriated money for educational purposes without setting up unduly restrictive measures of federal control; (*b*) since the population of the United States is extremely mobile, more so than ever before because of the wide ownership of cars and the improvement of roads (made possible by federal funds!), poor elementary schools in one state result in poorly educated children turning up in the secondary schools of another state; (*c*) the national need in this period of a grim struggle with Soviet imperialism in the age of rockets and thermonuclear weapons requires that *all* American youth be educated as well as possible; (*d*) in some states the taxing machinery has ground to a halt, and state funds are not available to the extent they should be to supplement the local taxes; (*e*) some ten or twelve states (mostly in the South) do not have the resources to raise sufficient state funds for education under any bearable system of taxation.

The opponents of massive federal aid, who for more than twenty years have controlled the action of Congress, argue somewhat as follows: (*a*) education is traditionally in the United States a local concern, and the greatest degree of central control that can be tolerated is control from the state capital; (*b*) if Congress appropriates annually any such sum as six billion dollars, a high degree of federal control is inevitable; (*c*) the control may take the form of inquiries by Congressional committees into educational affairs which should be the concern only of the states; (*d*) whatever may be written into the first authorization bill renouncing Congressional and federal influence, there can be no guarantee that a subsequent Congress will not tack a rider onto the appropriation bill which makes explicit one or another form of federal control (for example, the rider might refuse the funds to any state in which the schools were still segregated); (*e*) the federal budget cannot stand any such increase as is contemplated; (*f*) the needs of the schools have been vastly overestimated by the professional educators and the demands of teachers; what increases are needed can be met by state action.

The debate over massive federal aid for public schools promises to be one which will attract an increasing amount of public interest in the years immediately ahead. It is complicated by the variety of answers that can be provided to a simple question: If Congress is to vote large sums of money for public schools, how is the money to be divided among the states? Space does not permit me to analyze this highly important question in any detail. Suffice it to say that even those who are not opposed to federal aid on general grounds may be divided on the issue of the amount of money to be appropriated and the method of its allocation state by state. Of one thing only am I sure, in the next ten years either public education in many states will stand still or deteriorate still further, or the taxing machinery in many states will have to be vastly improved, or Congress will have to embark on the course of providing massive federal aid for the public schools in all or almost all states.

IV

DESEGREGATION

Since the opinions of the Supreme Court in 1954 and 1955 in regard to segregation, the status of education in the former Confederate states may be said to be uncertain. The seriousness of the situation may be estimated by the fact that many prominent citizens of Southern states are talking about setting up a system of privately financed schools in each locality where the Federal Court, in response to a suit, orders desegregation. The issue legally has been settled. Locally the response to the new situation creates a variety of issues which are essentially political rather than educational. It would appear that gradually as one suit after another is brought in Southern cities, towns, and school districts, completely segregated tax-supported schools will disappear. Whether for white children, private schools will take their place, as some now declare, is a matter for history to decide.

V

SHOULD EVERYONE GO TO COLLEGE?

Or Should Higher Education be Reserved for the Academically Talented?

Two separate issues tend to be confused in the discussion of the question whether all or almost all American youth should go to college. On the one hand, it is clear that for any one private institution the issue resolves itself into the question of what should be the criteria for admission. For publicly supported colleges and universities, on the other hand, a matter of public policy is involved. Each state or municipality which supports one or more universities or colleges must determine the conditions under which tax money is spent to provide education beyond the high school. In the last analysis, this is a political decision made by the voters in their election of the representatives who make the laws, collect the taxes, and distribute the public funds.

Let us consider first the question of who should go to college at taxpayers' expense — that is to say, who should receive essentially free education beyond the high school. Several states have adopted the policy of providing free education for all high school graduates who wish to avail themselves of the opportunity. California has a widespread system of local two-year junior colleges, a group of four-year state colleges, and a state university with many campuses. Ohio has no state-supported junior colleges but a number of state-supported four-year colleges. In both states any high school graduate can continue his or her education at public expense at least for a year or two.

In California's two-year local colleges, some students enroll in terminal programs and complete their formal education in one or two years. Others enroll in the equivalent of the first two years of the university. Those who successfully complete this academic work can then transfer to one of the several campuses of the University of California and enroll as juniors. The records show these transfer students do as well on the average as those admitted to the university as freshmen. In Ohio the enrollment in the freshman year of the state institutions is large, and in the many private colleges as well. However, a considerable fraction of those who enter the Ohio institutions drop out after one or two years of study. In some other states, extension branches of the state university provide locally for many of the needs met by the California junior colleges. There are a number of states in which admission to the tax-supported colleges and university (or universities) is more restricted than in Ohio and California. The citizens in any state may well debate what should be the state policy as regards tax-supported education beyond the high school. California or Ohio may be taken as a model if free post-high school education is to be provided for all high school graduates, though the history of the state will be often a determining factor as regards the practicability of any post-high school scheme. Those states in which admission to state-supported institutions of higher education is now restricted, must decide whether the institutions should raise or lower their standards.

Those who determine the admission policy of a private college or university face a continuing issue — namely, what standards should be set for admission. There are such a multitude of institutions offering four-year programs leading to a bachelor's degree that it is impossible to generalize about the present situation. At one end of the spectrum stand the so-called prestige colleges which are becoming more and more embarrassed by the flood of applicants for admission. At the other end are certain privately controlled four-year colleges which are not overcrowded and admission to which is in reality open to all who hold a high school diploma. Within many private universities parallel undergraduate programs are available in commerce or business, in teacher training, in engineering, in journalism, in nursing, in agriculture, in arts and sciences — to name only a few of the offerings. The requirements for admission and the standards for graduation cover a wide range. Wise guidance officers in the high school are well aware of the differences in admission policy among the hundreds of colleges. In those suburban communities where almost all parents want their offspring to enter a four-year college irrespective of academic ability, the well-informed high school guidance officer can guide almost all pupils into some four-year institution. Parental ambition to have the son or daughter enter a college with high admission standards can be modified in the case of children with a minimum of academic talent, provided the diagnosis is made early enough and the mothers and fathers are in close consultation with the school authorities.

It must be remembered that the American four-year liberal arts college is a unique institution. So, too, is the undergraduate liberal arts college of a university. As late as the 1820's the word "college" was used in the United States to designate a school intermediate between the elementary school and the university. As long as ability to read and write Latin and Greek were the recognized hallmarks of an educated man, the job of the college was to complete the study of the classics begun in school — not only the classics but mathematics too. It has been several generations since one could speak of a standard pattern for the curriculum of a four-year institution. This fact means that there can be no standard pattern of a college preparatory course. The engineering schools, to be sure, can and do lay down requirements for admission in terms of the mathematics that an entering student must have studied. Some colleges still have a few subject-matter requirements, but, as compared with fifty years ago, there are few subjects which must be studied in order to obtain admission to a college. The most selective colleges rely on a combination of the school record (the marks obtained and the school recommendation) and the new type of tests given by the College Entrance Examination Board. The standards for admission in terms of the developed academic talent of the applicant vary enormously from institution to institution. So, too, do the standards for graduation. The holding of a bachelor's degree may signify little more than four years' exposure to education. Many colleges have become more and more comprehensive, and undergraduates may specialize in fields such as journalism, home economics, business, and nursing. Those students who wish to study for the professions of law and medicine with few exceptions must usually have completed at least two years of an academic program in college. Many law schools as well as graduate schools of arts and sciences require the applicant to have already received a bachelor's degree. But admission officers are well aware of the fact that there exists a hierarchy of four-year institutions. Nothing is said publicly, but the college record of an applicant is judged in terms of what is known about the marking standards of the college in question.

No one fact differentiates European education from American more than the existence of the state examinations for admission to a university in Europe and the absence of any similar examinations in the United States. Here, the point at which a young person starts his or her professional training is far from clear. Future engineers enter an engineering school immediately on graduation from high school. Future doctors and lawyers often complete a four-year undergraduate course before starting to train for their professional work. Chemists, physicists, biologists, economists, future professors of the humanities, often major in college in the fields which, at the graduate level, they will study more intensively and in which they will eventually obtain a Ph.D. Some liberal arts colleges still restrict the range of subjects which an undergraduate may study. Only those which at the graduate level are recognized as falling within the competence of a faculty of arts and sciences are permitted.

The question has been repeatedly raised in the United States for a hundred years at least: "What should be a college program for an able student?" A rigid curriculum based on a working knowledge of Latin and Greek obtained in school was once the answer. Then came the triumph of the free elective system in which all *academic* subjects were treated as having equal value as part of a liberal education. In the last twenty years, the pendulum has swung back and many programs have been outlined in many colleges which are intended to provide a central core of the work of an undergraduate. There have been so many attempts to provide programs of general education that it is impossible to summarize the efforts. In many institutions the issue has been: How shall we provide a general or liberal education in addition to specialized education for those who attend our college? I should hazard the opinion that few, if any, communities of scholars are completely satisfied with the present answers.

VI

THE SECONDARY SCHOOL CURRICULUM

The public high schools and the private boarding schools which fifty or sixty years ago sent a good fraction of their graduates to college were often rightly designated as "college preparatory schools." During the last of the nineteenth and the first two decades of the twentieth century, something like a revolt of the schoolmasters took place. The teachers wished to be freed from the task of teaching their subjects according to a syllabus and be relieved of the responsibility of helping the less able students "cram" for the college entrance board examinations. This revolt coincided with the revolution in the nature of the public high school population. It became increasingly clear that there must be elective programs in school as well as in college, and that some of these programs must be of a practical nature. As a consequence of the change in employment practices (the abolishing of child labor), high school people faced a set of new problems. Professors of education who were disciples of Colonel Parker and John Dewey were ready to assist in the transformation of the high school curriculum. Instruction in foreign languages was cut back in many schools, leaving often an absurd residue of two years of Latin and two years of French or Spanish as the only possibility for even the brightest boy or girl. Mathematics and the physical sciences did not suffer the same sort of change, but the nature and quality of the instruction varied enormously from school to school. Art and music were added to the curriculum and increasing emphasis was placed on dramatics, the publication of a school paper, and various other activities which fifty years ago were strictly extracurricular.

Those who favored the new practices spoke in terms of the development of the "whole child," those who clung to the traditional curriculum spoke of education as a process of "training the mind" or developing the intellect. The issue is more usefully drawn if we turn to specific courses rather than use vague general phrases. On the one hand, there are some who feel that foreign languages, mathematics beyond algebra, and chemistry and physics are primarily subjects to be studied in college by the few who have a burning desire to master them; in the high school, sequential courses in these subjects might be available, but no guidance officer or school official should even suggest that able students might do well to elect these academic subjects. Educators who take this view are apt to talk in terms of the development of a well-rounded personality. At the other extreme stand a few critics of public secondary education who feel that a large proportion of a high school student body ought to be forced to study at least one foreign language and mathematics through grade 12 as well as physics, chemistry, and biology. There is less disagreement about the study of English literature and the development of skill in English composition. Probably both sides would agree that a considerable portion of time should be devoted to the study of history and the related social studies, but there would be issues as to the content of the social studies courses.

I find myself in an intermediate position between the two extremes I have described. To make my position clear I must emphasize the great differences between different communities. A high-income suburban town is one thing; a depressed, low-income district in a big city is quite another. The general education offered in the schools in each case may be essentially the same (English, social studies, some mathematics, some science), but the task of one guidance officer is the mirror image of the other's. And I believe the guidance officers are the key to the situation. In the last analysis I think every pupil (and his or her parents) should be free to choose or reject the kind of program advised by the guidance officer. Yet I think the study of a modern foreign language for four years, of mathematics for four years, and physics and chemistry should be urged on those who, judging by their records, appear to be able to handle these subjects. How large a proportion of a given school can profit from the study of *all* these subjects no one can say in advance. Various types of objective tests, together with the record in the lower grades, can help the guidance officer each year in advising a student as to his or her program. At least fifteen per cent of the high school population on a national basis have the capacity to undertake the kind of high school work to which I have been referring; in some schools many more. That an entire high school body can so profit probably no one would maintain. I fail to see any real issue as to the proportion who should be urged to elect a full academic program, since the matter can only be settled student by student in each school. There is an issue, however, between those who, like myself, would urge the counselors to urge the able students to elect foreign languages, mathematics, and science and those who believe the guidance officers should not seek to influence the choices made by the student.

A few words about the vocational or practical courses may be in order. Some critics of the American public high school take the position that the developing of skills marketable on graduation from high school is not a proper function of a secondary school. These reformers would eliminate all the shop courses, business courses, and home economics work in the senior high school and postpone instruction in these subjects to a two-year technical college. Whether the same people would close the vocational high schools in the large cities I am not sure. At all events, I cannot help believing that those who advocate the elimination of vocational work from the public secondary schools have not visited the high schools in industrialized communities or seen the work which is being done under the direction of vocational teachers. I am convinced that for certain types of students a purely academic course of study in grades 11 and 12 would be inadequate because a strong motivating force would be almost completely lacking. One has only to observe the students in good vocational courses to see the interest with which they pursue these practical studies. The serious attitude is carried over to the study of the academic subjects which occupy a half of the students' time.

The practical courses in grades 11 and 12 may or may not be financed in part by federal funds under the Smith-Hughes Act. Procedures differ from local board to local board and from state to state. There is urgent need for a review of the vocational courses financed by federal money and as I write (October 1962) a review is in process by a panel appointed by the President. The report of the panel as well as other studies of vocational education which may be undertaken in the near future will probably focus public attention on the many aspects of nonacademic courses in high school and their relation to the role of the school in preparing graduates to enter employment directly on leaving school. Closely connected is the problem of the high school "drop-out" and the unemployed youth in the slums of our large cities. In considering these issues, I would urge the layman to keep in mind the fact that any realistic appraisal of a high school curriculum must be related to the nature of the community being served. The small high school in a sparsely populated rural area is quite different from a high school in a congested slum of a city; and both are very different from the suburban high school from which ninety per cent of the graduates plan to enter a four-year college.

There are a whole host of issues of a more or less technical nature which arise when teachers and administrators talk about the curriculum. As an example, I may mention the practice found in many schools of grouping students in classes according to their ability in the subject being studied. This procedure has been both highly praised and soundly condemned by educators. Another issue on which professionals disagree is the point at which a child should leave a teacher who teaches all the skills and receive instruction by teachers who are concerned with only one subject such as arithmetic, or English, or social studies. The amount of time to be devoted to art and music and physical education, as well as the extent of the interscholastic athletic programs, are all issues on which educators disagree. To a large degree, these issues must be settled school district by school district, for they involve not only educational judgments but also community interests and may turn primarily on the amount of money available. The place of driver education is another issue of the same sort.

A final word is in order to remind the reader that there are many new developments in education at both the secondary and collegiate levels which are so new that appraisal is difficult. The use of television is one example. The use of team teaching in secondary schools is another; the role of teaching machines or programmed instruction still a third. Many issues will arise as these highly promising developments proceed. Clear answers to the questions raised will not be forthcoming, however, for a period of years.

VII

THE TRAINING AND EMPLOYMENT OF TEACHERS

Perhaps the most violent criticisms which have been directed against American education have come from professors in the liberal arts colleges or members of professional faculties of the universities. The main target of these attacks in many cases has been the schools of education or the faculties of education within the university. The dissatisfaction with the work of the professors of education has been expressed in many ways.

It is claimed by the objectors that, first, the courses in pedagogy, the history of education, the philosophy of education, and other courses offered by faculties of education are of little or no value. Second, the same professors who have given these courses to future teachers have been in the forefront of the progressive movement in education which, it is contended, has done so much to destroy American public schools (and not only the public schools). Third, it is said that the professional educators have persuaded the legislatures of all or almost all the states to require courses in their fields as prerequisites for certification to teach in public schools. Objectors deplore that, as a consequence of the state requirements, a student who may have graduated from a liberal arts college with high honors in history or chemistry or English is not able to teach in a public school unless further time is devoted to taking "education courses."

Perhaps no issue in American education has been filled with so much emotion as this war between professors in the faculties of education and the faculties of liberal arts; the hostility was to be found until a few years ago on almost every campus. Demands have been heard that the legislature remove all requirements for certification insofar as these requirements involve courses given by professors of education.

The grievance of the liberal arts professors that their students cannot be certified for positions in the public schools is based only on a partial truth. In some states it is possible for a student who graduates from a liberal arts college without taking any courses in education to obtain an emergency teaching certificate if the local school board wishes to employ such a person and certifies that an emergency exists. To obtain a regular certificate, however, the deficiency in the educational requirements must be met by attending courses in the afternoon or evening or in a summer school. The practice teaching which is an essential part of the instruction in all schools of education can, under these circumstances, be handled by the school system which has employed the teacher on an emergency certificate.

There are some signs that the battle between the professors of liberal arts and the professors of education is diminishing in intensity, though the fighting is by no means at an end. Professors of some of the liberal arts subjects and the professors of education and those actually involved in our public schools are meeting more frequently than they did a decade earlier. At least one successful meeting has been held in which former antagonists have come together with the avowed purpose of understanding one another. One example of the reconciliation is provided by the increasing interest of professors of physics, chemistry, biology, and mathematics in the teaching of these subjects in the schools; one large cooperative enterprise has been undertaken in which a new curriculum in physics has been successfully developed on the basis of cooperative effort, involving school people and professional physicists. The teaching of mathematics at all grade levels is being revolutionized by a similar procedure, and several new approaches to biology and chemistry have originated because of the efforts of college professors who are *not* professors of education. Yet in all these undertakings the members of the faculties of education have been ready and willing to lend a hand. This is particularly true of the highly successful summer institutes for science, mathematics, and foreign language teachers sponsored by the federal government. Therefore, unless all signs fail, the battle on the university campuses between the two faculties is in the process of being terminated.

There are many issues involved in the training and employment of teachers, however, which will remain even if peace is made between the professors of liberal arts and of education. One of these is the length of the education of the future teacher before he or she is ready to take the first full-time job. In California five years are required for secondary school teachers. Is this the answer which other states should adopt? Many states force both elementary and secondary school teachers to take courses during the school year or in the summer either by law or by relating an increase in salary to credits earned. Is this a good procedure? Many local boards provide a trial period of employment before the teacher's appointment is permanent. The details of such arrangements are subject to much argument. So too are proposals to pay the better teachers more than the others. In short, the whole problem of the recruiting and the employment of public school teachers and the salary schedule (which is far too low) is a complicated educational and political matter with which the United States must wrestle in the coming years.

25

America and Europe: Transatlantic Images

Melvin J. Lasky

> *"From a certain point onward there is no longer any turning back. That is the point that must be reached."*
> — Franz Kafka.

For the greatest part of the last three centuries, few Europeans, with the exception of those single-minded souls who were about to make their way across the Atlantic, found it necessary to think about America. But for Americans, Europe was from the very beginning that other soul that dwelt within their breasts. Europe was their past and their heritage, their teacher and their challenge as a new nation. No theme in American history can really be divorced from the background of Europe, whether it be foreign policy, the pushing-back of the frontier beyond the Mississippi and the Rockies, or the creation of an individual style in the national literature. Americans have not always understood this, possibly because they have been so preoccupied with the thing itself: with nostalgia for the old country, with bitter memories of the place of their trial and shame, with admiration for the richest civilization man had yet created, with hope that the New World would achieve something original and even fairer.

"The burden is necessarily greater for an American," Henry James said some eighty years ago, "for he must deal, more or less, even if only by implication with Europe; whereas no European is obliged to deal in the least with America."[1] Perhaps, he added, in a hundred, or even fifty years hence . . . ? Surely that time has come. In every European land, "America" has become a main theme of parliament and press, school, café, and household. We would seem to be at the beginning of some new epoch. Is it too melodramatic to think that what we have called Western civilization is now moving into a period of unprecedented partnership between Europeans and Americans, a period of some kind of "transatlantic community"?

In the United States of the fifteen postwar years there has not only been a new awareness of this problem but also the onset of a changing consciousness of "what it is to be an American" and of what attitudes a mature and "come-of-age" America is to take toward Europe and Europeans. American opinion has been in ferment. The country and its institutions are being regarded in a new way. In the past America was, alas, culturally dependent on Europe; now Europe is militarily (and not infrequently, economically) dependent upon America. As the editors of *Partisan Review* announced some years ago:

> America is no longer the raw and unformed land of promise from which men of superior gifts like James, Santayana, and Eliot departed, seeking in Europe what they found lacking in America. Europe is no longer regarded as a sanctuary; it no longer assures that rich experience of culture which inspired and justified a criticism of American life. The wheel has come full circle, and now America has become the protector of Western civilization, at least in a military and economic sense.[2]

The question which has fascinated me, in my own fifteen years in postwar Europe, is whether the wheel can ever break out of the traditional circle it has been making for centuries. *In Europe:* a Utopian pro-Americanism in times of adventurous hope, and then the turn to a grumbling anti-Americanism in times of stress. *In America:* a naïve and nostalgic pro-Europeanism when life was raw and difficult, and then the turn to a strident anti-Europeanism when prosperity made for power and national confidence.

There have been the beginnings of a new and encouragingly self-conscious "transatlantic dialogue" on this theme. European writers have been prepared to concede that what separates America from the mind of Europe is an angry self-assertiveness on both sides of the Atlantic. Is it "the impatience of youth" on the American side and "the resentfulness of age" on the European? Surely, since the Declaration of Independence the Americans had been looking across the ocean for inspiration; and when they were in Paris or in London, to be "cultured" obviously meant to be un-American or even anti-American. How could this fail to be pleasing to the self-esteem of Europeans? They felt themselves to be the center of civilization, and even when in terms of power and economics there was a time of bankruptcy a European intellectual could claim that "we had to borrow dollars from the U.S.A., but she still borrows our ideas. . . ." The disturbance in this balance of payments caused a transatlantic discord. Americans no longer care to sit at the feet of Europeans and are delighted to exchange their old role with generous grants to visitors to come and see and learn. The American way of life is no longer shamefacedly contrasted with the European; on the contrary, certain U.S. patterns are vigorously recommended if in politics there was to be stability and in economics efficiency and affluence. An observer remarked at the time of Marshall Plan enthusiasm, "Today it is Europe's intellectuals who are fumbling with their psyche: the Americans have all the answers pat."[3]

> This change is all the more distressing because neither side is fully conscious of it. Whether we are French or English or Scandinavian, we have forgotten how gloriously self-confident and how contemptuous of American ideas we Europeans still were even in 1938. We had the answers. Now we know that we haven't, and our new skepticism makes us rage against an American who thinks he has. He in his turn is quite oblivious of the intellectual somersault he has turned since the 1930's and resents our skepticism as defeatism. If you can't pay your way and have no idea how to save the world, he says, the least you can do is to listen to my lecture before you grab my dollars. . . . (*R. H. S. Crossman*)

But the Americans, as I have been saying, are no longer as "oblivious" as all that. An American poetess wrote some years ago:

> The American artist and intellectual must give over expecting the

> future to develop according to region or historic example. America is soaked with Europe, in any case; and there is no sign that Europe as it rebuilds itself, may not provide vitality, variety, and perspective for American life, art, and thought. For although Carthage never recovered after its furrows were sown with salt, Rome, like Troy, rebuilt itself innumerable times; and what may Europe not produce out of its present ruins? . . . (*Louise Bogan*)

There has been not only this strand of American confidence in Europe but also an understanding that with the coming of world power it would be disastrous for the United States to retreat into a narrow and self-satisfied cultural nationalism. There were even suggestions that, as American foreign policy tried to make a reality out of the hypothetical unity of Western Europe, so should American intellectuals attempt to realize the Goethean concept of *Weltliteratur*. At any rate, for the first time in centuries there was in the search for a transatlantic identity no glee and no malice, no flight from self nor heaviness of heart. "We cannot affirm America without reaffirming Europe and the West. Humans are beings with a history, a past; Europe is our past; and even God cannot will the past not to have been. . . ."

But if this is the point that had to be reached, and from which there may be no turning back, it was not always this way, for the past is the history of a strange transatlantic tension within the American soul, of glee and malice, of withdrawal and return.

THE NEW WORLD AND THE OLD

In the beginning there was the adventure, the discovery, the flight. America was created as a myth of hope and renewal, and it was only natural that Europe should be assigned the role of despair and decay. "I write the Wonders of the Christian Religion"—so the seventeenth-century Puritan divine, Cotton Mather, began his *Magnalia Christi Americana*—"flying from the depravations of Europe, to the American Strand. . . ." There was throughout this first century of American intellectual consciousness a prophetical identification of America with the judgment of righteousness. The greatest American theologian of the eighteenth century, Jonathan Edwards, argued that "the old world slew Christ; the new world, though it does not escape the brotherhood of sin and though its victory shall come in accordance with the dialectic of history, is nevertheless the hope of the world, if there is hope anywhere. . . ." Indeed, if the millennium is to commence anywhere it would be in America.[4]

In fact, the words of Bishop Berkeley (who visited Rhode Island for a few years in the early 1700's to help convert the Indians) echoed for generations through the American mind:

> Not such as Europe breeds, in her decay,
> Such as she bred, when fresh and young;
> When heavenly flame did animate her clay,
> By future poets shall be sung.
>
> Westward the course of empire takes its way . . .[5]

How could there be any doubt of the great future ahead? "Courage, then, Americans!" writes a Whig in 1768, "religion and science are on the wing to these shores. . . ." In 1770 Trumbull poetically entreats:

> Prove to the world, in these new-dawning skies,
> What genius kindles and what arts arise;
> What fav'ring Muses lent their willing aid . . .
> Here shall some Shakespeare charm the rising age,
> And hold in magic chains the listening stage . . .

In a poem of 1794 Timothy Dwight tells his countrymen:

> Cast around
> The eye of searching reason, and declare
> What Europe proffers, but a patchwork sway . . .
> Copy not from others,
> Shun the lures of Europe.

The classical faith of the eighteenth century in America is summed up by Noah Webster (of "Dictionary" fame) who demanded a purely American literature:

> Europe is grown old in folly, corruption, and tyranny. In that country laws are perverted, manners are licentious, literature is de-

> clining, and human nature is debased. . . . American glory begins to dawn at a favorable period, and under flattering circumstances. We have the experience of the whole world before our eyes; but to receive indiscriminately the maxims of government, the manners and literary taste of Europe, and make them the ground on which to build our systems in America, must soon convince us that a durable and stately edifice can never be created upon the moldering pillars of antiquity.

One plea is even recorded in the *North American Review* for a reversion to the Indian language and Indian ways if one were to be genuinely independent!

"What, then, is the American, this new man?" asked Crèvecoeur in the most famous paragraph of his *Letters from an American Farmer.*[6] He is the Western pilgrim who has left ancient prejudices and manners behind him; he is "a new man, who acts upon new principles; he must therefore entertain new ideas, and form new opinions"; he carries along with him what began long ago in the East, for he will "finish the great circle."[7]

The passions and energies of the American Revolutionary movement gave this Americanism an even more polemical note. "In no instance," proclaimed Thomas Paine, "hath nature made the satellite larger than its primary planet; and as England and America, with respect to each other, reverse the common order of nature, it is evident that they belong to different systems. England to Europe: America to itself! . . ."[8] And in his pamphlet *Common Sense* he formulated a pride in "the new World, which has been the asylum for the persecuted lovers of civil and religious liberty from every part of Europe" that was later to be symbolized in the Statue of Liberty in New York harbor.

Am I trying to suggest a permanent "anti-Europeanism" and "isolationism" in the American mind? Not at all. Men like Benjamin Franklin and Thomas Jefferson reveal the ambiguity of all these American pronouncements, and the pendulum-like shifts from a sense of American exceptionalism to a larger feeling of kinship with Europe "and the whole world." Franklin, especially, manifests neither the nostalgia nor the estrangement so characteristic of his compatriots. He took for granted the unity of civilization and the universal fraternity of thoughtful men. The difference between the Old World and the New was to Franklin a political and economic difference, not one of morals or basic culture. He had, of course, the American pride — traveling in Europe, he wrote in 1772, "had I never been in the American colonies, but were to form my judgment of civil society by what I have lately seen, I should never advise a nation of savages to admit of civilization. . . ." But this did not blind him that his political and social ideals were in ferment in Europe too, and he could report from Paris during the Revolution that "all Europe is on our side of the question," and that "it is a common observation here that our cause is the cause of all mankind. . . ."[9]

This was apparently a time of great pro-American feeling on the Continent. As Paine reported, "the face of America, moral and political, stood fair and high in the world. The luster of her revolution extended itself to every individual; and to be a citizen of America gave a title of respect in Europe." This feeling was reciprocated in America by a unique sense of international solidarity. "Old Europe will have to lean on our shoulders," wrote Thomas Jefferson to John Adams, "and to hobble along by our side, under the monkish trammels of priests and kings, as she can. . . ."[10] During the Revolutionary times (in France as in America) Americans sounded a flaming appeal:

> O ye that love mankind! Ye that dare oppose not only the tyranny, but the tyrant, stand forth! Every spot of the old world is overrun with oppression. Freedom hath been hunted round the Globe. Asia and Africa have long expelled her. — Europe regards her like a stranger, and England hath given her warning to depart. O! receive the fugitive, and prepare in time an asylum for mankind. (*Thomas Paine*)[11]

During periods of grave international crises, as for example the Napoleonic wars, even the apostles of isolation turned toward Europe. It was Jefferson who had preached that "our first and fundamental maxim should be, never to entangle ourselves in the broils of Europe." And it was Jefferson who in 1814 warned of the danger of allowing all of the Old World to fall into the hands of a single tyrant:

> . . . But is our particular interest to make us insensible to all sentiments of morality? Is it then become criminal, the moral wish that the torrents of blood this man is shedding in Europe, the sufferings of so

many human beings, good as ourselves, on whose necks he is trampling, the burnings of ancient cities, devastations of great countries, the destruction of law and order, and demoralization of the world, should be arrested, even if it should place our peace a little further distant? No. You and I cannot differ in wishing that Russia and Sweden, and Denmark, and Germany, and Spain, and Portugal, and Italy, and even England, may retain their independence.[12]

There are critics today who (apparently after a reading of Kennan or Niebuhr) bewail the element of "the moral crusader" in the American make-up; they overlook that behind it lies a special sense of responsibility of the New World to the Old which represents much of what is noblest in the American tradition.

THE TEMPTATION OF EUROPE

Goethe liked to talk about America. Sometimes he thought "it had it better," sometimes he thought of himself as a possible emigrant. But in the year 1824 (when the brother of Ralph Waldo Emerson made the Bostonian pilgrimage to Weimar) Goethe felt it was "too late" to seek refuge in America, "for there is now too much light even there. . . ." Emerson himself arrived in Europe a few years later; it was precisely the flight into darkness which was impelling Americans across the Atlantic, the "old-world character" of the continent where there was "not a house, not a shed, not a field that the eye can for a moment take to be American. . . ."[13]

Hawthorne, in whose work darkness and light were most sensitively recorded, was even more upset by the shadows of Europe. The walls of an old castle made him exclaim in his notebook, "Oh, that we could have ivy in America! What is there to beautify us, when our time of ruin comes?"[14] Another figure in what F. O. Matthiessen called "The American Renaissance" wrote: "We forgot that though the country was young, yet the people were old, that as Americans we have no childhood, no half-fabulous, legendary wealth, no misty, cloud-enveloped background. . . ."[15] Whitman, too, was not immune to the spell:

> So far, our democratic society . . . possesses nothing . . . to make up for that glowing, blood-throbbing, religious, social, emotional,

artistic, indefinable, indescribably beautiful charm and hold which fused the separate parts of the old feudal societies together, in their wonderful interpenetration. . . .[16]

And even in *Innocents Abroad,* Mark Twain notes:

> The change that has come over our little party is surprising. Day by day we lose some of our restlessness and absorb some of the spirit of quietude and ease that is in the tranquil atmosphere about us and in the demeanor of the people. We grow wise apace. We begin to comprehend what life is for. . . .

Could, then, the American become a European again?

> We have stood in the dim religious light of these hoary sanctuaries, in the midst of long ranks of dusty monuments and effigies of the great dead of Venice, until we seemed drifting back, back, back into the solemn past, and looking upon the scenes and mingling with the peoples of a remote antiquity. We have been in a half-waking sort of dream all the time. I do not know how else to describe the feeling. A part of our being has remained still in the nineteenth century, while another part of it has seemed in some unaccountable way walking among the phantoms of the tenth.[17]

Could, then, these Americans, these children of light, squinting, haunted, accustom themselves to the dark corridors of the Old World?

But the "thrill of strange emotion," as Hawthorne said, was there only "while you are still new in the old country. . . ." And, still new, the Americans were wide-eyed explorers. Jefferson had even put together an outline for friends who were going to Europe which he called "Objects of Attention for an American," and Item No. 7 reads:

> Politics of each country, well worth studying. . . . Examine their influence on the happiness of the people. Take every possible occasion for entering into the houses of the laborers, and especially at the moment of their repast; see what they eat, how they are clothed, and whether they are obliged to work too hard. . . .[18]

And when he himself was abroad he too sounded the note of

nostalgia and fulfillment — "Behold me at length on the vaunted scene of Europe! . . ." But he adds:

> You are perhaps curious to know how this new scene has struck a savage of the mountains of America? Not advantageously, I assure you . . . under pretense of governing they have divided their nations into two classes, wolves and sheep . . . experience declares that man is the only animal which devours his own kind; I can apply no milder term to the governments of Europe and to the general prey of the rich on the poor. . . .

And to this conclusion all the tourist-pilgrims came, sooner or later. Hawthorne's "delight at finding something permanent begins," as he says, "to yield to his Western love of change. . . ."

> . . . Better than this is the lot of our restless countrymen, whose modern instinct bids them tend always towards "fresh woods and pastures new." Rather than such monotony of sluggish ages, loitering on a village-green, toiling in hereditary fields, listening to the parson's drone lengthened through centuries in the gray Norman church, let us welcome whatever change may come, — change of place, social customs, political institutions, modes of worship, — trusting that, if all present things shall vanish, they will but make room for better systems, and for a higher type of man to clothe his life in them, and to fling them off in turn. . . .[19]

With the onset of the American restlessness, the temptation of Europe had lost its round. "What is there in Rome for me to see," complains Mark Twain, "that others have not seen before me? What is there for me to touch that others have not touched? What is there for me to feel, to learn, to hear, to know, that shall thrill me before it pass to others? What can I discover? Nothing. . . ." It was Van Wyck Brooks who remarked that Mark Twain, "writing of Europe, had cut the umbilical cord that united the still infant nation to the mother-culture. . . ."[20] America wanted to breathe alone, to speak with its own voice.

But youth was uncertain. "We are all the time wondering what is thought of us over there," Lowell wrote to Howells, "instead of going quietly about our business."[21] In his message to America, Tolstoy said: "And I should like to ask the American people why they do not pay more attention to their own voices . . . ?"[22] The answer was sometimes they did not hear them, sometimes they did not recognize them. Curiously enough, it was in the perspective from Europe that Americans first became aware of their own style and identity. Emerson had been wise enough to observe that "*we go to Europe to be Americanized. . . .*"[23]

> *Jefferson:* "Visit Europe; it will make you adore your own country, its equality and liberty, its soil, its climate, its laws, its people and its manners. . . ."
>
> *Hawthorne:* "I grew better acquainted with many of our national characteristics during those four years (in Europe) than in all my preceding life."
>
> *James:* "My native land, which time, absence, and change have, in a funny sort of way, made almost as romantic to me as 'Europe,' in dreams or in my earlier time here, used to be. . . . Europe had been romantic before, because she was different from America; wherefore America would now be romantic because she was different from Europe."

What an ironic fate for the Old World — not only to populate the New World, but to Americanize it to boot!

Emerson, like so many others before and after him, called for a Declaration of Intellectual Independence: "We have listened too long to the courtly muses of Europe. . . ."[24] Whitman was sensible enough to know that the "argument is not all on one side." Still,

> a calm man of deep vision will find in this tremendous modern spectacle of America at least as great sights as anything the foreign world, or the antique, or the relics of the antique, can afford him. . . . Shall I not vivify myself with life here, rushing, tumultuous, scornful, masterful, oceanic — greater than ever before known?[25]

"For who was our father and our mother?" cries Herman Melville in *Redburn* (1849).

> . . . Or can we point to any Romulus and Remus for our founders? Our ancestry is lost in the universal paternity, and Caesar and Alfred, St. Paul and Luther, and Homer and Shakespeare are as much ours as Washington, who is as much the world's as our own. We are the heirs of all time, and with all nations we divide our inheritance.

This, then, would seem to be the course of the dialectic, an almost deceptively simple thesis, antithesis, and synthesis: a partisan and nostalgic pro-Europeanism, a passionate and patriotic pro-Americanism, a cosmopolitan resolution.

TRANSATLANTIC PORTRAIT (I): COOPER

When James Fenimore Cooper sailed for Europe in the summer of 1826 he appeared to be the beginning of the fulfillment of a century-old dream for a great native American literature.[26] What could be more heroic, more epical than the Leather-Stocking Tales? Here — in *The Spy*, *The Pioneers*, *The Last of the Mohicans* — was the poetry of revolution, frontier, and Indian-fighting. Was this less noble than the warfare between Christian and Moor in the *Song of Roland*, or the founding of Rome in the Aeneid? As "the American *Scott*," he paid his respects to Sir Walter and remained on the Continent for seven years.

What never failed to shock him was the extent of European ignorance of America. The travel-books were inaccurate, prejudiced, and hostile.[27] Radicals often harmed the truth as much as Tories, for as Cooper observed: "Finding that things fall short of the political Elysium of their imaginations, they fly into the opposite extremes, as a sort of *amende honorable* to their own folly and ignorance."

It was the Marquis de Lafayette who first suggested the "transatlantic theme" to Cooper (and it proved to be the fateful element in his career for the next twenty-five years). Lafayette was the "grand old man" of French republicanism; he had fought as a general under Washington in the American Revolution, had been Vice-President of the National Assembly in 1789, had been liberated in Austria by Napoleon. He often thought of himself as "the Washington of France," and the "pro-Americanism" of his own liberal ideology (religious toleration, abolition of slavery, freedom of the press, parliamentary rule) was countered by the "anti-Americanism" of his critics and opponents. Cooper himself, in his years abroad, became an ardent and embattled defender of republican ideas. He was in Germany when the July Revolution broke out and the Bourbons were expelled from France in 1830, and he hurried from Dresden to Paris (much the same excursion as was to be made soon after by Heine). Paris was once again the Mecca of lovers of liberty, and when the Poles rose in revolt Cooper presided at mass-meetings in order to raise funds for the troops in Poland. (Edgar Allan Poe said he was going to Paris to join the Polish army.)

Early in their European friendship Lafayette had asked Cooper to write an account of his triumphal American tour. Cooper did not find the idea of a book of official speeches and celebrations especially attractive. But he was inspired by the idea of a book about America itself. It would "explain America to Europe, and show what a sane, balanced book about America by an intelligent, open-minded foreigner would be like." (In Scott's *Quarterly Review* the inherent inferiority of Americans had been so established that the only question which remained "open for discussion" was the cause: Was it the climate or the food?)

Cooper's book of 1828 — *Notions of the Americans: Picked up by a Travelling Bachelor* — is a distinguished American contribution to the transatlantic dialogue and happily betrays few of the vices of the propaganda tracts which in our own time prove so disorienting: it was no gray official apologia but a pamphlet of temperamental individuality. It had, of course, its one-sided moments: the omission of the Indian tragedy, the attempt to explain away Negro slavery on the grounds that Europeans instituted the slave trade, etc. The transatlantic dialogue is, on both sides, always in danger of degenerating into a debate with all the attendant vices of rhetorical trickery. But Cooper was honest, as witness a passage on "the poverty of material" in his native land (a passage which is echoed throughout American literature from Hawthorne to Henry James):

> There are no annals for the historian; no follies (beyond the most vulgar and commonplace) for the satirist; no manners for the dramatist; no obscure fictions for the writer of romance; no gross and hardy offences against decorum for the moralist; nor any of the rich artificial auxiliaries of poetry. . . . There is no costume for the peasant (there is scarcely a peasant at all), no wig for the judge, no baton for the general, no diadem for the chief magistrate.

Traveling in Italy, Cooper is captivated by the idea of a "cultural exchange" of the populations of Rome and New York for a year: "while the one party might partially awake from its dream of centuries, the other might discover that there is something valuable besides money. . . ." With this note Cooper began to cut the ground away from himself on both sides of the ocean: he convinced few Europeans, he pleased no Americans. This is, I think, one of the endless dialectical ironies which have caught Americans in Europe: Cooper was the difficult democrat in the Old World, and the fussy aristocrat in the New.

His novel of 1838, *Home as Found*, was inevitably a document of disillusionment. How could things but "fall short of the political Elysium" of the Cooper imagination abroad? He had returned to his own land "fatally cosmopolitan." The Europeanized family that set up house in New York, with its French furniture and Swiss servants, the children more continental than American, had no easy time. And the author began to delight in pointing out how much smaller the Catskills are than the Alps, or Trinity Church in Manhattan than St. Paul's in London. *Home as Found* was a picture of a narrow, mean, intolerant world, deprived of the graces of civilization. "Are you reconciled to your country?" was the question the returning traveler was everywhere asked. Cooper remained devoted to the ideal, but with the reality he was indeed irreconcilable. It had been bitter for him to discover that his own countrymen, as well as the Europeans, had failed to understand "the principles underlying American freedom." Cooper's theme in Europe, the superiority of American principles, became, after his return, the inferiority of American life. (A century later, as we shall see, this was reversed: the theme in America, the superiority of European principles for the generation of "expatriates," became — abroad — the inferiority of European life!) He felt himself to be "as good a democrat as there is in America," a partisan of democratic promise rather than a compromiser with social reality: a defender of "the real America."

The familiar and permanent themes are, in the words of one of his biographers: (1) "In Cooper's day and for long afterwards, every question about American culture involved Europe." (2) "It was the European trip that made Cooper self-consciously aware of the great American questions." (3) "The length of the trip itself presented a problem." (Jefferson had said that an American could safely live abroad only five years. Cooper meant to stay away for no more than the allotted period but overstayed his leave. He returned out of step with his country; he doubted, however, that he had fallen behind, as Jefferson said an American would, and suggested brashly that he had gone too far ahead alone.) (4) Was this a way of admitting that Europe had unfitted him for life in America? "Perhaps. But he never regretted his European adventure. To the end of his life he defended the American artist's right of access to Europe as part of his heritage. . . ."

TRANSATLANTIC PORTRAIT (II): ADAMS

Henry Adams was a twenty-year-old graduate of Harvard when in 1858 he sailed for Europe to study civil law (he did not know what this was, or any reason for his studying it) at the University of Berlin.[28] Two years were to go by before he would return to America (in the fall of 1860, just before Abraham Lincoln's election to the Presidency).

"What shall I say of this city?" Adams wrote from Berlin in November 1858. "Why, Lord bless my soul, I have got things enough to see and study in this city alone to take me two years even if I knew the language and only came for pleasure. The museums, picture galleries, theaters, gardens; there are enough to occupy one's time for the next six months. Then do the same with the half-million or so engravings. Lord! Such engravings!" But the young American was bored (and outraged) by the dull and medieval lecture-systems, went off afternoons tramping through the Tiergarten, and then departed with friends on foot for the south. He delighted in the honey and the *Glühwein* he was served in Thuringia, rushed through Weimar ("they bore you to death there with Goethe and Schiller").

Nürnberg was something else again, and he wrote to Brooks Adams:

> My amiable brother, what do you want me to say of this city. I hardly know how to express it all. Think me spooney if you will, but last evening as I wandered round in the dusk in these delightful old peaked, tiled, crooked, narrow, stinking lanes I thought that if ever again I enjoy as much happiness as here in Europe, and the months pass over bringing always new fascinations and no troubles, why then philosophers lie and earth's a paradise. We passed the day in a couple of great churches lying on the altar steps and looking at the glorious stained glass windows five hundred years ago, with their magnificent colors and quaint biblical stories. So fascinating these things are! . . .

> There's no use talking about it. Let it go! Nürnberg is Nürnberg. If I go on I shall be silly, even if I've not been already.
>
> So tomorrow we bid goodbye to Dürer and old Peter Visher, the churchs and the streets, the glorious old windows and the charming fountains and all the other fascinations of this city, and march on to Munich.

When time had gone by and the journey homeward was to be made, he thought of his father in Boston, son of the sixth President of the United States, grandson of the second President of the United States: "I am fully prepared to hear the Governor lay the fault of every failure and every error in my life to Europe. God Almighty could not get an idea out of his head that had once got in." And the idea was, of course, that Europe unfitted Americans for America. Yet the young Adams showed no lack of national pride, and his patriotism seemed none the worse off for all "the temptations of the Old World." — "I have never felt so proud as now of the great qualities of our people, or so confident of the capacity of men to develop their faculties in the mass. I believe that a new era of the movement of the world will date from that day which will drag nations up still another step, and carry us out of a quantity of fogs. Europe has a long way to go yet to catch us up. . . ."

This was the central article of the national faith. Charles Sumner, whose carriage young Henry Adams had chased after one evening on *Unter den Linden*, collected an array of brilliant prophecies about America that had issued over the centuries from the pens of eminent Europeans. "Westward the star of empire . . ." — but this star Adams did not chase. He and his brother Brooks were the first great pessimists in the American tradition. They lost faith in the national destiny; and they saw no real hope in the Old World, for the sickness of modern civilization was one.

> As far as we can see, if anything is radically wrong it must grow worse [this is 1894], for it must be in our system itself, and at the bottom of all modern society. If we are diseased, so is all the world. Everyone is discussing, disputing, doubting, economizing, going into bankruptcy, waiting for the storm to pass, but no sign of agreement is visible as to what has upset us, or whether we can cure the disease. That the trouble is quite different from any previous experience, pretty much everyone seems to admit; but nobody diagnoses it. Probably in a year or two, we shall pick ourselves up again, and go

> ahead, but we shall know no better what hit us. To judge from what I can gather from the *Economist* and other European sources of financial wisdom, Europe is rather more in the dark than we are. Europe and Asia are used to accepting diseases and death as inevitable, but to us the idea is a new one. We want to know what is wrong with the world that it should suddenly go to smash without visible cause or possible advantage. . . . Society here, as well as in Europe, is shaking, yet we have no bombs, no violence, and no wars to fear.

This was the brilliant dark surmise of the future in the nineteenth-century tradition of Nietzsche, Kierkegaard, and Burckhardt. For his part Adams was troubled by the problem of "publishing the pessimism of Europe," and so to "risk perverting the childlike innocence of America. . . ." His endless travels were self-confessed escapism. "Do you know," he writes from Mexico, "that I have traveled to every place on earth which travelers have described as most fascinating, in the hope of finding one where I should want to stay or return, and have found that Faust had a sure horse on the devil in his promise about the passing hour: *Bleibe doch, du bist so schoen!* Three days in any place on earth is all it will bear. The pleasure is in the movement, as Faust knew when he let the devil in to the preposterous contract. . . ."

With pleasure or not, movement brought him again and again to the Old World: "Europe is steadily drifting on some unknown shore which I want to see before I die." He did not quite hold out three days in Bayreuth ("I was nearly asphyxiated" — he was obviously of the school of Hanslick among Wagner-listeners). "Altogether," Adams wrote, echoing the mood of a despairing German liberal like Theodor Mommsen, "Germany gives me the sense of hopeless failure. In fact I have had more than enough of Europe, and I'm afraid my appetite for America is not voracious either. The world has lived too long. So have I. One of us two has got to go. For the public good, it had better be the world that goes, for at least I am harmless. . . ." To Brooks he offers the prophecy in 1898: "France must follow Spain to the seclusion of local interests; and Germany must merge in Russia. So we can foresee a new centralization, of which Russia is one pole, and we the other, with England between. The Anglo-American alliance is almost inevitable."

This new alignment haunted him, and he came back to it repeatedly. "In the long run — say in three generations more —

Russia and Germany, if they work together, are bound to be the biggest mass, in the most central position, unassailable to us, and able to overwhelm us at any point of contact." — "The sum of my certainty is that America has a very clear century of start over Russia, and that Western Europe must follow us for a hundred years, before Russia can swing her flail over the Atlantic. Whether she can do it then is no conundrum that I can settle. I imagine that my grandpapa [President John Quincy Adams], sitting here in his study ninety years ago, could see ahead to me now, better than I can see ahead to the year 2000; and yet it was not easy guessing even for him. . . ." This he wrote from St. Petersburg in 1901, before the events of the next period were to make him "half-crazy with fear that Russia is sailing straight into another French revolution which may upset all Europe and us too. . . ."

Still his sense of the *Untergang des Westens* was not primarily political, and many years before Oswald Spengler's illumination he wrote (in another letter to his brother Brooks, the complete record of which is surely the most depressing correspondence of modern times):

> I apprehend for the next hundred years an ultimate, colossal, cosmic collapse; but not on any of our old lines. My belief is that science is to wreck us, and that we are like monkeys monkeying with a loaded shell; we don't in the least know or care where our practically infinite energies come from or will bring us to. For myself, it is true; I know *no* care at all. But the faintest disturbance of equilibrium is felt throughout the solar system, and I feel sure that our power over energy has now reached a point where it must sensibly affect the old adjustment. It is mathematically certain to me that another thirty years of energy-development must reach an impasse.
>
> This is, however, a line of ideas wholly new, and very repugnant to our contemporaries. . . . I owe it only to my having always had a weakness for science mixed with metaphysics. I am a dilution of Lord Kelvin and St. Thomas Aquinas. . . . (August, 1902)

The Goncourts had also seen the threat of atomic destruction, but they had not taken it as seriously as Henry Adams. It depressed him to the point where he felt that not only his world but also his own life had been nothing but a failure, and it is in the spirit of that hopelessness that he wrote his autobiography, which was published after his death in 1918 and became the most remarkable document of its kind in American literature. Did he really please his friend Henry James by attributing all the trouble to the fact that "we were all improvised Europeans, and — Lord God! — how thin!"?

TRANSATLANTIC PORTRAIT (III): JAMES

If Henry Adams was a blow to American optimism, Henry James was the shock to literary America's nationalism.[29] How could it be that the most endowed literary figure of the time should go abroad, should become a "foreigner," should live and work as a European? This is a question which a more cosmopolitan America today has posed anew for itself and answered peacefully and satisfactorily, but for almost half a century (before and after James's death in London in 1916) it burdened the transatlantic consciousness of Americans. James himself complicated the issues, for his entire body of work — novels, short stories, travel-books, criticism, letters — is in some way concerned with Europeans and Americans, their relations and contrasts. If he had not existed, I would, at this point, have had to invent him, for he is that exquisite thing, the perfect turning-point in the spiritual tension between Old and New World. "Not till we are lost," Thoreau wrote in *Walden,* "not till we have lost the world . . . do we begin to find ourselves." Not till the American had become a European — as millions of Europeans had become Americans — would he be able to discover himself. T. S. Eliot, once writing about James (but obviously thinking of his own problem as well), said: "It is the final perfection, the consummation of an American to become, not an Englishman, but a European — something which no born European, no person of any European nationality can become. . . ." A Jamesian perfection it was, but hardly a "final" thing; it was rather a beginning of a new consciousness and the raising of the traditional transatlantic tension to a new and possibly higher level.

There is a touching scene in the papers of the James family: Bonn 1860, Mother and Aunt sitting in armchairs, the two sons Henry and William working hard on their German, and "Father who is walking up and down speaking of the superiority of America to these countries, and how much better that we should go home. . . ."

Henry James senior was a remarkable man. His two boys became most distinguished figures in American literature and philosophy; but as George Bernard Shaw once said, the old man "was the most interesting member of the family." (Perhaps the family itself is even more interesting: to be a member of it, someone once said, was enough; one needed no other country.) The old James had originally taken his children across the Atlantic in order "to allow them to absorb French and German and get a better sensuous education than they are likely to get here." It succeeded in making Henry and William the most cosmopolitan figures of their time, but the father "had gradually ceased to 'like' Europe." He found "an undeniable spiritual difference between Europe and America" — the Old World was the past, was exploitation, was servility. He warned his sons not to be enchanted by the historically picturesque, for he heard

> underneath it all the pent-up moaning and groaning soul of the race, struggling to be free. I am glad on the whole that my lot is cast in a land where life doesn't wait on death, and where consequently no natural but only an artificial picturesque is possible. The historical consciousness rules to such a distorted excess in Europe that I have always been restless there, and ended by pining for the land of the future exclusively. . . .

Henry James junior came to the opposite conclusion; pining for the land of the past, he settled in England in 1876 and remained there, returning once to gather material for a book on *The American Scene* and the only other times for deaths in the family. Perhaps he should have made the effort to be an "American Balzac," but the world of business in the U.S. was "a closed book" to him. "It's a complex fate being an American," he said. "To write well and worthily of American things one need even more than elsewhere to be a master. But unfortunately one is less! . . ."

Yet James never got away from "American things." All of his memorable international novels — *The Portrait of a Lady*, *The Europeans*, *The Ambassadors*, etc. — are devoted to the experiences of the new man ("Newman" is the hero's name in *The American*), or the innocent girl, Daisy Miller, the heiress of all the ages, in the dark corridors of European life. What could be less un-American than the tragedy of goodness and naïveté in an old world of greed and vice? His countrymen were very slow in discovering that America and

Americans do not come badly off at all! — even if James personally, poet of the moral dilemma, needed Europe, could not survive without it, for it gave him the shadow he needed to offset the "white American light."

A whole generation of Americans never forgave him. Critic after critic excommunicated him from the national heritage. One of the most influential critics in America, Parrington, has insisted: "He suffered the common fate of the *déraciné;* wandering between worlds, he found a home nowhere. It is not well for the artist to turn cosmopolitan, for the flavor of the fruit comes from the soil and sunshine of its native fields." And a recent standard college textbook noted: "It is not certain that H. J. really belongs to American literature, for he was critical of America and admired Europe."

Throughout his lifetime James had this problem out with himself (and with his family).

> The burden is necessarily greater for an American — for he must deal, more or less, even if only by implication, with Europe, whereas no European is obliged to deal in the least with America. No one ever dreams of calling him less complete for not doing so.

Perhaps in fifty years, he thought, the European "would have to reckon with our civilization as well. . . ."

William James appealed to him to make "the heroic effort" to return home:

> This is your dilemma: the congeniality of Europe, on the one hand . . . on the other hand, the dreariness of American conditions of life. . . . If you come your worst years will be the first. If you stay, the bad years may be the later ones, when, moreover, you can't change. And I have a suspicion that if you come, too, and *can* get once acclimated, the quality of what you write will be higher than it would be in Europe. . . .

"I know what I am about," he replied, "and I have always my eyes on my native land."

Was it, then, "a fatal mistake," as Van Wyck Brooks argued, to become an expatriate, a cosmopolitan? There were moments when even James thought so! He once confessed,

> If I were to live my life over again, I would be an American. I would steep myself in America. I would know no other land. I would

> study its beautiful side. The mixture of Europe and America which you see in me has proved disastrous. It has made of me a man who is neither American nor European. I have lost touch with my own people and I live here alone. . . .

But alone with his masterpieces! A youthfully patriotic America seized argumentatively upon these words, but who today can manage the naïve literary chauvinism which would exchange a bird in the hand for two in the patriotic bush? The brilliant revival of Henry James in America during the last thirty years has returned honor to the much-abused master, and is, I think, as much as anything a symbol of a new American maturity. "It is as if he had lived his life as unrecognized, unauthorized, undreamed-of ambassador of letters at large. America, England, France, Italy, Germany, Russia — he rounded them all and included them in his mission."

THE WHOLE WORLD FOR STAGE

"The wheels of the clock have so completely stopped in Europe," wrote Randolph Bourne in August 1914, "and this civilization that I have been admiring so much seems so palpably to be torn to shreds that I do not even want to think about Europe until the war is over and life is running again. . . ."[30] Other Americans, in their shock at the outbreak and the horror of the First World War, were even more bitter. The American Ambassador in London noted:

> The idea that we were brought up on, that Europe is the home of civilization in general — nonsense! It's a periodical slaughter-pen, with all the vices that this implies. I'd as lief live in the Chicago stockyards. (*Walter Hines Page*)[31]

The President in Washington was soberer. In his inaugural address of 1917, Woodrow Wilson declared: "The greatest things that remain to be done must be done with the whole world for stage. . . . We are provincials no longer. . . . There can be no turning back."

In Paris after the war Gertrude Stein told young Hemingway, "You are all a lost generation . . . ," and this became the inscription for his first novel and the name of a group of Americans who were to be transitional forces in the national culture. They were the adventurous young men in American history who went, not West, but East. "They do things better in Europe, let's go there." And off they went from Greenwich Village to Montparnasse — Hemingway, Scott Fitzgerald, John Dos Passos, E. E. Cummings, Ezra Pound, Hart Crane, T. S. Eliot, and so many others. Their dream was of an "escape into European cities with crooked streets. . . ." Their idea was "salvation by exile." These were the *expatriates*, and they waved to each other from the windows of passing trains in Europe. Malcolm Cowley, the historian of this generation, writes in *Exile's Return:*

> . . . at heart they were not convinced that even the subject matter of a great novel could be supplied by this country. American themes were lacking in dignity. Art and ideas were products manufactured under a European patent; all we could furnish towards them was raw talent destined usually to be wasted. Everywhere, in every department of culture, Europe offered the models to imitate — in painting, composing, philosophy, folk music, folk drinking, the drama, sex, politics, national consciousness — indeed, some doubted that this country was even a nation; it had no traditions except the fatal tradition of the pioneer. . . .[32]

What would that pioneer of American culture, Jefferson, have thought who 150 years before had said to Monroe: "While we shall see multiplied instances of Europeans going to live in America, I will venture to say, no man now living will ever see an instance of an American removing to settle in Europe and continuing there. . . ."[33] But perhaps he was wiser than he knew; for with the exception of Eliot, who, like James before him, remained to become a British subject, almost none of them continued there.

Because whatever it was that these Americans had "lost," none of them could find it permanently in Europe. The pattern was an old one — we have already seen it innumerable times — the old pattern of alienation and reintegration, of departure and return. Cowley's poems about movies and skyscrapers and machines begin to have a nostalgic note about them, and he discovered that "I had learned from a distance to admire America's picturesque qualities. . . ." The expatriates began to quarrel amongst each other. Was America really vulgar, vicious, a failure? Cowley once burst out —

> America is just as god-damned good as Europe — worse in some ways, better in others, just as appreciative, fresher material, inclined to stay at peace instead of marching into the Ruhr. As for its being the concentration point for all the vices and vulgarities — nuts. New York is refinement itself beside Berlin. French taste in most details is unbearable. London is a huge Gopher Prairie. I'm not ashamed to take off my coat anywhere and tell those degenerate Europeans that I'm an American citizen. Wave Old Glory! Peace! Normalcy!

America was, after all, their country and they began to feel a little homesick for it. The new generation of exiles came straggling back to New York.

> The exiles were ready to find that their own nation had every attribute they had been taught to admire in those of Europe. It had developed its national types — who could fail to recognize an American in a crowd? — it possessed a folklore, and traditions, and the songs that embodied them; it had even produced new forms of art which the Europeans were glad to borrow. Some of the exiles had reached a turning-point in their adventure and were preparing to embark on a voyage of rediscovery. Standing as it were on the Tour Eiffel, they looked southwestwards across the wheatfields of Beauce and the rain-drenched little hills of Brittany, until somewhere in the mist they saw the country of their childhood, which should henceforth be the country of their art. American themes, like other themes, had exactly the dignity that talent could lend them.

In 1930 when Sinclair Lewis was awarded the Nobel Prize he stood up as the spokesman of his generation of American writers: "I salute them with a joy in being not yet too far removed from their determination to give to the America that has mountains and endless prairies, enormous cities and far-lost cabins, billions of money and tons of faith, to an America that is as strange as Russia and as complex as China, a literature worthy of her vastness. . . ."[34] From Lewis himself to Faulkner, Thomas Wolfe, and Tennessee Williams, this can, I suppose, be considered as the achievement of the new generation; and this, in turn, made for confidence, for maturity, even for what Eliot called "the historical sense":

> The historical sense involves a perception, not only of the pastness of the past, but of its presence; the historical sense compels a man to

> write not merely with his own generation in his bones, but with a feeling that the whole of the literature of Europe from Homer and within it the whole of the literature of his own country has a simultaneous existence. . . .[35]

What this might mean for Americans, is that a historical sense of their attitudes towards Europe could possibly provide the opportunity to escape from the dead-hand of sentimental pieties.

One American scholar recently, troubled by the issues of "anti-Americanism," said:

> Most people are not able to stand personal criticism of themselves, especially when it emanates from strangers. Criticism of one's country, particularly if one is an American, is even less tolerable than criticism of oneself. Americans, more than any other people, seem to feel that a criticism of any of their country's institutions or ways constitutes a criticism of and an insult to themselves. A psychologist cannot help wondering whether this sensitivity does not betray a rather deep-seated insecurity — individually and collectively — which causes most Americans to respond in this way to such criticisms. This insecurity explains a great many things about Americans which foreigners see but which many Americans are so frequently unwilling to face. What look to the foreigner like arrogance and conceit are simply the overcompensatory devices by means of which the American is trying to compensate for his feeling of inadequacy and show that he is a "success.". . . (*Ashley Montagu*)[36]

In something of the same spirit an editor tried to face the "frightening misunderstandings" between Europe and America:

> For in Europe there has grown up a kind of myth about America, and it might one day be written that the free world destroyed itself because of it. It would not be the Big Lie of the Russians; only the fools believed that. It would be something much more inexplicable: the myth that for all our bathtubs and our cars and our skyscrapers we are without moral purpose; that we are the New Carthago — all money, no spirit; that we are, in short, a country without a soul.
>
> If America does not destroy this myth, it will destroy America. . . .[37]

And, finally, a few years ago this sensible (and already prophetic) thesis from Lewis Galantière:

The attempt to "spread Americanism" round the world is futile and offensive; to spread "understanding of America" is another thing.

I know of no revolutionary movement currently going on which, whatever its philosophic and ethical creed, does not have for its immediate pretext the material betterment of the life of the masses, East and West. In this art of material betterment, we of America are the leaders; and because we are, we are accused of materialism by those very non-Americans whose first purpose is a better material life for their compatriots. Those who thus accuse us, lose sight of the moral promptings behind our material system and assert that we have no culture, in the common sense of "refinement of taste," "acquaintance with the humanities," and so on. They do so because they judge us from the point of view of the culture of a bourgeois or aristocratic society, where nothing is easier than to run an avant-garde theater or magazine for a mere handful of "cultivated" spectators or readers, at the expense of underpaid printers, stagehands, and other workers.

Our critics are not aware that, as we tend materially towards a classless society, our cultural problem becomes a problem of culture for the mass, not for the few; that no European society has ever had to face the problem of, say, 100,000,000 people who possess the purchasing power to satisfy their impulse to entertainment and instruction. In a closed society, those millions could be ordered to read, hear, and see what their masters thought "culture"; in a democratic society, cultural despotism cannot be imposed; every movie producer, comic-book publisher, TV manager is free to solicit the patronage of those millions — and he does.

This is our problem, and Europeans must learn to understand that it is a problem which will face them as soon as their masses have the purchasing power as well as the freedom which our people enjoy. In the cultural domain, as well as in the material domain, America is a proving ground which Europeans ought to regard with sympathy and study with interest — not disdain as inferior to the dark and shabby world in which a Flaubert or a Dickens was produced. . . .[38]

Which leaves us, at the end of our documentary, with a number of questions. Was not the American notion of "exceptionalism," with all its unfriendly implications for Europe, the natural and understandable compensation for a strange transatlantic birth three thousand miles away from the Motherland? Was not the phenomenon of "expatriation" a unique tribute of a young society to an older culture? Is it sentimental piety on my own part to claim that the American tradition of "cosmopolitanism" is possibly the finest product of the national genius?

Perhaps the most significant fact of our time will be not, as Bismarck prophesied (with some characteristic continental envy and resentment), "the accident that in England and the United States the same language is spoken," but rather the fact that the Americans and all the Europeans, sharing as they do a libertarian ideal of a free and open society, were able in an epoch of historic challenge to communicate in a common tongue.

26

European Images of America

Marcus Cunliffe

IMAGE: *Artificial imitation of the external form of an object, statue (esp. of saint etc. as object of veneration); optical counterpart produced by rays of light reflected from mirror, refracted through lens, etc.; form, semblance; . . . simile, metaphor, idea, conception . . .*

IMAGINARY: *Existing only in imagination; (Math.) having no real existence, but assumed to exist for a special purpose (e.g. square root of negative quantity)*

(definitions from the *Concise Oxford Dictionary*)

IMAGINARY AMERICA

There is a vast literature of responses to America, more particularly of responses to the United States. Their precise nature has varied with time and circumstance, and according to the nationality, temperament, and social class of the observer. But much of the comment is repetitious; and some of the repetitions have such an astonishingly long history that they encourage a simple and summary form of classification. The notion of "images" frees us from too strict a regard for event or chronology. Let us start then with two elementary propositions and see where they lead.

The first proposition is that for most Europeans America has never existed. Instead of being a "real" place it has served as an image: a symbol, a Never-Never Land. How characteristic, indeed, that the whimsical Scottish dramatist J. M. Barrie should stock the Never-Never Land of his *Peter Pan* with figures of fantasy from the New World: Caribbean pirates and prowling Indians. The children who read Barrie in British nurseries took to bed with them another product of American folklore, the teddy bear, which derived from the near-mythical exploits of Theodore Roosevelt. What head of state in a European country ever made a comparable contribution to the dreams of early childhood? How characteristic, too, that the founder of the Boy Scout movement, Baden-Powell, should draw their name and some of their rituals from what he had heard of Red Indian life. Or that when the French writer of fantasies, Jules Verne, visited the United States with his brother just after the Civil War, they should make a special pilgrimage to the Fenimore Cooper region and address one another while there as "Hawkeye" and "Chingachgook."[1] James Russell Lowell remarked in 1869, "for some reason or other, the European has rarely been able to see America except in caricature."[2]

The second proposition, which these mild instances conceal, is that European images of America have rarely been dispassionate. Samuel Gompers, the American trade-union leader, said after visiting Europe in 1909 that its peoples saw his country through one of two mirrors, either convex or concave.[3] "Has the discovery of America been useful or hurtful to mankind?" — this was the title of an article published in 1784, typical of many of the period.[4] The question has been raised again and again ever since, in essentially the same form. It was still being asked in 1960 when the Oxford University Union debated the motion, "That this house holds America responsible for spreading vulgarity in Western society." America, which by degrees has come to signify the United States, not the whole hemisphere, has been one thing *or* the other: compliment *or* recrimination, adoration *or* detestation, boosting *or* knocking, the last best hope *or* an awful warning and a cautionary tale. Convex or concave, the image has been of a hypothetical place, so enveloped in didacticisms that the French traveler Georges Duhamel protested:

> I can't see the Americans for America. . . . Between the American citizen and me there rises I know not what monstrous phantom, a collection of laws, institutions, prejudices, and even myths. . . . I see a system rather than a people. Men, about whom I always feel an eager curiosity, in this country seem to me like pure ideograms, like the signs of an abstract, algebraic, and yet already fabulous civilization.[5]

The square root of a negative quantity. . . . Duhamel did not allow his confession of bewilderment to inhibit him. Nor have other commentators, for whom America has provided whatever generalization they happened to seek. Tocqueville's admission, "J'avoue que dans l'Amérique, j'ai vu plus que l'Amérique," could be applied to a hundred European theorizers on America. Sometimes they are hardly talking about America at all. Franz Kafka's friends in Prague were startled to learn from him in 1913 that he was at work on a novel entitled *Amerika,* though he understood very little English and had probably never met an American.[6] And despite its title, a recent French book, Lucien Lehman's "*Ces Cochons d'Américains!!*" (1954), turns out to be a vigorous essay on the defects of the author's own nation, with a few incidental references to the phenomenon of anti-Americanism.

One thing *or* the other. The point may be illustrated by listing examples of a heroic image of America, and then by presenting some of the contrasting, villainous images.

THE HEROIC IMAGE

The Earthly Paradise

The proposition that America has never existed as a real place for Europeans can be extended. We can say that the New World was invented before it was discovered. Mythology preceded exploration; and discovery happily fitted previous invention. In classical and in medieval legend there are persistent references to Atlantis; to the Hesperides; to Avalon; to the Blessed Isles: to some lost and perfect kingdom beyond the western seas. And we have the Garden of Eden, the earthly paradise from which sorrowful Adam was expelled. Columbus's Caribbean landfall in 1492 gave them all a possible, actual habitation. He himself was convinced, he wrote, that he had found "the terrestrial paradise." In Michael Drayton's poem *To the Virginian Voyage*, Virginia is described as "Earth's only paradise," still governed by the natural laws of the Golden Age. True, the early panegyrists of the New World, like the late ones, speak from mixed motives. They are often interested parties, promoters, advertisers. Yet they are not cynical liars: they are unable to separate fact from fancy when the two are so strangely conjoined.[7]

The Noble Savage

The natives of the new-found hemisphere (and of other, subsequently discovered territories, including the South Sea islands) likewise ministered to a European necessity. Columbus reported them to be virtuous and handsome. In the next century the picture was enlarged. "They seem to live," said Peter Martyr, "in that golden world of which old writers speak so much: wherein men lived simply and innocently without enforcement of laws, without quarreling Judges and libels, content only to satisfy nature, without further vexation for knowledge of things to come."[8] The American aborigines were thus converted into Noble Savages, free from the sins of sophistication that troubled European moralists in the seventeenth and eighteenth centuries. Full of natural dignity, integrity, and wisdom, the Noble Savage furnished an admirable contrast to the corrupt courtier or man of fashion in Paris and London.

By the eve of the American Revolution, sympathetic Europeans could assure themselves that the white settler in North America had absorbed some of the attributes of the aborigines. In the 1771 edition of *L'élève de la nature* (a Utopian novel first published in 1763, and avowedly inspired by Rousseau's *Émile*) the author, Gaspard de Beaurien, added a dedication to the "Inhabitants of Virginia":

> In that land which you inhabit and which you cultivate, there are to be found neither cities nor luxury nor crimes nor infirmities. Every day of your lives is serene, for the purity of your souls is communicated to the skies above you. You are free, you labor, and bring forth all about you, besides your abundant crops, a harvest of all the virtues.

> You are as Nature would wish us all to be. I therefore dedicate to you this portrait of a man whom I have conceived as formed by nature alone.[9]

Benjamin Franklin, "le bon Quaker," delighted Parisian society not merely on account of his sagacity and wit but also because he contrived to appear as a backwoods philosopher, a man whose wisdom was as intuitive, as much the result of an unspoiled environment, as that of an Indian chief. He fostered the view that he was by no means unique in his self-culture. "The famous Franklin has told us," said one French journalist, "that there is no working man in Philadelphia who does not read the newspapers at lunch time and a few good works of philosophy or politics for an hour after dinner."[10]

At this juncture Crèvecoeur published his *Letters from an American Farmer* (1782) and declared — with such an uncanny appropriateness that one is tempted to dismiss the passage as a fake concocted by some later propagandist — that a new type of man, the American, was in the making: a glorious amalgam of all types of men, actuated by new principles and behaving in new ways. In the expanded French edition, published a year after, Crèvecoeur took the idea still further. His sentiments indicate the tendency of Europeans to express their vision of America in oracular and theoretical terms. If this is not exactly what the American *is* like (and it was not for Crèvecoeur, a man well aware of frontier squalor, and so disturbed by the Revolution that he remained a loyalist), then it is at least what the American *ought* to be like, *must* become.

The Land of Liberty

The story developed with such an air of rightness that prophecy and destiny seemed to be identical. Success was deserved and therefore attained. The rebellious colonies secured their independence. The State of Nature became the United States, the Land of Liberty. "The genuine Liberty on which America is founded," declared the English writer Thomas Pownall in 1783, "is totally and entirely a New system of Things and Men."[11] Madame de Staël, one of Europe's dominant intellectual figures, toyed with the idea of transferring her *salon* to America. In England, Coleridge and his friends spoke of establishing their ideal "pantisocracy" in the New World.

While becoming the Land of Liberty, the United States produced two heroes for the world to wonder at. One was Franklin (whose autobiography, incidentally, was among Kafka's favorite books).[12] The other was the exemplary George Washington. Even the defeated British paid tribute to Washington's coolness and tenacity. The whole of Europe marveled at his subsequent patriotism and modesty, in retiring from military command, then in returning with obvious reluctance to lead the new nation as its first President under its new constitution, and finally in retiring unbidden into private life once more. "Virtue," according to Montesquieu, was a feature of republics, whereas monarchical societies valued "honor." He seemed to be correct. Washington's career revealed a republican morality of a standard rarely achieved even in the splendid days of classical antiquity.[13]

If Franklin and Washington were praised as virtuous statesmen, they were also celebrated as revolutionaries. The Land of Liberty haunted the imagination of European radicals. The American experiment was held to demonstrate that armed rebellion against authority was possible: citizen soldiers led by amateurs could beat professional armies. It was thought to prove that a federal republican democracy was a feasible form of government, though to conservative eyes this was the least workable and most objectionable of all blends of government. The United States stood for the right of revolution, for the likelihood of victory in revolution, and as the living exemplar of egalitarianism. So when the Russian radical Bakunin paid a visit to America in 1861, having escaped from Siberia, he carried back across the Atlantic a copy of the autograph of that great fellow-revolutionary, George Washington.[14] For liberals and radicals in Western Europe the United States was a perennial bench mark. In England, an exasperated Conservative member of Parliament said that the radical M.P. John Bright never contributed to a Commons debate without dragging in the United States.[15] Indeed the United States of the mid-nineteenth century occupied a place in the emotions of men such as Bright similar to that occupied seventy years later, in the emotions of their spiritual heirs, by the Soviet Union. It was, they insisted, a country founded on utterly novel and unimpeachably pure doctrine. Humanity had been given a fresh start and was no longer subject to the frailties of the Old World. In America everything was either perfect or perfectible. Hence, no criticism was applicable. For Bright and his associates it was truly the Land of Liberty when it guaranteed (in his words) "a free church, a free school, free land, a free vote, and a free career for the child of the humblest born in the land."[16]

It was this shining image that lured the potential emigrant. In leaving his own country he asserted his belief in the superiority of the United States. Even if he failed to find all that he dreamed of, his letters home tended to suppress the disappointment. How could he admit that he had duped himself? Even if like hundreds of thousands of others he eventually returned to the Old Country, the emigrant retained and transmitted his vision of an ideal place. In describing a village in southern Italy as it was during the 1930's, Carlo Levi speaks also for poor men in Greece and other parts of Europe:

> Their other world is America. . . . America, to the peasants, has a dual nature. It is a land where a man goes to work, where he toils and sweats for his daily bread, . . . where he can die and no one will remember him. At the same time, and with no contradiction in terms, it is an earthly paradise and the promised land.[17]

Europe's Future: Democracy

Even before the American Revolution the contrast between the "New" and "Old" worlds was explained as a contrast between the future and the past. "Westward the course of empire takes its way," according to Bishop Berkeley in 1726 (in what must be one of the most frequently quoted lines in the whole of literature). The English traveler Andrew Burnaby, who came to the colonies a generation later, remarked that

> An idea, strange as it is visionary, has entered into the minds of the generality of mankind, that empire is traveling westward: and everyone is looking forward with eager and impatient expectation to that destined moment when America is to give the law to the rest of the world.[18]

In 1776 the Abbé Galiani wrote from Naples to a friend in Paris:

> The epoch has become one of the total fall of Europe, and of transmigration into America. All here turns into rottenness, — religion,

> laws, arts, sciences, — and all hastens to renew itself in America. This is not a jest; nor is it an idea drawn from the English quarrels; I have said it . . . for more than twenty years, and I have constantly seen my prophecies come to pass. Therefore, do not buy your house in the Chaussée d'Antin; you must buy it in Philadelphia.[19]

The idea became more specific during the nineteenth century. The United States was in the van of progress, Europe's only hope lay in trying to follow in the same direction. In his *De la démocratie en Amérique* (1835, 1840), the most influential of all the European interpretations of the New World, Alexis de Tocqueville viewed the United States as a laboratory of egalitarianism, as Europe's probable destiny. It was a generous analysis. Yet he doubted whether the Union could long survive the centrifugal strains that threatened it. Sure enough, the Union did begin to break apart in 1860. But for Americanophiles such as John Bright the triumph of the North during the Civil War gave still another proof of the invincible power of the democratic ideal. Destiny could be defined as the inevitable victory of good causes. Who could now doubt the stability of the United States, the missionary force of its spirit, when it was able to overthrow so vast and militant a conspiracy? And when it also put an end to slavery — hitherto the one dark passage in an otherwise unblemished record? Fifty years after Tocqueville, in an equally generous but less conjectural testimony, *The American Commonwealth* (1888), James Bryce is also ready to interpret America as Europe's future:

> America has in some respects anticipated European nations. She is walking before them along a path which they may probably follow. She carries behind her . . . a lamp whose light helps those who come after her more than it always does herself.[20]

Bryce had to reckon with the sordid aspects of America in the Gilded Era. But he can explain these away as the mistakes of the pioneer grappling with the unfamiliar. They are temporary and incidental, not fundamental defects. On the whole Lord Bryce, we might say, has seen the future in the United States, and is quite sure that it works. To idealism have been added experience and stability. Unlike some other countries, America

> is made all of a piece, its institutions are the product of its economic and social conditions and the expression of its character. The . . . vehicle has been built with a lightness, strength, and elasticity which fit it for the roads it has to traverse.[21]

Heroes

In waging the Civil War, not only America but all the world acquired another, third hero in the person of Abraham Lincoln. Franklin, Washington, Lincoln: what European nation even in a history ten times as extensive as that of the young United States could claim a trio which held any comparable significance for mankind?

This strong, confident land was to offer two more possible candidates for world veneration during the twentieth century. One was Woodrow Wilson, the "Meester Veelson" who brought the prospect of a just and lasting peace to Europe, even if the hope was in vain. *Wilson, apôtre et martyr* — apostle and martyr! — was the title of a biography written by a Frenchman in 1933. The second man was Franklin D. Roosevelt, a leader who in the judgment of a great many Europeans (if with not quite so much unanimity among his own countrymen) could do no wrong. In the homes of the peasants of Lucania where Carlo Levi was summoned as a doctor, "what never failed to strike me . . . were the eyes of the two inseparable guardian angels that looked from the wall over the bed." These were the local Madonna, and F.D.R.:

> I never saw other pictures or images than these: not the King nor the Duce, nor even Garibaldi; no famous Italian of any kind, nor any one of the appropriate saints; only Roosevelt and the Madonna of Viggiano never failed to be present. To see them there. . . , in cheap prints, they seemed the two faces of the power that has divided the universe between them. . . . Sometimes a third image formed, along with these two, a trinity: a dollar bill, the last of those brought back from across the sea, or one that had come in the letter of a husband or relative, was tacked up, . . . like the Holy Ghost or an ambassador from heaven to the world of the dead.[22]

THE VILLAINOUS IMAGE

The discovery of America was an affront as well as a miracle: an affront to scholarship and morality. For each of the heroic images there has existed a hostile antithesis. Again, these hostile images often have little or nothing to do with a "real" America. Naturally enough, they are projections of European problems. Against the dream of an Earthly Paradise may be set the coarse invention called Cockaigne. The Noble Savage? — there is a contrary version, or what we might call the Ignoble Savage. The Land of Liberty has been depicted as something that could be labeled the Land of Libertinism. In place of the notion that America anticipates Europe's democratic future there is the alarmed conviction that the United States foreshadows Europe's fate — the fate pejoratively styled "Americanization." In contrast to the list of American world-heroes there is a list of American world-villains; and a list of world-martyrs, Americans whose sad experiences are cited as evidence of the cruelty and hypocrisy of the vaunted Land of Liberty. Each of these counter-images deserves a brief examination.

Cockaigne

The French *fabliau* of the thirteenth century, *Cocaigne*, may have been written to deride the fable of Avalon, the mythical island of the blest. In any case, to medieval Europe "Cocaigne" or "Cockaigne" represented an imaginary country, situated somewhere in the West, where no one need work or worry. The very landscape was made of food; birds dropped from the air already prepared for eating. (The Big Rock-Candy Mountain is a modern equivalent.) Cockaigne, also known as Lubberland, was a poor men's paradise and the fable has a certain charm.[23] But it is also a self-indulgent dream, of glut and gluttony, of life lived through the belly instead of the mind. I do not know whether America has often been explicitly identified with Cockaigne (though William Byrd of Virginia did refer to the back country of the early eighteenth century as Lubberland, perhaps in a somewhat different sense). But the notion clearly underlies European conceptions of American abundance, waste, and vulgarity. So the United States figures in nineteenth-century German and Norwegian novels as "a sort of dreary and vulgar fable-land, emancipated from the laws of probability."[24] Cockaigne is the medieval prototype of the Affluent Society, or at least of its sillier and nastier aspects such as the TV "give-away" show. The stupefied Flemish peasants whom Brueghel painted in his scenes of Cockaigne (Schlaraffenland) are the ancestors of the greedy, idiotic creatures caricatured today in *Mad* magazine.

The Ignoble Savage

To the European conservative preoccupied by the problem of achieving and maintaining order in society, or to the European scholar conscious of the gradual, difficult stages by which knowledge is accumulated: to such people the Noble Savage is a dangerous and preposterous myth. Can men be wise without study, without due reverence for the past? Can they grow intellect as a plant produces flowers, merely by being? "Don't cant in defense of savages," Dr. Johnson said irritably in 1784 to the more sanguine Boswell, when Boswell tried to tell him of the innate, untutored sensibility of men raised in a state of nature.[25] What *could* come out of a raw country like the United States? The answer of the Irish poet Thomas Moore, who toured there in 1803–04, was sharp:

> Take Christians, Mohawks, Democrats and all
> From the rude wigwam to the congress hall,
> From man the savage, whether slaved or free,
> To man the civilized, less tame than he,—
> 'Tis one dull chaos, one infertile strife
> Between half polished and half barbarous life.[26]

So much for Crèvecoeur and the eighteenth-century portrait of a land of simple, virtuous citizens destined to grow until the American example governed the universe.

The attack was mounted with more apparent scholarly precision in the work of Jean-Louis Buffon and Corneille de Pauw. What lessons did America hold for the naturalist? How could its species be classified? What of its aborigines? Buffon's *Histoire naturelle* (1761) and some other treatises argued that America's "newness," scientifically speaking, connoted immaturity. Animals and humans alike were inferior to those of the "Old" World, for climatic and other reasons. Moreover this handicap was not lessening but increasing. It could be traced in the degeneration of animal species, including breeds of cattle that had been introduced from Europe. It was evident in the life-cycle of the Indians, who decayed rapidly in physique and intellect after a seemingly vigorous childhood and adolescence. The deterioration, it was argued, affected the white settler in his turn. Peter Kalm, a Swedish scientist who traveled through North America in the mid-eighteenth century, believed that the colonists matured earlier and died earlier than did Europeans. De Pauw, following Kalm and Buffon in a series of essays — including a notorious contribution on the condition of America for the 1776 edition of Diderot's *Encyclopédie* — was sure that the colonists were less energetic and intelligent than their European contemporaries. "It has not been observed," he said, "that the professors of the University of Cambridge in New England have educated any young Americans to the point of being able to display them in the Old World."[27] The Abbé Raynal, in the first edition (1770) of his *Histoire philosophique et politique*, reproduced De Pauw's views, though he was later to modify them. Emphasizing the decadence of the English settlers, he asserted that

> their minds have been enervated like their bodies. Quick and penetrating at first, they grasp ideas easily; but they cannot concentrate nor accustom themselves to prolonged reflection. It is amazing that America has not yet produced a good poet, a capable mathematician, or a man of genius in a single art or a single science. Almost all have some facility in everything, but none has a marked talent for anything. Precocious and mature before us, they are far behind when we have reached our full mental development.[28]

So, in that most crucial year 1776, a European like De Pauw could maintain that mankind in America was suffering a fatal decline, through the insidious effects of heat and humidity. Though they have offered different explanations for the phenomenon, Europeans have kept on noting it ever since. Precocity and superficiality! — Raynal's observations have been repeated over and over, though without awareness of their parentage.

The Land of Libertinism

"The fever is in Europe, the remedy is in America," according to Voltaire. But some would turn the statement round. Consider for instance the old argument over the origins of syphilis. A Hessian soldier, stationed in South Carolina during the American Revolution, noted that the New World had conferred upon Germany the blessing of cheap food in the shape of the potato plant. "Columbus," he went on, "brought in exchange for this very useful food venereal diseases, a deplorable bargain for the Americans!"[29] We recognize here a classic confrontation: corrupt Europe, innocent and benevolent America. But others believe the opposite — that syphilis, unknown in Europe until the 1490's, was unwittingly brought back by Columbus's sailors through intercourse with Caribbean women.[30] (It has also been argued that though Europe owes the potato to *South* America, the vegetable was introduced in *North* America from Europe.) Here is the opposite confrontation. Unlucky Europe, tainted America — the place of contagion of every sort, physical, moral, ideological. From *this* virulent America of the European imagination spread not only the poisons of revolution and democratic misrule but also the social disorders of the frontier West, the plantation South, and the urban North. In fact the image dates from colonial days. America is the haunt of pirates in a far-from-cosy J. M. Barrie-ish sense. It is the dumping-ground for Britain's criminals and paupers, and continues to be the domain of Europe's outlaws, bad-hats, remittance-men, misfits. The Abbé Prévost's novel *Manon Lescaut* (1731) opens with a wagon-load of prostitutes who are about to be shipped to America (French Canada) in order to purify France. In George Eliot's *Middlemarch* the unspeakable Mr. Raffles is sent off to America with "an adequate sum," in the hope and expectation that he will "remain there for life." In this context "life" is an ambiguous word. "Life in the New World" has the ring of a prison sentence. (To the dismay of his patron, Raffles returns to England, explaining that "Things went confoundedly with me in New York; those Yankees are cool hands, and a man of gentlemanly feelings has no chance with them.") Raffles is dispatched to the America of Andrew Jackson, *circa* 1830. Half a century afterward the Scandinavian Hans Mattson writes:

> It cannot be denied that many among the higher classes in Sweden feel very unfriendly toward the United States, and it was even not long ago a common saying among them, "America is the paradise of all rogues and rascals."[31]

In this image, the United States was given over to libertinism. Sir Lepel Henry Griffin, a British observer who lacked the amiability of James Bryce, printed on the title page of his *The Great Republic* (1884) two harsh quotations that epitomize the tone of the book:

> — "The Commonwealth of Athens is become a forest of beasts."
>
> TIMON OF ATHENS
>
> — "O Liberté! que de crimes on commet en ton nom."
>
> JEANNE-MARIE ROLAND

In the America that Griffin saw and that others have scrutinized, whites gouged, stabbed, lynched, and dueled with one another. They committed still more brutal outrages upon the Negro. They hunted down the Indian. In their cities votes were bought and sold with shameless cynicism. Only in the remote, backward corners of Europe such as Sicily was there a comparable record of brigandage; Murder, Incorporated, in the twentieth century might be affiliated with the Sicilian *Mafia* but certainly had nothing to learn from it. From England the French language borrowed such peaceable nouns as *le weekend*, from the United States the altogether more stringent vocabulary of *le gangster*.

One scholar, Durand Echeverria, suggests that in France — and his theory would apply in part to other European countries — this kind of image of America has not changed except in detail from the eighteenth century to the present day. In books like Georges Duhamel's *Scènes de la vie future* (published in English as *America the Menace*, 1931) or Simone de Beauvoir's *L'Amérique au jour le jour* (*America Day by Day*, 1953) there is undoubtedly a predilection for the uglier sides of American life, including crime, miscegenation (or rather, its consequence), rape, drunkenness, and murder. Liberty or Libertinism? "I have in my pocket," says Duhamel, speaking of the American five-cent piece, "several of your small coins on which is stamped the word 'liberty.' And what do you see immediately under that word? The figure of a buffalo or an Indian. Oh, irony! They represent two free and spirited races that you have destroyed in less than three centuries."[32]

Europe's Fate: Americanization

Uncle Sham, Uncle Shylock: where it is not a question of American violence, the image is of a hypocritical, timid, joyless people, absorbed not in the pursuit of happiness — itself a vain quest, according to European critics — but in the even emptier pursuit of wealth. Charles Dickens popularized the expression "the Almighty Dollar" in his *American Notes* (1842). But the idea had long been in circulation. The Frenchman Louis-Félix de Beaujour, for example, offered an almost standard comment on the United States that he saw during the first decade of the nineteenth century:

> Virtue has been regarded as the guiding principle or principal strength of republics. That of the American Republic appears to be a frantic love of money. It is the result of the political equality which reigns there and which, leaving people with no other distinction except wealth, invites them to acquire it by every possible means.[33]

The protracted squabble over war debts after 1918 did a great deal to intensify the European image of America as Uncle Shylock.

By the 1850's, when the word "Americanization" came generally into European usage, it was not enough merely to deplore what was thought to go on across the Atlantic. This contagion too was spreading. Far from America taking over the tasks of civilization and pointing a better way for poor old Europe, it was now argued that Europe was the repository of a precious civilization and that this was being assailed by transatlantic barbarism. The image grew of a decadent, avaricious United States in which everything including love was standardized, homogenized, and dehumanized. Cash was the measure of worth, quantity had become a value. America was afflicted with consumption, in fact galloping consumption — not a medical but an economic and moral disease. Food was Fletcherized, production lines were Taylorized. Indeed with the advent of the automat and the assembly line the image became more precise. It was of a gadget and machine civilization, without savor or individuality. So in the inverted Utopia of Aldous Huxley's *Brave New World*, prayers were addressed not to Our Lord but to Our Ford.

And in the years after the Second World War both radicals and conservatives in Europe, who might find it difficult to agree on any other issue, could rally round the accusation that the United States was, consciously or unconsciously, tending to "coca-colonize" the rest of mankind. In *L'Américanisme et nous* (1958), Cyrille Arnavon contends that the attempt is deliberate and insidious — whether one examines the operations of NATO or of the United States Information Service, or even whether one takes into account the publication of a French edition of *Reader's Digest* (a perusal of which apparently stimulated M. Arnavon to write his book).

Such views drew additional ammunition from the fact that in the twentieth century radicals no longer looked to the United States for a lead. That role had been usurped, at least for a spell, by the Soviet Union. To the extent that the United States still symbolized the future, then, it seemed to stand for an anti-Utopia, rich and yet bankrupt. Apart from the dubious boon of "Americanization" the United States could be defined as a backward nation. That at any rate was the assumption in Harold Laski's *The American Democracy* (1948): lacking a left-wing political party, the United States was at a primitive stage of evolution and was bound to recapitulate the experiences of wiser if sadder European nations. Russian successes in outer space, since 1957, have reinforced the image of America as a nation that is no longer a dream and not even a *technologically* supreme nightmare.

Villains — or Martyrs

Five heroes — Franklin, Washington, Lincoln, Wilson, Roosevelt. But not quite everyone accepted these. The poet John Keats, writing in 1818 to his brother who had just emigrated to the United States, said:

> Dilke, whom you know to be a Godwin perfectibil[it]y Man, pleases himself with the idea that America will be the country to take up the human intellect where england leaves off — I differ there with him greatly — A country like the united states whose greatest men are Franklins and Washingtons will never do that — They are great Men doubtless but how are they to be compared to those of our countreymen Milton and the two Sidneys — The one is a philosophical Quaker full of mean and thrifty maxims the other sold the very

> charger who had taken him through all his Battles. Those Americans are great but they are not sublime Man — the humanity of the United States can never reach the sublime. . .[34]

If there was some dispute as to the stature of America's heroes, there was widespread agreement that America had produced villains for the whole world to shudder at, though of course none as horrendous as a Hitler. Perhaps it would be better to say groups of villains: the Robber Barons (Rockefeller, etc.), the Gangsters (Al Capone and the rest), the Demagogues (Joseph McCarthy especially), the Imperialists (headed I suppose by John Foster Dulles). There were too America's martyrs, the victims of national villainy, whose stories echo far beyond the borders of the United States: the Haymarket anarchists; perhaps Eugene Debs; certainly Sacco and Vanzetti, and the Rosenbergs, and Caryl Chessman.

From the faces in these galleries there builds up a total villainous image of the United States, an image which owes much to Marxist coloration and the recent stresses of the cold war but which had its first shadowy adumbration several centuries ago. It is of a gross, rapacious Uncle Sam, leering, fanged, squatting on money-bags, clutching the Bomb. We may set against it the Uncle Sam in a *New Yorker* cartoon of 1958. This one is a scrawny figure, in traditional stars-and-stripes regalia that hang loose upon him, stretched out upon an analyst's couch and declaring plaintively, "Everybody hates me."

CURRENT FASHIONS IN IMAGERY

It seems clear that the heroic image of America has tended to yield to the villainous image, and it might seem that the tendency will continue. Human beings are always dissatisfied in some degree with their own society. They therefore devise nostalgic or radical images of superior societies. The nostalgic images relate to bygone times and far-off places where life is simpler and purer than they conceive their own existence to be. The radical images usually relate to the future, or to some other contemporary society which has a special stake in the future, where the form of life already appears better than one's own and likely to become immeasurably better. Both of these kinds of image used to apply to the United States. The nostalgic one has now, we might think, almost vanished, while the radical one has lost most of its excitement. Large-scale immigration is at an end; we perceive the accidental relevance of Kafka's description of the Statue of Liberty, which — no doubt through sheer ignorance — he equips with a sword instead of a torch. In *The Irony of American History* (1952) Reinhold Niebuhr concludes that much of America's radical thunder has been stolen by Russia. Today the majority of even friendly assessments of the United States dwell upon its loss of nerve: *Americans Are Alone in the World* (1953), by Luigi Barzini, Jr., is a case in point. There is even something a little inert about *Image of America* (1959) by R. L. Bruckberger, an intelligent and well-informed French Dominican priest who sings the praises of American economic democracy in a way akin to the survey of the "permanent revolution" conducted by the editors of *Fortune*.

In the absence of either a nostalgic or a radical vision of America we may wonder whether *any* compelling image exists, other than that of bigness — of military and industrial mass, of the United States as the ponderous captain of Our Side in the dreary exchanges of the cold war. One perhaps, but not an edifying one: in an essay on "The Erotic Myth of America,"[35] the English anthropologist Geoffrey Gorer comments on the French appetite for sleazy novels like Boris Vian's *J'irai cracher sur vos tombes,* a work allegedly "traduit de l'Américain" but actually written by M. Vian. In such a genre, which also includes *No Orchids for Miss Blandish* (by René Raymond, under the American-sounding pseudonym "James Hadley Chase"), America is still a fantasy-land but of the most debased and vicious sort — "pays de cocagne," says Vian in his introduction, "la terre d'élection des puritains, des alcooliques, et de l'enfoncez-vous-bien-ça dans la tête."[36] A hundred years ago Frenchmen enjoyed Fenimore Cooper's lone wolf, Natty Bumppo. Now, it seems, they pass off as American their own morbid lone-wolf obsessions of killing and rape.

ANTI-AMERICANISM?

Articles that deal with external views of America are apt to slide into discussions of anti-Americanism. Why, the American reader asks, *why* such a lineage of error and hostility? He may be ready to concede that all human groups have fanciful images of one another, that these are usually out-of-date, and that they are almost invariably unfavorable. He may realize that "top-dog" nations, as Malcolm Muggeridge calls them, are particularly subject to misrepresentation, and that America must therefore expect to suffer from the *Schadenfreude* of a declining Europe. But having made these concessions he may still insist unhappily that the images of his country differ in kind, not merely in degree, from the images that European countries entertain of one another. To be "Anglicized" or "Hellenized" was for example never as dreadful, in general estimation, as to be "Americanized." Why must America serve as a scapegoat for Europe's own weaknesses? Why must Europeans blame America for imposing upon them a mass culture which they eagerly accept and even "improve" upon?

Many answers could be offered. There is no doubt that malice and envy play a part, as well as Communist propaganda. But it is useful to remind Americans of their own venerable tradition of xenophobia. Almost from the beginning the New World has explicitly repudiated the Old, defining its own virtues as the precise antithesis of the supposed vices of Europe. It has not often occurred to Americans, until lately, to consider whether this gratifying polarity was altogether true, or what reactions it might arouse in the breasts of the repudiated. "We will bury you" was the burden of America's message to Europe long before Mr. Khrushchev employed it in a different context. What is it like to be consigned to the graveyard of history when one does not *feel* dead? "Twisting the lion's tail" was once thought to be a reliable vote-raising technique for American politicians. What of the lion's own discomfort? If we were compiling a balance sheet of denigration, American Anglophobia would more than offset instances of British anti-Americanism. It is not surprising then that Europeans should retaliate: that they should pounce upon every discrepancy between American promise and American performance, especially when the promise is proclaimed with such grandiosity. American self-righteousness is reminiscent of that of the British, which did not endear them to Continental Europeans and which generated similar charges of hypocrisy. If the kettle did not claim to be quite so stainless, the pot might not search so eagerly for evidences of the kettle's blackness.

However, this sort of *tu quoque* debate is valueless for our immediate purposes, except that it leads to an important qualification — namely, that America has never been a "real," finite place to Americans themselves. There has always been a close correspondence between European *projected* images of America, and American *self*-images. The United States has been a fantasy to itself: something in process, something mysterious and abstract, a democratic vista, a "willingness of the heart," and so on. What ambitious assessment of his country by an American does not try to explore its fabled quality, its mission and meaning, its search for identity, its appeal to the future tense — in short the American Dream, which Americans refer to more often than Europeans do?[37]

Similarly, the American Nightmare is a prime domestic topic. If the heroic image is cherished by Americans, the villainous image has not been neglected. There is no anti-Americanism as eloquent as that of the native American. From the strictures of Federalist authors like Joseph Dennie, through the anger of abolitionists and of their Southern opponents, all the way down the decades to H. L. Mencken and his "booboisie," the Dos Passos of *U.S.A.*, the Henry Miller of *The Air-Conditioned Nightmare*, the cartoons of *Mad* magazine, or the Allen Ginsberg of *Howl:* throughout the history of the United States the villainous image has to a considerable extent been a home-produced product. Like European critics, but with a bitterer sense of disappointment, they have been irritated by the disparity between *ought* and *is*. American life does have repellent features, and Americans have said so with a fine ferocity. Are not Europeans entitled to do the same? If Sinclair Lewis wrote *Babbitt*, why should not C. E. M. Joad write *The Babbitt Warren* (an inferior book, alas)? Why should not Jean-Paul Sartre be allowed a play about lynching in the South (*La Putain respectueuse*) when William Faulkner has published a novel about France (*A Fable*)? Is Faulkner's France — or his South, for that matter — more "real" than Sartre's America? If an *Ugly American* by William J. Lederer and Eugene Burdick, why not a *Quiet American* by Graham Greene? Are the sadisms of Boris Vian different in any crucial respect from those of Mickey Spillane: do not the European and American publics derive the same same satisfactions from such literature?

REAL AMERICA

So far, we have suggested that

a) America has never been "real" for Europeans,

b) European images of America have usually been *either* highly favorable *or* markedly pejorative,

c) Pejorative images have prevailed lately over favorable ones,

d) America has never been quite "real" for Americans either: they too have expressed extremes of admiration and anger (consider the literary career of Mark Twain, moving in one direction — glorification to disgust; and of Dos Passos, moving in the opposite direction — disgust to glorification).

These reflections leave us nowhere very much, unless we add two other comments. The first has to do with the peculiar *efficacy* of the images I have enumerated. Most of them are manifestly unhistorical. Some bear palpable marks of prejudice: thus, Corneille de Pauw was in the hire of Frederick the Great, a monarch who was anxious to discourage emigration. Most versions of America, including that of Tocqueville, rest upon *a priori* reasoning. But no one has shown profounder insight than this French theorist, on the basis of his single visit to the United States. Surely we must conclude that he was correct to see in America more than America. Surely there is a poetic if not a literal truth in almost all the sequences of heroic and villainous images, and in their dramatic contrast. Even the views of De Pauw and Raynal on American precocity — silly, unscientific, Europe-oriented — have their relevance. We still catch the refrain: we hear it, for instance, in the much-quoted remark by Scott Fitzgerald that there are no second acts in American lives. In sum, these are surely "true" sets of images of a continent and a nation which has held in suspension all the extreme possibilities — hopes and fears alike — for the future of mankind under democracy, and which continues to enact them for itself and for much of Europe and the rest of the world, despite the apparent drastic qualifications of the present time. Only America has this symbolic function for Western society. Soviet Communism has never provided so wide a range; and if the American heroic image has become dulled, what are we to say of the Soviet image? The god that failed is Communism. The deities and devils of American democracy still fascinate Europeans.

Much of its high gloss may have gone, but its problems are of more immediate interest than ever.

In other words — to come to the second and final point — the images of America are now of *half*-gods and *half*-devils. The United States is less loved but more liked; more criticized but less hated. It has become more "real," and so our initial proposition is far less *apropos* than formerly. The relationship of America and Europe has greatly changed in the past half-century. The story is no longer of American repudiation and European condescension. The contest is no longer between America and Europe, nor even perhaps of America-plus-allies versus the Communist bloc. There are several blocs in today's world. North America and Western Europe are only two of them, yet two whose similarities are far greater than their differences. Both are highly industrialized and mobile societies. Their mutual involvements continually increase. We can still find absurd accounts of what America is presumed to be. But there is a growing number of expert European studies of the United States — of its politics, industry, history, literature, music, art, architecture. Europe's foremost living authority on the United States is Denis Brogan, and he is often compared with Tocqueville and Bryce. The comparison is just. But his tone is different. He *knows* infinitely more than Tocqueville did about the American scene, and considerably more than the esteemed Bryce. He is as capable as the next man of generalizing, but his approach is microscopic rather than macroscopic.

The great mythological and metaphorical European interpretations of America have ceased. D. H. Lawrence's *Studies in Classic American Literature* (1923) may have been the last of them. This does not mean that Europeans have ceased to talk about the United States in broad terms. It means that when they do so their authorities, their large labels, are all American. Current European magazines are crammed with observations on the Lonely Crowd, the Power Elite, the Organization Man, the Status-Seekers, the Affluent Society. Each is the coinage of an American author: David Riesman, C. Wright Mills, William H. Whyte, Jr., Vance Packard, J. K. Galbraith. For American literature, the grand theory is provided not by Europeans but by Americans: Perry Miller, Harry Levin, Philip Rahv, Richard Chase, Leslie Fiedler, Henry Nash Smith.

European images of America, always closer than is commonly

admitted, have now almost coincided with American self-images; and the Americans are the principal image-makers. The United States will continue to be a semi-mythical place for Europeans, but mainly to the extent that Americans see it thus. To the extent that the myth is rich, alive, and honest, so will be the European view. To the extent that it is commercial, vapid, and meretricious, so will it seem to Europeans. America will continue to be blamed excessively whenever something goes wrong. That is America's punishment and privilege for being an imaginary as well as a real country.

27

Japanese Images of America

Shigeto Tsuru

I

"If that double-bolted land, Japan, is ever to become hospitable, it is the whale-ship alone to whom the credit will be due; for already she is on the threshold."[1] Thus wrote Herman Melville prophetically in his immortal *Moby-Dick*, published in 1851, two years before Commodore Perry knocked at the door of that closed country in incidental search of ports of safety and supplies for American whale-ships. Until the arrival of Perry, Japan had been closed by the law of the land to the outside world for more than two hundred years except to Dutch traders through one small quarantined island off the port of Nagasaki.

By the time Perry came, the country had been seething with internal conflict between the forces of modernization and tradition. The catalytic effect of sudden contact with the West could easily be predicted to be enormous. Whatever image of America was then held by relatively well-informed Japanese may be guessed at from scattered accounts available in Dutch. This image was never articulated at the time in Japanese writing, but it must have been one which evoked, albeit vaguely, high expectations of opportunity, enlightenment, and progress. Otherwise it would be hard to explain, for example, the daring of Shōin Yoshida, the period's foremost ideological leader of modernization, who braved the strictest law of Tokugawa Japan to attempt a clandestine departure for America aboard Perry's flagship, the *Susquehanna.* One does not know, of course, how much difference it would have made to the subsequent course of Japanese history if Perry had acceded to Yoshida's wish. But the law-abiding Commodore declined,[2] and Yoshida was sent back to the shores for arrest and was later executed according to the law. Not all the attempts at illegal exit, however, were failures. The most notable success was that of Joseph Hardy Neeshima, a stowaway who arrived in Boston in 1864 and later became a founder of the earliest Christian university in Japan.

The image of America in the minds of Japanese up till the opening of ports by the Treaty of 1858 was probably a counterpart of the image of Japan as depicted, let us say, in the accounts by Marco Polo. It was that of a country unseen whose inhabitants had remained only an object of conjecture. As contact became established, naturally the first reaction was a series of unsophisticated impressions born of curiosity,[3] soon to be superseded by serious attempts at understanding specific trees in the forest but only later to be enriched by the seeing of the forest as a whole. Understandably, this evolution was punctuated by differing historical circumstances; successive images reflected the concrete needs of the persons concerned as well as the contingencies of the times. Thus it is convenient to divide the span of one hundred years, 1860–1960, into three more or less distinct periods for the purpose of surveying the historical evolution of the image of America held by Japanese.

The *first* period is the initial decade of the Meiji Restoration (1868–78), when the overriding consideration for Japan's political leaders was to learn from the West as much and as quickly as possible. In such circumstances we can speak of an image of America only in a somewhat restricted sense of the term. Only a very small percentage of the population had any direct concern with that image, and that in a most practical and concrete manner. The *second* period covers a longer stretch, let us say from the last decade of the nineteenth century to the defeat of Japan in the last war. This is the period which witnessed the remarkable rise and abrupt debacle of Japan as an imperialist power. Here new factors both in America and Japan contribute to the formation of the image, such as the coming of motion pictures, the U.S. policy on Japanese immigration, and Japan's sense of rivalry with the United States over China. In the second period the image of America naturally becomes more comprehensive, more varied, even conflicting, and engages the attention of a great many more people. Finally, the *third* period is ushered in at the date of Japan's surrender. From 1945 on, an incomparably large number of Americans have come to reside in Japan; and with the advancing process of acculturation the erstwhile sense of foreignness rapidly wanes. One might even say that a "shock of recognition" now traverses the Pacific as easily as the Atlantic.

II

The period of initial contact, which will be here dealt with somewhat sketchily, is characterized less by any outstanding example of Japanese contemplation of things American than by the hasty transplantation of typically American institutions onto the soil of newly developing Japan. The circumstances are not difficult to explain. Leaders of the Restoration, most of them in their twenties or thirties, were suddenly thrown into positions of responsibility. Although they had a fairly clear-cut idea of what they wanted to do, i.e., to modernize Japan at top speed without becoming a dependency of any Western power, most of them were, previous to the Restoration of 1868, little versed in the philosophy or in the arts of the West. Before they had time to learn or to contemplate, they wanted to modernize. This impatience accounts, for example, for the hasty adoption of the National Banking System after the American model on the recommendation of Hirobumi Ito, who visited the United States in 1870 and had only time enough to make a cursory study of the National Banking Act. It also explains various turnabouts, which took place after only a decade or two, in the choice of models for the Constitution, etc., from one country to another.[4]

Partly by accident and partly by design, certain aspects of the new reforms depended greatly, often exclusively, on the American model, and certain American writers and scholars played a prominent part in the early Westernization of Japan. To recount these developments will be indirectly to suggest the character of the image of America held by the Japanese at the time. Most prominent of American strands in the fabric of the new Japan was, without a doubt, the educational system which had to be created entirely anew. As early as in 1872, the fifth year of the Restoration, Arinori Mori, the first Japanese Minister to America and later a Minister of Education in the Japanese government, circulated an inquiry to a number of American educators asking their advice on how to build up the Japanese educational system. Thirteen of them responded, including Charles W. Eliot of Harvard, Theodore D. Woolsey of Yale, and William A. Stearns of Amherst; and their replies acted as seeds, as it were, on the virgin soil of educational opportunities in Japan.[5] One of the thirteen, David Murray of Rutgers University, was invited in 1873 to come to Japan as "Superintendent of Educational Affairs in the Empire of Japan and Adviser to the Japanese Imperial Minister of Education." For almost six years until January 1879, when he left Japan, Murray was a guiding spirit in the pioneering work of laying foundations for the universal education which contributed so much to the rapid development of modern Japan. His influence was eminently a healthy one, for, with his first-hand knowledge of the American system, he could, paradoxically enough, restrain the excessive zeal of his Japanese colleagues, some of whom, like Fujimaro Tanaka, wanted to copy the American system of federal noninterference too faithfully. Probably due largely to Murray's influence, the earliest Western books on education translated into Japanese were mostly of American origin. Among them, the most widely used are said to have been *Theory and Practice of Teaching* by David P. Page and *School Economy* by James P. Wickersham. Naturally, the pedagogic method adopted was also typically American at first, laying great stress on "object lessons." In this connection such books as Norman A. Calkins's *Primary Object Lessons* and Edward A. Sheldon's *Lessons on Objects* were immediately put into use. The earliest textbooks in schools were also nothing but the translations of such American books as the "School and Family" readers edited by Marcius Willson,[6] *The Progressive Primary Arithmetic* by Horatio N. Robinson, *Elements of*

Moral Science by Francis Wayland, *Parley's Universal History* by Samuel C. Goodrich, and *Primary Geography* by Sarah S. Cornell. Thus from the early days of new Japan names like George Washington and Benjamin Franklin, along with episodes from their lives, were commonplace in the Japanese household. In fact, Franklin's *Autobiography* was used quite early as a text in the education of the Imperial Household; and there remains on record a set of twelve Japanese poems, composed by Empress Meiji reputedly in 1875, matching twelve of the "thirteen precepts" of Benjamin Franklin.[7] Franklin's popularity symbolized the identification of America as a nation of practical wisdom. This, no doubt, was a quality which the Meiji Japan needed most. It was praised by a man like Yukichi Fukuzawa, the founder of Keio University, and came later to be all the more identified with the image of America as American influence receded towards the end of the nineteenth century.

Soon after the deliberate and systematic attempt at transplanting the American educational system to the new Japan, there was a spontaneous influx of American Protestants into Japan after the opening of the ports. These men, along with Japanese who returned from America as Christians, played an extremely important role in circles of higher education in the early years. Though the ban on Christianity, which had existed in Japan for more than two hundred years, was lifted soon after the Restoration (1873), it lingered on in spirit and practice for some time. It was this circumstance which forced the Protestant missionaries to work at first in a circuitous manner by engaging more in general education than in direct proselytization. It is difficult to assess the real effect which this sudden impingement of Protestantism had on the still semifeudal society of Japan. But at least on two reforms, that of education for women and of strict monogamy, its causal influence seems clear. Such movements as the campaign against prostitution, for penal reform, and for the establishment of orphanages are also traceable to American and Canadian missionaries of early Meiji years. Further, Americans who combined high scholarship with strong Christian character, though few in number, left indelible marks on the education of Japanese youths. Most notably, William Clark at Sapporo, Captain L. L. Janes at Kumamoto, and Samuel R. Brown at Yokohama inspired sensitive youths of the day; and the names of their Japanese protégés who later became prominent leaders of Japan present a catalogue which is unbelievably outstanding.[8] If we were to name a Japanese who could be said to have embodied the spirit of these Christians, it would be Joseph Hardy Neeshima, who after ten years' stay (1864–74) in America came back to Japan to found Dōshisha University in Kyoto. Until he died in 1890, Neeshima, more than any other Japanese, personified what was good in America in the eyes of Japanese.[9]

III

Lacking a comprehensive account by a Japanese depicting the image of America in the period of early contact between the two countries, we might consult Japanese literature to discover the American authors who commanded special Japanese attention. In this way we can infer the nature of the selection made by the Japanese who were interested in America and thus also the specific orientation which Japan's reading public received from the American literary world.

In eminence and popularity in the minds of the late nineteenth-century Japanese, few American authors came close to Washington Irving, Nathaniel Hawthorne, Walt Whitman, and Ralph Waldo Emerson. As a matter of fact, all four happened to experience special personal contact with those involved in the earliest intercourse between America and Japan in the mid-nineteenth century. Both Irving and Hawthorne were close friends of Commodore Perry and were among the first to read Perry's *Narrative of the Expedition*. Whitman was an eye-witness of the Broadway pageant[10] of the first Japanese diplomatic mission of 1860; that he continued his interest in Japan is evident from accounts in Horace Traubel's *With Walt Whitman in Camden*.[11] Finally, Emerson's association with Japan began when he appeared as a guest speaker at the reception in Boston for the famed Iwakura Mission in 1872.

Such associations, however, were incidental to the interest which Japanese took in the writings of these men. Of the four, probably Irving remained popular longest by virtue of *The Sketch Book*, which for about half a century no Japanese who studied English failed to sample. The affinity of the Rip Van Winkle story to one of the old Japanese fables, Urashima, may have had something to do with this popularity. Again, the theme of self-imposed celibacy, which can be gleaned from such pieces as "The Wife," "The Broken Heart," and "The Pride of the Village," seems to have had a special appeal to Japanese psychology. At any rate, no other American author had a wider and more appreciative circle of English readers in Japan than Irving. In the case of Hawthorne, many Japanese were familiar with his writings in the early Meiji years without knowing his name. For, as was mentioned earlier, *Parley's Universal History*, which had actually been written by Hawthorne, was in wide use as a textbook in Meiji Japan, as were the Swinton Readers, to which he also contributed. Hawthorne's *Biographical Stories* and *Twice-Told Tales* were also used widely as English textbooks; and, after Lafcadio Hearn began his lectures on American literature at the Tokyo Imperial University in 1898 and made a special point of praising the beauty of "Rappaccini's Daughter" in *Mosses from an Old Manse*, Hawthorne's reputation became all the more attractive to Japanese intellectuals. The introduction of Whitman to the Japanese public did not take place till 1892, the year he died; he was translated by Sōseki Natsume, the most eminent scholar of English literature as well as a novelist of Meiji Japan. Once Whitman came to be known, there was an explosive burst of interest in him. This interest has been sustained without abatement to this day, though among a restricted circle of intellectuals and literary men. The Whitman Exhibit, held in Tokyo in July 1953, probably could not be matched in any other non-American country in its scope and authenticity.[12] It is interesting to note that Whitman's reputation survived the critical comments of Lafcadio Hearn, who usually had a strong influence in shaping Japanese taste in English and American literature. The influence of Emerson on Japanese thinking was more pervasive than Whitman's though less enduring than Irving's. The mood of Meiji Japan was attracted, almost beyond reason, to an essay like "Civilization,"[13] the very title of which captivated the Japanese just emerging from the slumber of the exclusion period. Emerson's moralistic thinking was especially congenial to the Japanese, often having been likened, rightly or wrongly, to Wang Yang-ming's philosophy, which was quite popular among the intellectual leaders of the late Tokugawa Japan. As with Irving, Emerson's *Essays* was widely used as an English textbook and won a significant number of devotees around the turn of the century.[14] And if we extend the scope of our survey beyond literary figures, we find several other American names prominent in Japanese thinking in the period before the First World War. Such names as Theodore D. Woolsey, Henry George, Richard Ely, and William James cannot be overlooked in this connection.

Although the general impact of America on Japan was decisively the greatest among all the Western nations in the early years of the Restoration, it gradually gave way to European influences from the 1880's onward. Even the educational system, originally patterned after that of America, faced a reaction as early as 1880 when Fujimaro Tanaka was transferred from the Education Ministry to that of Justice. The educational reform of 1886 took Germany as its model, as the Meiji Constitution of 1889 was almost a replica of the Prussian Constitution. For scientific and cultural training in general, Japanese began to prefer Europe, especially Germany. Indeed, for a lengthy stretch of almost half a century from 1890 to 1940, we find only a handful of non-Christian Japanese who traveled to America with a serious intention of studying a scientific discipline. Instead, though by coincidence, a new era of Japanese-American relations began around 1895 when Japanese workers began coming to America in large numbers. The number of Japanese in America (excluding Hawaii) was estimated to be around 6,000 in 1895, but jumped to 35,000 by 1897, to 53,764 by 1904, and to 103,683 by 1908. After this date it declined through the effect of the Gentlemen's Agreement on immigration between the two countries.

Most of the immigrants came, not to escape from political oppression,[15] but to escape economic hardships at home. Few were under illusions as to the real opportunities which existed for Japanese in America. The name of a successful immigrant like Kinji Ushijima was much publicized even in grade-school textbooks in Japan at one time; but it was less to show that America was bountiful than to demonstrate that one could succeed in spite of the severe handicaps. The waves of anti-Japanese agitation on the West Coast, which gathered momentum after Japan's victory over Russia in 1905 and which culminated in the so-called "Anti-Japanese Immigration Act" of 1924, inevitably influenced the image of America held by Japanese at the time. While Japanese residents in America conscientiously redoubled their efforts, especially after 1924, to prove their assimilability into American culture (their failure in this regard had undoubtedly been a factor in the anti-Japanese agitation), Japanese at home increasingly shared an accusing attitude, saying that "Here is the richest country on the earth, which is unwilling to share its wealth with others." Mixed into such vague negative impressions was the positive identification of America either as a "mechanical civilization" (*kikai bunmei*) or as a "materialistic civilization" (*busshitsu bunmei*). Both terms connoted superficiality and the worship of Mammon. Such an image of America was most prevalent in the 1920's. "To become Americanized" was an epithet of opprobrium to a member of the intelligentsia. Even the vigor of American democracy in the period of the New Deal escaped the attention of most Japanese; for by then Japan was mortally preoccupied with her campaign of aggression, and the opposition within the country was necessarily far more radical than the New Deal. It is probably no exaggeration to say that the generation of Japanese who were born after the turn of the century held an extremely superficial view of America which remained more or less uncorrected until 1945.

IV

Probably more Americans than ever before came to Japan as tourists in the interwar years. At the same time American motion pictures gave an incomparably wider circle of Japanese contact with at least the cinematic version of American civilization. Trade between the two countries also prospered, though with some ups and downs. "Taylorism," the technique of scientific management, became a concrete issue between capital and labor in Japan. Baseball, the great American pastime, sank roots in Japan. In other words, America seemed everywhere in Japan in these years. Yet it is remarkable that there was no serious attempt at interpreting America's history, its society, or its culture in Japan in the interwar years. Yasaka Takagi in the field of constitutional and political history, Matsuo Takagaki in the history of literature, and Taihei Imamura in the study of American film comics were the notable exceptions. But even distinguished visitors from Japan to America usually went home empty-handed, leaving on record only cursory reactions of an impressionistic character. Tōson Shimazaki, the most prominent of lyric poets in modern Japan, made a leisurely trip through the Americas in the mid-thirties; but he preferred to write more and with greater enthusiasm on the southern continent than on the northern. That Japan's understanding of America was essentially superficial at the time became tragically evident when she embarked on her hopeless war against the United States in 1941.

In view of the low ebb in intellectual intercourse between the two countries, it may be instructive to summarize one of the few attempts made by a Japanese before the end of the Second World War at a comprehensive interpretation of America — an attempt by the author of the present essay. In 1943 I presented a picture of America as seen by a Japanese who had lived in America during most of the 1930's and who had returned to Japan after the war broke out. I had studied pragmatism under Max Otto at Wisconsin, social psychology under Gordon Allport at Harvard, and economics under a galaxy of Harvard Keynesians; but I tended always to guard jealously the intellectual attributes I had acquired in the turbulent atmosphere of the late 1920's in Japan. The analysis of the American scene which I presented first in 1943, was expanded into a longer essay immediately after the war.[16] Of this essay Shunsuke Tsurumi has written that it was one of the few Japanese commentaries on American life which transcended the circumstances of the war or the Occupation.[17]

After a disclaimer about the variety that exists among Americans, I venture to single out four distinctive attributes in their national character: (1) their confidence in the inherent power of an individual is very strong; (2) their criteria of value judgments tend to be one-dimensional; (3) their steps of pedagogy in general are continuous to the point of avoiding leaps of any kind; and (4) their canalization of human conduct is highly developed.

That confidence in the inherent power of an individual is strong is, we might say, an aspect of "rugged individualism." This confidence, no doubt, is related closely to the historical circumstances in which America developed. Alien to it is the following sociological insight of Schumpeter's: "Things economic and social move by their own momentum and the ensuing situations compel individuals and groups to behave in certain ways whatever they may wish to do — not indeed by destroying their freedom of choice but by shaping the choosing mentalities and by narrowing the list of possibilities from which to choose."[18] The idea that a society might evolve in accordance with laws to which individuals may unknowingly be subject completely escapes the comprehension of representative Americans. An expression like: "If you don't like it here, why don't you go back to where you came from?" can be heard only in a country where each man is considered to be the master of his own fate. Thus it was natural that the inclination to attribute unemployment to the laziness of the individual concerned lingered longest in America. In the realm of philosophy also, determinism was rejected and in its place developed the pragmatism of William James with its emphasis on the "will to believe." In Shunsuke Tsurumi's words: "There seems to have been a kind of pictorial image in the back of James's thinking — an image of a man standing alone, fully conscious of his physical body, at the end of the horizon with infinite possibilities open before him. He is free in the sense that he is not bound by any tradition or man-made laws; but, since he is also free of any material heritage from the past, he cannot be idle if he wants to live. The only things he can rely on are burning interests of all kinds which he is concretely conscious of within himself. He stakes everything on these interests and has no choice but to start an action with them in order to carry on his existence into the future."[19] Here is an image of a typical American whose confidence in the inherent power of an individual had to be strong.

That the criteria of value judgments tend to be one-dimensional does not necessarily imply that everything is measured in terms of monetary reward. It is rather an aspect of practical rationalism in daily life. An Oriental in America is often puzzled by the interrogation: "Are you happy?" For one, like a Japanese of prewar days, who was usually enmeshed in the hierarchical web of ethical codes, "happiness" would connote something extremely complex. He would easily be able to decide whether he was healthy, but would not use the word "happiness" in day-to-day circumstances. For Americans the feeling of happiness seems to connote any state of harmony between purposes and means to accomplish them. It can be clearly felt because it is a practical concept. Furthermore, when conflicting purposes arise, these can be visualized by Americans as rationally comparable, sometimes as even measurable in terms of monetary returns. Take higher education, for example. While a Japanese of prewar days would tend to regard it as an absolute value, Americans from early days were accustomed to treat it as an investment. A conflict of absolutes cannot be resolved unless the absolute of absolutes is postulated, as it was in feudal society. And just as their confidence in the inherent power of the individual reflected the Americans' resistance to determinism, the practical rationalism of Americans may be said to reflect their resistance to absolutes or to status of the kind that prevailed in feudal society. If American individualism is a manifesto of liberty, American resistance to absolutes is a manifesto of equality. This naturally opens the doors to the pluralism of William James and, with its emphasis on the practical comparability of values, to the instrumentalism of John Dewey.

That the steps of pedagogy in general are continuous to the point of avoiding leaps of any kind is a mark of democracy in communication in the broadest sense of the term. The Orient respects the tradition of Confucius, who said that he would not teach a pupil again unless the latter, upon learning from him one corner of the square, responded with three other corners on his own. There the essence of education had been thought to consist in an appropriate synthesis of continuity and discontinuity. In America, discontinuity is shunned as much as possible, and efforts are made always to be continuously in touch with the level of understanding of the pupil concerned. I remember an American historian of philosophy introducing the subject of Greek philosophy with the sentence, "The history of philosophy, like the stock market, has its ups and downs, now bullish and now bearish." Such a mode of expression might be used by someone seeking contact with lay readers, but would be most likely regarded as vulgar by the prewar Japanese. The method of "object lessons" in primary education, which, upon transplanting, had a short life in the early Meiji Japan, can also be said to be typically American in this connection. However, the attitude is not confined to the sphere of pedagogy. When one receives change at a store in America, the adding is usually done for the benefit of the customer. And although some Japanese have interpreted this practice as an indication of American weakness in mathematics, it is probably more correct to explain it in terms of the American respect for continuity. In everything, continuity at the point of immediate contact is important: for example, the tendency of Hollywood movies to condescend to the taste and interest of the largest common denominator, and of newspaper write-ups to be repetitive and plain. If attention can be held at the first impression, half the conquest is achieved. Therefore, in matters where an element of surprise serves to sustain the continuity of attention, the technique is highly developed for the particular purpose at hand, as in advertising which tends to be constantly novel and striking, and as even in women's make-up and material ornaments which are fashioned to be ever eye-catching. There is no doubt that this preference of concrete over abstract or of continuous over discontinuous has contributed greatly to the immense progress in America of practical arts of all kinds.

That the canalization of human conduct is highly developed is an aspect of the American character which is probably of more recent development. What it means may better first be conveyed through a concrete example. When one attempts to cross an intersection where traffic is heavy, one's problem is extremely simplified by the existence of appropriate signals. Without them, one would have to concentrate all the nerves at one's command and to look for an opening and make a dash, which incidentally was a common feature of city centers in prewar Japan. With signals, on the other hand, the relevant part of one's conduct is *canalized* into a limited set of extremely simplified sensory reactions. To stop on red and to walk on green and not to worry about anything else is a simple act of physical motion not much above the level of canine intelligence. A modern man is increasingly confronted with complex problems which place exacting demands on his entire being as an integrated bundle of physical and mental powers. If each problem required him to mobilize the entire bundle of such powers, he would soon be exhausted. If, on the other hand, devices are developed to enable him to meet each specific problem by the limited use of simpler physical and mental powers, the scope of his activities naturally expands. The mechanization in production processes is, of course, an aspect of the canalization. But the latter extends much farther afield. Whereas "a walking dictionary" was a common feature of most government offices in the prewar Japan, it is quite typical that America developed early a system of filing a store of information accessible to anyone who understands the system of classification. Where a master craftsman used to reign with his incommunicable endowment of skill, America started to separate out the elements in that skill and to deal with each element individually by means of far simpler devices. This characteristic approach has gone so far as to be applied to the question of "winning friends and influencing people," not to speak of the question of "how to look beautiful," although the traditional Japanese would say that artificiality is foreign to either deep-felt friendship or intrinsic beauty.

This, then, is a summary of the image of America by one Japanese in whom some strains of old Japan still remained.

V

Japan's surrender of 1945 ushered in an entirely new period in the history of Japano-American relations. The Occupation, which was mainly American, lasted for seven years. Even after the recovery of independence, American forces have continued to be stationed in Japan in large numbers. Meanwhile, thousands of Japanese have come to America for study, either serious or perfunctory. Many intermarriages have taken place. Economic intercourse is also far closer, not only in trade but also in the movement of capital and technology. One wave length in Japan is still reserved for a completely American radio broadcast; American magazines, *Time*, *Life*, and *Newsweek*, are accessible in air editions at every Japanese newsstand, while the Sunday summary section of the *New York Times* has a wide circulation among students and the English-reading public in general. American movies are more ubiquitous than ever; and popular American television programs, "westerns" in particular, are indispensable on Japanese TV. Professional baseball is ever more popular; and the postwar craze for things American brought in professional wrestling and American-type football in addition. Supermarkets on a small scale can now be seen in the shopping areas of big cities. There are few American new products which do not cross the Pacific in a month's time. The age of the automobile has also come to Japan in spite of the worst road system imaginable. The educational system was reformed to imitate the American pattern again; and the legal system, too, was strongly bent in that direction.

With such a background as this, one finds it difficult to speak of a single Asian image of America as being crystallized in contemporary Japan. Japan herself appears to be cleft into three heterogeneous generations: the oldest, born at the turn of the century or before but still influential in many walks of life; the middle-aged, in their forties or early fifties, in many cases casualties, either psychological or physical, of the war, now lacking confidence in themselves; and the youngest generation, a majority of whom have an outlook of life strongly tinged by American strains. The future, of course, is in the hands of this last group. It remains to be seen how much of what was once typical of Japan will become integrated into the evolving character of new Japan which, in its turn, will have incorporated the impact of America.

Just as the outlook is for an ever greater degree of assimilation of the American culture into that of Japan, the study of America in Japan has become, and is bound to become more so in the years to come, a viable field in itself. Whereas the prewar Japanese writings on things American were, with extremely few exceptions, amateurish or second-hand — second-hand in the sense that they tended to see America through the eyes of European experts — and whereas the image of America presented to the Japanese public in the war years was deliberately mendacious,[20] the area of American studies in the postwar era has blossomed forth with a vengeance, and it has come to command the interest of serious, able students in every field. Probably the first crop of such studies after 1945 was an ambitious five-volume work: *The History of American Thought*,[21] the fruit of organized research by the Science of Thought Study Group. This unique group consisted of scholars mostly outside the pale of traditional academicism in Japan. Although some were Marxist in methodology, what seems to be common among the members of the Group was not any peremptory *ism* for interpreting facts but rather an open-minded critical attitude on the subject-matter at hand. In fact, what united them appears to have been a keen awareness that in the prewar academic circles in Japan, America was never considered worthy of scholarly preoccupation.[22] The authors of these volumes were generally untainted by ideological cooperation with the militarist Japan and, probably more significant, remained unenthusiastic about the trend of Americanization in the postwar Japan. In this sense, their volumes represent that part of prewar Japanese scholarship which characterized the minority opposition of the time. One finds in these volumes penetrating and original studies on aspects of American thought, such as Shunsuke

Tsurumi's essay on "Communication" and Taihei Imamura's analysis of "Motion Pictures." Wading through these volumes, one is aware of the fact that the authors are not Americans, not because the treatment is too often sketchy or esoteric but because it shows the signs of digestion of American materials in a stomach, as it were, which is clearly different from America's.

Scholarly efforts like *The History of American Thought* will no doubt continue. By the time the decade of the 1950's had ended, it was plain that the Japanese scholarship on American affairs had taken firm roots with a degree of specialization and sophistication approaching that in the United States itself. With the progress in specialization, however, the orientation has become increasingly indistinguishable from that which prevails in America. It is as if studies on American problems in a Japanese university have become something akin to such studies in, let us say, a Canadian university. Yet, just as Canada today, which is as close as can be to America both in its geography and outlook, can and does have an image of America of its own, so Japan still looks toward America with a sense of foreignness which cannot easily be bridged. What enters here is an image of America in the broad, even historical, sense of the term. Above all, America presents itself as an undisputed leader in the camp of so-called "free countries" and as the most successful capitalist country in the world. It is characteristic of Japan today that this image does not produce a single unified reaction among her inhabitants. The majority applaud it and identify themselves with dominant attributes of America today. But a significant minority are disposed to find fault with certain policy manifestations of America's leadership in the postwar world. What is often termed "anti-Americanism" in Japan emanates from this group. But it is important to observe that this "anti-Americanism" has nothing to do with emotional bias against Americans as such. In view of its character, it should rather be identified as an attitude critical of certain American policies[23] especially as they impinge upon the political and economic life of Japan. It may sound paradoxical, but it stands to reason, that those Japanese who hold America's tradition and ideals highest happen to be counted in that minority. The time will no doubt come to set this incongruity aright.

Epilogue:
The One Against the Many

ARTHUR M. SCHLESINGER, JR.

In an epoch dominated by the aspirations of new states for national development, it is instructive to recall that the United States itself began as an underdeveloped country.

Every country, of course, has its distinctive development problems and must solve them according to its own traditions, capacities, and values. The American experience was unique in a number of ways. The country was blessed by notable advantages — above all, by the fact that population was scarce in relation to available resources. But the favorable ratio between population and resources was obviously not the only factor in American development. Had that been so, the Indians, for whom the ratio was even more favorable, would have developed the country long before the first settlers arrived from over the seas. What mattered equally was the spirit in which these settlers approached the economic and social challenges offered by the environment. Several elements seem fundamental to the philosophy which facilitated the rapid social and economic development of the American continent.

One factor was the deep faith in education. The belief that investment in people is the most essential way for a society to devote its resources existed from the earliest days of the American colonies. It arose originally from a philosophical rather than an economic commitment — from a faith in the dignity of man and from the resulting belief that it is the responsibility of society to offer man the opportunity to develop his highest potentialities. But, at the same time, it also helped produce the conditions essential to successful modernization.

Modern industrial society must be above all a literate society. Economic historians attribute two-thirds of the growth in American output over the centuries of American development to increases in productivity. And increases in productivity, of course, come directly from the size of the national investment in education and in research. J. K. Galbraith has rightly observed that "a dollar or a rupee invested in the intellectual improvement of human beings will regularly bring a greater increase in national income than a dollar or a rupee devoted to railways, dams, machine tools, or other tangible capital goods." These words accurately report the American national experience.

Another factor in the process of American development has been the commitment to self-government and representative institutions. We have found no better way than democracy to fulfill man's talents and release his energies. A related factor has been the conviction of the importance of personal freedom and personal initiative — the feeling that the individual is the source of creativity. Another has been the understanding of the role of cooperative activity, public as well as voluntary.

But fundamental to all of these, and perhaps the single most important explanation of the comparative speed of American development, has been the national rejection of dogmatic preconceptions about the nature of the social and economic order. America has had the good fortune not to be an ideological society.

By ideology I mean a body of systematic and rigid dogma by which people seek to understand the world — and to preserve or transform it. The conflict between ideology and empiricism has, of course, been old in human history. In the record of this conflict, ideology has attracted some of the strongest intelligences mankind has produced — those whom Sir Isaiah Berlin, reviving the gnomic saying of Archilochus, termed the "hedgehogs," who know one big thing, as against the "foxes," who know many small things.

Nor can one suggest that Americans have been consistently immune to the ideological temptation — to the temptation, that is, to define national goals in an ordered, comprehensive, and permanent way. After all, the American mind was conditioned by one of the noblest and most formidable structures of analysis ever devised, Calvinist theology, and any intellect so shaped was bound to have a certain vulnerability to secular ideology ever after. There have been hedgehogs throughout American history who have attempted to endow America with an all-inclusive creed, to translate Americanism into a set of binding propositions, and to construe the national tradition in terms of one or another ultimate, ranging from Natural Law to the Class Struggle.

Yet most of the time Americans have foxily mistrusted abstract rationalism and rigid *a priori* doctrine. Our national faith has been not in propositions but in processes. In its finest hours, the United States has, so to speak, risen above ideology. It has not permitted dogma to falsify reality, imprison experience, or narrow the spectrum of choice. This skepticism about ideology has been a primary source of the social inventiveness which has marked so much of our development. The most vital American social thought has been empirical, practical, pragmatic. America, in consequence, has been at its most characteristic a nation of innovation and experiment.

Pragmatism is no more wholly devoid of abstractions than ideology is wholly devoid of experience. The dividing line comes when abstractions and experience collide and one must give way to the other. At this point the pragmatist rejects abstractions and the ideologist rejects experience. The early history of the republic illustrates the difference. The American Revolution was a pragmatic effort conducted in terms of certain general values. The colonists fought for independence in terms of British ideals of civil freedom and representative government; they rebelled against British rule essentially for British reasons. The ideals of American independence found expression in the classical documents which accompanied the birth of the nation: the Declaration of Independence; the Constitution and Bill of Rights.

But it is important here to insist on the distinction between ideals and ideology. Ideals refer to the long-run goals of a nation and the spirit in which these goals are pursued. Ideology is something different, more systematic, more detailed, more comprehensive, more dogmatic. The case of one of the Founding Fathers, Thomas Jefferson, emphasizes the distinction. Jefferson was an expounder both of ideals and of ideology. As an expounder of ideals, he remains a vivid and fertile figure — alive, not only for Americans but, I believe, for all those interested in human dignity and human liberty. As an ideologist, however, Jefferson is today remote — a figure not of present concern but of historical curiosity. As an ideologist, he believed, for example, that agriculture was the only basis of a good society; that the small freehold system was the only foundation for freedom; that the honest and virtuous cultivator was the only reliable citizen for a democratic state; that an economy based on agriculture was self-regulating and, therefore, required a minimum of government; that that government was best which governed least; and that the great enemies of a free state were, on the one hand, urbanization, industry, banking, a landless working class, and all the other things which we know as characteristic of the modernization process, and, on the other, a strong national government with power to give direction to national development. This was Jefferson's ideology, and had the United States responded to it, we would be today a feeble and impotent nation. By responding to Jefferson's ideals rather than to his ideology, the United States has become a strong modern state, dedicated at its best to universal purposes of dignity and freedom.

Fortunately, Jefferson himself preferred his ideals to his ideology. In case of conflict he chose what helped people rather than what conformed to principle. Indeed, the whole ideological enterprise contradicted Jefferson's temper, which was basically flexible and experimental. The true Jefferson is not the ideological Jefferson but the Jefferson who said that one generation could not commit the next to its view of public policy or human destiny.

What is wrong with faith in ideology? The trouble is this. An ideology is not a picture of actuality; it is a model derived from actuality, a model designed to isolate certain salient features of actuality which the model builder, the ideologist, regards as of crucial importance. An ideology, in other words, is an abstraction from reality. There is nothing wrong with abstractions or models *per se*. In fact, we could not conduct discourse without them. There is nothing wrong with them — so long, that is, as people remember they are only models. The ideological fallacy is to forget that ideology is an abstraction from reality and to regard it as reality itself.

The besetting sin of the ideologist, in short, is to confuse his own tidy models with the vast, turbulent, unpredictable, and untidy reality which is the stuff of human experience. And this confusion has at least two bad results — it commits those who believe in ideology to a fatalistic view of history, and it misleads them about the concrete choices of public policy.

Consider for a moment the ideologist's view of history. The ideologist contends that the mysteries of history can be understood in terms of a clear-cut, absolute, social creed which explains the past and forecasts the future. Ideology thus presupposes a closed universe whose history is determined, whose principles are fixed, whose values and objectives are deducible from a central body of social dogma, and often whose central dogma is confided to the custody of an infallible priesthood. In the old philosophic debates between the one and the many, the ideologist stands with the one. It is his belief that the world as a whole can be understood from a single viewpoint, that everything in the abundant and streaming life of man is reducible to a single abstract system of interpretation.

The American democratic tradition has found this view of human history repugnant and false.[1] This tradition sees the world as many, not as one. These empirical instincts of American liberalism, the preference for fact over logic, for deed over dogma, have found their most brilliant expression in the writings of William James and in the approach to philosophical problems which James called "radical empiricism." Against the belief in the all-encompassing power of a single explanation, against the commitment to the absolutism of ideology, against the notion that all answers to political and social problems can be found in the back of some sacred book, against the deterministic interpretation of history, against the closed universe, James stood for what he called the unfinished universe — a universe marked by growth, variety, ambiguity, mystery, and contingency — a universe where free men may find partial truths, but where no mortal man will ever get an absolute grip on Absolute Truth, a universe where social progress depends not on capitulation to a single, all-consuming body of doctrine, but on the uncoerced intercourse of unconstrained minds.

Thus ideology and pragmatism differ radically in their views of history. They differ just as radically in their approach to issues of public policy. The ideologist, by mistaking models for reality, always misleads as to the possibilities and consequences of public decision.

The history of the twentieth century is a record of the manifold ways in which humanity has been betrayed by ideology.

Let us take an example from contemporary history. Much of the world today is oppressed by the insistence that it must choose between "capitalism" and "socialism." Yet the rise in the last generation of the mixed society — of the view that it is possible to give the state sufficient power to bring about social welfare and economic growth without thereby giving it power to abolish political and civil freedom — has revealed classical capitalism and classical socialism as nineteenth-century doctrines, left behind by the onward rush of science and technology. The world has moved beyond these obsolete ideologies toward a far more subtle and flexible social strategy. It is evident now, for example, that the choice between private and public means, that choice which has obsessed so much recent political and economic discussion in underdeveloped countries, is not a matter of religious principle. It is not a moral issue to be decided on absolutist grounds, either by those on the right who regard the use of public means as wicked and sinful, or by those on the left who regard the use of private means as wicked and sinful. It is simply a practical question as to which means can best achieve the desired end. It is a problem to be answered not by theology but by experience and experiment. Indeed, I would suggest that we might well banish the words "capitalism" and "socialism" from intellectual discourse. These words no longer have clear meanings. They are sources of heat, not of light. They belong to the vocabulary of demagoguery, not to the vocabulary of analysis.

So, with the invention of the mixed society, pragmatism has triumphed over absolutism. As a consequence, the world is coming to understand that the mixed economy offered the instrumentalities through which one can unite social control with individual freedom. But ideology is a drug; no matter how much it is exposed by experience, the craving for it still persists. That craving will, no doubt, always persist, so long as there is human hunger for an all-embracing, all-explanatory system, so long indeed as political philosophy is shaped by the compulsion to return to the womb.

The oldest philosophical problem, we have noted, is the relationship between the one and the many. Surely the basic conflict of our times, the world civil war of our own day, is precisely the conflict between those who would reduce the world to one and those who see the world as many — between those who believe that the world is evolving in a single direction, along a single predestined line, toward a single predestined conclusion, and those who think that humanity in the future, as in the past, will continue to evolve in diverse directions, toward diverse conclusions, according to the diverse traditions, values, and purposes of diverse peoples. It is a choice, in short, between dogmatism and pragmatism; between the theological society and the experimental society; between ideology and democracy.

This world civil war will come to an end when, and only when, the absolutists renounce their determination to make the world over in a single image, only when they accept a pluralistic destiny for mankind. The ideologists talk a great deal about peaceful competition. But, like all absolutists, they refuse — indeed, flee from — competition in the field where it really counts, that is, the competition of ideas.

One can go to New York or London or Paris and buy *Pravda* and *Izvestia* and Communist journals from the world over. But one cannot buy in Moscow any publications from democratic countries, except those put out by the local Communist parties. Not only is the *New York Times* forbidden but the *Manchester Guardian*, not only *Figaro* but *Le Monde*, not only the *National Review* but *L'Express* and the *New Statesman*. The works of Marx and Lenin are available everywhere in the West; the works of Mill, of Keynes, of Dewey, of William James, of nearly all the major social and philosophic thinkers of the West, are unobtainable in Moscow. After half a century of total intellectual control — after half a century of formidable construction and growth — the Soviet Union seems still afraid to expose Communist ideas to competition and challenge.

It appears even afraid to tell the truth about its own past. As a historian I sometimes feel that you can tell as much about a nation by the history it writes as by the history it makes. A half-century after the Russian Revolution, Russian historians are still not free to set down what really happened. The Communists appear recently to have abandoned their attempt to suggest that Trotsky in 1917 was an agent in the pay of Allen Dulles. But they are still a long distance from restoring him to his proper place in Soviet history. And Soviet officials constantly reaffirm the ban on peaceful competition in the realm of ideas. Coexistence with democratic social systems is deemed possible but coexistence with democratic ideas "impossible and unthinkable." Certainly, so long as the ideologists remain confessedly afraid of the free flow of ideas, even of deviant ideas within their own ideology, like the ideas of Yugoslavia, or Albania, or China, then it is unlikely that relaxation can ever come to our tormented world. Those who are convinced they have a monopoly on The Truth always feel that they are only saving the world when they slaughter the heretics. Their objective remains that of making the world over in the image of their dogmatic ideology. The goal is a monolithic world, organized on the principle of infallibility — infallibility of a single creed, a single party, and a single leader. Surely the only certainty in an absolute system is the certainty of absolute abuse. Injustice and criminality are inherent in a system of totalitarian dictatorship. The fact that one dictator admits the crimes of his predecessor is not enough to assure future justice.

The goal of free men is quite different. Free men know many truths, but they doubt whether any mortal man knows The Truth. They share the skepticism of Mr. Dooley, the American humorist, who once defined a fanatic as "a man who does what he thinks th' Lord wud do if He only knew th' facts in th' case." Their religious and their intellectual heritage join in leading them to suspect fellow men who lay claim to infallibility. They believe that there is no greater delusion than for man to mistake himself for God. They agree with Lincoln, who wrote: "Men are not flattered by being shown that there has been a difference of purpose between the Almighty and them. To deny it, however . . . is to deny that there is a God governing the world."

Free men accept the limitations of the human intellect and the infirmity of the human spirit. The distinctive human triumph, in their judgment, lies in the capacity to understand the frailty of human striving but to strive nonetheless. Freedom, as Brandeis said, is the great developer; it is both the means employed and the end attained. Freedom implies humility, not absolutism; it implies not the tyranny of the one but the tolerance of the many. Against the monolithic world, the American intellectual tradition affirms the pluralistic world. Against the world of coercion, it affirms the world of choice.

NOTES AND

FURTHER READING

INDEX

Notes and Further Reading

1. The American Revolution Considered as an Intellectual Movement

NOTES

[1] John Calvin, *Institutes of the Christian Religion,* trans. John Allen (sixth American edition, Philadelphia, 1932), I, 263.

[2] Cf. Frederick B. Tolles, *Quakers and the Atlantic Culture* (New York, 1960), p. 11; Babette M. Levy, "Early Puritanism in the Southern and Island Colonies," American Antiquarian Society, *Proceedings,* LXX (1960), 69–348.

[3] Perry Miller, *The New England Mind: The Seventeenth Century* (New York, 1939), pp. 398–431; E. S. Morgan, *The Puritan Dilemma* (Boston, 1958), pp. 18–100.

[4] In *The Eighteenth-Century Commonwealthman* (Cambridge, Mass., 1959), Caroline Robbins has identified and discussed this political tradition.

[5] Peter Laslett, "The English Revolution and Locke's Two Treatises," *Cambridge Historical Journal,* XII (1956), 40–55.

[6] On Whitefield, see Luke Tyerman, *The Life of the Rev. George Whitefield* (New York, 1877) and John Gillies, *Memoirs of Rev. George Whitefield* (New Haven, 1834). Originally published in 1772, Gillies's work was considerably expanded in later editions. On Whitefield in New England, see Edwin L. Gaustad, *The Great Awakening in New England* (New York, 1957).

[7] Charles Chauncy, *Seasonable Thoughts on the State of Religion in New England* (Boston, 1743), pp. 127, 151–168; *Boston Weekly News-Letter,* June 24–July 1, 1742; "Diary of Joshua Hempstead," New London Historical Society, *Proceedings,* I (1901), 379ff.

[8] On Edwards, see Ola Winslow, *Jonathan Edwards* (New York, 1940); Perry Miller, *Jonathan Edwards* (New York, 1949). On the New Divinity, see F. H. Foster, *A Genetic History of the New England Theology* (Chicago, 1907); Joseph Haroutunian, *Piety versus Moralism* (New York, 1932).

[9] *The Literary Diary of Ezra Stiles,* ed. F. B. Dexter (New York, 1901), III, 464. Cf. Conrad Wright, *The Beginnings of Unitarianism in America* (Boston, 1955), pp. 252–259.

[10] Stiles, *Diary,* III, 344, 438, 562.

[11] Rogers to Trumbull, March 17, 1783, Benjamin Trumbull Correspondence, Yale University Library.

[12] *New Haven Gazette and Connecticut Magazine,* July 31, October 9, 1788.

[13] See again Robbins, *Eighteenth-Century Commonwealthman.*

[14] E. S. Morgan, *Prologue to Revolution: Sources and Documents on the Stamp Act Crisis* (Chapel Hill, 1959), pp. 73, 91.

[15] Verner Crane, *Benjamin Franklin's Letters to the Press, 1758–1775* (Chapel Hill, 1950), p. xlii.

[16] Thomas Jefferson, *A Summary View of the Rights of British America* (Williamsburg, 1774); James Wilson, *Considerations on the Nature and the Extent of the Legislative Authority of the British Parliament* (Philadelphia, 1774); John Adams, *Works*, ed. C. F. Adams (Boston, 1850–56), IV, 3–177.

[17] Robert J. Taylor, ed., *Massachusetts, Colony to Commonwealth: Documents on the Formation of its Constitution, 1775–1780* (Chapel Hill, 1961), p. 45.

[18] Edmund C. Burnett, ed., *Letters of Members of the Continental Congress* (Washington, 1921–36), VIII, 206–210.

[19] Montesquieu, *Spirit of the Laws* (New York, 1949), p. 120 (Book VIII, c. 16).

[20] James Madison, *Writings*, ed. Gaillard Hunt (New York, 1900–1910), II, 361–369.

GUIDE TO FURTHER READING

The foregoing essay does not pretend to cover all the important intellectual developments that occurred during the era of the American Revolution. Some of the others are treated in Max Savelle, *Seeds of Liberty* (New York, 1948); Brooke Hindle, *The Pursuit of Science in Revolutionary America* (Chapel Hill, 1956); Michael Kraus, *Intercolonial Aspects of American Culture on the Eve of the Revolution* (New York, 1928); and *The Atlantic Civilization: Eighteenth-Century Origins* (Ithaca, 1949).

I have discussed some of the religious history of the period at greater length in *The Gentle Puritan: A Life of Ezra Stiles, 1727–1795* (New Haven, 1962). For a somewhat different view of the religious significance of the Revolution, see Perry Miller's brilliant interpretation in "From the Covenant to the Revival," in J. W. Smith and A. L. Jamison, eds., *The Shaping of American Religion* (Princeton, 1961), pp. 322–368. His *Jonathan Edwards* (New York, 1949) is the most searching study of that important figure. Alice Baldwin, *The New England Clergy and the American Revolution* (Durham, 1928) discusses the role of the clergy in spreading political ideas; and Carl Bridenbaugh, *Mitre and Sceptre* (New York, 1962) sets the colonial fear of bishops in a new perspective. On the history of the New Divinity a stimulating study is Joseph Haroutunian, *Piety versus Moralism* (New York, 1932).

Moses Coit Tyler surveys the writers on both sides of the struggle with England in *The Literary History of the American Revolution* (New York, 1897). The political ideas generated during that struggle are dealt with in Randolph G. Adams, *Political Ideas of the American Revolution* (Durham, 1922), and Clinton Rossiter, *Seedtime of the Republic* (New York, 1953). Irving Brant writes authoritatively of Madison's contributions in *James Madison: The Nationalist, 1780–1787* (Indianapolis, 1948) and *James Madison: Father of the Constitution, 1787–1800* (Indianapolis, 1950). The documents relating to the Massachusetts Constitution are collected in Robert J. Taylor, ed., *Massachusetts: Colony to Commonwealth* (Chapel Hill, 1961).

2. *The Rise of the Democratic Idea*

NOTES

[1] Wilfred E. Binkley, *American Political Parties: Their Natural History* (New York, 1959), chs. IV–VI.

[2] Cf. Robert E. Brown, *Middle-Class Democracy and the Revolution in Massachusetts, 1691–1780* (Ithaca, 1955).

[3] Louis Hartz, *The Liberal Tradition in America* (New York, 1955).

[4] For these slogans as they appear in the popular literature, see for example Joseph L. Blau, ed., *Social Theories of Jacksonian Democracy* (New York, 1947).

[5] Cf. Whitney Griswold, *Farming and Democracy* (New York, 1948).

[6] Cf. Donald Drew Egbert and Stow Persons, eds., *Socialism and American Life* (Princeton, 1952), Vol. I, chs. 4 and 5.

GUIDE TO FURTHER READING

For excellent general discussions of the writers involved here, see Vernon L. Parrington, *Main Currents in American Thought: An Interpretation of American Literature from the Beginnings to 1920* (3 vols., New York, 1927–30), and Richard Hofstadter, *The American Political Tradition and the Men Who Made It* (New York, 1948). For the international comparisons on the basis of which this essay rests, see Louis Hartz, *The Liberal Tradition in America: An Interpretation of American Political Thought Since the Revolution* (New York, 1955). A standard work on the battle between Hamilton and the democratic movement is Claude Bowers, *Jefferson and Hamilton: The Struggle for Democracy in America* (Boston, 1936). The Federalist tradition of John Adams is well described in Manning J. Dauer, *The Adams Federalists* (Baltimore, 1953), and the political philosophy of Adams is described in C. M. Walsh, *The Political Science of John Adams: A Study in the Theory of Mixed Government and the Bicameral System* (New York, 1915). Leonard D. White, *The Federalists: A Study in Administrative History* (New York, 1948) has cast new and significant light on the organizational aspects of Federalist thought. In connection with Jacksonian democracy, Charles A. Beard, *Economic Origins of Jeffersonian Democracy* (New York, 1915) remains an outstanding work. Charles M. Wiltse, *The Jeffersonian Tradition in American Democracy* (Chapel Hill, 1935) provides a good analysis of the Jeffersonian ideas. Arthur M. Schlesinger, Jr., *The Age of Jackson* (Boston, 1945) is a classic on the politics and thought of the Jacksonian movement, containing analyses of practically all the significant publicists of the era. Some of the fugitive material on the Jacksonian era is collected in the excellent anthology of Joseph L. Blau, *Social Theories of Jacksonian Democracy* (New York, 1947). The recent work of Marvin Meyers, *The Jacksonian Persuasion* (Palo Alto, 1957), is an interesting and subtle treatment of the intellectual history of the era. See also Glyndon G. Deusen, *The Jacksonian Era* (New York, 1959). In the last analysis, however, the greatest work on the movement of American democracy, not only during the Jacksonian era but in general, remains Alexis de Tocqueville, *Democracy in America* (ed. P. Bradley; 2 vols., New York, 1945).

3. The Classic Literature: Art and Idea

NOTES

[1] Gay Wilson Allen, *Walt Whitman Handbook* (Chicago, 1946), p. 277.

[2] Ralph Waldo Emerson, *Selected Prose and Poetry*, ed. Reginald L. Cook (New York, 1950), p. 472.

[3] Walt Whitman, *Leaves of Grass and Selected Prose*, ed. John Kouwenhoven (New York, 1950), p. 30.

[4] Emerson, pp. 336–337.

[5] Whitman, p. 510.

[6] Henry David Thoreau, *Walden and Other Writings*, ed. Brooks Atkinson (New York, 1937), p. 351.

[7] *The American Essays of Henry James*, ed. Leon Edel (New York, 1956), p. 72.

[8] *Masters of American Literature*, ed. Henry A. Pochman and Gay Wilson Allen (New York, 1949), I, 241.

[9] *The Novels and Tales of Nathaniel Hawthorne*, ed. Norman Holmes Pearson (New York, 1937), p. 243.

[10] Henry James, *Hawthorne* (New York, 1880), pp. 42–43.

[11] Philip Rahv, ed., *Literature in America* (New York, 1957), p. 17.

[12] James, *Hawthorne*, p. 43.

[13] Herman Melville, *The Confidence Man* (reprint, New York, 1957), p. 17.

[14] The reader will see that I am leaving out, arbitrarily, the large matter of European influences on our writers, such as that of the English and German romantics.

[15] *The Portable Melville*, ed. Jay Leyda (New York, 1952), p. 406.

[16] Whitman, p. 506.

[17] Lionel Trilling, *The Liberal Imagination* (New York, 1950), p. 9.

[18] D. H. Lawrence, *Studies in Classic American Literature* (reprint, New York, 1955), p. 184.

GUIDE TO FURTHER READING

Among the pioneering works that have formed our understanding of the pre-Civil War writers are D. H. Lawrence, *Studies in Classic American Literature* (New York, 1923); Van Wyck Brooks, *America's Coming-of-Age* (New York, 1915); and Constance Rourke, *American Humor* (New York, 1931). These works are still of primary importance, though they are all somewhat oracular, intuitive, and occasionally erroneous in detail. A fuller and more scholarly account of the classic writers, especially valuable for the relationships among them which it points out, is F. O. Matthiessen's standard work *American Renaissance* (New York, 1941). V. L. Parrington, *Main Currents in American Thought* (3 vols., New York, 1927–30) is still valuable for its account of the intellectual, especially the political, background of the literature. A standard though generally undistinguished work is the collaborative *Literary History of the United States* (New York, 1948). Leslie Fiedler, *Love and Death in the American Novel* (New York, 1960) contains many valuable insights. *The American Novel and Its Tradition* (New York, 1957), by Richard Chase, examines the nature of American fiction and traces its cultural origins.

Among the many books on single authors that may be recommended are: James Grossman, *James Fenimore Cooper* (New York, 1949); Henry James, *Hawthorne* (New York, 1880); Newton Arvin, *Herman Melville* (New York, 1950); Richard Chase, *Walt Whitman Reconsidered* (New York, 1955); Stephen Whicher, *Freedom and Fate: An Inner Life of Ralph Waldo Emerson* (Philadelphia, 1953); and Joseph Wood Krutch, *Henry David Thoreau* (New York, 1948). A useful guide through the large body of criticism and scholarship relevant to the classic writers is *Eight American Authors* (New York, 1956), edited by Floyd Stovall.

4. The Dissolution of Calvinism

NOTES

1 "Farewell to the Ministers of Geneva." Of the two reports of this oral farewell, I have used that of the minister Jean Pinant, as translated in *John Calvin, His Life, Letters, and Work*, by Hugh Y. Reyburn (London, 1914), pp. 315–317.

2 "Art," *The Complete Works of Ralph Waldo Emerson* (Boston, 1904), VII, 50. I am indebted to my colleague Robert W. Winter for his clarification of Emerson's theory of divine inspiration.

GUIDE TO FURTHER READING

Perry Miller's thirty-year study of the Puritans is one of the great explorations of American scholarship. The first two volumes of *The New England Mind, The Seventeenth Century* (Cambridge, Mass., 1939) and *From Colony to Province* (Cambridge, Mass., 1953), bring his story to the eve of the Awakening. *Errand into the Wilderness* (Cambridge, Mass., 1956) distills out its essence in smaller compass. In *Jonathan Edwards* (New York, 1949) Miller penetrates Edwards's Puritan and parochial language to his modern meaning. Herbert Schneider's succinct classic *The Puritan Mind* (New York, 1930; reissued as an Ann Arbor paperback in 1958) follows Puritan ideas from seventeenth-century England to nineteenth-century secularization in America. F. H. Foster, *A Genetic History of the New England Theology* (Chicago, 1907) concentrates more exclusively but still usefully upon the theological logic. In *Piety versus Moralism: The Passing of the New England Theology* (New York, 1932), Joseph Haroutunian, a sophisticated modern neo-Calvinist, laments that passing with much psychological as well as logical acumen. A literary man strongly attached to the Aesthetic Perception of high Puritanism, Chard Powers Smith, has told a less technical but richly elaborate story of religious disintegration in *Yankees and God* (New York, 1954), which carries things into the twentieth century. An older work, Williston Walker, *A*

History of the Congregational Churches in the United States (New York, 1894), is still very much worth reading. *The Beginnings of Unitarianism in America* (Boston, 1955), by Charles C. Wright, examines the liberalism bred in the Calvinist bosom. There are many acute studies of full-blown Unitarian and transcendentalist liberals and liberalism, but few of the liberal theology within the standard nineteenth-century denominations, partly because that liberalism was in many ways nontheological. Ethics and institutions have been easier to examine. But T. T. Munger, *Horace Bushnell, Preacher and Theologian* (Boston, 1899) remains a good introduction to this important figure; a more recent work is Barbara Cross, *Horace Bushnell: Minister to a Changing America* (Chicago, 1958). Perhaps the best reading is in books with a larger sweep: Walker on the Congregationalists; Smith on the long decline; and, luminously, H. Richard Niebuhr's *The Kingdom of God in America* (New York, 1937; reissued as a Harper Torchbook in paperback in 1959), relating theology to social expectations. As for revivals, Edwin S. Gaustad, *The Great Awakening in New England* (New York, 1957) narrates a few crucial years efficiently and sharply. Leonard Trinterud, *The Forming of an American Tradition: A Re-examination of Colonial Presbyterianism* (Philadelphia, 1949) studies that branch of Calvinism during the Awakening. A penetrating analysis of nineteenth-century revival psychology is to be found in Whitney Cross, *The Burned-Over District* (Ithaca, 1950). The reverberations of Calvinism in American political thought and practice, which I have underemphasized, have drawn much attention in varying moods. The relevant chapters of Vernon Parrington's *Main Currents in American Thought* (New York, 1927–30), particularly the first volume, register one mood. Its reverse is found in Ralph Barton Perry, *Puritanism and Democracy* (New York, 1944). In the relevant chapters of *Seedtime of the Republic* (New York, 1953), Clinton Rossiter offers a kind of compromise between Parrington's suspicion and Perry's admiration. Impulses to sample the sources themselves cannot be conveniently satisfied. Compact anthologies, comparable to those edited by Perry Miller on the early Puritans and the transcendentalists, are conspicuous for their absence — and desirability.

5. The Controversy over Slavery

NOTES

[1] Wendell Phillips, "Speech at Franklin Hall, May 12, 1848," in *The Pennsylvania Freeman,* June 8, 1848.

[2] *The Works of the Rev. John Wesley* (New York, 1826–30), X, 504.

GUIDE TO FURTHER READING

The first sources of information relative to this conflict of ideas are the reform newspapers, religious journals, and antislavery pamphlets. These are not readily available, but most students have access to the debates in Congress and in the Constitutional Convention of 1787. Opposing philosophies were summarized rather thoroughly by the political newspapers as the Civil War approached. The period was one of superior editorial writing, and the two following publications in the Beveridge Series of the American Historical Association are invaluable: Dwight L. Dumond, ed., *Southern Editorials on Secession* (New York, 1931), and Howard C. Perkins, ed., *Northern Editorials on Secession* (2 vols., New York, 1942). Excellent, but less likely to be available to most readers, are the following (short titles): Theodore D. Weld, *The Bible against Slavery* (New York, 1836), and *American Slavery as It Is* (New York, 1839); James G. Birney, *The American Churches the Bulwarks of American Slavery* (London, 1840); David Rice, *Slavery Inconsistent with Justice and Good Policy* (Philadelphia, 1792); [David Cooper], *A Serious Address to the Rulers of America* (Trenton, 1783); William Jay, *Miscellaneous Writings on Slavery* (Boston, 1853); Henry B. Stanton, *Remarks . . . before the Committee of the House of Representatives of Massachusetts* (Boston, 1837); William Goodell, *Slavery and Anti-Slavery* (New York, 1852); [Lewis Tappan], *Address to the Non-Slaveholders of the South* (New York, 1843); John Pierpont, *Moral Rule of Political Action* (Boston, 1839); E. M. Elliot, ed., *Cotton is King, and Pro-Slavery Arguments* (Augusta, 1860); George Fitzhugh, *Sociology for the South, or the Failure of a Free Society* (Richmond, 1852), and *Cannibals All! or, Slaves without Masters* (Richmond, 1857); and John Wesley, *Thoughts upon Slavery* (London, 1774).

There are numerous special studies by scholars in the field, readily available to students. Frederic Bancroft's work on slave-trading and colonization is pre-eminent and stands unchallenged today, in *Slave Trading in the Old South* (Baltimore, 1931), and in Jacob E. Cooke, *Frederic Bancroft: Historian* (Norman, 1957). Ulrich Bonnell Phillips, for years regarded as the master in the field of Southern history, but whose work is now rapidly being superseded, has two works still useful: *American Negro Slavery* (New York, 1929), and *The Course of the South to Secession* (New York, 1939). His "Central Theme of Southern History," in *American Historical Review*, XXXIV (1928), 30–43, is indispensable. Three of Phillips's students have done work in the field in an area which he himself preferred to ignore: Thomas E. Drake, *Quakers and Slavery in America* (New Haven, 1950) belongs in every historian's library. Gilbert H. Barnes, *The Antislavery Impulse, 1830–1844* (New York, 1933) was a pioneer work. It belongs on every reading list, but ignores the long history of antislavery activity before 1830, and suffers from a failure of the author to grasp the significance of political action. Dwight L. Dumond, *Antislavery Origins of the Civil War in the United States* (Ann Arbor, 1939) was the Commonwealth Foundation Lectures at the University of London in 1939. See also D. L. Dumond, *Antislavery: The Crusade for Freedom in America* (Ann Arbor, 1961); Kenneth Stampp, *The Peculiar Institution* (New York, 1956); and Stanley M. Elkins, *Slavery: A Problem in American Institutional and Intellectual Life* (Chicago, 1960). Two excellent analyses of the Southern philosophy are Jesse T. Carpenter, *The South as a Conscious Minority, 1789–1861* (New York, 1930), and William S. Jenkins, *Pro-Slavery Thought in the Old South* (Chapel Hill, 1935). Two more recent books worthy of close attention are Charles S. Sydnor, *The Development of Southern Sectionalism, 1819–1848* (University, La., 1948), and Clement Eaton, *A History of the Old South* (New York, 1949). Biographies of the two most powerful men in the antislavery movement are Benjamin P. Thomas, *Theodore Weld, Crusader for Freedom* (New Brunswick, 1950), and Betty Fladeland, *James Gillespie Birney: Slaveholder to Abolitionist* (Ithaca, 1955).

6. *Ideas and Economic Development*

GUIDE TO FURTHER READING

There is need for a restudy both of American economic history and of American economic thought in the light of what we have come recently to understand about the processes of economic development; in this connection, W. W. Rostow, *The Stages of Economic Growth* (Cambridge, Eng., 1960) is brilliant if occasionally schematic. Joseph Dorfman, *The Economic Mind in American Civilization*, especially volumes I and II (New York, 1946), offers a useful summary of technical economic thought in these formative years. For the role of public authorities in economic development, the following works are suggestive: Oscar and Mary Handlin, *Commonwealth: Massachusetts, 1774–1861* (Cambridge, Mass., 1947); Louis Hartz, *Economic Policy and Democratic Thought: Pennsylvania, 1776–1860* (Cambridge, Mass., 1948); Carter Goodrich, *Canals and American Economic Development* (New York, 1961). For a judicious review and critique of this literature, see R. A. Lively, "The American System," *Business History Review*, March, 1955. John C. Miller in his *Alexander Hamilton* (New York, 1959) and Broadus Mitchell in *Alexander Hamilton* (2 vols., New York, 1957–62) discuss the economic ideas of Alexander Hamilton *passim*. The student is also urged to examine Alexander Hamilton, *Papers on Public Credit, Commerce and Finance*, ed. Samuel McKee, Jr. (New York, 1934). For Jefferson's economic thought, see his *Notes on the State of Virginia* (a convenient edition is that edited by William Peden, Chapel Hill, 1955); see also the biography by Dumas Malone (3 vols., Boston, 1948–62). For a stimulating if exaggerated sketch of John Quincy Adams's economic nationalism, see Brooks Adams's "The Heritage of Henry Adams," in Henry Adams, *The Degradation of the Democratic Dogma* (New York, 1919). Jacksonian economic thought is considered from different viewpoints in Bray Hammond, *Banks and Politics in America, from the Revolution to the Civil War* (Princeton, 1957) and Arthur M. Schlesinger, Jr., *The Age of Jackson* (Boston, 1945). For Henry Charles Carey, see his *Past, Present and Future* (Philadelphia, 1848) and *Harmony of Interests: Manufacturing and Commercial* (Philadelphia, 1851); also the modern biography by Abraham D. Kaplan, *Henry C. Carey: A Study in American Economic Thought* (Baltimore, 1931). A modern study of the philosophy of internal improvements is needed.

7. *Social Darwinism*

NOTES

[1] Quotations from Spencer from *Social Statics* (London, 1850), pp. 323–326, 353.

[2] Josephine Shaw Lowell, "Charity Problems" (1896); reprinted in William

Rhinelander Stewart, *The Philanthropic Work of Josephine Shaw Lowell* (New York, 1911), p. 191.

[3] Lester F. Ward, *Dynamic Sociology* (New York, 1883), II, 251–252.

[4] Jane Addams, *Democracy and Social Ethics* (New York, 1902), p. 67.

[5] Jane Addams, *Twenty Years at Hull House* (New York, 1910), p. 297.

[6] Edward A. Ross, *Social Control* (New York, 1901), p. 423.

[7] Simon Patten, *The New Basis of Civilization* (New York, 1907), pp. 51–52.

GUIDE TO FURTHER READING

The only extended account is Richard Hofstadter, *Social Darwinism in American Thought 1860–1915* (Philadelphia, 1944). Relevant materials also appear in a larger context in the later volumes of Joseph Dorfman, *The Economic Mind in American Civilization* (New York, 1946–59). Spencer has an interminable *Autobiography* (London, 1904) and a *Life and Letters* (London, 1908) by David Duncan. On Sumner, see the biography by Harris Starr (New York, 1925) and the vivid *Reminiscences of William Graham Sumner* (New Haven, 1933) by his disciple A. G. Keller — both adulatory. The best analysis of Fiske's thought is in Milton Berman's biography (Cambridge, Mass., 1961). On authoritarian alternatives to Spencerian social science, see Donald Fleming, *John William Draper and the Religion of Science* (Philadelphia, 1950). William Rhinelander Stewart, *The Philanthropic Work of Josephine Shaw Lowell* (New York, 1911) contains a biographical sketch, with selections from her diary and correspondence and the text of her major writings. On Ward, see the biography by Samuel Chugerman (Durham, 1939). Jane Addams published two volumes of autobiography: *Twenty Years at Hull House* (New York, 1910) and *The Second Twenty Years at Hull House* (New York, 1930). On Cooley, see the biography and analysis of his thought by Edward C. Jandy (New York, 1942). Lillian Wald published the autobiographical *The House on Henry Street* (New York, 1915) and *Windows on Henry Street* (Boston, 1934); see also her biography by R. L. Duffus (New York, 1938). Devine's autobiography is *When Social Work Was Young* (New York, 1939).

8. The Triumph of Laissez-Faire

GUIDE TO FURTHER READING

The basic book is Sidney Fine, *Laissez-Faire and the General-Welfare State: A Study of Conflict in American Thought, 1865–1901* (Ann Arbor, 1956), a thorough, detailed, and judicious study. See also Joseph Dorfman, *The Economic Mind in American Civilization,* Vol. II (New York, 1946), especially on Amasa Walker and John Bates Clark. For the pre-Civil War period I have mentioned the three key studies — Oscar and Mary Handlin, *Commonwealth: A Study of the Role of Government in the American Economy: Massachusetts, 1774–1861* (New York, 1947); Louis Hartz, *Economic Policy and Democratic Thought: Pennsylvania, 1776–1860* (Cambridge, Mass., 1948); and James N. Primm, *Economic Policy in the Development of a Western State: Missouri,*

1820–1860 (Cambridge, Mass., 1954). On Veblen and his insights, see the selections from his *Theory of the Leisure Class, Theory of Business Enterprise,* and other writings on the industrial-pecuniary antithesis, in Max Lerner, ed., *The Portable Veblen* (New York, 1948). On Sumner and Burgess, see Charles and Mary Beard, *The American Spirit* (New York, 1945). John Moody's book, *The Masters of Capital,* is a volume in the *Chronicles of America* series, ed. Allen Johnson, Vol. 4 (New Haven, 1919). The Hacker reference is to Louis M. Hacker, *The Triumph of American Capitalism* (New York, 1940), which has a discussion of Carnegie. For Rockefeller, see Allan Nevins, *Study in Power: John D. Rockefeller* (2 vols., New York, 1953; 1 vol. abr., New York, 1959).

The best brief account of the Constitutional history of the laissez-faire period is in Robert G. McCloskey, *The American Supreme Court* (Chicago, 1960), ch. V, "Constitutional Evolution in the Gilded Age, 1865–1900." On Miller and the Slaughterhouse cases, Charles A. Fairman has done the basic biography — *Mr. Justice Miller and the Supreme Court: 1862–1890* (Cambridge, Mass., 1938). For Campbell's role see Walton H. Hamilton, "The Path of Due Process of Law," in Conyers Read, ed., *The Constitution Reconsidered* (New York, 1938), pp. 167–190. On Field, see two basic works, Carl B. Swisher, *Stephen J. Field: Craftsman of the Law* (Washington, 1930), and Robert G. McCloskey, *American Conservatism in the Age of Enterprise* (New York, 1931), which also includes studies of Carnegie and Sumner. For Cary, Goudy, Jewett, Evarts, Parsons, and Choate, as well as for Campbell and the whole group of Constitutional lawyers of the period, see Benjamin R. Twiss, *Lawyers and the Constitution* (Princeton, 1942), from which I have also drawn my material on Thomas M. Cooley's influence as a commentator.

For my own writings in this period of American Constitutional history, see my essays on "The Supreme Court and American Capitalism," "Constitution and Court as Symbols," "Vested Rights and Vested Interests," in my *Ideas Are Weapons* (New York, 1939), and the essay on "Minority Rule and the Constitutional Tradition" in my *Ideas for the Ice Age* (New York, 1941). For the role of Brandeis and Holmes in shaping or combating some of the judicial doctrines I have mentioned, see "The Social Thought of Mr. Justice Brandeis," in *Ideas Are Weapons,* and also my *Mind and Faith of Justice Holmes* (Boston, 1943; Modern Library Edition, New York, 1954). I have dealt with the concept of the freedom-property complex in *America as a Civilization* (New York, 1957), pp. 297–304; with the legal elite, pp. 426–452; with the Magnifico and the Puritan as types of the American business giant, pp. 274–284; and with the larger frame of American intellectual history, pp. 717–732 of the same book.

For the social thinkers of the Populist and Progressive periods, who attacked the laissez-faire system, see Morton White, *Social Thought in America: The Revolt Against Formalism* (New York, 1949; reprinted, Boston, 1957); Henry S. Commager, *The American Mind* (New Haven, 1950); Eric Goldman, *Rendezvous with Destiny* (New York, 1952); Richard Hofstadter, *The Age of Reform* (New York, 1955); and the section on "Laissez-faire Under Attack: Emergence of the Concept of the General-Welfare State," in Fine, cited above.

9. Science in America: The Nineteenth Century

NOTES

[1] As an example of the importance of including science among the indices of American international cultural relations, consider Nathaniel Hawthorne's reflection upon seeing an issue of Silliman's *American Journal of Science* on one of the desks in the Radcliffe Library at Oxford. It was, Hawthorne declared, "the only trace of American science, or American learning or ability in any department, which I discovered in the University of Oxford." Nathaniel Hawthorne, *The English Notebooks,* ed. Randall Stewart (New York, 1941), p. 413.

[2] Beaumont was able to obtain pure "gastric juice" from a human stomach and to observe the rate of secretion of this fluid under a variety of conditions. But he could not find a chemist anywhere in the United States who could analyze this material. America's foremost chemical authority, Benjamin Silliman, Sr., whom Beaumont visited in New Haven in 1833, later wrote him: "I regret that I can not contribute something important to our previous knowledge — there is much in physiology that eludes the scrutiny of chemistry." Silliman defended his ignorance by the statement that scientific phenomena were inexplicable by man and his science, and must be referred to the action of a divine power: ". . . all kinds of aliment may dissolve with the equally mild and simple gastric fluid, but who can explain the proximate, or even the ultimate, cause in any other way than by referring it to positive law of the Creator — often incomprehensible equally in his nature and his works." See George Rosen, *The Reception of William Beaumont's Discovery in Europe* (New York, 1942), p. 23; John F. Fulton and Elizabeth T. Thompson, *Benjamin Silliman, Pathfinder in American Science* (New York, 1947), p. 185.

[3] See Frederick B. Tolles, "Philadelphia's First Scientist: James Logan," *Isis,* XLVII (1956), 20–30; Conway Zirkle, *The Beginnings of Plant Hybridization* (Philadelphia, 1935).

[4] See I. B. Cohen, *Franklin and Newton* (Philadelphia, 1956), pp. 365–424.

[5] See I. B. Cohen, *Some Early Tools of American Science* (Cambridge, Mass., 1950).

[6] See Raymond P. Stearns, "Colonial Fellows of the Royal Society of London, 1661–1788," *Osiris,* VIII (1948), 73–121, reprinted in *William and Mary Quarterly,* III (1946), 208–268; Ralph S. Bates, *Scientific Societies in the United States* (2nd ed., New York, 1958).

[7] Professor Henry Guerlac has called attention to the fact that Tocqueville could not have been well informed on pure and applied science; the diary kept by his fellow-voyager, Beaumont, shows that Tocqueville did not even have contact with the major American scientists. A somewhat different picture emerges from visitors better equipped to understand science in America, such as a relative of Joseph Priestley's, John Finch. See I. B. Cohen, "The New World as a Source of Science for Europe," *Actes du IXe Congrès International d'Histoire des Sciences* (Barcelona-Madrid, 1959), pp. 95–130 (with bibliography), and especially p. 129 for Professor Guerlac's comments; also, George

Wilson Pierson, *Tocqueville and Beaumont in America* (New York, 1938), and John Finch, *Travels in the United States of America and Canada, Containing Some Account of their Scientific Institutions, and a Few Notices of the Geology and Mineralogy of Those Countries. To which is added, an essay in The Natural Boundaries of Empires* (London, 1833).

[8] Benjamin Silliman, *Elements of Chemistry in the Order of the Lectures Given in Yale College* (New Haven, 1830–31), p. 7.

[9] See I. B. Cohen, "Harvard and the Scientific Spirit," *Harvard Alumni Bulletin*, L (February 7, 1948), 393–398.

[10] Russell H. Chittenden, *History of the Sheffield Scientific School of Yale University, 1846–1922* (New Haven, 1928).

[11] See Andrew Denny Rodgers, III, *American Botany 1873–1892, Decades of Transition* (Princeton, 1944); also A. Hunter Dupree, *Asa Gray, 1810–1880* (Cambridge, Mass., 1959).

[12] Newcomb and Alexander Agassiz were first elected *membres correspondants* and then were advanced to *associés étrangers.*

It may be observed that in the twentieth century, prior to the Second World War, a number of Americans became *membres correspondants* and six were elected *associés étrangers:* Alexander Agassiz (1904), Hale (1904), Walcott (1919), Michelson (1920), Edmund Beecher Wilson (1928), and Simon Flexner (1937).

[13] In the early nineteenth century, many British men of science held that there had been a "decline" of science in England. Hence, one might guess that there might have been a "decline" of the same sort in America even had America not become independent from Britain. For a discussion of the topic in relation to American science, see I. B. Cohen, *Science and American Society in the First Century of the Republic* (Columbus, Ohio, 1961), pp. 9–11.

[14] I have omitted from this list three men who though associated with America were not elected to the Royal Society as American foreign members: David Hosack (1816), the New York physician who had been resident in London and was elected a regular Fellow rather than a foreign member, as was John J. Audubon (1838); and Louis Agassiz (1838), elected as a Swiss.

[15] See Paul H. Oehser, *Sons of Science: The Story of the Smithsonian Institution and Its Leaders* (New York, 1949).

[16] See Simon Newcomb, "Conditions which Discourage Scientific Work in America," *North American Review*, CLXXIV (1902), 153.

[17] See Charles True, *A History of Agricultural Experimentation and Research in the United States, 1607–1925*, U.S.D.A. Miscellaneous Publications, No. 251 (Washington, 1937), p. 66.

[18] See Merle M. Odgers, *Alexander Dallas Bache, Scientist and Educator, 1806–1867* (Philadelphia, 1947).

[19] See George Perkins Merrill, "Contributions to the History of American Geology," U.S. National Museum, *Annual Report . . . for 1904* (Washington, 1906), pt. 2, pp. 189–734; also George Perkins Merrill, *Contributions to a History of American State Geological and Natural History Surveys*, Smithsonian Institution, U.S. National Museum, Bulletin 109 (Washington, 1920).

[20] See A. Hunter Dupree, *Science in the Federal Government, a History of Policies and Activities to 1940* (Cambridge, Mass., 1957), pp. 216–217.

[21] See *Research — A National Resource*, Pt. II, *Industrial Research*, Report of the Science Committee to the National Resources Committee (Washington, 1938).

[22] John Tyndall, *Lectures on Light, Delivered in the United States in 1872–73*, with an Appendix (New York, 1873), especially the Preface (pp. 3–6), the "Summary and Conclusion" following the last lecture (pp. 160–183), and the Appendix containing Tyndall's remarks on February 4, 1873, at a banquet given in his honor. See also I. B. Cohen, "Some Reflections on the State of Science in America During the Nineteenth Century," *Proceedings of the National Academy of Sciences*, XLV (1959), 666–677.

[23] See Lynde Phelps Wheeler, *Josiah Willard Gibbs, the History of a Great Mind* (rev. ed., New Haven, 1952); also *The Early Work of Willard Gibbs in Applied Mechanics, Comprising the Text of His Hitherto Unpublished Ph.D. Thesis and Accounts of His Mechanical Inventions*, assembled by Lynde Phelps Wheeler, Everett Oyler Waters, and Samuel William Dudley (New York, 1947).

[24] See H. A. Rowland, "The Highest Aim of the Physicist" (Presidential Address, American Physical Society, New York, October 28, 1899), *American Journal of Science*, VIII (1899), 401–411; *Science*, X (1899), 825–833; *Bulletin of the American Physical Society*, I (1899), 4–16; *Johns Hopkins University Circulars*, CXLIII (1900), 17–20 (reprinted in *The Physical Papers of Henry Augustus Rowland*, collected for publication by a Committee of the Faculty of the University of Baltimore, 1902).

[25] Simon Newcomb, "Exact Science in America," *North American Review*, CXIX (1874), 286–308, and "Abstract Science in America," *North American Review*, CXXII (1876), 88–123. It is interesting to observe Newcomb's emphasis on the "basis of our requirements . . . [being] a better knowledge of the wants of science among those who give money for its promotion" and his emphasis that on "the material side we want nothing new at present; we require no increase in the number of our museums, observatories, or laboratories during the present generation."

[26] Rowland, *loc. cit.* Rowland was, of course, referring to the "Michelson-Morley experiment," renowned for its association with the theory of relativity.

GUIDE TO FURTHER READING

To date we have no adequate full-length study of science in America in the nineteenth century, although such a work is in preparation as part of a three-volume social history of science in America (from colonial times to the present) by Donald H. Fleming. In previous articles I have dealt with various aspects of the topics presented here, notably "Some Reflections on the State of Science in America During the Nineteenth Century," *Proc. National Academy of Sciences*, XLV (1959), 666–677; "The New World as a Source of Science for Europe," *Actes du IXe Congrès International d'Histoire des Sciences* (Barcelona-Madrid, 1959), pp. 95–130 (with bibliography); "La vie scientifique aux Etats-Unis au XIXe siècle," *Histoire générale des sciences*, ed. René Taton (Paris, 1961), III, 635–644; "American Physicists at War: I. From the Revolution to the World Wars; II. From the First World War to 1942," *American Journal of Physics*, XIII (1945), 223–235, 333–346.

Some of the basic problems are treated in Richard H. Shryock, *American Medical Research, Past and Present* (New York, 1947), and "American Indifference to Basic Research During the Nineteenth Century," *Archives Internationales d'Histoire des Sciences*, II (1948), 50–65. Of primary importance are the studies of A. Hunter Dupree: *Science in the Federal Government, a History of Policies and Activities to 1940* (Cambridge, Mass., 1957), with an extremely valuable guide to the primary and secondary literature; and *Asa Gray, 1810–1888* (Cambridge, Mass., 1959). Still valuable are the writings of George Brown Goode ("The Genesis of the United States National Museum," "The Origin of the National Scientific and Educational Institutions of the United States," "The Beginnings of Natural History in America," "The Beginnings of American Science," "The First National Scientific Congress") collected together with a bibliography in *Annual Report of . . . the Smithsonian Institution* for the year ending June 30, 1897.

The following biographies and special studies may be recommended: G. P. Fisher, *Life of Benjamin Silliman* (2 vols., New York, 1866); Donald H. Fleming, *William H. Welch and the Rise of Modern Medicine* (Boston, 1954); D. H. Fleming, *John William Draper* (Philadelphia, 1950); Edward Lurie, *Louis Agassiz, a Life in Science* (Chicago, 1960); Lynde Phelps Wheeler, *Josiah Willard Gibbs, the History of a Great Mind* (rev. ed., New Haven, 1952); Thomas Coulson, *Joseph Henry, His Life and Work* (Princeton, 1950); Paul H. Oehser, *Sons of Science: The Story of the Smithsonian Institution and Its Leaders* (New York, 1949); David Eugene Smith and Jekuthiel Ginsburg, *A History of Mathematics in America Before 1900* (Chicago, 1934); R. C. Archibald, *A Semicentennial History of the American Mathematical Society, 1888–1938* (New York, 1938); G. D. Birkhoff, "Fifty Years of American Mathematics," pp. 270–315 of *Semicentennial Addresses of the American Mathematical Society* (New York, 1938); Andrew Denny Rodgers, III, *John Torrey, a Story of North American Botany* (Princeton, 1942); Andrew Denny Rodgers, III, *American Botany 1873–1892, Decades of Transition* (Princeton, 1944); W. J. Hooker, "On the Botany of America," *American Journal of Science and Arts*, IX (1825), 263–284; Max Meisel, *A Bibliography of American Natural History, the Pioneer Century, 1769–1865* (3 vols., Brooklyn, 1924–29); George Rosen, *The Reception of William Beaumont's Discovery in Europe* (New York, 1942); William Jay Youmans, *Pioneers of Science in America, Sketches of Their Lives and Scientific Work* (New York, 1896); J. G. Crowther, *Famous American Men of Science* (New York, 1937); Bernard Jaffe, *Men of Science in America* (rev. ed., New York, 1958); Dirk J. Struik, *Yankee Science in the Making* (Boston, 1948); I. Bernard Cohen, *Some Early Tools of American Science* (Cambridge, Mass., 1950); Madge E. Pickard, "Government and Science in the United States: Historical Backgrounds," *Journal of the History of Medicine and Allied Sciences*, I (1946), 254–289, 446–481; Mitchell Wilson,

American Science and Invention, a Pictorial History (New York, 1954); Ralph S. Bates, *Scientific Societies in the United States* (2nd ed., New York, 1958); Raymond P. Stearns, "Colonial Fellows of the Royal Society of London, 1661–1788," *Osiris*, VIII (1948), 73–121, reprinted in *William and Mary Quarterly*, III (1946), 208–268; Frederick H. Getman, *The Life of Ira Remsen* (Easton, Penna., 1940); Edgar Fahs Smith, *Chemistry in America, Chapters from the History of the Science in the United States* (New York, 1914); E. F. Smith, *The Life of Robert Hare, an American Chemist, 1781–1858* (Philadelphia, 1917); George Perkins Merrill, *Contributions to a History of American State Geological and Natural History Surveys*, Smithsonian Institution, U.S. National Museum, Bulletin 109 (Washington, 1920); G. P. Merrill, *The First Hundred Years of American Geology* (New Haven, 1924).

10. Pragmatism and the Scope of Science

NOTES

This essay is reprinted in part from *American Perspectives*, edited by Robert E. Spiller and Eric Larrabee (Cambridge, Mass., 1961); by permission of the Harvard University Press.

1 For an illuminating consideration of this question, see Arthur W. Burks's essay introducing his selections from Peirce's writings in M. H. Fisch, ed., *Classic American Philosophers* (New York, 1951).

2 W. K. Clifford, "The Ethics of Belief," *Lectures and Essays*, ed. Leslie Stephen and Frederick Pollock (2nd ed., London, 1886), p. 363.

3 Charles S. Peirce, "The Fixation of Belief," *Popular Science Monthly*, XII (1877), 1–15; reprinted in *The Collected Papers of Charles Sanders Peirce*, ed. Charles Hartshorne, Paul Weiss, and Arthur W. Burks (Cambridge, Mass., 1931–58), V, 223–247.

4 William James, *The Will to Believe and Other Essays in Popular Philosophy* (New York, 1898), pp. 1–2.

5 *Popular Science Monthly*, XII (1878), 286–302; reprinted in *Collected Papers of Charles Sanders Peirce*, V, 248–271.

6 C. I. Lewis, *An Analysis of Knowledge and Valuation* (La Salle, Ill., 1946), p. 512.

7 *Ibid.*, p. 554.

8 W. B. Gallie, *Peirce and Pragmatism* (Penguin Books, 1952), p. 161.

9 William James, *The Principles of Psychology* (New York, 1890), II, 661, second note.

10 W. V. Quine, "Two Dogmas of Empiricism," *Philosophical Review*, LX (1951); reprinted in his *From a Logical Point of View* (Cambridge, Mass., 1953).

11 John Dewey, *Reconstruction in Philosophy* (New York, 1920), p. 137.

12 *Ibid.*, p. 138.

13 John Dewey, *Logic: The Theory of Inquiry* (New York, 1938), pp. 283–284.

GUIDE TO FURTHER READING

The reader who wishes to pursue the topic further is advised to begin with the works of the pragmatists dealt with in the essay. In the case of Peirce one should consult Volumes V, VII, and VIII of *The Collected Papers of Charles Sanders Peirce*, edited by Charles Hartshorne, Paul Weiss, and Arthur W. Burks (Cambridge, Mass., 1931–58). For the relevant views of James the two best books are *Pragmatism* (New York, 1907) and *The Will to Believe and Other Essays in Popular Philosophy* (New York, 1898). John Dewey's *Reconstruction in Philosophy* (New York, 1920), *The Quest for Certainty* (New York, 1929), and *Logic: The Theory of Inquiry* (New York, 1938) are the most important of his works bearing on the topic. C. I. Lewis presents his views in *Mind and the World-Order* (New York, 1929), *An Analysis of Knowledge and Valuation* (La Salle, Ill., 1946), and *The Ground and Nature of Right* (New York, 1955). W. V. Quine presents his in *From a Logical Point of View* (Cambridge, Mass., 1953) and in *Word and Object* (Cambridge, Mass., 1960).

For more extended discussion of topics related to the theme of the essay, see the following by Morton White: *Toward Reunion in Philosophy* (Cambridge, Mass., 1956); *Social Thought in America: The Revolt Against Formalism* (New York, 1949; reprinted with a new preface and epilogue, paperback, Boston, 1957); and "Experiment and Necessity in Dewey's Philosophy," *Antioch Review*, XIX (1959), 329–344.

11. The Realist Tradition in American Law

NOTES

This essay is taken in part from "American Legal Realism and the Sense of the Profession," delivered as the John R. Coen Lecture at the University of Colorado on April 7, 1961, and published in *Rocky Mountain Law Review*, XXXIV (1962), 123–149, and in *The Sovereign Prerogative, the Supreme Court and the Quest for Law* (New Haven: Yale University Press, 1962), pp. 3–44. I wish to thank the several publishers for their permission to use these passages here.

[1] M. deW. Howe, *Justice Oliver Wendell Holmes*, Vol. I: *The Shaping Years, 1841–1870* (Cambridge, Mass., 1957), pp. 280–286. See also Edmund Wilson, *Patriotic Gore* (New York, 1962), ch. 16; Francis Biddle, *Mr. Justice Holmes* (New York, 1943).

[2] O. W. Holmes, Jr., *Speeches* (Boston, 1934), p. 3. I should add that Holmes often spoke also to a somewhat inconsistent and Horatian theme, that the lonely scholar, Descartes, Kant, or Montesquieu, commands the future "from his study more than Napoleon from his throne." See, e.g., *Collected Legal Papers* (New York, 1920), pp. 32, 264, 269, 270–271.

[3] "Law in Science and Science in Law," in *Collected Legal Papers*, p. 224.

[4] See also *Collected Legal Papers*, p. 247.

[5] *Holmes-Pollock Letters*, ed. M. deW. Howe (Cambridge, Mass., 1941), I, 57.

[6] R. W. M. Dias and G. B. J. Hughes, *Jurisprudence* (London, 1957).

[7] Max Radin, *Law as Logic and Experience* (New Haven, 1940).

[8] H. L. A. Hart, *The Concept of Law* (Oxford, 1961), chs. 1–3.

[9] A. R. N. Cross, *Precedent in English Law* (New York, 1961); R. A. Wasserstrom, *The Judicial Decision* (Stanford, 1960), reviewed by Laymen Allen in *Yale Law Journal*, LXXI (1962), 1578. See Patrick Devlin, *Samples of Law-making* (Oxford, 1962), pp. 18–23.

[10] See C. H. S. Fifoot, *Judge and Jurist in the Reign of Victoria* (London, 1959), for a witty and ironic account of the process and its denouement.

[11] K. N. Llewellyn, *The Common Law Tradition: Deciding Appeals* (Boston, 1960), p. 38.

[12] O. W. Holmes, Jr., *The Common Law* (Boston, 1881), pp. 1–2.

[13] Jerome Frank, "A Conflict with Oblivion: Some Observations on the Founders of Legal Pragmatism," *Rutgers Law Review*, IX (1954), 425, 427.

[14] F. S. Cohen, *The Legal Conscience* (New Haven, 1960), p. 77.

[15] B. N. Cardozo, *The Nature of the Judicial Process* (New Haven, 1921), pp. 112–114.

[16] K. N. Llewellyn, "Some Realism about Realism — Responding to Dean Pound," *Harvard Law Review*, XLIV (1931), 1222, 1236. The formulation is almost exactly that of Dean Pound in one of his most famous and effective polemics, "Mechanical Jurisprudence," *Columbia Law Review*, VIII (1908), 605.

[17] Holmes, "Privilege, Malice and Intent," from *Harvard Law Review*, VIII (1894), in *Collected Legal Papers*, p. 117. See also, in the same book, the discussion of the uses of history in law as a means of setting us free, and of the problem of policy choice in law, pp. 224–242.

[18] G. H. Sabine, "The Pragmatic Approach to Politics," *American Political Science Review*, XXIV (1930), 865, 878. This view, essentially Gray's, was effectively criticized by Cardozo, *The Nature of the Judicial Process*, pp. 125–130.

[19] Alexander Pekelis, *Law and Social Action: Selected Essays* (Ithaca, 1950), p. 20.

[20] Llewellyn, *op. cit.* (supra note 16), p. 1236.

[21] Learned Hand, "The Contribution of an Independent Judiciary to Civilization," in *The Spirit of Liberty*, ed. I. Dilliard (New York, 1952), p. 172; and *The Bill of Rights* (Cambridge, Mass., 1958).

[22] Devlin, *Samples of Lawmaking*, pp. 18–22.

[23] Wasserstrom, *The Judicial Decision.*

[24] Herbert Wechsler, "Towards Neutral Principles of Constitutional Law," *Harvard Law Review*, LXXIII (1959), 1; reprinted as Chapter 1 of his *Principles, Politics and Fundamental Law* (Cambridge, Mass., 1961); H. M. Hart, Jr., "The Supreme Court, 1958 Term, Foreword, Time Chart of the Justices," *Harvard Law Review*, LXXIII (1959), 84, 98–125. A basis for views of this order is cogently outlined in H. M. Hart, Jr., and A. M. Sacks, *The Legal Process: Basic Problems in the Making and Application of Law* (tentative ed., mimeo., Cambridge, Mass., 1958). The issues raised by this series of controversies are discussed in my book, *The Sovereign Prerogative, the Supreme Court and the Quest for Law*, parts 1 and 2.

[25] Llewellyn, *op. cit.* (supra note 16), pp. 1223, 1236, 1254.

[26] *Ibid.*, p. 1240.

[27] Lon L. Fuller, *The Law in Quest of Itself* (Chicago, 1940).

[28] See Holmes, *Collected Legal Papers*, p. 310; Francis Biddle, *Justice Holmes, Natural Law, and the Supreme Court* (New York, 1961).

[29] Holmes, *Collected Legal Papers*, p. 307.

[30] *Ibid.*, p. 173.

[31] M. S. McDougal, "Fuller v. The American Legal Realists: An Intervention," *Yale Law Journal*, L (1941), 827, 834–835.

[32] Reviewed with insight in Iredell Jenkins, "The Matchmaker, or Toward a Synthesis of Legal Idealism and Positivism," *Journal of Legal Education*, XII (1959), 1. I have discussed these problems in "The Enforcement of Morals," *Cambridge Law Journal*, CLXXIV (1960), reprinted at p. 45 of *The Sovereign Prerogative*.

[33] Holmes, *Collected Legal Papers*, p. 170.

[34] This theme in the American literature corresponds to a world-wide revival of interest in the problem of standards for distinguishing good from bad law, stimulated by the spectacle of law under the circumstances of fascist and communist dictatorship. See C. J. Radcliffe, *The Law and Its Compass* (Evanston, Ill., 1960).

GUIDE TO FURTHER READING

The relationships between American thought about law and the larger literature of legal philosophy are sketched briefly but with a sure hand in Edgar Bodenheimer, *Jurisprudence, the Philosophy and Method of the Law* (Cambridge, Mass., 1962), and in *Salmond on Jurisprudence*, 11th edition, ed. Glanville Williams (London, 1957). The history and impact of American legal realism are assessed also in W. Friedmann, *Law in a Changing Society* (Berkeley, 1959); Julius Stone, *The Province and Function of Law* (Sydney, 1946); Karl N. Llewellyn, *The Common Law Tradition: Deciding Appeals* (Boston, 1960) and *Jurisprudence* (Chicago, 1962); and Alf Ross, *Towards a Realistic Jurisprudence* (Copenhagen, 1946).

Among the landmarks of the realist movement, in addition to the books and articles by Holmes, Cardozo, Pound, Llewellyn, and F. S. Cohen mentioned in the text, some of the most notable are Jerome Frank, *Law and the Modern Mind* (New York, 1930), using psychoanalytical ideas to explain the social authority of judges and of legal rules; Thurman Arnold's delightful and irreverent *The Symbols of Government* (New Haven, 1935), and *The Folklore of Capitalism* (New Haven, 1937); and Karl N. Llewellyn's early *Bramble Bush*, the outlook of which is somewhat modified in his two last books. Roscoe Pound's *Introduction to the Philosophy of Law* (rev. ed., New Haven, 1955) is a convenient short statement of his point of view. Edmond Cahn's *The Moral Decision: Right and Wrong in the Light of American Law* (Bloomington, Ind., 1955) is an original attempt to deal with the problem of values in law, faced earlier by F. S. Cohen. Lord Radcliffe's *Law and Its Compass* (Evanston, Ill., 1960), and A. P. d'Entrèves, *Natural Law* (London,

1951) powerfully express the outlook of the so-called "natural law" philosophers — those who stress the problem of criteria for judging the goodness or badness of positive law. This approach is developed in detail by F. S. C. Northrup, *The Complexity of Legal and Ethical Experience* (Boston, 1959), and in the writings of Messrs. McDougal and Lasswell, some of which are noted in the text. Their views are summarized in their famous joint article, "Legal Education and Public Policy: Professional Training in the Public Interest," *Yale Law Journal*, LII (1943), 203, and in M. S. McDougal, "The Law School of the Future: From Legal Realism to Policy Science in the World Community," *Yale Law Journal*, LVI (1947), 1345, and "Law as a Process of Decision: A Policy Oriented Approach to Legal Study," *Natural Law Forum*, I (1956), 53. Contrary views in their most influential modern form appear in H. L. A. Hart, *The Concept of Law* (Oxford, 1961); Alf Ross, *On Law and Justice* (London, 1958); and Hans Kelsen, *General Theory of Law and the State* (Cambridge, Mass., 1945).

12. Economic Thought and the New Industrialism

NOTES

1 I once amused a meeting of economists by pointing out that Crane Brinton's *Ideas and Men: The Story of Western Thought* (London, 1951) has in its index between Rhodes, Cecil, and Richards, I. A., no Ricardo, David.

2 David Ricardo, Thomas Malthus, the classical economists generally, and Karl Marx can be criticized for failing to stress the really important aspect of the nineteenth century — namely, the industrial revolution, which was going on and which, by shifting the schedules of their theoretical system, dwarfed the less important movements along the schedules on which they chose to concentrate.

3 Optimism and theology were in fact related, but they are logically distinguishable. Thus Malthus used religion to argue for the inevitability and rightness of poverty and the struggle against it.

4 While the thesis that List was an "exporter of the American system" stands up well when one looks at the additions to his thought after he left America, it is weakened somewhat by the consideration that he had already acquired some of his convictions *prior* to arriving in America at the age of thirty-six. — Joseph Dorfman, *The Economic Mind in American Civilization*, II (New York, 1946), 575–584.

5 If the citizens of a country desire such a goal, a good technical case can be made for protective tariffs. Certainly we cannot expect each consumer voluntarily to spend his money in such a way as to pull production into a diversified pattern — for the same reasons that we cannot expect individuals voluntarily to pay for the optimal pattern of "public goods" that they really want. And if the state is going to interfere with the pattern of production so as to protect domestic industry, it seems to me that a tariff (particularly an ad valorem tariff on a broad variety of similar products) is an even-handed, not-too-inefficient way of granting a subsidy.

[6] Academic freedom was notably absent in nineteenth-century America. Not only could one be excluded from employment in Pennsylvania for preaching free trade, but in the Harvard of the 1870's one could be switched from the teaching of economics to the teaching of history — a dire fate? — for unsound views on money.

[7] I used to have the vague notion that George was a good expositor of the Hume-Ricardian theory that land rent, being the return to a factor in inelastic supply, was not so much price determining as price determined and hence provided a good object for taxation in the sense of creating little dead-weight loss and siphoning off an "unearned surplus." But when a few years ago I looked for passages in *Progress and Poverty* to include in an anthology of readings in economics for beginning students, I was astonished not to be able to find any connected passages with a firm analytical structure.

[8] A long list of important economic scholars could easily be drawn up. It would contain such names as Frank W. Taussig, who in addition to making significant contributions to international economics was also a brilliant teacher and editor; H. J. Davenport, a formulator of rigorous economics, who was at the same time a man of strong social sympathies and the best friend Thorstein Veblen ever had; Allyn A. Young, whom we know from oral tradition to have been a keen and creative thinker but who, alas, has left in written form only a few suggestive fragments. His being called to an English chair was in 1927 a remarkable event — more remarkable than it would be today.

[9] This is not to deny that prior to the First World War America had many eminent mathematicians: Bôcher, Osgood, Moore, Bliss, and many others; and such eminent physicists as R. A. Millikan, A. A. Michelson, and many others. But it does assert that Germany, England, and France may have had an even greater number of luminaries. I believe I. I. Rabi is the source, too, for the story that up to the early 1920's the Göttingen library was content to take America's leading physics journal, *Physical Review*, in bound form *at the end of the year*. Contrast this with the present world status of the journal.

[10] After 1904 the Rhodes scholarships did provide a bridge between American students and English university life. But they were intended for leaders, not scholars, and they served to give a taste of undergraduate life rather than of graduate study.

[11] P. A. Samuelson, "Economists and the History of Ideas," Presidential Address before the American Economic Association at New York, N.Y., in 1961, printed in *The American Economic Review*, LII (March, 1962), 1–18. Lest this be misinterpreted as a plea for economics for the sake of economists, I suggest it be read along with my Stamp Memorial Lecture delivered in London a month earlier: *Problems of the American Economy* (London, 1962).

GUIDE TO FURTHER READING

Joseph A. Schumpeter, *History of Economic Analysis* (New York, 1954) is the gigantic posthumous work that any student of economics will have to sample: while dealing primarily with the history of analysis, Schumpeter comments widely on related intellectual disciplines; American topics are covered satisfactorily, but the relatively small space given to them by this erudite expatriate from Europe itself tells an important tale. Eric Roll, *A History of Economic Thought* (3rd ed., Englewood Cliffs, N.J., 1956) is a briefer and more popular treatment of some of the same matters Schumpeter deals with. Joseph Dorfman, *The Economic Mind in American Civilization* (New York, 1946–59) gives in five volumes a valuable survey of American economics and its relations to policy and social thought; the third and remaining volumes cover the period 1865–1933. Short selections from typical writers appear in H. W. Spiegel, *The Rise of American Economic Thought* (Philadelphia, 1960), along with a useful bibliography. Ben B. Seligman, *Main Currents in Modern Economics* (New York, 1962) is a recent comprehensive review of developments from 1870 up to the present time. Richard Hofstadter, *Social Darwinism in American Thought* (rev. ed., Boston, 1955) raises interesting problems for the economist interested in American ideologies. There is, however, no substitute for reading in the original some of the theories he describes. William Graham Sumner could never have been invented if he had not already existed, and today's student must read with his own eyes *Essays of William Graham Sumner*, ed. A. G. Keller and M. R. Davie (New Haven, 1934). Incredibly, Thorstein Veblen was once Sumner's graduate student. I suppose for the non-economist *The Theory of the Leisure Class* (New York, 1899, and many later editions) provides the most readable item in the Veblen menu. That Harvard University could in the same decade (the 1930's) house Thomas Nixon Carver and Alvin Hansen and J. Kenneth Galbraith shows the velocity of turnover in academic life: Carver's out-of-print textbooks are really more revealing than his vigorous essays, but anyone who would like to understand the ideology of the anti-Roosevelt Liberty League or of the National Association of Manufacturers may still read Carver's *Essays in Social Justice* (Cambridge, Mass., 1915). To round out the picture of contrasting American economic opinions, see Donald Drew Egbert and Stow Persons, *Socialism and American Life*, Vol. I (Princeton, 1952).

13. The Realistic Novel

NOTES

[1] *Journals of Ralph Waldo Emerson* (Boston, 1912), VII, 511–512.

[2] Henry James, *Partial Portraits* (London, 1888), p. 316.

[3] Henry James, *Hawthorne* (New York, 1880), pp. 42–43.

[4] *Ibid.*, p. 42.

[5] Henry James, *The Bostonians* (London, 1921), p. 34.

[6] Quoted in Ernest Samuels, *Henry Adams, The Middle Years* (Cambridge, Mass., 1958), p. 226.

[7] H. C. Vedder, quoted in Edwin H. Cady, *The Realist at War: The Mature Years of William Dean Howells* (Syracuse, 1958), p. 30.

[8] F. Scott Fitzgerald, *The Great Gatsby* (New York, 1925), p. 212.

[9] William Dean Howells, "Mark Twain: An Inquiry," in *My Mark Twain* (New York, 1910), pp. 170–171.

[10] Mark Twain, *Adventures of Huckleberry Finn* (New York, 1885), pp. 157–158.

[11] Samuels, p. 226.

[12] *The Letters of William James* (New York, 1920), I, 288.

[13] *The Letters of Henry James* (New York, 1920), II, 398.

[14] Henry James, *Letters to A. C. Benson and Auguste Monod*, ed. E. F. Benson (London, 1930), p. 35.

[15] *Letters of Henry James,* I, 30–31.

[16] William Dean Howells, *Criticism and Fiction* (New York, 1891), pp. 128–129.

GUIDE TO FURTHER READING

The most significant statement of American realism in its time is in the critical essays of Henry James on the theory of the novel and on contemporary novelists; a useful recent collection is *The Future of the Novel* (New York, 1956), edited by Leon Edel. *The American Essays of Henry James,* edited by Leon Edel (New York, 1956) is in its way equally informative on the rise of realism. Edmund Wilson's collection of American literary documents, *The Shock of Recognition* (New York, 1943) contains such essential works of and on this period as Howells's beautiful memoir, *My Mark Twain;* Henry James's book on Hawthorne; James's essay on Howells; and John Jay Chapman's essay on Emerson — a brilliant statement of what a later generation found so unacceptable in transcendentalism. There is a comprehensive selection of the best critical essays on Henry James in *The Question of Henry James*, edited by F. W. Dupee (New York, 1945), and there are helpful comments on James's early period in F. O. Matthiessen, ed., *The American Novels and Stories of Henry James* (New York, 1947).

There are excellent critical accounts of James, Howells, and Mark Twain in Richard Chase, *The American Novel and Its Tradition* (New York, 1957), and particularly incisive essays on *Huckleberry Finn* by Leo Marx and others in Charles Feidelson, Jr., and Paul Brodtkorb, Jr., eds., *Interpretations of American Literature* (New York, 1959). Leslie Fiedler's *Love and Death in the American Novel* (New York, 1960) centers on *Huckleberry Finn.* There is no really satisfactory critical work on Howells as a novelist, but Everett Carter, *Howells and the Age of Realism* (Philadelphia, 1954) is intelligent as well as sympathetic. There is a comprehensive collection of critical essays on Dreiser in Alfred Kazin and Charles Shapiro, eds., *The Stature of Theodore Dreiser* (Bloomington, 1955); and on Stephen Crane, both John Berryman, *Stephen Crane* (New York, 1950) and Daniel G. Hoffman, *The Poetry of Stephen Crane* (New York, 1957) are valuable.

14. The Intellectual versus the City

NOTES

This essay originally appeared in *Daedalus* (the journal of the American Academy of Arts and Sciences), Winter, 1961.

[1] Perry Miller, ed., *Consciousness in Concord* (Boston, 1958), p. 46.

[2] Henry James, *Hawthorne* (New York, 1880), p. 80.
[3] Harry Levin, *The Power of Blackness* (New York, 1958), p. 234.
[4] Alexis de Tocqueville, *Democracy in America* (New York, 1945), I, 289n.
[5] *Ibid.*
[6] Arthur M. Schlesinger, *Paths to the Present* (New York, 1949), pp. 223–225.
[7] Henry Adams, *The Education of Henry Adams* (Boston, 1918), pp. 7–8.
[8] *Ibid.*, p. 238.
[9] Henry James, *The American Scene* (reprint, New York, 1946), p. 77.
[10] *Ibid.*, p. 92.
[11] *Ibid.*, p. 84.
[12] *Ibid.*, p. 279.
[13] *Ibid.*, pp. 275, 280.
[14] *Ibid.*, p. 85.
[15] *Ibid.*, p. 86.
[16] *Ibid.*
[17] *Ibid.*, p. 115.
[18] F. O. Matthiessen, Introduction to *The American Novels and Stories of Henry James* (New York, 1947), p. xv.
[19] Ralph Barton Perry, *The Thought and Character of William James* (Boston, 1935), I, 351.
[20] *Ibid.*, p. 412.
[21] *The Letters of William James*, ed. Henry James (Boston, 1920), II, 264.
[22] *Ibid.*
[23] *Ibid.*
[24] Frederic C. Howe, *The City: The Hope of Democracy* (New York, 1905), p. 204.
[25] John Dewey, *School and Society* (Chicago, 1899), p. 9.
[26] Dewey, *The Public and Its Problems* (reprint, Chicago, 1946), p. 216.
[27] *Ibid.*, p. 213.

GUIDE TO FURTHER READING

The theme of this essay is more fully developed in Morton and Lucia White, *The Intellectual versus the City: From Thomas Jefferson to Frank Lloyd Wright* (Cambridge, Mass., 1962). The reader is also advised to examine the writings of standard American authors should he wish to pursue the topic further. For the earlier period Jefferson's *Notes on Virginia*, Emerson's *Nature*, and Thoreau's *Walden* are of course canonical; see also Hawthorne's *The Marble Faun* and Melville's *Pierre* for samples of their attitudes toward city life. For the period after the Civil War, see especially *The Education of Henry Adams* (Boston, 1918); Henry James, *The American Scene* (New York, 1907); William Dean Howells, *A Traveler from Altruria* (New York, 1894); Jane Addams, *Twenty Years at Hull House* (New York, 1910); Theodore Dreiser, *Newspaper Days* (New York, 1922); John Dewey, *The Public and Its Problems* (New York, 1927); Robert E. Park, *Human Communities: The City and Human Ecology* (Glencoe, Ill., 1952); Josiah Royce, *Race Questions,*

Provincialism and Other American Problems (New York, 1908); Frank Lloyd Wright, *The Living City* (New York, 1958).

Harry Levin, *The Power of Blackness* (New York, 1958) is very useful for the study of anti-urbanism in Hawthorne, Melville, and Poe; see also Leo Marx's interesting study, "The Machine in the Garden," *New England Quarterly*, XXIX (1956), 27–42; and Perry Miller's penetrating essay on romanticism, "Nature and the National Ego," in his *Errand into the Wilderness* (Cambridge, Mass., 1956).

The best historical account of the late-nineteenth-century American city is Arthur M. Schlesinger, *The Rise of the City: 1878–1898* (New York, 1933). Lewis Mumford's works, notably *The Culture of Cities* (New York, 1938) and *The City in History* (New York, 1961), restate many of the arguments leveled by major American intellectuals against the American city.

15. The Revolution in Higher Education

NOTES

1 In his excellent book, *Mark Hopkins and the Log* (New Haven, 1956), Frederick Rudolph examines the myth of the old college, as exemplified by Mark Hopkins and Williams College, judiciously but with disillusioning results.

2 Charles William Eliot, *Educational Reform* (New York, 1898), p. 105.

3 Quoted in Orie W. Long, *Literary Pioneers* (Cambridge, Mass., 1935), p. 166.

4 Cf. Andrew D. White: "I had, during my college life, known sundry college tutors seriously injured while they were doing police duty. I have seen a professor driven out of a room, through the panel of a door, with books, boots, and bootjacks hurled at his head; and even the respected president of a college, a doctor of divinity, while patrolling buildings with the janitors, subjected to outrageous indignity." *Autobiography* (New York, 1922), I, 348.

5 *Representative Phi Beta Kappa Orations*, ed. Northrup, Lane, and Schwab (Boston, 1915), pp. 160–161.

6 The size and wealth of an institution were in fact of vital importance to the quality of its achievement. George W. Pierson has pointed out that Harvard in this period was working with endowments that made even such rivals as Princeton and Yale "plain and poor." "American Universities in the Nineteenth Century: the Formative Period," in Margaret Clapp, ed., *The Modern University* (Ithaca, 1950), p. 80.

7 Practically all the new state universities of the West and South adopted a coeducational policy more or less as a matter of course. In 1880 fifty-one per cent of the colleges were mixed; in 1898, it was seventy per cent. The number of women students rose from about 2,700 to more than 25,000. By the turn of the century four out of five colleges, universities, and professional schools admitted women.

8 Eliot, *Educational Reform*, pp. 1–2.

[9] Samuel Eliot Morison, *Three Centuries of Harvard* (Cambridge, Mass., 1936), p. 358.

[10] Despite the clear preponderance of the German influence in the American idea of the university, some English influences persisted; they were especially strong in the better colleges and in some universities like Yale and Princeton. The English concern with the development of character in undergraduates and something that might be called atmosphere in the institutions is a noteworthy feature; as is the passion for imposing buildings, somewhat separated, if possible, from the urban community. An emphasis on teaching, as opposed to research, remains. In some institutions — notably, again, Yale and Princeton — the centrality of the college among the various parts of the university is an Anglo-American survival. So too is the aim of creating a broadly educated leadership, as opposed to a body of specialists. Finally, the English passion for undergraduate sports has survived and grown in this country — but with the unfortunate difference that the English emphasis on amateurism and broad participation has been supplanted with American commercialism and spectator sports.

[11] See the account of this transformation by Walter P. Metzger in Richard Hofstadter and Walter P. Metzger, *The Development of Academic Freedom in the United States* (New York, 1955), ch. VIII.

[12] Of course it should be clear that the universities were not the creations of a democracy, or of the faculties. In the main, they were created, or reformed, from the top down. They were triumphs of elite leadership, of enlightened autocracy. In the long run, they advanced academic "democracy" simply because they assembled faculties so large and so eminent that they had to be permitted in some considerable degree to govern themselves.

[13] Quoted in Morison, *Three Centuries of Harvard*, pp. 335–336.

[14] Cf. Andrew D. White on Yale in the 1850's: "Though the professors were most of them really distinguished men, and one at least, James Hadley, a scholar who, at Berlin or Leipzig, would have drawn throngs of students from all Christendom, they were fettered by a system which made everything of gerund-grinding and nothing of literature." *Autobiography*, I, 27.

[15] Morison, p. 347.

[16] Henry James, *Charles William Eliot* (Boston, 1930), I, 87.

[17] Fabian Franklin, *The Life of Daniel Coit Gilman* (New York, 1910), p. 80.

[18] Quoted by Dirk J. Struik, *Yankee Science in the Making* (Boston, 1948), p. 339.

[19] Quoted by F. C. Shattuck and J. L. Bremer in Samuel Eliot Morison, ed., *The Development of Harvard University, 1869–1929* (Cambridge, Mass., 1930), p. 558.

[20] Quoted in Logan Wilson, *The Academic Man* (New York, 1942), p. 175.

GUIDE TO FURTHER READING

The three books that most adequately plot out the course of college and university history are John S. Brubacher and Willis Rudy, *Higher Education in Transition* (New York, 1958), which traces educational development from

1636 to 1956; Richard Hofstadter and Walter P. Metzger, *The Development of Academic Freedom in the United States* (New York, 1955), which covers somewhat the same chronological ground and deals with a wide range of institutional and intellectual history; and Frederick Rudolph's excellent synthesis, *The American College and University: A History* (New York, 1962). George P. Schmidt, *The Liberal Arts College* (New Brunswick, 1957) is a readable scholarly history. Ernest Earnest, *Academic Procession* (New York, 1953) is a more informal work on the same subject. The best book on the history of the curriculum and curricular controversies is R. Freeman Butts, *The College Charts its Course* (New York, 1939). The first part of Richard Hofstadter and C. DeWitt Hardy, *The Development and Scope of Higher Education in the United States* (New York, 1952) deals briefly with university development in most of its phases. The documentation of these books will give any reader the key to the vast literature of educational history.

American Higher Education: A Documentary History (Chicago, 1961), edited by Richard Hofstadter and Wilson Smith, will give the general reader access to some of the most important sources. Anyone who wishes to understand the university revolution from original materials would do well to read Eliot's *Educational Reform* (New York, 1898), Gilman's *The Launching of a University* (New York, 1906) and *University Problems in the United States* (New York, 1898), and Andrew D. White's *Autobiography* (2 vols., New York, 1922), as well as other writings by leading educational promoters.

The institutional histories are very uneven. It is amazing to anyone who has not worked in the field how many American universities and colleges have had their histories written; it is amazing also how bad most of them are. To this generalization there are some indispensable and welcome exceptions. One hesitates to attempt a list, for fear of omitting a few good books that ought to be included; but among those of unusual value are the volumes by Samuel Eliot Morison on Harvard, George W. Pierson on Yale from 1871 to 1921, T. J. Wertenbaker on Princeton to 1896, Carl Becker on early Cornell, Merle Curti and Vernon Carstensen on Wisconsin, Daniel Hollis on South Carolina, Thomas Le Duc on Amherst, Frederick Rudolph on Williams, Robert S. Fletcher on Oberlin, E. P. Cheyney on Pennsylvania, P. A. Bruce on Virginia, and Hugh Hawkins on Johns Hopkins.

The literature of biography and reminiscence, embracing both presidents and professors, is helpful, and often of great interest. See among others: James Burrill Angell, *Reminiscences* (New York, 1912); E. M. Burns, *David Starr Jordan* (Stanford, 1952); James Mark Baldwin, *Between Two Wars, 1861–1921* (Boston, 1926); Nicholas Murray Butler, *Across the Busy Years* (New York, 1935); John R. Commons, *Myself* (New York, 1934); Joseph Dorfman, *Thorstein Veblen and His America* (New York, 1935); A. Hunter Dupree, *Asa Gray* (Cambridge, Mass., 1959); Fabian Franklin, *The Life of Daniel C. Gilman* (New York, 1910); G. Stanley Hall, *Life and Confessions of a Psychologist* (New York, 1923); Henry James, *Charles William Eliot* (2 vols., Boston, 1930); R. B. Perry, *The Thought and Character of William James* (2 vols., Boston, 1935); Walter P. Rogers, *Andrew D. White and the Modern University* (Ithaca, 1942); E. A. Ross, *Seventy Years of It* (New York, 1936);

Harris E. Starr, *William Graham Sumner* (New York, 1925); H. A. Yeomans, *Abbott Lawrence Lowell, 1856–1943* (Cambridge, Mass., 1948).

16. Foreign Policy: From Innocence to Engagement

NOTES

[1] Archibald C. Coolidge, *The United States as a World Power* (New York, 1908).

[2] *Addresses of John Hay* (New York, 1907), p. 120.

[3] Walter Millis, *Arms and Men* (New York, 1956), pp. 192 ff.

[4] The most persuasive proponent of the importance of this latter opinion is Walter Lippmann, who has the advantage that he himself did urge this very view in *The New Republic* in early 1917. But he does not succeed in making clear why nothing happened before unrestricted submarine warfare began, and everything afterward. See his *U.S. Foreign Policy, Shield of the Republic* (Boston, 1943).

[5] Ernest R. May, *The World War and American Isolation, 1914–1917* (Cambridge, Mass., 1959).

[6] W. L. Langer, "Peace and the New Order," in *Woodrow Wilson and the World of Today*, ed. Arthur P. Dudden (Philadelphia, 1957).

[7] Millis, p. 235.

[8] Address to Associated Harvard Clubs, Boston, Mass., June 4, 1946; quoted in *The Pattern of Responsibility*, ed. McGeorge Bundy (Boston, 1951), p. 18. It is not an accident that among the books which have developed this theme at length since 1952 a large number are by former members of Mr. Acheson's Policy Planning Staff.

[9] Reinhold Niebuhr, "The Illusion of World Government," *Foreign Affairs*, April, 1949.

[10] Trenchant criticism can be found in the work of Arnold Wolfers, Stanley Hoffmann, and Dexter Perkins.

[11] But one of the genuinely remarkable developments over the last generation is the increase, in the United States, of solid understanding of other parts of the world. Errors and misunderstandings are certain to recur, but it seems unlikely that there will be any so egregious as those which optimists of different stripes made in the 1940's in their assessments of Soviet Russia and Nationalist China.

[12] This essay was written in 1960, and it seems wrong in early 1963 to change its last sentence. Nor is it reasonable for me, as a member of President Kennedy's staff, to attempt an assessment of what he has achieved toward the ends I have described. But perhaps it will be agreed at least that his words and acts are already important for serious students.

GUIDE TO FURTHER READING

On the premise that events underpin thought, the reader is referred first to the standard diplomatic histories. There are at least three good ones: Samuel Flagg Bemis, *A Diplomatic History of the United States* (4th ed., New York, 1955); Thomas A. Bailey, *A Diplomatic History of the United States* (6th ed.,

New York, 1958); and Foster Rhea Dulles, *America's Rise to World Power, 1898–1954* (New York, 1955). The third gives the most attention to the thinking around the events. All three have useful bibliographies.

Second to the events are the actors. The public papers of Theodore Roosevelt, Woodrow Wilson, and Franklin Roosevelt are the most important printed evidence on the three most important men. Next come the standard biographies or autobiographies of these three and of Root, Taft, Lodge, Hughes, Stimson, Hoover, Hull, Hopkins, Truman, Vandenberg, and Acheson. On Eisenhower and John Foster Dulles there is really nothing good yet, though the sum of Dulles's speeches and writings deserves attention.

The thinkers who have been seriously influential are few. Certainly A. T. Mahan is one; his classic volume was *The Influence of Sea Power upon History, 1660–1783* (New York, 1890), but his essays on American problems are collected in several other volumes. Of later writers, the one with the most important total corpus of writing is Walter Lippmann, whose career as a major publicist begins before the First World War and continues today. His work, in its constant lucidity, its growing maturity, and its deep concern for responsible action, makes a sustained and illuminating commentary on problems of foreign policy; it never makes — and seldom tries to make — a theory. Among diplomatic historians one may use similar language for Dexter Perkins, whose wide range of writing is colored by sustained good will and pragmatic optimism. The works of both men are deeply American in temper.

Among other present-day writers the most influential have been George Kennan, Hans Morgenthau, and Reinhold Niebuhr; Kennan's several short books are steadily stimulating; the student of American attitudes will begin with *American Diplomacy, 1900–1950* (Chicago, 1951). Morgenthau's best work is *Politics Among Nations* (3rd ed., New York, 1960); a less convincing but stronger statement of his attitudes is *In Defense of the National Interest* (New York, 1951). Reinhold Niebuhr's comments are in many different places and often oblique; one good place to start is with *Reinhold Niebuhr on Politics*, ed. Harry R. Davis and Robert C. Good (New York, 1960).

The best general study of the way Americans have thought about foreign policy in the twentieth century is Robert E. Osgood, *Ideals and Self-Interest in America's Foreign Relations* (Chicago, 1953). For a general introduction before the student takes his thinker straight, and also for a steady series of sound and instructive comments, this book is invaluable; it is not so narrowly concerned with a single line of division as its title and its structure may suggest.

On military policy the best — almost the only — book is Walter Millis, *Arms and Men* (New York, 1956). On the history of attitudes toward international economics I am unable to suggest any good single work, and my own comments are little more than impressionistic guesses; the field needs attention.

The theorists of 1960, like the statesmen, are not yet easy to sort out, but a skillfully edited compendium on the thin topic of general theory is *Contemporary Theory in International Relations*, ed. Stanley H. Hoffmann (New York, 1960), while the best book on present problems of military policy is Bernard Brodie, *Strategy in the Missile Age* (Princeton, 1959).

17. American Moderns

NOTES

[1] *The Collected Essays of John Peale Bishop*, edited with an introduction by Edmund Wilson (New York, 1948), p. 75.

[2] From "Esthétique du Mal," in *The Collected Poems of Wallace Stevens* (New York: Alfred A. Knopf, 1954), p. 319.

GUIDE TO FURTHER READING

The quantity of criticism on this segment of American literature is so vast that only a few books can be listed here. Perhaps the best general survey of twentieth-century American fiction is Alfred Kazin's *On Native Grounds* (New York, 1942), a young man's book, exuberant, brilliant, and with some judgments (such as the depreciation of Faulkner) which the author has since repudiated. There is no really satisfactory history of twentieth-century American poetry, but sensitive appreciations can be found in Louise Bogan's *Achievement in American Poetry* (Chicago, 1951), and some information in *A History of American Poetry, 1900–1940* (New York, 1942) by Horace Gregory and Marya Zaturenska. Our best literary critic, Edmund Wilson, has first-rate essays on twentieth-century American writing in several of his collections: *The Wound and the Bow* (Boston, 1941), *Classics and Commercials* (New York, 1950), *The Shores of Light* (New York, 1952). Many stimulating general ideas concerning American literature can be found in Philip Rahv, *Image and Idea* (New York, 1949), and Lionel Trilling, *The Liberal Imagination* (New York, 1950). A good study of the American novel is Richard Chase, *The American Novel and Its Tradition* (New York, 1957). Philip Rahv has edited a useful collection of articles called *Literature in America* (New York, 1957).

Concerning the individual writers discussed in this essay the following books provide biographical material and critical discussons: Irving Howe, *Sherwood Anderson* (New York, 1951); James Schevill, *Sherwood Anderson: His Life and Work* (Denver, 1951); Philip Young, *Ernest Hemingway* (New York, 1952); Carlos Baker, *Ernest Hemingway* (Princeton, 1956); Arthur Mizener, *The Far Side of Paradise: A Biography of F. Scott Fitzgerald* (Boston, 1951); Alfred Kazin, ed., *F. Scott Fitzgerald, the Man and His Work* (Cleveland, 1951); Irving Howe, *William Faulkner: A Critical Study* (New York, 1952); Frederick Hoffman and Olga Vickery, eds., *Three Decades of Faulkner Criticism* (East Lansing, Mich., 1960); Olga Vickery, *The Novels of William Faulkner* (Baton Rouge, 1959); Frank Kermode, *Wallace Stevens* (New York, 1961); J. V. Cunningham, "Tradition and Modernity," in *Tradition and Poetic Structure* (Denver, 1960).

18. The Rise of Neo-Orthodoxy

NOTES

[1] Sydney E. Ahlstrom, "Continental Influence on American Christian Thought Since World War I," *Church History*, XXVIII, No. 3 (September, 1958), 7.

[2] H. Richard Niebuhr, *The Kingdom of God in America* (New York, 1937), pp. 167–168.

[3] The historian is Frank Hugh Foster. The quotation appears in Winthrop Hudson, *The Great Tradition of the American Churches* (New York, 1953), p. 253.

[4] H. Richard Niebuhr, p. 194.

[5] Paul Carter, *The Decline and Revival of the Social Gospel* (Ithaca, 1957).

[6] Will Herberg, *Protestant, Catholic, Jew* (New York, 1954).

[7] Martin Marty, *The Shape of American Religion* (New York, 1959).

GUIDE TO FURTHER READING

The sociology of religion in twentieth-century America is well discussed in Will Herberg, *Protestant, Catholic, Jew* (New York, 1954). The mid-twentieth-century aftermath of the Social Gospel movement is described in Paul Carter, *The Decline and Revival of the Social Gospel* (Ithaca, 1957). For a general introduction to Protestantism, with sections on developments in America, on Fundamentalism, Liberalism, and Neo-Orthodoxy, see John Dillenberger and Claude Welch, *Protestant Christianity* (New York, 1954). For a short, popular, readable introduction to contemporary theology, see Daniel Day Williams, *What Present-Day Theologians Are Thinking* (rev. ed., New York, 1959).

For more complete discussion of the major theologians, the volumes edited by C. W. Kegley and R. W. Bretall, in the Library of Living Theology, provide useful collections of essays on many aspects of the thought of Reinhold Niebuhr and of Paul Tillich in their respective volumes. Gordon Harland, *The Thought of Reinhold Niebuhr* (New York, 1960) is a good summary and commentary. There is now a useful one-volume systematization of Niebuhr's thought on politics, put together from his many writings: H. R. Davis and R. C. Good, eds., *Reinhold Niebuhr on Politics* (New York, 1960).

19. The New Economics

NOTES

[1] J. A. Schumpeter, *Ten Great Economists* (New York, 1951), p. 275.

[2] D. Riesman, *Constraint and Variety in American Education* (Lincoln, Neb., 1956), p. 60.

[3] J. M. Keynes, *Essays in Biography* (London, 1933), p. 183.

[4] Keynes, *The End of Laissez-Faire* (London, 1926), pp. 34–35; *Essays in Persuasion* (London, 1931), p. 300.

[5] S. E. Harris, *John Maynard Keynes: Economist and Policy Maker* (New York, 1955), p. 48.

[6] Keynes, *Treatise on Money* (London, 1930), II, 148–149; *Essays in Persuasion*, pp. 151–153; *The New Statesman and Nation*, July 7, 1923; and Report of Committee on Taxation and National Debt, 1923, *Evidence*, pp. 536, 538.

[7] Keynes, *Treatise on Money*, II, 154.

[8] Report of Committee Inquiring into Finance and Industry, 1931, Addendum I, p. 206.

[9] *The New Statesman and Nation*, February 4, 1933.

[10] Keynes, *General Theory of Employment, Interest and Money* (London, 1936), pp. 129–131.

[11] Keynes, *General Theory*, p. 120; *London Times*, December 28, 1937; and Committee on Finance and Industry, Addendum I, p. 206.

[12] Committee on Finance and Industry, Appendix C.

[13] S. E. Harris, ed., *The New Economics: Keynes' Influence on Theory and Public Policy* (New York, 1947).

[14] *The New Statesman and Nation*, April 1, 1933.

[15] D. B. Suits, *Economic Forecasting and Analysis with an Econometric Model* (mimeographed; July, 1961). What follows is based on this article.

[16] *Ibid.*, p. 13.

[17] *Ibid.*, pp. 7–8.

[18] *Ibid.*

[19] *Ibid.*, pp. 15, 34.

[20] Keynes, *General Theory*, p. 18.

[21] *Ibid.*, p. 362.

[22] Keynes, *Essays in Biography*, pp. 123, 140–141, 144.

[23] *Fortune*, February 23, 1950, and *New Republic*, July 29, 1940.

[24] Keynes, *The End of Laissez-Faire*, p. 38.

[25] *The New Economics*, pp. 191–192.

[26] *Ibid.*, p. 98.

[27] Keynes, *General Theory*, pp. 295–296.

[28] Keynes, *Treatise on Money*, II, 290–291.

[29] *New Republic*, February 20, 1935.

[30] J. K. Galbraith, *The Affluent Society* (Boston, 1958), p. 253.

[31] Keynes, *Essays in Biography*, pp. 170–171.

[32] In writing this section, I relied heavily on a symposium that I edited with the help of Paul Samuelson, "Mathematics in Economics," *Review of Economics and Statistics* (S. E. Harris, editor), 1954, pp. 357–386, with contributions by Messrs. Novick, Klein, Duesenberry, Chipman, Tinbergen, Champernowne, Solow, Samuelson, and Harris.

[33] *Review of Economics and Statistics*, 1954, p. 382.

[34] Schumpeter, *Ten Great Economists*, p. 97.

[35] Keynes, *Essays in Biography*, pp. 191–192, and *General Theory*, p. 298.

[36] A. C. Pigou, *Alfred Marshall and Current Thought* (London, 1953), p. 11.

[37] J. R. Hicks, "Linear Theory," *The Economic Journal*, December, 1960, pp. 690–699.

[38] *Review of Economics and Statistics*, 1954, p. 377.

[39] *Ibid.*, p. 376.

[40] *Ibid.*, p. 378.

[41] *Ibid.*, p. 374.

[42] *Ibid.*, p. 365.

[43] Items 2, 4, 5, 6 are especially dependent on mathematics.

[44] J. R. Hicks, "Linear Theory," *The Economic Journal*, December, 1960, p. 690.

45 W. W. Leontief, "Input-Output Economics," *Scientific American*, October, 1951, p. 1. (Reprint)

46 W. W. Leontief and others, *Studies in the Structure of the American Economy* (New York, 1953), p. 32.

47 Board of Trade and Central Statistical Office, *Input-Output Tables for the United Kingdom*, 1954, 1961.

48 "Demand Under the Microscope," *The London Economist*, September 19, 1953.

49 W. W. Leontief and M. Hoffenberg, "The Economic Effects of Disarmament," *Scientific American*, April, 1961, p. 9. (Reprint)

GUIDE TO FURTHER READING

Keynes's major work was the *General Theory of Employment, Interest and Money* (London, 1936). This book, far from an easy one to understand, nevertheless has been a spectacular success in attracting attention to Keynes's fundamental point that unemployment is a constant threat unless treated by adequate intervention by Government through monetary and fiscal policy. Keynes's influence would have been considerably less had not others clarified and amplified his work: L. R. Klein, *The Keynesian Revolution* (New York, 1947), A. H. Hansen, *A Guide to Keynes* (New York, 1953), and P. Samuelson, *Economics* (numerous editions) presented Keynes's position either with the aid of mathematics or through a simplified exposition so that those who were repelled by the difficult exposition in the original still had an opportunity to understand and then to be persuaded. *The New Economics*, ed. S. E. Harris (New York, 1947) was also helpful. An understanding of the evolution of Keynes's thought can be had especially from his *Essays in Biography* (1933) and R. Harrod's *The Life of John Maynard Keynes* (New York, 1951).

For an understanding of the rising status and use of mathematics in economics, the reader should consult a symposium on "Mathematics in Economics" in the *Review of Economics and Statistics*, 1954; W. W. Leontief and others, *Studies in the Structure of the American Economy* (New York, 1953); R. Dorfman, P. A. Samuelson, and R. M. Solow, *Linear Programming and Economic Analysis* (New York, 1958); J. R. Hicks, "Linear Theory," *The Economic Journal*, December, 1960; and S. Valavanis, *Econometrics* (New York, 1959).

20. Sources of the New Deal

GUIDE TO FURTHER READING

The essential sources are the works mentioned in the text — the relevant writings of Dewey, Croly, Veblen, and Beard. To these should be added *The New Nationalism* (New York, 1910) of Theodore Roosevelt and *The New Freedom* (New York, 1913) of Woodrow Wilson. Among secondary works, the following should be consulted: Morton White, *Social Thought in America: The Revolt Against Formalism* (New York, 1949; reprinted with a new preface and epilogue, Boston, 1957); Richard Hofstadter, *The Age of Reform* (New

York, 1955); Eric Goldman, *Rendezvous with Destiny* (New York, 1952); Charles Forcey, *The Crossroads of Liberalism* (New York, 1961); Roy F. Harrod, *Life of John Maynard Keynes* (New York, 1951); Arthur M. Schlesinger, Jr., *The Crisis of the Old Order, The Coming of the New Deal,* and *The Politics of Upheaval* (Boston, 1957, 1958, 1960, respectively).

21. The Contemplation of Society in America

GUIDE TO FURTHER READING

There is unfortunately no comprehensive, differentiated interpretation of the study of society in America. My own booklet, *The Present Situation in American Sociology*, which was published in 1948, is out of print and out of date but it remains, despite its sketchiness, the most comprehensive treatment. *Sociology in the United States of America* (UNESCO, 1956)) and Robert K. Merton *et al., Sociology Today* (New York, 1959) are two informative works on the period since the end of the Second World War.

The works of the older generation which are still worthy of perusal are: R. E. Park and E. W. Burgess, *Introduction to the Science of Sociology* (Chicago, 1921; 2nd ed., 1924), and Park's collected essays, e.g., *Human Communities* (Glencoe, Ill., 1952), and *Race and Culture* (Glencoe, 1950); W. I. Thomas and Florian Znaniecki, *The Polish Peasant in Europe and America* (2 vols., New York, 1927); C. H. Cooley, *Human Nature and the Social Order* (New York, 1902), and *Social Organization* (New York, 1909); John Dewey, *Human Nature and Conduct* (New York, 1922), *The Public and Its Problems* (New York, 1927), and *The Quest for Certainty* (New York, 1929); and finally, George Herbert Mead, *Mind, Self and Society*, ed. C. W. Morris (Chicago, 1934). The most interesting of the Chicago monographs were Frederick Thrasher, *The Gang* (Chicago, 1927); Louis Wirth, *The Ghetto* (Chicago, 1928); and H. Zorbaugh, *The Gold Coast and the Slum* (Chicago, 1929).

Harold Lasswell's best works were *Psychopathology and Politics* (Chicago, 1931); *World Politics and Personal Insecurity* (New York, 1930); and *Politics: Who Gets What, When, and How* (New York, 1936).

Lloyd Warner's views are summarized in *Structure of American Life* (Edinburgh, 1952). Elton Mayo and his ideas are best represented in *The Human Problems of an Industrial Civilization* (New York, 1933). His chief followers are T. N. Whitehead, *Leadership in a Free Society* (Cambridge, Mass., 1936) and F. J. Roethlisberger, *Management and the Worker* (with W. J. Dickson; Cambridge, Mass., 1939). Their works are ably summarized by George Homans in *The Human Group* (New York, 1950).

Paul Lazarsfeld has no single major work. One book which exemplifies his virtuosity is *The Academic Mind* (with Wagner Thielens; Glencoe, 1958). Robert Merton's most characteristic qualities are to be seen in his collected essays, *Social Theory and Social Structure* (rev. ed., Glencoe, 1957).

The main elements of the new outlook are to be seen in T. W. Adorno *et al., The Authoritarian Personality* (New York, 1950); Talcott Parsons and

Edward Shils, eds., *Towards a General Theory of Action* (Cambridge, Mass., 1951); and Talcott Parsons, *The Social System* (Glencoe, 1951).

22. *Modernity and Mass Society*

NOTES

[1] Some social statisticians at M.I.T., directed by Ithiel Pool, have elaborated the idea of "contact nets," and they have speculated, on the basis of some probability data, that any two persons in the United States, chosen at random, could find a mutual acquaintance in five steps.

[2] One of the elements that have facilitated the creation of a national society, as Mencken noted a quarter of a century ago, is the spongelike character of "American English," with its disregard for grammatical and syntactical precedents, its ability to borrow or invent new words, and its general uniformity throughout the country. See H. L. Mencken, *The American Language* (New York, 1940), p. 90.

[3] It is interesting to note that Henry Adams, lamenting in his own way the fragmentation of American life, gave a somewhat different picture than James in trying to account for the looseness of American life. "Down to 1850, and even later," he wrote, "New England society was still directed by the professions. Lawyers, physicians, professors, merchants were classes, and acted not as individuals, but as though they were clergymen and each profession were a church." It is the breakup of this sense of "clergy" (or what Coleridge called the "clerisy"), of the devotion of the well-educated to service, which Adams felt accounted for the corruption of American life. Henry Adams, *The Education of Henry Adams* (Boston, 1918), p. 32.

[4] For a discussion of the various uses of the term, see "The Theory of Mass Society," in Daniel Bell, *The End of Ideology* (Glencoe, Ill., 1960). Also, William Kornhauser, *The Politics of Mass Society* (Glencoe, 1959), and Leon Bramson, *The Political Context of Sociology* (Princeton, 1961).

[5] This was the mood of the more sensitive liberal critics as well. In 1955, Arthur Schlesinger, Jr., prepared a memorandum for the Democratic Presidential candidate, Adlai Stevenson, in which he argued that the problem for the Democratic Party domestically was to move, as he put it, from "quantitative liberalism," or the question of income redistribution, unemployment insurance, pension payments, and the like, to "qualitative liberalism," or the problems of urban sprawl, education, support for the arts, etc. The memorandum was circulated privately among an impressive number of writers and political figures, and finally appeared as an article in *The Reporter*, May 3, 1956.

[6] Dwight Macdonald, *Masscult and Midcult*, Partisan Review Pamphlets No. 4 (New York, 1961), p. 41.

[7] Mr. Macdonald's idiom itself needs explaining. In the early 1930's, the "tough" phase of American radicalism, the Bolshevik habit of compressing words — such as *politburo* for the political bureau of the Party, or *orgburo* for the organization bureau — caught on. Thus, the vogue of proletarian literature was known as proletcult. Mr. Macdonald, as the epigone of this radi-

calism (see his *Memoirs of a Revolutionist*), adopts this jargon for his own sardonic style.

[8] Hannah Arendt, "Society and Culture," in *Culture for the Millions*, ed. Norman Jacobs (Princeton, 1959), pp. 43–53. The argument is elaborated in Miss Arendt's *Between Past and Future* (New York, 1961), pp. 197–226.

[9] In an editorial essay for *The Dial*, June 14, 1919, reprinted in Thorstein Veblen, *Essays in Our Changing Order* (New York, 1934).

[10] "The Case of James Dean," by Edgar Morin, in *Evergreen Review*, No. 5; Edgar Morin, *The Stars* (New York, 1960); and the essay "Mass Culture in an Age of Baby-Geniuses," *La Nef*, April, 1958.

[11] "The only exception," he continues, "the Russian-Jewish Community of New York that plays so important a role in the cultural life of the city, proves the rule; for New York is not America, and this is one of the reasons why." Irving Kristol, "Table Talk," *Encounter*, October, 1955, pp. 60–61.

[12] The changing role of the little magazines provides a significant illustration of the metamorphosis in American culture. Originally, the little magazine represented a self-conscious protest against regnant literary taste and authority, and a vehicle for experimental and esoteric writing. It usually involved a coteric of individuals with a common viewpoint, and it was dedicated to personal self-expression. Above all, the little magazine was a product of the revolt against Puritanism, gentility, and vulgarity in American literature. Beginning around 1910, the revolt was symbolized by Harriet Monroe's *Poetry: A Magazine of Verse*, and Max Eastman's *The Masses*. Hoffman, Allen, and Ulrich, in their study *The Little Magazine* (Princeton, 1946), list only five periodicals before 1910 as deserving the appellation: one, *The Dial*, edited by Margaret Fuller and Ralph Waldo Emerson, appeared from 1840 through 1844 and, despite such contributors as Thoreau, Emerson, William Ellery Channing, and Theodore Parker, never had more than 300 subscribers at best; four of these periodicals were published in the 1890's.

In the 1920's there were over a hundred little magazines, most of them not surviving beyond an ephemeral existence of a year or two, most of them fiercely experimental, anti-bourgeois, and self-consciously rebellious against existing plutocratic and sexual conventions. These magazines were, however, important in providing a place for new writers. (Charles Allen, in an article in the *Sewanee Review*, has demonstrated that out of a hundred American writers who achieved significant reputations after 1914, eighty-five were first published in little magazines.) Despite a perhaps contrary impression, today *more* little magazines (over 300) are being brought out than ever before (see *The International Guide to Literary and Art Periodicals*, Villiers Publications, Ltd., London). But today the majority of these are academic, and sponsored in the main by university English departments; as a result, the bulk of the articles is critical rather than creative, and the editorship institutional rather than personal.

[13] I have elaborated this point somewhat in a short essay, "The Eclipse of Distance," in *Encounter*, April, 1963.

[14] As Paul Lazarsfeld points out, in commenting on a paper by Oscar Handlin on the difference between the folk art of the past and contemporary mass

culture: ". . . a careful reading of his contribution shows that what he means by folk art could have played only an occasional role in people's lives. What did they do on long winter evenings? Were they desperately bored? Or is boredom itself an experience which has developed in industrial society? From Handlin's personal remarks, one gathers that historians know very little about how people used to spend their time, so questions become speculations." In *Culture for the Millions*, p. xii.

[15] "The English uncultured are a brutal nation. . . . The brutality of the manners in the lower-class appears in the boxing, bear-baiting, cock-fighting, love of executions, and in readiness for a set-to in the streets, delightful to the English of all classes." Emerson, *English Traits* (New York, 1876), p. 63.

[16] Edward Shils, "Daydreams and Nightmares: Reflections on the Criticism of Mass Culture," *Sewanee Review*, LXV, No. 4 (Autumn, 1957), 586–608.

[17] "Notes on a National Cultural Policy," in *Culture for the Millions*, pp. 148–154. See, too, the testimony of Paul F. Lazarsfeld before the Kefauver Committee, reprinted in *Public Opinion Quarterly*, XIX, No. 3 (Fall, 1955).

[18] The one instance, perhaps of a genuine avant-garde today — a set of experiments far ahead of mass or even highbrow acceptance — is in music, where post-Schoenberg style, serial music, and electronic music have their devotees. But characteristic of *this* form of avant-garde is that, unlike earlier forms of "modern music" (e.g., Satie, Honegger, etc.), it is *not* allied to any form of generalized rebellion, but represents a serious and elaborate form of technical experimentation which is difficult for the untutored to follow.

GUIDE TO FURTHER READING

Arnold Hauser, *The Social History of Art* (New York, 1951); the most comprehensive study of the social setting of art from the early cave paintings to the movies. André Malraux, *The Voices of Silence* (New York, 1953); Malraux's provocative thesis is that modern graphic techniques make possible the "imaginary museum" whereby the art of cultures is now available to all, and in this fashion the contemporary definition and appreciation of culture becomes transformed. Jacques Barzun, *Classic, Romantic and Modern* (Boston, 1961); a discussion of Romanticism as a source of the modern idea of individualism. F. R. Leavis and Denys Thompson, *Culture and Environment* (London, 1933); one of the first and most sustained attacks on advertising, film, and the popular press, as breaking down tradition and the "organic community" of English life. Raymond Williams, *The Long Revolution* (London, 1961); a history, largely from English materials, of the growth of education, the reading public, and the changes in the novel and the drama as a result of the influence of mass culture. Richard Hoggart, *The Uses of Literacy* (London, 1956); a searching examination — and by now a modern "classic" — of the break-up of working-class culture under the impact of the mass media.

Clement Greenberg, *Art and Culture* (Boston, 1961); critical essays by a leading art critic of tendencies in painting in the last fifty years. It contains a seminal essay on "avant-garde and kitsch" which contrasts the acceptance of experimental and trashy art in popular taste. Harold Rosenberg, *The Tradition of the New* (New York, 1959); various essays by a leading critic which interpret, among other things, the "action painting" of the new abstract expressionists, and argue for a new theory as to what is the function of art. Wylie Sypher, *Loss of the Self in Modern Literature and Art* (New York, 1962); an explanation of the disintegration of the traditional representation of objects and figures in art and literature based on parallels in science. Meyer Schapiro, "Style," in *Anthropology Today*, ed. A. L. Kroeber (Chicago, 1953); a classic essay on the concept of "style" as unifying diverse elements of art and civilizations. Leo Lowenthal, *Literature, Popular Culture and Society* (Englewood Cliffs, N.J., 1961); diverse essays on the history of popular culture, especially valuable since so much of contemporary debate slights the historical perspective. Nikolaus Pevsner, *Pioneers of Modern Design* (New York, 1949); a history of changes in basic styles from *art nouveau* to the modern, functional style. Siegfried Giedion, *Mechanization Takes Command* (New York, 1948); the most comprehensive examination of the influence of technology on the social and aesthetic environment.

Norman Jacobs, ed., *Culture for the Millions* (Princeton, 1959); the best collection of essays available on the debate on mass culture; includes papers by Edward Shils, Hannah Arendt, Oscar Handlin, Randall Jarrell, James Baldwin, H. Stuart Hughes, and Arthur Schlesinger, Jr. Frederick Lewis Allen, *The Big Change* (New York, 1952); a social history of America from 1900 to 1950 with an emphasis on the change in living style and culture. Winston White, *Beyond Conformity* (Glencoe, Ill., 1962); attacks the idea that conformity predominates in America, and argues that the growing variety of American life will lead to cultural diversity. Orrin E. Klapp, *Heroes, Villains and Fools* (Englewood Cliffs, N.J., 1962); a discussion of the changing American character based on a socio-literary analysis of changing folk characters, popular heroes, and the like. Daniel Boorstin, *The Image* (New York, 1962); an effort to show how the graphic revolution and the mass media create "pseudo-events" and so distort the nature of reality. Oliver Larkin, *Art and Life in America* (New York, 1949); a social history of America told in terms of its painting, sculpture, architecture, and the minor arts and crafts. Herbert Marshall McLuhan, *The Mechanical Bride* (New York, 1951); a witty, off-beat analysis of the "hidden appeals" in advertising, comic strips, and the popular culture. Bernard Rosenberg and D. M. White, eds., *Mass Culture* (Glencoe, Ill., 1957); a potpourri of essays on the mass media and the arts, largely critical of American mass culture. Eric Larrabee and R. B. Meyersohn, eds., *Mass Leisure* (Glencoe, Ill., 1958); a collection parallel to the Rosenberg and White, above, with emphasis on the problems of leisure and consumption. Dwight Macdonald, *Masscult and Midcult*, Partisan Review Pamphlets No. 4 (New York, 1961); an all-out cannonade against middlebrow culture as pretentious, fake, and devitalizing of serious culture.

23. Science in America: The Twentieth Century

NOTES

[1] Carl Snyder, "America's Inferior Position in the Scientific World," *North American Review*, CLXXIV (1902), 60.

[2] Joseph Henry, "First Report of the Secretary of the Smithsonian Institution to the Board of Regents, December 8, 1847," *Eighth Annual Report of the Board of Regents of the Smithsonian Institution* (Washington, 1854), p. 135.

[3] Henry A. Rowland, "The Highest Aim of the Physicist," *Science*, X (1899), 825.

[4] Cited in A. Hunter Dupree, *Science in the Federal Government* (Cambridge, Mass., 1957), p. 309, from George E. Hale, "National Research Council Preliminary Report of the Organizing Committee to the President of the Academy," *Proceedings of the National Academy of Sciences*, II (1916), 508.

[5] R. A. Millikan, *Autobiography* (New York, 1950), p. 129. I am indebted to Mr. Stanley Goldberg for suggestions on the changing role of basic research in American science. His own study, "Basic Research — Myth and Reality," is now being prepared for publication.

[6] George Ellery Hale, "The National Value of Scientific Research," *Technology Review*, XVIII (1916), 811.

[7] E. B. Rosa, "The Economic Importance of Scientific Work of the Government," *Journal of the Washington Academy of Sciences*, X (1920), 341.

[8] Herbert Hoover, *The Vital Need for Greater Financial Support of Pure Research.* National Research Council Reprint and Circular Series, No. 65 (Washington, 1925), p. 4.

[9] Cited in A. Hunter Dupree, p. 349, from Henry A. Wallace, *Research and Adjustment March Together* (Washington, 1934), p. 2.

[10] See the two annual volumes: *Report of the Science Advisory Board, 1933–1935* (Washington, 1934–35).

[11] National Resources Committee, *Research — A National Resource. I. Relation of the Federal Government to Research* (Washington, 1938).

[12] Bernard Barber, *Science and the Social Order* (Glencoe, Ill., 1952), p. 76. Edward Y. Hartshorne, *German Universities and National Socialism* (Cambridge, Mass., 1937).

[13] Naval Research Advisory Committee, *Basic Research in the Navy*, I (Washington, 1959), 46.

[14] Irvin Stewart, *Organizing Scientific Research for War, The Administrative History of the Office of Scientific Research and Development* (Boston, 1948); James P. Baxter, *Scientists Against Time* (Boston, 1947).

[15] Vannevar Bush, *Science — The Endless Frontier. A Report to the President on a Program for Postwar Scientific Research* (Washington, 1945; reprinted 1960), p. 78.

[16] Quoted in National Science Foundation, *Basic Science, A National Resource* (Washington, 1957), p. 12.

[17] National Science Foundation, *Investing in Scientific Progress 1961–1970. Concepts, Goals, and Projections* (Washington, 1961).

[18] Gerald Holton, "Scientific Research and Scholarship, Notes Toward the Design of Proper Scales," *Daedalus*, Spring, 1962, p. 363.

[19] Bernard Barber, p. 118, and Ralph S. Bates, *Scientific Societies in the United States* (2nd ed., New York, 1958), pp. 194–195.

[20] Wallace R. Brode, "The Growth of Science and a National Science Program," *American Scientist*, L (1962), 15.

[21] *Ibid.*, p. 16.

[22] Don K. Price, J. Stefan Dupre, and W. Eric Gustafson, "Current Trends in Science Policy in the United States," *Impact of Science on Society*, X (1960), 189–190.

[23] National Science Foundation, *Federal Funds for Science*, X (Washington, 1962), 38–41.

[24] R. L. Meier and E. Rabinowitch, "Scientists Before and After the Bomb," *Annals of the American Academy of Political and Social Science*, CCXC (November, 1953), 119.

[25] Karl T. Compton, "The State of Science," in John Ely Burchard, ed., *Mid-Century: The Social Implications of Scientific Progress* (Cambridge, Mass., 1950), 28–29.

[26] C. P. Snow, *The Two Cultures and the Scientific Revolution. The Rede Lecture, 1959* (Cambridge, Eng., 1959).

GUIDE TO FURTHER READING

Among the most interesting sources for the social history of science in the United States in the twentieth century are the several reports to the Federal Government assaying the health of the scientific establishment and the responsibilities of government agencies. The two volumes compiled under the direction of Karl T. Compton, *Report of the Science Advisory Board, 1933–1935* (Washington, 1934–35), when read together with the three-part survey of the National Resources Committee, *Research — A National Resource*, I. *Relation of the Federal Government to Research*, II. *Industrial Research*, III. *Business Research* (Washington, 1938–41), give a real sense of the New Deal's attempt to rationalize scientific activity. The need for a National Research Foundation was the basis of the 1945 report by Vannevar Bush, *Science — The Endless Frontier. A Report to the President on a Program for Postwar Scientific Research* (Washington, 1945; reprinted 1960). This recommendation, which culminated in the establishment of the National Science Foundation in 1950, was given substantial support in the five-volume report prepared under the direction of John R. Steelman: The President's Scientific Research Board, *Science and Public Policy* (Washington, 1947).

Since its inception the NSF has been responsible for the publication of numerous studies assessing the nature and growth of the scientific community in the United States. Among them are: *Organization of the Federal Government for Scientific Activities* (Washington, 1956); *Proceedings of a Conference on Academic and Industrial Basic Research* (Washington, 1961); *National Science Foundation, 10th Annual Report* (Washington, 1960); *Federal Funds for Science*, I–X (Washington, 1952–62); *The Long-Range Demand for Scientific and Technical Personnel: A Methodological Study* (Washington, 1961); *Basic Research — A National Resource* (Washington, 1957); *Scientific Research and Development in Colleges and Universities, Expenditures and Manpower, 1953–54* (Washington, 1959).

The first detailed study of the developing relationship between science and the Federal Government was commissioned by the NSF and written by A.

Hunter Dupree, *Science in the Federal Government, A History of Policies and Activities to 1940* (Cambridge, Mass., 1957). The problems encountered in this relationship have been explored by Don K. Price, *Government and Science, Their Dynamic Relation in American Democracy* (New York, 1954), and more recently by J. Stefan Dupre and Sanford A. Lakoff, *Science and the Nation, Policy and Politics* (Englewood Cliffs, N.J., 1962).

One aspect of the development of science as a social institution is found in the historical study by Ralph S. Bates, *Scientific Societies in the United States* (2nd ed., New York, 1958). A more extensive survey of the same problem is found in the work by the sociologist Bernard Barber, *Science and the Social Order* (Glencoe, Ill., 1952).

The impact of war on science and of science on war in the United States has received treatment by several authors. A study of the First World War, with contributions by a number of the scientific participants, was edited by Robert M. Yerkes, *The New World of Science: Its Development During the War* (New York, 1920). Members of the Office for Scientific Research and Development were responsible for volumes in a series on Science in World War II. James Phinney Baxter, *Scientists Against Time* (Boston, 1947) dealt with the scientific and technical questions, while the organizational problems were recorded in a second volume by Irvin Stewart, *Organizing Scientific Research for War, The Administrative History of the Office of Scientific Research and Development* (Boston, 1948).

The momentous problems of building, and the decision to use, the atomic bomb have been treated by numerous authors asking different sorts of questions. The first volume of the new official history of the Atomic Energy Commission presents a full and fair account of the many details of the "birth" of the bomb: Richard G. Hewlett and Oscar E. Anderson, Jr., *The New World, 1939–1946*, Volume I, *A History of the Atomic Energy Commission* (University Park, Pa., 1962). One personal account of the building of the bomb has been written by the wartime commander of the project, Gen. Leslie R. Groves, *Now It Can Be Told, The Story of the Manhattan Project* (New York, 1962); another comes from one of the scientists in charge of the project, Arthur Holly Compton, *Atomic Quest, A Personal Narrative* (New York, 1956). Other interesting studies of the bomb and its aftermath include: Alice Kimball Smith, "Behind the Decision to Use the Atomic Bomb: Chicago, 1944–45," *Bulletin of the Atomic Scientists*, XIV (1958), 288–312; Robert Jungk, *Brighter Than a Thousand Suns, A Personal History of the Atomic Scientists* (New York, 1958); Erwin N. Hiebert, *The Impact of Atomic Energy, A History of Responses by Governments, Scientists, and Religious Groups* (Newton, Kansas, 1961); Robert Gilpin, *American Scientists and Nuclear Weapons Policy* (Princeton, 1962).

Several recent attempts to analyze the growth of science and suggest the implications for science policy include: Wallace R. Brode, "The Growth of Science and a National Science Program," *American Scientist*, L (1962), 1–28; Stevan Dedijer, "Measuring the Growth of Science," *Science*, CXXXVIII (1962), 781–788; Gerald Holton, "Scientific Research and Scholarship, Notes Toward the Design of Proper Scales," *Daedalus*, Spring, 1962, pp. 362–399;

Derek J. deS. Price, "Diseases of Science," *Science Since Babylon* (New Haven, 1961), pp. 92–124.

Stories of some of the recent work in science and of Americans who have made important contributions are told in Bernard Jaffe, *Men of Science in America, The Story of American Science Told Through the Lives and Achievements of Twenty Outstanding Men From Earliest Colonial Times to the Present Day* (rev. ed., New York, 1958); and in more popular form by the Editors of Fortune, *Great American Scientists, America's Rise to the Forefront of World Science* (Englewood Cliffs, N.J., 1961). The rise of American science in the twentieth century is related by one of the major contributors: *The Autobiography of Robert A. Millikan* (New York, 1950). An interesting comparative statement is provided by the German-born geneticist, Richard B. Goldschmidt, *In and Out of the Ivory Tower, The Autobiography of Richard B. Goldschmidt* (Seattle, 1960).

24. Contemporary Issues in Education

GUIDE TO FURTHER READING

I. THE CRITICS OF THE PUBLIC SCHOOLS. Arthur Bestor, *The Restoration of Learning* (New York, 1955); a vigorous and comprehensive attack on the education of teachers and the influence of professors of education on our public schools. Henry Ehlers and Gordon C. Lee, eds., *Crucial Issues in Education* (New York, 1959); an anthology containing selections from a number of different authors with differing viewpoints. C. Winfield Scott, Clyde M. Hill, and Hobart W. Burns, *The Great Debate* (Englewood Cliffs, N.J., 1959); this anthology, along with that of Ehlers and Lee, widely samples the controversial literature of the last five years; the two books are complementary. Paul Woodring, *Let's Talk Sense About Our Schools* (New York, 1957); a calm, reasoned examination of many of the intemperate criticisms of the schools.

II. CONCERNING CERTAIN CRITICAL ISSUES. David Fellman, *The Supreme Court and Education* (New York, 1960); a consideration of the legal aspects of both the religious issue and desegregation. Neal Gross, *Who Runs Our Schools* (New York, 1958); an analysis by a sociologist of the role of the school board, the superintendent, and various pressure groups. G. K. Hodenfield and T. M. Stinnett, *The Education of Teachers* (Englewood Cliffs, N.J., 1961); a summary of the issues involved in teacher education as developed from a series of national conferences designed to bring together the professors of the liberal arts and education. Don Shoemaker, ed., *With All Deliberate Speed* (New York, 1957); a somewhat dated though interesting account of the problems faced by the South and border states. Committee for Economic Development, *Paying for Better Schools;* a committee report involving a short discussion of the problems of federal aid, together with a proposal and dissenting opinions. Charles S. Benson, *The Economics of Public Education* (Boston, 1961); an excellent and thorough treatment of all the problems in financing our public schools.

III. OF MORE GENERAL INTEREST. George Z. F. Bereday and Luigi Volpicelli, eds., *Public Education in America* (New York, 1958); an excellent presentation of the major issues by a number of educational authorities. Martin Mayer, *The Schools* (New York, 1961); an interesting account of a number of aspects of education based on many visits to public schools by a free-lance writer. John W. Gardner, *Excellence: Can We Be Equal and Excellent Too?* (New York, 1961); a penetrating analysis of the basic issue in American education by the President of the Carnegie Corporation. Leland L. Medsker, *The Junior College* (New York, 1955); a description of one rapidly expanding segment of higher education. T. Lloyd Trump and Dorsey Baynham, *Focus on Change: A Guide to Better Schools* (Chicago, 1961); an important book for those anxious to see what imaginative reformers envision as the developing pattern of our schools. Arthur D. Morse, *Schools of Tomorrow — Today* (Albany, 1960); a report on nine new departures in educational practice of significance for the future; written for the layman.

IV. BOOKS BY THE AUTHOR ON EDUCATION. *The American High School Today* (New York, 1959); a report on a study of the widely comprehensive high school to be found in consolidated school districts and the smaller cities. *Slums and Suburbs* (New York, 1961); a report on the high schools to be found in the large cities and their suburbs. *Recommendations for Education in the Junior High School Years* (Princeton, 1960); a report. These three reports together contain thirty-four specific recommendations for the improvement of American public schools. *The Child, the Parent, and the State* (Cambridge, Mass., 1959); the last chapter gives a historical account of the changes in American secondary education in this century.

25. America and Europe: Transatlantic Images

NOTES

This essay originally appeared in *Encounter* (London), January, 1962.

[1] *The Notebooks of Henry James* (New York, 1947), p. 24.

[2] The symposium on "Our Country and Our Culture" appeared over several issues of *Partisan Review* (May–June, July–August, and September–October, 1952).

[3] R. H. S. Crossman, in the *New Statesman and Nation* (London), December 1, 1951.

[4] Perry Miller, *Jonathan Edwards* (New York, 1949), p. 326.

[5] Howard Mumford Jones, *The Theory of American Literature* (Ithaca, 1948), pp. 34–38. For similar passages, see Vernon L. Parrington, *The Connecticut Wits* (New York, 1926).

[6] St. John Crèvecoeur, *Letters from an American Farmer* (Everyman ed., New York, 1912), pp. 43–44.

[7] It would be wrong to think of this as a peculiarly American faith. In Europe's optimistic and Utopian nineteenth century the sharing of this vision

of a "grand America" was not rare. Cf. Yvonne French, *Transatlantic Exchanges* (London, 1951), pp. 203, 233.

"I think that whatever difficulties they may have to surmount," Herbert Spencer wrote in 1891, "and whatever tribulations they may have to pass through, the Americans may reasonably look forward to a time when they will have produced a civilization grander than any the world has known." At that time the American echo was a bit soberer — for William James says, "I suspect we have the bigger eventual destiny after all, and give us a thousand years and we may catch up in many details."

[8] Thomas Paine, *Writings* (New York, 1894), I, 92.

[9] Benjamin Franklin, *Letters,* January 13, 1772 (London), May 1, 1777 (Paris).

[10] Van Wyck Brooks, *The World of Washington Irving* (New York, 1944), p. 117n.

[11] *Common Sense.*

[12] Thomas Jefferson, *Writings*, ed. Lipscomb and Bergh (Washington, 1904–05), XIV, 43–45; XV, 477–480.

[13] *Conversations of Goethe with Eckermann* (Everyman ed., New York, 1930), p. 39; Ralph L. Rusk, *The Life of Ralph Waldo Emerson* (New York, 1949), pp. 107, 181.

[14] Mark Van Doren, *Hawthorne* (New York, 1949), p. 207.

[15] Horatio Greenough, in F. O. Matthiessen, *American Renaissance* (New York, 1941), pp. 145–146.

[16] Van Wyck Brooks, *The Times of Melville and Whitman* (New York, 1947), p. 267n.

[17] Mark Twain, *The Innocents Abroad* (New York, 1869), "Milan" and "Venice."

[18] Jefferson, *Writings*, XVII, 292.

[19] "Leamington Spa," from *Our Old Home* (1863), quoted in Philip Rahv, *The Discovery of Europe* (New York, 1947), pp. 201–202.

[20] Brooks, *Melville and Whitman*, p. 364.

[21] Lowell to Howells (1879), quoted in Brooks, *Melville and Whitman*, p. 240.

[22] Tolstoy's message to America (1901), cited in Matthiessen, *American Renaissance*, p. 172.

[23] This and the following three quotations can be found in: Merle Curti, *The Roots of American Loyalty* (New York, 1946), p. 145; Brooks, *Washington Irving*, p. 112; Rahv, *Discovery*, p. 178; F. O. Matthiessen, *The James Family* (New York, 1948), p. 310.

[24] "The American Scholar" (1837), in Mark Van Doren, *Emerson* (New York, 1946), p. 45.

[25] Brooks, *Melville and Whitman*, p. 239n.

[26] On Cooper, I have benefited from the researches of Robert Spiller, both in his biography, *Fenimore Cooper: Critic of His Times* (New York, 1931) and his anthology of *Representative Selections* (New York, 1936). Many references are to (and from) the excellent critical study by James Grossman (New York, 1949). Cooper's *The American Democrat* has recently been re-

printed (New York, 1956), with introductory material by Professor Spiller and H. L. Mencken.

[27] Were the Americans themselves always blameless here? Captain Marryat has written in his *Diary in America:*

> The Americans are often themselves the cause of their being misrepresented; there is no country perhaps in which the habit of deceiving for amusement, or what is termed hoaxing, is so common. . . . If they have the slightest suspicion that a foreigner is about to write a book, nothing appears to give them so much pleasure as to try to mislead him. . . . When I was at Boston, a gentleman of my acquaintance brought me Miss Martineau's work, and was excessively delighted when he pointed out to me two pages of fallacies which he had told her with a grave face, and which she had duly recorded and printed.

Fifty years later the novelist Stephen Crane raged in a letter home:

> They will believe anything wild or impossible you tell them. And then if you say your brother has a bath-tub in his house, they — ever so politely — call you a perjured falsifier of facts. I told a seemingly sane man at Mrs. Garnett's that I got my artistic education on the Bowery and he said, "Oh, really? So they have a school of fine arts there?"

For a more recent case, see the witty catalogue of Simone de Beauvoir's errors committed in her *L'Amérique au jour le jour* as recorded by Mary McCarthy (*Perspectives* 2, Winter 1953), who as one of Mme. de Beauvoir's New York guides must have, I suspect, done her share of misinformation.

[28] On Henry Adams, I have used and quoted from: *Henry Adams and His Friends: A Collection of His Unpublished Letters*, compiled by H. D. Cater (Boston, 1947); *Letters of Henry Adams*, ed. W. C. Ford (2 vols., Boston, 1930); *The Selected Letters of Henry Adams*, ed. Newton Arvin (New York, 1951). An extensive bibliography can be found in Elizabeth Stevenson's biography (New York, 1955).

[29] The best guide to the voluminous literature is *A Bibliography of Henry James* by Leon Edel and Dan H. Laurence (New York, 1957); there is a useful shorter list in D. W. Jefferson's *Henry James* (London, 1960). Invaluable is F. O. Matthiessen's *The James Family: A Group Biography* (New York, 1948), and the same author's edition of *The Notebooks of Henry James* (New York, 1947). The first volume of Leon Edel's James biography, *The Untried Years* (New York, 1953) and his book of *Selected Letters* (New York, 1955) are both helpful and important. I have also profited from F. W. Dupee's study of James (New York, 1951) in the American Men of Letters Series and his collection of various critical essays, *The Question of Henry James* (New York, 1945). The compilation of data by Simon Nowell Smith in *The Legend of the Master* (London, 1947) has given me many leads. I also recommend James's *The American Scene* (New York, 1946, with a notable introduction by W. H. Auden), *A Little Tour in France* (London, 1924), and the "Transatlantic Sketches" which I know only in the Tauchnitz edition (Leipzig, 1883) under the title *Foreign Parts.*

[30] Rahv, *Discovery*, p. 424.

[31] Letter of May 29, 1916, in B. J. Hendrick, *Life and Letters of Walter Hines Page* (New York, 1924).

[32] Malcolm Cowley, *Exile's Return* (New York, 1951), p. 94.

[33] Brooks, *Washington Irving*, p. 112n.

[34] Cowley, *Exile's Return,* pp. 297–298.

[35] T. S. Eliot, *Selected Essays* (London, 1932), p. 14.

[36] Ashley Montagu, *The Humanization of Man* (New York, 1962), p. 198.

[37] Russell Davenport (and the Editors of Fortune), *U.S.A.: The Permanent Revolution* (New York, 1951), p. 209.

[38] *The American Round Table* (New York, April, 1952); see also his "America Today," in *Foreign Affairs,* July, 1950.

GUIDE TO FURTHER READING

There is, alas, no satisfactory, comprehensive study of Americans on (and in) Europe. Philip Rahv has compiled an excellent anthology on "the Story of American Experience in the Old World," entitled *Discovery of Europe* (Boston, 1947), but the reader will have difficulty going on from there. It is regrettable (and perhaps revealing, for it suggests some strange inhibition) that American scholars have been rather less diligent about the transatlantic theme than Europeans. See, for example, Halvdan Koht, *The American Spirit in Europe* (Philadelphia, 1949) and Sigmund Skard, *The American Myth and the European Mind* (Philadelphia, 1961); and for a thoughtful British commentary which goes beyond these Norwegian studies, Professor Marcus Cunliffe's essay written for this volume and published in *Encounter* (December, 1961). If one thinks of the whole host of critiques of U.S. civilization and culture from European pens — ranging from D. H. Lawrence's brilliant *Studies in Classic American Literature* (London, 1922) to Jacques Maritain's *Reflections on America* (New York, 1958) — one is almost tempted to the conclusion that Europeans have been more interesting and penetrating on transatlantic themes than Americans have. At any rate, the examination of Old World attitudes to the New World is no poor starting point for American self-awareness.

On our specific theme of American attitudes to Europe, the reader might consult the various writings of Van Wyck Brooks, who has always been fascinated, even obsessed, by this problem. His five-volume "History of the Writer in America, 1800–1915," which he calls *Makers and Finders* (New York, 1936–52) — *The World of Washington Irving* (1944), *The Flowering of New England* (1936), *The Times of Melville and Whitman* (1947), *New England: Indian Summer* (1940), and *The Confident Years* (1952) — is rich in detail. See also his *The Dream of Arcadia* (New York, 1958), which is an account of "American Writers and Artists in Italy: 1760–1915." Only the title essay in Daniel Boorstin, *America and the Image of Europe* (New York, 1960) is relevant, but its incisiveness leads one to hope that this gifted historian will one day take up the subject at greater length. Charles L. Sanford, *The Quest for Paradise* (Urbana, 1961) is a suggestive study of "Europe and the American Moral Imagination." Professor Merle Curti has frequently explored aspects of this theme: see his *Growth of American Thought* (New York, 1943) and especially *The Roots of American Loyalty* (New York, 1946). Useful, if conventional, is Elizabeth B. White, *American Opinion of France* (New York, 1927), but rather closer to the kind of studies in transatlantic intellectual history which the subject is crying out for is Max M. Laserson, *The American Impact on Russia* (New York, 1950), particularly the pages on the experiences of Francis Dana, Henry George, Andrew White, and George Kennan. For the rest, the reader is advised to go to the novels, the poetry, the letters, the memoirs, and the biographies of the various writers mentioned in the text.

26. European Images of America

NOTES

1 Kenneth Allott, *Jules Verne* (London, 1940), p. 111.

2 From "On a Certain Condescension in Foreigners," quoted in Henry Pelling, *America and the British Left: From Bright to Bevan* (London, 1956), p. 161.

3 Pelling, p. 161.

4 J. Belknap, *Boston Magazine*, I (1784), cited in Michael Kraus, *The Atlantic Civilization: Eighteenth-Century Origins* (Ithaca, 1949), p. 5n. Other examples are given in R. R. Palmer, *The Age of the Democratic Revolution: The Challenge* (Princeton, 1959), p. 258.

5 Georges Duhamel, *America the Menace* (Boston, 1931), p. 42.

6 Franz Kafka, *Amerika* (New York, 1946), preface by Klaus Mann, pp. vi–vii. See also Richard E. Ruland, "A View from Back Home: Kafka's *Amerika*," *American Quarterly*, XIII (1961), 33–42.

7 The evolution of one aspect of this complex fantasy is traced in Loren Baritz, "The Idea of the West," *American Historical Review*, LXVI (1961), 618–640.

8 Quoted in Samuel Eliot Morison, *Admiral of the Ocean Sea: A Life of Christopher Columbus* (Boston, 1942), p. 232, from Richard Eden's 1555 translation. I have modernized the spelling.

9 Quoted in Durand Echeverria, *Mirage in the West: A History of the French Image of American Society to 1815* (Princeton, 1957), pp. 32–33.

10 Echeverria, p. 29.

11 Kraus, *Atlantic Civilization: Eighteenth-Century Origins*, p. 239.

12 Kafka, *Amerika*, afterword by Max Brod, p. 276.

13 Here is a typical reaction, by an English clergyman who visited the United States in the 1840's: "The Americans next-to-adore, with reason, the founder and father of his country. So pure, so disinterested, so exalted a patriot never adorned the annals of time. . . . How different a character is Washington to such charlatans as Bonaparte, and men of his class! and how equally different the issue of their work!" James Dixon, *Methodism in America* (London, 1849), pp. 46–47.

14 David Hecht, *Russian Radicals Look to America, 1825–1894* (Cambridge,

Mass., 1947), p. 57. In 1858 a Neapolitan history professor was put in jail by Ferdinand II for telling his students that George Washington was a great man, and a possible example for them to emulate. See Merle Curti, "The Reputation of America Overseas, 1776–1860," in *Probing Our Past* (New York, 1955), p. 195.

[15] Pelling, pp. 17–18.

[16] Pelling, p. 18.

[17] Carlo Levi, *Christ Stopped at Eboli,* quoted in Michael Kraus, *The North Atlantic Civilization* (Princeton, 1957), p. 162.

[18] Charles Sumner, *Prophetic Voices Concerning America* (Boston, 1874), p. 26.

[19] Sumner, p. 106.

[20] James Bryce, *The American Commonwealth* (2nd ed., London, 1889), II, 475.

[21] Bryce, II, 473.

[22] Kraus, *North Atlantic Civilization,* pp. 161–162. In Fascist Italy, the study of American literature became an oblique form of political protest among intellectuals. The first edition of an anthology, *Americana* (1941), was confiscated by the authorities. See Agostino Lombardo, *Sewanee Review,* LXVIII (Summer, 1960; a special issue devoted to Italian views on American literature), 367–368.

[23] See A. L. Morton, *The English Utopia* (London, 1952), pp. 12, 28.

[24] "America in European Literature," from Hjalmar H. Boyesen, *Literary and Social Silhouettes* (New York, 1894), p. 119. Boyesen, a shrewd observer, remarks (p. 118): "If I had told my grandmother in Norway that two and two made five in America, I do not believe it would have surprised her. She had seen what was to her a much more startling phenomenon. A slovenly, barefooted milkmaid named Guro, who had been in her employ, had returned from the United States, after an absence of five years, with all the airs of a lady, and arrayed in silks and jewelry which in Norway represented a small fortune. My grandmother was convinced that Guro . . . had crossed the ocean for the sole purpose of dazzling her, triumphing over her, and enjoying her discomfiture. For she had prophesied Guro a bad end, and she bore a lasting grudge against the country which had brought her prophecy to naught."

[25] Hoxie N. Fairchild, *The Noble Savage* (New York, 1928), p. 338.

[26] Fairchild, pp. 270–271.

[27] Echeverria, p. 11.

[28] Echeverria, p. 14.

[29] Kraus, *Atlantic Civilization: Eighteenth-Century Origins,* p. 18n.

[30] There is a full discussion of this problem in the two-volume edition of Morison, *Admiral of the Ocean Sea* (Boston, 1942), II, 193–218.

[31] Hans Mattson, *The Story of an Emigrant* (St. Paul, Minn., 1892), p. 298. The same opinion was apparently held by the upper classes in nineteenth-century Austria, for whom America was "a grand bedlam, a rendezvous of scamps and vagabonds." See Curti, *Probing Our Past,* p. 195.

[32] Echeverria, p. 281; Duhamel, p. 48. The villain-view of America, as it

obtained during the Civil War, is admirably expressed in an editorial of September 1862 from the Spanish newspaper *Pensiamento Español:* "The history of the model republic can be summed up in a few words. It came into being by rebellion. It was founded on atheism. It was populated by the dregs of all the nations in the world. It has lived without law of God or man. Within a hundred years, greed has ruined it. Now it is fighting like a cannibal, and it will die in a flood of blood and mire. Such is the real history of the one and only state in the world which has succeeded in constituting itself according to the flaming theories of democracy. The example is too horrible to stir any desire for imitation in Europe. . . ." Quoted in H. D. Jordan and E. J. Pratt, *European Opinion on the American Civil War* (London, 1931), pp. 250–251.

[33] "On a fait de la vertu le principe ou le principal ressort des républiques. Celui de la république américaine paraît être un amour effréné pour l'argent; c'est l'effet de l'égalité politique qui y règne, et qui ne laissant aux citoyens d'autre distinction que les richesses, les invite à en acquérir par toute sorte de moyens." Quoted in Richmond L. Hawkins, *Madame de Staël and the United States* (Cambridge, Mass., 1940), pp. 69–70. Hawkins points out that Mme. de Staël never did visit the United States: she merely invested money there.

[34] Maurice Buxton Forman, ed., *The Letters of John Keats* (4th ed., London, 1952), p. 234. Charles Wentworth Dilke was a warm friend of Keats's. D. H. Lawrence makes a similar charge against Franklin in his *Studies in Classic American Literature* (1923).

[35] *Partisan Review,* XVII (1950), 589–594.

[36] *J'irai cracher sur vos tombes* (Paris, 1946), p. 9.

[37] For example: "There are those, I know, who will reply that the liberation of humanity, the freedom of man and mind, is nothing but a dream. They are right. It is. It is the American Dream." Archibald MacLeish, on "The National Purpose," *New York Times,* May 30, 1960, p. 14.

GUIDE TO FURTHER READING

In addition to the material already cited, Antonello Gerbi, *La disputa del Nuovo Mondo: storia di una polemica, 1750–1900* (Milan, 1955) covers the whole hemisphere and is a work of considerable scope. Gilbert Chinard has published several studies of Franco-American relations. Among these, *Les Refugiés Huguenots en Amérique* (Paris, 1925) has a valuable prefatory discussion of the idea of America as a "mirage" for Europe. Franz M. Joseph, ed., *As Others See Us: The United States through Foreign Eyes* (Princeton, 1959) contains intelligent essays by Denis Brogan, Raymond Aron, and other contemporary observers, as well as an appendix on the concept of the national "image." Other collections of and guides to European opinions include Henry T. Tuckerman, *America and Her Commentators* (New York, 1864); John G. Brooks, *As Others See Us* (New York, 1908); Allan Nevins, ed., *America through British Eyes* (New York, 1948); and Oscar Handlin, ed., *This Was America* (Cambridge, Mass., 1949). Frank Monaghan, *French Travelers in the United States, 1765–1932* (New York, 1933) is a bibliographical guide. Michael Kraus's *North Atlantic Civilization* (Princeton, 1957), an Anvil paperback, has a handy selection of readings, e.g. from William T. Stead's *The Americanization of the World* (New York, 1901). Lucien Febvre and others, *Le Nouveau Monde et l'Europe* (Brussels, 1954), the transcript of a conference on the topic held in Geneva, has some good comments interspersed among the banalities.

Readers should not fail to consult Alexis de Tocqueville's extraordinary *Democracy in America,* which is available in a two-volume paperback edition (New York, 1954) with a long critical essay by Phillips Bradley. The circumstances of Tocqueville's visit and the character of his book are admirably described in George W. Pierson's *Tocqueville and Beaumont in America* (New York, 1938; also in an abridged paperback edition, New York, 1959). *Marie,* a novel dealing with slavery in America written by Tocqueville's companion, Gustave de Beaumont (1835), and full of other generalizations, has been recently translated (Stanford, 1958).

Among the mass of evidence on the reactions of particular countries, see: William Clark, *Less than Kin: A Study of Anglo-American Relations* (London, 1957); G. D. Lillibridge, *Beacon of Freedom: The Impact of American Democracy upon Great Britain, 1830–1870* (Philadelphia, 1954); Frank Thistlethwaite, *The Anglo-American Connection in the Early Nineteenth Century* (Philadelphia, 1959); R. H. Heindel, *The American Impact on Great Britain, 1898–1914* (Philadelphia, 1940); Leon D. Epstein, *Britain — Uneasy Ally* (Chicago, 1954), useful for its assessment of British opinion after World War II; Gilbert Chinard, *Volney et l'Amérique* (Baltimore, 1923); Seymour Drescher, "America and French Romanticism during the July Monarchy," *American Quarterly,* XI (1959), 3–20, on the hostile views of such men of letters as Balzac and Stendhal; Joseph E. Baker, "How the French See America," *Yale Review,* XLVII (1957), 239–253; Otto zu Stolberg-Wernigerode, *Germany and the United States of America During the Era of Bismarck* (Philadelphia, 1937); P. C. Weber, *America in Imaginative German Literature in the First Half of the 19th Century* (New York, 1926), interesting on Goethe and others; and Andrew J. Torrielli, *Italian Opinion on America as Revealed by Italian Travelers, 1850–1900* (Cambridge, Mass., 1941).

27. *Japanese Images of America*

NOTES

1 Herman Melville, *Moby-Dick,* ed. Alfred Kazin (Boston, 1956), p. 101.

2 Cf. *Narrative of the Expedition of an American Squadron to China Seas and Japan,* performed in the years 1852, 1853, and 1854, under the command of Commodore M. C. Perry, United States Navy, by order of the Government of the United States (Washington, 1856), pp. 485–489.

3 The earliest publication on America by a Japanese is *Hyōryū-ki* (*Accounts of My Drifting*), (2 vols., 1863), by Joseph Hiko, who on shipwreck was saved by an American boat in 1851 and spent several years in America before return-

ing to Japan. The earliest account of America by a highly educated Japanese on the basis of his first-hand observation is *Man-en Gan-nen Kenbei Shisetsu Nikki* (*Diary of Embassy Mission to America of 1860*) by Awajinokami Muragaki, who was a deputy in the first mission Japan sent to the United States in 1860.

4 Here a note of contrast might be inserted. In contrast to the improvising mood of Japan's Restoration leaders, Sun Yat-sen, the father of China's republican revolution, had a deep insight into the American form of government and had digested it thoroughly to develop his own political philosophy.

5 Mori edited their replies with his comments in a book published in English: *Education in Japan* (New York, 1873).

6 The translation was literal. Thus sentences like — "See the cat! It is on the bed. It is not a good cat, if it gets on the bed." — must have puzzled Japanese children, who were then entirely unacquainted with the Western type of bed.

7 "Chastity" is omitted for reasons unknown. See *Nichibei Bunka Kōshō Shi* (*The History of Cultural Relations between Japan and the United States*), IV (Tokyo, 1955), 173–177.

8 Among Clark's students were Kanzō Uchimura, Inazō Nitobe, Shōsuke Satō, Kingo Miyake. Among Janes's students were Hiromichi Kozaki, Danjō Ebina, Iichirō Tokutomi, Yūjirō Motora. And among Brown's students were Saburō Shimada, Shigenori Komai, Naoji Shiraishi.

9 Cf. Arthur S. Hardy, *Life and Letters of Joseph Hardy Neeshima* (Boston, 1892).

10 Cf. Whitman's poem: "A Broadway Pageant" (Reception of Japanese Embassy, June 16, 1860).

11 For example, Whitman read with a great deal of interest *Political Condition of Japan* (1888) by Tatsui Baba, himself an unforgettable character in the history of cultural intercourse between America and Japan.

12 Cf. Yasutake Fukumura and Rinya Yamamoto, "A Japanese Estimate of Walt Whitman," *The William Jewell Student*, Whitman Centenary Number (May, 1919); Shigetaka Naganuma, "Whitman's Influence in the Orient," *The Conservator* (June, 1919).

13 An essay by Emerson which is usually omitted from his collected essays nowadays.

14 Cf. Bunshō Jugaku, *A Bibliography of Ralph Waldo Emerson in Japan from 1878 to 1935* (Kyoto, 1947).

15 Some are said to have had the motive of escaping military conscription.

16 Originally the essay was a chapter in *Amerika Kokuminsei no Kenkyū* (*Studies on the National Character of Americans*) edited by Taiheiyō Kyōkai (The Pacific Association), 1943, and later was published in an expanded form as "Amerika-jin" ("The American") in a monthly journal: *Tenbō*, June, 1950.

17 See S. Tsurumi, "Nihon Chishiki-jin no Amerika Zō" ("The Image of America in the Minds of Japanese Intellectuals") in his *Amerika Shisō kara Nani o Manubuka* (*What Do We Learn from American Thought?*), (1958), especially p. 194.

[18] J. A. Schumpeter, *Capitalism, Socialism, and Democracy* (3rd ed., New York, 1950), pp. 129–130.

[19] S. Tsurumi, "Seirigaku·Igaku kara Ningenkan e" ("From Physiology·Medicine to the Image of Man"), in *Amerika Shisō Shi* (*The History of American Thought*), ed. Shigeto Tsuru, III (Tokyo, 1950), 115–116.

[20] Cf. S. Tsurumi, "Nihon Chishiki-jin no Amerika Zō" ("The Image of America in the Minds of Japanese Intellectuals").

[21] The first four volumes were published as *Amerika Shisō Shi* (*The History of American Thought*), (Tokyo, 1950–51); but the fifth volume appeared with the title *Gendai Amerika no Shisō* (*Contemporary American Thought*), (Tokyo, 1956). Shigeto Tsuru was the general editor for all the volumes.

[22] This point is mentioned in the Preface to the first volume.

[23] In particular, American foreign policy under Mr. Dulles appeared to the minority opposition in Japan as an attempt to make Japan, if unintentionally, a military outpost for the United States in the context of the latter's world strategy of containing the Soviet bloc. Establishment of a large number of military bases in Japan, the rearming of Japan in defiance of her constitutional provisions, and putting pressures to keep Japan alienated from the mainland China are some of the consequences which have been deplored by the minority opposition in Japan.

GUIDE TO FURTHER READING

Unfortunately, there are not many works in English in which Japanese present their images of America. The few that exist, therefore, should be regarded as samples rather than as representative. It is fortunate that Awajino-kami Muragaki's diary, *The Diary of the First Japanese Embassy to the U.S.A.* (Tokyo: The Foreign Affairs Association, 1958), exists in English translation, since his visit to America in 1860 was the occasion of the first encounter of a Japanese intellectual with the land and culture of the United States. Descriptions of America's impact on Japanese men of culture in the earliest years of Japanese-American contact may be found in *The Autobiography of Fukuzawa Yukichi* (Tokyo: Hokuseido, 1948); Kanzo Uchimura, *The Diary of a Japanese Convert* (New York, 1895); A. S. Hardy, *Life and Letters of Joseph Hardy Neeshima* (Boston, 1891); Yone Noguchi, *Japan and America* (New York, 1921); and Yone Noguchi, *The American Diary of a Japanese Girl* (Tokyo: Fuzambo, [n.d.]). Among the works by contemporaries, the following may be cited: Yasaka Takagi, *Toward International Understanding* (Tokyo: Kenkyusha, 1954); Chiyono Sugimoto Kiyooka, *But the Ships Are Sailing — Sailing* (Tokyo: Hokuseido, 1960); Gwen Terasaki, *Bridge to the Sun* (Chapel Hill, 1957); and Akira Ota, *A Garioan in the United States* (Tokyo: Hokuseido, 1955).

For an overall treatment of the subject the most informative work is Robert S. Schwantes, *Japanese and Americans* (New York, 1955), which contains a 40-page bibliographical essay. For the pre-Perry period, Shunzo Sakamaki, *Japan and the U.S., 1790–1853* (Tokyo: Asiatic Society of Japan, 1939) is useful. And for the postwar period, Kazuo Kawai, *Japan's American Interlude* (Chicago, 1960) and J. W. Bennett, H. Passin, and R. K. McKnight, *In Search of Identity: The Japanese Overseas Scholar in America and Japan* (Minneapolis, 1958) are to be recommended.

Epilogue: The One Against the Many

NOTES

This essay originally appeared in the *Saturday Review*, July 14, 1962, and is reprinted by permission.

[1] By "ideology" I refer to dogmatic systems of social and economic thought. Obviously most theologies inculcate a monistic view of the moral and religious destiny of man, but the Christian theologies, at least, are generally compatible with pluralistic views on social, economic, and historical issues.

Index

Index

Index